VOLUME 1

# Composition for the 21st ½ century

## Image-Making for Animation

VOLUME 1

# Composition for the 21st ½ century

## Image-Making for Animation

Thomas Paul Thesen

**CRC Press**
Taylor & Francis Group
Boca Raton London New York

CRC Press is an imprint of the
Taylor & Francis Group, an **informa** business

A FOCAL PRESS BOOK

CRC Press
Taylor & Francis Group
6000 Broken Sound Parkway NW, Suite 300
Boca Raton, FL 33487-2742

© 2022 by Taylor & Francis Group, LLC
CRC Press is an imprint of Taylor & Francis Group, an Informa business

No claim to original U.S. Government works

Printed on acid-free paper

DOI: 10.1201/b22148

International Standard Book Number-13: 978-1-138-74093-8 (Hardback)
978-1-138-74089-1 (Paperback)

**Visit the Taylor & Francis Web site at**
**http://www.taylorandfrancis.com**

**and the CRC Press Web site at**
**http://www.crcpress.com**

*This book is dedicated to Alexandra Jäth and my parents Luise & Ludwig Thesen.*

"Close your bodily eye, so that you may see your picture first with the spiritual eye. Then bring to the light of day that which you have seen in the darkness so that it may react upon others from the outside inwards"[1]

**Caspar David Friedrich**

[1]  *The Romantic Imagination: Literature and Art in England and Germany* (1996) by Fredrick Berwick.

# Contents

# Acknowledgments

I would like to thank the following people for helping me during the production of this book:

Katrin Albers (for her patience in reading and critiquing the final books), Monika Horstmann (for her advice in typographical matters), Melvyn Ternan, Emil Polyak, Patrick Smith, Giannalberto Bendazzi, Mia Goodwin, Michael Smith, Chris Longacre, Samuel Applegate, Charlie O'Sullivan, Steve Childers, George "The Tiger" Marinou (for his scientific critiques), Kinson Cheung, Park Seh Oh, James Batcho, and all my former students.

# Author

For more than 20 years, Thomas Paul Thesen's career has been about learning and understanding the complexities of art, animation, and image-making, both in still illustration, drawing and photography and the moving image. He has worked in the industry as a character animator and visual development artist for companies like Pixar, DreamWorks, and Sprite Animation Studios. He has also taught for many years at universities across Asia, the United States, and the United Kingdom.

To know more about his professional and personal work, visit http://thomasthesen.art/.

# The Reason Why I Wrote this Book

The point of this book is to encourage animation, film, and visual development enthusiasts to learn and keep learning about the complexities of image-making and animation in particular. This book obviously can never cover composition and design in its entirety; then the art form of image-making would be at its end and there wouldn't be anything artistically to add to it. So this book does not attempt to cover the field. It does nevertheless open possibilities, different creative thought processes, and encourage further studies and experimentation.

I have been studying illustration, art, animation, and film for quite a while now as a fan and geek, student and teacher. Image-making has so many facets that it is rather difficult to write general guidelines, as they can be often contradicted immediately. The scope of the art form and the commercial field of image-making and animation in particular is immense and allows one to indulge for years in the watching of moving drawings and characters on-screen alone, not even yet delving into the production of it. Doing this does teach artists much and provides a ground plane on which to build their own interpretation of the world surrounding them. It teaches them to appreciate the basics of image making like simple composition or how to create a basic concept, but it does not teach them the reasons behind it and what the artistic purpose of it is, and this is what this book tries to do.

Is animation a job or a passion or both? I myself chose animation because it is an art form that combines drawing, painting, film, music, storytelling, sculpture, etc., and because of its endless possibilities, its entertainment value, and especially its escapist abilities. That this does not all agree with the actual work in the animation industry is a given and one has to literally find one's own niche in the big picture. Most of popular animation, and never has animation been more popular than today, follows a strict conveyor-belt production pipeline, needed to cover all the complex steps to produce an animated film. This produces a high amount of technically excellent work, though creativity is often amiss and only once in a while one comes across a very unique show or feature that goes against the typical animation story line. After having seen so many animated features, one asks oneself what really is the purpose of animation these days. For that we need to go back to what animation is capable of in the first place: escapism and the creation of the unreal, unexpected, and exaggerated.

Why do students get into animation? Most of them do because they like animation and they grew up watching it. They like drawing (some of them), they like storytelling (some of them), and they enjoy being creative (some of them). It is a huge task in animation to learn the technical aspects, learning how to draw, to animate, to paint, how to compose, learn film language, and all the needed computer programs; it literally takes a decade to become a professional. One easily forgets in this forest of technicality and skills the reason for choosing this art form in the first place. Many are too early satisfied with creating something that moves instead of creating something that moves with a purpose. Transporting an idea, a message, and a worldview to share should be more important than a technique or the computer program used. Animation is an art form and as such needs an artist who has something to say. This doesn't have to be a huge world-changing message, but it should be a message that is worth working on day and night for a couple of months or sometimes years. Just recreating what others have done before a thousand times is only showing off one's technical abilities, which is important; however, it only covers a very small section of the entire art form that is animation and one can only appreciate so many fighting ninjas. Unfortunately, education is expensive and students very quickly want to get a job to make money and prove to themselves that they have "what it takes." For some, this is enough and they grow in their abilities while working in their jobs. Skills develop over time and if animation is chosen as an occupation or passion, there is much of life ahead to practice those skills. Others, though, go into animation for its artistic possibilities and its never-ending visual dreamscapes. Therefore, I want to provide the animation student or enthusiast with a compendium that contains not only the technical aspects of image-making for the moving image and particularly animation but also the reasons for choosing them and why they work in their imbedded and often abstract meaning. Everything we do is done for a purpose and the goal is always storytelling in its various shades.

When I was younger I always tried to figure out what people really meant when they were talking about "composition" or how images work. Every book always talked about it but there was rarely any in-depth explanation. There were some few details explained but not enough to really understand what composition actually is in its entirety. As a student in a class on medieval book illustration, I asked my professor how those paintings were done and how the color was produced in the eighth and ninth centuries. He just brushed me off and said, annoyed: "Why would you even want to know?" I still truly believe it is important to know how something is done in order to really grasp and appreciate it. In my entire education, there weren't really a lot of teachers which could tell me *how* an image worked and *how* I could use this knowledge in my work and *why* some painters and sculptors, animators or illustrators were considered so much better than others, aside their technical skills. It couldn't just be that their pictures were famous, and if they were famous, *why* were they famous?

So I went on a journey trying to learn everything that I was interested in and what I thought was important for an artist to know, to create art work for animation, film, and illustration. I realized very quickly that I would never cover the field that I thought I could cover, because it was just way too vast.

This book is a collection of all of those studies and some that I tried to grasp myself but couldn't really find anything worth a dime written on. Some topics might strike you as odd, but for me they seem important in order to open one's eyes to the visual happenings out there and push you to learn how to *see*.

Art making isn't a precise science; it is a constant exploration and is in continuous flux as you add new knowledge and disregard old, which will never give you a final result but will put you on a path that allows lifelong exploration.

What I tried to do in these two books was to not influence the reader with my personal style too much and to keep the illustrations as neutral as possible; however, I do also realize how difficult this is—any depiction will exert influence, so there is no neutral drawing ever. Nevertheless, you should not use my style as an example, but only the content of the text in relationship with the examples.

Neither does this book claim to be the only way of producing art or composing an image! Quite the contrary, as it is merely my own personal perspective and viewpoint.

## How to use this book[1]

This book has the best learning effect when all the movies, short films, or referenced artwork are watched, studied, and "experienced." Otherwise the impact of the learned information will be low. With online resources, it is very easy to watch some of the more difficult-to-find films and shorts, and I strongly recommend the accompanying visual experience along with the reading material. All the videos appearing in the book are available at www.routledge.com/9781138740921.

---

[1] Chapters 21 and 22 have been included in Volume 2 due to space reason but made topics of Volume 1 due to the significance of contents discussed in this volume. These two chapters have the same importance for both volumes.

# The role of animation

Animation is a visual medium and therefore of course uses mainly visual characteristics to transfer information from the artist to the audience. As animation is a hybrid between traditional art forms, like drawing, painting, design, and all existing graphic arts, it combines it with technological advances, storytelling, and film language. Yet one of the main building blocks in animation is the control and interpretation of movement and motion. Motion being described as a change in an object's location in connection to time, animation explores movement in terms of poses and timing in its characters and background, so movement not only within the frame but also from shot to shot. Since animation is created frame by frame, it has total control over every segment and aspect of each frame and its content. Animation can freely choose from any artistic expression mentioned above, combine all the existing arts into one, and has the ability to create visuals without limitation, as every frame can be controlled by the artist and pushed into the direction wanted. The only limitation is the technical feasibility and the imagination of the artist. Design characteristics like composition, perspective, color, texture, mood, light and shadow, or shape can all be pushed to the extreme. The image can either be hyperrealistic, realistic, cartoony, or completely abstract. That whole range of possibilities gives animation the advantage of creating images that are far beyond what photography or traditional film can do. In combination with film language and sound plus the control of motion, animation can create truly unique visuals. As animation develops along technology, we can't yet imagine what kind of visuals animation will give us in the future. The fast-paced development of the calculation abilities of game consoles and computers opens doors for a hybrid of animation and games that are going to be fantastic in their entertainment qualities and storytelling abilities. The audience does not just view the movie but is able to actively take part in the story process, influencing it and being in the story, being completely immersed in the experiences of a character and actually being that character. This not only pushes the involvement of the audience to another level but also requires more knowledge from the artist about how images work and how they are able to control the emotional impact of the story points and turn them into well-working images, entertainment, and in the best, yet rarest of outcomes: art. The following will hopefully help the reader to grasp the complexities of image-making, prepare for dealing more thoughtfully with the various aspects that create images, and answer the question of why we use these aspects.

# CHAPTER 1

# The Power of Images

We have around 35,000 years of art history from about 150 countries. All have different styles and interpretations of their world and every single one is a valid source of inspiration for us. But each individual piece of artwork is based on a culture, with its politics and religion, its people and environment that shaped this type of artwork at a very specific point in time. Art and design are always connected to historical events that influenced them. Art is a representation of that time frame and tells us visually how the people interpreted their world. Design and art is never timeless.

What can be taught in design is its technical side, the rules and the aesthetic of existing design in a historical context, what has proven to be successful. It is difficult to teach the artistic aspects of design because those are so often based on the personality of artists and how their work redefines what design and art can be. What design *will* be is completely open and cannot be taught.

This book does not intend to teach how design is done; no book really can. It can only teach rules that have been used for centuries. It is up to the designer to take all these rules and bend them, use them, change them, or completely disregard them, according to the project. If you just follow the rules strictly, the design will be rigid and banal. What you have to get into the design is your own personality and taste, thus creating an interpretation of what you believe adds to the existing design canon. You should always push what design has been so far and then open it up into a new direction.

If a book aims to teach you how to do design, then it has already failed, because how can something be taught that has still to be invented anew every single day? The artist's interpretation of existing design is what can make new design and, in the best scenarios, good design. Learning the rules of image making and using them in a personal and artistic way can lead to something that is creative and unique. Strictly following the rules might not be the right direction.

As animation artists, we deal with images on a daily basis; we dissect images and create characters that are usually for a general audience, as the purpose is either TV animation, feature animation, computer games, commercials, or characters for any other kind of commercial or social purpose. Because we work for an audience that has to accept our characters or environments, it is our task to create a design the audience is comfortable with. We don't want to repeat the same design idea over and over again but create a contemporary look that invites people into the world we created. This is a tricky task, to find a middle ground that is both new and known, interesting but familiar, so that the

design doesn't surpass the expectation and acceptance of the audience. This very audience usually seeks a look that somehow resembles images familiar to them, something they can relate to. The designer, on the other hand, often likes the unusual and the extraordinary, because that is what we, as artists, are usually looking for in our design. So these two extremes might clash at some point. Designers should not forget the audience when they are working on designs; they should create a look the audience can feel at home in. This does not mean that we should create only the obvious or what the audience wants. Quite the contrary! Animation is an art form and as such has the task to challenge people's views and push the boundaries of design and aesthetics in general. A middle ground has to be found, a middle ground where both artist and audience are satisfied. Animation in my opinion is not there to make money alone. Animation is there to explore the visual possibilities of the film medium and to explore storytelling in a graphic way or in a way that pushes reality to a new exciting level. When animation just tries to please, as we can often see in big productions, the outcome might not be as satisfying as it could have been from an artistic perspective. It can still obviously satisfy the audience from an entertainment point of view.

Is there such a thing as good design? I believe that there obviously is, but I can't really pinpoint any of it. Some design is successful because it is very detailed, intricate, and complicated, while others are just crude stick figures that exactly fit the story and therefore represent good design. Both can be great design; it depends on the project they are intended for.

In my opinion, animation is the strongest art form of the future and has power that we can't even fathom yet. It has the ability to create anything we can imagine, push the boundaries of the known, and create movies that make us wonder, if only the will to create the unique is as big as the financial forces that drive the industry.

## What is an image?

Every day, we are surrounded by such a vast number of images in magazines, movies, brochures, and commercials that we rarely ask ourselves what an image is and what it does explain to us on a subliminal level, that is, how the image and its aspects control us and our emotions, our thoughts and reactions. Images can provoke every emotion, from happiness to anger, hate to sadness. Every commercial uses all the aspects of image making to affect our desires and emotions in a profound yet simple way. Images have the strength to make us cry in just a couple of

**Figure 1.1**

René Magritte (1898–1967), *La Trahison des images* (*Ceci n'est pas une pipe*), 1929.

minutes (some in a couple of seconds), if done right. Therefore, if images have the power to evoke such strong emotions, the artist can control them and use all the aspects of image making to trigger exactly the desired emotion in the audience. Of course, this does sound a bit creepy; it has been and is still used for political messages that are less than advantageous. Therefore, every artist who deals with images also has a great responsibility for what the message of their artwork is. Leni Riefenstahl, for instance, should have thought twice about the content of her films before she created some of her stunning visuals for Adolf Hitler.

The root of the word *image* comes from *imago* (Latin), which means "likeness, copy." So an image is a representation of a situation in either two or three dimensions. It can be a drawing, painting, photograph, sculpture, object, glyph, graph, or map.

*The Treachery of Images* (*La Trahison des images*) from Rene Magritte (Figure 1.1) shows the risk of images and points out what they really are: only imitations of the real object but not the real object themselves. In Magritte's piece, you see a pipe, but the title underneath says that it is not a pipe. This seems like a contradiction because we do see a pipe. Nevertheless, the pipe in the picture is not a pipe, but just an image of a pipe; it is not the pipe itself. Pictures and images never show the real object. They are always just a representation or interpretation of the object. Even photography, which seems to create an exact replica of the portrayed object or scenery, is like any other image, just an interpretation of it. The color, composition, and mood, for instance, are all aspects of an image that influence its content. Ten people that photograph exactly the same object will create 10 different interpretations. Magritte's pipe is similar in appearance to a real pipe, but it is *not* the real pipe.

What influences the experience of observing images? Every image has a certain mood and content or story that evokes emotions in the viewer. Those emotions are influenced by our past and situations we experienced, which shaped us in one way or another. The emotions are also influenced by our knowledge. By looking at an image, we simply remember what we have seen before and the memory with the attached emotion comes back and thus influences the image looked at. It is our social and natural environments that shape our feelings toward images. Someone that grew up on a farm has very different feelings when looking at a picture of a field of wheat compared to someone that grew up in a metropolis. So every image is received differently by different people. Everybody has a slightly divergent emotion toward images. Swastikas, for example, have been symbols and decorations for thousands of years. But Figures 1.2 and 1.3 do tell different stories because we connect them to opposing historical and religious contexts.

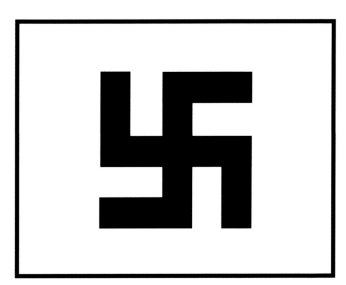

**Figure 1.2**

Hindu swastika: The evolution of the universe.

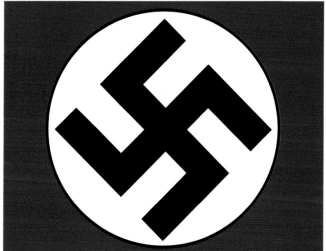

**Figure 1.3**

Nazi swastika: The symbol of the "creating, acting life."

Images change and their content is not fixed. With time, every image goes through a development because societies change and we always look at an image from our current perspective. We will never know how people looked at the Sistine Chapel at the time it was created, because we don't have the same experiences that would allow us to feel the same emotions. So every generation will see art anew.

## Connecting images

If you look at the swastika in Figure 1.3, that symbol immediately starts a flow of images in your head that are connected to World War II: significant political photos, concentration camps, soldiers marching in Nuremburg, and flags at the Olympics in 1936, but also less realistic interpretations like *Indiana Jones and the Last Crusade* (1989), *Captain America: The First Avenger* (2011), Marvel comics, or serious artistic dealings with the topic in the form of novels, music or paintings, sculpture, and installations. This type of swastika should make you uncomfortable because it is so strongly connected to a significant historical event of horrendous proportions. The design of the sign, its simplicity, and aesthetics are quite successful; however, we cannot possibly see it only from that aspect, as its context and meaning overshadow the design. What we can see in the example of the Nazi swastika occurs in every image we look at. Each image, as banal as it might be, tells a story. Some are rather complex and evoke a myriad of contradictory feelings; others are simple and easy to understand, but they all come in a historical context and are connected to an uncountable number of other images. The swastika in Figure 1.2, which is the Hindu swastika describing the evolution of the universe, lacks the connection to World War II and evokes different images of Buddhist and Hindu temples, of serenity and calm. Both swastikas are similar, but they tell completely different stories. An artist creating images needs to ensure that the story told is actually the story that was supposed to be told.

## Content

Figure 1.4 shows an advertisement from Pan Am's campaign for the introduction of the Boeing 707 for transatlantic flights in the early 1960s, a historical step in commercial air travel. The content is fairly easy to understand; there are no hidden clues and there is no complex subtext in the image. It is a print commercial, so by its nature it should be easily understood and read in a split second. But if you take a closer look at the picture, you can see more than just the airplane. The image clearly focuses on the jet engines, which provided a "beautifully quiet, vibration-free comfort at 600 mph," a unique and most definitely noteworthy feature of a commercial plane of the early 1960s. The size of the massive jet engines overpowers everything else in the image and their polished metal makes them appear clearly impressive and even slightly futuristic. However, they also feel safe as the passengers can even walk underneath them without hesitation

**Figure 1.4**

Pan Am.

(of course the passengers are very far away from the engines, but the flattening of the original three-dimensional image into a flat two-dimensional printed image allows the passengers to appear as if they were walking underneath the engine). Pan Am clearly provides safe and comfortable travel! There are various elements within the picture that give us hints of what emotionally we are supposed to feel. First, there is the metallic shiny surface of the airplane, which clearly defines the object as human-made and as clean, new, and solid. The huge wing of the plane covers nearly one-third of the entire image, thus providing some sort of roof that reminds one of a safe shelter for the passengers. Then there are the dominant jet engines, two of the four mentioned in the text. They look very powerful and are slightly intimidating in their size and complex design and in combination with the word "magic" just above their ability is impressive indeed! Then the blue sky, which we connect with words like "holiday," "depth," "air," "flying," "clean," "deep," etc., creates calm and comfort and the light clouds seem to slowly drift toward the left and also remind us of condensation lines of the airplanes. Then the group of arriving passengers, walking away from the airplane, seem calm and relaxed; they feel rested after the 6.5 hours flight to Europe, not stressed out and tired. The entire picture has one story: flying Pan Am is a safe, fast, and comfortable travel that also has an air of exclusivity to it. The connections between all these elements of the print commercial are very important as they tell the story the viewer is supposed to understand and feel. They open every image up in content and widen its meaning by providing different layers of information. The viewers will not necessarily fully "consciously think" about all the elements but will "subconsciously feel" them. In the case of an ad-campaign of course, only the positive connotations are of value, as the negative ones such as dangerous and expensive are not really a fit for an advertisement.

By presenting the jet engines with the passengers, we don't just get the information that the engine is powerful but that it is also already trusted and proven by many travelers as being safe, comfortable, quiet, and successful. The connection between the two elements therefore has various meanings and the information that we get from the image is beyond the mere visuals. It is not just an image of passengers stepping out of an airplane, but passengers that trust the new engine and step out of the plane after only 6.5 hours of magic.

The color of the Pan Am logo on the bottom of the page is the same as the color of the two lines of text underneath, which state that it is "the world's most experienced airline." The color connects compositionally the text to the logo and also to the blue in the sky. The logo is then in shape and position connecting with the smaller jet engine just above it, which in turn connects with the bigger jet engine on the left, connecting in shape and in content the two elements of Pan Am logo and futuristic engines, which is the message of the campaign.

The text also invites us to "Join the first Jet Travelers across the Atlantic." The words "Jet Travelers" are underlined, thus pointing out the passengers as being the first across the Atlantic. It is a new way of traveling!

The position of the engines is also noteworthy as they clearly go "forwards" and compositionally push toward the left like rockets. Their possible speed can already be imagined.

Much information is given in a simple ad like this, and we do not see just the airplane but an array of stories that evoke feelings and memories and create a longing. But the information is simple and easily understood. Everyone can understand the ad.

# Iconography and iconology

Erwin Panofsky was a German-born art historian whose main contribution was the interpretation of the iconography and iconology of European art. Panofsky (who mainly focused on Renaissance art) developed the idea of three different stages of the comprehension of art.

The first stage is the *primary* or *natural subject matter* and deals with the common understanding of the image, what is depicted without a deeper meaning: a fish is just a fish. It only deals with what is depicted on the simplest level: shapes, color, and light and shadow, which then are interpreted by the viewer as objects, characters, and locations.

The secondary or conventional subject matter deals with the meaning of what is depicted: its story; the relationship between the objects, characters, and location and what it all means; its *iconography*—the fish is a symbol for Jesus. This can only be grasped with a deep understanding of the subject matter and the knowledge of what is portrayed. That of course depends on the complexity of the image. We know, for instance, that a muscular man in a tight, blue outfit with a big *S* on it and a red cape is Superman. We also know that Superman comes with positive values, abilities, and superpowers and that only Kryptonite can defeat him. Someone that has never even heard of Superman would have no clue what this man is supposed to represent other than a tall, muscular man in a tight suit.

The third level is the tertiary or intrinsic meaning or content, the *iconology* of the piece, which deals with the piece of art in its historical context and how the time frame in which the piece was created influenced its style, meaning, story, etc.: why did the artist depict the fish in this specific way? Is there a connection to his time in terms of sociopolitics? But it also takes into consideration the artist's whole oeuvre and how it stands within the overall art historical context, how the sum of it can define it as an outstanding document of its time. The Superman comics would, therefore, be looked at in their relationship to the pulp magazines of the 1920s and the 1930s, the serial radio shows, the influences of movie stars and popular heroes of the time, the influence of politics and economics, and the personal history of the creators in relation to their artistic work.

An excellent example of complex iconography and iconology in animation is the work of Yuriy Norshteyn. His short film *Tale of Tales* (1979) is an intricate patchwork of different characters living through situations that are seemingly unrelated to each other. What is shown is not just the simple image but what the image represents. It all has a meaning that can tell a more complex and deeper story if one is looking for it.

Usually animation, especially feature film animation, is very straightforward and can lack a secondary meaning, which is a pity, as animation so easily lends itself to exaggeration and abstraction. It is the perfect medium for comedy, political farce, or even tragedy, all of which can have a deeper meaning despite a nonsensical, funny, or serious storyline. Animation can be entertaining *and* intellectually stimulating.

**More on Yuriy Norshteyn's *Tale of Tales*:**

Wells Paul, *Understanding Animation*, Routledge, London, 1998, pp. 93–97.
Kitson Clare, *Yuri Norstein and Tale of Tales, An Animator's Journey*, Indiana University Press, Bloomington, IN, 2005.

**More on the meanings of still life:**

Bryson Norman, *Looking at the Overlooked, Four Essays on Still Life Painting*, Reaction Books, London, 1990.

## Metaphorical meaning

Every image has a story to tell, no matter how banal the image might seem. Every detail in the image is therefore of importance, as they all affect how the story is interpreted and read. Pieter Claesz's *Still Life with Herring* (Figures 1.5 and 1.6) not only depicts an arrangement of plates and food on a table, which would be the natural subject matter, but has different objects with a dedicated meaning to them that as an assemblage tell a story, are an allegory with a religious meaning. The subject matter shows us a table with a typical Dutch breakfast of the 17th century of bread, fish, and a glass of beer. The colors are monochromatic, brownish, and earthen. They do not express strong and loud emotions but evoke quiet and calm, which fits the content of a modest meal. The soft and subtle lighting streams in from the above left and gives the image a solemn feeling. The composition is clear and geometric, the distances between the elements relate to each other, balancing out left, right, top, and bottom. The assembled objects follow a strict and geometric composition. Everything is placed with a purpose and meticulously composed for the effect of balance and readability. The right side is heavy with the weight of the dark table and glass of beer and balanced on the right with the bun and the weight of the shadow on the wall behind the table. The white belly of the fish serves in its bent position on the plate as a "connector" between glass and bun. The head points to the glass and its tail to the bun (Figure 1.6).

However, the iconography has a much deeper story to tell. The fish, in this case a herring, is a symbol for Christ at the last supper and can also be a symbol for food in the Lenten season before Easter, the time when Jesus died on a wooden cross. The cracked nuts symbolize again Christ, who died on a cross of nut wood; the bread is also a symbol for the last supper, etc. All these objects are not just randomly chosen but act as symbols for a religious story and only on the surface are an imitation of perfectly rendered objects. The breakfast, therefore, becomes an allegory with a religious meaning and invites contemplation by the viewer.

## Storytelling

The story told in an image is one that is led by the content of the image itself. Additionally, the image provokes other images of the artistic, social, and/or historical context and advocates references to even more images or occurrences. Artists can give as much information as they choose to guide the audience into a very direct and safe path to tell their story clearly, or they can keep viewers in the dark and let them figure out what the image is supposed to mean. Gregory Crewdson (1962–) is famous for his large-scale photographs that depict American life in a surreal and mystique way. His images of the series *Beneath the Roses* (2003–2005) remind us of movie stills, as they tell stories through their meticulously staged and large-scale setups (Figure 1.7). His use of cinematic techniques and aesthetics bring his images and stories to life. There is always some strange happening going on, some unexplainable situation, where people try to make sense of their environment but are often resting in thought and seem to be contemplating the moment. In particular, the complex and conscientious compositions, mysterious light sources, and choices of color lead to complex narrative patchworks with mostly vague stories. It is not just the broad image but the details that are spread throughout the set that give us clues to what is happening to the characters. The connections between the characters, objects, and locations allow various stories to develop in each photograph. But there are so many details that might shape the story that it is open for each observer to tell his or her own personal interpretation of the scene. Every viewer thus has a subjective story to tell, as we pay attention to specific details and connect them differently.

**Figure 1.5**

Pieter Claesz (ca. 1597–1661), *Still Life with Herring*, 1636.

**Figure 1.6**

**Figure 1.7**

Gregory Crewdson, from the series "Beneath the Roses," 2003–2005.

However, Gregory Crewdson's images are also referencing and influenced by the work of other artists, like the director Steven Spielberg, for instance. His early films, especially his science fiction–fantasy feature *Close Encounters of the Third Kind* (1977), are an obvious influence on Crewdson's work and aesthetics. Scenes chosen from Spielberg's movie compared with Crewdson's images show a clear connection between the two. Crewdson uses lights the same way Spielberg does. Light has a very significant meaning in *Close Encounters of the Third Kind* and also in Spielberg's feature *E.T., The Extraterrestrial* (1982). Light doesn't just illuminate the scene and create a mood but is also a character in its own right that has life itself, often representing an alien life-form and its presence, which in Crewdson's images is never pointed out as such but referred to through the obvious connection to Spielberg's movies. Therefore, those who are familiar with Spielberg's Hollywood productions read the photographs differently. Crewdson also refers to Edward Hopper (1882–1967) as a major influence, one of the most famous American painters of the early to mid-20th century. Hopper depicts daily American life, and his paintings show quiet scenes, people who are frozen in a moment, who seem to be lost in contemplation. There is never any action

but silence and thoughtfulness. The pictures of Hopper and Crewdson interest us because they don't reveal the whole extent of their stories. They obviously tell us something, but they don't tell us everything; that is what makes them so appealing. We want to figure out what those characters are pondering. They seem to be stuck in time. However, there are often not enough clues for us to fully understand their situation but only to wonder.

Another artist who does similar work in terms of cinematic scale to the ones from Crewdson is Canadian photographer Jeff Wall (1946–). His images are less obvious in the attempt to tell stories; however, their grand scale and presentation on light boxes also clearly reveal their connection to the cinematic screen. Wall restages scenes and moments he witnessed on the street and interprets them with nonprofessional actors. The photographs, also meticulously staged, are controlled on

**More on staged photography:**

Pauli Lori, *Playing the Part: A History of Staged Photography*, Merrell, London, 2006.

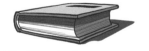

**Figure 1.8**

Jeff Wall, *Milk* (1984).

every level, producing a highly artificial moment, claiming through their crispness and quality to be shot on the spur of the moment. In the photograph titled *Milk* (Figure 1.8), the storytelling is reduced for a surreal effect and stunning composition. We see a young man seated on the ground looking to the right, holding a paper bag, out of which milk is sputtering. The juxtaposition between the seated man at rest and the violently moving milk makes no sense logically, because in order to get the milk spouting the man would have to move. But exactly that is the crucial point of *Milk* and it makes us wonder what the purpose of the image is. Jeff Wall in *Milk* gives

us an idea but does not reveal a story at all. He purposefully steps away from clear storytelling and presents a question rather than an answer.

The four examples of Pan Am, Claesz, Crewdson, and Wall show the extent of artists' power to tell a story the way they please: telling everything clearly as in the Pan Am ad, having a double meaning as in Claesz's painting, as in Crewdson's images telling a very visual story yet keeping it open for interpretation, or as in Wall's piece keeping the storytelling to a bare minimum and making it more about a wondrous event.

# CHAPTER 2

# The Purpose of Images

The first question that needs to be asked when starting a new drawing, painting, sketch, animation, or piece of art is:

- What is the purpose of the piece?
- What do I want to express with this image?
- What is the message or the idea?
- Who is the audience?

## What is the purpose of the animated piece?

People have different reasons why they are attracted to the study and production of animation and animation-related artwork, and all their reasons are of course valid; nevertheless, one should first think about the purpose of animation in general. There are two extremes to the spectrum, namely fine art and commercialism. Fine art comes with the experimentation and the exploration of the medium animation in an artistic playground, whereas commercialism comes with the goal of entertaining the audience through mostly traditional storytelling techniques that are expressed with character-driven animated visuals. Why is it important to contemplate these two extremes of animation and all the overlapping and intersecting possibilities in between? Animation is not necessarily either–or, not just commercial or just art. In the best possible outcome, it is both, because it is fully created by the human mind and not reliant on the natural world, as it can invent its own reality and infuse it with any thought construct. It is one of the most creative mediums, being a combination of drawing, painting, filmmaking, sculpture, architecture, and writing, and it can control every single element of its visuals and each single miniscule movement of its characters, objects, or abstract shapes. Because it can do all of that, it is also one of the most labor-intensive artistic mediums (aside from architecture) and thus comes with a responsibility that needs to be considered. Because animation is such a tedious artistic expression that contains so much control and labor, so much work on many levels, the produced piece, no matter how short, should have some content, some idea, something that is worth telling. I have seen so many characters and story lines that lack a purpose, lack a solid reason for being produced other than "it looks cool." Is animation just entertainment? Or is it merely there for its own sake as art? Because of the immense workload required to produce animation, there should always be a reason

for why this piece of animation is produced in the first place. The reason can be an important story, the exploration of a character's personality, the exploration of a thought, a technical exploration, or a technique. However, there should be a reason that justifies someone sitting down for weeks, months, or years to produce this piece of work.

This brings one to originality. It is so difficult in any field of art to be original. In animation, this is not different at all, quite the contrary. To make a living in animation, one needs to know the cliché of feature animation or TV animation to get a job, to be a small working wheel in the clockwork of animation production, which to function requires people that can turn out the *product* animation. However, one should never forget that animation is not just a product but also an art form. Animation can do much more than "entertain" and can be used in strong visuals that illuminate political thoughts, question social norms, or add to the world of fine art by exploring new ways of interpreting the world. William Kentridge's charcoal animation and John Edmark and Gregory Barsamian's use of zoetropes to create kinetic sculptures are just some examples of the wide range of animation and fine art. However, the large part of those fascinated by the field of animation see it as a product that will bring them a job in the industry and often forget that animation is not just a vehicle to produce entertainment. Every piece of art has a message and animation should always have one too. A message does not necessarily have to be a world-changing intellectual eye-opener but can be just a small and seemingly insignificant idea.

Only when you know beforehand what the purpose of the piece is, can you focus your attention on the final look and the effect you want it to achieve on the audience. What is the medium you are creating the artwork for? Is it fine art, illustration, storyboard, comic, film, development art? There are various media and all have their strengths and purposes (of course, the different media do overlap; there is no precise distinction). You should know the differences and strengths of each medium in order to use them purposefully and strongly and openly play with them. One aspect that all of the following media have in common is storytelling. They all deal with stories in one way or another. Without storytelling, those media could not exist, as their sole purpose is story and conveying information.

## Fine art and animation

Fine art does not have any rules or regulations other than what the artist wants the piece to be, which usually makes it a very personal and unique artistic expression, usually avoiding the general direction of entertainment aesthetics (of course, there are exceptions, like Gregory Crewdson, for instance). It can have the purpose of telling a story, dealing with a theme or topic, or dealing with an artistic problem to expand or question the viewing habits and viewing experiences of the audience, questioning common concepts of images or film/animation. For instance, the earlier-mentioned works of Gregory Barsamian, whose kinetic sculptures closed the gap between sculpture and animation, providing a three-dimensional version of an animated moment. On the surface, the sculptures themselves are only visual pieces that show a surreal and unique moment, but they have a deeper and more complex meaning to them. The piece of art is therefore twofold: it is on the one hand the physical piece that the viewer looks at, and on the other, often more importantly, it is also about its meaning on an intellectual and perceived level, how the audience reads the piece and reacts to it. Fine art, therefore, does not need to educate or entertain; it can if it wants to, but there is no requirement other than what the artist wants it to be.

Animation has more and more influence on sculpture and architecture nowadays as technology advances, and the movement of sculptures and architecture is now technically more feasible than decades ago. Kinetic elements on architecture, animation on huge screens and entire buildings are more and more visible in contemporary skylines.

## Illustrations

As the name already suggests, illustration "illuminates or clarifies" content. The illustration serves the purpose of clarifying through visuals the text, idea, concept, or any kind of project. It can be an illustration to explain how a washing machine works and also an illustration that accompanies a children's book or novel; it can likewise serve as an explanation on a webpage and can clarify how a new hotel will look like, and so on—there are different types of illustrations serving different purposes. An illustration for a children's book has a different complexity than an illustration for a political magazine. But they all should be fairly easy to read. *Explanatory or nonfictional illustrations* are precise and exact and should meticulously describe the content of the text and follow, if needed, scientific accuracy. *Nonfictional illustrations* also accompany the text visually and are an additional intellectual stimulus for the reader. It can go in the direction of fine art aesthetics, but it is usually not considered as fine art as it is an applied art. Both nonfictional and fictional illustrations visualize where the world has its limitations and can, because of their one-image nature, depict a moment in time, a prolonged time frame, or bring various points in time into one image. It is the immediate presentation of a visual situation that literature would need most often pages to describe, but illustration can show it in a split second.

Illustrations for fiction can leave room for interpretation. They should actually give the reader a stimulus to see the literal text

in a different light, see it from another perspective, push the reader's imagination, and not just represent what the reader has already read. Because of the fact that an illustration is mostly one still image, you have to tell the story or your interpretation of it on one page. That one image has to clearly demonstrate the relationships between the characters, objects, or situations. As the word *illustration* already implies, its purpose is to "clarify." If the image is difficult to read, it defeats the purpose. That said, you don't want the illustration to be too easy, because then it might be banal. You have to find a comfortable middle ground where the audience is stimulated but not overwhelmed, where the visuals do not merely show exactly what the reader just experienced in the text but give you more than that—a glance, a moment, character relations that go beyond the text, not adding content that the text does not contain, but expanding the given content and its emotional space.

Illustration is always the little brother of the text and has to be subordinate to it. The text is the key and leads the story; the illustration follows as a visual aid and stimulus. The text often does not need the illustration in fictional texts, novels, stories, poems, as they can stand on their own. The illustration, on the other hand, cannot or should not stand on its own. It is not a mere artistic expression; it is an artistic expression of the writer's imagination, done by the illustrator. The illustrator has to follow the pace and reality that the writer presents and expand on it visually.

Nonfictional illustration, being a more explanatory agent to begin with, is always in need of a text and often the text, in order to be clearly understood, is in need of the illustration. There is a much stronger bond between the two (political illustration does not necessarily need the text to work, but it needs a political context and a situation).

The key point is that illustration is always based on the text, cannot exist without it. An illustration that lacks a text is by definition not an illustration anymore but a mere artistic expression without a purpose other than being there for itself, making a statement. This is the point where art and illustration separate: Illustration has a purpose and is a craft that explains, illuminates, and describes. Fine art does not have that purpose, can stand on its own, and is not focused on the text as a basis for its existence.

## Comics or sequential art

Where illustration is a series of single images expressing a moment in time or a situation, comics tell stories in a series of panel drawings that express the storyline in various panels in a time frame or a series of time frames; it is, therefore, a semi-time-based medium. Comics combine literature, illustration, and aspects of film in order to give drawings a story and a character development in time, which illustration, because of its mostly single-image nature, lacks. The comic book or comic strip can offer filmlike possibilities. You can cut and can use space in a broader scope than illustration can; characters can develop in their personalities, you can have interactions between characters on a wider range, and you can develop a story that is more direct and complex than with illustration. The biggest advantage in comics, though, is dealing with time. Whereas illustration can only show time (or a sequence of actions) in one image, the comic has no time restrictions at all and can develop a full story line with character development that can stretch over an unlimited time frame.

Comics, however, do have overlap with many other media. In comics, you can use speech and dialogue, which overlaps with the medium of film. You can suggest movement with graphic compositions. You can play with the composition of a whole page to give emphasis to specific moments of the story. Comics are free of any design restrictions; they do not have to follow specific rules. Because of its story relationship to literature, its visual and time relationship to film, and in contrast its basis in drawing, illustration, and painting, the comic is a connection tool for the development of movies in the form of storyboards. Storyboards are very similar to comics; they are representations of the script and show the movie in a rough sketched form, with the use of film language. They help to suggest various visual possibilities of the script. However, storyboards sharing elements with comics does not make them comics!

## Development art

Development art for movies or games is technically illustrations; it clarifies the look of a movie, suggests visual possibilities, and clearly defines how characters, objects, and the environment of a movie can or will look like. The foundation for development art is, as for illustration, also the text, though in the form of a script. Without the script, development art has no purpose other than existing for its own sake. Development art is creating a visual world for a project, a script, or a game; it obviously has a purpose which is mainly for entertainment (and with it storytelling), therefore, often called *entertainment art*.

With development art, the director and the production team have characters, visual key moments, and main locations of the script at their disposal, which help them to channel their ideas and to come up with new creative ways to tell the story and understand the locations better, to logically approach the look of this new world and design. It is much easier to explore characters or environments when you see what they could look like. Though most of the development art ends up not fitting the movie, the development process is there to help the team approach the personalities of the characters and locations and to "find" the look of the world: it is constant trial and error. So development art is not just one or two images; it is a series of "styles" that show the evolutionary process of the look of the movie and finally end up with visuals that best express the script. The first idea is seldom the best idea. It has to be shaped and

strengthened throughout the development process, throughout which you try to be more and more precise and specific. You try to shape the details of your film's look, you think about how the world you are designing would actually work, how the characters inhabit the world, and how all of that makes sense in itself. Thus, development art has a specific and well-defined goal: to give an exact explanation of the world with drawings, paintings, maps, elevation drawings, and any other visual explanations for a given film or game project. It clearly shows the style of the movie and the exact proportions of the objects, landscapes, and characters. Development art in the end of the process should not leave any room for interpretation. It has to be as clear as possible in order to show the artists who work on the movie, game, or project how the final product is going to look like.

Visual development art is becoming a bigger and bigger aspect of film and game design and is also finding its way into interactive media, art, and entertainment. However, there is always a basis in the form of a text or script for the created imagery, and development art is not supposed to be presented on its own. As illustration, development art is not fine art but applied art.

## Education and animation

Education has a very special place in art and animation, as it has to follow a specific format to actually be educational. The age group that the piece is targeting is here of utmost importance as the various ages learn in very divergent ways and the amount and kind of information needs to be adjusted to the audience. Repeating information for younger children and using music and songs to engage them is a common tool to make information stick.

## Documentary animation

Documentary animation is becoming more and more popular and is used to visualize complex correlations. Animation is a very helpful tool for not only documenting events but also explaining complex relations. One of the first pieces of documentary animation was *The Sinking of the Lusitania* from 1918. The short was hand drawn frame by frame by none other than Winsor McKay, one of the fathers of animation and comics (who also produced the popular comic *Little Nemo in Slumberland* and the short film *Gertie the Dinosaur*). It is based on the sinking of the British liner RMS *Lusitania* by German submarines in World War I. Technically, these films are not really documentaries, as they express a version of the events but not the events themselves. When interview clips are used and then supported by animated visuals, the term *documentary* has a bit more validity, as one element of the film is clearly "real"; however, the visuals then still give it an artistic twist. For contemporary animated documentaries, check animator Patrick Smith's series from PBS, *Blank on Blank*, for instance.

**11**

## What do I want to express with the image?

Just drawing a piece is good for practice and excellent for improving one's skills; however, it does not give the piece a purpose and a purpose is what it needs to visualize the story and clarify with all its visual elements what the point of the story is. Without it, the image is random and serves no purpose other than presenting skills. Story is always the key element in creating images!

## What is the message or idea?

Aside from the story, there is the message: What is the meaning of the story? The meaning is not the story that is seen on the surface, but is what the story is *actually* about. *Lilo & Stitch* is not just about an alien coming to Earth and befriending a little girl. It is about how one stands up for the other, how friendship and family are crucial for comfort, safety, and mutual trust. These are the elements that guide and determine the story's direction, and are the foundation · of story, characters, background, and design. This is what was earlier described in art history as iconography and iconology (also check in Volume 2, Chapter 7, "Message or Theme").

## Who is the audience?

Be very clear about who the target audience of the image is and consider age group, knowledge required to understand the image, and purpose of the piece. Is it dealing with an already existing world like the *Star Wars* universe, or is the image showing a completely new world in which everything needs to be visually explained? If the audience is required to know much about the relationship between the characters and the entire story to begin with, then it can be assumed that many who don't know the initial setup of characters and the story's world won't grasp the full extent of the given storyline. For example, the feature film *Warcraft* from 2016, based on the computer game of the same name, had such an overload in information that it became a bit tedious for those audience members that did not know the storylines and characters of the original game the film is based on to clearly understand what was going on on-screen. Neither does everyone grasp the whole content of a religious image, as only the pious would have the requisite knowledge, which leaves out those without the background information, and so for them the images become decorative rather than informative.

## Case study: The look of a film "reversed" in the case of Pixar's *WALL-E* (2008)

Much of the information we receive from movie images on-screen affects us subconsciously. We absorb the information and usually quickly understand it, but we do not consciously process most of that information for the narrative to make sense. If we would, the amount of information given would be overwhelming, as it is not only the visual clues one must process but also the auditory information, the characters' information, the constantly changing emotions, moods, etc., which all contribute to the evolvement of a coherent and logical narrative. The continuous stream of information must be processed immediately. There are, in a simplified explanation, two ways the brain reacts to these sensual influences: through stimuli and perception. Stimuli generate physical responses that are immediate and subconscious. They are not causing an intellectual reaction; therefore, they do not carry a meaning. A visual stimulus, for instance, could be bright light causing the iris to close, allowing less light to enter the eye, an unavoidable and uncontrollable physical reaction to prevent damage to the retina. Perception, on the other hand, is the intellectual response to a given stimulus reaching the brain, which in turn then tries to make sense of it. The mind attempts to give the incoming information a meaning and interprets it, connects it with the previously received information and creates, in the case of movies, an ongoing narrative. The previously mentioned light stimulus would then result in the following: a sudden bright light on the cinematic screen, which had caused the character's and the viewer's iris to quickly contract (stimulus), might tell the story of the character on screen having entered a room and turned on the blinding light (perception).

Film contains images that are tweaked compared to reality for the reason of supporting a given narrative. This tweaking is already happening once the cinematographer chooses the framing of the shot. Cinematic images therefore can only interpret or mimic reality, thus create a "theatrical reality." Nevertheless, the viewer can react to a given stimulus from a cinematic image similarly to when experiencing the same stimulus in real life. We can thus use deliberately chosen stimuli in a film, to supply the artistic images on screen with an additional level of meaning and as a result, create emotions in the viewer. Paying attention to our own emotional reaction to distinct stimuli and the resulting perception, and then reusing them in the design of the cinematic image, allows a broader interpretation, widens the narrative's scope, and adds conscious and subconscious emotional possibilities. For instance, the intentional and artistic use of textures could add a level of comfort if clean or a level of discomfort when unclean. The immediate reaction to this stimulus of a clean or an unclean texture, being attraction or repulsion, raises, for instance, the question of why it is clean or unclean and how this information could further shape the narrative. In animation, we can push the "theatrical/cinematic reality" on screen even further, as we can design every single element, from the weather situation to the spoon in the cupboard, from the mood of the location to the characters' texture. Who are these characters supposed to be? Do they have a warm personality or a cold one? Are they comfortable to be around or uncomfortable? How can these feelings be expressed through textures?

Every design decision affects how the audience will not only react to the character or environment but also how the narrative reads through the use of the aspects of design. Following a perspiring character wearing a thick woollen Norwegian sweater on a tropical island will obviously affect the audience's comfort level and lead to a strong emotional response, influencing the meaning: why is the character wearing that sweater in the first place? On the animated screen, all these possible stimuli and resulting perceptions are under the control of the production team and can be (theoretically) perfectly designed to guide the audience's emotional reactions, their comfort or discomfort. Once we understand that every element on screen will affect the reading and interpretation of the narrative, we can use this to our advantage and purposefully place stimuli in the design. Done correctly, this will lead the audience on the intended emotional path.

To understand the scope of this possible embedded visual information in the form of stimuli in just two characters and the stories that evolve, we will dissect WALL-E and EVE from Pixar's feature WALL-E (2008). The design's visual clues and the resulting logical conclusions lead to the characters' personality traits, purpose, and backstory, based solely on their design.

The story of the movie is about a little robot, one of many, produced by a big company, in charge of cleaning up the rubbish humans left on planet Earth. The robot WALL-E is performing his daily tasks. All humans have left the uninhabitable Earth, and WALL-E shares his lonely life only with a cockroach. At some point, Earth is visited by an advanced robot called EVE. She has been sent by surviving humans living in a spaceship in outer space, to search for plant life on Earth. Finding it would be proof that Earth is once again habitable and ready for repopulation.

Looking at the character design of WALL-E, the words and phrases that describe him could be: *rusty, cute, dirty, color peels off, busy, compact, practical, yellow, construction job, solid, durable, scratched, self-sustainable, emotions, block shape, potbelly, cables, wheels with metal belts, joints, black and white striped safety lines, visible technical parts/joints, hydraulic pumps, connections, easy to repair, glasses/eyes/binoculars, visible screws, uneven terrain, bumps on the surface, buttons, childlike pose, playful, dreamy, trustworthy, not the wisest,* etc. There is already a huge amount of information we get by simply looking at the character and of course every piece of information is placed for a purpose, which is to explain the character visually in all his facets. The design describes not just his personality but also his purpose in life, his past and present, dreams, hopes, and parts of the storyline.

What other images are being triggered when looking at WALL-E? The whole concept of his design, the yellow color and black and

white stripes, is based on contemporary construction vehicles. This aesthetic gives the character a clear purpose and transfers one of the key points of the narrative: he is a construction robot intended to perform manual labor. The sole objective of trash-collection and compression, and the need for utmost practicability is clearly expressed in his square and boxy design. He must be compact to practically store away; he is solidly built, yet easy to repair; his eyes are big for locating trash (and to be easily readable in their expressions); his continuous track propulsion system is large and robust to move on rough terrain; his body is simple, yet practical, and does not contain any elements solely there for decorative purposes. He is self-sufficient, recharging through solar energy. Besides the parts crucial for his job and the ability to self-repair, nothing else is important for his existence. The design puts emphasis on those body parts that are the dominant for his task of collecting trash and everything in his design has a defined and clearly readable purpose. But because he has been working for quite a while, he is rusty; the color is peeling off; he has lots of scratches and bumps, has dirt all over his surface, has water and oil stains, and parts are bent and dented… he appears as a practical machine, built for hard work and in operation for a while, visualized in a design that is contemporary and therefore familiar. All these visual clues or stimuli and resulting perceptions, reveal aspects of his personality, his purpose, past and present.

WALL-E's opponent EVE is the exact opposite. The words that would describe her design could be *new, shiny, extremely futuristic, does not represent a robot in the traditional sense, no joints, precisely designed for slickness, surprising, cold, less warm emotions, egg shape, no wheels, flies mysteriously, blue eyes, feels colder, no gaps between fingers/arms, everything looks expensive, looks advanced.* She reminds of clinical environments, scientific research, white coats, septic rooms, knowledge, and precision. She is even wearing a protective "mask." seen in laboratories. Her flying makes her appear more advanced compared to WALL-E, who drives on chains and shakes and rattles. She floats gracefully, her arms hover beside her, and her head is not visibly connected to her body: all those attributes make her seem extraordinary. We do not know how she floats. There is nothing in our own technology that is capable of what she so magically accomplishes, thus we assume she must be from the future, a future with technology that we do not know of yet. Her name EVE says clearly that she is the first of her kind, the first of a new species. Her body shape is that of an egg: pure and white with the purpose of protecting unborn life and itself a symbol of life. Her shape resembles an egg because all the attributes that we connect with eggs express what the design team wants the audience to feel when they look at EVE: clean, safe, life, new beginnings. She is a robot designed to protect plant life and keep it safe in her body, and she herself represents a new beginning of life on Earth. Her facial expressions are not as friendly and open as WALL-E's. Despite her smiling eyes she feels less approachable, has less of an amicable attitude, which fits the personality of her character: created to perform a scientific task.

Both character designs visually express who they are and for what purpose they were built. There is a clear distinction between WALL-E's male geometric shapes with the purpose of construction work and EVE's female, round, organic shapes with the purpose of protecting life. Both are of course a blunt cliché, but they are juxtaposed by the male character WALL-E being the emotional one and the female character EVE being the colder and straightforward one.

This is the basic idea of character design that includes various stimuli in the form of design aspects, leading through logical conclusions to a character's narrative and trigger a wide emotional range of reactions and conclusions in the audience.

# Observe and understand

In order to develop characters and locations and be able to make them unique, one needs to learn to observe and find the extraordinary in the ordinary. We too often take the things that surround us for granted, without really looking at them, and not just looking but understanding them. We think we know what rain, snow, or trees look and feel like, how people act and behave, what fashions they wear, and how they interact with each other. Often, though, when we have to draw we fall back on using clichés and simple ideas, instead of creating a unique design with a specific emotion. But if we don't really study our environment on a daily basis and research it for every project anew, we will at some point only come up with clichés that don't really show anything new or exciting but will bore the audience with their repetitive look and feel. Observe what surrounds you and remember situations that were special, scenes that felt surreal and strange, different and noteworthy. Those are the moments that are so precious and important for us to remember. Use them in your own work. It is the exposure to the unusual in life that helps us to create.

There are so many visuals that we are confronted with on a daily basis that it is sometimes difficult to see images and understand them for what they are instead of just looking at them. In order to expand our visual library and knowledge, it is of utter importance to make it a habit every day to look at and study images and not just to let them pass our eyes but to understand their purpose and how they achieve their goals. On the contrary, it is not just a pleasure for artists to enjoy art and architecture, music and literature but a goal to understand it intellectually and grasp what it is meant to do, how it uses the elements of composition in relationship to its content and goals, and how it plays with them, explores them, and tries to find a new approach, pushing art and design to a new level. Plenty of artists have struggled with the same or similar visual problems we are struggling with today and found solutions that worked in their own time frame. Studying their work shows us how it can be done. Though to just look at the work is not enough; to understand its complexity in the context of its historical background is the key. If I just look at a still life from the 16th century without understanding its content and its message and how they reflect the life and religion of the time, most of what the painting is actually about will

just pass me unnoticed. The message is the key to its composition and its whole existence in the first place. Art is never just there for its beauty or uniqueness; then it would be mere decoration. Understanding the complexity of art teaches you why certain pieces are important and others can't reach the same status despite being technically advanced. Art always conveys a message, and that message is the basis for its conversion and its existence. Good art always tries to push an idea, a technique, or a certain intellectual concept. Without the urge to develop something new, the artist is a mere craftsman. It is the inner drive of artists to step into the unknown and new that makes them hopefully create something that hasn't been seen in this specific way before. The task should always be to see life and its complexity in a different light or to illuminate aspects of life in an artistic way, whatever that might be. In the end, it is about creating something new and pushing the idea of art and the interpretation of the current time-frame with its aesthetics and visuals towards the next step. A painting that is as well painted as the Sistine Chapel done today might not make a lot of sense, because it would be completely disjointed from its historical context, from its art-historical development, using its visuals without concern for the intellectual and historical basis. Art is not just sculpting, painting, or drawing; art is doing all that with a message that is rooted in its historical and social surroundings.

# Simplicity[1]

Simplicity is probably the most difficult concept for beginning students to grasp. They often want the most complex look that they have seen in movies, games, illustrations, and comics but do not yet grasp how simplicity is the very complex balancing of myriads of aspects to create an easily understandable piece of work that strives towards one goal: easy readability and understandability. Nevertheless, simplicity is a very important aspect not just for the beginning student but also the practicing professional artist. Simplicity does not necessarily mean that the image is going to be empty and the story plain or that the final image will be for toddlers. It means to focus on one idea, on one aspect of a story, and not five or ten different ones. All visual and story elements generally need to support only one idea. It is very easy for the audience to be confused by story lines that are not streamlined or design that is overly complex. For instance, how far the visuals can be reduced to a mere idea is shown by Derek Jarman's film *Blue* (Figure 2.1). In this film, Jarman deals with his fight with HIV/AIDS, how he loses his vision, loses friends who also die from AIDS, and his daily struggle with the disease, but he also reflects on his own mortality and art. From the first frame to the last, one only sees the color ultramarine blue and nothing else—an intense and soothing blue that envelopes the viewer in a deep and extraordinary color experience. The color is accompanied by a soundtrack, poems, anecdotes, and sexual stories of gay life and experiences that

---

[1] Also see Chapter 35, "Simplicity and Readability," in Volume 2.

**Figure 2.1**

Derek Jarman, *Blue* (1993).

are loosely connected with each other and present an intimate insight into Jarman's mind and life, more of a rich tapestry of moments than a continuous storyline. "In the pandemonium of image, I bring you the universal Blue," is a sentence spoken during the movie and sums up what Jarman tries to accomplish: the existence of myriads of images defies the need for creating more. While losing his own vision due to the complications with HIV/AIDS, it seems unnecessary and void of logic to create even more images, but blue represents the ultimate placeholder and has a much deeper meaning than any image could ever have as its simplicity allows interpretation to a much wider extent: "Blue is the universal love in which man bathes—it is the terrestrial paradise." Jarman has created images his whole life through film, art, and theatre. Now, facing blindness ends his visual existence, and the disease will cause his physical one to also vanish in time. The ultimate blue that Jarman chooses is very close to the French artist Yves Klein's International Klein Blue, developed in the late 1950s. Klein wanted to preserve the glow and pureness of the ultramarine blue pigment in the actual paint[2] and working with Edouard Adam developed a synthetic binder to maintain the pureness of the pigment's vibrancy. The meaning of Klein's blue in his artistic oeuvre is the representation of the *immaterial*, the *empty*, however, also *the human spirit and mind*. Blue therefore allows viewers to not only fully embrace the artist's image and world but also to bring theirs into the artwork by filling the empty. Both Jarman and Klein seek their own interpretation of the color and its emotional expression but also see it as a window into their world, a window that does

not push the audience into seeing a specific, preproduced image; they use their personal imagination and experiences to create their own visuals. Nevertheless, blue also comes with its traditional associations of serenity, calmness, peacefulness, and its rather obvious connection to the sky and ocean and thus a connection to depth or infinity. These connections cannot be eliminated, as they are the first and most basic associations one has when seeing the color blue. But the interpretation of the artist enriches and widens the obvious initial association and adds further meaning to the color. In Jarman's film, the color blue represents the void of images very much like in Klein's oeuvre, but it also represents death itself, giving it through the color a more positive and hopeful visual. He is concerned in his film with his vanishing vision and he exposes the audience to a very similar experience by denying them the traditional "film." The story, or rather the snippets of thoughts, develop images in the audience's own imagination instead of being satisfied with the artist's "forced" visuals in traditional film. Jarman intensifies this experience by using soundscapes that initiate the visuals, which are then furnished further by the imagination of the audience. This makes it the most personal experience of watching a movie, as the movie happens in one's mind and is different for every audience member; it even changes through time as the images change according to the experiences in one's own life.

The examples of Jarman's film and Klein's use of blue shows how simplicity can have in its most extreme a visual emptiness but still retain a complex intellectual meaning. Simplicity by no means implies just simplifying the image, but it means streamlining the various elements of the image, all of its compositional elements, the story, and its meaning, and guiding all elements towards one goal.

Not everything always has to be shown, though it has to be composed properly and with thought in order to be understood. Simplicity, therefore, isn't about just leaving things out; it is about leaving those elements out that don't contribute to the story (and thus to the artistic direction and the message). Additionally, it includes leaving those elements out that might be very essential to the story but do not increase suspense and the urge of the audience to find out what happens to the characters, their "need to know." By not showing everything, the artist increases the suspense or excitement of the audience. The audience wants to see something but the artist denies them elements to keep them interested. A famous example of this is Ridley Scott's science fiction–horror film *Alien* (1977), where suspense is mainly created by the lack of the monster in the image. The audience knows it's there but is as clueless as to where it lurks as the characters on-screen. Deciding what to leave out and what not to is a decision that can only be made by balancing the story, the art direction, the genre, the budget, and many other aspects.

For artists, on the other hand, simplicity is crucial for not overwhelming the audience with all the possibilities and

---

[2]  The pigments of many colors do lose some of their freshness when mixed with oils or other binders, so Klein, with the help of industrial chemist Edouard Adam, used a binder based on an artificial resin that keeps the glow of the pigment intact, especially the blue pigment of artificial ultramarine.

complexities of the work; it allows artists to concentrate on a few steps instead of many in the production of a piece of art. Simplicity also makes it easier for the audience to follow one story, not many. The problem with simplicity is that it is not very easy to implement—there is often complexity wanted in the design because it might give the image an artistic direction that is unique, new, different, or just fitting. Simplicity, like every other element in filmmaking, has to be balanced with all the aspects involved. An extremely complex story might be better understood if the image were simpler and didn't drag too much attention away from the comprehension of the story, or a simpler story could have complex images to be visually more challenging. But of course this is not a rule; it is a thought that should be checked once in a while so as to not lose sight of the overall project and its comprehensibility. Some images actually need complexity, need a very busy look to convince the audience of their content. For instance, a battle scene seemingly cannot be simple and reduced. However, it can be simplified in its composition, color, or lighting or by not showing it at all and just letting the characters talk about it.
Every design aspect allows simplicity!

## Simplicity and what can be omitted in order to not overwhelm the audience

This is a point that cannot be easily answered, as it depends on the style of the movie, the art direction, the storytelling, etc. Every movie design is an artistic endeavor and thus not really something that can be put into precise rules. The only rule for simplicity that is unshakeable is to omit everything that doesn't support the story itself and the main idea of the film/art piece/ illustration. For some films, this means a reduction of the visuals to the bare essentials (like the Spanish TV show *Pocoyo* by Guillermo Garcia Carsi), and in other films, it means to pack in so much action and information that the audience's eyes are bleeding by the end of the film (*Transformers* or *Pacific Rim*). Both are absolutely valid directions that can be fun and entertaining because they both create emotions, by either overwhelming the senses or stimulating imagination in the viewer to expand the visuals on-screen. What is incomprehensible, however, is when there are so many stories and elements in the image that draw attention, so many aspects of the character's personality that the audience needs to keep track of may lead them to miss what is actually important: the main story line. The result is that the filmmaker loses the audience, who at some point will just click themselves out of the film (exceptions like always apply). In order to keep the audience engaged, one has to reduce the visuals to only that information that assists and/or enhances the happenings of the story. Everything else should be omitted for the sake of understandability or clarity (and even that can be debated … Stanley Kubrick's *2001: A Space Odyssey* [1968] is a film that one barely understands, yet it is of utmost beauty and visual splendor, plus it triggers interpretations in one's mind en masse).

## Objects and information

We are now in a time period in which, once again, 3D viewing of images is popular and there is a notion that the more photorealistically an object is rendered or depicted, the more accurate it is. There is, therefore, the need for clarification of what an image can and cannot convey, what information we get through an image, and what information, even in 3D, is just not there (yet). The common notion is often that the more photorealistic an image is, the more trustworthy and accurate is its content, precisely because it is depicted realistically and looks the way we see it in person. Can we therefore say that a realistically rendered object gives us the most information about that object? The audience usually quickly understands what they are looking at in terms of the setup and the objects themselves (a cup is exactly that: a cup with its properties of color, material, shape, texture, content, lighting …). The audience also understands the story that those objects tell in relationship to each other (a cup with some toast right next to it and a low-placed, specific golden light usually means "breakfast"). The more the image matches our visual perception of how we actually see the world and matches our natural eyesight, the more we trust it as being genuine and accurate, mimicking nature. Therefore we always trust a photograph as the most accurate depiction (of course, knowing that there is forgery and effects in photography, too). We would not doubt a photo, though we would definitely doubt a drawing, as the drawing seems more of an artistic interpretation than the photograph. But is the object in the photograph exactly the same as it is in reality? Of course it is not; it cannot be, as the photo is already an alteration and interpretation of what we would have in the real object actually in front of us. So is there an image, or rather a *representation*, that exactly depicts what the object exists of with all its properties? That representation would have to show all the aspects of an object, show it in its entirety, not just a visual cliché of it. In a photograph we have the object defined by its shape, texture, color, style, volume, lighting situation, size, and location. But this is by no means all the information an object can give us. It is not just what we can see that makes an object what it is; it is also our haptic perception of the piece and the involvement of all our other senses that give us the full range of perception of what we are dealing with. Touching the object tells us something about its weight, its temperature, and how the texture feels. Aside from our haptic perception, for example, the object's history affects the image's content. How the object fits into a time frame, into a style or fashion is a major part of its story. Do we as an audience react to that time because we are personally involved in it, or is it a time frame that has nothing to do with us, because it is way in the distant past? A present-day person drinking from a cheap glass that he or she bought at a supermarket is quite different from the same person drinking from a Roman cage cup, a luxury item in its time in the 4th century AD. The cup itself in this story would change the content of the image

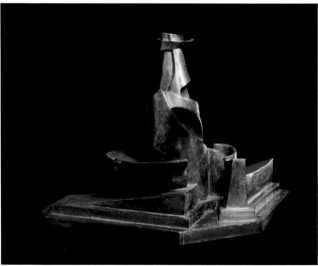

**Figure 2.2**

Alberto Boccioni, *Development of a Bottle in Space* (1913).

**Figure 2.3**

Alberto Boccioni, *Development of a Bottle in Space* (1913).

completely, as the cup comes along with its own historical time frame and value. We are so used to a common photograph and its information that we rarely ask ourselves what else there is to convey to describe an object aside from its visual superficiality. This is especially true nowadays, as 3D animation goes further and further into the photorealistic and even hyperrealistic look. The realistic look, however, is only one of many directions that a style in 3D could actually go in. For example, all surface textures in DreamWorks Animation's feature *Trolls* (2017) mimic the appearance of felt, so all surfaces, even skin, plants, and stones, are covered in felt or made of felt. This makes the entire film feel warm and cozy. We expect touching it must be comfortable and we feel welcome in this world.

Photographs only give a certain amount of information and only a particular kind, which is mostly superficial. They do not tell the viewer anything about the object's smell, taste, temperature, historical context, or its exact proportions from a three-dimensional point of view. There is always only one side of the object visible (if there is no reflection involved), and the inner structure of the object or its skeleton is usually hidden altogether. All that information is just assumed. If a bottle is depicted with a perfectly intact front view, the assumption is that the backside is also intact; however, the image itself does not reveal that information. The viewer makes the assumption that if the image shows the front intact, the back would also be intact. If the damaged part of the bottle were important information, we assume it would be shown in the photograph.

The goal of any picture is to give enough information about its content for the viewer to grasp easily what is depicted. Once we know what it is that we are supposed to be looking at, we

compare it to what we already know about that type of object and then fill in the gaps. When we see freshly baked bread in an image, we don't have to literally smell it to know how delicious its fragrance is. Nevertheless, there are visual possibilities that serve as metaphors for the delicious taste that we cannot (yet) convey as an actual olfactory experience—a bit of steam coming out of the broken bread, for instance. We can also show it with color, design, composition, lighting, texture, motion, and sound and of course good old storytelling with, for instance, the reaction of a person smelling the bread and smiling.

The struggle to broaden the range of the interpretation of the human form and the form of objects has kept artists busy for thousands of years and the 20th century has had its own interpretations. Umberto Boccioni, for instance, was a member of Italian Futurism, which declared in its manifesto in 1910 that the celebration and worship of old art is not only dangerous for the artist but outright destructive for creative output. Futurists celebrated contemporary "sculptures" of airplanes, steamships, and submarines,[3] which in turn had a strong impact on how the human form was seen and artistically interpreted. Boccioni himself wrote a *Technical Manifests of Futurist Sculpture* 2 years later and proclaimed, "The aim of sculpture is the abstract reconstruction of the planes and volumes which determine form, not their figurative value," and, "There can be a reawakening only if we make a sculpture of milieu or environment, because only this way can plasticity be developed, by being extended into space in order to model it. By means of the sculptor's clay, the Futurist

3  *Guido Carlo Argan, Propyläen Kunstgeschichte: Die Kunst des 20. Jahrhunderts,* Propyläen Verlag, Berlin, p. 80.

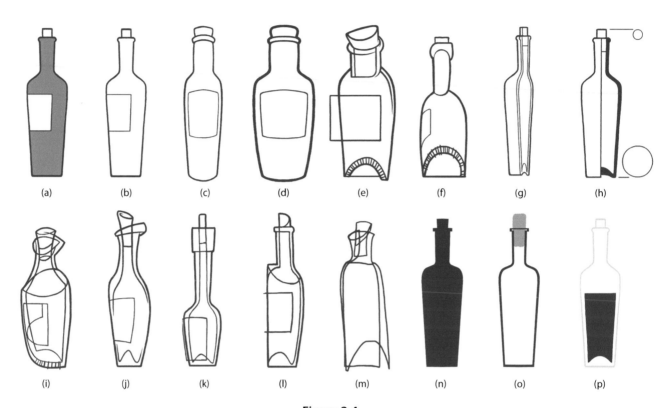

(a)  (b)  (c)  (d)  (e)  (f)  (g)  (h)

(i)  (j)  (k)  (l)  (m)  (n)  (o)  (p)

**Figure 2.4**

today can at last model the atmosphere which surrounds things."[4] For the Futurists, it was not important how an object actually looked realistically; they literally wanted to step away from realistic depictions to develop an artistic expression that was devoid of all art historical baggage, creating a new aesthetic that was based on modern technology and looking forward into the future instead of the past. Boccioni's famous sculpture *Development of a Bottle in Space* (Figures 2.2 and 2.3) is a stunning masterpiece about the three-dimensional interpretation of a bottle and how it relates to the "atmosphere surrounding it." The forms warp and flow, curve and break apart, only to reunite. It has movement and dynamism and, though very personal and subjective, still explains much more to us than the mere image of a bottle. Boccioni visualizes the unseen negative space by integrating it into the positive form of bottle, plate, and table. The object is deconstructed into geometric shards that flow into the surrounding forms of plate and table. The bottle, which is usually so easily defined by its simple silhouette, is broken into complex pieces that communicate with each other, giving birth to a new three-dimensional aesthetic. The information that Boccioni gives us by far exceeds that of a mere "bottle." It contains the entire concept and theory of the Futurist movement

and shows a bottle, a plate, and a surface through a very personal interpretation of the still life. We all know what a bottle looks like, so Boccioni plays with our knowledge and adds to that his vision of the concept "bottle." The breaking apart of the bottle's forms into its different components, its actual development in space is what elevates the whole sculpture to another intellectual level, raises questions, presents a theory rather than just giving us what we'd expect. The bottle is a means to an end to visually dispute sculpture itself, its purpose, three-dimensionality, and spatial expansion from a subjective perspective. But what would be an accurate depiction of a bottle? A photorealistic one or one where the artist expresses emotions and movement? In the lineup of miscellaneous interpretations of the same bottle in a simple line drawing (Figure 2.4a through 2.4p), each version gives us a different kind of information about a bottle. None of them, though, give us all the information required to grasp the bottle in its entirety and with its full range of information.

a. We see the overall shape of the bottle and the fact that there are different materials, interpreted by values. There is also a sticker on the bottle, but we can't see the bottle as an actual three-dimensional form, so we do not know if the sticker wraps around the bottle. We don't know the material, the thickness of the glass walls, the length of the cork, whether the bottle is round, or what is actually inside.

4 Umberto Boccioni, *Manifesto tecnico della scultura futurista*, in Robert L. Herbert (ed.), *Modern Artists on Art*, Dover Publications, Mineola, NY, 2000, p. 50. 1912.

b. This bottle does not show us different materials through value. We don't know that the cork is not part of the glass of the bottle's body.

c. The bulged body and the sticker wrapping around it give us a hint of the bottle being three-dimensional. The more voluptuous cork puts more emphasis on its form. Seeing the bottle in perspective, like a fish-eye lens, makes it very clear that the bottle seems to be dimensional, compared to Figure (a) and (b), in which the bottle could also be two-dimensional and flat.

d. This rather fat bottle suggests either pressure within the bottle or it being fairly heavy. The bottle feels much heavier than the one on its left, Figure (c) (however, a little bit of information about the material and the bottle quickly: it may be light as a feather—perhaps it is made of rubber and is inflatable. The lack of edges and its bulge make it a good example of design for toddlers or little kids, where no part of the actual object could potentially cause harm or injury.

e. This bottle shows a cubist approach: showing its various three-dimensional views in one drawing of the top, bottom, front, back, and side. We can see that the glass wall has thickness and that the bottom is probably round and has a texture on the outer rim. We can also see that the sticker is a rectangle, though we can't see that it wraps around the body.

f. This version shows us that the neck of the bottle is sitting on the body, that the neck has edges and round shapes, and that the sticker is actually wrapping around the bottle, but we can't really see the actual shape of it, which is so very clear in drawing e.

g. The bottle cut in half shows us that it is empty and that the cork neither stops right away nor goes all the way to the bottom. It shows that the bottom part is warped inwards and that the wall has various thicknesses. But we can't say for sure if the bottle is cut for clarification and demonstration purposes or if it actually looks like that.

h. This version is an archeological drawing, showing all of the information required to understand the three-dimensional form of the bottle, inside and outside. We know the shape, the thickness of the wall on every part, the bulge on the bottom, the size of the cork, the size of the bottom, that the bottle is actually round, that there is an outer wall and an inner emptiness. But we can't see the sticker and still don't know the material.

i. This drawing is a version that plays with the transparency of the bottle and has a personal approach in its actual shape. It gives us information about the bottle's transparency, its roundness (though not in its actual perfect form), it having a cork and the length of that cork, the sticker somehow wrapping around the body, and the texture on the bottom of the bottle.

j. Here we have a similar content like in image i. The bottle's shape is not realistic but is an interpretation. We have information about its transparency, the bottom part being warped, the neck having a thicker wall. We don't know

the actual size of the bottle, nor the size of the cork or the texture on the bottom.

k. This version puts emphasis on the neck more than on the body. The size relationship between body and neck makes this part of the bottle seem more important.

l. Drawing l explains to us the roundness and also edginess of the body. But we don't know exactly what the bottle's silhouette or shape looks like. It is rather the feeling of the little edge on the bottle's shoulder that is important, that is, exaggerated on the left.

m. This drawing was done in one continuous, uninterrupted line. There is much information missing, though it gives us the emotions and the "moment" the artist drew this image. It is not just about the bottle but also about the artist drawing the bottle and infusing it with his or her emotions during the drawing process.

n. The silhouette lacks much information and we don't really know if it is a bottle or not. It could also be a man in a long coat with a small head and hat.

o. This version gives us a hint about the density of the material: the smooth darker body of the bottle feels more solid, whereas the more organic cork feels softer and lighter, as the corners are rounded and the color muted. There is no clue about it being three-dimensional or empty, round, or what the bottom looks like.

p. Drawing p does not really focus on the bottle itself but its content.

# The inside of things

Every object consists of the design elements of shape and form, texture, size, and color, which all define the surface of the object, its outer appearance. But there is also the inside. This "skeleton" is as important for the object as its surface, as one does not exist without the other. A teapot is not just a heavy object made of porcelain but has a hollow body that is dark and cave-like, and its negative space is actually the whole purpose of the pot. The inside wall is covered in dark tea stains or is clean and shining white. While designing an object or drawing it, feeling the entire object with its inside *and* outside means grasping it completely and as a whole, understanding it as the object it is, not merely as a superficial cliché. This allows us to see the object in its entirety.

Considering the inside is even more important when drawing the human body, or any kind of body really, and paying attention to the outside, the skin, and forms only provides us with half of the information if the anatomy and the resulting weight distribution are not fully understood and taken into consideration (see Volume 2 of this book). The surface of skin and hair is only a small piece of the full scale of information that the figure-drawing model gives us and that one can see with a trained eye.

Knowledge of hip–shoulder movement or contrapposto, the position of the muscles and joints, fat distribution, and the spatial expansion of the body's forms in relationship with the happenings underneath is what will lead to a successful and solid drawing of the human body. This is true with everything we draw and design: we need to fully grasp the object, from the outside and the inside. Both are equally important, as without the inside the outside would be a mere shell!

Being able to dissect what we draw into its various elements helps us to first of all understand the object foremost in its physicality but also its personality. For instance, what is the difference between two teapots that look alike from the outside but whose insides differ, one being dark and dirty and the other clean and white? How can one show the inside on the outside? How do we feel about the one compared to the other? This emotion about the inside of the object needs to be incorporated into the drawing or design; it might not necessarily be clearly visible, but it will be hopefully felt by the audience, if the artist recognizes it in the first place and makes it an important point during the drawing process, the composition, and the overall information given in the entire final drawing. For instance, the teapot that is dirty could be half covered in shadow, could have a slightly different color, or could be closer to some dirt on the table. A building that is drawn and rendered is much more convincing when the artist knows what is actually in that building, what the purpose of it is, even if the outside does not necessarily reveal its purpose. But the subtle choices and interpretations of shapes and forms, colors and textures, the artistic "adjustment" of the visuals towards the very purpose is what might reveal the building's interior use to the viewer. An artist who just draws or designs "a building" isn't involved emotionally, whereas one who designs the same building with the interior in mind, its corridors, meeting rooms, plain storage facilities, cafeteria, and boring gray bathrooms, will incorporate his or her emotions into the exterior of the building and thus (hopefully) design visuals that are more expressive. Always feel the object and the characters you are drawing, be in the drawing!

# CHAPTER 3

# The Frame

To understand what a frame is and how it affects the image, we first have to define what an image actually is. An image can be a photograph, drawing, painting, or computer-generated visual that appeals to the visual sense of and evokes emotions in the viewer. It is either an exact rendition of an actual object, person, or environment or an artistic interpretation of it. Images are usually presented as a window into another space. The viewer looks onto a two-dimensional plane (even three-dimensional images are still obviously on a two-dimensional plane) that pretends to be what it is not: an additional reality, either flat, two-dimensional, or three-dimensional. To separate our reality from the artificial one, images have a defined border, which is usually geometric in shape with a very clear and accurate outline, which is the frame. The frame makes it very obvious to the viewer what is within this fake reality and what is not. Convention has defined the frame as being usually of a square shape, though any other shape is of course possible. A frame can be an actual frame of wood, metal, or plastic or a simple outline around an image and therefore visible as such, or it can be completely invisible if the frame is only defined by the border of the image. Figures 3.1 through 3.3 show the same visual, each with a different frame, and one can see the impact of the frame on its content. The image without a visible frame (Figure 3.1) still has the white paper surrounding it, which acts as its frame or rather as an opening into the other reality. White, which is less heavy in visual weight than black, lightens up the colors and makes the image seem to have less contrast and also makes the colors in the image feel slightly less vibrant. The white fights with the highlights of the image. The image with a black frame (Figure 3.2) feels very solid on the page, has more visual weight to it. The colors in the image seem more vibrant and have slightly more contrast because of the heavy black surrounding (though if an image lacks contrast, it can appear very pale

**Figure 3.1**

**Figure 3.2**

**Figure 3.3**

DOI: 10.1201/b22148-3

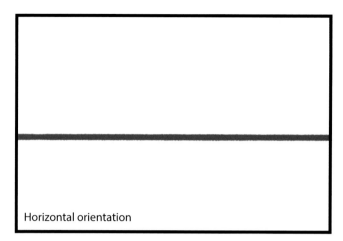

**Figure 3.4**

**Figure 3.5**

Giza, Egypt.

with the black around it). The heavy golden frame (Figure 3.3) also changes the colors, as the color of the frame will affect the colors in the painting. But with the frame being that heavy and wide and also golden, the presence of the frame itself, being precious and seemingly worth looking at, pushes itself into the foreground and takes away some of the importance of the image itself. The golden, overly decorative frame relates the picture to museum pieces, old castles, or even gaudy displays of kitsch. The frame always brings its own attributes and hidden agenda into the picture and affects its meaning, content, and importance. Whether the frame is white, black, colored, heavy and golden, or there is no frame at all, there is no neutral depiction of any image; there logically cannot be, since everything surrounding the image will affect its content. The physical space in which an image is viewed—for example, a museum, lobby, magazine, TV screen at home, or cinema screen in a movie theatre—has an effect on the viewer; there is no picture that stands on its own without being affected by its mode of presentation. The surrounding space will affect it. A museum will add to the image's value due to the often dignified atmosphere and the fact that most paintings/artwork in museums are precious, whereas the same picture displayed on a computer screen has a contemporary bias to it. There is no neutral depiction where the image alone expresses itself and presents its content without being affected by its mode of presentation.

For cinematic work, the most appropriate version would be a black frame, as movies are watched (well, actually, have been watched) mostly in dark theatres, where the screen's surroundings and black curtains act as the black frame. Thumbnail paintings in visual development are very often surrounded by a thick, black frame, which makes the colors appear more vibrant due to the strong contrast between the black and the content of the image; however, the best presentation always depends on the content.

Every picture needs space to breathe and to be able to define its own space without being crushed by another picture, texture, or object right next to it. The content and composition of a picture requires neutral space or a defined area in which it can unfold its design and compositional purpose. If there are two pictures too

close to each other, both compositions melt together, creating one joint composition. The more space there is between two pictures, the less their content associates with and affects each other's composition. Valid evidence of this is shown in Figures 3.7 and 3.8. Though not too close together, the vertical line in Figure 3.7 is elongated into Figure 3.8 and separates the two pillars from each other.

There is no composition that can deny the existence and effect that the frame has. There is no image without a frame, as the image *per se* serves as a deviation from our world and provides a glimpse into another reality. Even misshapen frames are still frames and come with their own compositional impact. The proposition of American pop artist Frank Stella's geometrically shaped frames, which deviated from the traditional square shape, shows how strongly those misshapen frames affect their content. An image without a frame would be the projection of characters and objects into our reality. This has started to happen in applications for phones where the image is projected over the environment. But even in those cases, the phone or tablet serves as a framing device. It'll take a while before the projection is frameless and works without the help of a screen. So for now the frame is still an integral part of the image!

## Horizontal orientation

When the horizontal sides of the frame are longer than the verticals, we have a horizontal orientation (Figures 3.4 and 3.5).

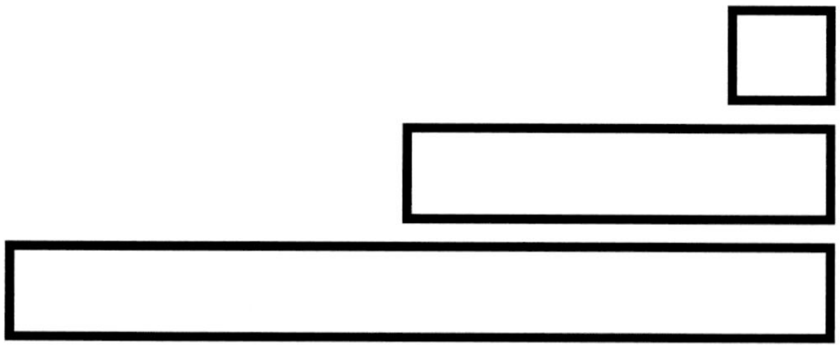

**Figure 3.6**

The longer sides of the image dominate the reading direction and force the eye to follow its direction left and right. Therefore, a horizontal orientation makes our gaze move along the horizontal lines rather than the vertical ones. The short sides, being subordinate to the long ones, often do not contain enough visual strength for the eye to explore this horizontal image vertically. The less the two sides vary in length, the less the eye is forced into a direction (Figure 3.6). The longer the image horizontally, the more intense is its power for the eye to pan across. The most stable picture in terms of vertical and horizontal equality would obviously be the square. The horizontal orientation lends itself to broad vistas and landscapes (Figure 3.5) and has a storytelling quality to it, since its orientation guides the viewer from one point to the next and so on. We feel that we can literally "go places." For example, look at Zhang Zeduan's (1085–1145) stunning scroll *Along the River during the Qingming Festival.*

## Vertical orientation

The vertical image has longer vertical frame sides than horizontal ones and is less prone to storytelling but more to heights and intimate situations compared to the horizontal image (Figures 3.7 and 3.8). Buildings, trees, and standing people are all accentuated by the vertical orientation, which also gives less space for us to move around (we can easily walk horizontally but

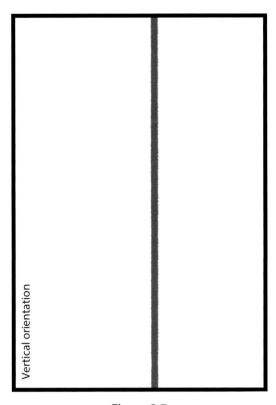

Vertical orientation

**Figure 3.7**

**Figure 3.8**

Luxor, Egypt.

**Figure 3.9**

Outside Dubai, United Arab Emirates.

cannot easily go up or down); it limits the visual freedom left and right but opens up the vertical space either up or down.

In an image with a vertical orientation but horizontal content (Figure 3.9), the image clearly restricts the eye from wandering left and right but forces the eye in this case towards the sun in the distance. However, the eye is capable of leaving the restrictions of the frame, as we know that the desert expands beyond the frame and obviously does not just stop there.

## Tilted horizon

When it comes to the horizon line, there are two possibilities: either the horizon is parallel to the lower frame or not. Being parallel to the frame gives the image stability and balance, as it is the typical perspective we have, which in turn makes us feel comfortable and safe (Figures 3.10 and 3.11). This is the natural state of experiencing the world around us: the horizon is always horizontal.

Once the horizon starts to tilt (Figures 3.12 and 3.13), the balance shifts and the image gains in tension, which can either be exciting or uncomfortable. We want the horizon to be horizontal

and our mind expects the image to be in balance. The dynamic that is created by the tilt is often used in commercials, music videos, and action sequences as the image gains in tension and helps the content to feel more exciting.

## Magnetism of the frame

As the frame affects the image, the content of the image is also affected by its position within the frame.

The frame consists of four sides within which the image is inscribed. Each position within the frame has its own compositional and emotional value. The most neutral position in the frame is the center, as the object, in the case of Figure 3.14a a blue dot, has the same distance towards each side of the frame (Figure 3.14b). Two objects that are close to each other develop a relationship. The closer the objects are, the stronger their attraction and connection is. The frame can be seen as an object that is in contact with its content, the blue dot. In Figure 3.14a, the attraction between frame and dot is very low, as the distance is the same in every direction and therefore the forces that act on the dot are very low. Once we move the dot left or right and the distance towards one side of the frame is reduced, the

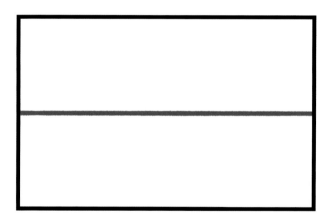

Figure 3.10

Figure 3.11

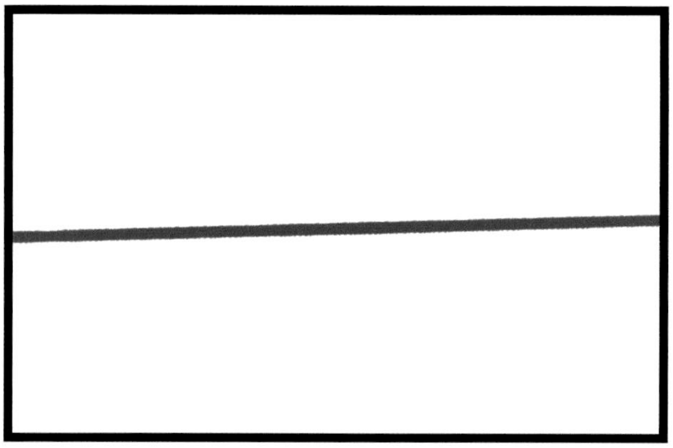

Figure 3.12

Figure 3.13

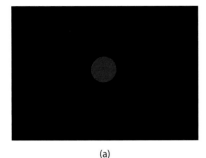

(a)

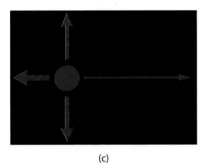

(b)

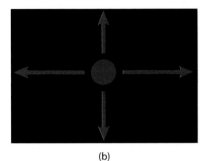

(c)

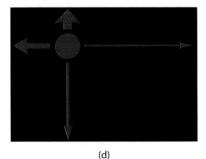

(d)

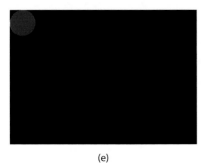

(e)

**Figure 3.14**

former neutral attraction starts to shift—that is, the shorter the distance, the stronger the attraction. In Figure 3.14c, the left side of the frame is gaining force while the right side is losing it. In Figure 3.14d, the upper side of the frame has the strongest drag toward the dot. This attraction is called the "magnetism of the frame," as the frame seemingly tries to drag the dot toward itself. In Figure 3.14e, the dot is in the corner, which is the position with the highest force, as the drag is coming from two sides, the upper side and the left side of the frame. The magnetism of the frame and the position of the object also affect the "movement" of the object in the frame. For instance, looking at the hot air balloon in Figures 3.15 and 3.16, debate about which balloon seems to go up and which one down. In the still image, there is a tendency of the balloon in the picture closer to the upper frame to move upward (Figure 3.16) and vice versa (of course this can always be overwritten by a contradicting story!).

It is recommended to not place objects or characters too close to the frame, as this not only causes the object to seemingly be dragged toward the frame but also starts to affect the depth of the image if the object touches the frame (also see the section "Overlap and Perspective" in Chapter 16). As mentioned above, the frame serves as a window into the scene that is depicted. Once anything in that image touches the frame, the idea of the window being an opening into the world behind the frame is destroyed. The viewer is not able anymore to see the world behind the frame as a separate dimensional universe but on the contrary sees it as a flat continuation of the frame itself. Avoid this happening and always either place objects and characters a little bit away from the frame or just let the frame cut into the object. Make a clear distinction between the frame and its content!

How strongly the magnetism of the frame can increase the forces within the frame is shown by Winslow Homer's painting *Northeaster* from 1895 (Figure 3.17). Homer, one of the most famous and prolific American painters of the 19th century, shows us simply a wave with its natural force and might breaking into the rocks on a beach. The wave coming in from left to right is cut off by a large rock that is placed on the bottom left, stretching toward the right. This movement of the rock forces our eyes towards the bottom right, which, being the corner of the frame and therefore already having a drag toward the outside of the frame, strongly drags the wave to the right (remember that the corner has the strongest forces in the frame). Additionally, we have the big white spindrift of the wave. Its shape also points toward the bottom right. Homer uses both the composition and the magnetism of the frame (or the corner as a compositional element) with purpose, to let us feel the power of the wave even more.

**Figure 3.15**

**Figure 3.16**

**Figure 3.17**

Winslow Homer, *Northeaster* (1895).

# Creating different frame shapes

Because there is a horizontal or vertical frame does not necessarily mean that we are stuck with a composition that only serves those horizontal or vertical orientations. The image of the Temple of Heaven in Beijing (Figure 3.18) gives us a composition within a composition. While covering up parts of the image with an arched entry, its unique shape creates a different frame for the temple and also shifts the focal point into the corner.

Film images are horizontal; there is nothing one can do about it. Getting used to composing for the horizontal frame is therefore an unavoidable necessity. But the horizontal orientation does not force us into strictly using horizontal compositions; we can still have a vertical orientation within the horizontal frame. By blocking parts of the screen with objects or architecture, we create a frame within a frame (Figure 3.19). This allows us to focus on one area within the frame. The blocks that create the inner frame can be any kind of object, architecture, fauna, character, color, or light and shadow.

In Andrew Dominick's beautifully shot feature *The Assassination of Jesse James by the Coward Robert Ford* (2007), the cinematography is done by Roger Deakins. He creates frames that follow the visuals of late 19th century photography, sometimes with distorting lenses creating stunning effects. The camera glancing through opening doors (Figure 3.20) reveals intimate and private moments that increase the distance between characters and audience.

**Figure 3.18**

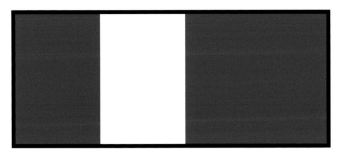

**Figure 3.19**

**Figure 3.20**

*The Assassination of Jesse James by the Coward Robert Ford* (2007).

**Figure 3.21**

*My Fair Lady* (1964).

**Figure 3.22**

*Citizen Kane* (1941).

The screenshot of George Cukor's *My Fair Lady* (1964) in Figure 3.21 shows another example of turning a horizontal frame into a vertical one. The cinematographer Harry Stradling accentuates the height of the character by placing flowers left and right of the frame and thus placing him in a vertical composition within the horizontal wide-screen frame. The blurriness of the flowers immediately forces the eye to the middle of the frame where the focus and the action are, and also comments on this scene's love song. Both compositions, Stradling's and Deakin's, divide the frame into three parts, where the focus is on the middle section.

An even more complex approach is seen in Orson Wells' *Citizen Kane* (1941) (Figure 3.22). In this shot, Kane's parents sign the contract that will change his life, and Kane himself, as a young boy, is playing all the way in the background in the snow. He is framed by the window in the center and therefore is visually emphasized in the shot. Additionally, he is surrounded by the people who are responsible for changing his life. This juxtaposition of the two actions allows storytelling on two different levels and continuously makes connections between the two groups. The seemingly insignificant boy becomes the center of the story!

# Vignetting images

Another way of manipulating the shape of the cinematic frame is *vignetting*, which happens either in the composition on set, in the camera by choice of a specific lens, or in postproduction. Vignetting emphasizes the focal point by reducing the outer areas in brightness, contrast, saturation, or focus (crispness). An image that gets darker closer to the frame and brighter closer to the center and/or focal point will naturally drag the eye towards the brighter areas. Our eye is by default drawn to the brightest, the most saturated, and the crispest areas. Vignetting is an additional tool for enhancing the focal point, though it should be used with care to not overdo it, as it then can easily look forced, especially if it is just a digital effect. Done with subtlety and care, it has a very powerful effect and gives the image the strength to draw the viewer in. This effect is not only a directional help for the eye but also a stylistic decision that evokes, for example, historical references to the beginning of photography and movie-making. In the aforementioned feature, *The Assassination of Jesse James by the Coward Robert Ford*, the cinematographer Roger Deakins uses heavy blur effects to give the feel and look of an old photograph. This in-camera effect is achieved with old wide-angle lenses mounted on the front of ARRI Macro lenses.[1] It reduces the importance of the unfocused areas in the image and allows us to step into the emotional

---

1  Interview by Stephen Pizzello and Jean Oppenheimer, *Roger Deakins, ASC, BSC explores the existential perils of the American West in The Assassination of Jesse James by the Coward Robert Ford and No Country for Old Men*, The American Society of Cinematographers, 2007. http://www.theasc.com/ac_magazine/October2007/QAWithDeakins/page1.php (accessed August 25, 2017).

**Figure 3.23**

*The Assassination of Jesse James by the Coward Robert Ford* (2007).

**Figure 3.24**

*The Assassination of Jesse James by the Coward Robert Ford* (2007).

state of the character in focus (Figures 3.23 and 3.24). The image distortion in the feature produces the dreamlike atmosphere of a bygone era when cameras were in their infancy. One is visually continuously tricked throughout the film into believing that what is being watched is not a modern-day recreation but an actual glimpse into the past. In some shots during the film, the image quality is blurry to the extreme, taking the characters out of the film reality and allowing them to enter a state of distance, surrealism, and a time gone by. The image turns from a merely storytelling vehicle to a level of pure visual emotion assisted by a melancholic musical score. Vignetting images can be a strong tool if used with a purpose that is not just the aesthetics alone.

## The round frame

As mentioned before, the shape of the frame has a major effect on the composition. The most common and practical frame shape

is a square or rectangle. A round (or oval) image is less common and has a very special position in art. In cinema, it has absolutely no impact, though for the sake of completeness it should be discussed. It is more difficult to compose images for a round frame, as much of what we are surrounded by is horizontal or vertical in its main orientation (architecture, standing people, trees …). In a round composition, the vectors, directions, and poses have to be inscribed into the round frame to not create a discrepancy between the two. As mentioned before, the frame is a window into another reality, though just opening up the frame toward a scene behind it that follows a strictly horizontal or vertical composition could be awkward (if it is not done on purpose). The compositional elements would probably go against the flow of the frame.

The two paintings from Michelangelo Buonarroti (1475–1564) and Sandro Botticelli (1445–1510) show two different solutions for composition within a round frame. Botticelli's *Madonna of the Magnificat* (1481) (Figure 3.25) meticulously succumbs to

**Figure 3.25**

Sandro Botticelli, *Madonna of the Magnificat* (1481).

**Figure 3.26**

Michelangelo Buonarroti, *Doni Tondo* (~1507).

the frame's shape and presents a composition in which every character and compositional element follows a concentric arrangement. On the other hand, Michelangelo's *Doni Tondo* (~1507) (Figure 3.26) has, aside from the triangular head positions of the holy family, the family inscribed in an oval, which leaves space left and right of the family. Michelangelo populates those spaces with nude young men and creates a foreground and background interaction, where the eye shifts between the two. Botticelli has the characters arranged outside the center and the background appears within the group, thus accentuating the painting's roundness, exactly the opposite of the *Doni Tondo*.

Film does not use the round frame as the actual shape of the screen, but it uses it as a frame within a frame. In early cinema, the round "frame" or better the dividing line between the round image shape and the surrounding black passe-partout was actually often used to focus on a certain action, emphasizing it for better understanding. It was also employed for either opening and closing the shutter of the lens to signify the end or beginning of a new scene or the beginning or ending of the film, called an "iris." The first artistic use of the round image can be seen in George Albert Smith's *As Seen through a Telescope* (1900), where the view through a telescope is simulated by a black mask mount in front of the camera to create a round frame. These early explorations were creatively developing film language and starting to firmly explore the possibilities of the new medium of film. The first film to actually use the round shape for its own strength, not as a cutting device (iris) or simulation of a telescope or microscope, was Marcel Duchamp's *Anemic Cinema* (1926), a Dadaist experimental film that uses spinning round plates with spiral designs and text to create a mesmerizing effect of three-dimensionality and a pre-op-art dizzying effect. In animation, the round frame is not much used, though there are some noteworthy films that use a round composition. First of all, it is the work of James Whitney (1921–1982) whose abstract works *Yantra* (1950–1957) and *Lapis* (1963–1966) are "the most widely known and admired of any abstract film(s)."[2] Whitney refers in his visuals to the mantra and the intoxicating allure of its central composition. The calm of the concentric movement and the ongoing change of pattern follow the complexity of mantras. The movement never reaches a goal, but the images are beautiful yet fleeting moments in time. The animation is very much based on a concentric composition and the technically necessary rectangular shape of the film image steps into the background. One dives into a vortex of colors, movement, and spirituality that invites deep and profound contemplation. A feature film that uses a rotund in its entire introduction is Richard Williams' *The Thief and the Cobbler* (1964–1993). The round frame shows a flight over the desert, reaching the Golden City and gliding through stylized clouds. The animation refers to the frame shape

in its movement and never loses sight of its roundness. Williams' introduction is a very unique piece of animation.

# The rectangular frame and its forces

The frame and its shape will always affect the content of the image, and the four sides of the rectangular frame are too strong in their visual forces to not be recognized by the eye and integrated into the composition. The horizontal bottom and top parts of the frame parallel the horizon line; the vertical sides always strengthen the gravitational forces in the image or the lack thereof. Therefore, we have four forces acting on the image: two horizontal and two vertical.

An example of a composition integrating the predetermined rectangular forces of the frame is Michelangelo Merisi da Caravaggio's (1574–1610) painting *David and Goliath* (1599) (Figure 3.27). The young boy David is shown over the corpse of his enemy Goliath, the giant Philistine warrior, on whose enormous shoulders and back David is kneeling. The severed head of Goliath is staring at us nearly in disbelief with the deadly mark of David's slingshot on the forehead responsible for the untimely death of the warrior. The small victorious boy is fastening a rope around Goliath's hair to carry away the severed head. The scene, despite its violent and brutal action,

**Figure 3.27**

Michelangelo Merisi (Caravaggio): *David and Goliath* (1599).

2  William Moritz, *James Whitney's Yantra and Lapis*, 1977. http://www. centerforvisualmusic.org/WMyantra.htm (accessed April 6, 2015).

**Figure 3.28**    **Figure 3.29**    **Figure 3.30**

**Figure 3.31**    **Figure 3.32**

is very intimate and David is not shown as the victorious and proud hero who slew the giant but rather as someone who had to fulfill a task out of necessity. The intimacy of the scene derives from the composition and the lighting, which gives us permission to look into a private box, a moment that is personal and just between David and his victim. David's head is covered nearly fully in shadow and we can only slightly see his sincere expression, lacking the triumph one would expect. The pose of David's body repeats three sides of the frame (Figure 3.28) and the right vertical side is the connection between David's and Goliath's heads. The leg, spine, and arm of David and the shoulder of Goliath mimic the frame's geometry. While the leg, arm, and back reflect the three sides of the frame, David's eyes are directly above the eyes of Goliath, establishing a strong connection between the two (Figure 3.29). The giant's head is

obviously much bigger than David's, which is surrounded by empty space. This breathing space allows the serenity of the image to develop and puts David into a calm and soothing space yet pushes the view toward the lower right, where the locks and the facial expression of Goliath create drama and a sense of uneasiness. Contemplation and death seem to emanate from the darkness of the background. David's left arm and leg are moving slightly toward the right, serving as vectors into the giant's head (Figure 3.30). Both heads are positioned in the corners; however, David's much smaller head is further away from the frame, allowing his head to be right above the severed head in the lower right corner. Goliath's head is also exposed to the magnetic forces of the frame. The tilt of it follows the diagonal of the frame, connecting David's right forearm with Goliath's head, especially the bleeding wound on his forehead (Figure 3.31).

Both characters are themselves inscribed in their pose into a square, not only repeating the frame shape but also referring to each other (Figure 3.32). The frame gives us a strictly confined space that the characters are nearly fully inscribed in. The giant's shoulders and head are inscribed in a rectangle of their own, making a distinct separation between him and David, between the living and the dead, the victor and the loser. Caravaggio gives us a composition that very much uses the frame with its predestined forces as the basis for the box the scene is placed in. The frame continuously communicates with the composition and the story.

## Open and closed frame

Open and closed frames are two different options for setting up the composition (mainly in film) in terms of what the image contains or reveals in relationship to the story. In the open frame, only small parts of the whole setting are revealed, which withhold information from the viewer. We concentrate on details that usually raise questions like, where are we? who is this? when is it? The closed frame, on the other hand, contains all the information that is needed to understand the image in its story. Nothing is hidden, all is revealed within the frame, which then answers the questions of where we are, who is in the set, or when the story takes place. Using both open and closed frames helps to create tension in a scene, illustration, drawing, or painting by keeping the audience informed and also entertained with suspense and active questioning.

### Open frame:

- Does not show the whole picture but provides only pieces and snippets of the location, characters, objects …
- Reveals information only bit by bit and thus keeps the audience guessing.
- Raises questions.
- Creates a location that is claustrophobic if not opened up by wide shots or following explanations.
- Can be more personal and intimate.
- Can create the idea of *pars pro toto* ("one part for the whole"): a crowd scene, for example, can be shown convincingly by only revealing part of the crowd that fills the whole frame and then extending the on-screen and offscreen space with sound of a large crowd.

### Closed frame:

- Is self-contained, as all the information to understand the shot or image is within the boundaries of the frame.
- The audience is informed about the goings-on in the image.
- Gives answers because it reveals the whole situation (though of course a closed frame can also function as a question as much as an open frame can be an answer).
- Opens up the claustrophobic and restricting space created by open frames.

- Objects that are cutoff by the frame in a closed frame extend the space even further as the audience assumes that the space is wider than the space the frame reveals (with cut-off foreground, middle ground, and background elements).

In film, once a closed frame reveals the action and setting and the audience knows what is happening in the shot, a cut to an open frame wouldn't have the same impact anymore. The audience already knows the answer. An open frame has the most impact at the beginning of a scene when the audience is still orienting themselves in the location and trying to figure out the story line of that specific shot or scene.

In the beginning of the famous scene from Steven Spielberg's *Jurassic Park* (1993) in which the *Tyrannosaurus rex* is approaching the stuck car in front of its enclosure, the offscreen space is what creates the suspense, as the *T. rex* is only heard but not seen. The water moving in the glasses, the reaction of the characters to goings-on outside the frame, the goat leg falling on top of the car—all the open frames in the scene are suggesting that there is something offscreen that the audience, as much as the characters, cannot see as of yet. This creates a claustrophobic feel, accentuated by the darkness, and also extends the intimate and safe situation in the cars to a dangerous world "out there." The open frame with the glasses on the dashboard keeps the audience guessing about what is out there. Well, not really "guessing," as we all know that they stopped in front of the *T. rex* enclosure, but we want to finally *see* the dinosaur! The closed frame later on answers that question by showing the *T. rex* standing next to the car. Suspense can be accentuated by question and answer and open and closed framing. Open and closed frames raise and answer questions, respectively. Nevertheless, of course that does not mean that an open frame cannot answer a question, nor that a closed one can never raise a question. They have a tendency to do so, but the final assessment of their effect is always connected to the imbedded story line, not solely the composition.

## On-screen and offscreen space in film

The film screen not only offers the space that is visually present in the image but can also refer to the space outside of the screen, which is invisible to the audience. This offscreen space is as important as what is actually seen on-screen and has a direct influence on the story and its suspense. Likewise, it underlines the mood of the scene: the image of a flower with the full sound of a big forest that is unseen on-screen is much more impressive than without. If the scene only shows the small space on-screen and the various shots are all medium close-ups and close-ups, the audience feels cornered and slowly claustrophobic. Offscreen space is, therefore, important to prevent spatial tightness. The audience needs some (imaginary) space to feel comfortable and the scene at some point needs to provide "breathing space." The lack of space and the creative use of this claustrophobia is a tool for horror films, where the restricted space heightens suspense. It is not just the offscreen space itself that is important but also the presence of beings in that unseen space, for instance, the alien in Ridley Scott's feature *Alien* (1979), that most often can't be seen but we know it is there. The rise of computer imagery does make it much easier to show the monster in its full glory and forces the audience to look at the dangerous beast. This takes away suspense but satisfies the human urge of curiosity.

# Offscreen space, suspense, and expectations

The frame is the window that allows us to view, observe, watch, and be emotionally involved in the story that goes on behind it. It seems simple enough: what is shown in the frame can be seen and affects the story; what is outside of the frame is invisible to the eye. But does the outside space that is beyond the frame equally affect the story? The space in an image consists of three parts: the on-screen space, which is restricted by the frame; the frame itself; and the offscreen space outside of the frame. Each part influences the other and cannot be seen as an individual and separate element. All three affect the story that is being told.

Imagine a shot of a desert with a thirsty woman walking on a sand dune. Obviously we know about a desert's vastness and know that there is a world beyond what we can see. We know that the sand dune is only one of many. The frame restricts the view and only allows a glimpse into the other world, but our knowledge widens that space: that there is more sand and more sky outside of the frame is logical. However, the story and its emotions depend on what is actually shown in the frame and what isn't, because both affect the imagination and also the expectation of what will happen next.

- If the camera pans in a very wide shot along the empty desert, we would expect the woman to be all by herself, because we can see a wide range of space and there is no rescue in sight; ergo she is alone.
- The second example of the same story point is a close-up: the emphasis lies now on the thirsty woman and not on the desert with its immense scale. If the camera only shows the woman in a medium shot, we concentrate more on her suffering and her possible slow demise than the actual desert, causing it to be a more intimate shot. In the close-up, the offscreen space would be secondary and smaller in its impact, though of course still in the mind of the audience. If the story has established beforehand that she is in a desert, the audience will constantly remember the location and her dangerous, deadly situation. If we do not know that she is in fact in a desert, then the close-up creates suspense indeed: we would not know where she is or if there is actually someone right next to her, outside of the frame.
- The third example follows her from dune to dune. The audience would hope as much as the thirsty woman that

behind each dune could possibly be rescue. The slow revelation of space behind each dune keeps us hoping, and suspense and tensions are high. The camera just stays at a close distance to her and follows her over each sand dune in the hope of finding water. The audience is kept as clueless as the woman. The offscreen space in this example therefore creates anticipation and excitement, whereas the pullback, wide shot, and pan would give confirmation of there being most probably no rescue (all of this can obviously change and be manipulated with a different set of shots or an outcome that is already known).

**Offscreen Space Can Be Defined by:**

1. Music and sound
2. Verbal or visual reference to offscreen spaces
3. Significant light source coming from offscreen
4. Establishing shot carrying its space through the scenes
5. Camera pan that is expected to be able to go on
6. Objects that are cut off by the frame

## 1. Music and sound[3]

Sound is a strong and independent agent and a very important indicator for offscreen space. Sound alone widens space, even without any visuals at all, like we saw in Derek Jarman's feature *Blue* (1993; Chapter 2, the section "Simplicity"), which has no images other than an ultramarine blue screen accompanied by a soundtrack. Sound elevates an image from a flat two-dimensional plane into a three-dimensional space. The two possibilities for sound in film are *diegetic* and *nondiegetic* sound. Diegetic sound is the sound that derives from the depicted location itself. Nondiegetic sound is an audible overlay over the reality on-screen (added music, voice-over, audio commentary).

On-screen sound adds realism and believability to the set. Offscreen sound does the same, though it widens the space. We don't have to see an airplane flying overhead; we only need to hear it to know that it is there. Just the sound of a bird and some wind in the leaves adds so much more space to the picture of a forest that we feel we are actually there. Just a bit of white city noise in the "background" and the restricted box of the frame is broken, letting the imagination widen the space drastically. Does nondiegetic sound increase the offscreen space? It depends on the content of the nondiegetic sound. If I see an image of a woman sitting on the lawn in a close-up and hear the soundtrack of the song "If You Are Going to San Francisco," then my imagination is already in San Francisco and images

---

3  Also see Chapter 19, "Music and Sound."

of the city flush into my head, adding space to the shot. In this case, the nondiegetic sound would evoke a bigger space in my imagination, which might reflect what the woman on that lawn is thinking about. But it additionally affects the space on-screen negatively, as it can reduce the space even more if she feels trapped in her current situation.

Sound is, like all the other elements that can be used to design a shot, strongly connected to the story and cannot really be seen independently from it.

## 2. Verbal or visual reference to offscreen spaces

Offscreen space can be suggested through characters and their relationship with happenings outside the frame: glances, conversation with unseen others, memories and events that are talked about, phone calls, pictures of other places—all refer to a world beyond the frame.

## 3. Significant light source coming from the offscreen space

We see a man at night walking through a dark alley. The light beam of a flashlight falls onto him and we immediately know that there is another person outside of the frame. The offscreen space, and with it the other person, is established through the flashlight.

## 4. Establishing shot carrying its space through the scene

The establishing shot introduces the available space in the beginning of the scene. This initial open space is then carried on unseen throughout the scene, but its presence is still felt and remembered by the audience. The space of the establishing shot lives on in the memory and imagination and can widen the on-screen space immensely. In long scenes, the offscreen space might have to be referred to again to not be forgotten.

## 5. Camera pan that is expected to be able to go on

A camera pan reveals offscreen space and can allow it to grow further, as the mind of the audience expects the revealed space to continue once the pan has stopped on-screen. It suggests that the shown pan is only a segment of the actual space surrounding the character.

## 6. Objects that are cut off by the frame

Cut objects also extend on-screen space. A table that is only half visible on-screen does not just end at the frame but obviously continues outside of the frame, which indicates that the space is bigger than what is seen on-screen.

# Case study: On- and offscreen space in Koji Yamamura's short film *Atama Yama* (2002)

*Atama Yama*, an animated short film by Japanese animator Koji Yamamura, is the surreal and grotesque story of a stingy man's head sprouting a cherry tree. The tree grows into a kind of bonsai tree on his bald head and people start gathering around the tree in cherry blossom season to celebrate, drink, and smoke. The man is getting seriously aggravated and rips out the tree, only to reveal a water hole that people use for swimming and bathing. This odd story is based on an old Japanese tale performed as rakugo,[4] a performance where the storyteller is seated on stage and tells the story only with a fan and a piece of cloth. The performer mimics the voices of the characters in the story, exactly what happens in Yamamura's short film with a voice-over. What makes this short so entertaining and surprisingly believable in its very odd story is how Yamamura uses composition and editing to convince the audience that the cherry blossom viewers are actually on the man's head despite the illogical size discrepancy. It is utterly convincing how this bizarre tale is visualized. Yamamura plays with on- and offscreen space and also with open frames to make this odd story a gem on-screen. He never shows a full shot of the people actually being on the man's head combined with his face and body underneath. There is only one camera pan that moves from the man's face onto his head where the group of people is gathering. The rest are close-ups and reaction shots of the man and then cuts to the people celebrating under the tree and again cuts back to the man's reaction. Yamamura shows us the real connection in the mentioned pan only once, which is enough for us to know what just happened and to believe it for the rest of the short film. After the setup, Yamamura only has to refer to it by the man looking up into the direction where the people are gathering on his head. It is a constant action → reaction and question → answer pattern that keeps us believing in the story. What is important, though, is the constant reiteration of the people's actions and his reactions; otherwise, the connection between the two would be broken and the audience would be confused about the goings-on. But the action does not have to result only in an emotional reaction of the man; it could also include movement that continues in the follow-up shot (match on action).

Examples for the connection of shots and the use of on- and offscreen space in *Atama Yama* are:

- Two men smoking under the cherry tree drop a cigarette → cut to the man's painful reaction.
- One man pees onto the tree because he is drunk and some of the pee flows down on the ground to the right → cut to a close-up of the man's head, where sweat is running down the man's right temple.

- In the shots under the cherry tree, petals are falling from the cherry blossoms → cut to the man's face, where we also see cherry blossom petals falling down.
- A drunken man kicks off his shoe, which falls → cut to the shoe falling into a cup of noodle soup → reaction shot of the man eating noodle soup.
- The man runs away in anger → cut to the bathers being thrown out of the pond.

Yamamura gives us many open frames of close-up shots of the man's head that extend the information on-screen in our imagination, and we always add the people to the offscreen space. The clues we are given are enough to enlarge the space and make the connection between the various shots that by themselves wouldn't suffice to tell the full story. It is the shot connections between both sides, man and people, that create the weird tale. For example, showing the man standing in the rain in front of a train track waiting and looking up toward the hole in his head, Yamamura gives us plenty of time to recognize the hole and to make the logical conclusion of it filling with water. After the shot in the rain, Yamamura transitions to black and then opens the next shot with a fish being pulled out of a pond and bathers enjoying themselves on a sunny day and we know that the people have come back to the man's head, which now houses a pond. There was enough time at the train track to actually expect exactly what is going to happen in the next shot. What kind of information Yamamura puts into the image is also crucial. There is no background to be seen when he cuts to the people and their actions other than the sky with clouds. The people are always on a curved surface mimicking the spherical cap of the man's skull. How the people actually get to the cap is never visualized; we just accept it because it happened in front of our eyes when we saw them walking (although we do not see their feet) and then arriving (we see them being on the cap). Additionally, the sound helps tremendously to keep the people's actions audible in the close-up shots of the man, by hearing them screaming and partying. The semi-diegetic sound carries its information over to the close-up shots. The rakugo storyteller also assists the images to make this odd tale believable. In the end, out of desperation, the man actually jumps into his own pond and falls repeatedly into himself in a rather nightmarish repetition. Yamamura gives us a surreal story that only works because of the perfect choice of elements of cinematic language. The right stringing together of shots makes this short an unforgettable cinematic experience.

---

4  Nancy Harrison, Koji Yamamura, *Vertigo Magazine*, January 1, 2006, Vertigo Issue 5 | November 2006.

# The polyptych

In art history, the polyptych is a frame option where multiple pictures are arranged into one piece, mostly used for religious paintings for altars and church pieces of the Renaissance. Usually there is a main theme, which is placed in the middle panel of the altar, and the secondary supporting panels are arranged around it. The most famous polyptych altars are the *Isenheim Altarpiece* (1512–1516) by Matthias Grünewald (13 painted panels and 1 wooden sculptural group) or the *Ghent Altarpiece* (1432) by brothers Hubert and Jan van Eyck, containing 12 panels. The altars come with various doors, which can be opened and closed, revealing different paintings for important festivals of the liturgical year. The most common types of polyptych are those with two panels (diptych), three panels (triptych), or four panels (tetraptych).

In cinema, the polyptych is called a *split screen* and is a very unique feature that is seldom used due to its very strong impact, yet it is still a fairly interesting artistic tool to consider. Usually there is only one narrative perspective presented on the cinema screen, but there is also the possibility of having various films play in one frame or various frames arranged next to each other, therefore, telling the story from different perspectives, either camera perspectives or character perspectives. The first use of the split screen (or, in this case, double exposure) was in the British Christmas short *Santa Claus* from 1898 by George Albert. Albert uses the technique to show two actions at the same time: two kids sleeping in their beds on the left of the screen and then on the right Santa coming down the chimney to bring presents. For 1898, this type of storytelling is quite impressive technically and conceptually. The next noteworthy use of the split screen is Abel Gance's mammoth feature *Napoleon* from 1927, which was in its third act projected with three projectors of 1.33:1 aspect ratio simultaneously to create one wide-screen with a massive ratio of 4.00:1, making it by far the largest aspect ratio in cinema history. The three screens often show three different images but also one very wide frame in some shots.

In 1958, director Stanley Donen used the split screen technique in his feature *Indiscreet*, a romantic comedy with Cary Grant and Ingrid Bergman with a very clever connection to the actual narrative. We see the two lovers lying in bed (each in their own in separate apartments) and talking on the phone with each other. The screen is split in half and the characters turn to each other while they are talking. It seems like they are in the same bed, but they are obviously also not, an artistic decision that has since been used in plenty of features and TV shows, especially romantic comedies (*When Harry Met Sally* from 1989, for instance).

The split screen, however, can also be used to double expose the film strip to have the same actor or actress appear twice in the image, like in Disney's feature *The Parent Trap* (1961), where the split of the screen is slightly blurred and covers the "cut" of the image in half. The camera exposes first one side of the frame, while the other side is covered and thus prevented from being exposed. Then the procedure is reversed and repeated. The outcome is one actor being seen twice in one frame. The same technique is still used today in order to have sharp focus on a foreground and background element in the same image. However, this use of the split screen is supposed to be unseen and does not show two different frames, each telling its own story.

In 1967, the National Film Board of Canada produced a very well-received multiscreen film installation for Expo 67 in Montreal at the Labyrinth Pavilion. The American magazine *BoxOffice* wrote the following on May 15, 1967, about the stunning visuals and the split screen:

> The cinematic effects of Labyrinth—the use of two enormous screens on wall and floor in the first chamber, are breath-taking. On the wall screen, one watches a steel worker straddling scaffolding 40 stories high. Simultaneously on the floor the screen gives a paralyzing sense of the drop. The human predicaments are all suggested in the Labyrinth. There is a birth in a Montreal Hospital (Ste. Jeanne d'Arc), death in Dorval, riots in Japan, traffic in New York, honeymooners in Niagara Falls, dancers in Ethiopia and rockets in Cape Kennedy. From this first chamber the viewer is funneled into a maze, a darkened, mirrored chamber of colored lights. The final chamber, with its five screens, is the most successful. It conveys a moving sense of man's possibilities of winning through peace.[5]

The obvious success and reaction to the project gave the split screen not only a contemporary artistic flavor but also public exposure, and the technique led to the very famous and rather stylish use of the split screen with multiple screens appearing and moving through the frame in Norman Jewison's *The Thomas Crown Affair* from 1968, a crime movie with Steve McQueen and Faye Dunaway. In the feature, during a game of polo, the screen is broken into multiple smaller frames and stripes, which move across the screen, making the game appear more exciting and dynamic. Because during the polo game, we see Dunaway filming McQueen on his horse, the idea of multiple screens within the screen makes sense from a narrative perspective. We feel as if we are, like her, looking through a viewfinder and trying to focus on the action.

By having various images within the screen through the technique of the split screen, their relationships will either show different aspects of one story or even create a new meaning, very much like the intellectual method in Sergei Eisenstein's montage theory. Two images grouped together will create an intellectual meaning that is beyond the meaning of either one of the images and can result in complex connotations.

Another very interesting film with a split screen was produced in 2000: Mike Figgis' experimental feature film *Timecode*. The screen is split into four segments, each of which shows a

---

5   NFB's Labyrinth Theatre Averaging 7,000-Plus Patrons at Expo '67. 1967. *Boxoffice (Archive: 1920–2000)*, 91(4), K-1.

continuous (unedited) 93-minutes film of the same narrative, but each segment having a different perspective. What makes this kind of cinema difficult to watch is, of course, the amount of visual information the audience has to focus on, which does not lead itself easily to relaxed storytelling. But it also has the advantage of showing various viewpoints and reactions of one actor in one quadrant to the action in another quadrant. Still, it is an exciting concept that can be used in a more subdued version, like in Tom Tykwer's *Run Lola Run* from 1998, in which the split screen is thoughtfully planned to provide information and let the characters' actions relate to each other. For example, we see Lola running on the right side of the frame, while her boyfriend Manni is waiting for her on the left. The relationship between the two characters' actions is what makes their reactions so much fun to watch and gives it additional suspense.

In animation, the split screen is used frequently by Dutch animator Paul Driessen. His short *The Boy Who Saw the Iceberg* (2000) has two screens. We see on the left side a boy's reality and on the right side his imagined story, which he has to start again and again because he is interrupted by adults. In *On Land, at Sea and in the Air* (1980), there are three panels in the frame, in which we follow various characters and a bird in odd situations on land, at sea, and in the air. *The End of the World in Four Seasons* (1995) has a whopping eight screens relating to each other. Each season has eight panels where comical moments of that season are played out. What works in Driessen's shorts is that the various actions never collide but always leave each other room to be seen. Additionally, the characters and their actions can affect the panels next to them, which leads to a highly entertaining and rather complex patchwork of film clips in Driessen's shorts.

# CHAPTER 4

# Aspect Ratio

The vast field of aspect ratios has so many variations that it is its own complex science. However, there are some that shaped cinema and helped to solidify specific aspect ratios in film history (see Figures 4.1 and 4.2, which compare the most important aspect ratios with each other). Throughout the first decades of moviemaking, the ratio was more or less set to 4:3, which was the ratio put in circulation by the Edison company in the mid-1890s and lasted until the beginning of the 1950s with slight changes in the precise size of the frame. The aspect ratio is the relationship between the height and width of a film frame, which can be expressed in various ways. The ratio 4:3, for instance, would define the length of the frame being four parts to three parts of the frame's height. On the other hand, 1.37:1 (which is the same ratio as 4:3, just calculated differently) indicates that the length of the frame is 1.37 times its height. Aspect ratios do not describe the actual size of the screen the film is projected on; it only specifies the frame's proportions. The first film ratio was "reintroduced" by W.K.L. Dickson in early 1891 for Thomas Edison's company for the Kinetoscope and was based on French scientist Jules Marey's chronophotograph device, which was patented in 1890, using the 1.33:1 ratio,[1] which was to become the ratio for the next 50 years of cinema. Edison, who was very concerned about protecting his company's developments and financial successes (not so much about the artistic possibilities of the medium film), had started the Motion Picture Patents Company (MPPC) in 1908 in order to discourage the infringement of his patents on film technology and projection. The MPPC represented all the major film studios and was very forceful in its actions. Its goal was to monopolize the industry in the distribution and use of film stock, filming and projecting of films, and distribution of films amongst its trusted members. This led to a famous court case, *US v. The Motion Pictures Patent Company*. In 1915, federal courts found the MPPC guilty of antitrust violations and stated in its verdict that it had acted "far beyond what was necessary to protect the use of patents or the monopoly which went with them,"[2] which ultimately led to MPPC having to pay injured parties triple damages.[3] After this major blow, the MPPC finally had to dissolve in 1918, the very same year

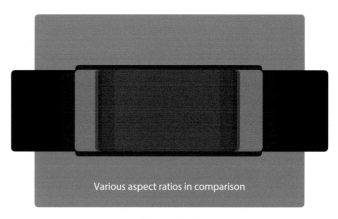

Various aspect ratios in comparison

**Figure 4.1**

Thomas Edison sold his company and left the filmmaking industry for good.[4] Nevertheless Edison's (partly Marey's) version of the film process had already been established in the industry and it remained the standard until the beginning of the 1950s. There were obviously still ongoing explorations by companies and inventors from the beginning of film, despite the 4:3 ratio having been established. Many companies in different countries tried again and again to market different ratios from the 4:3, the first being the Italian feature *Il sacco di Roma* from 1923, shot in 2.20:1 (only one sequence was actually presented in this wide format, not the entire film).[5] Many continued experimenting with different frame ratios, film strip sizes, and projection techniques (like anamorphic wide-screen or 3D viewing), but none of the experiments lasted longer than a couple of movies, despite some being promoted by major film studios. In 1925, for instance, Paramount released the Magnascope, a process where the projection lens magnified the image from 1:1 up to a 2:1 ratio depending on the capabilities of the theatre. Like Polyvision, the widest of all ratios of 4.00:1, only used in Abel Gance's *Napoleon* from 1927 in Act 4 (the rest of the feature is in the traditional 4:3), Magnascope was only meant to be used for specific scenes, not the entire movie. Magnascope's problem was the same one that many wide-screen formats in 35 mm are facing: the bigger the image is magnified, the more grain is visible on-screen, which results in a weaker image quality. In 1929, the Fox Film Corporation's Grandeur wide-screen format,

[1] Robert E. Carr and R.M. Hayes, *Wide Screen Movies, A History and Filmography of Wide Gauge Filmmaking*, McFarland & Company, Jefferson, MO, 1988, p. 1.
[2] U.S. v. Motion Picture Patents Co., 225 F. 800 (D.C. Pa. 1915).
[3] Charles Musser, *Before the Nickelodeon: Edwin S. Porter and the Edison Manufacturing Company*, University of California Press, Berkeley, CA, 1991, p. 471.

[4] Charles Musser, *Before the Nickelodeon, Edwin S. Porter and the Edison Manufacturing Company*, University of California Press, Berkeley, CA, 1991, p. 474.
[5] Robert E. Carr and R.M. Hayes. p. 3.

DOI: 10.1201/b22148-4

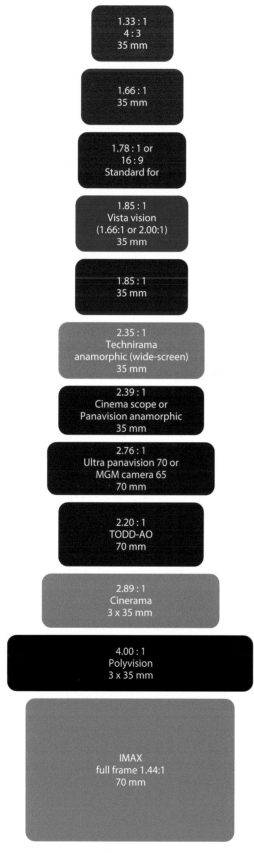

| 1.33 : 1 |
| 4 : 3 |
| 35 mm |

1.66 : 1
35 mm

1.78 : 1 or
16 : 9
Standard for

1.85 : 1
Vista vision
(1.66:1 or 2.00:1)
35 mm

1.85 : 1
35 mm

2.35 : 1
Technirama
anamorphic (wide-screen)
35 mm

2.39 : 1
Cinema scope or
Panavision anamorphic
35 mm

2.76 : 1
Ultra panavision 70 or
MGM camera 65
70 mm

2.20 : 1
TODD-AO
70 mm

2.89 : 1
Cinerama
3 x 35 mm

4.00 : 1
Polyvision
3 x 35 mm

IMAX
full frame 1.44:1
70 mm

**Figure 4.2**

with a 2.13:1 aspect ratio, solved this problem by using 70 mm film, twice the width of the popular 35 mm film used since the beginning of film, thus increasing the image quality drastically. However, 70 mm had also been used since nearly the beginning of film but did not catch on. There were also trials with sizes from 50 to 68 mm, which neither were successful on a wide commercial level. Fox Film Corporation's first feature in Grandeur was *Fox Movietone Follies of 1929*. RKO, MGM, and Warner Brothers all had their own wide gauge formats at that time; although none of these new technologies could establish themselves on the market, they had a lasting effect on the subsequent development of film presentations.

At the end of the 1940s, the invention of the home television set changed the landscape of cinema drastically. Households throughout the US were glued to their new TV sets and therefore stayed away from the cinema, because their entertainment was already waiting at home (in a rather modest quality and in black and white, mind you). Another incident was also responsible for the loss of the movie studios' income in Hollywood at the end of the 1940s: another lawsuit from the US Supreme Court, this time against Paramount Pictures. In the old Hollywood system, the movie studios had their own theatres and decided which movie would play for how long in which theatre by means of block booking. The US Supreme Court decided that this violated the Sherman Antitrust Act (which forbids companies from preventing competition) of 1890 and thus unlawfully created a monopoly. The studios were forced to abandon block booking, which created a major change in the Hollywood system. The studios could not force theatres to buy blocks of films anymore, which caused them to drastically reduce their output. Actors, directors, and staff needed to be let go, which led them into TV production work (for further reading, see Barnouw[6]). The audience followed their favorite actors to their TV screens and movie ticket sales plummeted. The movie studios, on the other hand, were looking for attractions that would bring back audiences with spectacles that could rival TV, and *Cinerama*, the first wide-screen extravaganza, was at the forefront of this development. The 1950s saw the development of many more wide-screen solutions like Superscope and Techniscope Super 35, Ultra Panavision, CinemaScope, Cinemiracle and Kinopanorama (both three-strip processes like Cinerama), Todd-AO and Dimension 150, Super Panavision 70, VistaVision, Technirama, Mayflies, Vistarama, and many others.[7] In addition to wide-screen, 3D viewing and the rather unsuccessful oddity of Smell-O-Vision were also explored.[8] In the 1960s, the hype of wide-screen was slowing down and many of the wide-screen cinematic processes slowly disappeared or scaled down their screens and simplified their filming or projection systems. The industry had settled on a couple of formats that seemed practical and financially reasonable like CinemaScope or Panavision.

6   Erik Barnouw, *Tube of Plenty: The Evolution of American Television*, Oxford University Press, New York, 1990.
7   Martin B. Hart (Curator), *The American Widescreen Museum*, established 1995. http://www.widescreenmuseum.com (accessed January 8, 2015).
8   Smell-O-Vision was produced by Mike Todd's son Mike Todd Jr. Mike Todd shot the rollercoaster scene in *This is Cinerama!* He was the producer behind the Todd-AO system and was formerly involved in the *Cinerama* project.

# 1952, the year that changed cinema!

The very first new wide-screen process was the above-mentioned Cinerama with its famous introductory film *This Is Cinerama!* Developed by motion picture engineer Fred Waller and recording specialist Howard Reeves, Cinerama was introduced to the public in a single cinema in New York at the Broadway Theatre, especially fitted with the Cinerama technology. It opened on September 1952 to stunned audiences who feasted their eyes on an enormous panorama screen of a 25-ft radius with an excellent sound system that presented film in an overwhelming quality.

slight overlap. The right projector presented the left image, the middle one the middle image, and the left projector the right image (Figures 4.4 and 4.6). The outer projector's light beams therefore crossed each other in the center. It had a seven-channel sound system of five speakers behind the screen and two on either side of the auditorium. The technology made it possible for the viewers to see not only the image in front of them but also what was in the corner of their eyes, expanding the field of vision tremendously and exposing the audience to a nearly real-life experience. Because of the deeply curved screen, the audience was fully immersed in the presentation. The setup of the three

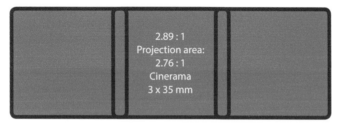

**Figure 4.3**

**Figure 4.4**

The audience was exposed to visuals they had never seen before and the success of Cinerama seemed a given. Because of Cinerama's complex filming and projection system, theatres needed to be retrofitted to play these spectacles; or special theatres were built, like the still surviving Cinerama Dome in Hollywood, Los Angeles. The Cinerama camera has three magazines that contain one film strip each and all shoot at a 46° angle to each other (Figure 4.6 shows the three cameras, A, B, and C, projecting on a curved screen where the three images slightly overlap, as can be seen in Figure 4.3). The film was shot at a speed of 26 frames/sec, and the image size on the 35 mm gauge was six sprockets high[9] (Figure 4.4) instead of the traditional four sprockets high on 4:3 ratio (Figure 4.5), creating a sharper image with less grain. It was projected onto a huge curved screen (146°) that was not a conventional stretched screen but consisted of 1,700 vertical, tightly mounted strips of fabric that prohibited the reflection of projection light onto the other side of the screen. The three films blended together into one film image with a

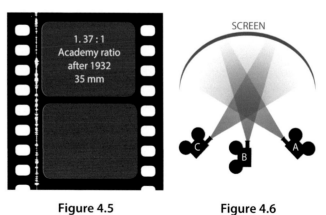

**Figure 4.5**　　　　**Figure 4.6**

cameras imitated human vision as closely as possible to cover an area 146° wide and 55° high. This projected field nearly covered human peripheral vision, combined with surround sound, which also imitated the ear's capability.[10] Nevertheless it did have its

9  Robert E. Carr and R.M. Hayes, *Wide Screen Movies, A History and Filmography of Wide Gauge Filmmaking*, McFarland & Company, Jefferson, MO, 1988, p. 13.

10  John W. Boyle, *And now...Cinerama*, American Cinematographer, 1952, Los Angeles, CA, pp. 480–481.

drawbacks: the camera itself did not have the ability to zoom, as there was only one lens inside the camera; the only option was a dolly shot, where the camera itself was physically moved. Due to the center of gravity of the camera being rather high, a camera tilt was also a challenge due to the weight of the camera. Nor was staging and blocking very practical, as the viewfinder of the camera was not easily accessible, making control of the composition difficult.[11] This did not lend itself easily to the Hollywood feature film techniques that had been established for decades but worked for more visual, plotless movies like documentaries or travelogues. Cinerama was also hugely expensive. Camera and projector, screen and film stock, and the extravagant yet excellent sound system made it a financially problematic projection solution, despite its great success. But it opened the toy box for film companies to lure the audience back into the movie theaters with new and exciting spectacles next to their other favorite pastime: TV. Only two features with a narrative story were ever shot with the Cinerama camera. The first was *The Wonderful World of the Brothers Grimm* (1962), with the taglines "Now Cinerama Tells a Story!" and "The First Dramatic Film in Fabulous CINERAMA," partly directed and produced by animation veteran George Pal. *The Brothers Grimm* is the only feature that contains animation in Cinerama. Henry Levin directed the film, George Pal the sequence "The Cobbler and the Elves" with his famous *Puppetoons*, a stop-motion animation technique with facial replacement puppets. Cinerama shot its second and last narrative feature, *How the West Was Won* (1963), which boasted spectacular views, beautiful compositions, and a scope that was proof of what this process is actually capable of. From then on, it was decided that the format did not support the narrative structure of a feature film and the process was used for documentaries and travelogues only. All other narrative feature films that were presented in Cinerama were shown in Cinerama theatres but were neither shot with the three-magazine Cinerama camera nor projected by three projectors. Stanley Kramer's *It's a Mad, Mad, Mad, Mad World* (1963) was shot in Ultra Panavision 70 but transferred to Cinerama for special presentations and premiers. The British production of *Khartoum* (1966) was shot in Ultra Panavision 70 and only shown for its world premiere at the London Casino Theatre in 70 mm in the Cinerama theatre after the three-strip projector had been replaced by a regular 70 mm projector.[12] Stanley Kubrick's *2001: A Space Odyssey* (1968) was transferred to various cinematographic processes, including Cinerama, but shot with Panavision cameras and lenses.[13] Cinerama had its biggest success in its first 10 years, through around 1962.[14] There has been a small revival of this specific process because three of the theatres are still in existence and

operating and presentations still happen. The last film shot with the original three-magazine cameras was the 12 minutes documentary *The Last Days of Cinerama* in 2012.

## Aspect ratio change during the film

The aspect ratio that is chosen at the beginning of a production is the one used throughout the film … well, mostly. There are some films that change the ratio during the presentation of the feature. This can be an interesting change in the scale and grandeur of the film and be successful once there is a relevant reason for the change relating to the story. Disney's *Brother Bear* is one successful example of this. The film changes 24 minutes into the film from a regular wide-screen ratio of 1.75:1 to an anamorphic ratio of 2.35:1. The change is rooted in the story and visually interprets the protagonist Kenai's change from his human form into a bear. The landscape becomes grander, wider, and emanates opulence. Accompanying the ratio change is a shift in color and style. Saturation is increased, the characters become cartoonier, and the animals can talk. It is seemingly more "fun" to be a bear.

Another film that uses a change in ratio during the film is *The Simpsons Movie* (2007), which changes from 1.85:1 for the Itchy and Scratchy intro to a ratio of 2.35:1 for the rest of the feature. The wide-screen format of the feature compared to the TV show ratio of 1.38:1 or 1.78:1 (HD TV) is more cinematic and grander, giving the audience the feeling of scale and importance.

In Disney's *Enchanted* (2007), the frame rate change happens at the beginning, and it flips from 2.35:1 after the title to 1.85:1 when the animated sequence starts. Giselle, a princess-to-be, lives in Andalasia, an animated fairy-tale world that has only very happy endings. Through an evil plot, Giselle gets displaced into contemporary New York (the ratio goes back to the original 2.35:1) and she falls, after some mishaps, for a modern-day-prince: a handsome doctor. At the end of the film, when Edward and Nancy, two other characters, are getting married in Andalasia, which is again animated, the film does not change into the initial smaller ratio from the beginning.

Disney's animated short film from 2013, *Get a Horse*, seemingly has a frame ratio change from the academy ratio of 4:3 in black and white, with the characters of the Disney shorts of the end of the 1920s populating the screen, to the wide-screen format of digital 3D of 2.35:1. However, the film actually never really changes ratios, as the beginning of the short shows a film presentation in a movie theatre, which is revealed once Mickey pops from the screen onto the stage, very much like Buster Keaton's famous *Sherlock Jr.* (1924) or Woody Allen's spectacular *The Purple Rose of Cairo* (1985), all blurring the border between audience and characters on-screen. Mickey himself "changes" the ratio of the image on-screen by pushing away the curtain on stage, but the actual ratio of the short does not change; only the ratio within the short changes. The view of the screen within the movie theatre stays the same.

[11] *The Last Days of Cinerama* (2012); Documentary short directed by Mike Celestino, Robert Garren.
[12] Roland Lataille: Cinerama. http://incinerama.com/ctcasino.htm
[13] IMDB: 2001: *A Space Odyssey*: http://www.imdb.com/title/tt0062622/?ref_=nv_sr_1; retrieved 6th of February 2018.
[14] John Belton, Introduction, Widescreen, *Film History*, Vol. 15, No. 1, (2003), pp. 3–4.

# Important aspect ratios

Figure 4.7

1.33:1: The standard aspect ratio for films from the beginning of the development of film was 4:3 or 1.33:1. Developed by William Kennedy Dickson and Thomas Edison in the early 1890s (based on French scientist Jules Marey's[15] chronophotograph device, which was patented in 1890, using the 1.33:1 ratio), it kept its importance until way into the 1990s, mostly due to the 4:3 TV screen size, introduced in the 1940s. Dickson's film strip, camera, and projector design was chosen over many others that were developed at the time, but Edison's wide distribution and aggressive protection of his patents and devices[16] gave him a business advantage. His films and technology had already made their mark, as he also suppressed competition from other companies. In 1909, the Motion Picture Patent Company declared the 4:3 image ratio in 35 mm with four perforations per frame as the standard in the industry (which obviously did not stop the further development and invention of other presentation methods and film sizes and even 3D viewing) (Figures 4.7 and 4.8a). This ratio was used until the appearance of sound in 1928, which needed to be displayed right next to the image to keep the synchronization of sound and image accurate. The soundtrack cut into the image on the left, reducing its size to about 1.19:1, which was a rather tall aspect ratio and not a very practical size for the already existing 1.33 projection screens in the theatres. All film companies wanted to go back to the initial 1.33 ratio and in 1932 the Academy of Motion Arts and Sciences decided that the official aspect ratio would now be 1.375:1. In order to fit the image on the 35 mm film strip, it was reduced in size, which slightly widened the separation strip between the frames (Figure 4.8b). The new standardized aspect ratio was named the *Academy ratio*. Most features produced through the 1950s, presented on a TV set, were shown in their original aspect ratio and not cut to fit the TV screen, as TV had the same or a similar aspect ratio as films for cinema. Other features, mainly produced after 1953, that did not fit the 4:3 ratio were often heavily cut on both sides to force them into the 4:3 ratio to be able to be played on TV, drastically changing the composition and with it the impact of the frames.

(a)                              (b)

Figure 4.8

## Examples of 1.33 and 1.37

### US Animated Features

- *Gulliver's Travels* (1939)
- *Mr. Bug Goes to Town* (1941)
- All Disney features through 1955
- *Fritz the Cat* (1972)
- *Coonskin* (1975)
- *Aristocats* (1970)
- *The Rescuers* (1977)

### European Animated Features

- *The Adventures of Prince Achmed* (1926)
- *The Snow Maiden* (1952)
- *Animal Farm* (1954)
- *The King and the Mockingbird* (1980)
- *The Wind in the Willows* (1983)
- *Gwen, the Book of Sand* (1985)
- *Gandahar* (1988)

Figure 4.9

---

[15] Étienne-Jules Marey (1830–1904) is one of the pioneers of photography and cinema. Especially in animation he is famous for his motion studies of animals and humans (Chronophotography) where various phases of the movement are recorded and the movement then studied. Marey's photographic studies are an invaluable source of information for motion studies. In 1882 he invented the chronophotographic gun which was able to shoot 12 consecutive images per second, which were then recorded on one photo (see Figure 4.9).

[16] Kirsten Anderson Wagner, *Schirmer Encyclopedia of Film*, Thomson Gale, Farmington Hills, MI, p. 181.

**Figure 4.10**

1.66:1: The mentioned success of TV sales in the US and the general change of American lifestyle in the 1950s caused people to stay at home watching TV rather than visiting movie theatres. This started a competition between film studios to outdo each other with bigger and better projection options that could rival the home entertainment system. In 1953, the film studio Paramount released the feature *Shane*, which was shot in the traditional 4:3 ratio; however, when presented in theatres the image was cut on the top and bottom to achieve a 1.66:1 ratio. This format was also printed on 35 mm film stock. To achieve the wider format, the 1.66 image needs to be shrunk to fit the 4:3 frame (Figure 4.11). European feature animation is mostly shot in a 1.37 or 1.66:1 ratio.

Most of the following aspect ratios that are wider than the traditional Academy ratio of 1.375:1 are still printed on a regular 35 mm filmstrip, with the image being four perforations high. This results in a higher granularity because the image is actually reduced in size within the 4:3 field to achieve the wider image.

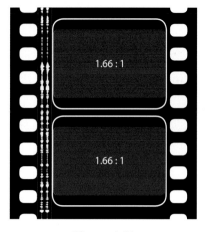

**Figure 4.11**

**Examples of 1.66:1**

**US Features and Shorts**

- *Oliver and Company* (1988)
- *Nightmare before Christmas* (1993)
- *The Lion King* (1994)
- *Pocahontas* (1995)
- *James and the Giant Peach* (1996)
- *The Tell-Tale Heart* (1953): UPA short (United Productions of America)

**Japanese Animated Feature**

- *Hakujaden: The Tale of the White Serpent* (1958)

**European Animated Features**

- *Asterix the Gaul* (1967)
- *Yellow Submarine* (1968)
- *Asterix and Cleopatra* (1968)
- *Fantastic Planet* (1973)
- *Allegro Non Troppo* (1976)
- *The Twelve Tasks of Asterix* (1976)
- *Watership Down* (1978)
- *Asterix and Caesar* (1985)
- *The Triplets of Belleville* (2003)

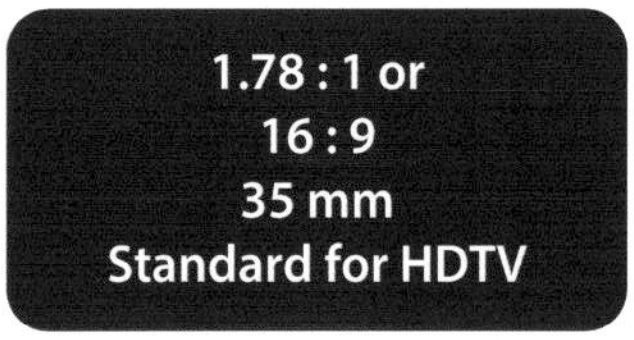

**Figure 4.12**

1.78:1: The ratio 1.78:1 or 16:9 is the standard for HDTV, which translates into 1920×1080 pixels per frame in its digital form. In the beginning of the 1980s, Kerns Powers found that by using all popular aspect ratios and laying them on top of each other, the area covered by all of them was exactly 1.78:1 (and they also fit into an outer rectangle of again a 1.78:1 ratio). Since 2008, 16:9 has been the standard aspect ratio for laptops and computer screens. This aspect ratio on 35 mm film (see Figure 4.13) has the sound track also on the left and its 16:9 image is likewise shrunk to fit into the 4:3 frame.

The ratio 1.75:1 was mainly used in the mid-1950s by Warner Brothers and MGM for some of their features, but Disney has also used this aspect ratio by cropping some of its features produced in the Academy ratio 1.37:1 to achieve the 1.75:1 ratio for theatrical presentation or DVD release.

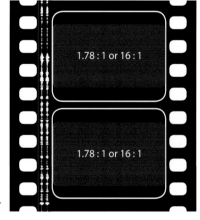

**Figure 4.13**

**Examples of 1.75 or 1.78:1**

**Feature Animation 1.75:1**

- *The Jungle Book* (1967): 1.37:1 (negative ratio); 1.75:1 (intended ratio)
- *101 Dalmatians* (1961)

**Feature Animation 1.78:1**

- *Rock-A-Doodle* (1991)
- *The Care Bears Movie* (1985)

**Figure 4.14**

1.85:1: In 1953, Universal released the 1.85:1 ratio (Figure 4.14), which was wider than Paramount's 1.66:1 but also shrunk the size of the frame to fit into the 4:3 field, which makes the image even smaller, thus reducing its quality. Now the 4:3 image size of four perforations is shrunken to three perforations in height in this widescreen ratio (Figure 4.15). Ultimately Universal's ratio was the one that proved itself to be the most successful in the industry and is still widely used in feature film.

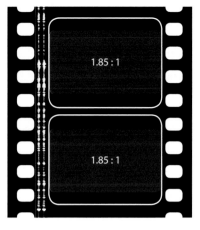

**Figure 4.15**

## Examples of 1.85:1

### US Animated Features in 1.85:1

- *1001 Arabian Nights* (1959) (UPA)
- *Gay Purr-ee* (1962) (UPA)
- *Heavy Traffic* (1973)
- *Wizards* (1977)
- *Lord of the Rings* (1978)
- *American Pop* (1981)
- *Heavy Metal* (1981)
- *The Last Unicorn* (1982)
- *Time Masters* (1982)
- *The Secret of NIMH* (1982)
- *Fire and Ice* (1983)
- *The Adventures of Mark Twain* (1985)
- *The Great Mouse Detective* (1986)
- *An American Tale* (1986)
- *Roger Rabbit* (1988)
- *The Land Before Time* (1988):
  1.37:1 (negative ratio);
  1.85:1 (intended ratio)
- *All Dogs Go to Heaven* (1989)
- *Little Mermaid* (1989)
- *Shrek* (2001)
- *Ice Age* (2002)
- *Shark Tale* (2004)
- *Madagascar* (2005)
- *Corpse Bride* (2005)
- *Over the Hedge* (2006)
- *Open Season* (2006)
- *Coraline* (2009)
- *Hotel Transylvania* (2012)
- *Frankenweenie* (2012)
- *The Boxtrolls* (2014)

### US Animated Shorts in 1.85:1

#### Disney Roger Rabbit Short Series

- *Tummy Trouble* (1989)
- *Roller Coaster Rabbit* (1990)
- *Trail Mix-Up* (1993)

#### UPA

- *Magoo's Problem Child* (1956)

### European Animated Features

- *Time Masters* (1982)
- *Fantastic Mister Fox* (2009)
- *The Illusionist* (2010)

### Japanese Animated Features

- *Be Forever Yamato* (1980)
- *Wings of Honneamise* (1987)
- *Akira* (1988)
- *Ghost in the Shell* (1995)
- *Steamboy* (2004)
- *Summer Wars* (2009)

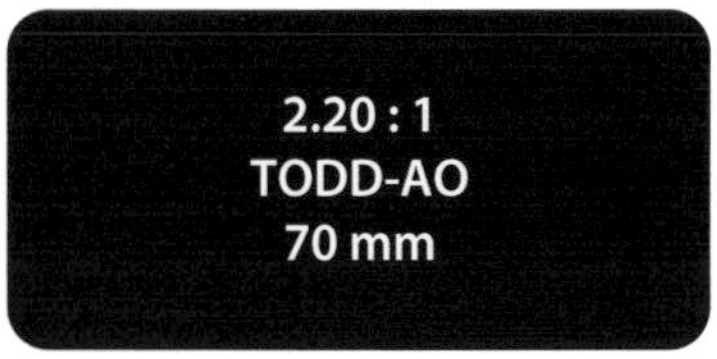

**Figure 4.16**

2.20:1: Mike Todd, the producer of the Todd-AO system, was initially involved in the Cinerama project and was responsible for producing the European parts of the promotional short film *This Is Cinerama!* The tremendous costs of the Cinerama process and its problem of the two visible seams of the three images on-screen led Mike Todd to look for a cheaper and more feasible presentation technique that involved similar outcomes with a more affordable price. Dr. Brian O'Brien, optical scientist and head of research of the American Optical Company, developed a new system for Mr. Todd, which they called *Todd-AO*. Its quality was in many ways superior to the other systems, as its film stock image was much bigger, resulting in a higher image quality (instead of the 35 mm filmstrip, Todd-AO had twice the width, resulting in a 70 mm film stock). The first feature shot with the new system, which was a nonanamorphic process that did not squash the image but kept its original width, was a film version of Rodgers and Hammerstein's famous and very popular musical *Oklahoma!* in 1955, which was shot both in Todd-AO and CinemaScope. Those two different versions could play in all theatres, those that were equipped with the Todd-AO system and those that played the CinemaScope version on regular screens. It is not the exactly same film in the two different formats; it is actually a slightly contrasting film, as each had to be adjusted for its own compositional needs. Todd-AO had a much wider field of vision compared to CinemaScope lenses, and in *Oklahoma!* the filmmakers did not use the full visual range that Todd-AO was actually capable of. The scale of *Oklahoma!* was topped by the second feature in this new system: *Around the World in 80 Days* (1956), based on Jules Verne's famous adventure story. *Time* magazine described the film in 1956 with enthusiasm:

> To top it all off Producer Todd took his picture on the world's largest film—exactly twice as wide (70 mm) as the normal Hollywood stock—and has projected it on one of the world's largest indoor screens—a vast concave gullet that opens almost as wide as *Cinerama*, and possesses much of the same power to suck the spectator out of his seat. Not content with that, Todd flooded this huge surface with a light almost twice as intense as any ever seen on screen before, and so hot that the film has to be refrigerated as it passes through the Todd-AO projector.[17]

The *Todd-AO* system uses 70 mm film and has a height of five sprockets per image, which is shot in 65 mm and then copied onto 70 mm, leaving room for the six-channel sound on magnetic stripes along the sides of the sprockets (very much like the Cinerama setup with seven channels of sound; see Figure 4.17). The wide-angle lenses for this system shot widths of 37°, 48°, 64°, and 128°[18] (compared to the 148° of Cinerama),

**Figure 4.17**

which is enormous and allowed an extremely wide horizontal field of vision.[19] It nearly shot a width with one lens that Cinerama achieved with three side by side. The realism of its image was a result of the size of the image itself on the 70 mm film, which resulted in superior sharpness. Also the film, to avoid flicker during the projection, was projected with a higher frame speed of 30 frames a second.

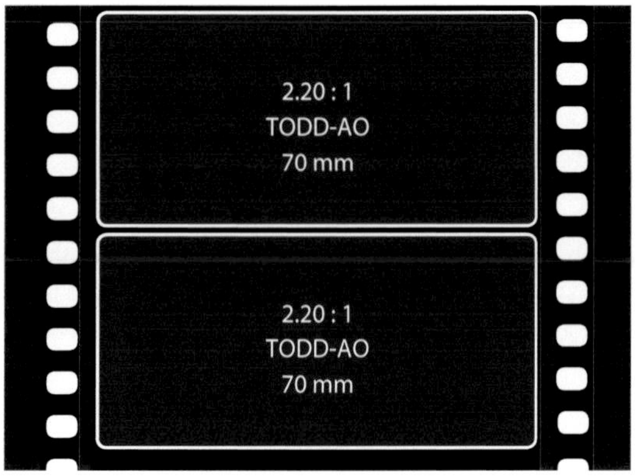

This speed was only kept for the first two feature films (the third film was a short subject, *The Miracle of Todd-AO* from 1956) and then reduced to the common 24 frames, as the higher speed heated the film so much that it needed to be cooled while being projected. Where Cinerama uses a very curved screen for its projection, in the beginning Todd-AO used a slightly curved screen, though it shifted to the regular flat screen from 1958 onwards. Because of the screen's curvature either the projector had to be on screen level to not distort the image or, in case of the projection booth being higher than the screen, the distortion had to be eliminated within the print; the image on the film stock was skewed in order to compensate for the distortion on screen. Around 20 films were shot with the Todd-AO system before it lost to its competitor IMAX at the beginning of 1975.

---

[17] Time. October 29, 1956, Vol. 68 Issue 18, p74. 4p.

[18] The Todd-AO Process: An Examination of the Type of Equipment That is Needed to Film and Project this New Super Wide Screen Process; Written by: American Optical Company/ The Todd-AO Coroporation. Printed in Theater Catalog 1955-56, and prepared for in70mm.com by Anders M. Olsson, Lund, Sweden, http://www.in70mm.com/todd_ao/archive/process/index.htm (accessed October 16, 2015).

[19] In an interview with Roy Frumke, Mike Todd, Jr., stated interestingly in 1995: "O'Brien was a brilliant optical scientist, but while they spent millions on lenses and the optical printer and all that crap, a guy by the name of Ned Mann went out and bought Leica still camera lenses for about $800, adapted them to the camera, and that's what we ended up using for all the Todd-AO demonstration footage. And it cost nothing. Even the original cameras weren't created by O'Brien; they were the modified Fearless Superfilm cameras. Joe Schenck told us about them, and we found them out in an army studio on Long Island. So it was all bullshit. Some of *Oklahoma!* was shot with Leica lenses, some with Todd-AO lenses, and they had to discard most of the 128 mm bug-eye lens footage because O'Brien's optical printer never worked. But almost all of *Around the World in 80 Days* was shot with cheap lenses, and the results were great because of the 70 mm film." from http://www.in70mm.com/news/2004/todd_jr/interview/index.htm (accessed October 16, 2015).

**Examples of Todd-AO**

**US Animated Feature**

- *Who Framed Roger Rabbit* (1988)

**US Live-Action Features**

- *Oklahoma!* (1955) (30 frames/sec)
- *Around the World in 80 Days* (1956) (30 frames/sec)
- *Porgy & Bess* (1959)
- *Cleopatra* (1963)

- *The Sound of Music* (1965)
- *The Bible* (1966) (Italian and US production)
- *Star!* (1968)
- *Hello, Dolly!* (1969)
- *Airport* (1970)

**British Live-Action Feature**

- *Those Magnificent Men in Their Flying Machines; or, How I Flew from London to Paris in 25 Hours 11 Minutes* (1965)

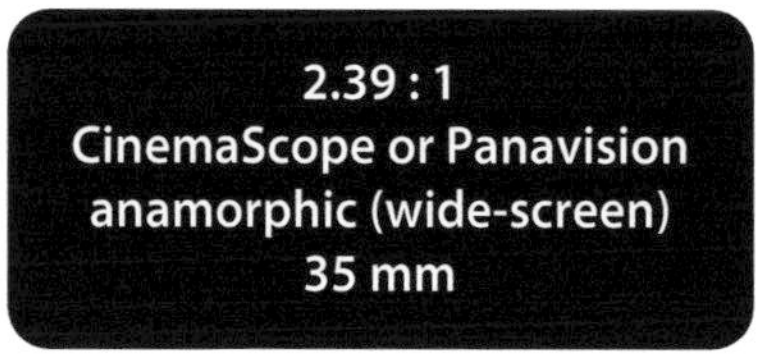

**2.39 : 1**
**CinemaScope or Panavision anamorphic (wide-screen) 35 mm**

**Figure 4.18**

2.39:1: Patented in 1927 by French inventor Henri Chrétien, the anamorphic wide-screen technology came to fruition just 3 weeks after Chrétien saw Abel Gance's *Napoleon* in its Polyvision format. Chrétien had already worked on anamorphic lenses for years but saw their potential in cinema after Gance's feature. His anamorphic system, called *Hypergonar*, was supported by the French film studio Pathé, which tried for a couple of years to promote the new system to the public. This was not very successful, as viewers did not seem to be ready for yet another major change in cinema after the introduction of sound 1 year earlier.[20] With a new name and by a new film company CinemaScope was (re-)introduced to cinema audiences on the 16th of September 1953[21], with the movie *The Robe*, by Twentieth Century Fox. Chrétien's process was taken from the shelves because of the success of Cinerama and the movie studios realized that the public was very receptive to a new cinematic experience. By using an anamorphic lens that squashes the image during the shoot and using the opposite lens to stretch the image again while projecting it on-screen, the final image presents itself in the correct dimensions (Figures 4.20 and 4.21). The advantage of CinemaScope is that the full area of the 4:3 field on the filmstrip is used and the image not shrunken, which raises the image quality and gives a better picture. Because of its use of 35 mm film stock CinemaScope was very successful in the theatres, as the projectors did not need to be changed and only anamorphic lenses needed to be installed. The actual aspect ratio for CinemaScope changed throughout the years due to the sound stripe being changed from an additional filmstrip with magnetic sound that was synced to the CinemaScope image (in the year 1953 it was 2.66:1) to the soundtrack being on the same filmstrip (still in 1953: 2.55:1). It continued to change to a 2.35:1 (see Figure 4.19) presentation in 1955 with various sound stripe options and in 1970 to a final 2.39:1 aspect ratio to provide a black space between frames for better projection.[22]

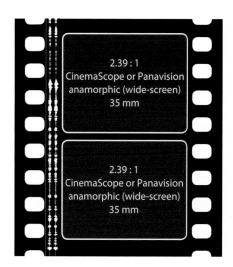

**Figure 4.19**

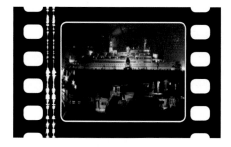

**Figure 4.20**

**Figure 4.21**

---

[20] Jean-Jacques Meusy and Alan Williams, Henri Chrétien, Bernard Natan, and the Hypergonar, *Film History*, Vol. 15, No. 1 (2003), pp. 11–31.
[21] John Belton, Introduction Widescreen; *Film History*, Vol. 15, No. 1 (2003), pp. 3–4.
[22] The American Widescreen Museum; Cinemascope: Facts on the Aspect Ratio, http://www.widescreenmuseum.com/widescreen/cinemascope_oar.htm (last modified by December 23 2017).

Vertical Orientation

# CinemaScope in animation

The first animated short done in CinemaScope was Disney's *Toot, Whistle, Plunk and Boom* in 1953, directed by Ward Kimball. In March 1954, in an article in the magazine *Films in Review*[23] Kimball discussed the advantages and disadvantages of the new wide-screen format for animation in particular. He explained that the new wider format made some of the old animation equipment obsolete as new animation discs had to be designed to fit the wider animation paper.

**Examples of 2.39:1**

### US Animated Features in CinemaScope

- *Lady and the Tramp* (1955)
- *Raggedy Ann & Andy: A Musical Adventure* (1977)
- *Anastasia* (1997)
- *Titan A.E.* (2000)
- *Brother Bear* (2003): partly 1.66, partly 2.35
- *The Simpsons Movie* (2007); Itchy and Scratchy part shot in 1.85:1
- *WALL-E* (2008)
- *Shrek Forever After* (2010)
- *ParaNorman* (2012)

### UK Animated Feature in Panavision

- *The Thief and the Cobbler* (1964–1995, unfinished)

### US Animated Shorts in CinemaScope MGM

### Droopy

- *Millionaire Droopy* (1956)
- *One Droopy Night* (1957)
- *Sheep Wrecked* (1958)
- *Mutts about Racing* (1958)
- *Droopy Leprechaun* (1958)

### Tom and Jerry

- *Pet Peeves* (1954)
- *Touché, Pussy Cat!* (1954)
- *Southbound Duckling* (1955)
- *Pup on a Picnic* (1955)
- *That's My Mommy* (1955)
- *Tom and Chérie* (1955)
- Starting in 1956–1958, all Tom and Jerry shorts were shot in CinemaScope.

### US Animated Shorts in CinemaScope by Disney

- *Toot, Whistle, Plunk and Boom* (1953)

### Disney's Donald Duck

- *Grand Canyonscope* (1954)
- *No Hunting* (1955)
- *Bearly Asleep* (1955)
- *Beezy Bear* (1955)
- *Up a Tree* (1955)
- *Chips Ahoy* (1956)
- *How to Have an Accident in the Home* (1956)

### Disney's Humphrey the Bear

- *Hooked Bear* (1956)
- *In the Bag* (1956)

### US Animated Shorts in CinemaScope by UPA

- *Gerald McBoing! Boing! on Planet Moo* (1956)
- *When Magoo Flew* (1954)
- *The Fifty-First Dragon* (1954)
- *Magoo's Canine Mutiny* (1956)
- *Magoo Beats the Heat* (1956)
- *Magoo's Puddle Jumper* (1956)
- *Meet Mother Magoo* (1956)
- *Magoo Goes Overboard* (1957)
- *Magoo Breaks Par* (1957)

### US Animated Shorts in CinemaScope by Terrytoons

- Flebus (1957)
- *It's a Living* (1957)
- *Gaston's Baby* (1958)
- *The Juggler of Our Lady* (1958)
- *Springtime for Clobber* (1958)
- *Dustcap Doormat* (1958)
- *Signed, Sealed, and Clobbered* (1958)
- *Sidney's Family Tree* (1958)
- *Foofle's Picnic* (1960)
- *Tree Spree* (1961)
- *Honorable Cat Story* (1961)
- *Home Life* (1962)
- *Tea House Mouse* (1963)
- *Spooky-Yaki* (1963)
- *Search for Misery* (1964)

---

[23] Ward Kimball, Cartooning in Cinemascope, *Films in Review*, March 1954, New York City, NY, pp. 118–119.

All the other departments also had to learn or figure out ways of dealing with the wider scope, especially the layout department, which needed to adjust the character action and composition on a wider frame.

Ward Kimball: "In CinemaScope, *cartoon characters* move, not the backgrounds. Because there is more space, the characters can move around without getting outside the visual angle. They can also move around in relation to each other. In CinemaScope cartoon characters no longer perform in one spot against a moving background *but are moved through the scenes*."[24] CinemaScope provided simplification because fewer shots and cuts were required as the characters moved in more continuous actions on a wider set. Because of the wider backgrounds, more characters could be shown in one shot (unless the film were later cropped to smaller ratios).

One film in particular used 2D animation as a special effect to great success in CinemaScope: Fred M. Wilcox's live-action sci-fi feature *Forbidden Planet* (1954). In this science fiction drama, the special effects are exceptionally well done, and in particular the alien monster is unusually convincing for a film of that era. Drawn in 2D by Joshua Meador (special effects animator from Disney and one of the four artists in Disney's documentary *4 Artists Paint 1 Tree: A Walt Disney "Adventure in Art"* from 1958), the effects animation of the fiery red and credible "monster of the subconscious" showed what else 2D animation was capable of in CinemaScope's scale.

# Japanese feature animation and Toeiscope

In 1958, the Japanese film company Toei projected its first live-action feature in Toeiscope, which was licensed by CinemaScope.[24] Toei Animation, a branch of Toei, released its first feature and with it Japan's first animated feature in color in 1958: Taiji Yabushita's *Hakujaden* (*The Tale of the White Serpent*), which was shot in the 1.66:1 aspect ratio. Toei Animation's second feature *Shônen Sarutobi Sasuke* (*Magic Boy*) (1959) was the first animated feature that was shown with the Toeiscope projection system and presented in the 2.35:1 ratio. *Saiyûki* (*Alakazam the Great*), in 1960, was the second. Many of the features since then have been shot in 2.35:1 ratio. Hayao Miyazaki, though, Japan's most famous animation director, has shot all his films in the 1.85:1 ratio. Toeiscope is licensed by CinemaScope but, instead of the 2.39 ratio, it uses 2.35:1.

## Examples of Wide-Screen

### Japanese Studio 4°C in 2.35:1

- *Tekkonkinkreet* (2006)

### Toei Animation's Cinematographic Process: Toeiscope, 2.35:1

- *Saiyûki (Alakazam the Great)* (1960)
- *Gulliver's Travels beyond the Moon* (1965)
- *The Little Norse Prince* (1968)
- *Flying Phantom Ship* (1969)
- *The World of Hans Christian Andersen* (1968)
- *Puss in Boots* (1969)
- *30,000 Miles under the Sea* (1970)
- *Ali Baba and the Forty Thieves* (1971)
- *Mazinger Z vs. The Great General of Darkness* (1974)
- *Taro the Dragon Boy* (1979)
- *Aesop's Fables* (1983)

### Chinese Animation in 2.35:1

- *Nezha Conquers the Dragon King/Prince Nezha's Triumph against Dragon King* (1979)

---

**CinemaScope article:**

David Bordwell, *Poetics of Cinema*, (1st ed.). Routledge, New York, NY, 2007.

---

24  Ward Kimball, Cartooning in Cinemascope, *Films in Review*, March 1954, New York City, NY, p. 119.

> 2.76 : 1
> Ultra Panavision 70 or
> MGM Camera 65
> anamorphic (wide-screen) 70 mm

**Figure 4.22**

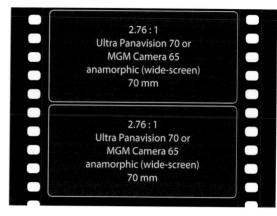

> 2.76 : 1
> Ultra Panavision 70 or
> MGM Camera 65
> anamorphic (wide-screen)
> 70 mm
>
> 2.76 : 1
> Ultra Panavision 70 or
> MGM Camera 65
> anamorphic (wide-screen)
> 70 mm

**Figure 4.23**

2.76:1: Ultra Panavision or MGM Camera 65 was shot on 65 mm film stock and therefore had a better image quality to begin with. Where most of the other wide-screen ratios used 35 mm and fit the image into the 3:4 field, Ultra Panavision used a 70 mm filmstrip for projection, which provided twice the scale compared to 35 mm. The film was shot on 65 mm and then projected on 70 mm. The additional 5 mm difference contained four soundtracks that displayed a six-channel stereo sound on four magnetic sound stripes. Ultra Panavision used an anamorphic lens with a 1.25× squash of the image and stretch while projecting it again on the screen, which can be seen in the different sizes of the frame in the projection size in Figure 4.22 compared to the squashed frame on the film stock in Figure 4.23. Ultra Panavision 70 or MGM Camera 65 was introduced in 1957 and lasted until 1966, when it finally ran out of fashion.

**Examples of Ultra Panavision 70**

***US Live-Action Feature Films***

- *Ben Hur* (1959)
- *How the West Was Won* (1959), shot in Panavision and Cinerama
- *Mutiny on the Bounty* (1962)
- *It's a Mad, Mad, Mad, Mad World* (1963)
- *Khartoum* (1966), filmed in Panavision 70 but presented in single-projector Cinerama

> 4.00 : 1
> Polyvision
> 3 x 35 mm

**Figure 4.24**

4.00:1: Polyvision was by far the widest of the flat-screen cinematic aspect ratios for feature films (only superseded by Disney World's 12:1 ratio Circle-Vision 360°, which does not show narrative feature films). In Polyvision, three projectors were placed next to each other to project the massive 4.00:1 format.[25] It was only used once for Abel Gance's *Napoleon* in 1927. The film was projected in the first two parts in the regular 1.33:1 format, and only the last part was projected with three 1.33:1 frames next to each other. Polyvision is technically not a wide-screen format, as it consists of three different images of a 3:4 ratio that present a montage of scenes, where the middle frame is the narrative frame and the left and right one the accompanying "mood" frames,[26] therefore, rather a triptych. The Polyvision frames show only in a couple of shots one continuous image that consists of three slightly overlapping projections (Figure 4.25). The effect, however, is not fully convincing, despite its awe-inspiring grandeur, as the final images do not always overlap correctly.

**Figure 4.25**

---

[25] In *Wide Screen Movies*, Carr and Hayes mention an aspect ratio of 3.66:1.

[26] Robert E. Carr and R.M. Hayes, *Wide Screen Movies, A History and Filmography of Wide Gauge Filmmaking*, Mc Farland and Co. Inc., Jefferson, NC, 1988, p. 4.

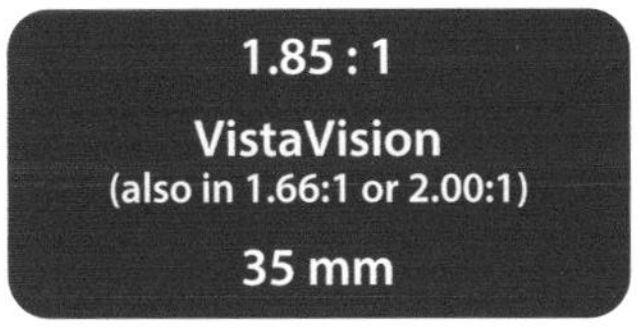

**1.85 : 1**

**VistaVision**
(also in 1.66:1 or 2.00:1)

**35 mm**

**Figure 4.26**

1.66:1, 1.85:1, and 2.00:1: In 1954, Paramount responded to CinemaScope with their own ratio: VistaVision. Where all the other wide-screen technologies we have been looking at so far used the filmstrip in the traditional presentation of the sprockets being vertical, VistaVision had the same 35 mm film stock but turned it horizontally and had the image also horizontal. The advantage is a much bigger field size on the same 35 mm film. Usually VistaVision is unsqueezed and shot and projected without an anamorphic lens, thus giving a sharper picture at a 1.66:1 ratio. However, there was also the possibility of making the image wider with anamorphic lenses, bringing the image up to a ratio of 2.00:1. Paramount stated in 1954 that it considered a ratio of 1.66:1 to be the perfect size and the initial CinemaScope ratio as too wide for its height. VistaVision could be shot in 1.66, 1.85, and the aforementioned 2.00:1 aspect ratio (Figure 4.27). The soundtrack was optical and the film image was much clearer and crisper than its competitors. Because of the longer filmstrip (the horizontal position of the image on a 35 mm filmstrip made the image occupy eight instead of four sprockets' length), VistaVision needed to be presented at a higher speed, which caused many technical problems during the projection, which made it less practical.

Nevertheless, VistaVision was heavily used in special effects shots due to its bigger size and better image quality. For special effects, multiple filmstrips have to be copied over and over in the optical printer (where two or more film images are copied onto one) in order to transfer all effects shots together onto one final image. Every generation of film loses quality during the copying process, which means that if 35 mm film were used in the traditional vertical orientation, after several runs through the optical printer, the image quality would be insufficient for presentation. But because VistaVision had a much bigger field size, after several copy phases the picture quality was still good and precise enough for a traditional vertical 35 mm print.

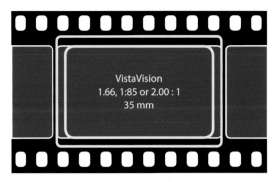

**Figure 4.27**

**Examples of VistaVision's Use for Special Effects in US Features (Excerpt)**

- *Star Wars* (1977)
- *The Empire Strikes Back* (1980)
- *Tron* (1982)
- *Star Trek: The Wrath of Khan* (1982)
- *Return of the Jedi* (1983)
- *Back to the Future* (1986)
- *RoboCop* (1987)
- *Who Framed Roger Rabbit* (1989)
- *Back to the Future Part II* (1989)
- *The Abyss* (1989)
- *Indiana Jones and the Last Crusade* (1989)
- *Back to the Future Part III* (1990)
- *Forrest Gump* (1994)
- *Jumanji* (1995)
- *Contact* (1997)
- *Men in Black* (1998)
- *The Matrix* (1999)
- *The Mummy* (1999)
- *Gladiator* (2000)
- *The Perfect Storm* (2000)
- *The Mummy Returns* (2001)
- *Spider-Man 2* (2004)
- *Batman Begins* (2005)
- *The Dark Knight* (2008)
- *Watchmen* (2009)
- *Inception* (2010)
- *Harry Potter and the Deathly Hallows, Parts 1 and 2* (2010, 2011)
- *Interstellar* (2014)

**Japanese Animated Features**

- *Lupin III: The Mystery of Mamo* (1978)
- *Urusei Yatsura 2: Beautiful Dreamer* (1984)[27]

---

[27] http://en.wikipedia.org/wiki/List_of_VistaVision_films (last edited by December 23, 2017).

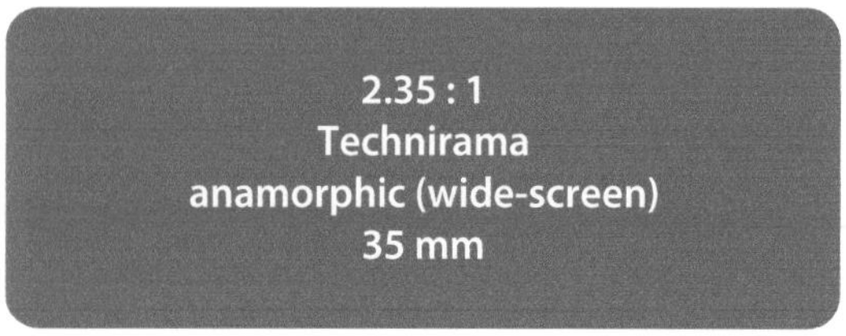

2.35 : 1
Technirama
anamorphic (wide-screen)
35 mm

**Figure 4.28**

2.35:1: Technirama is very much the same as VistaVision, but brought to the audience by Technicolor instead of Paramount. It uses the same horizontal orientation of the filmstrip with an equal image length of eight sprockets (Figure 4.29). Technirama, though, did use an anamorphic lens to stretch the image to a 2.35:1 aspect ratio on the cinema screen, making it wider than VistaVision.

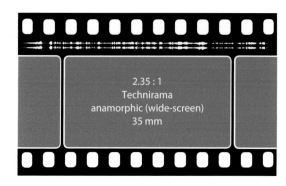

2.35 : 1
Technirama
anamorphic (wide-screen)
35 mm

**Figure 4.29**

**Examples**

**US Animated Features in Technirama**

*   *Sleeping Beauty* (1957), in its full negative aspect ratio of 2.55:1, its Technirama cinematic presentation of 2.20:1 and its CinemaScope presentation of 2.35:1
*   *The Black Cauldron* (1985)

**Books on aspect ratios, wide-screen cinema, and television:**

Robert E. Carr and R.M. Hayes, *Wide Screen Movies, A History and Filmography of Wide Gauge Filmmaking*, McFarland and Co. Inc., Jefferson, MO, 1988.

Belton John, *Widescreen Cinema*, Harvard University Press, Cambridge, MA, 1992.

Charles Musser, *Before the Nickelodeon: Edwin S. Porter and the Edison Manufacturing Company*, University of California Press, Berkeley, CA, 1991.

Erik Barnouw, *Tube of Plenty: The Evolution of American Television*, Oxford University Press, Oxford, 1990.

**Figure 4.30**

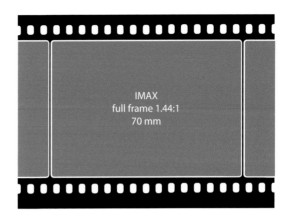

**Figure 4.31**

1.43:1: In September 1929, the Fox Film Company introduced the Grandeur[28] system at the Gaiety Theatre on Broadway in New York to audiences. The film was *Fox Movietone Follies of 1929* and was the start of a 2-year-long production of wide-screen movies by Fox. The new system used 70 mm film for the presentation (in a different perforation than today's 70 mm format). Due to its expensive nature and the raging Great Depression, the system was not profitable and was stopped after a couple of features, all done by Fox. Other Hollywood studios like Warner Brothers, MGM, and Paramount were also investing in larger formats from 55 mm up to 70 mm,[29] though none of the studios could agree on a wider format that would become the standard. The 70 mm filmstrip was used by Ultra Panavision and Todd-AO in the mid-1950s; however, both used the filmstrip vertically. IMAX, developed in 1970, uses the filmstrip horizontally, thus increasing the field tremendously. In 1970, director Donald Britain from the National Film Board of Canada presented the very first true IMAX film at the Expo in Osaka: *Tiger Child* at the Fuji Group Pavilion.[30] The first permanent IMAX theatre opened in 1971 at the Ontario Place in Toronto, Canada. IMAX film stock does not contain any soundtrack area, as it wants to keep the image size as big as possible, to not jeopardize its crispness. The soundtrack is on an additional 35 mm magnetic film that is locked to the film image (very much like Cinerama used to do at the very beginning of its success). The IMAX image size is 15 sprockets in length (Figure 4.31), making it significantly larger

than any other wide-screen format (four times bigger than VistaVision!). However, in its aspect ratio, IMAX has a rather traditional size of 1.43:1, but can be widened to 1.89:1 or 2.39:1.

The number of films that have been shown in IMAX cinemas is very extensive, though most of them are documentaries and travelogues and only a small number are feature films. Again, this scale seems less of a fit for a narrative film than for visual spectacles; however, IMAX does show narrative films on a regular basis.

**Examples of IMAX Features**

**US Animated Features in IMAX**

- *Fantasia 2000* (1999)
- *Treasure Planet* (2002)
- *The Polar Express* (2004)

**Reissues of Animated Features in IMAX**

- Beauty and the Beast
- *The Lion King*

**Regular Features in IMAX (Not Necessarily Shot with an IMAX Camera)**

- Harry Potter franchise released for IMAX, shot in Panavision
- *Interstellar* (2014), which actually used the IMAX cameras for many shots

[28] David Coles, Magnified Grandeur: The Big Screen 1926–31, *70 mm: The 70 mm Newsletter*, Vol. 14, No. 64 (2001), pp. 4–8.
[29] 70mm Is Born, Dies, and is Resurrected; Martin Hart (curator): http://www.widescreenmuseum.com/widescreen/wingto1.htm (accessed January 15, 2015).
[30] IMAX's Chronology of Technological Events (Reprinted courtesy of IMAX Corp.) http://www.ieee.ca/millennium/imax/imax_chronology.html (accessed January 13, 2015).

# Case study: Widescreen and composition in *Disney's Sleeping Beauty* (1959)[31]

**Supervising director:** Clyde Geronimi

**Production design:** Ken Anderson, Don DaGradi

**Sequence directors:** Les Clark, Eric Larson, Wolfgang Reitherman

**Color stylist:** Eyvind Earle

**Backgrounds:** Dick Anthony, Frank Armitage, Al Dempster, Ralph Hulett, Bill Layne, Fil Mottola, Walt Peregoy, Anthony Rizzo, Richard H. Thomas, Thelma Witmer

**Layout:** Ray Aragon, Tom Codrick, Basil Davidovich, Don Griffith, Victor Haboush, Joe Hale, Jack Huber, Hoomer Jonas, Ernie Nordli, McLaren Stewart, Chuck Jones (uncredited)

*Sleeping Beauty* was the 16th feature-length animation production by Disney Studios and is nowadays praised as one of the most beautifully designed features ever produced, as well as the most lavish. Its scale and unique design make it for sure an outstanding film. *Sleeping Beauty* continues the series of Disney using European fairy tales as a basis, starting obviously with *Snow White and the Seven Dwarfs* in 1937 after having tackled many other fairy tales in short films throughout the 1930s. Disney's second feature, *Pinocchio* from 1940, based on the story of Pinocchio by Carlo Collodi, published in an Italian teen periodical, can loosely be called a fairy tale, as a fairy actually does appear in the story. The third fairy tale was in 1950: *Cinderella*. *Alice in Wonderland* is based on a novel, *Peter Pan* on a stage play, and finally *Sleeping Beauty* in 1959, based on the Brothers Grimm's and Charles Perrault's documentations of traditional German and French tales. The writing of *Sleeping Beauty*'s screenplay started in early 1951 and the film's release was continuously postponed from 1955 (the initially planned release) all the way to 1959, which made it not only the longest feature in production to that point but also the most expensive[32] (it supposedly cost $6 million).[33] However, every penny that was spent can be seen on-screen, as the lushness of its images is unsurpassed. The overall complexity of the production, its scale, and overall design crowns *Sleeping Beauty* as a gem amongst animated features. Disney created his own interpretation of the fairy tale of the young princess Briar Rose, cursed by the sorceress Maleficent to die from pricking her finger on a spindle on her 16th birthday. With the help of three fairies, the curse is decreased from death to sleep and they raise Briar Rose in the nearby forest in safety, away from the court and away from danger. On her 16th birthday, though, despite all care,

she is stung by a spindle and falls into a deep sleep. Prince Phillip, who met Aurora in the forest just before her birthday, makes it his task to save and marry her. After a long fight with Maleficent, Phillip prevails, and Aurora is saved.

The development of the feature proceeded differently than the features that had been produced at the studio before. Whenever Walt came into story meetings for *Sleeping Beauty*, his mind was occupied with other projects that seemed more important to him at the time (the Disneyland theme park or TV productions that very much helped to bring in revenue for the company), so much so that the development of *Sleeping Beauty* suffered from neglect on his part. As Disney himself was the head of the studio and everything had to be signed off by him in order to continue the development of the film, any delay or even halt did immensely affect the production. Artists and staff attending the meetings on *Sleeping Beauty* remembered not only the pressure Walt was under from other projects but also his overall neglect and lack of detailed attention to the feature. Producer Harry Tytle wrote years later that Disney "seems to be tired, has so much on his mind; he didn't give this the treatment he would have in years past, where he'd go in for a couple of days and fine-tooth comb the whole picture … He hit more from a broad aspect than from small specifics, like he used to."[34]

Disney's interpretation of the original tale of Sleeping Beauty comes with many changes that leave only the basic framework of the story. Unfortunately, the final story structure is a bit bumpy at times, as Disney focuses on aspects that are not in the book and are extended in the film version for no apparent reason other than bringing entertainment. The drinking feast between King Stefan and King Hubert seems out of place and just hinders the flow of the story, as "charming" as it might seem. In addition, the cake baking, and dress-making scene is overly extended to give more room to the entertaining and warm-hearted fairies, but it does not really bring the story forward. The story also lacks some logic in key scenes. Although Aurora has lived with the fairies in the forest for 16 years, they still don't know how to bake a cake or make a dress, despite having lived on their own for over a decade and cared for Aurora without using any magic. What did they eat back in the woods? Bark? Then, when Aurora is being brought back to the castle on her 16th birthday, the fairies leave her by herself to grieve, despite knowing that this is the day when she is supposed to be stung by the spindle, the day for which they had been hiding her for 16 years! These, let's call them "minor" faults, do seem strange in a massive production like this, though they do not reduce the pleasure of watching the film, as the visuals and the entertainment make up tenfold for the faults.

---

[31] Due to the fact that the Disney Company did not release the copyrights for images of this feature to be used in this educational section, which would have tremendously helped the understanding of the discussed composition, it is necessary for the reader to check and compare widescreen images from the movie alongside the text to fully grasp the design.

[32] Michael Barrier, *Hollywood Cartoons: American Animation in its Golden Age*, Oxford University Press, Oxford, 1999, pp. 554–555.

[33] Bob Thomas, *Disney's Art of Animation, from Mickey Mouse to Hercules*, Hyperion, New York City, NY, 1997, p. 105.

[34] Harry Tytle, *One of "Walt's boys," An Insider's Account of Disney's Golden Years*, Airtight Seels Allied Production, Royal Oak, Mission Viejo, CA, 1997, p. 219.

Just to mention some of the major accomplishments of *Sleeping Beauty*: it has the most complex color line work in cel animation, the biggest frame with 70 mm Super Technirama wide-screen, and the most detailed backgrounds in the group of animated Disney features. These accomplishments compensate for some of the flaws in the story.

Nevertheless, the story development was not the only difficulty that the feature dealt with from the beginning on—the design also created major challenges for the involved parties. Disney himself was always very fond of visual development artist Mary Blair's work, so much so that he wanted her sensibility and design to appear in the features on-screen, not only as a visual development artist working for the production behind the screen. He wanted a film that *looked* like Blair's work. Though of course *Alice in Wonderland* (1951), *Peter Pan* (1953), and some short films contain traces of her style, there is not much left of her work in the final screen image, as Walt himself admitted. His decision to give Eyvind Earle, a background painter and designer at the studio since 1951, the stylistic direction of *Sleeping Beauty* was made clear by his statement from an earlier preproduction meeting: "For years and years I have been hiring artists like Mary Blair to design the styling of a feature, and by the time the picture is finished, there is hardly a trace of the original styling left. This time Eyvind Earle is styling *Sleeping Beauty* and that's the way it's going to be!" Despite Disney's obvious statement, the question is why he gave Eyvind Earle the overwhelming authority to decide the feature's look and background design (Earle is actually named in the credits of the film as the color stylist). Earle had already worked on various features and shorts as the background painter at the studio. However, it was his personal style that struck Disney as unique enough to try a new approach for the visuals in *Sleeping Beauty*. At the time, Earle had a style that was different from the typical Disney style and thus his work could be considered a new direction for the film's look, as it had worked years previously with Tyrus Wong's on *Bambi*. Before Earle started at Disney, he had worked successfully as a designer of greeting cards and could look back at 20 years of painting experience and exhibitions that allowed him to develop his own style, far removed from any animation style. Additionally, what Walt was tending toward was more illustrative visuals rather than the typical animation visuals. Once Disney had decided that Earle would be responsible for the look of the film, he focused his energy on other projects, especially Disneyland, which demanded his full attention. Animated feature films were not the focus for Walt anymore. They took a back seat for the company's planned future due to the high costs and lengthy production time, which was caused partly by Walt's very own lack of commitment. Frank Thomas remembered, "We were on that (*Sleeping Beauty*) for five years, and that was all because we couldn't get Walt to come into any of the meetings. You'd eventually get him, but you couldn't move anything."[35]

---

[35] Michael Barrier, *The Animated Man: A Life of Walt Disney*, University of California Press, Berkeley, CA, p. 272.

## Design

Disney Animation had already been creating "illusions of life" for about 25 years with organic flowing shapes and naturalistic movement in the characters and dynamism in the organic line itself. The curved line was the basis of everything that Disney had been doing since the Alice shorts in the early 1920s. That changed with the dawn of modern animation, which was initiated by United Productions of America (UPA), the animation company from Los Angeles that pushed animation design to the next level and allowed modern ideas of art and design to impregnate the often rather conservative animation designs of the rest of the animation business. Art aesthetics (and also commercial illustration) were so far removed from what animation design was doing at the time that it was just a matter of time until someone connected the two and brought a new sensibility into commercial animation that was modern and fresh. UPA started in the mid-1940s with various short films (*Hell Bent For Election*, 1945; *Private Snafu: A Few Quick Facts: Fear*, 1945; *Brotherhood of Men*, 1946) that explored the idea of pushing animation design away from the industry leader's naturalistic approach towards a more stylized design that not only speaks to the visual senses but also the intellectual. UPA's achievement cannot be overestimated, as it single-handedly allowed a very different style to dominate animation from then on. In the 1950s and 1960s, UPA's animation aesthetics led the field and its influence still surrounds animation production nowadays. Their success in the 1950s was immense in short films and commercials. The Disney Studios could not close its eyes to this development and therefore had to adjust its direction ever so slightly. In some shorts, like *Toot, Whistle, Plunk and Boom* from 1953 or *Pigs is Pigs* from 1954, the Disney designers went down the visual path that UPA had opened. Nevertheless, Disney shorts always stayed on the visual surface with their use of modern design, as they changed the visuals but not how the visuals were intertwined with the intellectual basis of the story. UPA interpreted freely in their better shorts with shapes and colors, textures, and the character animation style the visuals for a specific story so that it all culminated in one unique and strong artistic concept. Each concept was based on the visual and intellectual representation of that very story, not the mere naturalistic depiction of it, and thus every UPA short film has its very own style that evolved out of that specific story. Disney, on the other hand, saw the development in 1950s style only from a visual perspective; thus they changed the look of the films slightly but didn't see the additional potential that the modern design had in terms of its sensibility towards how the audience can be manipulated with the "feel" of semi representational visuals or nonrepresentational colors. The full UPA approach to modern design never really took hold at Disney Studios, which always spoke to the masses in terms of stylized naturalism. *Sleeping Beauty* is a film that still is in the same realm as all the other Disney features, as it is representational in its depiction of nature, slightly less so than, for example, *Bambi* or

*Snow White*. It is much more stylized in shape and form and also in its depiction of space and perspective. As Walt Disney stated in 1935 during the preparation of *Snow White and the Seven Dwarfs* in a letter to Don Graham:

> The point must be made clear to the men that our study of the actual is not so that we may be able to accomplish the actual, but so that we may have a basis upon which to go into the fantastic, the unreal, the imaginative—and yet to let it have a foundation of fact, in order that it may more richly possess sincerity and contact with the public. A good many of the men misinterpret the idea of studying the actual motion. They think it is our purpose merely to duplicate these things. This misconception should be cleared up for all. I definitely feel that we cannot do the fantastic things, based on the real, unless we first know the real. This point should be brought out very clearly to all new men, and even the older men.[36]

This states clearly that Disney never wanted to make a copy of life. It was never his goal to come as closely to real life as possible but to give a version of it and, as he said, "to create the fantastic, the unreal, the imaginative." *Sleeping Beauty* is still in exactly the same visual realm as described by Disney but does not go as far as UPA pushed its design. The evolvement for modern design in the 1950s that took over the animation field worldwide was heavily toned down for *Sleeping Beauty* in order to fit the tradition of nearly 20 years of Disney features. The final film is a bridge between the sensibility of old illustrated books and European fairy tale visuals and a contemporary design that also looks forward and incorporates the development that UPA initiated. The outcome is in parts a stunning example of the best of what hand-drawn animation is capable of.

The film's story is set in the 14th century and the artists chose the *Très Riches Heures du Duc de Berry*, painted by the Limburg brothers from 1412 to 1416, the *Unicorn Tapestries* (1495–1505; Metropolitan Museum of Art, New York), and *The Lady and the Unicorn* tapestries (ca. 1500; Musée National du Moyen Âge, Paris; see Figure 4.32) as their main source of inspiration for the look of the film. Layout artist John Hench provided the initial idea to use European medieval art for the basis of the film's visuals.[37] Earle mentioned in an interview with Richard Allan on July 15, 1989, that he wanted "stylized, simplified Gothic, a medieval tapestry out of the surface wherever possible … Everything from the foreground to the far distance is in focus. That gives you more depth."[38] Once Eyvind Earle was put in charge of the overall film design by Walt Disney himself, he developed a style that was very much based on European and Persian book illustration,

**Figure 4.32**

*The Lady and the Unicorn* at the Musée National du Moyen Âge in Paris.

the abovementioned tapestries, and Laurence Olivier's feature film and Shakespeare adaptation of *Henry V* from 1944,[39] which uses the *Très Riches Heures du Duc de Berry* in some backgrounds as a basis.

When compared to the source material that Earle used as inspiration, there is one composition that Earle seemed to have followed in his backgrounds repeatedly and that is that of the six tapestries of *The Lady and the Unicorn* (Figure 4.32) at the Musée National du Moyen Âge in Paris (not to be confused with the *Unicorn Tapestries* in the Cloisters of the Metropolitan Museum of Art in New York, which impressed John Hench to the point where he suggested them as a style direction to Walt Disney). The tapestries of *The Lady and the Unicorn* have very similar compositional components that can be found again in most of Earle's background designs for *Sleeping Beauty*. The strong focus on horizontals and verticals (Figure 4.33), the very center and also left and right off-center, plus the vertical elements on the very left and right of the frame corners can all be found as significant compositional fields in Earle's backgrounds. It is not just a similarity between the two that can be traced back to medieval art in general but a very strong connection to this one compositional concept in all six of the tapestries.

Earle uses the precise visual description in renaissance art and Persian illustration to describe the fairy tale forest in miniscule details. Nevertheless, he does not just copy the art but interprets it with a modern sensibility and creates something new and unique. The modern geometric and shape-oriented design

[36] Shaun Usher, *Letters of Note*; "How to train an animator" by Walt Disney, http://www.lettersofnote.com/2010/06/how-to-train-animator-by-walt-disney.html (accessed August 25, 2017).

[37] Michael Barrier, *Hollywood Cartoons*, Oxford University Press, 2009; New York, NY, pp. 556–557.

[38] Bruno Girveau, Lella Smith, and Pierre Lambert, *Once Upon a Time: Walt Disney, the Sources of Inspiration for the Disney Studios*, Prestel Publishing, Munich, 2007, p. 132.

[39] Bruno Girveau, Lella Smith, and Pierre Lambert, *Once Upon a Time: Walt Disney, the Sources of Inspiration for the Disney Studios*, Oxford University Press, Oxford, 2006; Girveau writes, "… Laurence Olivier's film of *Henry V* (1944), whose reconstructed settings for both the interiors and exteriors were extensively used in the development of *Sleeping Beauty*," page 234.

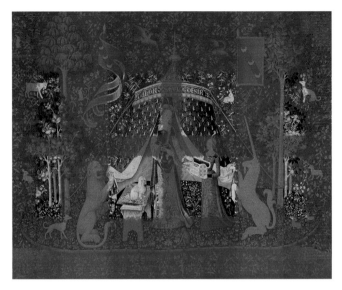

**Figure 4.33**

is combined with the flat perspectives, the flat colors, and geometric composition of the mentioned tapestries and book illuminations and develops a style that still impresses with its complexities today. However, in Earle's own words, his influences seem more widespread and have a surprising randomness, though also a refreshing playfulness:

> And since it's obvious that the Gothic style and detail evolved from the Arabic influence acquired during the Crusades, I found it perfectly permissible to use all the wonderful patterns and details found in Persian miniatures. And since Persian miniatures had a lot in common with Chinese and Japanese art, I felt it was OK for me to inject quite a bit of Japanese art, especially in the close-ups of leaves and overhanging branches.[40]

This treatment of nature is most apparent in the famous forest scene (Sequence 8, 00:22:36), where Briar Rose meets her dream prince for the first time. The lush forest looks like an English garden design of the 18th century. Everything is cut and trimmed for the highest compositional impact and breathes the artificiality of controlled nature of famous European Baroque gardens or even Japanese gardens. *Snow White*'s and *Bambi*'s forests are natural settings that emanate organic life and depict freely growing and untamed nature. *Sleeping Beauty*'s forest is a gigantic park setting that is well groomed daily and kept clean of any fallen leave that might disrupt the composition and spoil its innocence. Earle not only used the design and look of medieval art but also chose a painting technique similar to that of illuminated manuscripts of the 14th century. The colors are layered, and the forms create their dimensionality through tedious textures and suggested light and shadow that sculpt them dimensionally, though do not necessarily give them a realistic look. Earle's backgrounds are also layered in color and

light, starting with the simple composition of the shapes in plain colors and then adding the textures and details on top. His paintings do not have any movement within the color that derives from the brush stroke or from adding color strokes with slightly different hues onto the canvas to simulate a vibrating effect. Earle's colors are very even and flat, which allows the flat cel animation to fit in beautifully. In one of the instructional paintings he did for his colleagues to teach them how to paint "Earle" style, one can see the technique he used step by step, starting with the broad shapes, then using a sponge to give the shapes texture, and then adding the additional detailed textures to strengthen depth, perspective, and light and shadows.

## Composition

At the beginning of the 1950s, cinema had to compete with television to keep audiences in the theaters instead of watching television at home. TV was becoming more and more common in modern households and the movie industry responded with the "experience film" by expanding the scale of the cinematic screen and giving the audiences a visual thrill that they could not have at home in front of their still rather modestly sized TV sets. There had been wide-screen ratios in cinema before but none that really caught on for very long. For the feature *Lady and the Tramp* Disney decided to use the popular wide-screen ratio CinemaScope to make his film more attractive to audiences. *Lady and the Tramp* was shot in 1954 as the first animated feature in CinemaScope 2.35:1 aspect ratio. The layout artists and animators had to learn how to deal with the different frame ratio of 70 mm wide-screen, which was a hugely different frame compared to the earlier used ratio of 1.33:1 or 4:3, as not just the screen was bigger but the artwork the artists were animating and drawing the layouts on also had to be wider. *Sleeping Beauty* was the second of Disney's animated features shot in wide-screen, but this time Disney used 70 mm Technirama with the same 2.35:1 ratio for prints and an even wider ratio for the original negative: 2.55:1. Burny Mattinson, an animator on *Sleeping Beauty*, discussed in an interview the reasons for the decision to shoot again in the wide format:

> CinemaScope was the new wave at the time and we had just done *Lady and the Tramp* which was originally to be done in standard 35 mm frame. Walt said "let's capitalize on CinemaScope" and we added the wider aspect into the designs. So, when it came to *Sleeping Beauty* he wanted to make it bigger and better and said "let's go with 70 mm" because he was trying to make a true classic. In fact he asked that we design this design as a moving tapestry.[41]

The choice to again shoot in this exceptionally wide format brought major problems to the overall production. Again, animator Burny Mattinson:

[40] Eyvind Earle, *Horizon Bound on a Bicycle; Autobiography*, Eyvind Earle, 1991.

[41] *Burny Mattinson Talks about Maleficent from Sleeping Beauty*, http://movieweb.com/burny-mattinson-talks-about-maleficent-from-sleeping-beauty/ (accessed April 19, 2017).

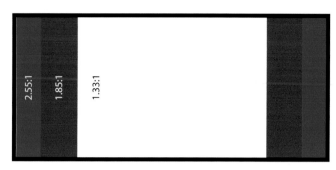

**Figure 4.34**

It caused a lot of problems, due to the fact that instead of working with 16″ paper, we were working with 48″ paper lengths—it slowed us down considerably. More mileage background-wise and character-wise meant more space to move a character across the screen. We had to put everything on a single frame which meant more drawings. Everything was twice as time-consuming.[42]

The enormously wide formatted frame had to be filled with interesting images that despite the width have characters that wouldn't feel lonely and lost in the huge horizontal stage. In order to increase the presentability of the final film, the composition had to follow two formats: the 2.55:1 ratio for the Technirama presentation and also a smaller format for regular movie theatres that were not equipped with the specific projectors needed to project the Technirama format. The layout artists and animators, therefore, had to be careful to place the action in the field ratio of US cinematic presentations since the 1960s, which was 1.85:1. The most important character action, though, was still in the 1.33:1 field within the wide horizontal Technirama field, leaving nearly half of the frame vacant of character animation and significant background information most of the time (Figures 4.34).

To compose the backgrounds, there are three compositional pairs of blocks in the frame plus the horizontal and vertical centers (Figure 4.35)[43] (a compositional framework we have seen in the tapestries of *The Lady and the Unicorn* in Figures 4.32 and 4.33). Those elements are not rigid in every shot of *Sleeping Beauty* but can be pushed left or right and up or down in order to balance the composition; however, they always appear in pairs, very rarely on their own. The four elements are two horizontal stripes that are above the lower and below the upper frame (blue); one pair of vertical stripes that is left and right off-center (purple); and one that is close to each outer frame (red) and additionally the horizontal and vertical center (turquoise). These pairs can shift left and right and vary in width and thus give a wide range of possibilities for the different needs of the

compositions. To reduce the immensely wide Technirama frame, Eyvind Earle places trees, objects, architecture, etc., in the vertical red blocks, which very much lessen the frame's width and also help to invite the viewer into the image, as they serve as either framing devices or provide a perspective drag into the image, like a theater scene. Considering the immense difficulties of such a wide format, the resulting final film image is rather stunning, not just from an artistic standpoint but also from a technical one. Though Earle did fight his battles at the Disney Studios to get his vision onto the screen to the best of his abilities, the result seems to prove him right at times.

Earle's backgrounds are most stunning in the forest sequence (Sequence 8, 00:22:36), directed by Eric Larson. It is the famous moment when Aurora is singing about her dream prince to a group of forest animals and afterwards actually meets him in

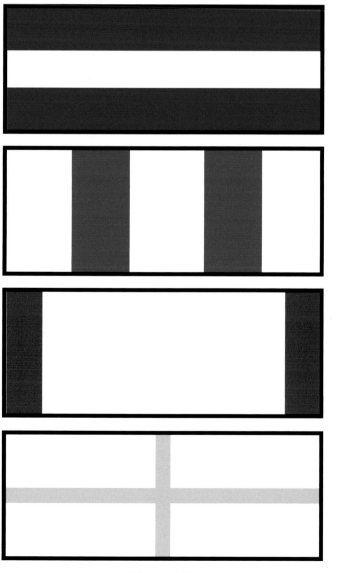

**Figure 4.35**

---

[42] *Once Upon A Dream: Burny Mattinson on Sleeping Beauty's Maleficent*, http://animatedviews.com/2008/once-upon-a-dream-burny-mattinson-on-sleeping-beautys-maleficent/ (accessed April 19, 2017).
[43] This is from my own observation, not a style or planned layout rule that the film followed!

person. The sheer scale of this sequence is everything and more of what Disney was capable of in terms of complexity. A stunning piece of animation indeed. The character's movements fit in style and position perfectly into the backgrounds, the story is delightful in those scenes, and the flow and grace of the overall character animation is utterly fluid.

Earle's background colors tend to be slightly desaturated. On the other hand, the characters that are in front of the backgrounds have very vibrant colors and separate successfully from their ground. It is difficult to comprehend that the animators at the Disney studio rejected the design because of the characters supposedly not reading well enough in front of the backgrounds. "He lacked the mood in a lot of things," director Clyde Geronimi said of Earle in 1976. "All that beautiful detail in the trees, the bark, and all that, that's all well and good, but who the hell's going to look at that?"[44]

Clyde Geronimi, one of the four directors on *Sleeping Beauty*, does have a point when you look at an animated film only from the perspective of characters and character-driven action, where the background is there to create a mood, take the supporting role, and provide a stage for the characters.. However, there is also another option and that is the background being a character itself that the audience can be enveloped by. A lush and detailed background can also have its own unique appeal that does not necessarily distract from the action of the characters. All the details don't have to be seen at all times, but they surely will be felt. That gives the scene a richness that is likewise a valid design direction. The characters' design in *Sleeping Beauty*, their outline, color, and movement allow them to stand on their own perfectly well, not being overshadowed by the complexity of the backgrounds, and additionally the difference in texture of background and characters lets them read very well indeed. Yet animator Frank Thomas stated: "… we had to find designs that enabled us to get some kind of life in the characters, but still recognize that they would have to 'work' against the busy detail of the backgrounds and hold their own graphically regardless of the choices Eyvind made for the colors of the costumes."[45] What is different in animation compared to illustration is the fact that movement will always separate the character from its background as movement overwrites all design elements and will attract the eye, despite the business of the texture. *Sleeping Beauty*, though, does have backgrounds that sometimes lack the warm and cozy Disney mood and feel cold and in the worst cases uncomfortable (partly because of the texture). Those are often the ones that contain architecture, especially the castle of King Stefan, Aurora's father. In some scenes, the castle feels very uninviting and has a cold atmosphere because of the treatment of the stone walls and the dark and dull or heavily desaturated colors. However, in other shots the architecture is

beautifully rendered and does look comfortable and inviting, despite its dominating texture, as shown in the long panorama shot at 00:44:38. Where the forest feels almost magical, the castle appears strange and distant. This can be seen in the first moments of the film, when the parade walks towards the castle gate to celebrate the birth of Aurora (00:03:00–00:03:11 and the follow-up shot 00:03:12–00:03:24). The choice of color in these shots is very different from earlier Disney features and also immensely different from the forest scene (Sequence 8). It does not emanate the joy of a celebration of the happiest day in King Stefan's and Queen Leah's lives. The characters' skin color is greyish pale and by contrast the fabrics have a saturation that in some parts explodes out of the frame. The colors here are nearly nonrepresentational, whereas in Forest Sequence 8, they are representational. This celebration could have been a successful sequence if the colors expressed a happier and more inviting mood. The distribution of textures is also somehow unconventional or often unsuccessful in the architectural backgrounds of that scene (especially in the shot beginning at 00:03:12). Comparing them with the images of the forest, the two seem to originate from two different films. The stone textures are mechanical, the river and grass in the background have no texture at all but just a very airbrushed look to them that lacks perspective and depth, and light and shadows are also strangely placed. This just lets the background fall apart in that section and it does look unsophisticated, especially compared to the heavy texture in the stones of the bridge, which separates from its surrounding like in a collage. In the forest backgrounds, this does not occur, because there is subtle texture even in the distant areas. Texture is well distributed with balance and perspective in mind. After Eyvind Earle left the production of *Sleeping Beauty* before the film was finalized, the backgrounds were reworked and airbrush was added by Gerry Geronimi to lessen the impact of the texture.[46] Whether those airbrushed parts are the ones that got added after Eyvind Earle left the production is difficult to determine. But it is very obvious that Earle felt very much at home with natural settings as compared to architectural ones (in his later personal career he focused almost solely on trees and landscapes). The discrepancy between the backgrounds ranges from excellent to lesser quality, and one can only speculate which backgrounds were done by Earle and which by his staff or were altered altogether.[47]

Most of the backgrounds follow the pattern mentioned in their main compositional elements, which are mostly horizontals and verticals that are placed very similarly from background to background (Figures 4.35 and 4.36). The balance is not just positive space balanced with positive space, but also positive versus negative space, which makes the images less rigid and provides

[44] Michael Barrier, *Hollywood Cartoons*, Oxford University Press, Oxford, p. 558.
[45] Michael Barrier, *The Animated Man: A Life of Walt Disney*, University of California Press, Berkeley, CA, p. 272.

[46] Michael Barrier, *Hollywood Cartoons: American Animation in its Golden Age*, Oxford University Press, Oxford, 1999, p. 558.
[47] By no means am I hinting at the idea that all the successful backgrounds are done by Earle himself!

Figure 4.36

them with a very pleasant tension (e.g., the background at 00:29:31, the moment when the owl wears the prince's cape; after the camera has zoomed out, the big tree on the right is being balanced by the negative space on the left at the exact same distance from the center). There is some rigidity in the background paintings, as they have mostly geometric shapes that only appear organic due to their textures, but it always appears as a style that is pleasant and enticing, especially those in Sequence 8.

The composition in this shot (starting at 00:29:24 and ending at 00:29:31) follows the mentioned pattern or compositional grid before and after a camera move. The camera zooms out at 00:29:29, and we can see that the beginning of the shot (00:29:24) has the same compositional foundation as the ending frame of the zoom (00:29:31). This whole idea of basing every shot on a compositional scheme seems rigid, though is a very smart move, because it gives all the images a structural foundation that changes ever so slightly to not allow sameness to sneak in. The flexibility of the compositional pattern is mostly possible because of the extra wide frame and can be seen in other live-action feature films with the same wide aspect ratio (especially the gorgeously composed epic Western *How the West Was Won* from 1962).

## Layout

The character animation is strictly confined to the 1.33:1 aspect ratio within the wider 70 mm Technirama format. The composition of the widescreen backgrounds supports in its design and layout the narrower action frame. If the full width of the screen were used for the character animation, then the film would be limited to a theatrical 70 mm presentation and could not be cut for TV or other narrower media, because the characters would be cut off. Limiting the characters' actions to a smaller frame firstly allows presentation in every medium

from 70 mm down to a 1.33:1 aspect ratio and also helps to reduce the width of the frame visually. The sides of each frame in *Sleeping Beauty* are occupied by objects, architecture, and trees and do not contain any crucial information or character animation. In the following examples this relationship between the narrower aspect ratio of the character animation and the wider backgrounds is explored.

The first to be examined shot has no camera movement and we just focus on the position of the character within the wider frame. In the second shot of Sequence 8 (00:22:46–00:22:51), a little bird sits on a branch, sees Aurora, and then flies towards her. The main action happens within the middle third of the frame and thus is roughly contained in the 1.33:1 frame ratio. Compositionally in the beginning of the shot, the bird's position is enhanced by the fir cone just above, which makes this position visually significant. The eye is immediately drawn to the cone and the blue bird, so the audience does not have to search for the action when the shot starts. The bird is sitting on the part of the branch that additionally has a geometric tilt down, right underneath the tip of the cone. The second position of the bird's action (00:22:49) is right in the middle of the frame, where the branch has its high point. The third position (00:22:49) is as far from the center as the first position and is again on a low point of the branch. The bird's position is exactly diagonally opposing the position of the cone, juxtaposing it horizontally and vertically. The composition of the background keeps the stage for the character empty, which helps it to read better. The tree on the right blocks off the image and guides the eye in combination with the cone, which serves as a downward arrow, the branches to the left of the cone, and the tangle of fir needles towards the image's lower left, where Aurora is walking (off-frame) and where the bird leaves the frame.

In the second example shot, there is a subtle diagonal camera movement. The shot begins at 00:26:56 and ends at 00:27:04, and the slight diagonal camera pan is accompanied by Aurora walking downwards through the forest with the birds following her. Her movement is slightly downhill, and the composition and camera follow that direction. Again, the character action is limited to a much narrower frame ratio and the movement is supported in the background by the at 45° angled light rays, and the branches and roots, likewise accentuating the diagonal. The background and middle ground support her path and angle of movement. The warm colors of the ray of light attract the eye, so the focus is on Aurora's face. The brightness of her hair and blouse of course contribute to her clearly being the focal point (however, the red bird is rather dominant in its saturation). Aurora's overall movement from the first to the last frame in this shot is a reflection of the stage's shape and directional tilt in the background.

This very strong relationship between background composition and character action can be seen in many of the shots, even, as seen in the previously discussed shot, when including camera movement. The following example shot, starting at 00:28:12 and ending at 00:28:16, shows a long, yet quick camera pan, beginning with a full shot of a squirrel that sees the prince's clothes in the distance and ending with the squirrel's visual goal, the very cape and hat, in the same position. The direction of the background is obviously from left to right, as the branch serves as an unmistakable arrow to the right. The tree trunk at the beginning of the pan, which occupies the whole left side of the frame, closes the image on that side and pushes the attention of the viewer to the right, where we assume the prince's clothes to be located. The part where the squirrel recognizes the prince's cape in the squirrel's second position at 00:28:14 has an emptier background, and the sky brightens up behind the character, thus pointing out this significant moment. As in the example with the bird on the branch in the second shot of Sequence 8, the squirrel is right on top of the bend in the branch, this time off-center, pushing the eye further left. Though looking at the distribution of the squirrel's visual weight, the tail and the body of the squirrel balance each other out with the pivot being right in the center of the frame. The squirrel's eyes at 00:28:14 appear in the same position in the frame as the prince's red cape at the end of the shot.

In the fourth example, the animals are dressed up as the dream prince and swaggering towards the left. The shot starts after the zoom-out at 00:29:30. The action is in the center of the frame and the camera pans from right to left during the animals' walk. The emphasis on the vertical compositional elements at the very left and right of the frame (the tree-trunks and the negative spaces in between) are balancing each other at the beginning of the pan as much as they do at the end of the pan. Likewise, the rectangular bush behind the characters' action is in the beginning of the pan right in the middle of the frame, whereas at the end of the pan it is perfectly juxtaposed by the vertical and horizontal lines of the trees on the left. Thus,

the compositional foundation is maintained throughout the entire pan.

The composition in *Sleeping Beauty* is a perfect example of the extent to which the layout can be pushed in order to make the image read well with (and also without) the character animation. The purpose of layout is exactly that: composition that succumbs to the emotion of the story point and to the action in the shot.

What always struck me as odd in *Sleeping Beauty*'s layout, though, was the movement of the townspeople or the lack thereof in the architectural settings. Aside from the main characters, there is barely any movement in the people that attend the birthday party or any of the events at the castle, for that matter. The town always feels like it is a stage for the main characters and they are the only ones that are actually alive in that place. Everyone else is just a cutout paper board positioned to fill the stage. This is what really underlines the rigidity of the architectural settings, because there is no life in them. If there is some movement, then it is the flags that are blowing slightly in the wind. Of course, it would have meant a fair amount of work and expense to let all the townspeople move ever so slightly, but it would have added believability to the castle and the difference between the castle being alive on the one hand and asleep on the other. Maleficent's dilapidated castle feels more alive than king Stefan's, because her minions scuffling, running, and jumping around.

## Lighting

The lighting in the backgrounds most often falls in from the upper right at approximately 45 degrees. It does not matter if it is daylight in the forest (see Figure 4.37), daylight outside in the castle's yard, or moonlight, the angle and direction in every background is more or less the same. Some interiors, however, have an undefined direction, like in the fairy's hut. In addition, there are some backgrounds in the forest where the light comes from the opposite side. Nevertheless, this unity in lighting provides yet another design element that all the images succumb to. The light and shadow are usually not too strong in contrast but rather soft and subtle; therefore, they do not attract too much attention. In many backgrounds, the lighting is very vague and there is more of a form-rendering aspect to the light than a mood created by the incoming rays, which often does not have a specific source.

In the forest backgrounds, there is in certain parts a connection between the angle of the incoming sunlight and the angles of tree parts, shapes of stones, or other elements. The angle of the light rays are thus intensified without showing too much of the light itself, and the amalgam of light and layout makes a pleasant connection.

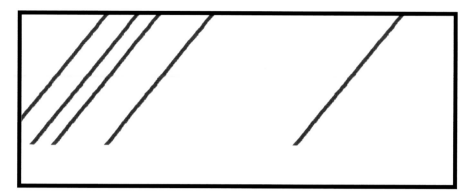

**Figure 4.37**

Lighting in the architectural backgrounds is often less defined and more vague, as often no direct source of light illuminates the setting. The light is more form-descriptive instead of actually creating a strong light and shadow mood in the background; however, the light rays are still visible. In Maleficent's throne hall, the light has no specific source, unless a green fire is seen. The light, a green and yellow glow, has Maleficent herself in the center, but the light does not emanate from her.

Light and shadow is generally applied in many of the backgrounds as a strong design element, thus supporting the compositional foundation, rather than solely creating a mood.

## Modern design in *Sleeping Beauty*

How does *Sleeping Beauty* fit into the oeuvre of Disney's features? Most of the features from the studio, as this one does, display a very unique visual style, which is a response to its time and its creators. Therefore, *Sleeping Beauty*'s style is as much a representation of the 1950s, with UPA's influence clearly visible, as *101 Dalmatians* is, with the invention of the Xerox technology and its stellar rise to success at the very end of the 1950s. Design is never just design but always a representation of the political and social climate at the time or even the deliberate lack thereof. *Sleeping Beauty* reflects the struggle of the Disney Studio to bring modern design into their features. They did it successfully in their shorts with *Toot, Whistle, Plunk and Boom* (1953) and especially *Pigs is Pigs* (1954), but *Sleeping Beauty* takes this direction and adds the complexity of realism and naturalism to the mix, which is an extraordinarily difficult task as the modern design revolution is the opposite of realism, highly stylized with reduced graphics and shapes, something that does not lend itself easily to a Disney feature film. Walt wanted to recreate the success of *Snow White* as the company's flagship project by choosing yet another well-known fairy tale. This type of story done in the "traditional Disney style" demanded a heroine and a hero that were realistic, not cartoony characters and this in turn suggested a naturalistic background design containing two aspects: elements from modern design and also characters who were stylized, yet realistic humans in look and character animation.

Style-wise, the medieval tapestries and also the work of the Limburg brothers were the perfect amalgam for this direction: stylization plus realism with a different (or false) use of two-point perspective. Translating this style into hundreds and hundreds of backgrounds was a battle for designer Eyvind Earle, to say the least. A battle to achieve the needed accuracy and consistency of a very new and different aesthetic (compared to what the company did before) and also, as many records and interviews with artists working on the feature prove, a battle amongst the artists who so strongly disagreed with Earle's decisions. Eyvind Earle achieved what has to be acknowledged as a success in finding a composite between traditional Disney feature style and a modern 1950s sensibility in composition and dimensionality. It is not and would have never been a feature that could actually translate the UPA aesthetics into a feature film (even UPA wasn't particularly successful in translating their short film style into features, when considering their two features *1001 Arabian Nights* in 1959 or *Gay Purr-ee* in 1962). Disney artists had obviously not shut themselves out of the stylistic development outside their studio walls, quite the contrary: it had influenced their designs early on. This is especially visible in Ward Kimball's *Toot, Whistle, Plunk and Boom* and his documentary features for Disney's TV show, though the change at the studio came slowly and not at all with a boom and was limited mostly to Ward Kimball's work, Disney's short-lived commercial department, or the TV productions. Eyvind Earle, having worked on both shorts *Toot, Whistle, Plunk and Boom* and *Pigs is Pigs*, was obviously right at the forefront of this development and probably for Walt Disney the right man for the job. Earle's work is more accessible in terms of it not being too modern but integrating modern elements into traditional and recognizable images.

One can already see in *Alice in Wonderland* from 1951 that the artists had integrated modern design very successfully by allowing some of the sensibilities of Mary Blair's development work to shine through the final screen image (flat colors, less accurate perspectives, and an unconventional color scheme), though this was again a comedy with stylized and cartoony characters, not a semiserious story line that required a different, less cartoony approach, as *Sleeping Beauty* did.

Earle's work on *Sleeping Beauty* in hindsight is a huge success and a partial failure at the same time. The work falls into two categories: nature and architecture. The natural depictions, as discussed earlier, succeed in almost every background, and the architectural ones often fail as backgrounds for animation purposes; however, there are also some successful ones where the color and texture do work beautifully. This is a very broad statement, and of course there are exceptions to the rule. Earle did what animation needs to do: open up the aesthetics of animation and explore and update Disney feature animation, which was a bit stuck in its ways at the time and not innovative or experimental enough in its feature films compared to the developments outside the studio. Exploration by its very nature will sometimes be successful and sometimes not. However, by exploring you will always push the limits of what animation is capable of as an art form. Years later when the Disney Company was in another deep pit of lack of creativity and inventiveness, the artists came up with the glorious idea of using the "Earle style" for another one of their features: *Pocahontas*. Earle's understanding of the two-dimensional plane and the graphic qualities of it, which works so beautifully in some of his designs, does not work as successfully in *Pocahontas*. Hand-drawn animation does not require a three-dimensional space but can use its two-dimensionality as a benefit in creating graphically and compositionally focused images instead of recreating a space in three-point perspective. That is where *Pocahontas* failed in its visuals: the background designers just use the idea of texture here and there where they deem it a fit and ignore the geometric flatness of Earle's designs, which comes with a composition that has purpose and focus, where every part in the image serves the whole. Most backgrounds in *Pocahontas* lack artistic refinement and sophistication and are often plain and conceptless, wanting to recreate the grandeur of *Sleeping Beauty* but not able to fully submit to the strictness of the two-dimensional plane with its graphic rules (this is about the backgrounds, not the character animation!). This is where the overwhelming backgrounds of Eyvind Earle come in as the work of an artist, a unique approach that, whether you approve of his visuals or not, shows character and personality combined with artistic knowledge and a compositional sensibility that is refreshing. Earle understood 1950s design and used it wisely for a Disney feature film. Feature animation is an art form and should always be treated as such: pushing boundaries.

The struggle Eyvind Earle experienced with his art direction at Disney Studios was not an easy task and did affect him staying at Disney. He worked for Disney Studios for only 7 years and left in March of 1958, before *Sleeping Beauty* was finished, to accept a job at John Sutherland Motion Picture Company in Los Angeles, where he designed the lush short film *Symphony in Steel* in his style. He kept working in animation for a couple of years, doing TV holiday specials and commercials. Nevertheless, after 15 years in animation, he went back to concentrating full-time on his very successful painting career. Looking at Eyvind Earle's later work,

the focus is most definitely on nature—uniquely shaped trees with overwhelming decorative textures and flowing hills. There is much dramatic light and shadow play and natural moods are often depicted through fog and interesting settings. The light, like in the backgrounds for *Sleeping Beauty*, still comes in from a 45° angle most of the time (in some very dramatic lighting situations, though, the shadows are very long and dominate the composition). His paintings never reveal the brush, never reveal their material, and thus are the opposite of what nature is: they are constrained, geometric landscapes with every single detail painted. They lack the looseness of the brush, the suggestive qualities that can make nature paintings of Impressionism so real, vibrant, and graspable. Earle's work does not seem to have a message in any of his paintings, no critique or opinion, but just quiet contemplation. This can cause the images in the worst case to tend towards decoration instead of fine art and in the best case present a very unique surreal landscape that draws the audience back to nature with its quiet moments and graphic qualities. Earle's work is cold and distant, often with an odd and unexpected color range, sometimes with a warm and pleasant beauty. It always feels otherworldly but never really fully organic. It often has a feel of high-definition images that are detailed to the last leaf and lure the viewer in to visually explore their cleanliness. Though the images invite, they would never allow one to step in, as that would disturb their untouched composition.

## After *Sleeping Beauty*

Because *Sleeping Beauty* was such an immensely expensive feature, costs for the films afterwards were reduced and ways sought to cut costs. One of the departments that was always costly (and especially in *Sleeping Beauty*) was the ink and paint department, where mostly women worked on transferring the animation drawings to cels in delicately colored line work. In order to eliminate this step, the Xerox process was developed to a stage where it could be used to transfer the drawings onto cels via the Xerox machine. The first film that used the Xerox technique was the short film *Goliath II* (1960), directed by Wolfgang Reitherman, a very charming story of a tiny elephant whose gigantic elephant father is the leader of the herd. Because of Goliath's miniscule size, the father does not care for his son, who in turn tries to impress his father, which in the end he succeeds at. Where *Sleeping Beauty* mostly succeeds in its design, *Goliath II* does not work. It does follow the design of *Sleeping* Beauty very loosely but only in parts and is not very consistent in its dealing with dimensionality. Sometimes it is very flat and sometimes renders everything dimensional, so the film does feel very much like a collage of styles. The characters are three-dimensional and their animation is cartoony and form-oriented. Strangely enough, the crocodile from *Peter Pan*, which was animated in 1953, appears in *Goliath II* in exactly the same way, even with the same movement. The same is true for the elephants and them bumping into each other. This very scene appears again in *Jungle Book* in 1967 and the design of the elephants is more or less the same. So Goliath, despite its very charming story, is an assemblage of Disney styles and animation over a time period of 14 years and it really shows. Everything is in it and nothing seems to really fit. Under the keen observing eyes of Eyvind Earle, this might not have happened (yes, this is blunt assumption!), but he was already long gone working on other assignments in another studio. Where *Sleeping Beauty* mostly succeeds in its depiction of nature, *Goliath II* does not, as it packs too many styles into the short without considering a strong

concept that everything has to follow and succumb to: character design, layout, background design, character animation, and a fitting color design. In the background design, the discrepancy between shape and form is too strong and thus the characters often do not fit into the environment, as they are obviously fully dimensional.

The first feature that used Xerox was *101 Dalmatians* in 1961 and its design was the complete opposite of *Sleeping Beauty*. All the design problems of *Goliath II* were gone and a style was developed that made *101 Dalmatians* yet another design smorgasbord of epic proportion!

**More on Sleeping Beauty:**

Ioan Szasz, *Awaking Beauty: The Art of Eyvind Earl*, Weldon Owen Publishing, San Francisco, 2017.

**More on Disney's Ink & Paint Department:**

Mindy Johnson, *Ink & Paint, The Women of Walt Disney's Animation*, Disney Editions, Glendale, 2017.

# Case study: compositional pattern in Cinerama's narrative feature *How the West Was Won* (1962)

**Segment directors:** John Ford, Henry Hathaway, George Marshall, Richard Thorpe

**Cinematography:** Wiliam H. Daniels, Milton R. Krasner, Charles Lang Jr., Joseph LaShelle

Previously, we have discussed the effect the extension of the projection screen had on the development of cinema in the 1950s and 1960s with its widening aspect ratios. Aside from the "event-character" that cinema regained, the wider screen demanded an aesthetic adjustment, affecting the composition of this much larger given space on screen. Specifically, the widescreen format of Cinerama, which inaugurated the fad for wider screens in 1952, had an immense ratio of 2.89:1 and therefore had so much additional space in need to be not only filled with visual information but also doing it in an arranged, easy to read, and aesthetically pleasing cinematic design. The interesting compositional solution for these wider images of Cinerama is going to be discussed in this section, with the example of Cinerama's second and last narrative feature film *How the West Was Won* from 1962/ 63[1]. Cinerama's technique of projecting three 35 mm filmstrips horizontally to mimic the full width of one apparently continuous image, caused two seams to appear on screen due to the necessary overlap of the images (see Figure 4.38). The slightly different coloration of the three filmstrips[2] and their marginally inaccurate overlap did not lead to one perfectly congruent image, but an image in which the two seams were still visible. The three projectors C, B, and A (see Figure 4.6) projected their image onto the curved Cinerama screen from left to right as images A, B, and C, as seen in Figure 4.38, with the two seams as the overlapping areas. These seams were not a significant problem in documentaries and travelogues that Cinerama started out with, but became a challenge in narrative films, the first of which being *The Wonderful World of the Brothers Grimm* from 1962. To lessen the visual disturbance and distraction of these seams for Cinerama's two narrative features, the image was during the film-shoot already composed with these distracting seams in mind, and consequentially affected the composition and notably the staging of the characters. The solution for eliminating or at least reducing the seams' visual disturbance was either to camouflage them mostly with architectural pieces, trees, poles, or any kind of vertical elements with no narrative significance, or to avoid the seams and their immediate vicinity for the staging of the characters altogether. Actors draw the audience's attention and therefore they must not be placed onto or into the proximity of the seams, as the

slightly inaccurate overlap would blur the characters' focus, which is most likely their faces, and thus would impair their legibility. The vertical seams were hence for the most part unsuited for the placement of character action. Consequentially, the actors' staging is following a compositional system which avoids the seams. Preference is given firstly to the middle area of the entire image (panel B), and secondly to the outer areas left and right of the two seams (panels A and C), overall keeping the action in the middle of each of the three panels. There are distinct compositional arrangements in the film which are repeated throughout and some of which I want to discuss in the following. Nevertheless, I must point out that the film has recently been restored, and the seams are mostly removed through digital image manipulation and the additional color correction equalized the three different panels, providing an image that is superior to the original. Nevertheless, the seams can be detected by the compositional placement of mentioned vertical elements, and the lack of characters in these areas, plus the very accurate placement of the characters within the three panels.[3]

The simplest character placement is one character in the middle of one of the panels, as can be seen in Figure 4.39. The centrality of the character within the panel is often used in the film, either in the middle panel B, or in panels A and C. Though often on their own in one single shot, supporting additional characters appear in the other panels. At the beginning of the film, at timecode 00:10:34, the composition displays this most basic compositional pattern, where the focus lies in the middle of the shot, in this case a mid-shot of the cargo master. The seams in the example are for the most part covered by the vertical edges of the cargo master's booth, and the character appears right in the middle of panel B. What we can see in this shot is apparent in all the film's compositions, which is the strict focus on image balance, where the left and right elements are placed in opposing pairs, balancing each other, and providing the image with compositional calm, an overall harmony and evenly balanced image weight. The middle, in this case the cargo master, serves as the pivot point of the image's weight. For instance, the tree on the left (panel A) of the cargo master's booth is balanced by a group of people on the very right (panel C), both having the same distance from the vertical frame. The heavy visual weight of the tree on the left, due to its darkness and size, is much higher than the visual weight on the right, being open and airy, which requires a compositional adjustment. Consequentially, to avoid

---

[1]  The film was released in late 1962 in the United Kingdome and in early 1963 in the United States.
[2]  The chemical process of film development was not accurate enough to provide perfectly equal color on various filmstrips.

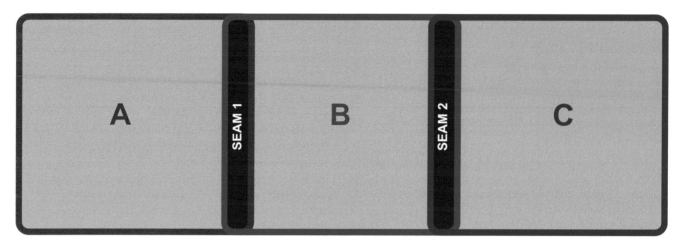

Figure 4.38

Figure 4.39

an imbalanced composition, the resulting light weight of the very right is weighed down by the larger group of people at the right side of the cargo master's booth, which is juxtaposed by the light visual weight of the single boy sitting on the left of the booth in the shadow, resulting in a perfectly balanced image that has the same visual weight on both sides, yet has enough tension in the various elements' differences in color, light and shadow, size, etc., to not appear rigid. It is not the single elements on the left or right, but the wholeness of all elements' visual weight and their additional differences that constitutes the interplay between balance and tension.

The second possible character arrangement has two characters in the middle of a panel (see Figure 4.40). One single character can be enlarged in a panel to a mid-shot or even a medium close-up and still not reach with the shoulders into the two seams left and right, which would blur that part of the character and thus be visually distracting. For two characters standing next to each other in one single panel and still be unaffected by the seams is only then a possibility if the characters either step back for a medium full shot or full shot (the further the characters step back from the camera, the more characters can fit into the panel without overlapping each other). Once the character comes closer to the camera, the characters must either step into each other's personal space to avoid penetrating with their shoulders the seams, or they must overlap each other (see Figure 4.41). This "overlap" can also be interpreted as an over-the-shoulder-arrangement in one panel.

The feature *When the West Was Won's* apparently rigid compositional concept still allows a wide range of possible character placements in the three panels and their compositional communication. Two simple examples, Figures 4.42 and 4.43, just give a glimpse into the vast possibilities available for the various arrangements. These two examples have all three panels filled with character/s, but of course there is also the option of two or even just one panel to be equipped with communicating characters, keeping the other panel/s empty. Character-empty panels, nevertheless, require compositional elements, like architecture, nature, sky, to balance out the weight of the opposing character-panel/s.

**Figure 4.40**

**Figure 4.41**

**Figure 4.42**

Figure 4.43

We are dealing with film, in which the composition is continuously changing not simply within the shot itself, but the composition of the present shot will replace the previous composition and will then in turn be replaced by the composition of the following shot. Hence all compositions relate to each other sequentially, produce a "travelling composition" that flows from shot to shot. Cutting from one shot's composition to a shot with a very different composition can create a harsh and interruptive cut, whereas cutting from one to another shot, which incorporates elements from the previous composition can provide a smoother, more comfortable, or even seamless cut. The feature *How the West Was One*, because its shots are based on such a rather strict compositional foundation with the three panels A, B, and C, as seen in the previously discussed images, maintains a rather smooth shot flow through its responses of one shot's composition to the next. For instance, replacing from one shot to the next a panel *with* characters (positive space) with a panel *lacking* characters (negative space), allows the composition to maintain its basic and strict foundation based

on the three-panel structure, but also permits a communication between the shots, responding to balance and tension. The shot composition in Figure 4.44 has panel A containing the negative space of the shot, and B and C being the positive-space-panels, with C having the highest visual weight as the characters overall volume outweighs B's. A possible follow-up shot can be seen in Figure 4.45, in which the previous negative space in panel A is replaced with a character, whereas B and C are now empty. Those two empty panels can be equipped creatively with background or foreground elements that support the shot's composition, balance, and weight, yet at the same time react to the previous shot's composition. If done in every panel thoughtfully, this will establish enough tension and balance for the shot, follow-up shots, and the entire scene to read harmoniously. Characters talking to each other in consecutive shots can thus be arranged in a fashion that utilize all three panels communicating with each other within the shot itself (see Figures 4.39, 4.40, 4.41), and additionally one can experiment with, for instance, positive and negative spaces that replace each other in the follow-up shots.

Figure 4.44

**Figure 4.45**

Having all shots follow such a strict arrangement as seen in these various examples has the disadvantage of repetition, but the advantage that shots can more easily be connected in editing, as they all share the same compositional structure. Despite the apparent rigidity of the compositional framework of the feature *How the West Was Won*, there is much playfulness in its various shots, so much so, that some are rather complicated not just because of their compositional business but also the activity of the actors. Many shots in the feature are filled with many characters in fore-, middle-, and background, providing further arrangement options, all following the three-panel structure. Some of the shots are rather complex and contain more than one focal point. One interesting shot composition can be seen in the shot with timecode 01:55:22, where the main action with two characters talking happens in the middle panel B. The two men are shot in a medium full-shot, whereas the supporting panels A and C each contain a one-point perspective (a bar with a hallway on the left and a bar-counter with people on the right). Both panels' vanishing points strongly attract attention, and at the same time frame panel B and balance the whole composition in a rather dizzying fashion, as the eye wants to pay attention to all three panels at the same time. The follow-up shots likewise serve rather complex character staging situations, with the actors being placed in different distances from the camera and additionally providing through their actions various areas of interest. This complexity can render the shot/s challenging for the viewer but also add/s commotion and suspense.

The feature's previously discussed compositional "rules" that lead to its visual concept can be easily detected in every shot and scene:

- The seams are most often covered by vertical architectural or natural elements.
- The characters are placed within the panels A, B, and C, staying away from the seams.
- Each shot's composition responds to the succeeding shot's composition.
- Opposing compositional elements on the left and right of the frame's sides are paired for balance and tension.
- Positive and negative spaces alternate as much as light and dark, or busy and calm.

The features *The Wonderful World of the Brothers Grimm* and *How the West Was* Won are exclusive in them following the division of the screen by three to succumb to the unique projection technique needs of Cinerama, thus producing their conceptual and consequentially epic format. The limitation of the Cinerama projection technique led to an interesting compositional solution, conceiving one-of-a-kind cinematic visuals that so clearly reflect the vast widescreen exploration of the mid-20th century.

# ASPECTS OF DESIGN

John Hubley and Zachary Schwartz (UPA):

> We have found that the medium of animation has become a new language. It is no longer the vaudeville world of pigs and bunnies. Nor is it the mechanical diagram, the photographed charts of the old "training film." It has encompassed the whole field of visual images, including the photograph. We have found that line, shape, color, and symbols in movement can represent the essence of an idea, can express it humorously, with force, with clarity. The method is only dependent upon the idea to be expressed. And a suitable form can be found for any idea.[48]

## Aspects of design in the single shot and scene

Knowing all the options there are for designing images is already covering most of what is needed. The rest of the design work is balancing all those options (which are mentioned in the list on the right) and finding the fitting ingredients in the correct balance to tell the story. These can only be possibilities, as there is no correct final. Design is not like math, where you get a final answer that is either right or wrong (simply put). Design is never right or wrong (sometimes it actually is wrong) but has a tendency towards being successful or not. Composing means arranging parts or components to create a whole. The components or aspects are all equal in their importance and none is superior to the other. They work together, not on their own! The communication between them is what gives an image complexity and weight, which in the end benefits its reading and understandability. The following is a list of all the aspects that are there to be used to design a *moving image or a single shot*: they are for the film image. However, other than the last two aspects, movement and music and sound, they all also apply to the still image, illustration, or concept work based on a story. There is no need to use all of them, though there is a need for all of them to be examined upon their ability to support the story point.

**The following aspects of design in film, explained in Chapter 5 onwards, are:**

5. Composition

6. Character staging and film-language

7. Vectors

8. Directions

9. Shape and form

10. Mood

11. Size

12. Depth

13. Light and shadow

14. Color

15. Contrast

16. Perspective

17. Texture

18. Movement

19. Music and sound

20. Variation

Simplicity and readability (Chapter 35, Volume 2)

Believability (Chapter 36, Volume 2)

---

[48] John Hubley and Zachary Schwartz, Animation Learns a New Language, *Hollywood Quarterly*, Vol. 1, No. 4, (1946), pp. 360–363.

# CHAPTER 5

# Composition

Composition is the first of the 18 *aspects of design*, as all the other aspects are part of composition and support its lead. This also means that composition itself is part of all of the following Chapters 6–20, plus Chapter 35, "Simplicity and Readability," and Chapter 36, "Believability," both in Volume 2.

Composition in visual arts is the arrangement of the pictorial elements in order to create a well-balanced and effective image that, with the use of psychology, geometry, color, and all the other aspects of design, interprets and visualizes the intended story point. It is very similar to a musical composition where the conductor arranges many instruments in order to achieve a pleasant piece of orchestral music, puts all the instruments in order of importance, but only allows those to audibly step forward that have an important role at that very moment. Visual artists use the design elements to compose images. The pictorial elements in the frame can be arranged with subtlety and accuracy to achieve what we need the image to express story-wise *and* emotionally: emotions we want to evoke in the audience. The artist can control how the image is being read. Composition is the foundation of images and the underlying structure that holds everything together. This function makes it the most important part of image-making, because firstly it is the controlling basis of every element in the image and secondly it contains a substantial piece of the storytelling that affects the viewers psychologically and of course emotionally. Composition can subconsciously lead the viewers on a path through the image, affect their emotions, and influence their reading and thus understanding of the image. All images contain stories; there is no exception. Without the proper understanding, the purpose of the image, to tell stories, is obviously obsolete. Images serve the function of transporting either an idea, a message, or a story from artist to viewer, so artists need to know what they want to convey. Nevertheless, this is by no means only one-directional. The interaction between artist and viewer always goes back and forth and can be affected by either party's input. Artists have to know how to interpret a specific story point and have to predict how the viewer might react to the composition. They have to play with viewers' expectations but always surprise them with a new and unexpected direction. The artist's role of creating emotions in the viewer's mind, then, only works properly when the artist has an insight into what viewers can understand and what they are willing to accept visually. Viewers, on the other hand, are only able to grasp the full content of an image or shot if they have the educational background and age that allows every aspect and intellectual layer of the image to be read clearly. Some aspects might be easy to grasp; some

others are more difficult and require very specific knowledge. Therefore, images can have different levels of information and also different levels of readability and understandability. Not every piece of information an image has is crucial for its understanding. Irony or sarcasm can be obvious for one viewer but completely ignored by another, though the story itself needs to still be understood by both. Some images are meant to be for toddlers; others are meant to be for scientists in chemistry who deal with complex molecular structures. Knowing this, the artist should always make the image as simple as needed to be understood by many, yet add more information in additional levels to not be too banal for those who are seeking more in the image than most. The image or composition by no means needs to be intellectually overloaded with information but can just mean that in a kids' show the characters that can fly are always shown in the upper part of the frame, whereas all walking characters are always shown in the lower part of the frame. This is an extremely simple idea; however, it creates a compositional restraint upon which a style could be built.

Every visual decision should be made with a purpose. As composition is the main design aspect in images, all the other aspects have to be subordinate to it. Any design aspect that does not follow the main direction possibly weakens the image, diluting its message and ultimately negatively affecting the understandability. Composition itself is not an easy task. There are so many possibilities and points to consider that it takes quite a while to be able to let it speak for you and express what you wanted. But it is also one of the most rewarding tasks, as it allows complexity and thought that can be tied in with the story and create some unique directions.

Composition is never a solid and straightforward procedure but always a tedious and open field that can change constantly and has to be adjusted even if only little changes are made. Everything in the composition relates to each other and shifting one element in the frame affects all the other elements. The goal of composition is to arrange the objects in the frame and to create a balanced visual that accentuates the area of importance, the focal point. In a three-dimensional setting, when

**More on composition:**

Arnheim Rudolf, *The Power of the Center: A Study of Composition in the Visual Arts*, University of California Press, Berkeley, CA, 2009.

Herbert Zettl, *Sight Sound Motion, Applied Media Aesthetics*, Thomson Wadsworth, Belmont, TN, 2008.

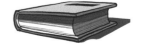

**Figure 5.1**

**Figure 5.2**

**Figure 5.3**

**Figure 5.4**

**Figure 5.5**

**Figure 5.6**

we walk through a city taking photographs, we can just stroll around and find various arrangements through the viewfinder that underline the initial concept, if there was one, or we can explore and find an arrangement that expresses exactly what is needed. In the six photographs in Figures 5.1 through 5.6, a temple area in Thailand, it is not determined what the focal point is yet or what should be expressed about the site. It is rather a play with the area, compositional photographic sketches to find the actual focal point or the composition that is the most interesting. The area consists of four dominant elements. The big tree in the background, the temple behind it, the reflecting pond, and the Naga snake that encircles the pond and ends in a five-headed corner piece. This example is to explain what elements can be arranged and the effect this has on the composition and the importance of each piece.

1. In the first image, the tree and the five-headed Naga are juxtaposed with each other, creating a strong diagonal. The sides of the pond open up like scissors and determine the tree as the important element in the frame (Figure 5.1).
2. The tree and the Naga are on the same vertical, creating a pillar that is accentuated by the reflection of the tree in the pond. The image's weight is very heavy on the left side, as there are very few elements on the right side to balance the image (Figure 5.2).
3. The vertical is shifted to the right for a better balance in the image. Compared to Figure 5.2 the composition is less heavy on the left; however, the edges of the pond are touching the frame (see the section "Magnetism of the Frame" in Chapter 3) (Figure 5.3).
4. In this composition, the overall direction in the frame is a diagonal from the tree in the back to the lower left (the reflection of the tree also pushes towards the left), accentuated by the diagonal right wall of the pond (Figure 5.4).
5. Slightly less emphasis is given to the tree in the background, which pushes the focus onto the pond, rather than tree and Naga (Figure 5.5).
6. Obviously, the focus is on the Naga and the tree has less importance. However, the composition is also very heavy on the left and the geometric quality of the pond is lost, plus the lack of water and reflection gives the image less texture and makes it also look dry, less inviting (Figure 5.6).

By walking around the pond and trying out various possibilities, by shifting all the elements around and weighing them against each other, a composition evolves that brings all or most positive points together and accentuates the focal point in the best light. Each composition has advantages but also disadvantages. The question is: what is the purpose of the given scenery? What is the focus of the image? Tree, temple, Naga, or pond? What story needs to be told? What mood has to be expressed? Without answering these questions the "correct" composition cannot be determined.

# Purposes of composition

**The various purposes of composition are as follows:**

- Create a structure for the content of the frame
- Create a focal point
- Improve the readability of the image
- Tell the story visually
- Structure the image into levels of importance
- Support a pleasing aesthetic
- Enjoy the game of composing complex visuals
- Positive and negative space, breathing space
- Create tension and balance
- Create paths for the viewer to observe the image
- Arrange the characters in relationship to the story and each other

# Create a structure for the content of the frame

As previously mentioned, composition is the arrangement of the visual elements in the image and a framework for everything else to succumb to. The arrangement of the elements not only create a pleasing visual but also make intellectual connections that assist the artist in expressing complex ideas. In Caspar David Friedrich's painting *Winterlandschaft* ("Winter Landscape") (Figure 5.7) from 1811, the artist shows us a quiet and calm landscape with trees and a Gothic cathedral in the gloomy distance during wintertime. The three trees are close to the spectator and are interspersed with two big boulders. In the middle, a man is resting by leaning with his back on the stone; we can see he left his crutches in the snow on the right. In front of the tallest tree stands a cross with a crucified Jesus, which the traveler is praying to. In the distance between the trees, rising out of the winter fog, the silhouette of a cathedral is slightly visible through the winter haze. Friedrich's painting looks quiet and composed and has a very arranged feel to it. But he composes the elements with such ease and subtlety that it does take a while to actually figure out what liaisons between the elements he established in order to reach a visually calm composition. To understand the basis of the composition, it is recommended to reduce the major pieces in the frame into simple geometric shapes and find a structure in or connections between them (Figure 5.8). Immediately, one can see that the two symmetrical triangular shapes of the

**Figure 5.7**

Caspar David Friedrich: *Winterlandschaft (Winter Landscape)*; 1811.

**Figure 5.8**

dominant geometrical shapes, not only in the trees, stones, or the cathedral but also in the background planes that are cutting into the frame from left and right. The tree in the middle and the stone and small tree on the left enclose a negative space that the cathedral is inscribed in. At the cross section of negative space, tilted horizon, and the symmetrical axis of the cathedral is the entrance gate, right between the two trees. Following the tilted horizon from the entrance on the left to the right we reach Jesus' head. The cross is also facing the opening gate of the cathedral, being slightly turned towards it. This connection between gate and head could be interpreted as that the believer goes through Jesus' words into the sanctity of the church. And that is exactly what the traveler is doing.

The colors are chosen very carefully and extend the geometric basis of the composition into the world of texture and mood. The contrast of trees, stones, and snow is so strong that the impact of each in the composition is immense. The shapes read extraordinarily well. The solid realness of trees and stones is contrasted with the aerial and dream-like depiction of the cathedral, which is more of an unreal vision, an imaginary building for the believer instead of a structure of stones. There is very clear distinction between the real world and the sacred world. The latter is believed in rather than fully visible. The traveler has to

taller tree on the right and the cathedral relate to each other and balance each other out. The smaller tree is right in their middle, marking the center of the image and also having the same height as the small side towers of the cathedral, repeating them. The boulders on the left and in the middle add variation and tension and frame the cathedral. Triangles are the

**Figure 5.9**

**Figure 5.10**

**Figure 5.11**

**Figure 5.12**

believe in the existence of God without ever seeing a clear image of him. There is a faint aura around the upper part of the cathedral, which allows it to read better. The color in both sky and cathedral has a gradient in it from top to bottom for better contrast between the two. However, it also pulls the eye upwards into the light, which is a symbol for God. Throughout the whole composition, many elements strengthen the structure by making connections. They are creating the arrangement and order that gives the composition balance and tension. Figure 5.9 shows how the entrance at the gate serves as a center from which various vectors and lines spread out: the stone's shape and tilt in the middle connects with the gate, the connection of the tips of the two trees is on one line towards the gate, the tip of the cathedral is perpendicular to the gate, and the tilt of the horizon line refers back to this center. Figure 5.10 explores the curves in the trees and the swoop of the branches, which results in the eye travelling upwards to the left towards the

cathedral. All four curves go through either Jesus' or the hiker's heads. Figure 5.11 explores the relationship between the triangle of cathedral, stone, and hiker and how distances correlate to each other. The distances are not random; they follow a strict scheme, which gives the composition an orderly, geometric, clean look. Figure 5.12 shows the distance between the two right trees and the cathedral. All in all, this seemingly simple image boasts complexities and religious symbolism. The two crutches of the man praying that he left behind while walking to his resting place can be seen as the worldly problems that one can leave behind when putting one's faith in Jesus. The silence and melancholy of this scene and the surreal appearance of the cathedral let this painting from Friedrich seem like a metaphor for an idea rather than a depiction of reality. Everything in the painting is related to each other and has meaning. This is mainly achieved by the rather complex framework of the "magic" of composition.

# Create a focal point

The focal point is either the point or the area of interest in the image, the center of the composition (not the center of the frame!). There is usually one focal point in cinematic images, but there can be as many as needed in other media. Look-and-find pictures have many focal points and still work beautifully. Nevertheless, these are rare exceptions and usually every image should have only one focal point, where the main idea of the image takes place, where the action is, or where the main story point happens. If you have more than one focal point, it is difficult for the audience to understand what the specific story point is, who the main character is, what the story is actually about. In still images like fine art or illustration, it is easier to understand the content if there is more than one focal point, as there is more time to observe the image. However, there is usually then one primary focal point and secondary ones that do not fight with the significance of the primary focal point. In movie shots, it is actually quite difficult to understand an image that has several areas where action takes place, unless the time for observation is sufficient to grasp the relationship between the various focal points. A still image doesn't have any viewing restraints in terms of time. We can look at the image as long as we want to. In movies, the time is limited, and we usually do not stop the film and try to understand the composition. The current shot is replaced very quickly by the next shot and so on. Especially in complicated images with lots of details and information, you want to help the audience to figure out quickly where to look at and what the story is about, without them getting lost in insignificant details. The focal point can be accentuated with all the elements of composition: strong colors attract attention, bright light can be a guide for the eye, perspectives or vectors lead the eye, etc.

In Adolph Menzel's (1815–1905) enormous painting *Eisenwalzwerk* ("Iron Rolling Mill") (158 cm × 254 cm), he shows us the hard and strenuous work in an iron rolling mill (Figure 5.13). We can smell the smoke and feel the hard work. The image emanates heat as a result of the intense warm colors. There are so many men in this image that we wouldn't really know where to look were it not for the focal point in the image, with the hot iron being the brightest spot, slightly right of center. (Aren't you already annoyed by that red dot on the page? That's how strong the focal point should be in the frame!) Interestingly enough, the area where the hot iron is located is the calmest one in the painting. Everywhere else is action and bedlam: men working, wheels turning, heavy smoke, and pipes and pillars create a forest of metal and heat. The story is about the metal itself; that is what the composition tells us. The metal is the primary interest; the workers are secondary, though they fill the entire frame with their actions, surrounding the metal,

worshipping it. It is literally the life "around" the metal. We are immediately drawn to the brightest area with the hot iron and then slowly spread outwards. The movement of the glowing liquid leads directly into the face of the man on the opposite side of the oven. His intense facial expression is what connects us emotionally with this worker (Figure 5.14). Menzel shows us dozens of workers, but there is only one that we clearly connect with. He is the only one whose face is free of any obstruction of shadow, arms, or their big forge tongs. Further outside, we can see men eating, washing themselves, and doing all sorts of work in the mill. Menzel superbly achieves the focus on one area; he gives us an armada of characters to marvel at but only one character to connect with emotionally. The painterly treatment of the different areas on the canvas very much accentuate the focal area. The characters surrounding the center of the hot iron are all painted very clearly and precisely and the light that is emitted by the hot iron gives a very strong contrast to the characters. The further the characters are from the light source, the less contrast there is and the more blurry the men are painted, which makes them appear slightly out of focus. This is an aesthetic that reflects early photography, where the lenses had the tendency to blur the outer areas of the frame slightly, putting the focus into the middle of the frame. This strongly pushes the eye to the center where there is detail, precision, light and shadow, strong contrast, and of course a warm light source. We have one focal point but dozens of other scenes that are interesting. This is effective in a painting where we have time to observe each character, follow the entire production of metal, and even witness the characters in the lower right corner eating their lunch.

The focal point needs to be so strong that none of the other design properties will affect it and possibly push the image's focus onto something else. Figures 5.15 through 5.18 show how the flatness of the first image (Figure 5.15) keeps the focus on the round ball, and there are two layers of information: the level of the blue ball and then the level of the black squares behind. The arrangement of the black squares pushes down towards the blue ball on a two-dimensional plane. Figure 5.16 has a suggestion of perspective, which shows through clear overlap and tonal perspective and also gives a clue about the tilt of the ground plane, suggesting a three-dimensional space and therefore strengthening and pushing towards the focal point. Figure 5.17 has even more perspective through the size change of the squares and the gradient, again strengthening the perspective push towards the blue ball. However, just changing the color of the right square in Figure 5.18 destroys the perspective that has supported the blue ball and the focus is immediately on the red square. Small changes within the composition therefore can overthrow the focal point.

**Figure 5.13**

Adolph Menzel, *Eisenwalzwerk (Iron Rolling Mill)*, 1872–75.

**Figure 5.14**

We have just dealt with the focal point in the still image but have not yet discussed the moving image. The still image has a composition that does not change; thus, the focal point is obviously also still. All the compositional elements can be planned precisely for that one image. The moving image has its focal points continuously move inside (and sometimes even outside) the frame, depending on the position of the action. A walking character, for instance, will not constantly stay in the same place on-screen but move around. The background composition therefore needs to support the character's position. This makes designing for the moving image a lot more complicated because every shot needs to be designed with the moving focal point in mind. Film deals with fluctuating compositions and continuously changing focal points. A film can be seen as a string of images, each with their own composition that constantly changes. Each shot relates to the shot right next to it, before *and* after. In the film strip in Figure 5.19, which is supposed to show shots, not frames, Shot 3 would relate to Shots 2 and 4. Its composition is to be considered in the composition of Shots 2 and 4 (sometimes even Shots 5 and 6). For example, in Shot 1 (Figure 5.20), the movement goes from the upper left of the screen to the lower right. Shot 2 takes this position and holds it; the viewer's eye focuses on this position. Shot 3 also starts with the focal point in the same position and then it moves to the lower left. Thus, the changing focal point has a continuous path from shot to shot, which is uninterrupted (in this simple example). However, in Shots 5, 6, and 7 the focal point jumps from shot to shot into a different position.

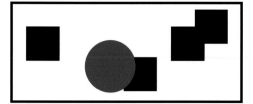

Figure 5.15

Figure 5.16

Figure 5.17

Figure 5.18

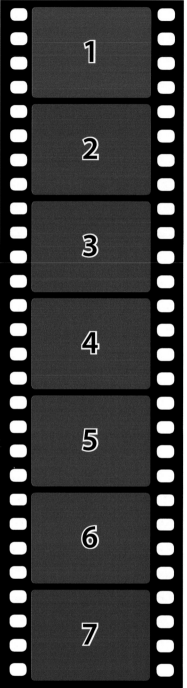

Figure 5.19

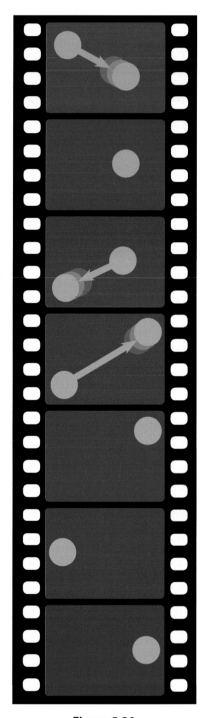

Figure 5.20

There are various options for dealing with focal points from shot to shot and how they connect shots or disconnect them:

- **The focal point in one single shot stays the same (Figure 5.21):** There is no movement within the shot; the focal point does not change.
- **The focal point in one single shot changes (Figure 5.22):** One shot with movement in it. The movement will always attract the eye, so the focal point can easily be located if it is connected to the movement. If the focal point is stagnant but there is movement around it, then it could be difficult to locate the focal point.

- **The focal point stays the same from one shot to the next (Figure 5.23) (Video 5A):** The focal point is in the same position from Shot 1 to Shot 2. The eye is already fixating on the area of the first focal point. When the cut happens, the eye is still in

that area; this keeps the eye in the right spot but can make the composition of the entire scene monotonous if done too often.

- **The focal point changes position from one shot to the next (Figure 5.24) (Video 5B):** This creates a significant and harsh cut in the flow of the scene and can be distracting. The interruption in the visual flow, though, can be used to either highlight a specific shot or to start a new scene. It can also add action and dynamics to a scene

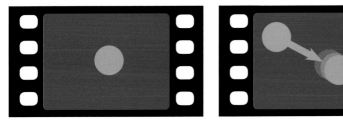

Figure 5.21                    Figure 5.22

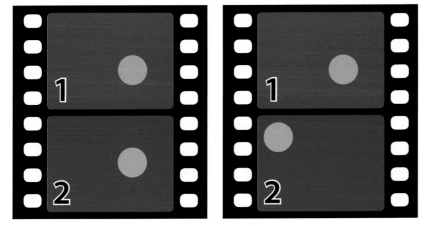

Figure 5.23                    Figure 5.24

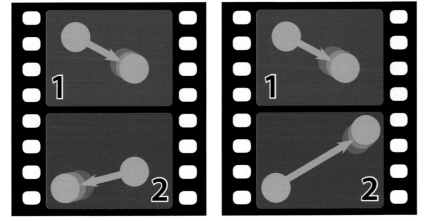

Figure 5.25                    Figure 5.26

itself for use in music videos, action sequences, significant shots that are highlighted through harsh transitions.

- **Two focal points in one shot:** Two people are talking to each other and our eyes go naturally from one to the other, following action and reaction. The interaction between the two is a very obvious occurrence that is easy to follow. If our eyes are on the right side of the frame following the main character, though, and something happens on the left side of the frame, then we wouldn't really recognize it. Our eyes have to first be guided towards the left, and once we look left then the important action can take place.
- **A continuously moving focal point with constantly changing backgrounds (Video 5E):** The movement of the focal point dominates the frame and the background steps literally into the background, because the eye follows the focal point from shot to shot. This can of course also be switched, by letting the movement of the background dominate the scene or both.

The aspect ratio of the frame also has an impact on the focal point. On a 4:3 frame it is easier to find the focal point, as the area is narrower. If the ratio is 2.85:1 and one is sitting in the movie theatre in the first row, finding the focal point might be a challenge and get easily tiring.

That does not necessarily mean that in cinematic visuals there is always only one focal point. The focal point can quickly switch from one to the next. In Vittoria de Sica's masterpiece *Bicycle Thieves* (1948), a story of a father and son trying to find the father's stolen bicycle, has one scene where the two having had a fight, are physically distant but slowly throughout the scene move closer to each other again. They walk through a street with a row of trees separating their path and are still angry at each other. At the end of that shot, the boy crosses over into the path of his father, the first step of them making up. In

the final shots of this scene the father and son are next to the river talking to each other (Figure 5.27), but in the background a young couple enters the image at the time when father and son are burying their feud (Figure 5.28). There is of course only one primary focal point in the image, which is the father and son, being the center of the whole story. Though the couple entering the scene means a great deal to the story as we now can see that "love" has returned. De Sica gives the image a secondary focal point, which supports the story of the primary one but does not push itself into the foreground. It is a subtle subliminal

in which the audience has to actively find the focal point (music video, action movie).

- **A moving focal point matches the one in the next shot (Figure 5.25) (Video 5C):** The matching moving focal point makes it much easier to follow the action on-screen. There is a flow that is just disrupted by the replacement of the background; the focal points stay the same. This creates a very smooth transition from one shot to the next.
- **Moving and not matching focal points (Figure 5.26) (Video 5D):** This is the same idea as in Video 5B, only with moving focal point. It creates dynamics and action and lends

**Figure 5.27**

**Figure 5.28**

Vittorio de Sica: *Bicycle Thieves* (1948).

message that has a great impact. We don't have to consciously see something but can also "feel" that something else is going on in the image that our subconscious can recognize and therefore touches our emotions and becomes embedded into the story. The focal point changes briefly from father to couple, just enough to release a feeling of comfort. It works because the couple only adds flavor to the shot but does not affect the actual story.

# Create a focal point through the rule of thirds and the golden section

The rule of thirds is a compositional grid that takes the focal points within the image out of the center and places them onto a preproduced grid (see Figures 5.31 through 5.36). The rule of thirds is a simplified version of the golden section (or *golden ratio*, *divine section* or *ratio*, *golden proportion*, or *golden cut*),

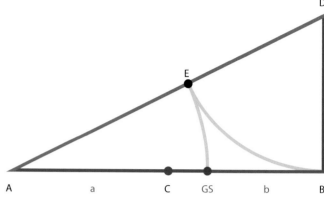

1. Draw line A-B, cut in half and achieve C.
2. Draw a perpendicular onto B with the length of CB and achieve D.
3. Connect D with A.
4. Draw a circle with D as center and a radius of DB onto AD and achieve E.
5. Draw a circle with A as center and a radius of AE onto AB and achieve GS, the golden section.
6. AGS= a; GSB=b.
7. **a + b** is to **a** as **a** is to **b**.

**Figure 5.29**

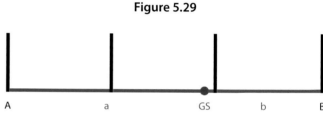

Dividing the line AB however into thirds does roughly hit the point GS.

**Figure 5.30**

precisely dividing the image into a perfect and harmonious relationship. The golden section has been used for centuries and is calculated mathematically or constructed geometrically; it is used in architecture, painting, and most other visual arts. Aesthetically, the golden section is the most comfortable and "perfect" division in art and allows the image to attain tension between its parts. Figure 5.29 shows the construction of the golden section and the relationship between two distances a and b. Mathematically, the golden section is explained as follows: a + b is to a as a is to b. The Greek letter φ (phi) represents the golden ratio and is numerically expressed as 1.618033987…

However, dividing line AB in Figure 5.30 into three segments does give a similar result to the golden section, and this is where the rule of thirds is a more practical and quick solution, not fully accurate, but close. How this can be applied in composition is shown in the examples in Figures 5.31 through 5.36. Figure 5.31 has the simplest composition but still combines two different compositional devices: the rule of thirds on the one hand and the central vertical on the other. Thus, the focus is on the sun in the middle and the division between sky and sand is on the upper line of the rule of thirds. However, the closest sand dune is right on the horizontal center and thus the image combines the rule of thirds and horizontal and vertical center. This composition is the most

**Figure 5.31**

**Figure 5.33**

**Figure 5.35**

**Figure 5.32**

The rule of thirds not only focuses on the three sections, but still also can have the two middle lines, horizontal and vertical centers, as important elements within the composition.

**Figure 5.34**

Not only can the focal point be placed on the vertical and horizontals but also any element within the frame that seems important for the composition can align with the grid to give the image order.

**Figure 5.36**

The rule of thirds can also be extended into a grid of fours (or more), depending on the aesthetic preferences. However, this also affects the golden ratio and the readability of the image.

quiet in the lineup. Figure 5.33 is more complex, as the elements do not perfectly line up with the squares but only has important parts here and there that collide and meet with the grid. The flag on the left is balanced by the prayer flags on the right. The composition uses neither the horizontal nor the vertical centers as guidelines. Figure 5.35 is the most complex, as it combines all the previous devices in one image. All the elements are arranged in a way that accentuates the center, corners, rule of thirds and fourth. This makes the most complex composition also the busiest. Using a grid of fours, however, also does change the golden ratio!

**Figure 5.37**

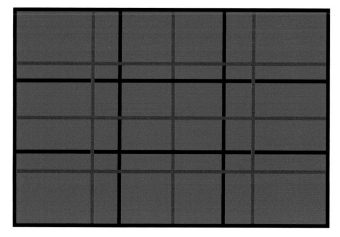

**Figure 5.38**

## Rule of thirds in the cinematic frame

In film the vertical frame is obviously nonexistent; only the horizontal frame is in use, which lends itself easily to the two different divisions of thirds and fourths, creating either nine or sixteen squares (Figure 5.37 and 5.38). With the grid of fourths, the center is included in the grid, whereas in the grid of thirds it is not. As we have seen earlier, balance is an option not a necessity in the frame, as an imbalanced shot can be balanced by the following shot, creating balance in the entire scene rather than the single shot. This advantage in the film image allows for a variety of options. Each cinematographer has his or her own preference for which compositional grid to use (or any other compositional arrangement, as obviously more are possible). What makes these two grids very user-friendly for the cinematic composition is their simplicity, which allows easier editing later on. If most shots follow a basic compositional grid, the succeeding shots will match in their composition more easily (by no means easy!), and editing for a continuous flow of the scene can be achieved. However, of course the characters and backgrounds do change during a shot, so the compositions need to be planned out. Shots can be edited together, as they already share a common grid (in theory, the praxis is more complex).

## Gestalt theory

Another possibility for arranging the elements in the frame and accentuating the focal point next to the golden section or rule of thirds is gestalt theory, which takes more of the object's aspects into account like size, color, distance, etc., and discusses which elements drag attention but also which elements connect. This theory greatly helps in the arrangement and visual weight of objects or elements and thus benefits the position of the focal point. Gestalt theory was developed in the 1920s in Germany by psychologists Max Wertheimer, Kurt Koffka, and Wolfgang Köhler. Max Wertheimer describes his gestalt theory: "The basic thesis of gestalt theory might be formulated thus: there are contexts in which what is happening in the whole cannot be deduced from the characteristics of the separate pieces, but conversely; what happens to a part of the whole is, in clear cut cases, determined by the laws of the inner structure of its whole."[1] It is much easier for the mind to see the sum of the image's parts than it would be to see all the individual parts by themselves. Grouping parts in order to understand the whole image is much quicker than seeing its single elements and then trying to make sense of it. Gestalt theory might seem unnecessary for animation; nevertheless, it is indispensable for clever visual decisions and can be the basis for drawing itself, as all of its laws do not just apply to the overall arrangement of elements within the drawing but also to each single stroke or line. Also, all the principles do appear here and there throughout this whole book in one way or another. Gestalt theory is therefore crucial in design!

How do those principles fit into animation or image making? The principles *per se* are most often described as abstract shapes in relationship with each other, which is what I also will do in the following explanation. However, one has to replace the shapes with objects, characters, or environments to really get their impact on the image or moving image.

## There are eight laws of grouping in Gestalt theory

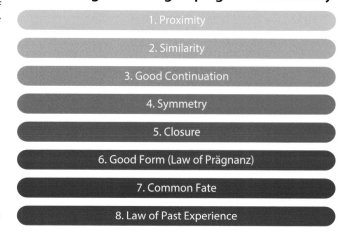

1. Proximity
2. Similarity
3. Good Continuation
4. Symmetry
5. Closure
6. Good Form (Law of Prägnanz)
7. Common Fate
8. Law of Past Experience

1  Max Wertheimer, Lecture at the Kantgesellschaft (Kant Society), Berlin (17 Dec 1924), "*Über Gestalttheorie*," as taken down in shorthand. Translated by N. Nairn-Allison in Social Research (1944), 11, 91.

## 1. Proximity

The idea behind this principle is that our eye assorts objects into groups depending on their proximity to each other. Closer objects have an attraction to each other, whereas the further away they are the less their attraction impacts the grouping. This always depends on the number of objects in the frame and their relationships. We see the whole rather than the details; we would see a forest first and then the trees. This makes it much easier for the mind to observe our surroundings, as grouping objects simplifies the image instead of seeing all of the objects at once. In Figure 5.39a, all the blue squares have the same distance from each other, so we perceive first a big square and then its single elements. In Figure 5.39b, there are two rows of squares grouped together as their proximity changes compared with Figure 5.39a. In Figure 5.39c, the eye organizes the squares into vertical columns, as they are closer vertically than horizontally, and in Figure 5.39d we have three groups of two, three, and four squares and those groups also form a triangle.

## 2. Similarity

This principle allows the eye to sort objects into groups based on their design aspects like shape, color, form, size, light and shadow, texture, direction, etc. The similarity principle uses the physical attributes of objects to relate them to one another. In Figure 5.40a through (d), I arranged the squares according to their color and obviously also their proximity. Which one dominates can be controlled with the design aspects. In Figure 5.40c or (d), the eye can easily group the red squares and blend out all the other squares.

## 3. Continuity

This principle seems rather obvious and is more based on logic, though it is inherently imbedded into our perception. Objects that overlap each other are seen in our mind as whole, not interrupted (Figure 5.41). However, if seen from a more abstract perspective, the eye groups lines and shapes together that have the same or a similar curvature and direction and sees them as one piece. The attributes of the object don't have to be the same in order to be seen as one line, shape, or form. The eye connects objects with different design aspects if their direction or any other aspect is the same or similar.

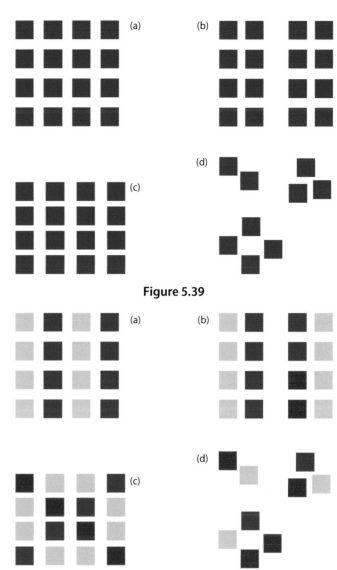

Figure 5.39

Figure 5.40

## 4. Symmetry

The law of symmetry states that the eye is able to perceive objects as being symmetrical and containing a center. In Figure 5.42, we see two groups of shapes that are symmetrical instead of six different shapes. The eye sees immediately that the three different shapes are mirrored on the other side. Objects do not necessarily have to have the same shape, form, color, or texture in order to be grouped together based on their symmetry.

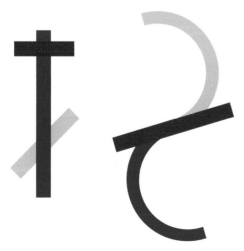

Figure 5.41

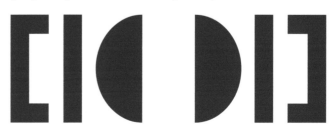

Figure 5.42

### 5. Closure

With closure, the mind fills gaps in the visual information that are necessary to see the whole (Figure 5.43a). Objects that are missing parts or details are in the viewer's mind completed, which is why we understand very rudimentary drawings that depict the world in lines. Drawings are always just a fragment of the whole image and still our mind clearly understands their message. We don't need to draw each single window in a skyscraper in order to know that they are there. Less information actually makes it visually more interesting when it comes to drawing. The reduction is visually appealing and challenging for the mind. In Figure 5.43b, we can see three shapes, or is it two shapes, because the triangle is inscribed into the rectangle? Closure also helps us to distinguish shapes from each other that otherwise group.

### 6. Good Form (Law of Prägnanz)

*Prägnanz* is the German word for "pithiness" or "clarity" and in gestalt psychology means the simplification of complex structures into simpler, easier to understand visuals. In order for us to understand convoluted images, we eliminate details or group them to focus on the overall whole first instead of being distracted by unimportant elements. We organize forms or shapes into groups of similar or same color, texture, size, etc., and therefore simplify the load of information to more easily understand the image and look for the important information instead of being confused with the information as a whole. Figure 5.44 shows three different colored shapes that also create as a negative shape a white triangle. We do not pay much attention to the white separating lines between the shapes but quickly see the white triangle (Figure 5.45).

### 7. Common Fate

With common fate we bring, compared to the previous six laws, movement into the perception. Every object moves on a path that in animation we call an *arc*. Cars that drive with the same or a similar speed on a highway are seen as one group of cars, not single cars. The eye connects all those objects that share the same or a similar movement, speed, or direction and organizes them into one group. In **Video 5F**, we see three groups of dots, not nine dots. The dots share three different directions, so we see three groups. We simplify the image in order to not be overwhelmed with information. An example in animation for common fate is the famous scene in *Lion King* where the wildebeest are stampeding down the ravine towards Simba. They are seen as one big wave of animals, not as hundreds of single ones.

### 8. Law of Past Experience

Objects that have been seen together or in relation to each other are most likely to be connected again in a new visual experience. For example, if I see a group of objects—a hammer, a wrench, an apple, and a bun—I will obviously group the tools into one group and the food into another. The same happens with shapes, forms, colors, etc.

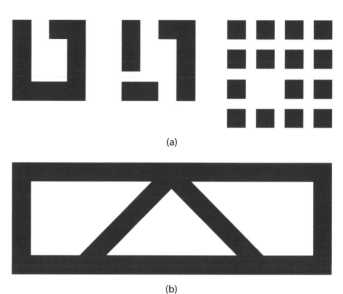

(a)

(b)

**Figure 5.43**

**Figure 5.44**

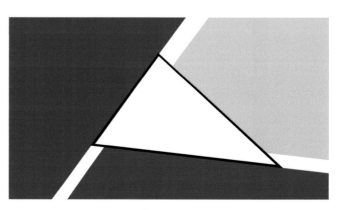

**Figure 5.45**

# Improving the readability of the image

Each image contains lots of visual information and every part affects the story in one way or another. All this information could just be spread throughout the frame randomly and it would be up to the viewer to make sense of what the frame contains. This can be an interesting and intellectual challenge, but it does take time and concentration in order for the audience to make those important connections between all these bits and pieces and figure out what the story behind it is. One task of composition is to channel this huge amount of information and present it to the viewer in an understandable and simple visual arrangement, clarifying what is and what is not important. Composition is crucial in getting the right message across and not overwhelming the viewer with various stories that do not support the main point (two or more story points in one image are possible in film, though they have to be well planned out to be understood).

## There are various options for improving the readability of images

### Simplicity
Most important of all, of course, is simplicity and the reduction or proper arrangement of visual information. Less information means less time needed to read the picture. Without simplicity in design and story, the content of the images can be too overwhelming and not clear enough to be understood quickly. If it is the style direction to compose consuming images, then the content has to be arranged by levels of importance that obviously tell the viewer what is the primary and what the secondary information.

### Aspects of design
Secondly, we have the aspects of design to guide the eye to the important parts or lead them on a path that elegantly tells the story. They can also be used to hide information that is insignificant. The aspects of design are composition, shape and form, vectors, directions, color, contrast, light and shadow, perspective, size, texture, depth, movement, music, and sound.

### Objects/Characters in the image and their importance
The readability of the image is greatly improved by the controlled arrangement of objects and characters in terms of their importance. Primary characters and objects have to always be placed in the focal area, supported by all the aspects of design. Secondary characters or objects (like furniture, pictures, objects that relate to the story, etc.) are to be placed to support the main action and must never without a reason drag attention towards themselves. Secondary characters or actions can, however, come with their own imbedded meaning and therefore can, if desired, affect the story, comment on the main action, or even tell their own subplot, yet should never interrupt the main plot without a solid reason.

# Tell the story visually

Composition seems to be a rather technical field that does not lend itself to clear storytelling. *Color, light and shadow, shapes, size*, etc., are all rather technical terms. This is the part where a more abstract thought process comes in handy. A simple example should demonstrate the storytelling ability of composition. Figures 5.46 through 5.48 show the same character walking happily towards the right. All three pictures have a shape above the character. The position of the shape, which is obviously part of the overall composition (arrangement of the elements within the frame), has a clear impact on how we read the image. Figure 5.46 has a heavy shape above the character, right on top of his head. It could fall at any moment onto his head, and like the Celts who were supposedly afraid that the sky might fall (see *Asterix & Obelix* for clarification), we should be afraid that it actually might happen and thus crush our happy little friend. Pushing the shape towards the front of him makes us concerned that it might fall when he reaches it (Figure 5.47), whereas if it is behind him we know that the danger has passed and there is an actual visible reason for him to be happy (Figure 5.48). This is a rather

**Figure 5.46**

**Figure 5.47**

**Figure 5.48**

simple composition but shows how it can tell or contribute to the story. The shape can be really anything; it does not have to be an actual object or architecture. It can be a dark color, a shadow, texture … the important thing is what it does to our perception of the space and how it then affects the story. Exceptions of course here make the rule!

Every design aspect can do the same and affect visually what the story tells us literally. How the artist uses those design elements in the composition to enrich and support the story is of course a very personal decision and depends on the artist's sensibility and to what extent he or she wants specific image elements to step forward or backward, intellectually and/or visually. As image makers we cannot rely on text or sound to tell the story; we need to find a way of interpreting visually in the frame what the story is about. The difficult part starts when more abstract personality traits have to be visualized, like the character being insincere. How do you visualize "insincere"? You cannot just let someone in the shot say: "Oh, by the way, our main character is insincere." The solution is color, shape, overall appearance, and the balance of personality traits against those of other characters. Every single literal point can be translated into visuals; that might not be easy, but it can be done and the composition is no exception.

## Structure the image into levels of importance

Composition can also create layers of information either through the arrangement of the elements or through the design aspects. We have already seen this in the composition of Friedrich's *Winterlandschaft* (Figure 5.7), where there is the obvious story of the wanderer resting, but then there is the deeper meaning that is only possible to grasp by understanding the composition. The main elements that drive the story should be dominant, whereas the secondary elements or characters should step back. This does not define the position of the characters in the frame, and neither does it suggest a specific arrangement!

The illustration of the children's book *The Moles* (Figure 5.49), based on a Korean fairy tale, is about two young moles falling for each other and wanting to stay together. The parents of one of them, though, have other plans for their offspring and try to find the best spouse there is, and it is not the one their kid already chose. The illustration uses the idea of "levels of importance" by creating two different levels in the illustration that are stacked. The level of the parents shows the actual story point of them asking the Buddha for advice. However, the front level of the two young moles across from each other reminds the viewer of the overall storyline. The big Buddha is giving his blessing to the mole on the right, who is the one that wants to marry the mole on the left. The blessings are shown by the statue's lotus leaves, creating the shape of a heart just above the right mole's head. The image has connections between all the elements and tells the story visually. Everything in the image has a purpose and is positioned for a reason.

## Support a pleasing aesthetic

This is honestly the most wishy-washy point of them all. What is pleasing to one isn't necessarily pleasing to the next, and what I find amazing today, in 20 years I might find old-fashioned, badly done, or pedestrian. Aesthetic comes with knowledge of art history, animation history, film history, and the expertise and experience of what good design can be in relationship to the technique that is used and of course how it is used creatively. But it can also come from someone who has no training or knowledge in art at all and exactly because of that creates something new and amazing. Then something or someone comes along and again proves all of it wrong and presents the opposite and still is aesthetically pleasing. Judging design and with it composition is an extremely difficult task, as the question is, from which perspective are you judging it? From an artistic perspective, an economical one, a unique, personal one, or from a merely technical one? What is good design/composition and a pleasing aesthetic? Obviously, it cannot be answered

**Figure 5.49**

from a subjective perspective, but we have to look into the relationship between image, story, purpose, and technique.

These questions should help to define this (or make it even more confusing):

**Does the composition visualize the story convincingly?** The psychological impact of the composition needs to reflect the story's needs. How does the composition "feel": cramped, loose, busy, solitary, exciting, threatening, happy, sad …? It is the job of the composition to interpret the story in images that clearly relate to the characters and their personalities described in the script. The visuals need to represent the story; otherwise, the discrepancy will affect the believability of the world. However, this is also not clearly definable, as it is an artistic point and thus allows an endless range of possibilities and needs to be judged case by case.

**Is the composition unique and interesting or does it just copy existing clichés?** An aesthetic that is old and overused can lower the emotional response of the audience, but it can also evoke an emotional response if it triggers a positive memory of one's own childhood or history. The aesthetic of Cartoon Network's cartoons of the mid-1990s (for instance, *Dexter's Laboratory*), which partly followed the style of UPA cartoons from the 1950s and 1960s literally reanimated an era of design long gone. It created a relationship with animation history and brought back a style, of which composition can be part.

**What artistic time frame does the film or image follow and does the composition reflect that?** A film that is set in ninth century Europe might follow a compositional arrangement used in medieval illustrations instead of using all the compositional techniques from today. Restriction often forces one to come up with creative solutions (see Tomm Moore's feature animation *The Secret of Kells*).

**Who is the composition for? What target audience is to be addressed and what is the purpose of the entire piece?** The aesthetic of a film needs to be seen in relationship to its audience and what aesthetics they are capable of understanding. Simplicity geared towards small children is of course not subject to the same aesthetic judgment as a feature film for adults.

**What compositional rules does the film follow?** The rules of image making are plenty and have developed over hundreds of years; they have proven themselves aesthetically pleasant for the viewer. The aesthetics of a production can follow these established rules, which however will not necessarily make the film aesthetically pleasing, as it depends on the artist's skills. The production can also go against those rules and because of it create a new piece of work that is visually interesting and unique; however, it needs to be conscious about doing that. Modern composition and aesthetics allow many forms of visuals; there isn't a clear definition of *right* or *wrong*, only of working or not working within the chosen field. American feature animation on a grand scale usually follows a certain aesthetic, as does European or Japanese animation. They only partly overlap.

**What aesthetic direction does it follow and how does that visually relate/interpret the story?** There are obviously many aesthetics out there that all have their own rules and values. It is impossible to name them all, as there are not just genres, but subgenres, films that are based on books, games, older shows, the style of an illustrator or animator, other cultures that have a completely different aesthetic, etc. If the design of a show mimics the style of, for example, Russian folk art, but the story has nothing to do with Russia or folk art, then there might be a bit of a discrepancy that isn't convincing. However, it could also be an interesting approach, to mix styles and cultures and let the audience find the connection. Needless to say that the connection has to be explainable by the artist and done on purpose.

**What is the budget and how is it used to create the visuals on screen?** A film with a low budget has to be judged from a different perspective than a feature with an enormous budget. Don Bluth's *The Secret of NIMH* (1982), for example, cost about US$7 million and is aesthetically grand in style and celebrated for its visual splendor, compared to *The Little Mermaid* (1989), which cost US$40 million but is by no means five times more elaborate or five times more intricately composed. However, scale has an impact on the aesthetic but does not necessarily have an effect on the aesthetic quality or value of a piece.

**Is the goal making money, being artistic, or both?** These goals rarely go together; nevertheless, there are of course films that have successfully combined the two. Tim Burton's *Nightmare before Christmas* (1993) is one of them. It does not follow the typical feature film design of the time, instead producing a new visual experience that is artistic and creative, yet still sellable to a broad audience, and thus recouping the great costs of such an immense production. It is not very practical to just think of the artistic outcome of an $18 million production; you still need to communicate with the general public and entertain them, so that the money spent comes back in through ticket sales. However, a small, short film that is privately funded can have an artistic direction that is free from the need for ticket sales and thus explore a much wider range of visual possibilities and storytelling styles.

**What is the experience of the viewer?** Aesthetic judgment comes not only from the sensory experience itself, which is subjective *per se*, but also from knowledge and broad exposure to the field. If one only sees one Japanese woodblock print, one will probably find it beautiful and aesthetically pleasing, but an extended exposure and additional professional study of the different artists in the field, the study of the hundreds of years of production, will of course affect one's judgment. The initial aesthetic judgment might dramatically change: what caused a positive emotional reaction at the first viewing might after some study and acquired knowledge cause the opposite emotion, as now broader knowledge will put the piece into a different category. Aesthetic judgment is therefore always connected to a certain time frame and the experience and knowledge of the viewer.

Nevertheless, the following is a list of movies that I myself find aesthetically important for one reason or another—and, yes, the list constantly changes:

> *The King and the Mockingbird · Wallace & Gromit · Pinocchio · Ernest & Celestine · 101 Dalmatians · UPA shorts · Bambi · Fantasia · Dumbo · Sleeping Beauty · Nightmare before Christmas · Akira Spirited Away · Yellow Submarine · My Neighbors the Yamadas · The Thief and the Cobbler · Prince Achmed ·* Hubley shorts, especially *Adventures of an \* · The Wind in the Willows* (British stop motion version) *· Winnie the Pooh* (Russian Version) *· The Corpse Bride · Kung Fu Panda · Up · Ratatouille · How to Train Your Dragon · Robots ·* Brothers Quay short films *· Tekkonkinkreet · Triplets of Belleville ·* Len Lye's *Free Radicals ·* Oskar Fischinger's *Alegretto ·* Richard Condi's *The Cat Came Back ·* Brothers Lauenstein's short film *Balance ·* Short films by Yuriy Norshteyn *·* Short films by Te Wei *·* Short from the Shanghai Studios: *The Monkeys That Wanted to Steal the Moon · Boy and the World · Zootopia*

## Enjoy the game of composing complex visuals

Composition is not just about creating a foundation for the image and a basis for the story. It is so much more than that … if you want it to be. There is no limit to the complexity if the project allows for more intricate, sophisticated designs or intellectually challenging visuals. The fun in composing can be the cerebral stimulation and trying to involve the audience in a communication that has the main story point as a basis but spreads out from there into different directions and creates a network of comments that can tell any story to those that are willing or able to read them. The artist can make the audience not just follow the basic story but be in a dialogue that consists of additional shades of the story, substory, or message. Multiple levels of information challenge the viewer in the second or third viewing and an image becomes richer in storytelling and artistry. It is always possible to challenge yourself with a witty or complex composition that brings a new reading to the table and shows the story point in a different light. The possibilities are endless! It depends on how much time you want to spend on the composition and how many ideas you have (and of course who the audience is). In Caravaggio's (Michelangelo Merisi) painting *The Incredulity of Saint Thomas* (1601–1602) (Figure 5.50), we see Jesus leading Thomas' finger into his wound as proof that it is him who resurrected. The heads of the four men clearly depict the shape of a cross in the middle of the frame (Figure 5.51). This shape not only groups them but also makes an intellectual and visual connection to Jesus' death on the cross. His resurrection is proof of his status as the son of God. The means of his death and the symbol of Christianity is therefore already present in the composition. Shape and form within the composition can add intellectual clues for the further understanding of the image.

In film and animation, we are dealing additionally with movement, so intricate compositions with an imbedded

meaning, like in Caravaggio's painting, are more difficult to achieve but not impossible. Most compositions are representational, show clearly what is needed for the storytelling, and are less open for interpretation. However, there are movies that do use composition to express core elements of the story and represent an idea or even a message in the overall compositional style. An interesting example is the cinematography of Otto Heller in Sidney J. Furie's 1965 Cold War espionage thriller *The Ipcress File*. What makes Heller's compositions so striking is that he uses many camera angles that are uncomfortable, heavily tilted, objects cover the characters, the actors are placed in unusual positions within the frame, and the overall visibility is reduced. The basis for this is the

**Figure 5.50**

Michelangelo Merisi (Caravaggio): *The Incredulity of Saint Thomas* (1601–1602).

**Figure 5.51**

main character's poor eyesight, which is reflected in the visuals. The skewed compositions tell us of a warped reality, of an unusual situation, and let us see reality from literally a very new perspective. The audience as much as the main character learns to *see* their world differently. The unique style of composition therefore has a message of its own and affects the emotional response of the audience. Another example in animation is DreamWorks's feature *Madagascar*, which has a case study on this chapter.

## Positive and negative space, breathing space

How we fill the space within the frame has an impact on the audience's response and can, with the help of all the other design aspects, create a space that is either tight or spacious. Positive space is the form or shape that is occupied by characters and objects (sometimes parts of the environment), whereas negative space is the space surrounding the positive space. Too much positive space will make the image feel claustrophobic, loud, narrow, dense, but also exciting and thrilling. Much negative space can have the opposite effect of the image feeling quiet, sporadic, sparse, but also relaxing and intimate. However, with positive and negative space there is a bit more to it. For instance, if we zoom into the character very close and the character fills the entire frame, it is claustrophobic, but also intimate. As always: exceptions make the rule! I just talked about Caravaggio's painting *The Incredulity of Saint Thomas*; just imagine the four characters, who define the positive space, being accompanied by ten more in the background, filling the empty, negative space behind them. The feeling of intimacy and quiet would be replaced by tightness and business and the frame would feel overcrowded. The very point of the intimate and subtle action of Thomas putting his hand into Jesus' wound would be lost and turned into a public event. (The feeling of quiet in Caravaggio's painting is, of course, also supported by the characters' actions and emotions, as well as the colors, lighting, etc. Here, we are just talking about the filling of the space!) It is the background and its sparseness that accentuates the privateness of the affair. Whether an image needs this empty space or not depends on the story. Most pictures play with empty space because it gives the picture a calm that lets the eye and the intellect rest for a while and provides needed contrast to the busy areas. This is called

### Lewis Carroll
"Jabberwocky"

'Twas brillig, and the slithy toves
Did gyre and gimble in the wabe;
All mimsy were the borogoves,
And the mome raths outgrabe.

"Beware the Jabberwock, my son!
The jaws that bite, the claws that catch!
Beware the Jubjub bird, and shun
The frumious Bandersnatch!"

He took his vorpal sword in hand:
Long time the manxome foe he sought -
So rested he by the Tumtum tree,
And stood awhile in thought.

And as in uffish thought he stood,
The Jabberwock, with eyes of flame,
Came whiffling through the tulgey wood,
And burbled as it came!

One, two! One, two! and through and through
The vorpal blade went snicker-snack!
He left it dead, and with its head
He went galumphing back.

"And hast thou slain the Jabberwock?
Come to my arms, my beamish boy!
O frabjous day! Callooh! Callay!"
He chortled in his joy.

'Twas brillig, and the slithy toves
Did gyre and gimble in the wabe;
All mimsy were the borogoves,
And the mome raths outgrabe.

**Figure 5.52**

"breathing space," an area balancing out the lively parts of the frame with its quietness to provide tension on the one hand and ease on the other. Sometimes we need areas in the frame that lack visual information but allow the image to breathe, to give it some air, and to help the viewer not to be overwhelmed and the image not to feel claustrophobic. We can either choose to keep parts of the image empty or emptier and focus the attention towards the foreground elements and let the background be just a secondary visual that supports the foreground but does not have a significance in terms of information, like in Caravaggio's painting, in which the background is just a dark gradient.

In the illustration for Lewis Carroll's poem *Jabberwocky* (Figure 5.52), the focus is on the son and his vorpal sword looking at the empty space in front of him where the Jabberwocky is expected to appear. The entire composition flows round from the son to the negative space. The relationship between negative and positive space therefore helps tell the story and creates tension. However, the empty space has a shadow on the ground, showing that the Jabberwocky is about to appear, filling the empty space with a creature of our imagination. Of course, the accompanying text has to follow the overall curves and the flow of the composition;

otherwise it would destroy the effect of it. Text should always appear in an area that is quiet, just for the practical reason of being able to read it.

Nonetheless, empty space can be omitted if the picture is supposed to excite and stimulate with action. A painting of a great battle has less empty or negative space as it is about an aggressive military deed, a planned mess that causes confusion. Albrecht Altdorfer's (1480–1538) huge and famous painting *Alexanderschlacht* ("The Battle of Alexander at Issus") from 1529 has sweeping movements not only in the fighting armies but also movement and grandeur in the sky and landscape (Figure 5.53). There are very few quiet moments in the depiction of Alexander's battle; tension and excitement is everywhere we look. Even the sun, moon, and the entire atmosphere take part in this dramatic scene with broad, exciting clouds. Not only the armies fight; the whole world is in for the action!

Another example where empty space is left out on purpose is look-and-find picture books, like the work of German illustrator Ali Mitgutsch, which invites the observer to get lost in the image and search and look, find new activities over and over again, and never get bored. The mere point of look-and-find pictures is to present something that is packed and emanates the excitement of never being able to explore all the actions on the page. It never ceases to be fun. But even in those busy pictures there is some structure; it is not a random arrangement but is composed to make it easier to observe to give each action enough room and guide the eye on a path.

Positive, negative, and breathing space need to be balanced according to the story's needs. The balance between action and reticence is what brings tension into the frame. How busy or empty the image should be depends of course on the story and its interpretation.

The challenge sometimes is to have negative or empty space but not make it look empty. Subtle textures or simple pattern allows these areas to not appear empty.

## Create tension and balance

Composition helps the viewer to understand the image and makes it easier to quickly see what is of importance and what is secondary. The other purpose is to create harmony in the image with shapes and weight, colors and textures, to distribute the content in the frame in order for the image to be balanced. There are two forces in the frame that always struggle with each other and that need to be equally considered: balance and tension. Too much balance and the image might be too quiet; too much tension and the image falls apart. All of this is connected to the story, as the story dictates if the image needs to have more balance or more tension. There is absolutely no rule for that, but it is often a personal preference of what "feels" right. But a mere "feeling" doesn't help, so we have to find at least a direction of how to deal with tension and balance.

**Figure 5.53**

Albrecht Altdorfer, *The Battle of Alexander at Issus*, 1529.

## Tension and visual weight

Figure 5.54 has a ball in the exact center of the frame. There is no tension between the distances of the four sides and the ball. It is perfectly balanced in the middle of the frame. This image is quiet and calm, expressing either confidence, stability, or exposure (more on the interpretation of this in Chapter 6, "Character Staging and Film Language"). It is a definite statement of the presentation of the ball with no hesitation. Figure 5.55 has the ball slightly shifted to the right, which adds tension as the forces between the distance from left to right have changed. There is now a very different relationship between the ball and the space on the left and on the right. This tension has an effect on the content, as the stability is now gone. The eye wants to shift the ball back into the middle and therefore active involvement of the audience begins. We are all of a sudden part of the content and not just a bystander. Figure 5.56 has the ball not only shifted right but also pushed up, which adds even more tension from all four sides but also has a certain randomness to it, as it lacks the remains of order that Figure 5.55 still has. Shifting the shape too much towards the frame, like in Figure 5.57, the opposite side on the left starts to feel empty and the created tension is very strong without being balanced by another element appearing on the left (and the magnetism of the frame starts to really impact the composition).

In the image from Caspar David Friedrich, *Winterlandschaft* (Figure 5.7), which we discussed earlier, the composition is very geometric and arranged and all shapes are obvious and clear. The center tree marks with its tip the central axis of the painting. The tree to the right is as far away from the center as the cathedral in the background and repeats its shape. This is the balance where the same or similar shape appears on the left and right of the center. However, the shape repeats but its content does not, which adds additional tension in color, contrast, texture, and object, one being a tree and the other a cathedral. The stone and tree on the far left do not have their counterparts on the right, which also causes tension. The whole composition is still very well balanced, soothing, and calm. This is where the visual weight comes in to balance out the tension. Observe the two triangles of right tree and cathedral. The tree is much heavier visually than the cathedral because of its texture, color, and contrast. The cathedral, because of its lack of contrast and its airy look, is lighter. The shapes balance each other out but the visual weight does not. By adding more weight onto the left (the small tree and stone), the scale of the images' weight on each side is even again. The visual weight of the snow in the foreground is much heavier than the snow planes on the right in the middle ground, which lack contrast. However, the snowy planes on the right are on a scale more extensive than the small hill in the front left. In this case, balance is achieved through weighing size with color and contrast. Shapes, textures, colors, light and shadow, etc., always affect one another; they form complex relationships and influence each other's space and visual weight. When you get a feeling for how complex the tension and balance can be

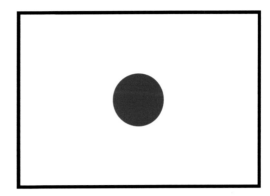

**Figure 5.54**

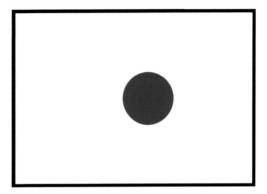

**Figure 5.55**

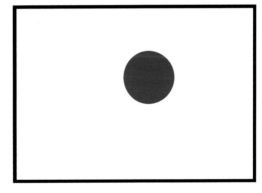

**Figure 5.56**

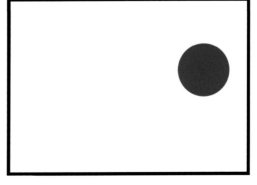

**Figure 5.57**

in an image, you start to see the image not as a mere painting but as a distribution of shapes, colors, and movement that all together create the composition. Nevertheless, all the pictorial elements constantly vie for dominance, creating a vibrant tapestry of artistic movement.

## Balance and visual weight

As much as an image needs tension, it also needs balance. Figure 5.58a has a simple composition of a ball at the far left of the frame. The right side is completely empty. There is tension in the image because the eye is attracted to the left, but there is nothing on the right that balances it out. The ball has so much visual weight (Figure 5.58b) that it tips the image over and it feels as if the ball drags down the left side. Visual weight does not relate to the actual weight of the depicted object. If the white ball were a balloon, its visual weight would still be heavy and drag down the left side of the frame. To avoid the tilt of the frame, another object can be positioned on the right to give the image more stability, like in Figure 5.58c. However, this does change the story, as now there is a strong relationship between the two shapes. Too much balance can take away the tension that an image also needs. What can be done in order to keep the balance, yet still have tension, is to not only choose objects to balance out the frame but use color, light and shadow, texture, or any other aspect to balance out the frame—anything that helps to not make the image tilt too much (Figure 5.58d). For images that require text to be added into the frame, this also needs to be considered, as text itself has its own visual weight. See Figure 5.59 for more information.

In Shohei Imamura's film *Intentions of Murder* (1964) (Figures 5.60–5.63), cinematographer Shinsaku Himeda creates unique compositions with balance, yet still keeps the tension. The focal point in all three images is either on the far right or far left, or

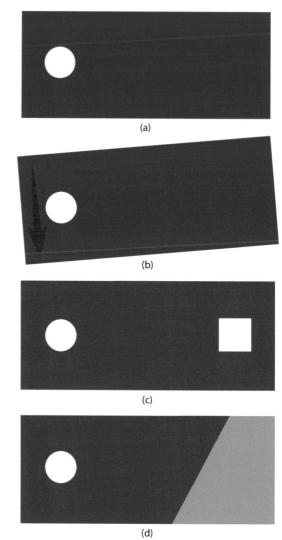

(a)

(b)

(c)

(d)

**Figure 5.58**

Image and text:

This could be the position where the text for the story would appear in the illustration. The text-field has its own visual weight that needs to be considered when designing the composition for a book-illustration. By keeping parts of the illustration empty for the imbedded text, the final image will be balanced when the text or any other needed graphic information is finally inserted. If the text however covers all the negative space, then again the image can feel cramped and overcrowded.

**Figure 5.59**

off-center right/left, and he always places "something" on the opposite side to establish the needed balance. But in every image the compositional element that he places on the opposite side is what also gives the image tension because it has a different shape and different visual weight. A lid lamp, a shelf with vases, or a sign saying "Matsushima" visually balance the action but don't take away the importance of the focal point. Both sides relate to

each other compositionally and have the possibility to also relate intellectually, but it is very clear where the focus lies.

Nevertheless, balance does not need to be symmetrically obvious as in the mentioned examples, but can be rather complex by taking weight, color, contrast, and position into consideration in an abstract composition that deviates from storytelling and focuses just on the design aspects without them representing reality or interpreting reality. In Piet Mondrian's painting *Composition with Yellow, Blue, and Red* (Figure 5.64), the composition is balanced because of the weight and distribution of the colors. We have a red bigger rectangle in the lower right (with a tiny one on the right frame) and a yellow rectangle in the upper left corner. The red feels heavier compared to the yellow as its luminance is lower. Mondrian balances the red with a light blue rectangle on the left, which adds more visual weight to the left side. He adds additional tension to the painting by not adding a black outline to the blue rectangle, which seems to separate the blue from the solid structure of the canvas and creates its own level, allowing it to be behind the black framework. The framework itself is balanced on the left and right, as both sides have the same amount of four black verticals next to the middle of the frame. It is the two black horizontals underneath the red square that create tension. The tiny red square on the very right connects with the blue line. The yellow and the small red square also point towards the offscreen space, as they seem to expand outside of the frame. Abstract art can follow the same compositional options or rules but without the narrative storytelling that relates to the natural world.

**Figure 5.60**

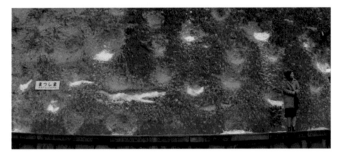

**Figure 5.61**

**Figure 5.62**

**Figure 5.63**

Shohei Imamura: *Intentions of Murder* (1964).

**Figure 5.64**

Piet Mondrian, *Composition with Yellow, Blue, and Red*, (1937–1942).

# Create paths for the viewer to observe the image

Various reading paths in a picture are designed by the artist to guide the viewer's eyes from one part of the image to another and thus tell the story bit by bit. Through a well-designed composition, the artist can highlight important parts and visually tone down less important ones for the sake of storytelling. This is one of the main points of composition, to determine which elements in the image are worth accentuating and which elements need to be subdued for the image to be understood the way it is intended. In Caravaggio's (Michelangelo Merisi, 1571–1610) painting *The Entombment of Christ* (1602–1603) (Figure 5.65), the realism of the scene is typical for Caravaggio's art: realistic, painful, and heartbreaking. He pushes the emotions, not only of the characters but also of the audience, to its limits and creates paintings that never leave one neutral. One is always involved in the rough realism that are by other contemporary painters often sugarcoated for aesthetic reasons. Caravaggio came out of Italian Mannerism and opened the path for the Baroque movement. He included in his paintings a stunning sensibility for light and shadow in an intensity not seen before. He avoids embellishing the entombment, is as realistic as possible, and even transports the ancient scene into the seventeenth century for the viewer to be even more affected and also involved by the contemporary interpretation. The characters are down to earth, real people with dirty feet and worn clothing. We can feel the finger of Saint John touching Jesus' wound, feel the sting of the sweaty, dirty fingers in the wound and the texture of the open flesh. Also, the weight of the corpse is apparent, causing us to not just see this scene as a mere painting but as a burial scene that we are actually witnessing. The easy readability of the painting can be contributed to Caravaggio's masterful handling of composition (and obvious painting skills). The vast number of paths and vectors he creates of the burial of Jesus' limp body make it very easy for the viewer to observe and follow one character after another, as they lead from one to the next, only to end up in Jesus' face where the paths continue along his arm into the grave (Figure 5.66). Jesus seems to point down into his dark resting place, showing what is about to happen. There are various reasons why Jesus is the focal point of the painting compositionally. Firstly, he is horizontally placed compared to everyone else standing. Then he is the character closest to us. Additionally, the area that most often drags the attention first is the brightest in the image. Light or bright colors are most often the focus. In Caravaggio's painting, Jesus is the brightest of all the characters, which fits his Christian role of being the "light." His pale skin has the tone of death and dominates the frame from the first glance. He is in between the living and the grave, making him the one that separates life from death, again noting in visuals the Christian message. The second focal point is Nicodemus, the man in the middle, who carries Jesus's legs and looks straight at us. The original painting in the church of Santa Maria in Vallicella[2] was hung above eye level and therefore Nicodemus is looking down at the viewer. The eye contact drags one into the image right from the start and creates an emotional connection to this intense scene; one is immediately involved in the story. The man's modest attire and dirty feet make him one of the common people and allows the poor devotee to feel close to Jesus and his entourage, who also were all commoners. From Jesus's position, one can now wander through the canvas and bit by bit grasp the story and the relationship between the portrayed people. There are various compositional ideas in the painting (Figures 5.66–5.69) that are stacked on top of each other in order to form paths and vectors for this complex and challenging composition to evolve. The movement of the poses of Maria of Clopas raising her arms in mourning to heaven, down to Saint John, is very similar to frames in an animated sequence (Figure 5.67).

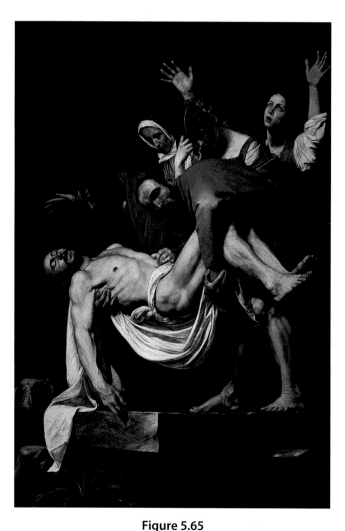

**Figure 5.65**

Michelangelo Merisi (Caravaggio): *The Entombment of Christ* (1602–1603).

2   The original is in the Vatican; a copy hangs in Santa Maria Vallicella.

**Figure 5.66**

**Figure 5.67**

**Figure 5.68**

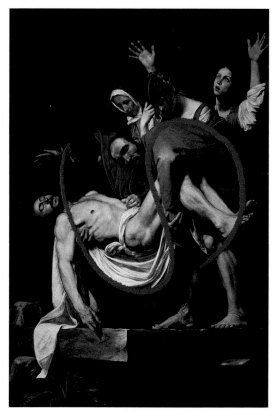

**Figure 5.69**

Every character bends down more towards Jesus in cascading poses. This sequential depiction allows movement that leads the eye so effectually towards the dead. Figures 5.58 and 5.59 show how the eye follows circular paths to continuously be forced to go around in the image and not stay still. Caravaggio packs his images full of vectors and connections and they make his pictures, even in the details, look composed and arranged; but because of his immense compositional skills the images are never rigid or stiff but always organic and "natural."

In animation these paths can be a bit trickier, because we are not just dealing with one image but an image that is changing continuously. The layout of the frames has to be meticulously planned out from the first to the last key frame of the scene, so that no character covers important information in the frame during their performance. However, the position of each character, their character animation and emotional impact, their relationships to each other, and their poses must not disrupt the design of the shot. In Richard Williams' film *The Thief and the Cobbler*, this is often solved very gracefully and always in a compositionally interesting manner. Williams uses the shapes of the character's poses, which he distorts oftentimes freely, to serve the purpose of the character animation *and* the composition. This leads visually into the addressed characters and thus creates strong vectors where the eye wanders back and forth (Figures 5.70 and 5.71). He frequently makes use of positive and negative space (Figures 5.72 and 5.73) to invent new and interesting compositions that do not follow the well-worn paths of typical feature film animation. In Figure 5.72, Zigzag is talking to King Nod and offering him a lady from Mombasa. While he is talking, through his positive body shape and his position in the frame he gives way to the action in the negative space around him, which by itself creates an interesting rotund within the frame. However, the image, whose reading direction is screen left, does not seem cramped with information, because Williams leaves the very left side of the frame nearly empty, to give the image breathing space and allow the hand to be fully recognized in its silhouette. The strong movement from Zigzag's black shoulders downwards and up to his hand is rather unanatomical, though also highly effective. Note the arrangement of the group in the background from Zigzag's eyes downwards to the left towards his hand and then back up again through the shortest adviser in the front towards Zigzag's face. Williams molds the characters' shapes mainly for the enrichment of the composition and its visual impact and therefore takes full advantage of the possibilities within animation.

**Figure 5.70**

**Figure 5.71**

**Figure 5.72**

**Figure 5.73**

Richard Williams' *The Thief and the Cobbler*; (1964–1992).

# Case study: Disney's steps into the modern world in *Pigs is Pigs* (1954)[3]

**Director:** Jack Kinney
**Layout artist:** Bruce Bushman
**Background artist:** Al Dempster
**Background artist:** Eyvind Earle
**Layout artist:** John Wilson

When UPA started to push animation design with its award-winning shorts in the 1950s, many animation companies worldwide followed its lead. Disney's role was always to design films that took reality as the base and give it a twist. This is rooted in nineteenth century illustration, which Walt Disney himself was trying to transfer onto the screen before the 1950s. Art movements like impressionism, surrealism, expressionism, Dada, or abstract expressionism, to name a few, were not something that Disney artists usually used as reference material, or if they did it did not trickle down through the development process ending up on-screen. One of the very few contemporary fine artists who was invited to Disney was Savador Dali (1904–1989), brought in to work on a short film called *Destino* from 1945 to 1946, a surrealist film that was not finished until 2003. What Disney developed in the 1930s and 1940s was immensely important for the animation industry, and the films that were designed and created range amongst the masterpieces of cinema, though one thing has to be understood: Disney interpreted nature and used design as a vehicle for the story and for storytelling. He never used an abstract idea to be visualized in animation. In the section *Toccata and Fugue*, a sequence in *Fantasia* (1940), Disney hired abstract animator and artist Oskar Fischinger to design an abstract interpretation of Johann Sebastian Bach's music. Compared to Fischinger's own short films, which are truly abstract and have no relationship to the real world, the *Fantasia* sequence is not an abstract film at all. What Fischinger intended to appear in the film is not what ended up on-screen, as the Disney artists changed most of Fischinger's abstract designs to representative shapes and colors, which is the opposite of abstract film, whose purpose is the negation of the representational world. Oskar Fischinger writes about his Disney experience:

> I worked on this film for nine months; then through some "behind the back" talks and intrigue (something very big at the Disney Studios) I was demoted to an entirely different department, and three months later I left Disney again, agreeing to call off the contract. The film "Toccata and Fugue by Bach" is really not my work, though my work may be present at some points; rather it is the most inartistic product

of a factory. Many people worked on it, and whenever I put out an idea or suggestion for this film, it was immediately cut to pieces and killed, or often it took two, three or more months until a suggestion took hold in the minds of some people connected with it who had their say. One thing I definitely found out: that no true work of art can be made with that procedure used in the Disney Studio.[4]

What we see in the short is flying violins, waves, clouds, and various other objects that defy the abstract nature of the piece. Disney films never wanted to be art; they wanted to be entertainment on the highest level (despite their often kitschy and emotionally over-the-top Broadway-tune sensibility). Technically, it is very difficult to reach the quality produced at Disney. However, what should be understood is exactly that: Disney films are not concerned about a unique artistic approach to image making. Their product is an always beautiful image that entertains in the most intricate and crafted way possible. Some Disney artists rejected this idea of realism having to be the basis of animation and later on, after the Disney strike of 1941, left the company, which led to the founding of the animation company UPA. Their approach to animation developed into a completely different one compared to Disney's. UPA is famous for its animation design, though it should be more famous for its animation concepts and the rigorous implementation of those ideas into the design. UPA pushed each design to its utmost limits. That can be seen in films like *Gerald McBoing-Boing* (1950), *Rooty Toot Toot* (1951), *Willie the Kid* (1952), *Christopher Crumpet* (1953), *Fudget's Budget* (1954), or even *The Tell-Tale Heart* (1953). Each UPA short has a different sensibility and design that fits only that one short and was not repeated in any of the other UPA shorts. It would be wrong to compliment UPA on all levels, as the style of their shorts derived from ideas that the art world had already dealt with for quite a while. Nevertheless, UPA brought those artistic sensibilities of fine art into animation. John Hubley and Zachary Schwartz, two of the founders of UPA, wrote about animation in 1946:

> The significance of the animated film as a means of communication is best realized in terms of its flexibility and scope of expression. It places no limitations upon ideas; the graphic representation grows out of the idea. The broadest abstract theory may be treated in a factual manner and made interesting, clear, and memorable through the use of movement and sound. All degrees of the general and particular are within its normal scope because anything that the brain can conceive can be expressed through the symbol.[5]

---

[3] Due to the fact that the Disney Company did not release the copyrights for images of this short film to be used in this educational section, which would have tremendously helped the understanding of the discussed composition, it is necessary for the reader to check and compare screen images from the short film alongside the text to fully grasp the composition.

[4] William Moritz, *Optical Poetry, The Life and Work of Oskar Fischinger*, Indiana University Press, Bloomington, IN, 2003, p. 85.
[5] John Hubley and Zachary Schwartz, Animation Learns a New Language, *Hollywood Quarterly*, Vol. 1, No. 4 (1946), pp. 360–363.

Where Disney uses style as a beautiful and often stunning cover for its subjects, in the shorts of UPA, style is the core of the piece. The style follows the idea strictly and succumbs in every aspect to this idea unapologetically. What the story requires, the style of UPA shorts will provide visually with a modern sensibility. This is what makes those UPA cartoons so special. It is not only their entertainment value (or some might say their lack of it—you can't please everyone) or their unique design, it is the conceptual approach and often undeniable artistic honesty in their visuals that impresses.

UPA's designs were all the rave, and every studio followed their lead; however, Disney himself was not too fond of the influence of UPA's style. Walt Disney told artist T. Hee after having worked at UPA and then returned to Disney: "Damn it, T., even if the critics do say that my art is like Christmas cards, it makes a hell of a lot more money than the things you've been doing over at UPA!"[6] The Disney Company adjusted in a few of its shorts and features to a style of a much smaller studio. Some of their short films during that time have a design approach that has UPA and modern design not only as a direction but outright visually adores it! One of the shorts is Ward Kimball's *Toot, Whistle, Plunk and Boom* from 1953, 2 years after UPA director Robert Cannon's game-changing short film *Gerald McBoing-Boing* and John Hubley's short film *Rooty Toot Toot*. Disney animator Ward Kimball, who was an admirer of UPA's work and had visited the studio frequently, wanted some of its aesthetics to enter the Disney style. His short film *Toot, Whistle, Plunk and Boom* is a bit of a mish mash of two styles that are neither traditional Disney design nor a style that finds its own language next to UPA's sensibility. It very much just follows the design that had been becoming popular in animation and illustration (in the sections of the teacher's lessons, for instance); its songs and music are not adjusted to the modern design but still are very prosaic and homely. Nevertheless, it did win the Academy Award for best animated short film in 1954. Another Disney short film at that time that followed UPA's aesthetic and artistic lead was Jack Kinney's *Pigs Is Pigs* from 1954. Kinney was one of Disney's most prolific directors of shorts and features but was also an animator. He directed, for example, the hilarious *Der Fuehrer's Face* with Donald Duck (1942), always counted amongst the best animated shorts.

The charming story of *Pigs Is Pigs* tells us about Flannery, a station master who receives a box of guinea pigs that is being picked up by customer McMorehouse. The pickle is that the charge for pigs is 48 cents but for pets only 44 cents. McMorehouse refuses to pay 48 cents, as he claims his guinea pigs are pets, not pigs. This disagreement between Flannery and McMorehouse has to be solved now by going through

the official route of the railway. This means that the guinea pigs stay at the station till the quarrel is solved. They start to multiply immediately and produce hundreds of thousands of offspring.

In the design of *Pigs Is Pigs*, Disney did an exceptional job in using the surface layer of a UPA approach, its design language, and applying it to its complex Disney look of beautifully crafted design. The backgrounds are very well executed, the characters unique and fit their personality, the color design is still mostly representational yet fits the stylization. Nevertheless, the entire design never goes as far as any of the UPA shorts but always stays in the very safe field, which is modern but does not push any boundaries other than the ones from Disney itself. It never does the next step of trying to visualize the content of the story: multiplication of guinea pigs, which is only shown literally, never intellectually. As beautiful and stunning as the design is, it lacks a deeper meaning, which, for example, UPA's *Fudget's Budget*, from the same year (1954), most definitely has, where every aspect of the design deals with the rather dry topic of calculation, which is visualized in the backgrounds, colors and characters. *Pigs Is Pigs* is therefore beautifully executed entertainment, nothing more and nothing less, but does not relate to the artistic meaning of its own visual abstraction.

## Possible design rules in *Pigs is Pigs*

In order to design an entire short film that looks congruent in all its elements, rules need to be applied to prevent the characters and backgrounds from deviating aesthetically from each other. The following points suggest compositional guidelines that are clearly visible in the short's images.

## Overall design

- Less organic in composition and shape language and more geometric.
- Suggested perspective, with skewed planes that avoid right angles. Foreground and background planes occasionally fight for dominance due to tangents. This flattens the space, which is of course the goal.
- Few lines in the architecture or in objects are parallel. Lines are mostly slightly off. However, in order to break perspective, lines can be parallel instead of tapering towards a vanishing point or flatten the entire space. The main goal goes towards flat space rather than full perspective.
- Architectural lines are not realistic and follow neither one-, two-, or three-point perspective but are a mix of the three.
- If perspective is used, then it is broken by allowing some lines to miss the vanishing point.
- Focus on horizontals and verticals in the composition.
- Use of only straight or curved lines without too much tension (symmetrical curves). S-curves are avoided but are used sparsely in details.

6  Abraham Adam, *When Magoo Flew, The Rise and Fall of Animation Studio UPA*, Wesleyan University Press, Middletown, CT, 2012. from Hee, interview by Gray, 13 and 20 April 1977.

- Objects and characters are only shown in three-quarter, side, or front view, which keeps the perspectives very limited (very much like in the architecture).
- Pattern or texture should keep the image flat, not create perspective (texture is mostly used in the main office's wallpaper and the ceiling of the station, then partly on the railway gravel).
- Colors are kept plain without much visible brush work; gradients are sparsely used.
- As much variation as possible: variation in composition, shapes, color, and movement within the restraints of the style.
- Shadows only if they are part of the design (timecode 00:05:00; there are no shadows for the characters). Shadows are not used to create perspective but to enhance the composition with its focal points.
- Shadows have a defined outline with a distinct geometric shape.
- Diagonals are few and if they are used their compositional strength is lessened again by horizontals.

## Composition

The composition succumbs to the main idea of modern animation design: the geometry in the visuals provides the image with balance in most frames. It follows a strict framework that most of the visual elements succumb to (see Figure 5.74). It is the division of the frame into four vertical zones (red and blue) and six horizontal zones and the middle of the frame (purple, yellow, and green). The composition can be based on a grid like that proposed, which the composition incorporates with positive and negative spaces or any elements that might fit a position within the grid. Not every background follows it in all parts, though. Some, for example, follow the horizontal yellow and green lines and the vertical blue lines but do not

follow the purple ones. This is only a suggested grid that I myself observed; others are of course possible! For the impact, the grid has on the composition, see Figures 5.75 through 5.80 with their accompanying explanations.

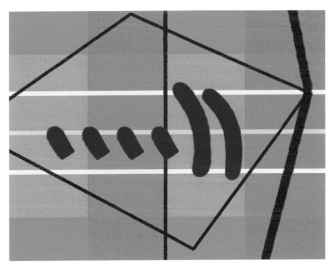

**Figure 5.75**

Composition at 00:04:24 (Figure 5.75): In some of the backgrounds, a tilted square is used to fill the frame in the middle (Compare shot composition of Figure 5.75 with shot 00:05:00, Figure 5.76). The character's diagonal tilt is in its movement strictly horizontal, going towards the left corner of the box. A nice weight distribution between right side of two big guinea-pigs and four small ones on the left in this composition.

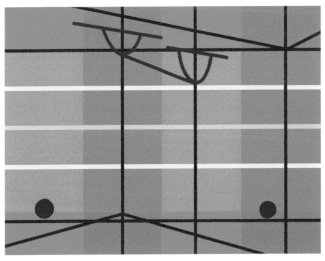

**Figure 5.76**

Background Composition at 00:05:00 (Figure 5.76): There is a good juxtaposition between empty space and busy space on the walldesign. The extreme size-difference between window and characters are what makes this background very unique. But it still follows the compositional framework and the mirroring shapes (character on the lower right and sign on the respective left).

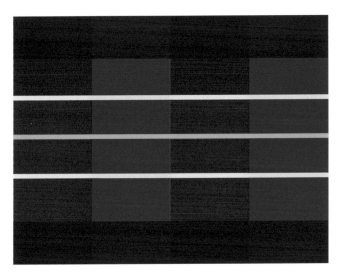

**Figure 5.74**

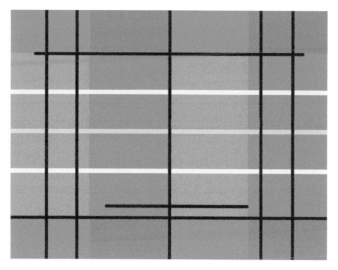

**Figure 5.77**

Composition at 00:05:39 (Figure 5.77): The characters balance each other out on the left and right. Two characters left with light clothing have as much compositional weight as the one character dressed in black on the left. The characters appear in the right and left section of the suggested grid.

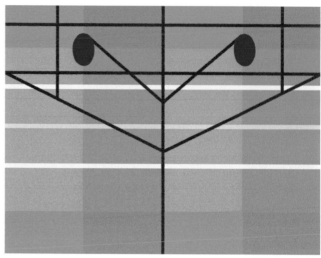

**Figure 5.78**

Composition at 00:06:47 (Figure 5.78): The pose of Flannery goes with the positioning and direction of the orange sign and the lamp behind him. The violin's direction flows into the orange sign on the back-wall and Flannery's geometric head and hat connect to the lamp on his left. The pile of guinea pigs has no color- only size perspective that keeps the image flat. The focus on the center of the frame is obvious and balanced out by negative and positive space on the back wall.

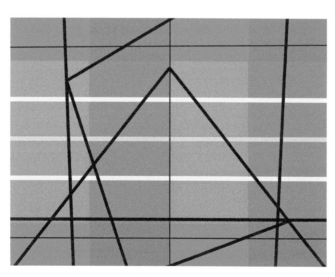

**Figure 5.79**

Background composition at 00:07:39 (Figure 5.79): In this fake one-point In this fake one-point perspective, the geometric floor-pattern and the lower part of the doors are tapering towards a vanishing point in the middle of the door. The upper part of the doors, however, create a strong horizontal that passes the vanishing point. The fake light & shadow that is suggested by the tilted square in the middle enhances the focal point, serves as a frame within a frame, but also helps to break the perspective of the hallway.

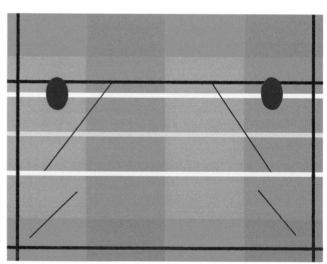

**Figure 5.80**

Composition at 00:07:50 (Figure 5.80): Despite this background being very busy with the "million-and-one" guinea pigs it has the same balance as all the other backgrounds, framed with tree and telephone pole and the two houses left and right. The color perspective is there but in a much-reduced contrast. The color in the foreground is slightly warmer than the warm grey in the background. Thus, depth is achieved by atmospheric perspective, but also at the same time reduced by the choice of colors which flatten the image and allow the guinea pigs to stand out.

The layout of the short was done by John Wilson, who had worked on some shorts at UPA (uncredited animator on *Gerald McBoing-Boing* and *Christopher Crumpet*; production design, uncredited, on *Rooty Toot Toot*), so he was probably familiar with the design procedures at UPA. Also, Eyvind Earle, who would later be credited as the "color stylist" of *Sleeping Beauty*, worked on *Pigs Is Pigs* as a background artist.

Overall, the backgrounds do vary slightly in their depiction of space but not enough to be distracting. They still seem to visualize the same reality. In most backgrounds, we can see a strong emphasis on balance. Special interest is given in the composition to the right and left sides of center and their corresponding partners, across or mirrored. But none of the backgrounds are completely balanced; they always have some parts that break the symmetry and keep the composition from being rigid. Overall *Pigs Is Pigs* is an excellent short film and its design is a true gem amongst Disney's shorts from the same time. What makes it so exceptional is its will for exploration; it pushes the artistic developments of UPA into the traditional work of the Disney Company and does an excellent job. *Pigs Is Pigs* was nominated for an Academy Award and its director Jack Kinney did actually work for UPA after his career at Disney, directing the rather "interesting" feature *1001 Arabian Nights* with Mister Magoo in 1959, at the same time Disney's *Sleeping Beauty* was released, one low and one high point of the rival companies.

## Arrange the characters in relationship to the story and each other

How the characters are positioned within the frame obviously has an impact on how the audience will read and understand the characters' status and their relationship to each other. What the character's relationship is, if a character is submissive or dominant, and if the characters communicate with each other or not, all can be expressed via composition and staging. The following explains, in a case study, how the four characters in Dreamwork's feature *Madagascar* (2005) not only have a strong compositional concept for the entire feature, but also express the various story moments and emotions of each character through their position within the frame.

## Case study: Geometric composition in DreamWorks' *Madagascar* (2005)

DreamWorks' feature film *Madagascar* is an excellent example of several elements of a feature film representing one conceptual idea and strictly following it in design, composition and layout, and animation. In *Madagascar*, it is *geometry* that is the key conceptual word that finds its way into the visuals. The story is of four animals who live in the New York Zoo and one day follow zebra Marty, who is sick of being trapped in a pen, to Africa. He wants to go back to his roots and experience "the wild." After an uneventful yet cramped journey on a container ship, the four are washed up on the shore of Madagascar, where they learn how to survive in the wild and redefine their friendship. The characters loosely follow the group relationship and dynamic of the four main characters in the sitcom *Seinfeld*, or as Michael Barrier puts it:

> The four leads inevitably call to mind the four leads in Seinfeld, but they're not analogues for Jerry and Elaine and the others; their oddities simply fit together in a similar way. These are characters who, like the Seinfeld gang, do not compensate for one another's weaknesses but simply prop one another up.[7]

Each of the characters is assigned a unique shape that is unmistakable. Production designer Kendal Cronkheit about the four characters:

> They work almost like puzzle pieces that can link together. Alex is an inverted triangle; Gloria is a circle; Melman is a tall, skinny stick; and Marty is a cylinder. They are different from one another in silhouette, but are based on the same design [aesthetic], which was exaggerated proportions with sharp graphic shapes and details.[8]

The four are quadrupeds, yet Alex the lion and Gloria the hippopotamus are bipeds throughout the film, which allows them more humanlike poses and actions (though Alex turns into a quadruped once he "goes wild"). The choice for the design, to go back to the cartoons of the golden age of American animation and use a stylized design instead of the, at the time, more common design in computer animation, is explained by Cronkheit: "We had done the *Shrek* movies hyper-realistic but the treatment here suited the idea of doing something different, where we could also stretch as artists."[9] The strong emphasis on horizontal, vertical, and geometric shapes/forms was influenced by Warner Brothers cartoons from the 1940s and 1950s and also by illustration from the same era. The style and character design by Craig Kellman is very much influenced by this style, and he stylistically repeats it in many ways. His work is close to the illustrators he works off of, like Ed Benedict, J.P. Miller, and Martin Provenson, who in the 1950s refined a very common, worldwide illustration style. Ed Benedict was character designer for Hanna-Barbera studios and designed characters for TV shows like *The Flintstones* and *The Ruff and Reddy Show*. His character designs are what Amid Amidi called "highly sophisticated, containing that indefinable drawing quality that gives a drawing charm and personality."[10] Illustration and animation design from the 1950s is highly shape based and reduces characters to their basic geometric components, which contain the essence of that specific animal's or human's form and personality. The shapes are occasionally pushed to the extreme, not even resembling in the least the actual animal's shape, but strangely enough still read very well. Kellman uses the styles of the mentioned illustrators and animation designers and replicates it, creating undoubtedly charming characters that push the animation design of the 1950s into contemporary computer graphics (CG) three-dimensionality. One of the main rules in 1950s design that he frequently applies, next to strong simplified shapes, is the straight-versus-curved rule, where a curved line is juxtaposed by a straight line in order to provide variation in the line work and shapes of the character. That can create pleasing, stylized results, where the line itself has solidity in the straight line but also an organic flow in the curved line. This prevents the lines and shapes from being too even and therefore plain. Kellman's design follows strictly fixed rules that result in a 1950s aesthetic that is very pleasant to look at and beautifully designed, though it does not explore a new and personal direction. He does not use the style of the 1950s as inspiration but repeats it and then translates the characters into a three-dimensional form with a sophisticated look. Nevertheless, the animal characters in *Madagascar* are beautifully interpreted and every part of their bodies has an edgy and geometric form language, which is never rigid but always alive through dynamic poses and very fluent lines of action. Their personalities work perfectly against each other and create a lively dynamic. This cannot be said about the human characters, who do not fully follow the same rules in their design.

[7] Michael Barrier, *Bright Little Island*, 2005. http://www.michaelbarrier.com/Commentary/Madagascar/Madagascar.htm (accessed April 13, 2015).

[8] http://www.emol.org/film/archives/madagascar/production1.html (accessed August 26, 2017).

[9] Jerry Beck, *The Art of Madagascar Escape 2 Africa*, Insight Editions, San Raffael, CA, 2008, p. 16.

[10] Amid Amidi, *Cartoon Modern, Style and Design in Fifties Animation*, Chronicle Books, San Francisco, CA, 2006, p. 40.

More realistic in comparison to the animals, they seem to come from a slightly different movie.

This pushing of the design in a 1950s direction is not only applied to the actual look of the film but also in the character animation that pursues the extreme squash and stretch of a Warner Brothers cartoon or a Tex Avery character, where the rules of nature are pushed to their limits. For computer animation this was not a new direction, as squash and stretch had already been explored in Pixar's *The Incredibles* (2004), which had flowing and very convincing cartoony character animation. However, *The Incredibles* did not yet go to extremes in its animation style, as that would have not fit its design direction. *Madagascar* pushed its design, as mentioned above, towards the geometric and found a character animation style worth exploring despite its technical complexities. Director Eric Darnell:

> The principles of squash and stretch, and taking animation to an extreme, have been around for decades. And with the computer, sometimes doing the kind of things that are so simple when you draw—like taking a character's head and just stretching it out this way or that way—can actually be a complicated technical procedure.[11]

The character animation uses poses that are also geometric in their core elements. Even Alex's, Melman's, and Marty's tails are often shaped as meanders instead of curls to underline the theme "geometry." The poses themselves follow 1950s style in playing with straights and curves. The character animation is snappy, in line with the animation style of Warner Brothers and Tex Avery, with its quick movements alternating with holds, putting emphasis on the juxtaposition of fast versus slow. The quick timing in the character animation fits the design; they both visualize the idea of an edge. Michael Barrier on the character animation style: "… what used to be called shooting from pose to pose—that is, a character moves from one pose to another with only a few frames in between."[12]

In the layout the composition very strictly follows circles, horizontals, and verticals. The famous shot of the group huddled together on the beach of the island (Figure 5.83) is a good representation of the entire geometric layout.

[11] Jerry Beck, *The Art of Madagascar Escape 2 Africa*, Insight Editions, San Raffael, CA, 2008, p. 18.
[12] Michael Barrier, Bright Little Island, 2005. http://www.michaelbarrier.com/Commentary/Madagascar/Madagascar.htm (accessed April 13, 2015).

The importance of vertical and horizontal, of the center and also the strong balance in the frame is what drives the layout. What is striking in the sequence of the four arriving on the shore of Madagascar is the simplicity of the composition. In every shot it is reduced to its basics; there is nothing that complicates or disturbs it. Clarity is what drives geometry.

In the following, I'll discuss the geometric shot compositions of the beginning of the scene when the group arrives at the beach on Madagascar.

**Figures 5.81 and 5.82:** This is the iconographic image of the characters' heads huddled together in a trapezoid arrangement. The idea is very effective in its simplicity and the characters' eyelines are all on the same curve, producing geometrical order.

**Figures 5.83 and 5.84:** The trapezoid shape in Figure 5.81 is translated into the same trapezoid shape of the group being inscribed in Figure 5.83. The characters appear in the same position as before. Pushing the characters together makes it more obvious that they are a group in a hostile environment. One entity against nature! The beach strictly follows the horizontal.

**Figures 5.85 and 5.86:** The tree line has a slight tilt from each side towards the center (similar to the trapezoid

Figure 5.81

Figure 5.82

Figure 5.83

Figure 5.84

Figure 5.85

Figure 5.86

**Figure 5.87**

**Figure 5.88**

**Figure 5.89**

**Figure 5.90**

**Figure 5.91**

**Figure 5.92**

**Figure 5.93**

**Figure 5.94**

**Figure 5.95**

**Figure 5.96**

shape in the previous figures), which forces the eye into the middle towards the characters' position. A subtle arrangement of trees surrounds the travelers and creates an entrance into the forest that is framed by two tall palm trees. Camera angle and horizon are both low to increase the size and height of the majestic Madagascar jungle. The big baobab tree slightly off-center accentuates the middle but gives tension to the composition.

**Figures 5.87 and 5.88:** The group is still one big shape, though Melman's body and head balance the right half of the frame. The visual weight of the characters on the left are the same as Melman's visual weight on the right.

**Figures 5.89 and 5.90:** This composition already anticipates the composition of the next shot but also refers to the trapezoid shape of the group in the beginning of the scene. The tilt of the character's eyes towards the upper left is the same as the tilt in the tree line in Figure 5.91. The character's height in Figure 5.89 appears in three tree crowns in Figure 5.91 in the same position, transporting this composition into the next shot.

**Figures 5.91 and 5.92:** The upwards drift of the characters is parallel to the tilt of the trees.

**Figures 5.93 and 5.94:** The trees are vignetting the characters, placing them into the same position as in the previous shot. This can only be achieved if the characters are positioned very carefully for them to appear in the very same constellation but shot with the camera turned ~180°. Usually, the characters would be mirrored if shot from the opposing side, which means Melman would be on the left instead of the right. Careful placement and correct camera positioning, though, can create an arrangement that repeats the position of the characters in the two shots. The camera angle is high: the characters feel miniscule and trapped in nature. The group of Gloria, Alex, and Marty has the same distance from the frame as Melman. The log on the beach prevents the characters from easily going into the jungle. However, the leaves that are close to the camera serve as vectors leading into the jungle.

**Figures 5.95 and 5.96:** Melman's head is still in the same position as in the previous shot. His eyes in particular are at the same height and position in the frame.

**Figures 5.97 and 5.98:** The exact positioning and size of the objects and distances in the shot make this shot very geometric. Melman's leg is as far away from the middle as the stone's edges on the right and his hoof is on the same tilted line as the bottom of the stone. The slight tilt in the sand pushes the eye upwards, towards the forest, which is again repeated in Melman's slight head tilt in the next shot.

**Figures 5.99 and 5.100:** Melman's head is inscribed into the frame; his ears are parallel to the verticals of the frame. The slight tilt of his head correlates with the tilt of the beach.

**Figures 5.101 and 5.102:** The characters still take part in the strong trapezoid shape from earlier shots. The camera angle and horizon are low. The characters are slightly off-center left, compared to Melman's eyes in the previous shot, which are off-center right.

**Figures 5.103 and 5.104:** The characters are starting to break up as a group. Alex is getting worried about ending up in a jungle, or even worse: San Diego! Marty's and Gloria's body poses and lines of action are slightly bending away from Alex, allowing him to be the center. The height of sand and water are equal.

**Figures 5.105 and 5.106:** There is a balance between the position of Marty's body and neck and the position of the tree trunk, which both have the same length and distance from the frame. The jungle

Figure 5.97

Figure 5.98

Figure 5.99

Figure 5.100

Figure 5.101

Figure 5.102

Figure 5.103

Figure 5.104

Figure 5.105

Figure 5.106

**Figure 5.107**                    **Figure 5.108**

background is darker and greener in front of Marty's head, which allows the face to read better and drags the eye into the jungle. Behind Marty's mane, the jungle is busier in color and shapes. The background is cut into three vertical elements: behind Marty's head it is busy and colorful; in front of Marty's head the jungle is darker and drags the eye in; the right third is as long as the tree trunk in the sand and has two trees that define its square shape. This right third repeats the left third with Marty's curved mane.

**Figures 5.107 and 5.108:** Melman marks with his body the center of the frame and is also the center of Alex chasing Marty. Alex's line of action of is in unison with Marty's line of action. Because of the strong squash and stretch, Alex's body shape is pointing towards Marty like an arrow. The background's horizontal is right in the middle of the frame.

Certain compositional rules are becoming obvious in this short dissection of the different shots in *Madagascar*.

- Geometry is the key to every shot, focusing on strong horizontals, verticals, and the middle of the frame.
- Simplicity is important for every shot. Characters, objects, and nature are to be reduced to simple shapes and blocks, not dragging too much attention to themselves but always serving the composition.
- Diagonals are only used if they connect the characters.
- Melman's long neck should always be used as a connecting agent for the group and not just be there without purpose.
- The line of action of the characters should either work with each other or against each other, according to their emotional relationship at that moment of the story.
- Whenever possible, use the characters as one entity, not as single characters.

# CHAPTER 6

# Character Staging and Film Language

In the previous chapter, we saw how characters and objects in the composition can be reduced to geometric blocks that refer to each other. The characters in *Madagascar* not only relate within the shots but spread across multiple shots through their assigned positions or movement. The characters do not need to show up in an assigned position to have an impact on the story of a shot; as long as it has been made clear in previous shots that a position belongs to one character, his or her position can transcend throughout the scene. This is more of a subtext than a clear storytelling device but is nevertheless very effective. The result is a fluctuating composition where not only the characters themselves affect the story but also their assigned positions. This chapter will explore why characters can be placed in a particular position and what the meaning or interpretation of that position is or can be.

The frame can be seen as a box in which objects and characters move around and connect like people and/or furniture in a room. Which position would you take if you were stepping into a room that you did not know? The center position or the corner? This obviously depends on one's confidence and the overall situation, but usually people would wait standing close to a wall, as it is a safer position compared to waiting right in the middle of the room. With our backs to the wall we can see what is in front of us, but we do not need to care about what is behind us, as the wall protects our backs: simple survival instinct! Seeing the frame as a room is practical in approaching "staging" from an abstract and emotional perspective rather than positioning the characters randomly. It gives possible meaning to the positions.

In the following, I want to discuss the various possibilities of how to frame characters and what message we get through their position in the frame. For reasons of simplicity, I use the top view of a room and leave out perspective, as this adds another level of complexity to staging that will be dealt with later on.

In Figure 6.1, the dot is in the center of the stage. It is exactly in the middle, which means that the distance to each side of the frame is the same. The position is balanced and no side of the frame has more attraction. The position in the middle accentuates the diagonals as the dot connects with each corner of the frame (Figure 6.2). This connection of the various elements within the frame leads us to what is called *psychological closure*, where points within the frame connect and create a shape or form. A single point in space has nothing to relate to other than the corners of the frame. There is otherwise no connection, no direction, and no movement as the point is just resting in itself. Two points start a relationship and thus create an invisible line between each other. The eye connects the two points and fills in the gap, which is the line. Three dots create a triangle (Figure 6.3), four would create a square, and so on. We call this completion of a shape's or form's minimal information by the eye *psychological closure*, which is based on the Gestalt theory, where the whole is bigger than its details. The shape/form created is also called "Gestalt" (Figures 6.3 through 6.5). This phenomenon is important for the following explanations and will appear again here and there.

We always interpret the position within the frame and give it a meaning. If one would describe the emotion of the dot in the middle, it could be either *confident* or *scared*, depending on the story that we want to associate with it. Those two emotions obviously contradict each other, so the spot itself in the middle doesn't exactly pinpoint a specific emotion but leads to a story, and with the story comes the emotion attached. If the position in the center is analyzed, the distance of the dot to the frame is the same in each direction. The questions we have to ask first in this example are, what does the frame stand for? Is the frame only a limitation of our view without any physical substance, enclosing the dot emotionally or intellectually but not revealing the entire space of what is outside the frame? Or is it an actual wall-like structure that encloses the dot physically? Both are significantly different concepts that change and shape the interpretation of the dot's emotional state. Additionally, it is important to consider what is actually inside the frame and what is happening outside of it that might affect the

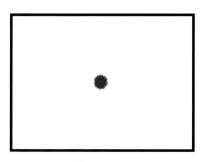

**Figure 6.1**

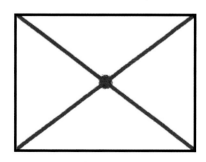

**Figure 6.2**

DOI: 10.1201/b22148-6

Psychological closure

**Figure 6.3**

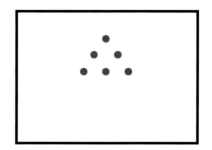

**Figure 6.4**

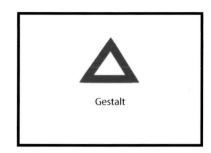

Gestalt

**Figure 6.5**

inside. The space around the dot in Figure 6.1 is massive, making the dot feel either self-dependent and confident by standing strong in the center or it could also be interpreted as alone and maybe even scared, as it is exposed in the middle of the stage like an actor with stage fright, with the audience being offscreen. Thus a frame reveals not only the character but also the space around the character, and both interact with each other. In this first example, the space being overwhelming and the character very small, the negative space dominates the frame and becomes significant, either decreasing the importance of the character or pointing out his or her insignificance. There is never just one explanation or interpretation! A new story can overwrite the initial interpretation and prove the opposite to also be true. However, it is the search for an interpretation that helps to determine a good position for the character that is based on logic and reason. That the opposite can most often also be true only makes the search more exciting. A discussion starts and one has to evaluate the pros and cons of the current staging.

In Stanley Kubrick's *2001: A Space Odyssey* (1968), dead center is the perfect place for the onboard computer HAL 9000 to appear (Figure 6.6). The scene is about the conversation between David and Frank, the two astronauts, talking about HAL's recent mistakes and the need to shut him down to secure their lives and the mission. HAL, being in the center of the frame, only seen as a tiny red eye, is still the center of attention, although we are listening to the conversation of David and Frank. The composition lets the two astronauts talk to each other, though their heads are slightly tilted, so they have to look up to see each other. Their tilt, however, points towards HAL, who is literally the center of the conversation and the center of the image.

**Figure 6.6**

Stanley Kubrick, *2001 A Space Odyssey* (1968).

Putting him in the most neutral position in the frame also makes him the strongest character in the shot and the most dangerous, when we consider the conversation between David and Frank and its result. More examples of how the center of the frame can be practically used in storytelling can be seen in examples Figures 6.7 and 6.8, from David Lean's *Lawrence of Arabia* (1962).

## Central arrangement

The center of the frame expresses two very different emotions in the two shots in Figures 6.7 and 6.8: the humbling scope of the desert, where man is insignificant, and in the second shot the strength of man to survive in the desert. The position itself does not give a clear emotion; only in relationship with all the elements of composition and the story information will it affect and visualize the required mood and story.

The second position (Figure 6.9) shows the dot being placed in the upper left corner. This position makes the dot feel somehow more timid and less confident. The corner position allows the character the widest overview over the room if the frame represents the wall. On the other hand, if the frame defines an on-screen space without boundaries towards the offscreen space, meaning there is no wall, then this position would be a very dangerous one, as the threat to the character could be just outside the frame, hidden from the viewer and also hidden from the character, leaving him exposed to whatever might hide offscreen. The movie *Alien* (1979) plays with the idea of a threat from the offscreen space. We know there is a threat somewhere outside of the confined space on-screen, but we cannot see it. The position in Figure 6.9 could also be interpreted as giving the character curiosity if he wants to know what is outside of the border of the frame. Additionally this very high position within the frame is also one of strength and superiority, if the character is "on top of things." This can be seen more clearly with other characters in a group, which we will address in a moment.

Figure 6.10 shows two dots across from each other, both at the same distance from the frame. They are the same size and shape; neither seems more important. They obviously relate to each other. Our eye connects the two dots and adds an invisible bridge between them (Figure 6.11): psychological closure! In the shot of Murnau's masterful

**Figure 6.7**

David Lean's *Lawrence of Arabia* (1962). In Lean's film, the desert itself is a character; it overwhelms with its sheer scale and size; its humbling power and life-threatening force constantly play their part in the story. The image shows Lawrence and his Bedouin guide Tafas riding through the desert. The emotional impact is a humbling one. We are stunned by the size of the mountains and the scale of the desert, which spreads before us with its impressive natural force. The image is uplifting with an accompanying bombastic musical score.

**Figure 6.8**

David Lean's *Lawrence of Arabia* (1962). In this figure, the approaching character's intent is not revealed yet; we don't know if the character of Sherif Ali is good or bad or will have any significance to the story at all. The character's continuous approach describes him as strong and imposing, because he triumphs over the relentless and sizzling heat of the desert. He is a survivor in this barren land. This image feels more dangerous, despite the small size of the character.

**Figure 6.9**  **Figure 6.10**

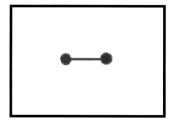

**Figure 6.11**  **Figure 6.12**

**Figure 6.13**

F.W. Murnau: *Sunrise: A Song of Two Humans*, 1927.

feature film *Sunrise: A Song of Two Humans* (1927), we see the protagonist of the story at night contemplating in front of the full moon, waiting for his lover, a visiting "femme fatale" from the city he is having an affair with (Figure 6.13). The two are planning to get rid of his wife by drowning her in the lake. In this foreboding shot, the man is waiting in the reeds for the woman to arrive. The juxtaposing shapes of his head and the moon, the bright, coldly glowing disc in its clean shape compared to his black silhouette and rough outline allow many interpretations of what is about to happen and what both could represent. The simplicity in this shot, and the sole focus on moon and head, makes these two relating shapes read all the stronger.

Figure 6.12 has three dots aligned in one line horizontally. They are at exactly the same distance from each other; however, the ones on the outside have problems communicating, as there is the middle character in between. If the three dots are arranged differently and placed in the shape of a triangle (Figure 6.14), the group structure is stronger than it was before; now all three members can equally "talk" to each other (Figure 6.15). In the triangular arrangement, the relationship between all three seems equal, as the distances are very similar (Figure 6.16); nonetheless, the one on top could be singled out because it is placed above the other two, making its position more dominant, whereas the ones underneath do feel more submissive. If we want two of the three dots to be grouped into one unit, we have to bring them closer to each other, in order to strengthen their connection. The closer the characters are to each other, the stronger their connection is; the further they are apart, the weaker the connection. In Figure 6.17, it is very clear which pair is connected

**107**

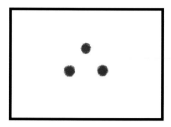

**Figure 6.14**

**Figure 6.15**

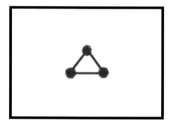

**Figure 6.16**

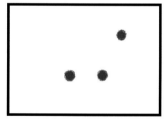

**Figure 6.17**

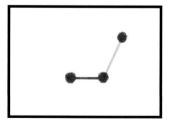

**Figure 6.18**

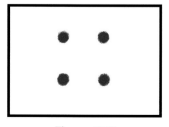

**Figure 6.19**

and which dot is the odd one out. The single dot relates slightly to the pair, but in a much weaker connection compared to the one of the group (Figure 6.18).

Figure 6.19 has four dots in a square arrangement; there are six possibilities for communication, because they don't just communicate on the outline of the square but also across each other (Figure 6.20).

Another possible arrangement of four is shown in Figure 6.21. It depends in this arrangement on how the four dots are grouped. Figures 6.22 through 6.24 suggest three different ways of having a group of three and one character being not part of the group (other than that, it would just be Figure 6.20 with a different arrangement).

In Figure 6.22, the character on top seems to be the dominant one. It has the strength in the composition and dominates the other three. If the singled-out character should be the weak one, the position underneath the row of three would put it into the submissive position. The next example, Figure 6.23, suggests a similar arrangement: The single character is now in the weak position, as it is nearly surrounded by the three. This makes the group of three appear more threatening (or protective, if that is the storyline).

The grouping in Figure 6.24 makes the singled-out character on the left have seemingly no connection to the group of three, as they seem to face the other way. Their arrangement opens up towards the right, so their backs could be turned to the single character. Through the rules of the Gestalt Theory, Chapter 5, "Composition," we know that we can group characters via size, color, shape, textures, movement, and past experience. For examples, on the arrangement of three and four characters in relationship with storytelling, see again example Figures 6.26 and 6.27 from David Lean's *Lawrence of Arabia* (1962).

The more characters we add, the more interactions are possible, which can make it difficult for the story to be easily understood. Who is in charge, which character is the one that the story is following, and how can the arrangement of the characters support the composition? If we want to emphasize the middle dot being the dominant one, the character can be enhanced via the aforementioned aspects of color, size, shape, etc. This will surely point him out as the focal point. Every different arrangement or change in the dot's design aspects that visually separates him from the others allows a new interpretation of the relationship the dots have towards each other and therefore the story that is being told. In Figure 6.25, size obviously makes the middle dot stronger and more dominant. What was the case in Figure 6.23, that the dot in the same position was the weaker one, in Figure 6.25 changes and the bigger dot seems to be the stronger one (obviously again the story could overwrite that!). Any change will affect the story being told!

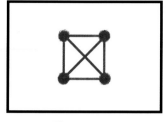

**Figure 6.20**

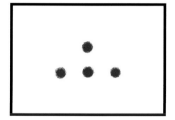

**Figure 6.21**

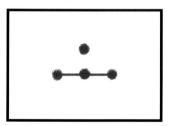

**Figure 6.22**

**Figure 6.23**

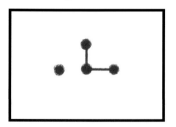

**Figure 6.24**

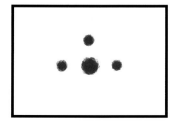

**Figure 6.25**

**Figure 6.26**

Three character arrangement in David Lean's *Lawrence of Arabia* (1962). Lawrence and his guide Tafas are left and right of a well and waiting for the arrival of Sherif Ali, in the distance between them. The similar size of Lawrence and Tafas groups them together, though Sherif Ali is the center of attention, despite his miniscule scale. The closeness of the two outer characters to the frame opens up the negative space between them and focuses our attention towards Sherif Ali, who is at the same level as Lawrence's and Tafas' heads. Adding the well into the shot makes the position of Tafas much more dominant than the position of Lawrence on the left but also connects the well with the arriving Sherif Ali. (Tafas is going to be shot by Sherif Ali because he took the water out of the well; Lawrence is still an outsider.) And this is what this scene is about: the fight for water in the desert, symbolized by the well in the middle.

The change of distance between the dots, as mentioned before, changes their bond. The closer the characters are to each other, the stronger their connection. The previous arrangement allowed some interpretation, because the distance between the dots was exactly the same. In Figure 6.28, there is obviously a grouping of three characters, and one is singled out. The various possibilities of the grouping shown in Figures 6.22 through 6.24 don't work as easily anymore, as the three dots on top have a much stronger bond.

Breaking up the arrangement and creating a more loose positioning of the dots still relates them to each other, and it is still apparent which dots group into units (Figure 6.29), though in this arrangement there is the issue of the three right dots having the same distance to each other. But because of the two upper dots being very close, creating one group, the two right lower dots instinctively also group together. To clarify this, the units can be separated slightly, as shown in Figure 6.30.

Characters not only relate to each other through their distance but also their orientation, which is one of the most dominant

**Figure 6.27**

Four-character arrangement in David Lean's *Lawrence of Arabia* (1962). In this shot, we can clearly see the grouping of the four characters. Lawrence and his guide create one group and the two camels the second. However, in this shot the distance of the guide to the camel and Lawrence are very similar. Observe how the height of Lawrence's head and the head of the camel are the same, being both on the horizon line. What makes the people and the camels group is (aside from them being obviously humans and camels) their color. The humans are beige, the camels darker.

ways of leading the audience's attention towards something or someone on- or offscreen. In the examples in Figures 6.31 and 6.33, the characters either relate to each other within the group and the single character being the outsider (Figures 6.31 and 6.32) or as a group facing the one singled out (Figures 6.33 and 6.34). The communication between the characters in the two examples is very different. Where in Figure 6.31 the emphasis lies in the communication within the group, in Figure 6.33 the communication is between the group and the single character. The forces between the two possibilities are very different, which also dramatically shifts the focal point from lower left off center in Figure 6.31 to the upper right off center in Figure 6.33.

In an even bigger group, the main character has to be pointed out in order to be seen as the important player in the story. This can be achieved through either singling out the character and putting a distance between him and the group or by changing his attributes to indicate him as the focus. In Figure 6.35, the main character is obviously the one in the middle surrounded by the group. It is difficult to see any other character from the group as the focus of the image. Nevertheless, by just changing the color and contrast of the group, as in Figure 6.36, it completely shifts the importance: now the focus is on the character on

More on arranging characters in the frame:

Katz Steven, *Film Directing Shot by Shot: Visualizing from Concept to Screen*, Michael Wiese Productions, Studio City, CA, 1991, pp. 121–275.

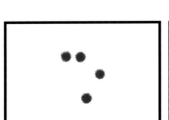

**Figure 6.28**          **Figure 6.29**          **Figure 6.30**

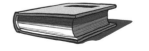

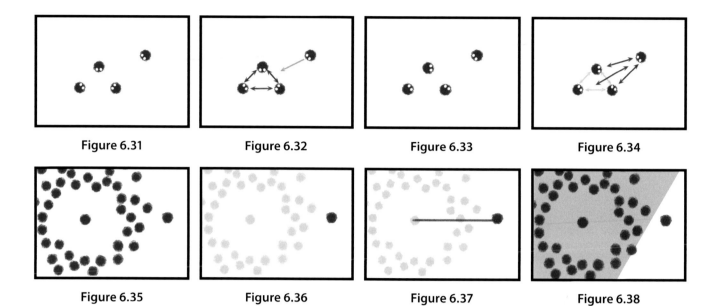

| Figure 6.31 | Figure 6.32 | Figure 6.33 | Figure 6.34 |

| Figure 6.35 | Figure 6.36 | Figure 6.37 | Figure 6.38 |

the right. Our eye immediately goes towards the dot on the right instead of the character in the middle of the group. But both the dark blue dot and the dot in the middle are on one horizontal line (Figure 6.37), which makes them relate to each other and create a connection, which is the beginning of a story between the two.

How can the focus of the middle character be shifted towards the character on the right without changing the contrast of the group? Let a shadow fall over the group and the sunlight strikes the character on the right (Figure 6.38). This would lead the eye from the left to the right. Light and shadow is always a helpful tool to enhance a position or bring a character forward (and again, with the other aspects of design this can be broken once more).

Rembrandt van Rijn (1606–1669) used this spotlight idea quite often in his paintings to single out certain characters and render them more important through light. In his painting *The Night Watch* (1642) (Figure 6.39), he gives us a rather complex composition of characters who are all active, yet the focus is obviously on the two characters in the front, Captain Frans Banning Cocq and Lieutenant Willem van Ruytenburgh, surrounded by 14 of their men, the militia group Kloveniers, a group of able-bodied men who could defend the city or assist in case of riots. The color scheme of the two leaders in the front separates them effectively from the background, one being dressed in black velvet, the other one in a yellowish-white silk outfit that is much brighter than most of the other characters. The only other two characters that really stand out are the little girl or angel peeking from behind of one of the soldiers and the man dressed in red in front of the girl, who symbolizes the Kloveniers. The light brightens the girl up to such an extent that she is not only immediately visible but also balances out the white outfit of Willem van Ruytenburgh. Putting both of the men into the front and center of the painting makes them

perspective-wise the tallest characters and puts them in the most dominant position. Additionally, the light hits both of them and brightens them more than any other character in the background, aside from the angel on the left. They are painted with much more detail and attention to texture. In particular, the fine lace and stitching on Cocq's and Ruytenburgh's clothing is so delicately painted that it immediately catches the eye. Comparing the main characters with the ones surrounding them, there is much less detail, less focus, less light and contrast in most of the characters. There is the juxtaposition of two men on the left and right side of the frame, who are also lit up and accentuated by light, color, and contrast. The composition of the various objects in the image, the guns, spears, arms, bodies, etc., are meticulously planned out to let the captain and the lieutenant be the center and focus of the painting. Rembrandt balances all the design elements exceptionally well and creates an experience full of life that seems to move. There is so much complexity in the composition that one can actually study it for hours and constantly find new interesting relationships between the depicted elements and characters.

Another example of an interesting arrangement of characters is Auguste Rodin's *The Burghers of Calais* from 1889 (Figure 6.40), which he sculpted for the city of Calais to commemorate six burghers who sacrificed themselves for the welfare of the city in the year 1347. The six men are standing on ground level with the viewer, only slightly elevated on a plinth. They are showing signs of emotional distress of sacrificing themselves by going towards a possible execution, not knowing yet that their lives will be saved. As Rodin wants the audience to be able to observe the six men on ground level, be "amongst" them, he created a movement that goes clockwise around the plinth they are standing on. The arrangement is compiled of six "sculptures in the round," which means that they are not meant to be observed from only one angle but seen from every position. The orientation of the men

**Figure 6.39**

Rembrandt van Rijn, *The Night Watch* (1642).

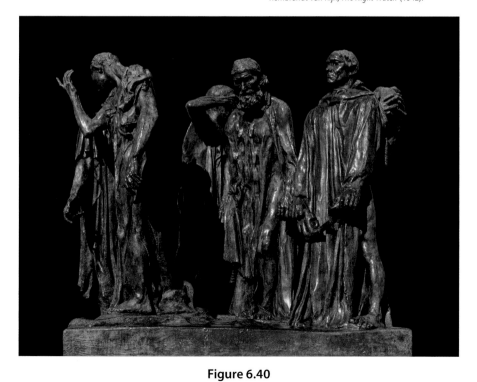

**Figure 6.40**

Auguste Rodin: *The Burghers of Calais* (1884–89).

**Figure 6.41**

creates a circular movement of the whole group (Figure 6.41, which shows the group from a top view), and each character that is on the outside of the plinth pushes the viewer further to the next statue and so on; there is a clear and continuous motion with most of the men going forward. There is only one more character in the middle of the group, who fills the inside of the arrangement, giving it the density it needs. This middle character is also turning with the clockwise movement of the group and his front is open towards the gap between the two outer characters left and right of him. A viewer walking around the sculpture will be able to look straight into the face of the man in the middle when he reaches the opening. Each figure is a piece on its own, yet they still work as a group, because they constantly refer to each other's movement and create a motion and direction that the viewer instinctively follows.

## Relationship with each other and the audience

Another aspect in staging is the relationship of the character on-screen with the audience and their emotional connection. The character on-screen is seldom encouraged to break the "fourth wall,"[1] which means to cross the boundary between the "reality" on screen and the reality in the auditorium. As soon as the character starts to be aware of the other world outside of the screen and reacts to it, the audience is personally integrated into the story. Breaking the wall for no purpose, for example, one of the actors looking into the camera by mistake, acknowledging, by looking into the lens, the camera as physically being there, is thus proof that the film is fake, not its own reality. However, this can also be used as an artistic device as in Chuck Jones' *Duck Amuck* (1953), when Daffy Duck starts to address the audience: they start to believe in the character on-screen being alive in his animated reality. Daffy Duck behaves like he is a regular actor who has a contractual agreement to fulfill. This makes him believable as not just an animated character but as an animated character who lives within the animated reality by the very nature of its artificial technique. Animation is always an obvious fictitious product, where the audience at any stage knows that the happenings on-screen are fake. But by letting animated

Figure 6.42

Figure 6.43

Figure 6.44

Figure 6.45

---

[1] **Fourth Wall**
The fourth wall is an imaginary wall between stage or cinema screen and audience. The characters on stage or on screen do not interact verbally or via eye contact with the members of the audience or acknowledge them in any way; their action happens in a surrounding that is removed from our reality. "Breaking the fourth wall" refers to the practice of letting the characters on stage or screen react to the audience and involve them either in a conversation or make comments about the story. Woody Allen's *Purple Rose of Cairo* (1985) uses this idea for the entirety of its story. The female character in the film watches a film herself and one character of the story on-screen steps out into the auditorium and runs away with her. The breaking of the fourth wall can be a very strong artistic device to integrate the audience actively into the story and also make the characters on-screen be aware of themselves being characters on a screen, like Daffy Duck in Chuck Jones' famous short *Duck Amuck* (1953).

characters talk to the audience members and address them personally, allowing them to have a consciousness of themselves actually being animated characters, gives them, precisely because they are breaking the fourth wall, believability as living and breathing characters.

Figure 6.46

Figure 6.47

Figure 6.48

Figure 6.49

The following examples show how one character can either have a visual connection with the audience or not. With two characters we have the same possibilities, only that the two can relate to each other *and* the audience, which makes it more complex.

## One character

Figures 6.42 through 6.45 show a character turning, and each position has another story imbedded. The connection to the audience is reduced the further the character turns, till in Figure 6.45 there is no connection at all. It feels like the character is looking into the future or past and we are partaking in this reflection.

Example: At the very beginning of Woody Allen's *Interiors* (1978), we have a husband reflect on his relationship with his wife, the mother of his three daughters. We only see the man from the back, looking down from a skyscraper into Manhattan. We are strangely involved in the man's personal accounts of his wife's behavior and their life together, yet also emotionally removed from him as we can only see his back.

## Two characters

Two characters facing the audience (Figure 6.46) puts them in the most exposed arrangement. It feels like they are being "presented" to us, ready to be judged. Of course, this can be a weak or a strong position depending on the storyline. It also suggests that they are indifferent to each other (in this case because they are rather far apart). The more the right character turns towards the left in Figure 6.47, the more intense the relationship becomes. The right one is nevertheless the active one in this communication between the two, whereas the left one is passive, because he isn't paying attention to his counterpart. This is obviously very important for storytelling in terms of how the two characters interact with each other, who is the active and who the passive player, who the dominant and who the submissive. With little changes in the arrangement, the relationship can shift completely (Figure 6.48 and onwards). Once the left character turns towards the right one, the connection between audience and character is broken and the bond between the two starts getting stronger. The moment they are facing each other, the attention and communication on both sides is equal (Figure 6.50). The audience is now not part of the communication anymore but a watching bystander. A very dismissive arrangement is seen in Figure 6.51, where the left character has his back towards

Figure 6.50

Figure 6.51

Figure 6.52

Figure 6.53

**Figure 6.54**

**Figure 6.55**

the audience and ignores the character on the right. He actively turns away from the audience *and* the character on the right.

Once the characters turn their backs to the audience (Figure 6.52), they lose their visual connection with each other and also lose the connection with the audience, which is the most neutral position in terms of emotions. The audience cannot see the facial expressions of the characters and neither can they see each other's. There is no emotional bond whatsoever. However, what this arrangement gains is that the two characters now seem to look forward or backwards in time, look into the future or past, seem to experience a moment together, reflect and contemplate. The last possibility is that one faces the back of the other (Figure 6.53). This position shows either indifference from both or intense interest from one but total disinterest from the other (and of course one more option, that both of them are just waiting in line and have no relationship whatsoever). With light and shadow, color, and all the other aspects of design the two characters can now be either made the focal point or step back in importance in addition to their positioning to each other (Figure 6.54 or 6.55) and the various camera angles. The possibilities of staging the characters are literally infinite!

# Staging of characters in the cinematic frame

In storyboarding and film, composition works slightly differently than in illustration or fine art, as we have already seen in the

previous chapters. It is not just one image that needs to be designed but a series of images with the additional motion of the characters and camera movement throughout the shots. A shot's composition is always based on the previous shot, as it should take over the focal point and continue with the same or a similar focal point in the next shot (exceptions always apply, as it is the intended cinematic effect that is important!). Cinematic composition thus contains a compositional flow, which the audience should be easily able to follow. In terms of character placement in a continuous shot flow, there are a couple of rules that are worth learning, as they help to keep the characters' relationship logical throughout the scene:

## Action axis for two players (180° Rule)

When positioning the camera on the set for a dialogue scene, one has to be cautious about where to place it. The goal for the two characters is to always face each other in the final scene when communicating. To have them continuously facing each other from shot to shot, the camera has to be placed with caution to ensure the continuity needed. To achieve this, each character occupies one respective side of the screen, regardless of whether one or both characters are in the shot (Figure 6.56 with its corresponding Camera Position 1 in Figure 6.61). This position of the turquoise character on the left and the blue character on the right is maintained throughout the scene as long as the camera stays within the red half circle in Figure 6.61, which covers 180° of the entire space (hence the 180° rule). The shots from Camera Positions 1–4 show the character Turquoise on the left and the character Blue on the right, despite the camera moving from left to right within the space. In the editing process, every shot can be easily cut together with any other shot from Positions 1–4, and the characters will always keep facing each other. To achieve Shots 1–4, the camera needs to be placed within the semicircle on one side of an imagined line between the characters. Once this "action axis" is established, the camera can take any position within the marked red area and all the shots will technically and logically match in the editing. If the camera steps over the action axis (Camera Position 5 and Figure 6.60), the characters will change their assigned positions in the frame: now Blue is left and Turquoise is right, which in the editing process would result in the characters switching sides from one shot to the next. This of course causes confusion in the viewer, who expects each of the players to occupy one side of the frame in this specific time frame of the scene. However, if the camera travels actively, without a cut, from one side of the action axis to the other side and the viewer can see the two characters switching sides, a new line of action is established and the sides that the characters occupied visibly change. As long as the audience can see how the switch happened, they will understand the newly established positions of the characters. This change can happen as often as needed if the camera shows the change or the characters themselves actively move from one side to the other in one shot. Of course, there are moments when the immediate switch from

**Figure 6.56**

**Figure 6.57**

**Figure 6.58**

**Figure 6.59**

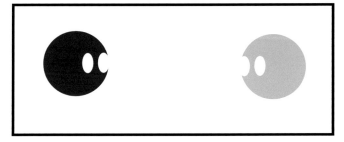

**Figure 6.60**

one side of the action axis to the other is wanted as an artistic or emotional tool, for example, to purposefully confuse the audience or add dynamic in an action scene. Yet this has to be done with knowledge of the resulting confusion. However, there are some directors who do not always care about the line of action, like, for example, Japanese director Yasujiro Ozu. His films still read perfectly well.

## Action axis for three players

Three players have, all in all, six possible action axes, though most of them do not make much sense when considered for what is needed in the scene (Figure 6.62). How the action axis is chosen depends on how these three characters are to be grouped: three people independently from each other, or two as a group against one. The story will determine what grouping is needed, which character is the main player in the story, and which the bystander. Only because the main player is the focus of the scene does not mean that the main player also has to be the focus visually. Showing the bystander's reactions to what is heard

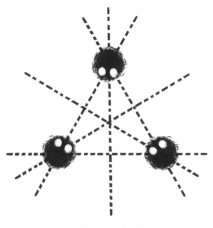

**Figure 6.61**

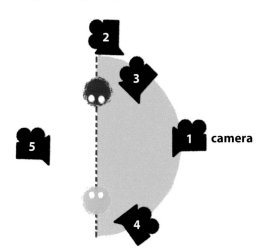

**Figure 6.62**

Six possible action axes with three players.

from the conversation between the other two can give the scene the needed "spice" it needs to emotionally read better. This is where the creativity and sensibility of the filmmaker comes in. But the camera still has to follow the requirements of the action axis to not confuse the audience.

Figures 6.63 and 6.64 suggest the action axis to be established between Players I and II. Player III is the listening bystander. Which side of the line of action is chosen depends on how the bystander is to be included into the shots: with facial expressions clearly visible, like in Figure 6.63, or less visible in Figure 6.64. In Figure 6.63, the facial expressions of the bystander are easily incorporated into the frame as his or her front is exposed to all possible camera positions. In Figure 6.64, they are not. He or she is either out of the shot if we frame the other two or we only see the back of his or her head. Figure 6.63

has the option to include Player III into most of the shots, whereas Figure 6.64 can only include him or her in some shots and then only either from the side or the back of the head. There are some positions, though, that give us a side view, with the other two included in the shot.

The questions that should be asked when choosing the action-axis:

- Who is talking to whom?
- Who is/are the main player(s) and who is a bystander?
- Whose facial reactions need to be seen in the shots?
- What visual impact do I need for the composition/narrative?

## Example 1

Figure 6.65 chooses the left side of the action axis and again has Player III as the bystander, whose facial expressions and reactions in this theoretical scene are deemed important for the conversation between Players I and II. Player I is still the main player and Player II is secondary. The three positions of Cameras 1, 2, and 3 propose different shots within the 180° semicircle, and we can see in Figures 6.66 through 6.68 how all the shots have the characters talk to each other in the correct direction. The main player, Player I, is always facing right, addressing Player II, or both Players II and III. If Camera 3 is turned too much, then we end up with a shot like Figure 6.69, which causes the main player, Player I, to appear in Player II's position but still looking right. This might be slightly confusing, though the character is still talking into and facing the correct direction (this option can be used as an artistic device). Nevertheless, Camera 4 is outside of the 180° semicircle but it is still clear of who addresses whom as long as all three are in the shot. This position would work despite the camera being out of the semicircle *because* we see the main player from the front. He or she is the center of attention and as long as

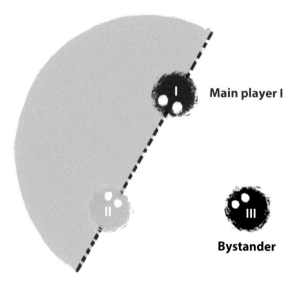

**Figure 6.63**

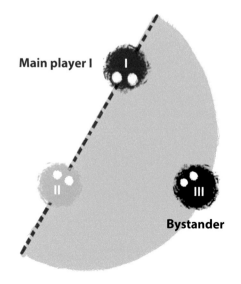

**Figure 6.64**

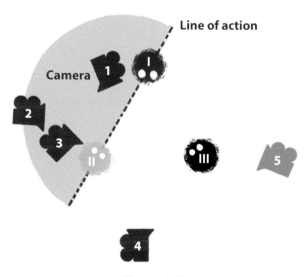

**Figure 6.65**

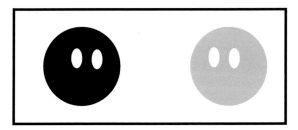

**Figure 6.66**

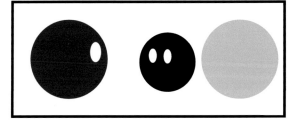

**Figure 6.67**

**Figure 6.68**

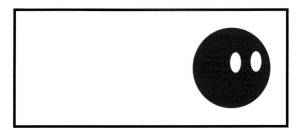

**Figure 6.69**

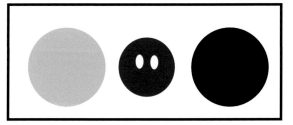

**Figure 6.70**

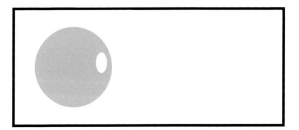

**Figure 6.71**

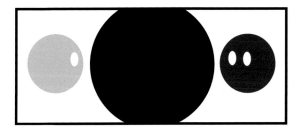

**Figure 6.72**

image in Figure 6.71. Now Player II is facing the right instead of the left. Cut into a scene with shots from Cameras 1–3 the players do not face each other anymore, which is a break of the logical continuity of the scene. The logic fades when we shoot with Camera 5 with the shot in Figure 6.72, where the main player in blue all of a sudden faces left, instead of right. Therefore all shots left of the line of action can be edited into a scene without the change of direction, whereas Figures 6.70 through 6.72 include a change of direction of the characters on-screen. Cutting those shots into Figures 6.68 through 6.69 causes the characters to switch sides. Regardless of the line of action, though, some shots can still be considered if the arrangement of the characters is still clear and the previous shots allow the switch. Once the arrangement of two or three characters is established and the audience knows the position of the characters within the set, then switches can be accepted by the audience (I say *can*, not *will*, as it always depends on the story being told and how it is told).

A good practice to understand the logic behind the three-dimensional relationship of characters in the frame and their changing positions is by cutting out a wide-screen rectangle from a piece of cardboard to mimic the camera's viewfinder. This can be done as a simple framing device to compose three objects, placed in a triangle on a table, in the cardboard frame. While circling around the table in order to find shot possibilities, the liaison between the three objects shifts continuously and their positions change from left to right and vice versa. What needs to be understood is the three-dimensionality of the setup, where the positions of the objects in the frame are not a constant but change in size and position depending on the location of the camera. This seems logical and simple but is more of a challenge than one might think when there are more than two players involved.

that is clear, this shot still works (Figure 6.70). Once we shoot Characters II or III with Camera 4, the directions the characters are facing is a potential problem. For example, if Camera 4 is turned to the left to take a close-up shot of Player II we get the

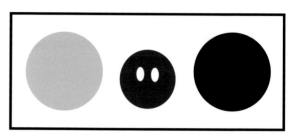

**Main player**

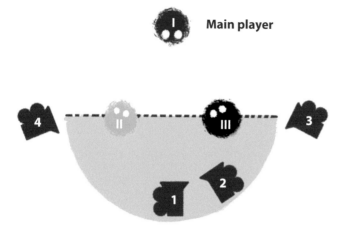

Figure 6.73

Figure 6.74

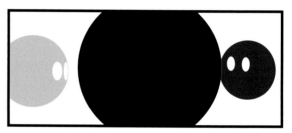

Figure 6.75

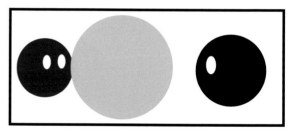

Figure 6.76

## Example 2

A fourth possibility for placing the action axis is shown in Figure 6.73, which has the line between Players II and III and gives us very good shot positions into the face, and therefore the expressions, of main Player I (Camera Positions 1 or 2). This setup, however, shows no facial expression for either Players II or III. We can only see the back of their heads or a slice of their three-quarters back view. The placement in Figure 6.73 would only work if the focal point of the conversation were the main player's face and the expressions of Players II and III were of no importance, but the visual weight of their heads might be (to frame the speaker or make him feel intimidated by the big-sized heads; this is often used in interrogation shots, where the police officers' faces are of no importance, but the interrogated one's reactions are key).

The action axis can always be broken during the conversation by simply moving the camera in the shot. Then the audience witnesses the change actively on-screen, as mentioned before. The camera position can also be changed once the audience is familiar enough with the setup of the characters to accept a significant change, even a switch of sides, though this depends on the actual scene and how it reads. In some scenes it works; in others it does not. Which shots can be combined with each other to create a logical shot flow depends on the story, how much information is already given, and how much is still needed. The action axis is a guideline that has to be kept in mind at all times, but it is not a 100% strict rule that can never be broken. If it fits and works, why not? Whether it actually is comprehensible depends on the shots before and after, the information that the audience has received already, and how the scene reads as a whole in its timing, its composition, its story, etc. If breaking the rule would fit the content of the scene or a break would still allow the scene to read well, then there is nothing wrong if the reason makes sense and does not confuse the audience.

Figure 6.77

It is not advised, though, to break the rule without fully understanding its impact.

## Main player and one unit

There is also the option of grouping Players II and III into one unit, treating them as one player, and letting the line of action run between them (Figure 6.78). All the rules of two players then apply.

## Letter patterns of two and three characters

The arrangement of two or three characters in the frame allow, aside from the aforementioned options, the

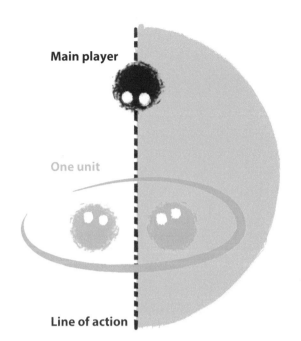

**Main player**

**One unit**

**Line of action**

**Figure 6.78**

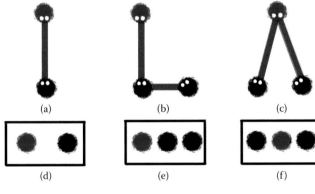

(a)  (b)  (c)

(d)  (e)  (f)

**Figure 6.79**

As seen, however, the arrangements have different narrative and emotional foundations.

## Groups of more than three

More than three players in the group can be placed in the frame by always having the action axis between the main player and the group or one specific character from within the group who the main player is talking to. In any group, there are usually two people talking to each other. It does not happen very often that 10 people talk to each other at the same time. Once one character finishes speaking, the conversation shifts to someone else, then maybe two address each other, and so on. The characters, to avoid confusion, can be arranged into two or three groups that the main player is then talking to or two groups

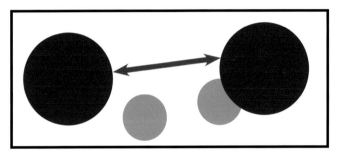

**Figure 6.80**

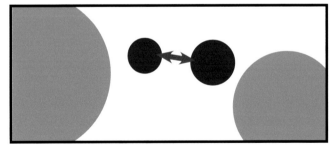

**Figure 6.81**

letter patterns (Figure 6.79). There are three different options: I-, L-, and A-patterns, which include not only the directions in which the various characters are facing each other in Figure 6.79 but any other variations. The I-pattern (see Figure 6.79a) has two characters interact with each other, which includes all the options talked about in Figures 6.46 through 6.55. The arrangement can look like the frame in Figure 6.79d. The L-pattern (see Figure 6.79b) has the three characters grouped into two: the two black characters and the blue one next to them as seen in Figure 6.79e. The black character is in the frame next to the two, which means he is not clearly separate. The A-pattern (see Figure 6.79c), however, has the blue character surrounded by the two black ones in Figure 6.79f. A camera movement can change the L-pattern into an A-pattern, so the arrangement is for clarity and to describe the placing of the various characters.

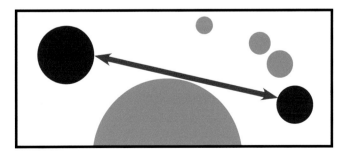

**Figure 6.82**

**More on letter patterns:**

Katz Steven, *Film Directing Shot by Shot: Visualizing from Concept to Screen*, Michael Wiese Productions, Studio City, CA, 1991, p. 176.

that address each other. What is important in bigger groups is that the audience always knows who is talking to whom and where they are located within the group. Most of the members of the group are filling the screen to either suggest congestion or to guide the eye towards the two talking. In the example Figures 6.80 through 6.82, it is obvious who is conversing with whom, as the main characters are marked by dark blue. The other light blue characters enhance the connection between the two (Figures 6.80 and 6.81) or interrupt the connection (Figure 6.82). Comparing the simple abstraction of the characters with a shot from *Brave* (timecode 00:09:46) one can clearly see the curve in the heads of the characters and it is obvious who is leading the conversation—who is the active one and who the passive ones.

## Questions that should always be raised when composing shots with multiple characters

- Which composition reflects the emotional impact of the story moment?
- How should the visual weight be distributed within the frame in order to support the narrative?
- Where are the characters to be placed within the set to get the composition that conveys the emotional needs?
- How is foreground, middle ground, and background used to create perspective or avoid it?
- What is the relationship between the characters in the shot?
- What is the role of each character in that very moment?
- Who or what is the focal point of that very moment in the conversation?
- Is the shot an action or reaction shot?
- How can the composition be enhanced for visual interest?
- How can the inactive players within the group be used as elements to create vectors that guide the eye towards the active players?
- How can the inactive players within the group be used with their facial expressions or poses to support the conversation?
- How can the background elements be used to enhance the position of the main players?
- How can the shot be designed to spark the interest of the audience?

## Examples for group composition

The group composition again has several possibilities: the group as a whole is the center of attention and no one character in particular is important, or one or several characters in the group are the focal point. The compositional difference is drastic, as both immediately have to show what the message of the image is and who is the focal point. In case of the group being important, the composition has to be well distributed to not have characters stand out, not have empty spaces or parts that draw attention. Of course, there can be a general direction of

**Figure 6.83**

*Portonaccio Sarcophagus*; Roman, 190–200 AD.

**Figure 6.84**

**Figure 6.85**

the group to either point towards the focal point in the image or to a point in the offscreen space. But this has to be carefully balanced in order to achieve the desired effect. There can also be a subcomposition within the group that points out specific characters, though the whole direction is still intact. Randomness should be avoided and the characters need to be placed purposefully in the shot, if one wants the scene to read easily. Even extremely busy compositions that seem overcrowded with people have a compositional fundament that controls the image. In the Roman *Sarcophagus of Portonaccio*

(190–200 AD; Figure 6.83), the composition is certainly complex and rather difficult to comprehend. The compositional structure many characters are inscribed in, is not easily seen because of the business in the relief. The sarcophagus depicts a general's campaign for Emperor Marcus Aurelius, showing a battle of Roman forces against tribesmen from the north. Unfinished in its carving, it is the most important person's face that is missing: the general's in the middle of the sarcophagus' front piece (slightly off-center left), the one commissioning the work. The center of attention is the general on his horse, riding to the right. The rest of the group, soldiers and northern tribesmen, are seemingly loosely assembled around the general. The hostile tribesmen are distributed on the lower half of the composition and the Roman soldiers in the upper half, clearly showing who is dominant and who submissive (or which of the two fighting parties commissioned the piece). The composition is well planned out in its even spread of objects and characters. Weight or directions give the relief a very busy, yet also balanced arrangement. In Figure 6.84, the characters and their movements are highlighted to see which parts on the left and right relate to each other, balance each other out. The concentric movement's center is the general's horse's triangular head. Underneath, in Figure 6.85, we can see which character and pose is reflected on the opposite side again for balance. The business of the intertwined characters obviously works in its hectic and deadly depiction of a battle scene. The bodies seem to wind and struggle in a frame that is too small for them. The confinement underlines the insanity and claustrophobia of the scene and heightens the resulting honor of the general having probably won the battle. What seemed random in the beginning reveals after thorough study a manifold of symmetrical poses and complex compositional relationships.

An easier approach to the group composition is a less busy arrangement where the main character is clearly the center of attention and the group is there to point this out. Group composition in animation often takes this easier road, as adding movement to the group makes the scene overwhelmingly complex. Simplicity and clarity are the goals and can be seen in many scenes of Pixar's *Brave* (2012).[2] Though there are many group shots in the film, there is always a clear center of attention. The eye is attracted to movement and characters moving even just slightly will drag the audience's eyes towards themselves. In the first example of the feature (timecode 00:18:31), the three kings are lining up in front of their soldiers, which is already a clear visual statement. However, the left character moves and therefore the stage belongs visually to him, despite all characters occupying the same amount of screen space; the middle character is only seemingly the more important one (which gives away his personality in the composition, rather than his importance in the actual story point). It is the movement in this balanced composition that definitely points out the left character as the center of attention (however, movement can also be used to draw the attention away from the obvious main character within the shot for comedic or narrative purposes).

In the second example (timecode 00:24:11), the composition makes it clear that King Fergus is the center, because of the

building "framing" him, rendering him important. The other characters on the left are arranged in a half circle to push the eye towards the right. Also the background hill, whose peak seems to be above Fergus's head, right where the gable of the roof is, accentuates his position. It is interesting in this shot which character is juxtaposed with what or whom and how that can be interpreted: Fergus is as far from the frame as the other three kings on the left. Merida, sitting on a chair to the right of Fergus, is balanced out by a tall tree on the left. She is going to be the stability of the kingdom, not her father.

At 00:18:45, the crowd with spears and banners moves the attention upwards to the king. The crowd is forming a very clear triangular shape, whose peak is Fergus and his family.

In the fourth example (timecode 01:05:01), the composition is geometric and clear. Princess Merida is the center of a composition that groups the three clan leaders and her in a trapezoid shape, which is repeated by each of the king's subjects. Merida, being the "leader" of all the clans, like her father Fergus, is dressed in a green outfit and her bright red hair makes her dominate all the others in the image. The shadows that are cast are going away from Merida, serving as vectors between the clan leaders and their soldiers and also serve as arrows towards the center. The light from the candelabras left and right don't seem to have much impact on the lighting in the shot as the main light comes from the center above. Light can enhance and strengthen the shot and does not always have to be perfectly logical if the composition reads better otherwise.

Group compositions are much easier to grasp if the group itself is considered as a shape instead of a whole bunch of people that have to be positioned. Start with the broad composition and its shape and emotional impact, and then once the broad shape is defined, position the characters that are important and drive the story. Afterwards the poses and details of the other characters can be refined. Always start with the big shape and then work your way down to the details.

Film images must be composed in a simple fashion to be quickly read and understood. Paintings on the other hand can have a more intricate arrangement, as the audience has more time to read the sophisticated structure of the often tediously arranged elements. To what extent the complexity can be pushed in a painting, yet still maintain a rather simple foundation, shows Peter Paul Ruben's painting *The Four Continents* (also referred to as *The Four Rivers of Paradise*), painted ca. 1615 (Figure 6.86). The painting illustrates the four continents with their respective rivers as allegories. On the very left is Europa, with the river Danube, followed to the right by Africa with the river Nile, America in the back with the Rio de la Plata, and on the right side of the group is Asia with the river Ganges. All characters are carefully arranged for them to lead toward each other, allowing an easy reading of the intended compositional flow, purposefully linking the individual elements. Every character is connected in their

[2] Due to the fact that the Disney Company did not release the copyrights for images of this feature to be used in this educational section, which would have tremendously helped the understanding of the discussed composition, it is necessary for the reader to check and compare the widescreen images from the movie alongside the text to fully grasp the compositions.

122

pose to the next, every arm, leg, and direction is deliberately designed to lead to and thus highlight another element. This detailed arrangement allows the eye to constantly move from one allegory to the next and never rest for too long.

All heads are organized in a horizontal S-curve (or more precisely, in the shape of a pretzel; see, for instance, Figure 6.82 where the heads are arranged in a simple curve). On the right end of that curve, the river Ganges' left arm is leading the viewers' eyes back into the middle of the composition, directly to the continent of Africa, as does the right arm of the river Nile, whose embracing arm ultimately leads into Africa's face. She is the only main character who the viewers can directly connect with, as she is "breaking the fourth wall" and draws them into

the scene. Aside from the main characters' heads who occupy the upper half of the painting, there are more subtle elements that assist that main compositional curve and broaden it, allowing the main composition to affect and include the lower part of the painting with the animals. For instance, the Asian river Ganges' vertical leg directly points towards the tigress' head, the representative animal of Asia. His pose is juxtaposed by the Nile's posture, whose left arm is in its flow smoothly leading into the tail of the crocodile, the animal of Africa. Despite the apparent intricacy of the composition, with all the various characters being linked, the focal point of the painting is Africa, as it is her who is bridging the gap between painting and reality, between painter and viewer.

**Figure 6.86**

Peter Paul Rubens: *The Four Continents* (ca. 1615).

**More on storyboarding, cinematic composition, film-language and cinematography:**

Katz Steven, *Film Directing Shot by Shot: Visualizing from Concept to Screen*, Michael Wiese Productions, Studio City, CA, 1991.

Katz Steven, *Film Directing: Cinematic Motion: A Workshop for Staging Scenes*, Michael Wiese Productions, Studio City, CA, 2004.

Gustavo Mercado, *The Filmmaker's Eye: Learning (and Breaking) the Rules of Cinematic Composition*, Focal Press, Waltham MA, 2010.

Christopher Kenworthy, *Master Shots Vol 1–3: 100 Advanced Camera Techniques to Get an Expensive Look on Your Low-Budget Movie*, Michael Wiese Productions, Studio City, CA, 2003.

Joseph V. Mascelli, *Five C's of Cinematography: Motion Pictures Filming Techniques*, Silman-James Press, Hollywood, CA, 1998.

John Alton, *Painting with Light*, University of California Press, Berkeley, CA, 1998.

# Case study: Arranging characters in relationship to the story, composition, and editing in Polanski's *The Fearless Vampire Killers* (1967)

**In order to understand the following, you must watch the scene from Polanski's feature.**

The film image deals with composition in a very similar yet simpler way than a painting does; however, it additionally adds the aspect of movement and editing to the mix. As I discussed earlier, no shot in a scene can stand on its own as it always refers back to the shot(s) before or prepares for the shot(s) after. There is a continuous flow that must never be neglected other than for an artistic, valid reason.

In 1967, Roman Polanski, who had been successful with surreal horror movies, released his feature vampire comedy *The Fearless Vampire Killers*, which was very different from his earlier films *Repulsion* (1965) and *Cul de Sac* (1966). *The Fearless Vampire Killers* is a horror comedy very loosely based on the story of Count Dracula and the silent movie *Nosferatu* from 1922 by director F.W. Murnau. Polanski's feature is noteworthy for various reasons, one being the extraordinary character inventions of actor Jack MacGowran as Professor Abronsius, Alfie Bass's interpretation of the innkeeper Yoine Shagal, and many others, which are all deliciously over the top. Polanski wanted to create a fairy tale rather than a traditional horror movie, and he succeeded in the tone and mood of the film having the look and the feeling of a Central European setting; it is so very well executed as an interpretation and exaggeration, not a representation. The feeling of the various locations all have a mood that is unmistakably Central European.

The comedy part, however, is not to everyone's taste because it isn't straight out funny or farcical but is quiet in its funny moments, much like the comedies of Buster Keaton. It is the little character moments of the actors that make the film funny and quirky. There is a dreamlike quality to the film in the narrative, the characterization, its gorgeous and illustrative visuals, and its unusual music. In particular, the production design by Wilfrid Shingleton and the cinematography by Douglas Slocombe elevate the film to a sometimes surreal quality that is exquisite.

The story is of Professor Abronsius and his disciple Alfred, both from the University of Königsberg (today's Kaliningrad), travelling into the heart of Transylvania for scientific studies on bats and vampires. In a village, Alfred meets Sarah, who he falls in love with but who is also unfortunately going to be bitter by the head of the vampires: Count Krolock. Sarah's father, innkeeper Yoine, tries to rescue his daughter from the fangs of the count but is also bitten and joins the undead as a Jewish vampire. At the nearby castle Alfred and Abronsius meet Count Krolock and his son, who is smitten with Alfred. They find Sarah and try to leave with her, but the army of old and ancient vampires chases the trio through the dusty and dilapidated castle, until …

When the film was released in theaters, there were two different versions: the European version, which is Polanski's version and the one still shown, and then another version for the US market, which was changed and edited again by the production company MGM and released as *The Fearless Vampire Killers, or Pardon Me, But Your Teeth Are in My Neck* as a cinematic farce. The US version was a huge flop, whereas in Europe the film is still celebrated as a cult movie, so much so that it has also produced a very successful stage musical. Not until the 1980s did Polanski again address a topic that was more entertainment and "illustrative" when he shot *The Pirates* (1986) with Walter Matthau as the infamous, repulsive, and gross pirate Thomas Bartholomew Red, also a character worth watching (despite the film being a bit, well … odd?).

In the following pages, I will explain via a scene of the feature how the characters in the frame relate to each other but also how the shots connect and how all of it visualizes the narrative. For instance, the characters take a spot in the frame, which is their designated position for part of the scene (for example, Alfred is in the shot on the right side of the frame and continues that preferred position throughout). This position is the same position of that character in the next shot or the shot afterwards. Characters nevertheless do not have to appear in a shot physically at all times to be connected to their position. The spot can be empty of characters, but still the audience remembers that this position was reserved for that one character, who still lingers on in the mind of the viewer. This can quickly change by just allowing another character to appear in that position. From then on, it is reserved for the new character, until there is yet another replacement. The next couple of pages explain the shot connections and reasons for each cut, plus the positions of the characters in the frame and how it all connects to the narrative. All the aspects of design are of course integrated into the composition, which does make it a bit complex; you might want to watch the scene again, then go back and read the following once more.

**SHOT 1**

**Figure 6.87**

**Figure 6.88**

**SHOT 2**

**Figure 6.89**

**Figure 6.90**

**SHOT 3**

**Figure 6.91**

**Figure 6.92**

Beginning shot 1 (Figure 6.87)

The first shot in this scene introduces the two characters and their action: putting on their skies.

The camera tilts up and shows both of them with Abronsius in the middle and Alfred on the right, slightly facing left, opening the frame towards the following action. Their group composition gets interrupted by Shagal, who jumps between them. The A-pattern of the character constellation is changed by Shagal moving to frame-left and turns the grouping into an L-pattern, which unites the two vampire-hunters again into a group. Focus is on Shagal as he is the acting and moving character in the image. The other two are more or less inactive at the end of the shot, just being stunned about what just happened.

End of shot 1 (Figure 6.88)

CUT

Beginning of shot 2 (Figure 6.89)

Shagal is in the middle of the frame now, appearing in the very spot of Professor Abronsius from shot 1. Shagal's former position is occupied in shot 2 by the wooden gate on the left. The negative space between Alfred and Abronsius in shot 1 fills a tree trunk and Alfred's former position is still filled with architecture (positive and negative space replace each other). The eye line from shot 1 stays on Shagal's height in shot 2. Shagal turns around and stays in the middle of the frame while he runs away through the gate in the middle. At the end of the shot Shagal is running off to the right towards the tree (remember the exact point of Shagal in the frame when the cut happens).

End of shot 2 (Figure 6.90)

CUT

Beginning shot 3 (Figure 6.91)

Our eyes follow still the direction of Shagal towards the right and ending up in Alfred's face, reading his stunned expression. His body appears exactly in the position of the tree in the previous shot and Professor Ambronsius appears in the position of the gate on the right. An A-pattern is achieved by the combination of shot 2 and shot 3. Shagal is as a ghost-image still in shot 3 as his ending-position in shot 2 was the middle of the frame and that is where he is still as an "invisible character" that both Abronsius and Alfred are looking at.

The two fearless vampire hunters are leaving the frame to the left, the mirrored direction of where Shagal ran off and also the same direction that Shagal was running off in shot 2. Alfred is taking over Abronsius, he is slightly faster while leaving the frame.

End of shot 3 (Figure 6.92)

CUT

**S H O T 4**

**Figure 6.93**

**Figure 6.94**

**S H O T 5**

**Figure 6.95**

**Figure 6.96**

**S H O T 6**

**Figure 6.97**

Beginning of shot 4 (Figure 6.93)

We see Shagal, who had been cut in shot 2 right in the middle of the frame, again appears in the middle of shot 4's composition, scuffling up the hill through the snow. The two fearless vampire hunters that left the frame at the end of shot 3 towards the left come into the frame again from the left following Shagal in the middle of the frame, which becomes the area of interest (usually characters that leave the frame come into the next shot from the same direction they had left). Alfred comes into the frame first, because he was seemingly the first leaving the frame in the previous shot.

The previous shot 3 had Abronsius as a compositional element on the left and Alfred on the right, which is now replaced by the hut and barn on each side. The bottom lines of the two buildings point towards the focal area in the middle where Shagal disappears in the distance.

End of shot 4 (Figure 6.94)

**CUT**

Beginning of shot 5 (Figure 6.95)

Shagal is seen tiny in the distance. His path through the snow from lower corner left towards the middle right is still an after-thought of the path and tilt the two vampire hunters came into the shot 4. The middle of the frame is accentuated by the three trees in the distance, a reflection of the three characters. Two trees build one group "following" one tree on the right in front of them. The positive space in shot 4 on the left and right are now the negative spaces in shot 5.

Shagall disappears behind a hill and the two hunters come this time from the right into the frame, which gives variation to the entry in the previous shot. The two skiers are driving in the middle of the frame towards the three trees.

End of shot 5 (Figure 6.96)

**CUT**

Beginning of shot 6 (Figure 6.97)

Slight change in perspective and closer to the hill, Shagal is following a path in the snow around the hill on the left. He appears right in the spot he would be in if he would have continued running in shot 5. His position is exactly the same but the environment shifts. Alfred swoops in a long curve from the left into the scene and then changes direction. During the swoop Abronsius steps into the frame also from the left and stops right of where Shagal is in the far distance connecting again the professor with Alfred, instead of Alfred and Shagal which we have already witnessed. Because the professor is facing right, he has Shagal in his back, establishing again the bond between himself and Alfred.

Abronsius is looking at Alfred who is stopping right off center waiving for him to come down the hill. Shagal is still running in the distance, now on a long curve.

End of shot 6 (Figure 6.98)

**S H O T 7**

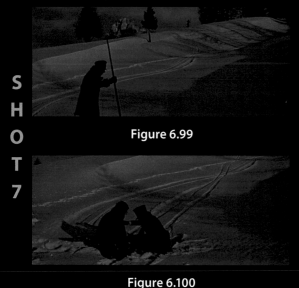

**Figure 6.99**

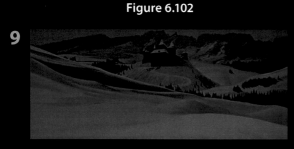

**Figure 6.100**

Beginning of shot 7 (Figure 6.99)

Switch of position: shot from Alfred's point who is looking up at Abronsius skiing down the hill. The two characters switch their positions from the previous shot: Alfred is in Abronsius' position, just lower and the professor in Alfred's position, but higher (the shadows are still right to left, same as in the shot before, though the shadows should logically be vice versa as the camera switched position).

Abronsius drives down the hill and smashes into Alfred; both get up and while they stand up...

End of shot 7 (Figure 6.100)

**CUT**

**S H O T 8**

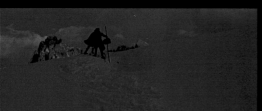

**Figure 6.101**

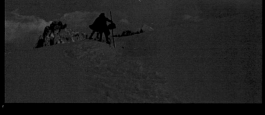

**Figure 6.102**

Beginning of shot 8 (Figure 6.101)

...we see both of them climbing up the hill in exactly the same vertical, though in a different height.

The two vampire killers are stopping seemingly stunned left off center and are looking into the distance at something which seems to be positioned in the middle of the frame.

End of shot 8 (Figure 6.102)

**CUT**

**9**

**Figure 6.103**

Beginning of shot 9 (Figure 6.103)

In the position where both of them were looking into in the previous shot, we now see the sinister castle of Count Krolock right in the upper center. The slanted hill from shot 8 is now tilted the opposite direction, providing variation within the composition.

End of shot 9

**CUT**

**10**

Beginning of shot 10 (Figure 6.104)

Close up of the castle still in the very same position as in shot 9, though from underneath, which makes it appear more powerful and ominous. The closer view of the castle also suggests that the two vampire hunters will walk towards it.

End of shot 10

# Camera shots and angles

## Terminology

### Take

The term *take* is reserved for live-action footage and contains the time frame from the beginning of a recording to its uninterrupted end. Once the camera stops recording, the *take* is over and the next *take* can begin (in a professional recording, the *take* is started with the clapper board, which contains the information of production title, director, camera, date, scene, and take number). If the camera shot is a very long, uninterrupted *take*, it's called a *long take*. The *take* is the unedited shot. There are features that have been shot in one *take* but only since the introduction of the digital movie camera. Traditional movie cameras were only able to shoot up to 11 minutes, whereas digital cameras can, with great technical difficulties, shoot an entire feature film. However, many films that are seemingly shot in one *take* are stitched together digitally.

### Shot

Once the *take* is edited for use in the scene, it is called a *shot*. For traditional film, the *shot* has a defined time frame, whereas in animation or special-effects heavy films *shots* can also have an extended time frame or any other visual that is not interrupted by a cut. It is therefore a piece of film that is not interrupted by any kind of cut that replaces the entire visual content of the frame. (Figure 6.105 for instance shows various shots that distinguish each other from the distance between camera and object. Further shot categories are going to be explained on the next couple of pages).

### Scene

If a *shot* is a word in the film, a *scene* is a sentence. It is usually confined to one location and contains the action happening in that location during a defined period of uninterrupted time (exceptions apply). Once any of the parameters of time, locale, or character setup change, the *scene* usually changes.

### Sequence

A film, which is a relatively long piece of visual storytelling, has various chapters called *sequences*. They are smaller divisions of the larger unit, *film*. The *sequence* itself consists of various scenes that usually group together into a distinct period of events.

## Shot categories

For functioning and logical cinematic storytelling, one needs to know the various shot options and how each shot expresses a certain idea, emotion, or is technically helpful for the story to be expressed. There is a vast amount of shots that can all be grouped into four categories.

EXTREME
CLOSE-UP

MEDIUM CLOSE-UP
FULL CLOSE-UP
WIDE CLOSE-UP

CLOSE SHOT

MEDIUM
CLOSE-SHOT

MEDIUM SHOT

MEDIUM
FULL-SHOT

FULL SHOT

**Figure 6.105**

## The Four Different Shot Categories

1. Distance from the Object

2. Content

3. Camera angle

4. Camera movement

129

## 1. Distance from the object

### Extreme wide shot

More or less the establishing shot, except that the *extreme wide shot* does not have to be at the beginning of a scene but can be placed anywhere (Figure 6.106). As the *establishing shot*, the extreme wide shot gives the image a sense of scale and grandeur that not only widens the screen but also gives the characters a relationship to their environment beyond their immediate surrounding. Emotions from the characters cannot be seen, as the characters are much too far away.

### Very wide shot

Closer to the actual setting than the extreme wide shot, the *very wide shot* has the character still far away and does not yet fill the screen vertically (Figure 6.107). The character can be seen in his or her environment, expressing a strong relationship between the two. The emotional facial expressions of the character are still difficult to see clearly, so the emotional state has to be expressed either by the pose or the overall mood of the background (Figure 6.107).

### Wide shot, long shot, full shot

The character is fully visible in the frame and cropped at neither the feet or head. The *wide shot* shows enough of the background to keep the setting in frame and constantly emphasizes the correlation between the character and environment.

### Mid shot, three-quarter shot, American shot

The *mid-shot* shows the character from above the knees or the lower waist up, allowing the face with its detailed emotions to read much better than in the wide shot. The camera is closer to the character and therefore establishes a more personal connection. The distance to the character is still comfortable. It is also called the *American shot*, due to the convention in American Westerns of including the gun on the upper thigh.

### Medium close shot

This shot starts above the waist (Figure 6.108). The closer the camera zooms towards the head, the better the emotions can be read and the closer and more intimate the relationship between audience and character is. The comfort level starts to change at the point where the comfort distance between the character on-screen and the audience is broken. Then the character is fully exposed emotionally and the distance to the character is very intimate (usually this distance is only allowed for very close family members or lovers).

### Close-up

The full head-shot allows for the most subtle facial expressions to be seen (Figure 6.109). This shot has to be used carefully, as it has the most intimate distance and carries a strong emotional weight. In a regular conversation, the *close-up* is reserved for intense emotions, as the comfortable distance between audience and character is penetrated.

**Figure 6.106**

Fleischer's Superman series, *The Bulleteers*, 1942

**Figure 6.107**

Fleischer's Superman series, *Superman*, 1941

**Figure 6.108**

Fleischer's Superman series, *Superman*, 1941

**Figure 6.109**

Fleischer's Superman series, *Superman*, 1941

### Choker

The *choker* is a specific close-up shot where the character's head is shown from the eyebrows to underneath the mouth.

### Extreme close-up

Very close to the character's face, the *extreme close-up* reveals a character's innermost feelings. It is as close as the audience can be to the character and therefore it shows not just the character's partial emotions but also his "inner dialogue" and thoughts. It does not necessarily have to show the character's eyes, but the extreme close-up usually contains parts of his face. It is an unusual shot that does not allow for very precise facial expressions, as the camera is too close to reveal all of the face. This kind of shot can also be a detail of an object and then is referred to as the "insert shot."

### Cut-in

The *cut-in* shows other parts of the character up close (Figure 6.110). It gives more information about the previous emotion or action and specifies the previous shot or shots (or prepares for the following shots). For example, someone picks up a phone; the next cut, showing the hand grabbing the phone, would be the cut-in.

### Cutaway

The *cutaway* shot contains another part of the location that is not the characters. It can be, like the insert shot, an image that interprets or comments the previous shot. In live-action footage, the cutaway shot is used by the editor, for instance, to eliminate unwanted footage in a shot or scene in order to cover up the cut. The cutaway therefore helps to achieve a seamless edit.

### Over-the-shoulder shot

The camera looks over the shoulder of one of the characters, revealing from their point of view what is to be seen (Figure 6.111). It includes the character physically and emotionally in the frame. (It is most often used in dialogues where you don't want to continuously show the characters from the side talking to each other but have other perspectives that help to break up a possible visual monotony.)

### Noddy shot (mostly for TV interviews)

This shot shows a character who is listening and reacting to what is said or being asked. This shot again helps to integrate the character into the conversation and have them react to questions and comments. It also helps the editor to get a seamless flow in a scene when full scenes have to be cut for audio reasons, footage quality, content that has to be cut out, or any reason that requires certain parts of the shot to be cut. The Noddy shot also helps the audience to get a full experience of the conversation and be involved in the talk.

### Point-of-view shot

This shot is from the character's viewpoint and reveals what he can see of the location. Films based on games, for instance, play a lot with the point-of-view shot, as it mimics the game play in the feature.

## 2. Content

### Establishing shot

The *establishing shot* introduces the audience to the location in the beginning of a scene. It broadly presents the setting, time of day, locale, and mood (Figure 6.112). Additionally, it can interpret the overall emotional exposition of the scene in metaphorical visuals. The establishing shot has the ability to bring grandness into the scene by showing the scale of the environment and not allowing the offscreen space felt in the scene to be tight or even claustrophobic. TV series add establishing shots within the show in order to widen the offscreen space and allow the imagination to go beyond the often tight studio setting. Leaving out the establishing shot gives the viewer a sense of tightness that can be very uncomfortable at times if the space on-screen is rather small and/or cramped.

### Insert shot

An *insert shot* is a close shot of an object that visually explains, comments, or interprets the moment of a scene or is

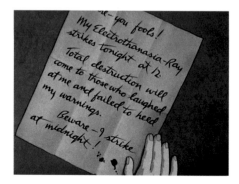

**Figure 6.110**

Fleischer's Superman series, *Superman*, 1941

**Figure 6.111**

Fleischer's Superman series, *The Bulleteers*, 1942

directly related to the content of a character's speech. It is useful for breaking up a speech or long shots and giving visual stimulus to the audience other than the character continuously talking. Those shots can strongly impact the interpretability of a scene and additionally give it a metaphorical spin.

### Reaction shot

The *reaction shot* is used to cut to the reaction of the character in a conversation or action; a glance from him or her, a subtle movement or gesture that does not contain any spoken word from the character (Figure 6.113). It is a reaction to something or someone. These shots are crucial in making a connection between the characters and showing their thoughts and reactions to each other and allowing them to comment the scene nonverbally.

### Weather shot

This shot shows the weather situation, which can relate to the story point and visually explain the emotional state of the characters.

## 3. Camera angle

### Bird's-eye view

The scene is shown from a point very high above (Figure 6.114). The camera "flies" above the characters and suggests an omniscient perspective. The viewer sees the characters in their environment, sees them as miniature characters struggling with their seemingly "small" issues. They are part of a whole.

### High angle

The camera is not positioned as high as in the bird's-eye view but is still above the characters (Figure 6.115). The "godlike" perspective of the bird's-eye view shot is replaced by a more modest one that is less omniscient yet still looks down at the characters from a perspective that expresses understanding of the situation by the audience. As we saw in David Lean's *Lawrence of Arabia* (Figure 6.7), the miniscule characters can also, because of their small size, feel mighty, as they are capable of defeating the desert.

### Eye level

The camera mimics the most natural position of human vision and gives the feeling of being directly involved in the action (Figure 6.116). The *eye level shot* integrates viewers into the scene and makes them invisible participants. Though it might lack originality in perspective, it is the shot that is used most in film, as it has the ability to draw the viewer back into the story on a more personal level. At exactly what height the camera is placed depends on the director. For instance, in Spielberg's *ET: The Extraterrestrial* (1982), the camera was at the eye level of the

**Figure 6.112**

Fleischer's Superman series, *Superman*, 1941

**Figure 6.113**

Fleischer's Superman series, *Superman*, 1941

**Figure 6.114**

Fleischer's Superman series, *Superman*, 1941

**Figure 6.115**

Fleischer's Superman series, *The Arctic Giant*, 1942

children rather than the grown-ups. And in the films of Japanese director Yasujiro Ozu, the camera is often placed very low on the ground (or sometimes even lowered into the ground).

### Low angle

For the *low angle* shot, there are two options: the camera is either placed very low to show the character upwards and incorporate the area above and behind the character into the shot or the camera is kept horizontal at a very low level (Figure 6.117). The Japanese director Yasujiro Ozu, previously mentioned, is famous for using low angles in his features on a continuous basis in order to bring the audience down to the level of his characters sitting on a Japanese tatami-mat, creating an eye level shot of about 80 cm off the ground. The low angle shot always either expresses an omnipotent character who is strong physically or mentally or determined, or it shows the character in distress with the head lowered; the camera can then look directly into the face of the character.

### Oblique angle, canted angle, and Dutch angle

In this shot, the horizon line is not parallel to the frame but tilted (Figure 6.118). This causes uneasiness and discomfort but can also give the image dynamic and a sense of movement. We explore the world mostly from a horizontal perspective, which urges us to straighten a frame that is crooked on the wall, and it makes us uneasy when we see an image with a tilted horizon. This can be used effectively in shots that are action-driven and emotionally intense, where the world is literally out of balance. These kinds of shots are often used in action scenes, music videos, and commercials.

## 4. Camera movement

The moving camera adds liveliness and dynamic to the shot and the movement can push the story actively forward in a physical or metaphorical direction. In this kind of shot, the audience is experiencing the three-dimensionality of the setting and its possibility for exploration. If the camera moves too much, it can be disorienting and confusing, as one has to get an idea of the location and the characters in relationship to each other, which can be difficult with a continuously moving camera. What needs to be clear is that the camera moves with a purpose! There always needs to be a well-defined reason for *why* the camera is moving and what the effect is on the narrative!

(For clarity and understanding, please look up the film examples mentioned in the following.)

### Pan

The *pan* is the horizontal movement of the camera, which is fixed to the ground. There is only the rotational movement of the camera's fixed axis. It underlines the horizontal orientation of the cinematic frame and has a very story-driven feel to it. It invites the audience to explore the scenery from a standing

**Figure 6.116**

Fleischer's Superman series, *The Magnetic Telescope*, 1942

**Figure 6.117**

Fleischer's Superman series, *The Mummy Strikes*, 1943

**Figure 6.118**

Fleischer's Superman series, *The Mummy Strikes*, 1943

position and is a movement that mimics the head's turn left and right without changing one's position. It is often an observational view.

### Track

In a tracking shot, the camera moves on a track horizontally and changes its own position continuously. The camera moves along the x-axis. The tracking shot does not necessarily have to be on a straight line but can follow the subject on a curved line, meandering through the scenery. The camera literally "goes places," as it actually moves through the scene with the viewer. The perspective changes and the audience is actively taken from point A to point B.

## Dolly

The *dolly* shot changes the physical distance between the subject and audience and the camera moves along the *z*-axis (into the frame). The dolly shot has more of an intense impact than the zoom, where the perspective does not change but only the size of the subject on screen. With reduction or expansion of the distance, the audience feels as if it is actually getting physically away from or towards the subject and increasing or decreasing our emotional connection to the character or the entire scene (usually at the end of the scene).

## Crane

The *crane* shot is another aerial shot with a controlled path. The camera is mounted on a crane that is balanced with a counterweight, allowing the cameraman with the heavy equipment to have a very smooth and steady movement. It is similar to the tracking or dolly shot, only with the addition of *y*-axis involvement, as the camera can go high above the scene into any position needed. The camera can freely move on the *x*-, *y*-, and *z*-axes. This shot has the broadest range of movement of all camera shots and its emotional impact is very strong, as the shots it creates are unusual in perspective and give the scene a smooth and calm grace. On the other hand, they can also follow the action easily and change perspective during the shot, giving the scene unique visuals.

## Tilt

The camera *tilt* is a rotation around its axis up and down; it destabilizes the shot with its content. The eye wants to straighten the image, and the tilt can make the audience uncomfortable. It also adds dynamic and movement to the image. But it can also simply be the viewpoint of someone who is looking up or down.

## Handheld shots

The *handheld shot* is a very nervous shot that has a strong active component. The continuously slightly shaking image suggests hectic movement, involvement in the scene by the audience, and "being right in the middle of the action" as we follow the camera operators in their paths. Often used to intensify action scenes, the handheld camera shot adds dynamic, hectic, nervousness, and also stress and tension to the image. It has a very "real" feel to it that often relates to a documentary style. An example is Daniel Myrick and Eduardo Sánchez's *Blair Witch Project* (1999).

## Steadicam

The Steadicam, a camera stabilizing brand, removes the movement caused by a walking or running camera operator and gives, compared to the handheld shot, a very smooth and stable movement. It removes the nervousness that can occur in handheld shots and provides a calm movement even if the terrain is rough.

## Zoom

Technically the *zoom* is not a camera movement, as the camera itself does not physically move, but the lens only changes the perspective. The zoom reduces the visual but not physical distance between camera and object. The camera stays in place; the lens creates the illusion of bringing the subject closer to the camera (zoom in). The perspective does not change, but the lens can distort the image. This shot points out the focal area and strongly emphasizes its importance (or the opposite, in zooming out).

## 360° shot

Developed by German cinematographer Michael Ballhaus, in the 360° shot the camera circles around the subjects and creates a slightly dizzying feeling. The continuously changing background and perspective of the characters makes this a very dynamic and active shot. Examples can be found in Rainer Werner Fassbinder's film *Martha* (1974) or Martin Scorsese's film *Time of Innocence* (1993).

## Dolly zoom, vertigo effect

This kind of effect is achieved by zooming into or out of the subject while the camera simultaneously dollies towards or away from it. The size of the subject remains the same on-screen, while the background changes in size in relationship to the subject. Examples can be found in Alfred Hitchcock's *Vertigo* (1958), Martin Scorsese's film *Goodfellas* (1990), and Steven Spielberg's *Jaws* (1975).

## Helicopter shot/drone shot

This shot is obviously filmed from a helicopter and shows the scene from a very high angle, which includes the bird's-eye shot explained earlier and the high angle shot. The helicopter shot is used for elaborate establishing shots or shots that end a scene or sequence to give it scope (when not part of the narrative because the characters are in an actual helicopter). An example is the beginning of Stanley Kubrick's *The Shining* (1980).

# Editing

Designing the film does not end with the visuals within the shot, like lighting or camerawork, but continues with how the various shots are then arranged. Do they flow smoothly from one shot to the next or do they harshly replace each other; is the narrative easily understandable or a complex meandering of information? Next to the visuals, editing is the strongest artistic tool for shaping the film in its narrative structure and keeping the audience continuously interested in the given narrative, yet it is one of the most complex and difficult tools to understand. Editing is not just putting one shot next to the other and following the logical flow of the story, but it has endless possibilities for not just telling the story from various perspectives but also affecting how the audience will receive the information needed to understand the story. It can be a highly intricate network of images that interlock and provide information piece by piece.

The editor chooses those takes that convey best the script content or contain the best acting and then cuts it down to a shot. This shot is then edited together with other shots in order to build and arrange a visual narrative, which is the scene. Editing is the art of assembling various shots into one scene to create the illusion of a narrative, temporal, and spatial consistency. It is also important in the editing process to allow the scene to flow and let the audience be immersed in the story instead of being aware of the shot's connections and their artificiality. The editing of a film is not only an important cinematic art form that is crucial for successfully telling the story but can also be part of the film's style.

The way the shots are assembled has a direct effect on the reading and the interpretation of the scene. Withholding information or playing with the audience's knowledge about the story makes editing the most important visual storytelling device at the end of the film production, as it is the editing that determines tension, suspense, informational flow, stylistic direction, common or unique storytelling style.

The example in Figure 6.119 explains this a bit more: there are three panels that tell a story. One panel shows a man walking down the street, the second panel shows a wristwatch, and the third panel shows a cup of coffee. From three panels, six different arrangements can be made (more if one of the shots is shown twice). Each of the arrangements tells the story from a slightly different perspective. It is obviously about a man going somewhere, about coffee being drunk, and about the time. What determines the details of the story, for example whose watch it is and who actually drinks the coffee, or whether the coffee is an actual coffee or just imagined or wanted, depends on how the various shots are arranged (and further details within the shots). There are two devices that need to be considered at all times when deciding on the arrangement of the panels: *question and answer* and *suspense*.

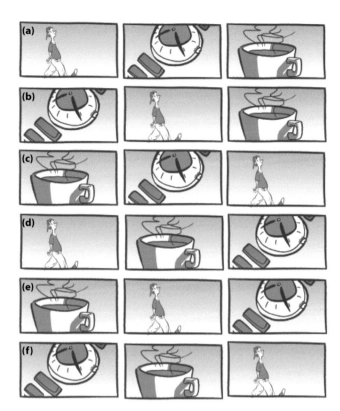

**Figure 6.119**

## Question and answer[3]

Every image either raises a question or answers one. So in the first example (Figure 6.119a, Panel 1), the question would be: who is walking down the street and why? The answer is given in the next panel: a watch. We do not know who this watch belongs to. It can either be the walking man's (if we have already seen him wearing it or if he raises his arm to look at it) or someone else's. So the answer might be either "I'm late!" or "When is he coming?" The second panel, however, also asks its own question: why is the time important? The question is given in the third picture: a coffee. So it now depends on the second panel and who this watch belongs to, to determine whether the cup of coffee is one that the owner of the watch is drinking or wants to drink once the walking man arrives. If, however, the watch belongs to the walking man, then it could mean that he is looking at his watch and thinking about whether there might be enough time to have a cup of coffee. Therefore, how the exact story is being told depends on further details in the image and information that has been given earlier or will be given later on. Every version of the arrangement in Figure 6.119 (a)-(f) can either connect the objects with the man or with the unknown person, if there is one. The arrangement also determines where the emphasis in the story is. Is the focus on the time, the coffee, the walking man,

3 For more information see Katz Steven, Film Directing Shot by Shot: Visualizing from Concept to Screen, Michael Wiese Productions, Studio City, CA, 1991. Chapter 7.

or the invisible character? And this is where editing comes in: how does the editor arrange all the shots to create an interesting visual narrative. Each version of the examples seems similar; however, what differs are the details, the length of the shots, the lighting, colors, the subtleties in the camera position, *and* how it all is arranged. All of it will affect how the audience will read the scene. In Figure 6.119b, for instance, the watch starts the scene, so it seems important. In Figure 6.119c, the emphasis is on the cup of coffee, so the meeting or the coffee itself is important.

If the lighting situations of all three images are clearly different, then obviously the watch would not belong to the walking man but also would not be in the same place as the cup of coffee.

## Suspense

*Suspense* does not just mean suspense of the type in a horror movie, for instance, but is also needed in a romance or a musical or any other genre to give the audience a reason to keep watching the story. Suspense is actually needed in any kind of story at any moment of the narrative. It is crucial for the audience to be continuously interested in the narrative. If all the information is already given in the first minute of the feature film, why bother to watch it? Information is obviously given throughout the entire feature bit by bit from its beginning to end but is also in the smallest segments of the film: its shots and their arrangement. Information needs to trickle down for the audience to beg for more and want to keep watching the story through every moment of the film. Too much continuous suspense, however, and the audience is just constantly on high alert, which can desensitize and ultimately bore. Too little suspense and the film can also be boring.

Designing the storyboard means to explore and shuffle the panels and try out each single possibility in order to find the best solution, one that creates suspense and is the most exciting version of that moment in the film's developing narrative. Which example in Figure 6.119a through (f) would have the most suspense? That can obviously only be said with the full story in mind and the purpose of that piece of board in the overall narrative.

## Editing can be divided into three categories:

1. Editing styles

2. Matches

3. Duration

### 1. Editing styles
Editing styles again are divided into the following classifications.

  a.  Continuity style
  b.  Montage
  c.  Elliptical editing

**Continuity style (also called *Hollywood classic style*):**
This style of editing is the most significant style for storytelling in today's feature films. It tells the story with spatial and temporal continuity the way events happen, one after the other. It is a very logical way of editing that strictly follows the timeline and the events in one spatial setup. Temporal jumps can happen from one scene to the next but not from one shot to the next. Within a scene, temporal and spatial continuity must be maintained. For instance, a scene in which the character is in a spaceship traveling through time and space can also be edited in the continuity style as long as the temporal and spatial continuity that the characters themselves experience is maintained. Eyeline match, the 180° rule, match on action, and diegetic sound, for instance, are all editing tools to maintain the feeling of continuity within a scene. Various editing techniques can also disrupt the continuity and put in question the temporal or spatial continuity. Parallel editing or a jump cut can connect two separate times and places and interrupt the continuity.

Continuity style editing was developed in the early years of cinema and Georges Méliès, Edwin S. Porter, and D.W. Griffith contributed to the development of seamless editing. Porter's *The Great Train Robbery* from 1903 is one of the first films that uses crosscutting, where two events occur at the same time in different locations and are combined via editing for greater suspense. In particular, American filmmaker D.W. Griffith experimented with the connection of various shots to create a seamless visual narrative, which can be seen in his questionable feature *Birth of a Nation* (1915) and *Intolerance* (1916); both are significant features in cinematic history and brought visual storytelling to a new level with innovative narrative techniques.

### Montage
By juxtaposing two shots with two contrary visuals, the viewer will see a relationship between the two and create a story or emotion that goes beyond the individual shots. Any two images will be connected by the viewer and a story will result. The shots don't have to relate temporally or spatially for the viewer to come up with an interpretation. The main idea of montage was developed by Lev Kuleshov (with his students through the Kuleshov effect) and Sergej Eisenstein in the 1910s and 1920s. Eisenstein (1898–1948) was a Soviet film director and film theorist, one of the main representatives of the Russian montage technique. The goal was to experiment with the relationship between images and by juxtaposing them to develop a language that evokes themes, reactions, political and social messages, symbols, metaphors, or simply emotions in the viewer. Russian montage after Eisenstein has five artistic methods of combining shots and stimulating a response in the audience.

  1.  **Metric**: The editing follows a specific number of frames (based purely on the physical length of the shot) and cuts to the next shot no matter what the image contains. Metric montage is the most basic technique of connecting shots to result in an emotional response by the audience.

2. **Rhythmic**: Rhythmic montage is a variation of metric montage, as it takes the shot's length based on its content and movement within the shot. It also includes cutting based on continuity and proposes visual continuity from shot to shot.

3. **Tonal**: Tonal montage deals with the emotional content of the shot, which is affected by content, light and shadow, or general mood.

4. **Overtonal/associational**: Overtonal montage is the combination of metric, rhythmic, and tonal montage to further suggest complexity.

5. **Intellectual**: Creates an intellectual meaning by juxtaposing different shots. A story or political meaning can develop in the mind of the viewer by having images follow each other that do not have anything in common. The viewer connects them and draws a conclusion.

Film examples for Russian montage are as follows:

- Sergei Eisenstein: *Battleship Potemkin* (1925)
- Sergei Eisenstein: *October* (1928)
- Dziga Vertov: *Man with a Movie Camera* (1929)

Kenneth Anger's short film *Scorpio Rising* (1964) is a masterful example of how far one can push the idea of montage by juxtaposing documentary and found footage and thus expanding on the original meaning of each of its single elements. Aside from relating images to each other, Anger also uses popular music to additionally tint the story ironically, sexually, or intellectually. This creates a complex framework of elements that comment, explain, or compare. *Scorpio Rising* is an experimental "documentary" in which Anger explores the biker subculture of Brooklyn in the early 1960s and juxtaposes shots, for instance, of bikers working on their precious bikes with a boy playing with a toy bike or scenes of a biker preparing to go out and edits them together with shots of Jesus from an early silent feature film, therefore giving the shots an ironic touch or obvious comment. Anger's film can be seen as an early "music video" as he freely cuts images together with musical hits from the early 1960s and uses popular music to further greatly enhance his montage technique. Music is an integral part of the filmic experience of *Scorpio Rising* and has as much value as the image itself. Anger uses images that have by themselves a surprise value, like the swastika, skull, the over masculinity of some of the characters, drugs, and seeming brutality. Though in combination with the music and lyrics, the meanings of the images change and allow an often sexual, homoerotic meaning or social comment. Many themes are touched upon: religion, stardom, fan-cult, biker culture, comics, American B-movies, homoeroticism, drugs, hypermasculinity, Nazism, etc. It is rather difficult to find an overall leading theme within the short film, which is its strength, as it denies easy interpretation and explanation but suggests a cacophony of themes and emotions.

### Elliptical editing

In this editing technique, the connected shots suggest an event from which parts are omitted in order to shorten the time of the scene and condense its content. The actions in the scene don't necessarily have to be restricted to a certain time or location but can show the development of an action through time. Elliptical editing is included in many scenes, as most narratives need shortening by omitting unnecessary information. For example, a man goes to a store. The camera might show him picking up his bag and keys, locking the door, and then in the next shot we see him walking down the street and reaching the store. We would not want to see him perform every single little action, follow him for 20 minutes all the way down to the store, and then continue with the story. Most of the action is cut out and only the basic framework of the action is left, enough for the audience to understand the narrative. Elliptical editing, however, goes a step further and condenses a longer time period into a short segment. An example is Jessie's memory in Pixar's *Toy Story 2* (1999) in the form of the song "When She Loved Me," about being abandoned by her original owner, Emilie. The scene includes all the happy times with Emilie but also the final separation and Jessie's emotional breakdown.

### 2. Matches

Matches can also be divided into three types.

a. Eyeline match
b. Graphic match
c. Match on action

### Eyeline match

For the audience to get the impression of following the action on screen logically and being part of the on-screen character's own visual perception, the eyeline match helps them to see what the character sees. For example, a person looks to the left, and the next shot would then show what he or she is looking at. However, we expect the object/character/visual goal to be on the eyeline, already suggested in the first shot, as shown in Figure 6.120. The character's eyes create an invisible line, the eyeline, on which, either on- or offscreen, the visual goal logically has to be located. The following shot needs to show the visual goal on that eyeline (Figure 6.121) in order for the audience to believe in the illusion. The eyeline in the first shot and the matching visual goal in the second shot give the illusion of a real connection.

### Graphic match

The graphic match uses shapes and forms of the same kind and replaces them from Shot 1 to Shot 2 using their visual and/or intellectual qualities to cover up the cut.

One of the most famous graphic matches appears in David Lean's *Lawrence of Arabia*, where Lawrence's match (the actual match to create a flame with!) is replaced by the hot rising sun.

**Figure 6.120**

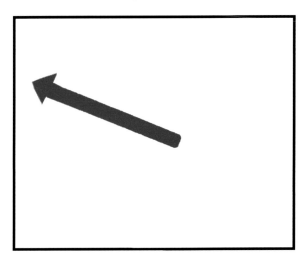

**Figure 6.121**

**Match on action**
This editing technique is the most commonly used to edit action sequences and general movement throughout continuous shots **(Video 6A)**. The movement is shown from one perspective and then the cut happens during the movement, followed by a shot from another perspective showing the continuation of that very same action from the same point at which it was interrupted. This allows uninterrupted movement through various shots.

**3. Duration**
Duration is likewise divided into three types.

  a.  Long take
  b.  Overlapping editing
  c.  Rhythm

**Long take versus planned sequence**
Any shot that is above about 1 minute long can be called a *long take*, though this depends on the era or style of the film. Action films are obviously much faster paced than a romance or

documentary. The immense technical complexities of long takes is what makes them rather rare in film history, and long takes of above 11 minutes were not possible before the rise of digital cameras. A film with only one take is, for example, *The Russian Arc* from 2002, directed by Alexander Sokurov, consisting of one continuous shot of 96 minutes. The camera moves through the Hermitage Museum, the former Winter Palace, in St. Petersburg and explores its history through various stories, an extraordinarily complex feat. Of course, this is very unusual, as the complexity of shooting a long take of 1.5 hours is immense. Every part has to be meticulously choreographed and planned ahead to avoid mishaps. A less lengthy scene is in Kenji Mizoguchi's period drama *Ugetsu* from 1953: in one scene in the hut at the end of the film, Genjurō finally comes home to see his wife Miyagi and their son. The camera comes into the empty house, follows Genjurō towards the fireplace, where all of a sudden, his wife and son are waiting for him. The scene is breathtaking as the set changes literally in front of one's eyes without a cut.

Further examples:

  •  Alfonso Cuarón: *Children of Men* (2006)
  •  TV show: *True Detective*; Season 1, fourth episode, "Who Goes There" (2014)

**Overlapping editing**
In this editing style, the action is repeated for greater impact. It can be repeated from different angles or repeated in parts of the previous shot. This style is used sometimes in action films to lengthen the duration of the action itself and to allow the audience to become immersed further in the events and aesthetics of the explosion, the fighting moment, or the result of a fight: the final blow. By repeating the final moment the audience was waiting for, the "triumph" of the hero or the "final blow" can be enjoyed and the time of the triumph is extended. Overlapping editing does have a strong impact, though it can also take the audience out of the continuity of the film, as it emphasizes its artificiality.

**Rhythm**
The length of each of the shots and their rhythmical relationship with each other creates a rhythm. Often the music and sound are either the basis of that rhythm or enhance it; however, it can also use the rhythmic movement within the shots. This technique obviously is heavily used in music videos where the music has an integral part. Rhythm can heavily influence the feel of a scene and its impact on the audience, as the speed of the shots and the shot selection have an effect on suspense and flow.

# Various editing techniques
## Cheat cut

The cheat cut is a logical mismatch between shots within a scene for the sake of compositional impact. In a scene from Vincente

Minelli's film *Meet Me in St. Louis* (1944), the cheat cut happens when a woman is on the phone with her family sitting behind her at a table. She is in a position where the camera couldn't possibly film her, as the wall the phone is mounted on would obstruct the view. By tilting the wall with the phone and allowing the woman to talk while the whole family is in the background watching her, we have a strong relationship between the phone and everyone in the room, which is the comedic basis of the conversation: the family's reaction to what the conversation is about. For the sake of composition, the logic of the set is sacrificed, and the cheat cut allows visuals that are not logical but serve the purpose of the story.

## Crosscut/Parallel editing

The crosscut combines two actions that happen in different locations at the same time in one scene. The actions don't have to necessarily relate to each other in terms of their story; they can also relate in terms of their interpretability and give an ironic twist to one element of the scene. The crosscut can create suspense, expectation, tension, or an unusual interpretation.

Examples:

*   D.W. Griffith: *Intolerance* (1916)
*   Christopher Nolan: *Inception* (2010)

## Cut-in and cut-away

The cut-in shot is much closer to the action, whereas the cut-away is further away, as the name says. Both shots don't have to contribute with their content to the action itself (they can be used as a technical device for the editor to cover unusable parts of the take, for example) but can intensify the mood of the location or also intensify the emotional connection to the character.

## Dissolve

Two scenes "melt" together in a very soft edit. The last part of the shot dissolves into the first part of the next shot, showing the two images simultaneously. This can either be a very smooth transition from one scene to the next, or it can also connect two shots by linking their visual content and therefore having them comment on each other.

## Iris

Most often used in old black and white films of the silent era, the iris is an opening or closing frame that emphasizes the focal point. It can either open a shot by highlighting the main character or location or end a shot by narrowing the focus onto a character.

## Jump cut

This is a very obvious cut that happens when the characters stay in the same position of the frame but the background or the

camera position itself slightly changes, or the characters change position but the background stays the same. This rough-looking edit takes away the fluidity of a scene and interrupts the visual flow. It can be used to either make an obvious break in a scene or to intensify a moment. It is often used to suggest a character's daily actions in the same location over a long time period. The jump cut was always considered a mistake in film editing until the 1960s, when Jean-Luc Godard first used it as an artistic device in his feature *Breathless* (1960). The film needed to be reduced in its running time and during the process the jump cut developed and gave the scenes a nervous and contemporary feel. The most famous jump cut is in Stanley Kubrick's *2001: A Space Odyssey* (1968). An ape throws a bone into the air, the bone spins around, and the following cut then shows a spaceship with the same shape turning in space. Another feature that uses the jump-cut very successfully in its title-sequence, as here the technique relates to its narrative, is Woody Allen's feature *Deconstructing Harry* (1997).

## Establishing shot and re-establishing shot

The *establishing shot* introduces the audience to the location in the beginning of a scene. It broadly presents the setting, time of day, locale and mood. Additionally, it can interpret the overall emotional exposition of the scene in metaphorical visuals. The establishing shot has the ability to bring grandness into the scene by showing the scale of the environment and not allowing the offscreen space felt in the scene to be tight or even claustrophobic. TV series add establishing shots within the show in order to widen the offscreen space and allow the imagination to go beyond the often-tight studio setting. Leaving out the establishing shot gives the viewer a sense of tightness that can be very uncomfortable at times if the space on-screen is rather small and/or cramped. The re-establishing shot reintroduces the establishing shot during the scene to either show the changed positions of the characters or to finish the scene from a wider perspective, showing a "result."

## Shot and reverse shot

These are two shots that are linked with each other to most often create a realistic sense of an ongoing conversation or communication with two or more characters. It is like watching a conversation between two characters as the bystander and just turning the head towards the respective speaker. This technique is often used in conversations; however, it can have a "TV feel" to it if not broken up once in a while. A good example for playing creatively with the shot–reverse shot pattern is Jan Pinkava's short film (by Pixar) *Geri's Game* from 1997. The character Geri, an older man, plays chess against himself and the camera shows Geri walking from one side of the table to the other in order to cover both players' positions. The camera shows Geri actually walking over to the other side, yet cuts this repeated action shorter and shorter shot after shot, omitting more and more information until the audience is convinced that Geri is now actually two older men playing chess instead of one.

## Wipe

In the wipe, either one shot pushes out another shot from left/right or up/down or a line swipes one shot away and reveals another shot underneath. An interesting film that plays with wipes in many creative ways to mimic a comic language in film is Ang Lee's *Hulk* from 2003. The aesthetic of a comic is translated both in wipes/transitions and split-screen shots into live-action feature film in endless, very creative variations.

## Superimposition

One shot is superimposed onto another shot, showing both at the same time. The visual content of the two shots comment on each other. An example is *Tuesday with Morrie*, directed by Mick Jackson (1999).

**More on editing:**

Katz Steven, *Film Directing Shot by Shot: Visualizing from Concept to Screen*, Michael Wiese Productions, Studio City, CA, 1991.
Walter Murch, *In the Blink of an Eye, A Perspective on Film Editing*, Silman-James Press, West Hollywood, CA, 2001.

# CHAPTER 7

# Vectors

The composition is an arrangement of elements that interpret the narrative in visuals. The various compositional elements lead the eye towards the focal point and thus make it much easier for the viewers to orient themselves from shot to shot and quickly read the content of the frame. Vectors, now, are visual devices that assist the eye in being sometimes guided, sometimes forced towards that very focal point or other significant elements within the frame. These vectors can define which elements are important for the story, which characters relate to each other or to objects, and how the eye is supposed to "walk" through the frame from point to point. Vectors can be seen as a street system through which the eye wanders through the image, a street system that the artist builds. The streets are predetermined and tell the eye where to go and where to stop and observe something important. They can be incredibly helpful in explaining visually a complex liaison that otherwise would be rather difficult to tell. For instance, how does one know that a ball belongs to a specific child in a group of 20 without showing it too bluntly? Vectors can do the job very subtly without the viewers realizing they are being manipulated.

## Vectors that point towards the focal point

Claude Monet's painting *The Magpie* (Figure 7.1), painted in the winter of 1868–1869, is very interesting in its use of vectors in pointing out the actual magpie. The bird is tiny and without the artist's compositional skills the viewer probably would not find the bird's position very quickly. In this light-filled winter moment, the shadows on the snow are painted with a blue tint, very different from the contemporary conventions of painting shadows black and dark. This painting is one of the earliest paintings in art where shadows are treated as not just areas that lack light but areas that also are filled with a different kind of light. *The Magpie* therefore has a significant role in art, as it literally helped to open up the world of light and shadow on the canvas.

The focal point in the scene is obviously the magpie on the left. The clearest compositional element that points out the significance of this focal area is the break in the horizontal wall,

which not only marks the focal point through its brightness in light but also in the verticals and horizontals of the wooden gate, signifying its otherness. The contrast between the dark wall and the bright island of light amidst the horizontal wooden gate is so strong that the eye cannot but be dragged towards it. The broad blocks of architecture, wall, and flora (Figure 7.2)

**Figure 7.1**

Claude Monet: *The Magpie* (1868–69).

**Figure 7.2**

DOI: 10.1201/b22148-7

**Figure 7.3**

**Figure 7.4**

# The five kinds of vectors

## Index vectors

Index vectors
are lines that are
clearly going in
one direction, defining with them not just a connection between
two parts but also giving them a clear direction.

## Graphic vectors

Those vectors
do not have a
direction, but
only suggest a
path that can
be followed
either left or right. That path is a line or shapes, colors,
textures … that the eye follows one by one.

## Continuing vectors

One vector follows
another and
creates a chain of
vectors that lead
into one direction.
Continuing vectors are the ones where the eye walks on a path,
clearly going from one point to the next.

## Converging vectors

Two or more vectors
go towards each other
and create tension.

## Diverging vectors

Two or more vectors
go away from each
other. These vectors
can, for example, show
a strong aversion
in the pose. If the
character holds the glass of wine, but rejects it and looks the other
way, the diverging vectors would accentuate this dislike.

# Vectors that don't work

In the photograph in Figure 7.5, we see two pavilions in the
gardens of the Forbidden City in Beijing (Figures 7.5 and 7.6).
The focus of the picture should be the building in the lower
left, but the vectors tell another story, as they point towards the
negative space in the sky, making *it* the focus. The sweeping

create two big shapes that taper towards the focal point
but also are darker in contrast and richer in detail. There are
three additional trees on the right that diminish in size and
detail, guiding the eye left. The wall itself also diminishes in
size towards the gate. Left of the bird there are three shapes
that decrease in size towards the magpie (Figure 7.3). These
different compositional ideas point out the significance of
the area around the magpie. What would be the vectors in
this image? Everything that leads towards the focal point
(Figure 7.4) suggests some of the various possibilities. Not
all of the suggested vectors point directly to the magpie
but into its vicinity, the general direction of the focal point.
This makes the image less rigid and gives it a more loose and
realistic appeal, rather than feeling mathematical and overly
planned.

Vectors do not have to be defined only by objects or architecture
but can also be defined by colors, textures, light and shadow, and
their separating lines.

Figure 7.5

Figure 7.6

curvatures of the ends of the roof have tremendous impact with their movement. They force the eye into the empty area of the picture, which defeats the purpose. The vectors are so dominant that the eye constantly moves into the sky, even when one tries to stay focused on the architecture, the visual forces of the roof push the eye upwards (Figure 7.6). These vectors don't work, as the focal point should be the pavilion, not the sky. Of course, if the sky is the focal point, then obviously the vectors would be perfect.

## Vectors that connect objects

Vectors not only give a direction, but they also connect objects and characters with each other and thus affect storytelling. In the illustrations in Figure 7.7a and (b), it has been determined that the focal point is the blue ball at the edge of the old-fashioned TV set. The diminishing size of the objects in Figure 7.7b create a strong graphic vector towards the blue ball, connecting it with the group. In Figure 7.7a, there is no connection. The created vector that leads away from the ball interrupts the connection that was "friendly" in Figure 7.7b and has become "unfriendly" in Figure 7.7a.

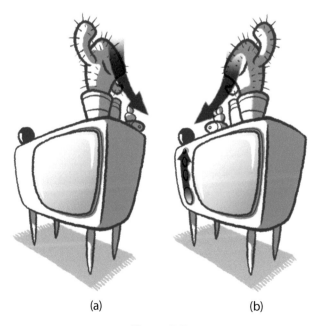

(a)            (b)

Figure 7.7

Vectors not only connect but can also separate. In Figure 7.7a, the blue ball is still the focal point because it is surrounded by nothing, which points it out as unique and thus attracts the eye. However, the strong vector of the cactus and its henchmen leads away from the ball, drastically reducing its significance, whereas in Figure 7.7b they enhance the ball's position.

The relationship between objects is more complex, however, and its direction can be controlled through various elements for which Figure 7.8a through (d) shows a couple of examples. In Figure 7.8a, the four objects are arranged in size next to each other with the same distance. The created vector's direction is not necessarily determined (despite the biggest cactus on

the left dragging the attention, the actual direction of the vector is unclear). There is also a slight movement because of the more slender shape of the left cactus and the decreasing height and increasing width of the objects.

In Figure 7.8b, the distances between the objects increase towards the right, which can affect the magnitude of the vector but does not affect its direction. Figure 7.8c changes the contrast between the four objects, which clearly pushes the focus towards the left, whereas in Figure 7.8d the focus is pushed towards the right. Contrast therefore strongly affects the direction of the vector. Because of a change of contrast, the eye sees the objects as not having the same distance towards the viewer. In Figure 7.8c, the

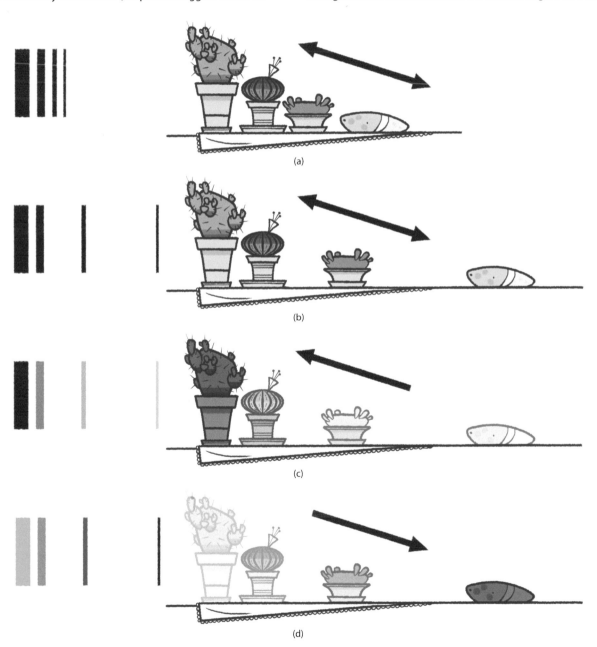

(a)

(b)

(c)

(d)

**Figure 7.8**

**Figure 7.9**

**Figure 7.10**

Utagawa Hiroshige: *The Famous Sight of Mount Fuji on the Left* (1847–52).

leftmost cactus is clearly closer to the viewer than the stone on the right. Depending on the various distances of the objects to the viewer, this line can either be straight or curved, adding movement to the composition. In Figure 7.8d, this is simply reversed, allowing the singled-out stone on the right to step into the foreground. Where in Figure 7.8c the distances between the objects actually support the object by diminishing in distance towards the focal area, in Figure 7.8d the objects increase in distance towards the stone, which does fight the smooth movement towards the stone. There are two forces fighting against each other: contrast and distance.

## Vectors that do not point towards the focal point

Figure 7.7a already explored a vector that goes against the intended precise focal point, so vectors do not have to point directly at the focal point but can also assist in defining an area of interest. In Utagawa Hiroshige's woodprint *The Famous Sight of Mount Fuji on the Left* (1847–1852) from his series *The Tokaido Road—The Fifty-Three Stations* (Figure 7.9), we see a group of travelers walking along the Tokaido Road next to a row of pine trees. Some strong vectors, created through the perspective of the trees and the street, open up the upcoming path of the travelers (Figure 7.10). The trees end halfway through the image, revealing an open field, which not only allows the famous view towards Mount Fuji but also gives the travelers breathing space on their road ahead. The vectors here do not point towards the focal point, which is obviously Mount Fuji, but frame it. The mountain is therefore not the exact focus but the famous sight within a moment of a group of travelers, which makes Fuji-san the primary focus, the travelers the secondary.

**Figure 7.11**

**Figure 7.12**

Alfred Sisley: *Boat in the Flood at Port Marly* (1876).

# Vectors and architecture

The perspective lines of architecture in a one-, two-, or three-point perspective mostly serve as vectors with a high magnitude that have a very strong effect on the reading of the image and the path the eye is guided on. In particular, one-point perspectives have this strong drag into the vanishing point. However, this can be used as an advantage to put emphasis on or around an area in the frame. Alfred Sisley's *Boat in the Flood at Port Marly* from 1876 (Figure 7.11) has the overwhelming architecture of the house of a wine merchant on the left dominate the scene (the image is very heavy in its visual weight on the left). The strong perspective lines of the house's vanishing point lead into the seemingly empty area of the flood; however, obviously the flood is the very point of this quiet scene. By having the perspective lines of the house go towards the right, the eye is constantly pushed right and cannot stay on the building without wandering into the area of the flood (Figure 7.12). Other elements are also important, like the vertical corner of the house accentuating the two men in the boat, just in front of the house. However, they serve as secondary information: the flood is compositionally the focal point.

Another artist who gleefully played often with unusual perspectives was Gustave Caillebotte, who in his famous painting *Paris Street; Rainy Day* (1877) confuses us with a very strange and utterly complex composition that is rather captivating because of its uniqueness (Figure 7.13). We see a Parisian couple walking towards us and away from Place de Dublin in Paris, at the time a newly constructed intersection, following Baron Haussmann's famous spacious redesign of old Paris into a contemporary metropolis. There are various compositional arrangements in the painting that overlap each other and thus create a complex assemblage of contemporary and fashionable Parisian life of the bourgeoisie. The image is divided in half by the green lantern in the middle serving as the axis of the frame, separating the three Parisians close to the observer and the view on the left into the street life. The horizon line is literally on the eyeline of the man (Figure 7.14), who is just off-center to the right. Many elements of the composition mirror each other, with the lamp in the middle, and thus create a balanced arrangement that still has a lot of tension as Caillebotte balances negative with positive space and also small versus big. The star-shaped structure of the street layout and the resulting pizza-slice-shaped building has two vanishing points within the picture frame. The right vanishing point is just slightly off-center and the couple's eyes are looking directly at it (red arrows in Figure 7.15), whereas the left vanishing point is just about within the frame (blue arrows in Figure 7.15). The perspective lines of the left building serve as extremely strong vectors, pulling the view towards the couple's face but also pulling it away to the left, as it can be seen as a vector with two directions. The tilt of the couple's head, the slight tilt of the umbrellas all push the view into the street of Paris, constantly forcing the viewer's eye left and right.

**Figure 7.13**

Gustave Caillebotte: *Paris Street, Rainy Day* (1877).

**Figure 7.14**

**Figure 7.15**

# CHAPTER 8

# Directions

Directions deal with the overall orientation of the image and its imbedded or suggested movement. Directions are not to be confused with vectors. Where a *vector* is part of the image, a compositional aid to point towards the focal point (or other important elements in the frame) and assist the reading of the image in its details, the *direction* is the overall movement in the frame, assisted often by the orientation of the frame itself: horizontal or vertical. Vectors can assist directions but do not have to. It is the combined vectors and forces that together drive the image's direction. A car going to the right on a horizontal street would have the car itself as a motion vector going to the right and the direction of the image would obviously also be right. A car going to the right on a horizontal street with a person in the car pointing backwards would have the car as a motion vector going to the right;

the person's pointing hand is nevertheless an index vector to the left and the direction in the entire image would be horizontal with the main forces going to the left as this is the direction the person forces our view into (characters usually overwrite the movement of objects, as we relate to characters more). In Caspar David Friedrich's painting *Das Eismeer/The Sea of Ice* (1823–1824) (Figure 8.1), the direction is defined by the movement of the ice floes. The painting has a very busy composition with seemingly no specific direction. There are piles of ice floes that are pushed into each other and banked up skywards. The highest peak of the middle spike reaches up with its sharp penetrating needle and marks the main direction of the painting. There is a directional flow in the floes that goes along the lower horizontal frame (the white lines in Figure 8.2) and swoops upwards, mainly through the bigger triangular

**Figure 8.1**

Caspar David Friedrich: *Das Eismeer* (The Sea of Ice) (1823–24).

DOI: 10.1201/b22148-8

**Figure 8.2**

floe on the right, just underneath the crushed ship, which directs upwards through many other smaller vectors towards the upper spike mentioned earlier. Above the triangular shape further to the right is the carcass of a capsized shipwreck, which got slowly buried under huge plates of ice. This sinking ship is marked with the name HMS *Griper*, which was one of the ships sailing in 1819 on a Northwest Passage expedition, a sea route through the Arctic Ocean. The HMS *Griper* never sank nor did it get crushed, so Friedrich's interpretation of the voyage is fictional. The lack of nature and life and also the scale of the ship next to the enormous ice floes makes the disaster of the ship, which is obviously not the center of the image, even more dramatic. The ship itself is not important in this lifeless northern part of the world. Its scale is insignificant compared to the gigantic plates of ice, which are overwhelming in their strength. The directional flow of the entire image is from the lower left corner towards the right frame and then upwards to the spike (assisted by the distant peak on the left side of the frame).

Directions in cinema are limited to a horizontal orientation, of course; nevertheless, there can be other directions in the overall content of the frame. In a film shot, there is also the camera movement that affects directions. A horizontal

orientation of the frame can, with a long camera tilt upwards, turn the direction of the frame vertical, and one must never forget the strength of the additional offscreen space. In addition, the orientation of the frame can change according to the movement within the frame.

## Directions in animation

The direction of the frame in animation is usually already determined, as the action happens in a horizontal cinematic aspect ratio, which always will have an emphasis on the horizontal orientation, left to right or vice versa. However, within this rigid framework the direction is affected by either the composition in the frame, the movement on- or offscreen (surround sound does affect the space in the viewer's mind), or a combination of both, plus the movement of the camera. In still images, obviously movement can only be suggested through the arrangement of the various elements, but in film images movement is split into camera/background movement and the movement of characters and objects. The direction of the character is affected by the tilt of the horizon. It not only changes the composition but obviously also changes the

**Figure 8.3**

**Figure 8.4**

**Figure 8.5**

**Figure 8.6**

**Figure 8.7**

**Figure 8.8**

effort of the character in Figures 8.3 through 8.5. It is seemingly more difficult for the character to run up the hill than down the hill, despite it being the same character. The same can be done with background elements that either accentuate the character's direction or hinder the character in his or her movement (Figures 8.6 through 8.8). The strictly vertical lines in Figure 8.6 seem to slightly hinder the character's effort and speed compared to the same image without the vertical lines in Figure 8.3. The forward tilting vertical lines in Figure 8.7 seem to make it easier for the character to run, whereas the backwards tilted lines in Figure 8.8 seem to go against the character's movement and it takes more effort to run. In animation, there is a strong relationship between character movement and the setting. The character's path is already predetermined and can be integrated into the set design to either support or hinder the character's path. Often the background already shows in its arrangement of the various elements where the character

will be moving within the set. The movement of the character can therefore define the accessibility of the set, very much like in a computer game: if the player isn't supposed to walk his character into a certain area of the environment, it is blocked with an object. How far this relationship between character action and background design and layout is pushed depends of course on the design direction. Camera pans and camera movement provide good possibilities to use the design in supporting the general direction of the movement. Because in animation the entire background can be fully controlled in its design, it is possible to adjust the set to the movement of the character and allow the background to push or drag the character through the set via correctly placed elements. For instance, in fast-paced action sequences, the background elements can be tilted in order to enhance the feeling of speed. This can be seen in the reconstructed background by Philip DeGuard and Maurice Noble (Figure 8.9) taken from

**Figure 8.9**

Warner Brothers: *To Beep or Not To Beep* (1963); Directed by Chuck Jones; Layouts by Maurice Noble; Backgrounds by Philip DeGuard.

**Figure 8.10**

the Warner Brothers' cartoon *To Beep or Not To Beep* (1963), in which the entire path of the character moving from right to left is reflected in the positioning and tilt of the various elements in the landscape (Figure 8.10). The entire landscape keeps the movement of the coyote in mind, who is pushed by a spring on a bolder painfully towards the left. The short also has, next to the colored tilted elements shown in Figure 8.10, heavily tilted cactuses serving as a background for the speeding Road Runner, again exaggerating the actual movement of the character.

## Possible directions in a horizontal orientation

The following examples should help to see the composition not only in its individual elements but also in its overall impact on the frame and where the audience's eyes are pushed towards. The eye can either rest comfortably within the frame or seek, because of the direction in the frame, action points outside of the frame. For example, a character who looks in a close-up onto an object that is located offscreen will greatly support the direction to the offscreen space with his or her glance. The space will then increase and include the offscreen space into the happenings on-screen.

**Figure 8.11**

This image has no direction; everything is a mess and there is not one direction that dominates. The composition is all over the place, which creates a feeling of unease and nervousness.

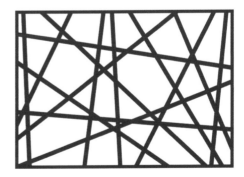

**Figure 8.12**

This composition also has no specific direction, though the image is much more controlled and less busy. Example: Willem de Kooning, *Attic*, 1949.

**Figure 8.13**

By placing a line with a stronger amplitude (in this case, a thicker line), the alterity of the line makes it more important in its direction than the smaller busy lines. The nonexistent direction from the image above changes into a slightly tilted horizontal direction. The more dominant aspect in the image, in this case the thicker line, will determine the main direction.

**Figure 8.16**

The composition is very controlled and geometric. There is a curved direction that leads to the upper right, to a point that is offscreen, but can also lead to the accumulation of the lines in the upper middle, where the image has the strongest tension. It feels as if the eye gets sucked into the upper right in a screwing motion. The inclusion of the z-axis here can be very beneficial.

**Figure 8.14**

Here, the direction is obvious; however, the lines are not in perfect order and it is unclear if the direction is going right to left or left to right. There is a loose and curved movement, organic and busy, yet not stressful. The loose organization calms the composition slightly down and gives it a comfortable flow.

**Figure 8.17**

The direction is loosely pointing into the upper right because of the converging lines. The point of interest is offscreen, upper right. There is an organic feel to the arrangement. However, the movement could also come from that point of interest and go away towards the left, depending on the story or further design aspects involved.

**Figure 8.15**

The direction is going towards or coming from one specific point on the upper right, offscreen. The magnitude of the movement is increased as the lines strive towards the corner of the image. The slightly arranged lines make the image organic, yet busy. It is organized but not completely calm.

**Figure 8.18**

The direction is clear, but there is not one point offscreen that the lines point towards; it has a general vertical direction.

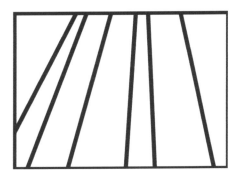

**Figure 8.19**

This composition is organized and calm. There are just a couple of lines that define the direction clearly and unmistakably as vertical. This type of image occurs in an architectural perspective with a clear one-point perspective, for instance. The point the lines converge towards lies outside of the frame.

**Figure 8.22**

In this controlled composition, the lines go along with the frame horizontally. The geometry in the composition gives the image an artificial and unorganic look, which can be highly increased if the lines have the same length. The direction is unclear and can be left to right or vice versa.

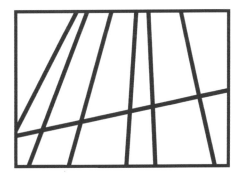

**Figure 8.20**

Because of the otherness of the horizontal line, its direction is more important than the vertical lines. In this image, which direction is dominant depends on the magnitude of each direction. If this were an architectural setting in a one-point perspective, the viewer's attention could be brought back from the offscreen vanishing point, which the eye is drawn towards in Figure 8.19, and the horizontal line would then overwrite the importance of the offscreen space.

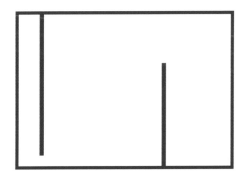

**Figure 8.23**

Reducing the number of lines to just two also defines the direction clearly. As there are only two lines, the direction is vertical. Less information changes the magnitude of the direction, not the direction itself.

**Figure 8.21**

The lines are clearly going towards a point that is on-screen, not offscreen. The focal point is inside the frame. However, if the direction of each line is going outwards (an explosion, for instance), the direction can also move away from the center, not towards it.

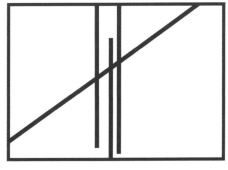

**Figure 8.24**

The direction can be controlled by the number of lines defining a direction. The more lines, the stronger the magnitude of the direction. Nevertheless because of the "otherness" of the diagonal line, it can drag attention towards itself and thus can also define the direction. In this case, it depends on the magnitude of each compositional component to determine which one will ultimately define the direction.

# Layout for 2D animation

To get the story points set up as sharply as possible and to dramatize with camera angles and choice of long-shot, close-up and so on, the flow of the story. You were really the director's arm on the visualization of the film.

**David Hilberman, on his job as a layout artist at Disney[2]**

*I personally find it very helpful to understand technically how layout for 2D animation has been done in the past on actual paper as it seems to make more sense in its use in computer programs if the traditional approach on paper is understood in its details and required accuracy.*

*Many students when working on their short films claim for instance that "the character just walks down the street" and that will take the character four seconds. But very few go into the details in their planning and know how many steps it actually takes, how fast the character needs to walk, how fast is the camera tracking alongside the character, how fast do the buildings in the background need to be moved in order for the perspective to work? Much of it is just set aside and not dealt with, but all of it is needed in order to create a shot that makes not only visually sense but also sense in terms of story-telling and emotional impact. Therefore the following is important!*

Often the question arises of what layout actually is. Layout seems to be the topic in animation that everyone is very happy to avoid and is the unicorn amongst all animation topics … the mysterious creature that is out there but no one has ever dealt with. Layout is definitely a topic that many like to ignore, as it is rather tedious and does not seem to have the glorious reputation of character animation or character design, for instance. Although the first can be true, the latter could not be more incorrect. The more one deals with layout, the more fascinating the topic becomes; it is the refinement of the single shot and scene and deals so much with visual perception and how the audience will ultimately not just see the final image but also how they will understand it. In 2009, I was in Osaka visiting the Studio Ghibli Layout Exhibition. It was an unusual exhibit, as layout is not what one would expect to see in a museum and definitely not 1,300 pages of it! It was room after room filled with layout drawings from all the Studio Ghibli films and the exhibition, because of its great success and public appreciation, has been travelling the world and spreading "layout joy" to the general public. It was the first major exhibit of this art form on an overwhelming scale. Some of the layout drawings covered entire walls because of their size. What made this exhibit so enticing is the variation within the topic and the detail into which the artists at Ghibli dove into to put most of the information of one shot into usually a single layout drawing.

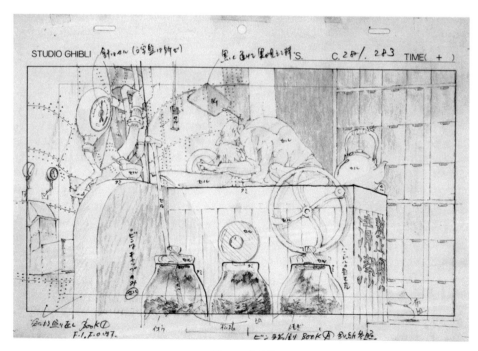

**Figure 8.25**

Layout drawing of Studio Ghibli's *Spirited Away* (2000). We can see the red line separating the character-movement from the background and also the areas where the characters actions intersect with the props, like the glass containers on the floor.

---

[2] John Canemaker and David Hilberman, *Cartoonist Profiles*, Vol. 48 (December 1980).

**Figure 8.26**

Layout drawing of Studio Ghibli's *Spirited Away* (2000). Here we see again the red lines that determine where Chihiro's shoes intersect with the background and we also see the perspective of Chihiro in the back of the shot and the front. Also light and shadow are indicated in blue.

In his book *Setting the Scene: The Art and Evolution of Animation Layout*, Fraser McLean describes *layout* as "… the marriage of storytelling and composition; it is the art of placing moving storytelling images within a frame so that they can unfold before us in real time." I would add that it is the blueprint of the artistic and technical information of every shot in order to provide the best visual storytelling for the animated shot. Layout is not equally done in every studio worldwide, as every company has its own procedure and each studio defines it in a different way. 2D layout can be very different from 3D layout in its technical details. Therefore layout is not, like most topics in animation for that matter, the most precise of animation topics. But there is a common direction amongst most of the studios and in the following I provide a general overview.

In an animated film, the process of creating the story flow by connecting different shots to compile a scene is reversed compared with that of a live-action film. In live-action, the camera and the actors are of course on the actual set, ready to repeat the shots as often as needed. The camera operator chooses the camera position that best conveys the content of the script. He or she can have different camera setups to shoot the scene from various angles. The actors on the set have the possibility to deliver different versions of their scene and improve the impact of their acting by repeating their part again and again until the director is satisfied with the results. This can produce a high number of different shot options for a particular part of the script. In the editing

process, the editor and director have then various shots to choose from, to edit the best possible scene. In animation, the actual production is reversed. We cannot create 10 different versions of each shot and then pick the best for the scene. That would by far exceed the finances and work force of an animation company. The live-action movie set is already built and it is not overwhelmingly expensive to shoot various shots in the existing set (however, it is obviously expensive to build the set in the first place and hire the various people for the production). In 2D animation, for instance, every new shot has to be animated and painted from scratch; the background has to be designed, planned, drawn, and then painted, which results in very high costs for each new shot. Therefore, every single shot has to be precisely planned out before it is passed on to the next department. The final story-boarded shot, the designed characters and assets, and the final layout of the shot have to be solid and well developed before they go to the next stage in production.

### Steve Childers, layout supervisor at Warner Animation Group and Sony Pictures Imageworks, on layout

*I got into layout through scene planning on traditional (hand-drawn) animated features. By the time I entered the industry, camera work was transitioning to a digital process and no longer meant moving a physical flatbed incrementally, by hand, beneath a down-shooter. Software was developed that allowed us to take scanned animation levels, layer them in a computer, and then work out the camera mechanics before rendering. Rough layout artists at that time provided drawn reference for composition, sizing, and movement, but for the most part were not yet involved in executing moving animatics.*

*That changed with the advent of full CGI features. Suddenly, the layout department was also responsible for creating sequences of roughly blocked-out characters and camera moves with sensible "real world" lens choices. For someone like myself with limited drafting abilities (certainly nowhere near what I witnessed among the 2D layout artists), this was my chance to develop the skills for this exciting part of the animation process. I love the "big picture" aspect of CG layout—we are able to make multiple iterations at the sequence level before the process gets down to the extremely detail-intensive shot work that comes next. Working from story boards, sometimes we have a very clear vision of what to create, and other times they serve only as a launching board for new ideas, new cutting patterns. At various times, we get to play director, cinematographer, and editor as we seek to answer questions that may not always be apparent in the script or boards: does the story make sense? will the emotional beats resonate? can an audience follow what is happening? are we making the best artistic choices?*

*The goal of the layout department is to provide the director and creative leadership the best possible version of their project. It's an exciting process of sharing ideas and playing with the building blocks that create a foundation for the entire show. In most cases, no one outside the production sees the actual rough layout reels, and they aren't much to look at—little or no facial expression, unblinking eyes, characters that "slide" instead of walk. But the "hidden" work done here literally "sets the stage" for the beautiful artistry that will be added by the downstream departments.*

## Difference between storyboard and layout

Storyboard drawings are very loose sketches, only showing the most basic information to get the rough idea across. The purpose of storyboarding is to see what helps the story to be understood in a visual way with the use of film language, what shot supports the story flow, and how suspense can be maintained. It is much easier to determine the flow of a scene with loose sketches, where your attention is focused on the basics, than with refined drawings, where all the little details demand attention. In storyboard drawings, the composition of characters versus background, props, furniture, etc., is on a very basic level, if it is there at all. Precision in background details is not the point of storyboarding! It must not be concerned with the exact look of the background, because that is not its purpose. A sketch with the basic information transports the story point of the shot; it shows what rough composition helps the narrative and the mood to progress and what shots interrupt it, create suspense or expectation. Storyboards are developed with trial and error by shifting and changing the drawings quickly. Simplicity is the key of this constant flux. The final layout, on the other hand, needs detailed drawings to explain the shot in all its intricate details. Having to design the whole environment and all its pieces on one page, it is crucial to be as precise as possible and to refine the composition as much as needed. It is also necessary to support the movement of the animation with well-composed backgrounds and vice versa. The background must leave room for the animation to take place but should also support the action. The importance of layout cannot be overstated in animation! Without accurate layout pages, the information needed for every department to understand the shot is lacking.

**Figure 8.27**
Layout drawing of Studio Ghibli's *Spirited Away* (2000).

Every production starts with the storyboard, which, if it works, will obviously have to be refined at some point. In order to make the process of the production as smooth and effective as possible and for the information to be transferred from one department to the next, the animator, the background painters, the camera operator, etc., need precise instructions for those shots to fit the animation style, keep the mood once established for the entire scene, and be still logical in its story. It is crucial that the style of the movie be maintained in every shot, in every piece of animation, and in every background by all the artists involved. This is the point where the layout information is a very important tool in the process. Layout gives those instructions to every department, following the style guide and the storyboard meticulously, plus adding all the information that every department needs to know in order to produce the shot exactly as intended. The storyboard is already a rough version of the film; the layout therefore is the refined version of the storyboard pages with technical instructions and the final design of the backgrounds, architecture, props, and characters in 2D animation and with the correct position and path of the characters in the 3D set with all the needed assets and props in a computer-animated production. The layout needs to keep the freshness of the loose and often very appealing storyboard sketches and translate them into a "blueprint" version of the film. Where the storyboard suggests the backgrounds in a sketchy form and provides only rough information on characters and environment, the layout refines this and provides a final version in the planning process. It deals with pleasing compositions, character posing, the logical flow and length of the shots, the correct positioning of props, furniture, characters, etc., and in the end delivers all this information to the departments that follow in the production. Layout is the phase of the movie where every single shot has to be deconstructed and meticulously thought through. There has to be logic behind every movement of the character, every environment, and every camera movement. If a character is walking to the left and the clouds behind him are moving to the right in one shot, and in the next shot the character is still walking to the left but the clouds all of a sudden accompany the movement of the character, it will appear as a mistake on-screen, which is confusing to the audience and therefore interrupts the story flow. Even if it is not immediately recognized as a mistake, subconsciously the audience will "feel" the mistake. We can detect flaws in images on a subconscious level; they make us uneasy and often feel "wrong" even though we cannot immediately pinpoint why. The layout department has to be adamant in avoiding mistakes. We all remember scenes in movies in which we got taken out of the story just for a second by thoughts like: where has the glass gone that the character just placed on the table? Wasn't the tie leaning to the left in the last shot? Was there not a red car behind the main character? All these little mistakes require attention and result in a thought. They take attention off of those parts in the image that are essential to the story, even if only for a split second. The viewer has to quickly decide whether the mistake actually is a mistake or if it belongs to the story line. Mistakes in the layout can also cause very high costs. Faults get carried over from department to department, and in the end only the final shot might reveal the mistake. Then the entire shot has to be either fixed or redone. Accuracy therefore is not just a matter of storytelling but also a financial aspect.

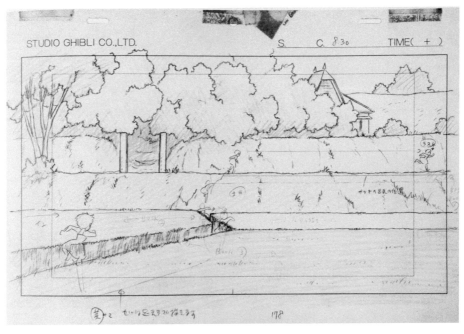

**Figure 8.28**

Layout drawing of Studio Ghibli's *My Neighbor Totoro* (1988). The path of Satsuki through the fields is indicated by various key poses in red.

Whenever we look at a new image in the movie, we have a split second to orient ourselves in the two- or three-dimensional setup of the scene. We have to decide where the characters are, where the camera is placed or from which viewpoint of the set we are observing the scene, where the light is coming from, etc. We then have to locate the main character and read their expression, listen to the dialogue, and put that piece of information into the context of the whole story. Besides that we have to listen to the music, which gives us yet more information about the scene. Those are just the basics of the image; color, composition, mood, light, and certain image styles give us even more information. There is a whole lot to be processed by the viewer and much of this information is dealt with on a subconscious level. Therefore, it is crucial for the scene to be as clearly and easily understandable as possible. All information that does not directly support the scene or the movie has to be eliminated.[3] The layout department has to make sure that every aspect of the layout is correct, so that the audience can focus on what is really important. In addition, it is the responsibility of the layout department to provide this information as easily understandable as possible.

## What information does layout convey?

Every animation studio has its very own way of producing a movie and there is no exact rule for anything … unfortunately. Some of the following is not used by all studios in their layout production; it is just a guideline for what *can* appear on a layout drawing or as layout information in a CG production.

## Technical information

- Production title and company name (usually on the top left or right or bottom right).
- Scene and shot number (top right).
- Shot length (top right).
- Aspect ratio and field size (12 fld, 16 fld or HD fld).

## Camera instructions

- Camera view.
- Camera movement (zoom in/zoom out; pan, etc.) (Figures 8.29 and 8.36).

[3] There are nevertheless movies in which secondary action goes on in the background to enrich the created world of the movie, to give more information about the world in general, information that is not necessarily number one in importance to the story. For example, in the *Harry Potter* movies there are plenty of scenes where the magical world is shown through little objects or scenes here and there in the background, which do sometimes take the attention away from the main story line, but they serve as gimmicks, to make the image even more interesting and to give the audience the feeling of magic being everywhere. It can work in favor of the movie to enrich it but can come across as a trinket that drags much attention and seems "presented" rather than subtly placed. The attention should always be on the main characters and them dealing with their situation.

- Camera timing instructions: how long is the camera stagnant, how long does the camera movement last (accompanied by the animation spreadsheet).
- Angle at which the camera rotates.
- In 3D movies, the camera instructions are much more detailed, due to the closer relationship of 3D movies to live-action and the much broader range of camera possibilities (this includes any information that defines further the camera, the shot type, the camera lens, any camera simulation that needs to be done in CG).

## Background instructions

- How many parts or layers the background consists of: for the simulation of depth, backgrounds are layered (the split backgrounds can be presented on different layout pages, to show the separation more clearly).
- Overlay: the part of the background that lies above the layer of the character animation.
- Underlay: the part of the shot that lies in between background and character animation.
- Information about where the character's action might conflict with the background. In this case, the background might need to be split, and background parts then overlap the character animation instead of being behind the characters (Figures 8.25 and 8.26).
- Instructions for all the movement in the frame: character animation, special effects, and such can be marked with different colors (this is important for the background painter in order to know what belongs to the background and what to the character animation).
- Separate colors might be used to distinguish between background, characters, effects, overlay/underlay, light and shadow… (Figure 8.25)
- Information on props: every object that is touched or moved by the character in that shot must not be painted into the background. It needs to be animated by the animation department. The layout needs to be clear on this information.
- Direction and type of the light source.
- In hand-drawn animation, at some studios the entire design of each background falls under the supervision of the layout department. It is responsible for the actual arrangement of the objects within the set and the final line drawing of the background.

## Animation instructions

- Character animation path: shows the exact path of the character in the environment (Figures 8.28 and 8.36).
- In some shots, the layout department gives instructions on the step length of the characters and where the characters put down their feet.
- Suggestion of key poses, which are often guidelines. However, in TV productions those suggested poses can

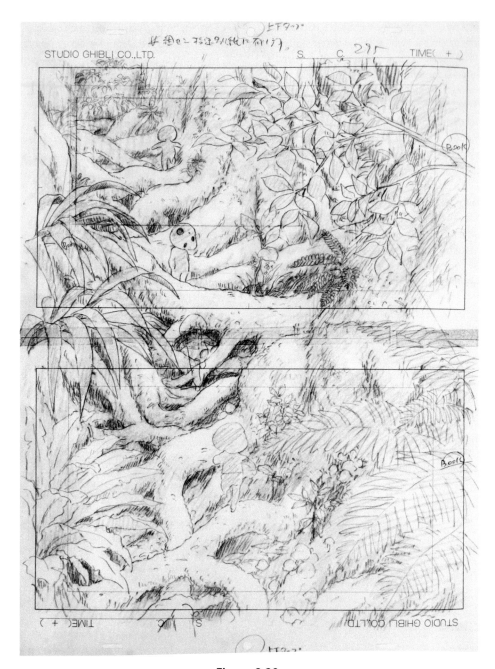

**Figure 8.29**

Layout drawing of Studio Ghibli's *Princess Mononoke* (1997). We see the path of the forest spirits walking upwards and can also see the camera movement with initial and final frame.

already be the key poses for the animation and have to be followed closely (Figure 8.28).
- Character animation perspective: shows the perspective changes of the character within the environment. This is quite important for the character animator to know the exact scale of the character. It is not always apparent in the background what the size changes of the character will be if there is perspectival change.
- Facial expression suggestions to the animators.

- Special effects animation: smoke, rain, clouds, glows, fire, rain, ripple effects, water drops, reflections, etc., can be determined in a different color.
- Definition of the ground plane and the contact of the characters with their environment: in order for the animation to be placed correctly in the environment, it is of utmost importance that the layout be precise, so that the animator can take the layout as an exact reference for the ground level or any background elements that are in direct contact

with the character (like a wall the character leans on, or stairs he steps on). If the layout in that area is not accurate, the animation is bound to float and the contact between ground and character will be unstable.

- Light and shadow information for the character: the shadows are usually also clearly marked with a different color.
- In case, the background is very detailed and additional information for the character animation has to be shown, a second piece of animation paper is placed on top of the layout and the character information is put on the second sheet.
- The layout sheet also tells the animator where the design of the character or prop is to be found in the workbook (the book that has all the information on props and characters).

## Animation fields and field sizes for 2D animation

In the beginning of the development of animation, the audience was stunned for a while by the fact that a drawing could move by itself on-screen. The movement of the character was enough to keep the attention of the audience for a short while, and for a simple piece of animation this still might work. However, the more complicated the animation process became, the more refined the production of each shot had to be. In particular, the introduction of the camera movement needed to be translated from a live-action approach into 2D animation. Once we want the camera to explore our imaginary world on the paper, we need to be able to define where the camera should start out and where it should end. When we draw on the animation paper, we can't see yet what section of the paper the camera in the final movie is going to show. In live-action, the viewfinder in the camera clearly clarifies what part of the set is chosen and the cinematographer can design the shot composition by looking through the camera. In traditional animation, we don't have that possibility on paper. We have to find a way of projecting the viewfinder onto the paper, so that we can see the final composition as it is going to be presented on screen. For this purpose we use "field guides" in animation, which are grids printed on plastic sheets. It is also a system that allows the camera operator who will shoot the animation to find an area on the animation paper with utter precision. The *animation grid* is a preproduced and standardized field of rectangles that are all marked by numbers to make finding an area on the field guide easy and accurate. There are many different field guides depending on the aspect ratio of the animation or the type of production, TV, or feature animation (Figure 8.30).

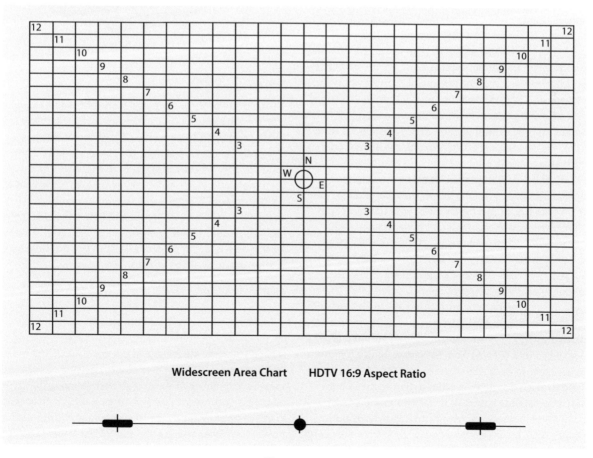

**Widescreen Area Chart**     **HDTV 16:9 Aspect Ratio**

**Figure 8.30**

Figure 8.31

We have the common formats of 10-field paper (8 ½″ x 11″), 12-field paper (10 ½″ x 12 ½″) and 16-field paper (13 ½″ x 17″). Then there are the longer formats, which are used for camera pans and backgrounds, called *wing* and *scope paper* or just *pan paper* (double-pan [2 pan]: 12-field paper [10 ½″ × 25″], 16-field paper [13 ½″ × 33″]; triple pan [3 pan]: 12-field paper [10 ½″ × 37 ½″]; quadruple pan [4 pan]: 12 field paper [12 ½″ × 64″])

The animation paper itself is always punched to keep the animation registered and to avoid it from shaking when shot under the camera or scanned in. Without the proper adjustment of each drawing, it would be more than difficult to have a smooth and precise movement. In order to keep the animation in place, the paper is adjusted by a peg bar, which is a three-pin bar that consists of two outer rectangular pins and a round pin in the middle (Figure 8.31). This specific three-pin peg bar has the ACME standard registration (ACME stands for this specific type of registration, which became somewhat of a standard in animation production worldwide). There are two different versions available: top bar and bottom bar. The top bar is for top-registered animation and the bottom bar for bottom-registered animation, meaning that the punch of the paper is either on the top or the bottom of the animation paper (and yes, you can just turn the paper around). Usually bottom-registered animation is used for character animation (it is much easier to "roll" through the animation pages and see the rough animation). The peg bar itself is attached to the animation disc, which also comes in different sizes: 12- and 16-field discs (Figure 8.32). The difference is the size of the drawing area; 16-field discs of course provide a bigger drawing area. On the peg bar is a ruler (i.e., on the better discs) with the center pin being 0 and then increasing in number towards both ends, up to 9. The measurement is done in inches and every inch is divided into 20 parts, so every half inch has 10 subdivisions (in layout you have to use those measurements on the peg bar, as a regular ruler has its inches divided differently). The rectangular pins of the peg bar are located at 4 inches left and right from the center pin. All this information is the same on the field guides that only have additionally the grid printed on. The 12-field guide counts 12 fields from the center, which is marked with a small circle, to each side of the guide. The 16-field guide has 16 fields in each direction. In order to find an area on the field guide there are the letters W, N, E, and S printed next to the center, which stands for West, North, East, and South (Figure 8.30). "3F S" means go three fields south from the center. One field has a rectangular size of 1″ × 0.75″, which is about 2.5 cm × 1.9 cm.

Figure 8.32

## Camera Zoom

The field size of 12F is the entire frame of the 12-field paper, which is the biggest possible field on that paper. If the camera needs to zoom in, the field the camera zooms into has to obviously be smaller than the 12 field we started out with. For example, the camera can start at 12F (FLD or F = fields) and then zoom into position (Pos) 5F, which means the field would decrease from 12F to 5F. In the layout this information would look as shown in Figure 8.33. The center of the two fields, 12F and 5F, has not changed, but it still needs to be indicated in the written version on the layout page as a C with a line through, for center. Written out, it would be as follows:

Zoom in from Pos(A)12F ₵

to Pos(B)5F ₵

What if you want the camera to not just zoom in but move upwards: zoom in from 12F to 5F and have the camera at the same time move up 3F on your artwork? Moving the camera up on the artwork means you move the camera north of center. In this example (Figure 8.34), the camera would start at frame position A (black), which is the start of the camera zoom, with a 12F at center, and end up at position B (in red) with 5F 3N, which marks the end of the camera zoom.

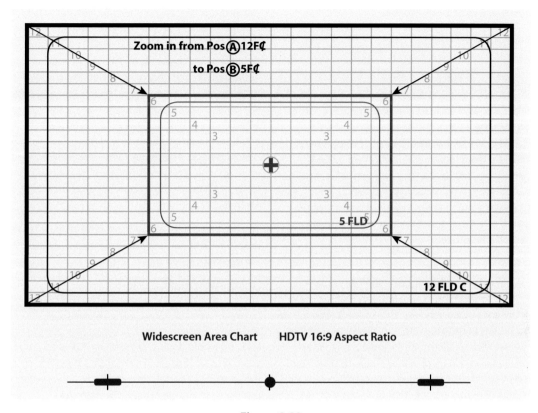

Figure 8.33

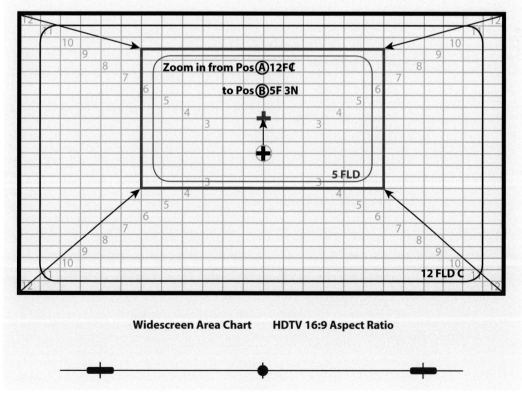

Figure 8.34

In the written version it would look like this:

Zoom in from Pos(A)12F ¢

to Pos(B)5F ¢ 3N

The position letter is always encircled to avoid confusion with other letters on the layout page! The field frame of position A would be indicated in the layout drawing with the color black, frame B with red, and the next camera position would be C in blue; then it starts again with black, then red, then blue, etc. The whole camera movement would look like Figure 8.37. It indicates the frame size of each position in the lower right corner of the frame; it also specifies with arrows that the camera zooms from position A to B, from black to red.

What happens now with your drawing when you zoom into the drawing from position A to end up at position B? Because you enlarge the drawing by zooming in, you not only enlarge the image but also the lines of the drawing. The thickness of the lines thus increases. This has to be taken into consideration, and the line has to be adjusted to still fit the style. Additionally, when using a 5F-sized field in which there will be character animation, the animator can only animate (on paper) to a certain size with precision and detail. Whether it is practical to animate or not

depends on the scale of the character in the field. The same is true for the 12F and oversized characters. It might be worth considering if a full character on 12F takes more time to animate than the same character on 10F. The artwork of background and character can only be enlarged to a certain extent, before it is distracting to the audience. The weight and thickness of the line of the character animation has to fit the background, and when either one is too heavy the image starts to look wrong and the audience will notice that it is actually a drawing that has been enlarged. All this has to be judged on a case-to-case basis, and it also depends on the style of the animation and the shot. However, it needs to be approached with caution and a sense of aesthetics.

The next step is to not only move the camera upwards 3F into position B, but also west 2F; then your camera instruction would look like this:

Zoom in from Pos(A)12F ¢

to Pos(B)7F ¢ 3N 2W

and you would end up 3F north and 2F further west (left) with your camera. The layout then shows the different field frames like in Figure 8.35. Do not forget to draw in the centers of each new position and connect them with an arrow!

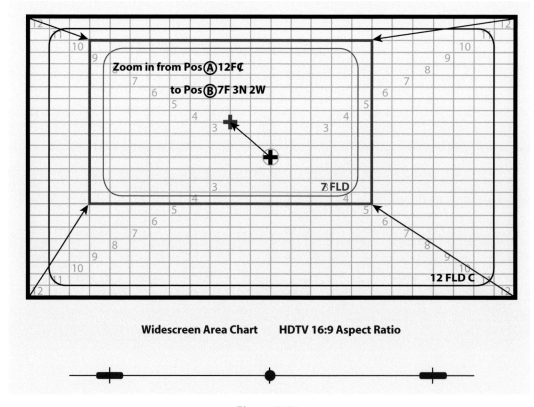

**Widescreen Area Chart**    **HDTV 16:9 Aspect Ratio**

**Figure 8.35**

## TV field guides

If you have to animate for a TV wide-screen format, the HDTV wide-screen guide is used, with a 16:9 ratio (or 1.77:1). This format is now more standard for TV animation and has replaced the 4 × 3 (1.33:1) ratio with its 12-field size, which is based on the Academy aspect ratio, which has been used since the silent film era and was then taken over by TV. The 4 × 3 16F field guide is the same ratio as the 12F one but provides a bigger working area, so the chart allows obviously a 16-field frame. Because of its bigger size, the center is not the same as the center point on the 12-field guide. It is further north and so the center always has to be indicated in the layout drawing!

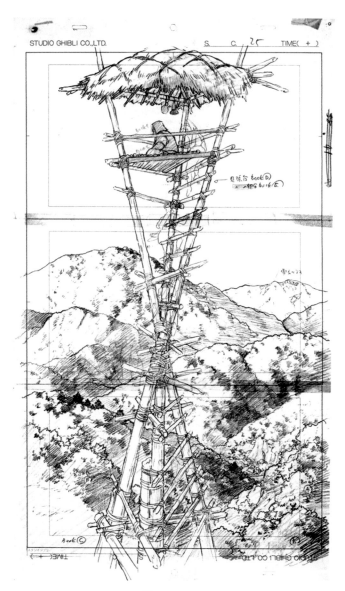

**Figure 8.36**

Layout drawing of Studio *Ghibli's Princess Mononoke* (1997). We see Ashitaka's path climbing upwards and his key poses along the way.

There is one aspect you have to keep in mind for TV: all those different formats give you a guideline of what section of your animation will be seen on-screen. But because there is still the problem of different TV types and different broadcasting systems, the final image is not presented exactly the same on every TV. Panels next to the inside of the frame can be cut off. In order to avoid important pieces of the action of your animation being trimmed, there is a TV-safe area within the frame, in which the animation will always appear on every TV. This TV-safe area is sometimes shown on the field guide, or you can purchase yet other charts that indicate for every field size the safe area, which always gets shown on every TV everywhere. In the examples in Figures 8.33 through 8.35, they are included in the frames of positions A and B.

The example in Figure 8.37 shows a zoom in from position A to position B and then a zoom out to position C. Frame C is drawn in blue.

## Limitations

If your field is seven fields large and located in the center and you need to move the field west for six fields then your seven field's frame would end up outside of the 12-field guide. You can only move the field as far as the 12 field-guide allows it. The solution for this is as follows:

- Either to change the move to only five fields west.
- Or push the center of your starting position A east one field, giving you enough space to pan west six fields.
- Or if absolutely necessary, change to a larger pan paper, which in this case would not make much sense, because shifting the center of your seven-field frame east is an obvious and simple solution.

## Camera pan

The camera pan (Figure 8.38) on pan paper (which is nearly three times the length of regular animation paper) makes it a bit more complex, as there are now three centers instead of just one. The centers of positions of A, B, and C are now indicated with Pos Ⓐ, Ⓑ, and Ⓒ on the bottom of the page; the starting and ending positions of the pan are marked with red lines and the words *start* and *stop* in red on the bottom of the layout page. Additionally, the information about east and west is obsolete, as a pan only mentions the north and south directions; left and right is indicated in relationship to the new created centers. For example, if Position B's center is 1 inch (1″) right of center (also see Figure 8.39), which is written as follows:

Pos Ⓑ 1″ LO C

That is where the trick comes in. If the center is right, it is referred to as *left* and vice versa. What needs to be understood is that

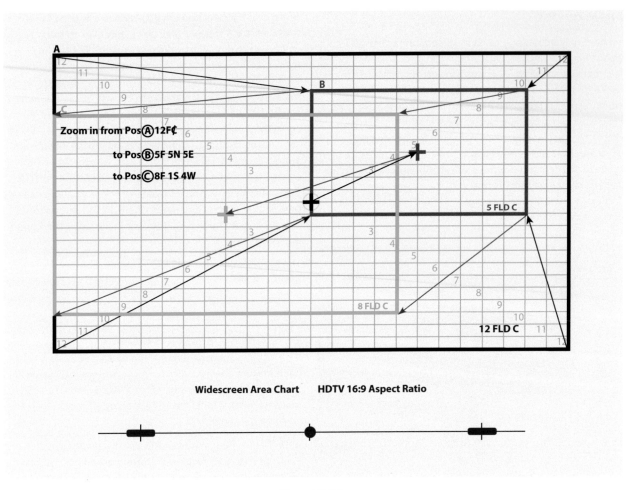

Zoom in from Pos(A)12F¢

to Pos(B)5F 5N 5E

to Pos(C)8F 1S 4W

5 FLD C

8 FLD C

12 FLD C

Widescreen Area Chart    HDTV 16:9 Aspect Ratio

Figure 8.37

The following image 12 shows a camera-pan on a sheet of pan-paper. The additional complexity here is that the center of each position changes, so we have now 3 new centers, which are marked on the bottom of the page with Pos A , B and C.

Written out the pan looks like this:

**While pan left Zoom in from Pos(A) 8F ¢**

**to Pos(B)7F 2S, 1' LO¢**

**then pan left Zoom in from Pos(C) 5F 6S, 5' LO¢**

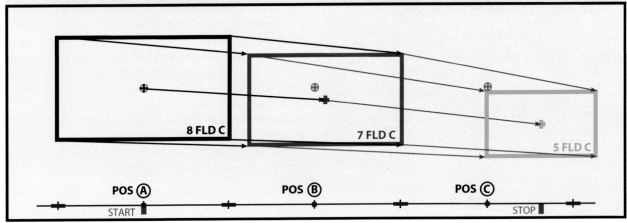

8 FLD C

7 FLD C

5 FLD C

POS (A)

POS (B)

POS (C)

START

STOP

Figure 8.38

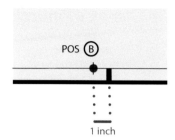

**Figure 8.39**

the center is on the layout page right, but the actual animation paper under the camera is moving left for the pan. All the camera information on the layout page is for the camera personnel, and they need to know which direction the paper will be moved. The camera itself is not moving, but the paper underneath is shifted to simulate a camera move. So, if a camera move is to the right, the paper underneath the camera has to be shifted to the left in order to get a pan to the right. In writing this would be: LO (left of) and RO (right of).

This isn't all; unfortunately, it is even more complex … much more! Because we are not only dealing with one layer (in our case, one background) but several layers of which the animation can consist: background (BG), underlay (UL), animation (ANIM), overlay (OV), effects layers …

- Background: the lowest layer of the final image
- Underlay: the layer between background and animation
- Animation layer: the layer with the character animation, effects animation, etc., which can be additionally split into various layers
- Overlay: the layer that is placed over the animation layer

There can of course be more than four different layers. There can be several UL, several animation layers, etc., depending on the complexity of the shot.

What we have to keep in mind is the complex movement of not only one layer but the movement of several layers and their relationship with each other to simulate parallax (meaning that objects that have different distances from the viewer move at different speeds if the viewer moves horizontally). For example, we have one background and one underlay. The background consists of a simple landscape with mountains and the underlay is a house. The camera view would be from a passing car, looking at the house. If both layers, BG and UL, are moved at the same speed across the camera's viewfinder, the resulting image would be a simple pan, where the house is locked into the background and the viewer in the car would see a very flat background with no simulation of depth. If the speed between the house layer and background are varied and the house moves faster than the background, both layers are separated and the house would appear as what it is: an object in front of the background moving faster from the car's perspective driving by. The further away the

object is from the moving car, the slower it seems to move. The sun in the far distance seems to stand still in the sky, whereas the trees close to the car pass the car window with incredible speed.

What could make things even more complicated is if we want a camera movement that simulates this view out of the car: a person looking out the window looking around at the landscape, observing it. Now we would have to not only move all the different layers, but we would have to change the field position within the pan. All this has to be calculated precisely for each separate layer, so that the speed of each piece of art looks correct. Today the use of computer programs makes it much easier to deal with those issues, but it is important to understand in theory how it has been shot under a traditional animation camera.[4]

Books on layout:

Fraser McLean, *Setting the Scene: The Art and Evolution of Animation Layout*, Chronicle Books, San Francisco, CA, 2011.
Walt Disney Animation Studios the Archive Series, *Layout & Background*, Disney Editions, Glendale, CA, 2011.
Mike S. Fowler, *Animation Background Layout: From Student to Professional*, Fowler Cartooning Ink, Canada, 2002.
Mark T. Byrne, *Animation: The Art of Layout and Storyboarding*, Mark Byrne Publication, Ireland, 1999.

---

4   Without the papers of Mike S. Fowler the topic of layout would have been a complete mystery to me. For the full story on layout: Mike S. Fowler, *Animation Background Layout: From Student to Professional*, Fowler Cartooning Ink, Canada, 2002.

# Case study: The complexity of the multiplane shots in Disney's *Pinocchio* (1940)[4]

**Supervising directors**: Ben Sharpsteen, Hamilton Luske

**Sequence directors**: Norman Ferguson, T. Hee, Wilfred Jackson, Jack Kinney, Bill Roberts

**Conceptual design**: Gustav Tenggren

**Art direction**: Ken Anderson, Hugh Hennesy, John Hubley, Dick Kelsey, Kendall O'Connor, Charles Philippi, Thor Putnam, Terrell Stapp, McLaren Stewart, Al Zinnen, Bruce Bushman, Arthur Heinemann, Charles Payzant

**Special effects department**: Bob Jones, Wah Ming Chang

**Camera effects technician**: Bob Broughton

**Layout**: Bruce Bushman

**Backgrounds**: Claude Coats, Merle Cox, Ray Huffine, Ed Star, Dick Anthony, Eric Hansen, Mique Nelson, Art Riley

> *Because of the success of* Snow White, *we went overboard trying to make* Pinocchio *the best cartoon feature ever made.*
>
> **Wooly Reithermann on *Pinocchio*[5]**

When the Disney artists finished *Snow White and the Seven Dwarfs* in 1937, critics and audiences were stunned and praised the feature for its lush and unique look, its technical achievements, the creation of magical cinematic moments, and that the Disney artists had finally elevated American animation to an art form in its own right. Up to that point, and especially with the release of *Snow White*, the company had produced films that conquered many of animation's great challenges. The Disney company had successfully developed convincing character animation with believable emotions, effects animation, animation storytelling in a short film format (and started to conquer features with *Snow White*), animation design with an aesthetic basis in nineteenth century book illustration, refinement of all the principles of animation, and finally, adding yet another level of realism to the Disney box of tricks: the development of the famous multiplane camera (Figure 8.40), developed at the Disney studios in 1934 by production manager Bill Garity and Ub Iwerks (who had developed his own version of a horizontal multiplane camera before 1934).[6] At the time, film critic

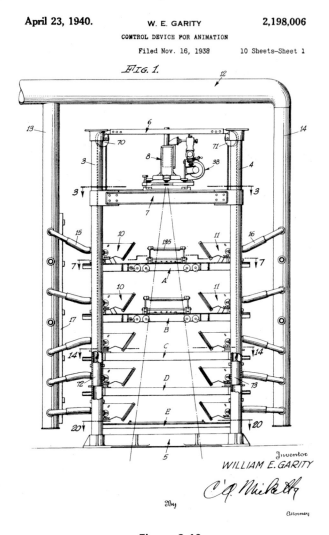

April 23, 1940.

W. E. GARITY    2,198,006

CONTROL DEVICE FOR ANIMATION

Filed Nov. 16, 1938    10 Sheets—Sheet 1

*FIG. 1.*

*Inventor*
WILLIAM E. GARITY

*Attorney*

**Figure 8.40**

Richard Schickel[7] saw the multiplane camera as the logical visual extension to Disney's art. Sound in 1928 and color in 1933 had already added more realism to the earlier black and white cartoons. Schickel wrote: "The multiplane camera thus becomes a symbolic act of completion for Disney. With it, he broke the last major barrier between his art and realism of the photographic kind."[8] This new camera setup simulates parallax at its basis, the visual perception that objects close to the camera move with faster speed compared to those objects further away. The US patent number for this "control device for animation" was filed on November 16, 1938. The patent itself was granted on April 21, 1940, the year Disney's

---

4   Due to the fact that the Disney Company did not release the image copyrights for the feature "Pinocchio" to be used in this educational section, which would have tremendously helped the understanding of the discussed compositions and shots, it is necessary for the reader to check and compare the various shots from the movie with the text to fully grasp the design. The time-codes provided relate to Disney's Blu-ray 70th Anniversary Platinum Edition (2009).

5   Gary Arnold, Pinocchio: Disney Animation at Its Peak, *The Washington Post*, December 22, 1978, Friday, Final Edition.

6   Mark Langer, The Disney-Fleischer Dilemma, in Steve Neale ed., *The Classical Hollywood Reader*, Routledge, Abingdon, 2012, p. 310.

7   Richard Schickel, American film critic, author, and documentary filmmaker, born in 1933.

8   Mark Langer, The Disney-Fleischer Dilemma, in Steve Neale ed., *The Classical Hollywood Reader*, Routledge, Abingdon, 2012, p. 311.

second feature, *Pinocchio*, was released. The multiplane camera was not just invented on the spot, though, and Walt Disney probably did not invent it himself.[9] The idea of the camera goes all the way back to the camera setup for Lotte Reiniger's silhouette film *Prince Achmed* in or before 1926 in Berlin/Germany.  The camera setup Reiniger used, however, is a simple version of the one Disney Studios later patented and called the *multiplane camera* (one can even go further back in time, as the idea of creating depth from two-dimensional layers can be found in the leveled and painted backgrounds on a traditional theater stage). Berthold Bartosch, working with Lotte Reiniger on *Prince Achmed*, also used a similar setup for his animated short film *L'idee* from 1932.

Ken Anderson, animator and designer at Disney, talks about the first steps of developing the new camera after Walt Disney ordered him to create more dimensionality with an actually animated background and its interaction with the characters for the short film *The Three Orphan Kittens* from 1935.

Ken Anderson in an interview with Dave Smith:

> *Ken Anderson*: He [Harold Helvenston] was the expert on lighting multiple levels with balance. Walt then put Jimmy Algar to modeling a foreground of trees in clay. He also had me draw three additional levels of trees—each one farther away than the preceding one. He was trying for three dimensions. Jim modeled one plane—of the multiplane—and I painted three others on glass planes. We then built an arrangement that was a horizontal setup on sawhorses, behind a platen which held the animation. Bill Garity was the mastermind of this procedure. He was both the business manager and engineer. Cy Young was the effects animator. He did the character animation in the scene. It was a scene from Snow White of the witch going through the forest. Our planes were of glass— six or seven feet long. They were mounted to slide on horizontal carriages, which were supported by sawhorses. The longest panes of glass were closest to the camera, because they moved faster and traveled farther than the more distant ones. When the three-dimensional clay trees in the foreground moved past the camera it was very real, because it was apparent that they turned showing three sides of each tree. The planes were a foot and a half apart. The speed of each plane was figured by Bill Garity. He had to interpret the supposed distance from one level of trees to the next by their size and number of feet into inches and speed. The speed was predetermined by the walking witch on each frame of film. One particularly frustrating thing was trying to paint the clay trees, for the paint wouldn't stick to the plasticine.
>
> *Dave Smith*: This was all before *The Old Mill*, then.
>
> *Ken Anderson*: Yes …[10]

But the development of more dimensionality in 2D animation was not only a topic at the Disney studios. In 1936, the Fleischer Studio filed a patent for their Setback Camera or Stereoscopic Process that allowed the cel animation to be shot in front of a three-dimensional set built with vertically staggered layers, which is a similar concept to Disney's multiplane camera that had the artwork horizontally staggered. Fleischer's setup, however, had a three-dimensional set behind the animation layer, instead of two-dimensional paintings, and with a vertical instead of a horizontal orientation. Fleischer's patent dates from the 15th of September, 2 years before Disney filed its patent. Both inventions were heavily publicized in the media at the time as technical innovations to improve each studio's output. Disney and Fleischer were competing on a continuous basis on technical advancements in their films[11] and Max Fleischer, for example, had already experimented with sound from 1924 to 1926 in his *Song Car-Tunes* series, in which the De Forest Phonofilm Optical Sound on Film technique was used. There was strong competition between the two studios and in the beginning Fleischer had much success with his characters Koko the Clown, Betty Boop (the most popular character at the time), and especially Popeye. On the Disney side, the multiplane camera and its stunning results were promoted for *Snow White* in order to show the advancements of Disney Studio's filming techniques.[12] In an article in the magazine *Modern Mechanics*, the camera was called a "monster camera." "It was always my ambition to own a swell camera," says Walt Disney, "and now, godammit, I got one. I get a kick just watching the boys operate it, and remembering how I used to have to make 'em out of baling wire."[13] Disney himself still promoted and explained the camera in 1957 in his TV show for ABC. There was obviously much deserved pride involved. The cost of Disney's new toy was estimated at the staggering sum of $75,000 (a stunning $1.45 million today). The multiplane camera had a 14 ft iron framework with up to seven shelves that were placed horizontally underneath the camera, which was mounted on top of the iron giant.[14] Each level could carry one animation layer, background layer, or effects layer and had its own lighting setup that could be adjusted. It also had its own system of wheels to move each layer left or right with absolute accuracy. The camera could, instead of just shooting one animation cel right on top of the background from above, shoot through various levels of artwork (background layers and various character layers). The shifting of each level left or right was along the direction of the peg bar, the registration pins that keep the animation in place, thus allowing utmost exactitude. The new camera had many advantages. First and foremost, though, the illusion of

---

[9] Though Joe Grant remembers in his interview with Michael Barrier from October 1, 1988: "One of his (Disney's) hobbies was getting new effects, new ideas into what he was doing. Just like his multiplane and all that sort of thing. That's all his."

[10] Didier Ghez, Walt's People Volume 9, in Didier Ghez (Ed.), *Talking Disney with the Artists Who Knew Him*, Xlibris, Bloomingdale, IN, 2010, p. 120.

[11] Mark Langer, The Disney-Fleischer Dilemma, in Steve Neale ed., *The Classical Hollywood Reader*, Routledge, Abingdon, 2012, p. 313.

[12] The magazine *Modern Mechanics* had articles on the use of the multiplane camera as early as January 1938 and also in 1944.

[13] Mouse & Man, *Time*, 0040781X, Vol. 30, Issue 26, *Time Magazine*, December 12, 1937.

[14] Mouse & Man, *Time*, 0040781X, Vol. 30, Issue 26, *Time Magazine*, December 12, 1937.

parallax, space, and depth were the most valued benefits - depth not only through complex camera movements but also in still images where the image was divided into foreground, middle ground, and background. By focusing on any one level the rest of the image would appear blurred, giving the illusion of field of depth. The multiplane camera required more than five camera operators, as each layer had to be adjusted incrementally for every frame in order to simulate camera movement in the final shot. The overall movement had to be mathematically calculated for each level so that in the end the speed of each would produce the parallax simulation that was striven for. If shadows were used in the shot, each exposed frame had to be rewound and exposed again with the shadow layer to achieve the transparency of the shadow on the ground plane. The wizardry of the multiplane camera was very successfully applied for the first time in the short *The Old Mill* (1937), and it proved itself inestimable in simulating three-dimensionality. It allowed the image to leave the flat, two-dimensional drawing and painting and added not only realism to the film but also believability. In *The Old Mill*, the multiplane camera was used for zooming in and out, dollying in and out of the image, and panning left, right, up, and down. The difference between zoom and dolly is that in a zoom the different elements of the image don't change in perspective (so there is no parallax in the image), whereas in a dolly shot the elements do change, which makes the dolly shot a true multiplane shot. Out of all the shots in *The Old Mill*, roughly a third seem to have been shot with the multiplane camera with its perspective advantages, whereas the other two-thirds are regular shots without a separation of the backgrounds into various levels. Out of the 30%, half are still shots and in half of the shots the camera is moving and used to its full glorious visual advantage.

The feature *Snow White*, released in the same year as *The Old Mill*, was intended to prove animation's entertaining abilities beyond the traditional short subject. However, that required more development in various areas, like design, effects animation, animation technology, character development, and emotion and mood to keep the story going for 1.5 hours (approximately 10 times the length of a short film!). It was clear that the short format with its continuous flow of gags would not suffice for the feature to be convincing. Disney did have critics who questioned the project of producing a feature film, because they doubted not only that anyone would be able to (or even want to) watch animated characters for 1.5 hours but also that animated characters would have the emotional depth needed to carry the story along. Despite all odds, the result was obviously convincing enough for the film to be praised from all sides. Nevertheless, it was not only the characters that contributed to the success of the film. The multiplane camera helped immensely to establish the mood of the locations and open up the image, adding space and "air" to some shots, enough to affect the feature as a whole. The shot 3B (time-code 00:12:15 – 00:12:29) with Snow White being led by a group of animals

through the forest towards the dwarfs' cottage excellently proved what the artists and technicians at Disney had mastered in terms of camera movement, character movement, layout, timing, rhythm, mood, and color (see more about this shot in Chapter 19, "Music and Sound" case study *Snow White and the Seven Dwarfs* (1937): Rhythm in scene 3B). It is astounding to witness the artistic and technical step from *The Old Mill* to *Snow White*!

Not yet satisfied with its achievement, the next feature that Disney Studios produced was yet another step in terms of complexity of camera movement and dimensionality on-screen. Disney's recipe for success was that he and his artists were never satisfied with what they accomplished but always strived for another level of complexity to improve the quality of their products. *Pinocchio* isn't really a step but another leap forward, one that still today seems impossible. Where *Snow White* is beautiful in its camera work, *Pinocchio* is nothing short of spectacular. The complexity is indeed astounding, and as a contemporary critique stated in 1940 in *Time* magazine:

> *Pinocchio* (Disney-RKO) is the world's third full-length cartoon movie.[15] It is Disney's second, and in every respect except its score his best. In craftsmanship and delicacy of drawing and coloring, in the articulation of its dozens of characters, in the greater variety and depth of its photographic effects, it tops the high standard *Snow White* set. The charm, humor and loving care with which it treats its inanimate characters puts it in a class by itself.[16]

*Snow White*'s huge success and its incoming revenues allowed Disney to spend even more on *Pinocchio* and create a lavishly decorated universe that boasts technological and artistic achievements. Woolie Reitermann (director and animator at Disney) remembers:

> We experimented with new techniques, embellished the artwork with tremendous time-consuming detail and modeled the characters to give them roundness and dimension. We even threw out a lot of costly animation, which is something we can't afford to

**Books on *Pinocchio*:**

Carlo Collodi: *The Adventures of Pinocchio*, 1883.

J.B. Kaufmann, *Pinocchio: The Making of an Epic*, Weldon Owen, San Francisco, CA, Incorporated, 2015.

John Canemaker, *The Lost Notebook: Herman Schultheis & the Secrets of Walt Disney's Movie Magic*, Weldon Owen, Incorporated, San Francisco, CA, 2014.

Ray Pointer, *The Art and Inventions of Max Fleischer, American Animation Pioneer*, McFarland & Company, Jefferson, NC, 2017.

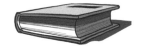

---

15  *Snow White* is the world's first hand-drawn animated feature film and Fleischer Studio's *Gulliver's Travels* from 1939 the second. The first animated feature film that has survived is Lotte Reiniger's *The Adventures of Prince Achmed* (1926). The *actual* first two animated feature films in film history (though they did not survive and thus there is no proof) are Quirino Christiani's *El Apóstol* from 1917 and *Sin dejar rastros* from 1918.

16  *The New Pictures: Time*, Vol. 35, No. 9, p. 70. 2 p, February 26, 1940.

do today … The camera boys were so creative with their angles and use of a dozen planes for a 3-D effect, they ran up a bill of $25,000 for a half-minute shot … Walt eventually had to blow the whistle and try to conserve on the spending. [17]

*Pinocchio* is decorated with elaborate multiplane shots that mimic luxurious live-action crane shots: the camera flies over the town, passes through gateways, and even follows the characters walking and singing through the town from a bird's-eye view. These shots are amongst the most complicated shots in any of Disney's features up to today, as the planning and artistry of those shots (some even with character animation) are a mathematical and artistic tour de force. The multiplane shots are placed perfectly throughout the film to add some magic in moments when it's mostly needed. Though one misconception should be clarified: the Disney films might have been shot under the multiplane camera but by no means is every shot a "multiplane shot," as this would be financially infeasible and due to their complexity impractical for an entire production. Traditional animation shots (zoom and pan) are still the norm in *Pinocchio* and all other Disney films, as they had been used since the early *Alice Comedies* in the mid-1920s. The multiplane shots are rare and only there to impress with their lavishness or to add a visual reminder to the aspired dimensionality, but were never applied on a continuous basis. In Disney's shorts up until 1937, most shots were without any camera movement at all. If the camera moved, then it was mostly horizontally without a zoom. Very few times did the camera move vertically, as the animation table was set up for a horizontal pan only, not a vertical one. But exceptions were made when needed for a short film's specific story point to be visually enticing. The slow opening of the screen's space also benefited from bringing animation technology forward and adding novelty to the shorts. For example, at the end of the storm that blows the concert members into the sky in *The Band Concert* from 1934, is a shot where the background moves vertically behind the animation layer for quite a while. This makes the storm's vertical power much more convincing. An example of an exceptional horizontal camera move is in *The Three Orphan Kittens* from 1935, in which we see the three kittens walk on a mirrored, polished, and spotless clean tile floor. When they walk, the camera tracks along and the tiles on the floor, the furniture, and parts of the wall are animated in a perspective change while the kittens are reflected in the tiles. For *The Three Orphan Kittens* Disney wanted a dimensional approach and asked animator Ken Anderson (later the designer of *101 Dalmatians*) to push the depth in the background and also the interaction of the characters with the set. Ken Anderson remembers:

> Walt found out that I knew perspective early on in my animation business, so he sidetracked me and said: Ken, I want these three little kittens (which is a picture I was doing assistant animation on)

the three little kittens to go across the kitchen floor and jump up on a step into the living room and there is a grand piano. And he said: animate these little kittens and the floors all moving and the walls, everything is moving. I did all that and it was all painted on cels and he loved it. He thought it was a really good try.[18]

This shot is obviously a gimmick in the short film and does not really need to be there in its splendor, but it was an exploratory trial to see whether and how it would work, and the finished shot most definitely adds an "ahhh" effect for the audience even today. The same shot concept with the animated floor and the panning camera can be seen in *Snow White* in the house-cleaning sequence. There was obviously exploration done at the studio for various camera possibilities to simulate dimensionality and space, aside from the typical, though very practical, right and left pan.

In *Pinocchio*, some shots were shot under a newly developed version of the multiplane camera, the so-called universal multiplane camera crane, that was actually much closer to Fleischer's stereoscopic setup, as it too used a vertical arrangement of the background plates instead of the horizontal one; this means that the camera would track horizontally into the vertical plates rather than shoot downwards like in the former multiplane setup. The new camera is mentioned in a promotional article about the feature in the magazine *Popular Mechanics*, issue 73 from January 1940:

> Cameras considered the last word when *Snow White* was filmed have been improved or replaced by new types. Among the most important is the type of universal camera crane, a development whereby instead of using a vertical method of shooting, as on the original Disney multiplane camera, the camera dollies into a scene or away from it, on the same principle as motion-picture photography in a live-action studio. The backgrounds which can be used on this camera are twice as big as those which could fit in the original multiplane setup.[19]

As mentioned above, for the new camera setup of the universal multiplane camera crane, huge backgrounds were vertically positioned. The immense size of the backgrounds was needed due to the scale change of those pieces of art farthest away from the camera and of course if there was much camera movement involved. In order to fill the entire frame of the camera with all the different background plates, the painting had to be bigger the farther it was away from the camera. The previously mentioned shot '3B' (time-code 00:12:15 – 00:12:29) of Snow White running towards the dwarfs' cottage is mostly a horizontal right to left movement (the camera follows her on the path towards screen left), which could be achieved with the multiplane camera because the height of the paper fit the height of the layer trays underneath the camera (remember that the trays could only move left or right, so horizontally, but not vertically!). The "new" universal multiplane camera crane in *Pinocchio* was actually used for the

---

[17] Gary Arnold, Pinocchio: Disney Animation at Its Peak, *The Washington Post*, December 22, 1978, Friday, Final Edition.

[18] Disney Family Album: Ken Anderson; documentary 1984.
[19] Popular Mechanics, Color Shooting in Fairyland, *Popular Mechanics*, Vol. 1, No. 73 (January 1940), pp. 16–24.

most elaborate camera movements, as the backgrounds were just way too big to fit into the older camera setup. This allowed the swooping camera flights that make those shots so light and graceful, as there was now the possibility for much bigger-scale artwork and a movement of the camera in every direction without limitation. Despite the presence of the multiplane camera and the new universal multiplane camera crane, as mentioned before not every shot in *Pinocchio* is a multiplane shot. Once in a while a shot appears that has depth to remind the audience of the realness of the world. Nevertheless, it is not just the big swooping shots that add depth to the image but the layout and colors also contribute to a strong sense of dimensionality. Many backgrounds and also some of the development work, mostly by Gustav Tenggren, have objects in the foreground that are cast in shadow and thus allow a levelling of the image into dark and light zones that will immediately create depth without using expensive multiplane shots. The strong contrast between foreground elements, middle ground, and background already produces enough dimensionality without the need to divide the background into separate layers. With the use of overlap of characters and objects, this can create a very convincing feel of spatial extension. Up until 1935, Disney's shorts were rather lacking in depth and did not yet have the color qualities that opened up the shot into three-dimensional space. The vivid colors of the shorts after 1933 still lack contrast compared to the work a couple of years later. Depth started to be much more of a concern in the *Silly Symphonies* during 1935 with the above-mentioned short *The Three Orphan Kittens* (released in October 1935). This short is the first one where perspective seems to be an actual concern in terms of the background paintings. From that point on, the *Silly Symphonies* have more contrast, which in turn creates depth. The short *The Country Cousin* (release date August 1936) marks another step in adding even more depth, as the contrast is again increased. The development ends with the short *The Old Mill*, released in October 1937, exactly 2 years after *Three Orphan Kittens*. *The Old Mill* has the strongest contrast in the films of Disney to that point, which shows the learning curve of the artists and their understanding the subtleties of image making not only in terms of animation but in terms of fine art illustration of the quality of Arthur Rackham or Hermann Vogel, whose works served as inspirational pieces for the development of *Snow White* during the same time of 1935–1937. On the other hand, there were concept artists of the caliber of Albert Hurter, Ferdinand Hovarth, and Gustav Tenggren (who himself had already worked in the style of Arthur Rackham long before his employment at Disney in 1936), professionally trained illustrators, who were responsible for translating a very romantic European illustration style into animation for *Snow White*. The strong contrast of those illustrations obviously had an impact on the short film production and not only on Disney's first feature. Tenggren himself was hired at Disney in 1936 and worked on the backgrounds of *The Old Mill*. The productions improved drastically in image quality in terms of color, contrast, composition, and depth from 1935 to 1937, and the feature *Pinocchio* marks a glorious high point in Disney's goal of

bringing the rich European illustration style onto the silver screen. "Several technical problems were solved before *Snow White* went on the road, but it was too late for changes and the lessons learned then will benefit fairyland's second full-length Technicolor production, *Pinocchio*,"[20] was written in a 1940s *Popular Mechanics* article. Additionally to the field of depth created by the separation of the background elements for the multiplane camera there is also the option of prepainting the focus into the background, which was done in parts of *Fantasia* (1941) and notably in *Bambi* (1942), to mimic Tyrus Wong's art style. Therefore, the simulation of depth is not exclusively created by the multiplane camera, but the camera is one more option for the artists to create the illusion of romanticized reality, though a very complex and pricey option. As Mark Langer rightfully states, "… the Multiplane camera and the Stereoptical Process were used infrequently after a few years, which suggests that they were more of a dead end than the road of progress. The economic consequences of using such expensive technologies simply did not justify their continued use."[21]

## The Schultheis notebook and the multiplane shots in *Pinocchio*

In 1990, a set of notebooks were discovered in Los Angeles written by Herman Schultheis, who worked at the Disney Studios for about 2.5 years during the production of *Pinocchio*, *Fantasia*, *Bambi*, *The Reluctant Dragon*, and *Dumbo* (plus the shorts *Farmyard Symphony*, *Mickey's Surprise Party*, and *Donald's Penguin*). Schultheis' broad knowledge of optics, chemistry, physics, electromechanics, and photography made him a perfect fit for the effects department at the studio, which required, due to the continuously rising need for new special effects, experts who could tackle very complex tasks in a creative way and find feasible solutions. Schultheis was also responsible for the duty of documenting events at Disney and doing research trips for some of the feature films. During his time at the studio, he assembled in his own time a notebook of 146 pages that explained, sometimes in great detail, the technical procedures of the special effects developed for some of the shots of the above-mentioned feature films. The discovery of Schultheis' notebooks, which were literally found in a drawer, gives us an invaluable insight into how some of the shots were done, as the studio itself had not deemed the preservation of the technological procedures of its effects department of worth at the time. Before the discovery of the books, the knowledge of how those complex effects were achieved, especially for *Pinocchio* and *Fantasia*, was considered lost. In his notebooks, though, Herman Schultheis describes, for example, on four pages with detailed pictures the entire setup of the shoot of the elaborate camera movement of the opening of Scene 2 from *Pinocchio*, the most elaborate camera movement

[20] Popular Mechanics, Color Shooting in Fairyland, *Popular Mechanics*, Vol. 1, No. 73 (January 1940), pp. 17–24.
[21] Mark Langer, The Disney-Fleischer Dilemma, in Steve Neale ed., *The Classical Hollywood Reader*, Routledge, Abingdon, 2012, p. 316.

ever produced at Disney in 2D animation. The notebooks serve as priceless historical records, giving us a glimpse into the complexity and importance of the effects department. Without the endless effort of dozens of specialists, the features would not have been as visually stunning as they are. It is by no means just the animators and artists who create the film, but also the technicians and special effects crews who worked relentlessly finding creative solutions of how to turn storyboard ideas into actual working shots of magical beauty. What the notebooks reveal is that some of the multiplane shots that appear in the features were not shot under the patented multiplane camera but were rather shot on the aforementioned vertical provisional camera setup constructed out of metal and wood, the so-called universal multiplane camera crane. All in all, Schultheis writes in his notes approximately 16 pages about the production of *Pinocchio*.

The following five pages of the notebooks are most important for the discussed camera movements and all give valuable information about the technical and artistic procedure of the shots. The five pages follow each other in the notebook on pages 57–64, from which pages 59 and 61–64 are examined. There are some more pages on *Pinocchio* spread throughout the notebook.

**Page 59:** This page deals with the night scene when Jiminy hops over to Geppetto's store (time-code 00:03:10 – 00:03:22). Schultheis explains the two different versions shot: the black and white version with drawings and then the full color final version. The black and white version has layers but no middle layer, though the length of the footage is noted for each section of the shot. Not just the feet of film but also the exact frame number are accurately noted. The actual picture of Geppetto's store, which fills most of the screen when Jiminy hops over, is not the background painting but the overlay painted on glass. The background is the interior of the store that is brightly lit. In between background and overlay is a diffused, airbrushed glass plate that pans while the camera is getting closer. This shot is most surprising because of it mimicking Jiminy's jumping through the means of the camera also hopping up and down and Schultheis even shows a chart, which he calls a "zigzag" chart, that was used to create the hopping effect.

**Page 61:** This is the beginning of the in-depth explanation of the: "Going to School" shot (time-code 00:26:50 – 00:27:43) that is the most famous of multiplane shots in general. Schultheis writes on the page an explanation:

> In the multiplane camera, backgrounds are broken down to various levels for three-dimensional effects. The different levels are moved at different speeds. The cameras used for shooting cartoons can be moved only up and down but not sideways, therefore the scene has to be moved. To obtain a pan move the camera stays stationary while the background is moved in the opposite direction at a fraction of an inch per exposure. A vertical pan is similar to up + down movement

of the camera. A diagonal pan follows an angular path. The universal multiplane camera moves similar to a regular camera on a dolly.[22]

At the bottom of the page he continues:

> The clock tower is on the front glass level, which is first used as animation level. Animation: Bell ringing, pigeons flying at about 25', all objects on this level are out of field. The glass is removed. The village tower and rooftops are on the next level. At about 63' all objects on this level are out of the field and the level can be removed. The next level (village square) is used for animation: kids playing, etc. This level has a clear glass section (in the arch). The camera trucks through this section (at about 69' this level can be removed) and we arrive at the last level (with animation).[23]

This explanation by Schultheis is priceless, as it is an exact account of how the "Going to School" shot was achieved.

**Page 62:** Schultheis continues with the "Going to School" shot: "While the camera trucks in, glass level after glass level is removed and illumination change, thus caused, is compensated. The first tests were made with paper drawings in pencil."[24] There had obviously been tests done, like in the night scene (time-code 00:02:50 and ends at 00:03:09), to see how this complex shot would turn out. Additionally, it is quite interesting that light changes caused by the removal of the planes needed to be adjusted.

**Page 63:** Shows in sections the entire final "Going to School" shot in photographs.

The notebooks can be either seen at the Walt Disney Family Museum in San Francisco or purchased as a facsimile in:

Canemaker John, *The Lost Notebook: Herman Schultheis and the Secrets of Walt Disney's Movie Magic*, The Walt Disney Family Foundation Press, San Francisco, CA, 2014.

**Page 64:** This page is quite fascinating as it shows pictures of not just the entire setup of the different glass panels in their wooden frames but also shows a truck from *Fuller Paints*, a company specialized in paint and glass (it also notes on the truck that "they last"), delivering the huge paintings to the effects department for the shoot.

In particular, the photographs of technicians or artists carrying these precious paintings into the effects department show the reality of the actual production and are proof that those backgrounds are more than just a magical image on a cinema screen.

[22] Canemaker John, *The Lost Notebook: Herman Schultheis and the Secrets of Walt Disney's Movie Magic*, The Walt Disney Family Foundation Press, San Francisco, CA, 2014, p. 182.
[23] Ibid.
[24] Ibid, p.183.

## Introduction shots of seq 01.0, scene 6

**The following can only be clearly understood with the actual film clip at hand. The complexity of the visuals cannot be fully explained in words. This shot starts at timecode 00:02:50 and ends at 00:03:09.**

The beginning of *Pinocchio* is as magical and spectacular as one wishes it to be for Disney's second feature film. The story of the marionette Pinocchio, however, does not very accurately follow Carlo Collodi's original story, and Jimini Cricket has visually not much in common with an actual cricket, plus there are some story points that are a little weak (that a dove brings Pinocchio the message of his father's whereabouts seems a tad too simple), but the cast of entertaining characters, the stunning visuals more than make up for its tiny shortcomings. Jiminy Cricket opens the book that tells Pinocchio's story and introduces us to a picture with a night scene in an alpine village. The moon and the starlight bathe the scenery in cold blue light and while the stars are twinkling, the camera stops once the entire frame is filled with the night sky, probably for technical purposes: the background of the town stays the same, but there is a slight blurry transition where the two different shots are connected either in the camera alone or both in camera and by changing the setup of the background plates (or is this also because of the light adjustment that needs to be done after the removal of the front glass plate, mentioned by Schultheis in his notebook?). The camera carries us over the roofs while Jiminy tells us that his travels took him to a "quaint little village …" The camera swoops all the way through Jiminy's introduction over the roofs. That is when the second layer of the background comes in with weather vanes and chimneys, roofs, and a tower painted on a glass overlay. Once these cover the entire vertical of the screen, the backgrounds are exchanged and left of the tall tower the second layer of roofs appears, tilting downwards onto Geppetto's shop. The perspective of the last panel is skewed, as the camera must make a convincing change in height from first being above the roofs and then on street level in front of Geppetto's shop. The houses' roofs on the right side of the shop can be seen slightly from a top angle. The shop itself, nevertheless, is seen perfectly from the front. Because of the darkness of the entire scene, this rather brave perspective change works perfectly fine and does not reveal its skewed lines at all. The camera stops on the cobblestone street just a small distance away from Geppetto's shop, to which Jiminy hops over to peek into the golden lit room.

It is such a perfect introduction to a fairy tale that one cannot imagine it any other way. The background of the town at night is painted on one big panel in the shape of a curve with its perspective slowly changing towards the left. It was already being considered as a camera movement in Tenggren's conceptual piece of this shot. Many elements of Tenggren's illustration appear in the final shot: the direction of the image, the compositional flow from the bright star in a curve towards

Geppetto's shop in the lower left, and during the movement there are tower and weather vanes passing the camera to create depth. It must have been astounding for audiences to witness these shots in 1940 when visuals of this quality and scope in full color had never been seen before. It still takes one's breath away today! The layout drawings that were done to develop the shot show that there might have been another approach considered, with the camera going through the town on the other side of Geppetto's house and coming in from the left, instead of flying over the roofs and then coming in from the right to dolly towards the lit window. Both layout drawings of this complex shot that still exist, show Geppetto's house at night with a brightly lit room from the same perspective. That architecture is a constant. There are actually less layers under the camera involved than one might expect in terms of depth going from the foreground all the way back to the mountains. But there is no separation of mountains and town. Neither is there a separation of mountains and village in the opening shot of Scene 2. The artists and technicians understood that the strongest effect of parallax happens with the objects that are closest to the camera. The shift of levels far away between, for example, sky and mountains is so miniscule that it is first of all extremely difficult to achieve because of the tiny increments of movement from frame to frame and it also is negligible if broad movement in the front drags the attention. The curved background painting of the night-scene that the camera is swooping through is getting covered slowly by an overlay painted on glass with weather vane and chimneys and then a tower that covers the entire vertical of the frame, so that the switch of the final background's perspective can happen unseen (time-code 00:03:02). This second part of the shot with the cobblestone street towards Geppetto's shop only has one layer. So all in all the entire shot consists of three layers, two full paintings and one layer on glass. After the cut, the shot when Jimini hops towards the shop, likewise contains of three layers, but this time the main layer is the overlay painted on glass with an open window, revealing the interior of Geppetto's room.

This is the moment where the camera clearly shows that it is not just a neutral observing agent but the character Jiminy hopping over to the shop. The nice addition is that the camera itself is hopping. To make the change from the flying camera to the hopping character's eye clear, there is a cut after which the camera is closer to Geppetto's shop than it was before. Without it, it could indeed have been difficult to convince the audience that the swooping camera flying over the roofs before, was actually not Jiminy but an invisible eye (despite being a cricket, Jiminy cannot fly in the movie). When the camera is simulating Jiminy's hops, the perspective representation of outside and inside the shop, each one on a separate layer, is astounding as both layers are time-delayed for parallax, simulating the depth of Geppetto's lit room. This is a creative and unique use of the multiplane camera crane. The explanation of the lighting and setup of the shop is beautifully documented in Schultheis' notebook as mentioned earlier. Surprisingly enough we see on a photograph the actual size of the painting of Geppetto's shop on a glass plate and it is really big, much bigger than expected. We learn that in the color version an additional airbrushed glass layer was panning between the interior and exterior layers of the shop. By moving the airbrushed gradient it diffused the image behind it. The closer the camera came towards the windowsill, the less of the gradient blurred the interior. We also see two different lighting situations in the photographs: one with the back layer lit and one with both layers lit.

## Opening shot of scene 2:

### "Going to School" (time-code 00:26:50 – 00:27:43)

Another scene, also a flight over town, clearly stands out for its complex camera work and in creating the perfect three-dimensional feel of two-dimensional artwork that has never been achieved again in this sophistication and technical perfection in a finished feature film.[25] It is the opening shot of Scene 2, when Pinocchio is about to go to school. The camera flies along a bell tower and slowly zooms into the little town where Geppetto lives and works, but this time at daytime. We pass houses and people, fountains and trees, even go through an arch onto the marketplace. The self-confidence of the Disney crew can be seen in every inch on-screen, in every color and shape, in the perfect amalgamation of character animation and backgrounds. The flawless perspective changes along the flying camera from the bell tower down to Geppetto's front door. A camera movement that is so smoothly presented that one does not even realize its tremendous difficulties in being achieved is a gem in cinema indeed. The Disney artists playfully guide the audience's attention. The leading of their eyes from one point to the next is so effortless that it does never register that there is heavy manipulation involved.

The following will dissect the scene and find the visual and artistic choices that lead to this successful shot.

### Composition, layout, and character movement

The shot consists of six different background layers plus additional character animation layers in between:

- Animation layer: doves and bell
- Upper layer 1: bell tower
- Upper layer 2: tree and stone wall
- Upper layer 3: fence and round tower
- Upper layer 4: two buildings in perspective
- Animation layer: townspeople
- Background layer 5: this is the actual background with the whole town and mountains

- Animation layer: kids running to school
- Underlay 6: final background with Geppetto's house

This shot was also not shot under the multiplane camera but the universal multiplane camera crane with artwork being placed vertically in front of the camera due to the massive size of the backgrounds. Layout artist Thor Putnam with his team was responsible for this shot, which was first tested using pencil sketches and then finally shot between October and November 1939.[26]

The shot opens with the bell tower and guides our eye screen right (time-code 00:27:02) to the roofs of the village. The left of the tower is empty of architecture and does not offer as much visual attraction as the right. The sloping mountains in the background let the image read from upper left to lower right. The doves on the bell tower accentuate that direction to the right ever so slightly. They do not just plainly fly to the right but allow the eye to wander and enjoy the beauty of the painting, as their movement happens in slopes, just giving the "idea" of moving lower right.

In the next part (beginning at time-code 00:27:05), the camera pans down along the houses and trees and then slowly tracks into the center of town (beginning at time-code 00:27:11). The center itself is already marked as such through its light and otherness amongst the houses. At the very beginning of that camera pan, the path that leads into the square one wanders along the white fence at the lower right and then down the path towards the square in a zigzag path. Objects and architecture are placed on both sides of the frame to block off the sides, keeping the eye focused on the center of the frame. Outside the center it is rather dark, vignetting the town square. The camera at that moment pans to the right (time-code 00:27:11), but once the big tree covers the right side of the frame with its strong trunk, the camera seems to avoid its dominance and changes its path and dollies into the city. The birds slowly disappear once the camera starts to push into the next part of the background. When the camera pulls in further (beginning around time-code 00:27:17), a frame within a frame appears: the tower on the left, the diagonal rooftop on the bottom, the roof above the center: all frame the marketplace in a staggered perspective. The market square has two openings: the left one is a small arch, the right one a squared opening into the second market square where Geppetto's house is located. Once the camera is on the first marketplace (the second one comes after the camera goes through the squared opening), two boys come in from the lower left with a little dog. Next to them is a man carrying a rake. From the upper left, a baker walks down with some bread under his arm. He is just about to pass through the small arch. The character animation starts exactly

25 There is, however, Williams' unfinished *The Thief and the Cobbler's* complex camera work.

26 J.B. Kaufman, *Pinocchio: The Making of an Epic*, Weldon Owen, San Francisco, CA, Incorporated, 2015, pp. 146–150.

after the upper layer leaves the frame and is removed. The camera goes towards the small arch and the squared opening is at that point off-screen. First, we see the kids and the baker coming in. Immediately our eye is drawn to the kids with the dog, as there is just more action and movement compared to the baker's walk. Secondly, the geese enter the frame, shifting the attention to the lower right, while at the same time the camera starts a change in direction likewise towards the right. The strongest force in the image, however, is the camera's movement, and every other movement within the frame is usually subordinate to it. The relationship between characters and camera, composition and color leads the eye step by step through the market square, though still allowing the eye to wander to a certain degree. Now (time-code 00:27:27) the camera is going through the squared opening into the next market square. It is interesting to mention that the underlying background painting of the second marketplace, seen through the squared opening on the right during the track-in (time-code 00:27:17), is not changing in perspective in relationship to the layer of the first marketplace on top, they are thus both still part of the same painting layer. This second market square is very different in its architectural design from the very same second market square shown slightly later during the continued track-in at time-code 00:27:26. What first was a simple house corner with two buckets, changed into a much more elaborate row of houses with architectural details, doors, and windows. The foreground architecture of the squared opening and the architecture of the second market square seen behind have now been separated into two shifting layers. Once the camera pans right and shifts its focus onto the second background, the camera pulls through the squared opening. Right afterwards, the background Panel 5 is removed and the multiplane shot turns into a regular, though large-scale, one-layered background pan to the right. However, in this instance the character animation starts before Panel 5 is removed. The camera is about to go through the gate when a little boy comes out of the door on the left, stops, turns around, and blows his nose in his mother's kerchief and gives her a kiss, then runs off to the right (time-code 00:27:30) and stops at the fountain. The two women in the doorway push the view also towards screen right, as does the pupil coming out of the alley and the old man on the corner. Nevertheless, the direction of the movement splits here. Despite the main direction of the group of kids being to the upper left, where the school is located, their movement goes against the camera panning to the right; the dominance of the camera in the shot makes the goal Geppetto's house. The focus shifts and we know that the house is now important, neither the kids nor the city anymore. The ending frame (starting at time-code 00:27:41) shows Geppetto's shop in a composition that does not focus on broad diagonal movement anymore but slowly dollies towards the shop, balancing the composition and focusing on the center when the camera finally stops. It then cuts to the door opening and Pinocchio appearing excited about his first day at school.

We were successfully introduced to the setting in an elaborate and immensely complicated establishing shot. Throughout this exquisite piece of cinematic magic, one small character moment is exchanging another and the various characters never conflict but always allow each other to be fully understood by the viewer. First it is the doves, then the kids and the baker on the square, then the geese drag the eyes to the lower right, then the boy's nose is getting blown, then we go from the kid out of the alley to the old man or we stay with the boy who is running to the fountain. Either way, we will end up at the fountain, as that's where the action is for a short moment. We are watching a boy's head getting dunked into the water and then follow all the kids to school till we finally switch directions and go along with the camera to the right. After the scene at the fountain, there is no group scene anymore; we are just watching kids run by, which allows us to change focus from the kids and the town towards the main entrance of Geppetto's house, this being enhanced by zooming into the door and creating a very strong compositional focus. At every stage, the entire shot gives us something to marvel at. There is no moment that is plain or boring. Either the beauty of the background or character movement keep one visually amazed at each second of the camera move.

## The future of the multiplane camera

After *Pinocchio*, the multiplane camera was frequently used in Disney's features *Fantasia* and *Bambi* on yet another huge scale. But later features were not as elaborate anymore. There is the famous flight over London in *Peter Pan* where there are four layers of clouds, plus the character layer and the background painting of London from above, which all create a real feel of depth and actual flight. However, the overall use was limited to specific shots. The last film that was shot with a multiplane camera was *The Little Mermaid* in 1989, though it wasn't shot under Disney Studio's own camera but by an outside contractor. Afterwards the work of the multiplane camera was done by computer programs that are much easier to use and changes are quickly performed. However, this also makes the shots themselves less precious.

As beautiful as multiplane shots are and as elaborately as they have been produced in cinema animation, they do somewhat clash with the rest of the shots that are not as lavishly presented. In some films they fit in better than in others. The more dimensionally the backgrounds are painted, the more the multiplane shots fit. The less realistic they are, the more the multiplane shots differentiate in style from the shots surrounding them. The concept of the design being flat and graphic should not clash with the camera mimicking three-dimensionality. Both have to have the same goal: either flat or deep. For example, *Alice in Wonderland*'s (1951) multiplane introduction shot is somewhat awkward, as one can clearly see the separation of the flat layers that just shift on top of each other. Because of the design of *Alice in Wonderland*, which pays more attention to its two-dimensionality, the shift of the layers points out their actual flatness, whereas in *Pinocchio*, because the background simulates depth in the paintings already, the multiplane shots are an extension of the concept of dimensionality, rather than fighting it. The shots should avoid dragging attention towards their otherness and seamlessly fit into the scene. The more Disney joined the direction of 1950s design, the less the multiplane shots seemed to fit. They are still beautiful to look at, though. Nevertheless, *Sleeping Beauty* works better, as the design is geometric and shape-oriented 1950s design, though the textures and the lighting create a sense of dimensionality, so the multiplane shots fit much better into the concept and the flow of the film, yet still do drag attention to themselves. There is always the goal to let the multiplane shots be part of the whole, but in the end they are effect shots that appear as such. *101 Dalmatians*, with its spectacular design, has very few multiplane shots and rightfully so. The ones that appear in the film aren't really adding anything to the visuals but only step out of the overall concept and do not seem necessary. The multiplane had its run and despite its limited use produced magical moments for animation that elevated the features to a whole new level of expertise and beauty. It was mostly those shots that contributed to the feeling of scale and allowed the films to be of a truly cinematic scope.

Ken Anderson has the real reasons behind the multiplane, which are obviously much more valid. He responds to a question about the use of the multiplane camera in Disney's feature *Robin Hood* from 1973:

> Practically none. Only where economically feasible because no longer are people amazed by three-dimensional effects. And they never really were, but we had to try everything. Walt always wanted to try everything. Always what has grabbed people is that they were able to believe. They could get carried away if the personality development was correct and the situations were strong. They could actually be carried away to believing that these drawn things were actually in existence and were really happening. If they get sucked into it, it doesn't matter if it is three-dimensional or flat or what the heck. Walt's original drive was to make it as real as possible, which to him meant not seeing any drawn lines. He would have loved it if we could have rendered each character as round as you can get with a photograph.[27]

Walt Disney would probably then have loved CG animation …

# Composition and thumbnail drawings

Don't fall into the trap of wanting to design a specific image that you already have in mind! If you stick to that idea too much you don't allow yourself the flexibility of being able to adjust the composition to what it needs to be instead of what you want it to be. The practice of drawing in thumbnail drawings a story moment, or a shot that depicts the action, is only one approach to come up with an interesting composition. This can be an approach that repeats ideas because you only let your conscious mind create the visuals and that is often cluttered with images that you "like" because you have seen them before and want to recreate them. A more creative approach is to trick your imagination and make it invent visuals that your conscious mind would have never come up with: you need to waken the deeper regions of your mind and let your imagination wander on paths that allow anything to happen. In Wim Wender's film *Till the End of the World* (1991), a story in which people get addicted to their own dreams, which they record at night and watch obsessively during the day, a sentence is mentioned that exactly describes this state where the mind is entertaining itself: "You're now looking at the human soul … singing to itself … to its own god!" It is like a stroll through fantasia and you just walk through it and decide which image and idea is worth chasing after and which is not. This is the ultimate state of the creative mind, a state in which it creates visuals that flow continuously and you just have to follow the path. This might all sound like esoteric bogus, but it is actually a very real state of mind if you allow it to happen. You will step into this state if you focus on your work and really concentrate, allow your mind to be just in the moment of the environment that you want to create. Focus on the smells of that place, the air, the sounds, the entire feel of it. Any disruption will stop your mind from creating and you have to start all over again. It is a meditative state that helps you to be as creative as possible. After a while you will be able to get into this state much more easily and you will be able to imagine images without much effort. But this needs to be practiced. And there are obviously myriad other ways of being creative; only because one works for me does not mean it'll work for everyone! There are more ways than just one to be creative and the more possibilities you have at your disposal, the more variety you can bring into your daily creative routine. Much of this goes back to a specific way of drawing, especially our beloved thumbnail drawings. There is something that happens in the mind that deals with unfinished drawings in a very creative way, because the mind projects something into the unfinished line work that is not yet in there. The mind steps into a conversation with the drawing and this communication is what fuels the creativity. The mind is feeling the drawing, not just drawing the drawing. The finishing comes later when the mind needs to come in and make decisions that are very rational by deciding which of the elements of composition are the ones that would help the image and which could be neglected. Of course, that does not mean that once the thumbnail drawings are done, this creative flow does not happen anymore; it can always happen and is helpful at any stage of production. But the thumbnail stage is the one where ideas get born and that is the most important stage. Refining those ideas and finishing them in an aesthetically pleasing and unique finished painting takes work, talent, and knowledge. However, a painting does not have to be polished

---

[27] Didier Ghez, *Walt's People Volume 9, Talking Disney with the Artists who knew him*, Xlibris, Bloomingdale, IN, 2010, p. 133.

**Figure 8.41**

Thumbnail drawings are the most crucial starting point in any creative production! They must never be ignored as they provide in a short time a wide range of ideas. These drawings from my sketchbook above are about 4cm wide and explore fantastical background ideas for a short film project.

and beautiful in order to be amazing. These are two different things altogether. Someone can have very poor drawings but still have superb ideas. And another can have technically stunning artwork but in the end have nothing to say.

## Abstract thumbnail drawings

Then there is yet another approach to creativity: the abstract thumbnail. For example, a character is in psychological distress. I could just show him in his room being distraught, have some proper lighting that underlines his feelings, remember a situation in my own life when I was distraught, and let all this lead my composition. But I could also approach it from the abstract perspective and figure out in thumbnail drawings what *distraught* actually might look like in abstract shapes. Is it a calm composition? A busy or confused composition, where lines go in all directions? Where is the image's weight? Is there a big weight on top of the character or is the character on top of the weight? Are shapes penetrating the character or is he in an empty space? What needs to be done is to translate the emotions of that very moment in the script into weights, shapes, and light and shadow and to feel them as blocks that are threatening the character, helping him, assisting him, fighting or caressing him. Express all that in simple arrangements of shapes and then "feel" which one is the one that describes the situation the most: from an abstract perspective! Be careful with picking those thumbnails that describe a space with furniture or graspable objects and architecture. Because we are dealing with storytelling, there will be a story in those abstract thumbnails; it is inevitable and actually wanted. The goal is to not lock down the shapes to actual objects but to allow them to be anything in this process. Focus on the drawing and let your mind replace the shapes with actual objects, design elements like light and shadow, textures, colors, or situations, but also keep it open for further interpretation. The abstract shapes allow the mind to find possibilities of what the thumbnail *could* be. A long square could be a tree, could be architecture or a leg that is really close to the camera, could be a shadow or a positive or negative shape. An already defined image with objects, furniture, and architecture is so fixed and definite, it denies the mind to go into any other creative direction. In a defined thumbnail your mind is already set and you do not allow yourself to be truly creative. An abstract thumbnail drawing that lacks details, on the other hand, gets you started with the composition and provides an open frame with the right emotional expression ready to be filled with any stories, objects, architectures, shadows, and characters. Where the tiny thumbnail drawing does not allow refinement, as it is not possible to put details into the miniscule drawing, the abstract thumbnail stops the draftsperson from thinking too realistically and too often then getting stuck in an idea even before the creative process has started. Practice with abstract thumbnails will help you tremendously in not just designing a background but designing a composition that has a purpose and an emotional basis. The point is to find a composition that expresses in an abstract way the essence of the story and the emotional state of

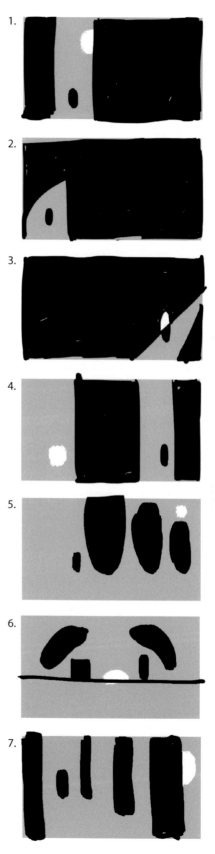

**Figure 8.42**

8.

9.

10.

11.

12.

13.

14.

**Figure 8.43**

the character. With a simple sketch, there is already a lot to be seen and an emotional base is established. The question is which one of the thumbnails expresses most the story point. This has a lot to do with how the shapes in the frame relate to each other and how they affect each other's space. Let us go through a couple of abstract thumbnails to find out what the shapes can express and how their visual weight and contrast influence the emotion.

All of the following explanations are of course just my interpretations and can be easily overwritten by a different interpretation. This can only be a broad simplification with the purpose of creating ideas, not presenting the "truth."

1. The heavy black to the left and right of the character provides only a small space that he can occupy. It is open to the sky and half the light source is showing. What those black shapes are is at this point unimportant, as they can be anything. The point in the composition is that there is something there that minimizes the space of the character and creates a shaft upwards. The character is in a semi-safe zone that is lit and is surrounded by some solid space that is dark and unknown.

2. He is in a very dark space that allows no light. The shape he is inscribed in only makes it possible for him to escape downwards. He is pushed down by the weight of the darkness above him, and the triangular shape surrounding him also pushes him down and out of the frame. His space is disconnected with the right (mirroring the curved shape would connect it with the space on the right).

3. The character is in a dark space that he passes through. The light top and the dark bottom of his body suggest that the darkness surrounding him does not swallow him completely. He is either coming towards us or walking away. The exact direction is not yet determined.

4. Two gigantic shapes are pressing the character into a small shaft. The shape on his left is so big and heavy that it seems to cut the character off from the light and the open frame on the left. Either direction he chooses, he is bumping into black. He feels slightly trapped.

5. Again the character on the left is blocked from the light source; however, the three big round shapes seem comfortable, not threatening. The character is not in a perfectly stable situation, though he is much more comfortable compared to Image 4. The huge shape right next to him, however, does feel unstable. Minor problems might have to be solved for him to reach the light.

6. The character on the right is protected and in a comfortable space, balanced and calm.

7. The character on the left has a path in front of him that he has to conquer. Light is far away and blocked from his path. He seems to come towards us (because of the strong perspective and the shapes left and right of the frame dragging him forward?). The shapes on the left or right prevent the character from leaving the screen. He has to come forward and face the problem.

8. This composition with the strict row of same shapes and a big light source being cut off suggests stability that is slightly off. The empty space suggests that something in the regularity is missing. Because the character is positioned exactly in the mirrored position of the empty spot, there is a relationship between the two. Nevertheless, the round shapes are comfortable and soothing.

9. The character on the left is in an open space with lots of emptiness surrounding him. Behind him is a solid that seems to protect him from the back. The light is coming from behind him, creating a long shadow. This feels as if the character is going into a new chapter, though bringing with him his past (if the character is going towards the right). If the character is moving towards the left he is going towards the light, leaving behind something (the emptiness might suggest loneliness?). Though the solid mass on the left seems to prevent him from getting into the light easily or prevents us from following, it could also suggest that getting into the light is final; the wall is a separation between the here and now and the future.

10. The character is half covered and has an open space behind him with a light source in the lower right. The light source is either coming up or going away. The character is in a safe zone, though nearly completely absorbed by the darkness. The light suggests either hope or the lack of it, depending on the movement of the light source. The light source does not have to be the sun; it can be a streetlight, a car light, or even a candle very close to the camera. It can be a person or an object … seeing the shape as a placeholder allows the visuals to fluctuate tremendously.

11. The character is in front of a light source, which causes a long and strong shadow. The character feels exposed and the situation seems final.

12. The darkness above oppresses the character and weighs on him. However, the light source is on his level and therefore there is hope. But because the black shape is already bigger than the grey one underneath, it seems as if the available space for the character is getting smaller. There is still enough space to leave.

13. This composition suggests a very strong balance and stability, though also a threat from outside, that the character is shielding himself from. There is some comfort in this composition.

14. This strong "explosive" shape around the character suggests either strength coming from the character as he pushes the darkness away, or that the darkness starts to press down with spikes towards the character, reducing his small space even more. The shape of the spikes suggests violent action or a threat.

15. The character is in a small space where shapes are spreading outwards, suggesting strong movement away from the character. The character feels extroverted and exposed but there is some joy and happiness in the frame.

16. This composition is making the character appear introverted. All the movement protects the character and keeps the emotion within him. This could also be interpreted as being threatening and violent.

15.

16.

17.

18.

19.

20.

21.

**Figure 8.44**

17.  This character is in a very safe place but is surrounded by chaos. The lack of order and balance creates an uncomfortable mess; nevertheless, the character is still safe and not affected by the chaos as of yet.

18.  The movement of the three large shapes towards the character gives not just a path or vector towards the character but also, because of its soft, round shapes that are seemingly weightless, lifts the character up. This composition is rather lighthearted and comfortable.

19.  The character has overcome the dark space and light is in sight, or the character is just about to be swallowed by the darkness if the light is vanishing. Because of the overwhelming visual weight of the black, the second interpretation is more likely.

20.  Trapped behind bars, the character is far away from light and comfort. He isn't in immediate danger but is not in a safe place. His position up high makes the character feel light.

21.  The character is surrounded by darkness, though a circle of light is still protecting him, giving him safety. But there is a problem next to him that might cause his fall.

The exploration of these ideas can obviously go on forever because the possibilities are endless. But after a while you get an idea of what would actually work for the scene and what wouldn't. The composition develops itself and tells you what is the right direction if you listen and think about the content of the frame and what the shapes and weights express. However, there is not very often a definite right or wrong, as it always depends on the story that is attached! How all these shapes are interpreted and turned into positive or negative shapes is open. The advantage of starting out with an abstract approach of thumbnails is that you detach yourself from trying to copy reality or a version of it and concentrate on what the pure composition would allow you to do to tell the story with the strongest emotional impact and the biggest amount of variation. Thinking abstract opens up so many more options visually than realistic images would do. You see different things in an abstract picture, because the shapes and forms can easily morph into something else. The shapes are placeholders for ideas. Image 19, for example: the dark shape underneath the character could be a hill that he is walking on, or it could be a sunbathing person very close to the camera at a beach, and in the distance you see another character walking. It could also be a car, or a huge aircraft with the round shape on the right being a turbine of another aircraft. Anything is possible because the abstract simplicity of the shapes allows your mind to wander and invent visuals that you would have never come up with on the spot. Abstract thumbnails pushed further are an excellent tool for storyboarding.

More on thumbnail drawings in Volume 2, Chapter 11.

# CHAPTER 9

# Shape and Form

## Composition of the various elements within the frame

Composition applies not only to the elements within the frame but also to the elements themselves and how they are composed and relate to each other in groups. All the points that have been discussed in composition relate equally to architecture, furniture, flora, and overall nature in the whole and in detail.

### Staging and furnishing of the set

There are two points that need to be considered:

- Aesthetics
- Logic and practicality

Aesthetics deal with the artistic interpretation of the story and the look of the space, whereas the logic deals with how the space is used in a practical way, how the different elements, rooms, furniture, etc., are distributed to create a space that can be lived in or is believable (for more on the logic of the set, See Volume 2, Chapter 36, "Believability").

Your location or set staging works very similar to the composition on a canvas. To achieve an interesting composition with the various elements in a two- or three-dimensional environment, all the parts have to be seen as relating to each other and then balanced out for the best aesthetic and logical/practical effect according to the story point. Staging has the task of simplifying the visual information and guiding the eye towards what is important and what is not. Figure 9.1 shows how objects relate to each other by changing their composition. The first example (Figure 9.1a) is just a plain tree with a plain and simple house next to it. There is nothing special or interesting about it. Both have straightforward shapes, the same height, and have geometric and symmetrical details. They are placed next to each other, have a similar volume, and the perspective is limited, the roof nearly touching the tree's crown, thus creating a tangent. Tree and house have just a minor relationship with each other and only give the information of "tree" or "house," but their lack of unique details do not specify them further. It is a cliché of a tree and a house with no personality. The second image (Figure 9.1b) has the tree taller than the house, which already makes a difference.

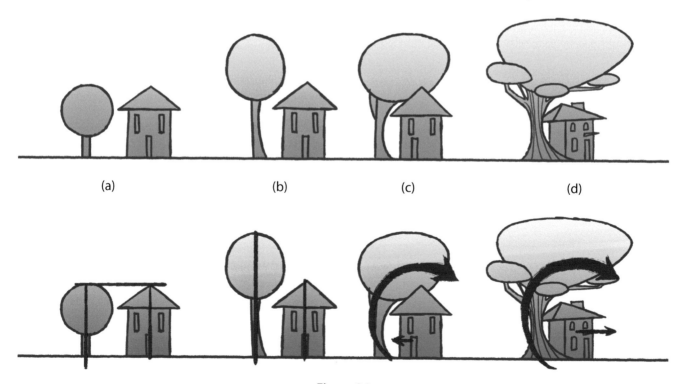

| (a) | (b) | (c) | (d) |

**Figure 9.1**

DOI: 10.1201/b22148-9

**Figure 9.2**

The trunk of the tree is not as parallel as in the image before, giving it a hint of naturalness, but the two are still just standing next to each other without communicating. The tangent is removed and perspective is at least possible but not apparent. In Figure 9.1c, the tree has a more interesting shape and bends over the house, seemingly giving it protection and therefore establishing a dialogue between house and tree. The door of the house is shifted closer towards the tree, which makes the house open up to the left, whereas the tree opens to the right. The hint of overlap of roof and crown suggests perspective, opening the three-dimensional space. However, the house seems more important, as it is in the foreground. Figure 9.1d has more details, more interesting shapes, and both tree and house open towards the right, thus having one common direction. All shapes in this fourth drawing have variation and the objects are balanced, though they still have some tension. This is just a simple example with two parts. However, if you

look at the relationship between house and tree, Chapter 6, "Character Staging and Film Language," comes in handy, plus Volume 2, Chapter 5, "Relationships." All the points that are discussed about characters and how they relate to each other can be easily applied to the relationship between objects. You just need to define the personality in the tree and the house in Figure 9.1a through (d) and then explore their relationships.

Add other parts: clouds, forest, mountains, streets, a lake, etc., and you get a vast amount of possibilities. There is no right or wrong in the examples in Figure 9.1. All have their purpose depending on their usage and target audience, the style that is required, and the story that has to be told. But the more the parts relate to each other and create a storytelling relationship, the more complex the image would be and the more content you can put into it (Figures 9.2, 9.4, and 9.5, for instance, use the composition of all the elements in the frame to create movement towards the right and have one overall shape that leads the eye). The simpler the arrangement in the image, the better it is understood and the more iconic it can be.

How this affects a single object can be seen in Figure 9.3. The two TV sets are nearly the same; however, (a) is busier than the other because its composition is not as arranged. Some minor parts are not lining up, thus creating a composition that feels slightly more uneven and out of balance. The difference is miniscule, but it does have an effect on how we feel about the object. Neither one is right or wrong; they both just have a different purpose. (a) might fit into a room that is more cluttered, whereas (b) might fit into a room that is clean and tidy.

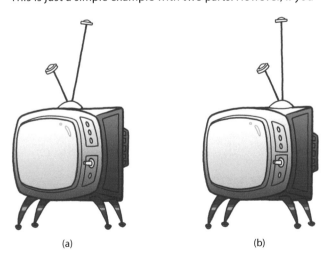

(a)                              (b)

**Figure 9.3**

There are five compositional aspects that can be played with when designing objects, furniture, flora, etc. (there is obviously also texture, light and shadow, and all the other aspects of design, but the five mentioned affect the foundation of the object compositionally):

1. Shape and form

2. Direction and movement

3. Strength and force

4. Weight

5. Tension and compression

As every picture has a composition with an arrangement of elements that follow the story point, all the objects that it consists of can likewise be designed with a compositional idea in mind; therefore, the composition as a whole can reappear in its details. The first step is to determine what the purpose of the given object is and how it relates to the overall composition. The shape then follows the direction of the established composition. (The shape can follow but does not have to. It is a style decision if it does!) In Volume 2, which deals with designing characters, there is a whole chapter on shape (see Volume 2, Chapter 12, "Shape") and most of it applies to objects also, in a loose sense. However the characters are kind of an entity on their own that relate to the environment but are not fixed to a specific area; they can freely move around the space. Objects other than vehicles are usually locked into a clearly defined compositional arrangement that only changes by changing the camera position. A tree or a house, for instance, doesn't just walk away. Therefore, shape has a different meaning in character design compared to shape in object design. Nevertheless, there are most definitely aspects in the chapter on shape that will make the following more logical. So please read Chapter 12 in Volume 2. Shape is the one foundation we can play and be creative with the most and the one that includes direction,

**Figure 9.4**

**Figure 9.5**

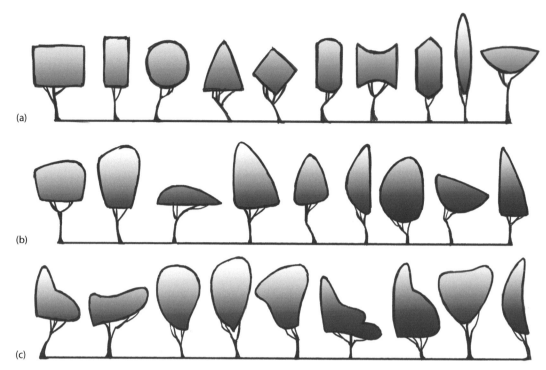

(a)

(b)

(c)

**Figure 9.6**

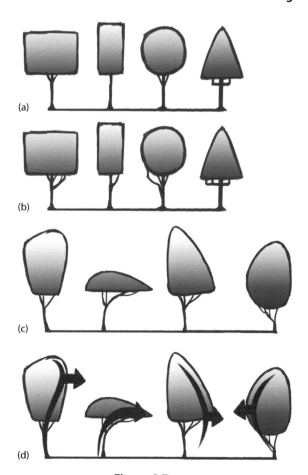

(a)

(b)

(c)

(d)

**Figure 9.7**

tension, weight, and of course exaggeration; however, it is also one that is difficult to grasp. The range reaches from realistic to cartoony, all the way to abstracted, and gives us endless options to be inventive with. As you can already see in the choice of words *realistic*, *cartoony*, and *abstracted*, the shape can assist in defining the style direction of the object, with exaggeration as one of the tools. Designing shapes does not only mean to play with the whole shape and see its silhouette change but also to play with the shapes inside of the object. Everything in the object consists of shapes, and the relationship between them is what gives the final object an interesting and hopefully unique look. Every part in the composition is important and every part affects the whole. I personally find it very helpful to inscribe a character into the object to give it personality. It does not matter if it is a tree or a stone; making shapes react to each other and letting them communicate is incredibly helpful in finding "meaning" in an object that is usually rather emotionless. The following will help to understand this.

The five aspects of shape (1. Shape and Form, 2. Direction and movement, 3. Strength and forces, 4. Weight and 5. Tension and compression; see also Volume 2, Chapter 12, "Shape") similarly apply to objects.

## 1. Shape and form

Shape is one of the most important aspects in any object, organic or inorganic. It not only defines the "character" of the object but also its "personality" to an extent. Let us look at the three different options of simple tree shapes.

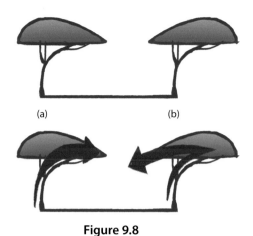

**Figure 9.8**

## Symmetric examples

The symmetry in the examples in Figure 9.6a is obviously juxtaposed by the asymmetric trunks and branches, which make the trees look like they have been pruned for a park. There is some organic feel to the trees, as they are not as rigid as those in Figure 9.7a, where the trunks are just straight. The trees are very balanced in both figures; however, in Figure 9.6a, the trunks clearly show a movement to hold up the crown.

## Asymmetric examples

As Figure 9.6b shows, the less geometric the crown is, the more organic it feels by still maintaining a feeling of control and clarity. The lack of bilateral symmetry allows these crowns to be more natural.

## Organic examples

As evident in Figure 9.6c, organic shapes feel the most natural. However, some of the shapes are so unusual for trees that they

can feel slightly odd. The last tree on the right in Figure 9.6c seems to want to bend towards the tree to the left of it.

## 2. Direction and movement

The direction of the object means its orientation and where it faces. A symmetrical object is usually seen from the front/side view, which means there is no defined direction yet, as we can see in Figure 9.7a. Trunk and crown are both seen from the front, causing a clear bilateral symmetrical object that has no direction (however, the last example in row (a) has a direction upwards, as the crown looks like an arrow). Small changes in the trunk, however, can suggest a direction, as we can see in Figure 9.7b. The orientation of the additional branch gives more emphasis to one side of the object; hence a direction is established. Once we have an asymmetrical or organic shape, there is often a clear direction the shape "flows" into (Figure 9.7c and (d)). This can be enhanced through trunk and branches, serving as vectors that additionally accentuate the direction (Figure 9.8a). However, if neither trunk nor crown follows the same orientation (Figure 9.8b), the direction can be slightly confusing, and then which element will dominate depends on the magnitude of each. This can also cause a very interesting tension within the object and thus be used as an advantage (in the example in Figure 9.8b, however, the weight of the crown is now very heavy on its right side, making the tree seem to tilt and fall to the right).

## 3. Strength and forces

The two forces that act from or on a shape are external and internal forces. Every shape or form has imbedded forces that define its spatial expansion or where the shape seems to want

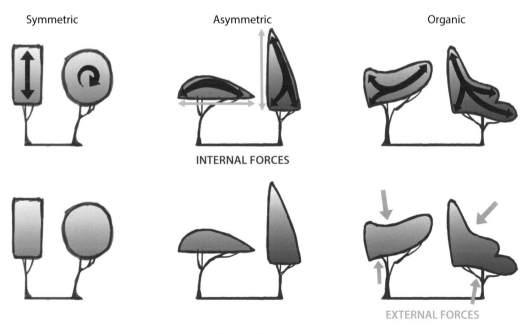

**Figure 9.9**

to expand towards. Those are the internal forces. The three different shape types of symmetric, asymmetric, and organic in the example in Figure 9.9 demonstrate how those forces can act on the shape of the crown itself, without the trunk. The symmetric shape has few internal forces acting, which makes the shape rest in itself and appear calm. The asymmetric shape has more internal forces that stretch and bulge the shape. (The green arrows visualize the tension in the straight line, which the symmetric shape does not have, as everything is straight. There is no juxtaposition between curved and straight line.) The organic shape has various forces within itself and it can feel like something wants to break free from the shape. There are few symmetric or asymmetric shapes that have external forces, but the organic shape is exposed to them. They seem to press against the shape from the outside and thus squash and stretch the shape. Forces obviously go hand in hand with the direction and movement of the shape.

## 4. Weight

The weight of the object can express an emotion, which usually connects with a character or cliché that we are familiar with. The emotional expression of the carpet in Disney's *Aladdin* (1992) is an example where the simple shape of a square interprets human poses and expresses what the carpet feels at that very moment. This can be extended to any kind of object: mimicking a human pose and then making the object feel strong, sad, happy, heavy … In the example in Figure 9.10a, the tree's overall shape seems to go up, Figure 9.10b's shape to go slightly down (or stay horizontal), and Figure 9.10c to droop down. This can be interpreted in human emotions as strong and proud for the tree in Figure 9.10a, heavy and struggling for that in Figure 9.10b, and being crushed under the weight and sad in Figure 9.10c (obviously the emotion can change with the story attached!). Weight therefore can express emotions. Where is the main weight located within the shape? How does the object react to the distribution of the weight? Strong enough to carry the weight easily, or not strong enough and struggling with the weight?

The distribution of weight can also say something about the stability of the object and how it can hold itself up (Figure 9.11a through (d)). The pivot point of the object tells us if it is in balance or not (see Volume 2 on Chapter 20, "Pivot Point"). The weight on either side of the pivot point needs to have the same volume in order to be in balance. Figure 9.11a has stability, and the volume of the crown is evenly distributed left and right of the pivot. The further the pivot is shifted, the less balance there is within the object. Figure 9.11b still has enough balance to be fully convincing in its stability. The trees in Figure 9.11c and (d) have so much imbalance that it feels like they are toppling over. Considering the weight and balance of the object and relating it to a human emotion or pose can give the object personality and character and in combination with all the other background elements greatly enhances the mood in the image.

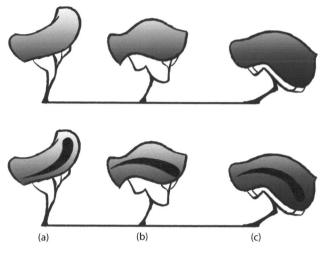

**Figure 9.10**

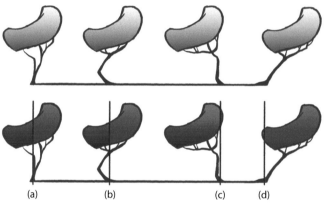

**Figure 9.11**

## 5. Tension and compression

Tension and compression happen as a result of weight and the distribution of the internal and external forces: action and reaction. They are both visual keys for the movement within the shape and also the physical reactions to its own weight. But tension and compression can also affect an object–object relationship, where one object reacts to the forces of the other, like in Figure 9.12. In the case of the simple tree in Figure 9.13, we need to consider tension and compression separately in crown and trunk, as the trunk reacts to the weight of the crown. Figure 9.13a through (c) visualize the tension and compression within the shape itself and how its weight causes the crown to gradually droop down. Where there is action, there is also reaction; where there is a force, there is a counterforce. Thus there are three options: the counterforce is stronger than, equal to, or weaker than the force. In Figure 9.13a, the inner strength within the shape lifts it up, whereas in Figure 9.13c there is not enough strength to hold up the crown, so its shape droops. Either way, the

**Figure 9.12**

## Body ratio

The more variation there is within the design, the more interesting it can be (see Figure 9.14 where the same tree only has slightly different branches, which clearly affect the tree's "personality"). The first step, however, is to recognize that the elements within the design actually do exist in the first place. Figures 9.15 shows how the trunk and crown as two different elements can be squashed and stretched and thus create a tension within the design. Another example could be Figure 9.16 where the tip and end of a pencil do relate and juxtapose. If both elements are the same in length, the design is very balanced, which can cause the object to be plain in some cases. A difference between the two is needed to give the object an inner tension. The magnitude of that tension is the key. How much is too much and how much is too little? This needs to be discussed on a case-by-case basis. However, one should always be aware of the different elements relating to each other. Figure 9.16a, for instance, has the tip of the pencil as a quarter of the length of the entire eraser, whereas Figure 9.16b has both elements with the same length; Figure 9.16c and d increase the tension between the tip and eraser dramatically.

tension within the shape causes the shape to bulge, either from its own strength in Figure 9.13a or from the lack of it in Figure 9.13c. The reaction of the trunk that holds up the crown also has three options to react to the weight of the crown: the tree trunk either is strong enough to hold up the crown (Figure 9.13d), just balance it (Figure 9.13e), or succumbs to the weight of the crown (Figure 9.13f) and bends down. Tension and compression are the result of the various forces acting upon the shapes of the object.

This is by no means just a matter of organic shapes but can also be used in any object. However, this does go hand in hand with the level of cartooniness in the style and its exaggeration (Figure 9.12), in which the tree seems to push the house away; tension and compression cause squash and stretch. But it always includes action and reaction.

## Grouping of objects

Figure 9.17 shows a location where the objects are arranged in a composition that points towards a certain spot, which would be the "stage" of the character in animation. The various objects create graphic, index, and continuing vectors and play with positive and negative space to make it clear to the audience where the character is expected to appear. Always consider how several objects group and create a single shape! Everything that is placed within the set has an impact on the grouping and the overall composition.

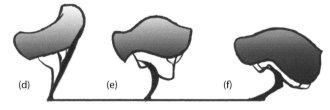

TENSION & COMPRESSION

**Figure 9.14**

**Figure 9.13**

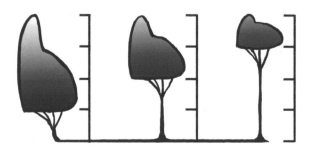

**Figure 9.15**

187

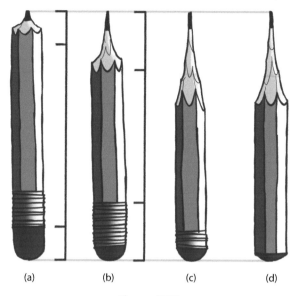

(a)　　　(b)　　　(c)　　　(d)

**Figure 9.16**

# The procedure of object design

The task was to design piles of stones that are strange and slightly surreal. It all starts, as always, with good, old thumbnail sketches (Figure 9.18a). They give you the quickest results and the widest variety of shapes and are a great starting point for your work. Do as many as you need to get a "feeling" for the shapes themselves and how much exaggeration the object demands to reach a level of stylization that fits the story and mood. The next step is the refinement of the thumbnails (Figure 9.18b), where the qualities of those sketches that seem to work are quickly explored. This "refinement" does not mean at all to just trace the drawing; it means to find the shapes that work within the object and enhance them with all the other shapes surrounding it—to explore shapes/forms, weight, directions, forces, tension and compression, and the ratios between the significant elements. The process of refining is often misinterpreted as cleaning up the drawing, but the cleanup is not going to happen for a while, as the first steps are to develop a working composition within the object itself and that does take time. What those compositional ideas could be is demonstrated in the examples in Figure 9.18e through (g), where the following points are deemed important: overall shape of the object (Figure 9.18e), directions within the object itself (Figure 9.18f), and shape variation inside of the object and how the shapes communicate with one another (Figure 9.18g; also see Figure 9.19). If one only traced the lines to clean up the thumbnail drawing, the actual comprehension of the subtle communication between those lines, shapes, tension, and balance would be neither felt nor understood. One would only consider the outside of the object without feeling the inside, its movement and intrinsic energy, the relationship of positive and negative space, the juxtaposing sizes and visual weights, and all the forces that struggle within the object. All those have to be determined, exaggerated, and weighed against each other while the drawing is refined. Without feeling it, there is no emotion in the drawing! Only when all those points are considered in the design can the final drawing happen (Figure 9.18c and (d)).

**Figure 9.17**

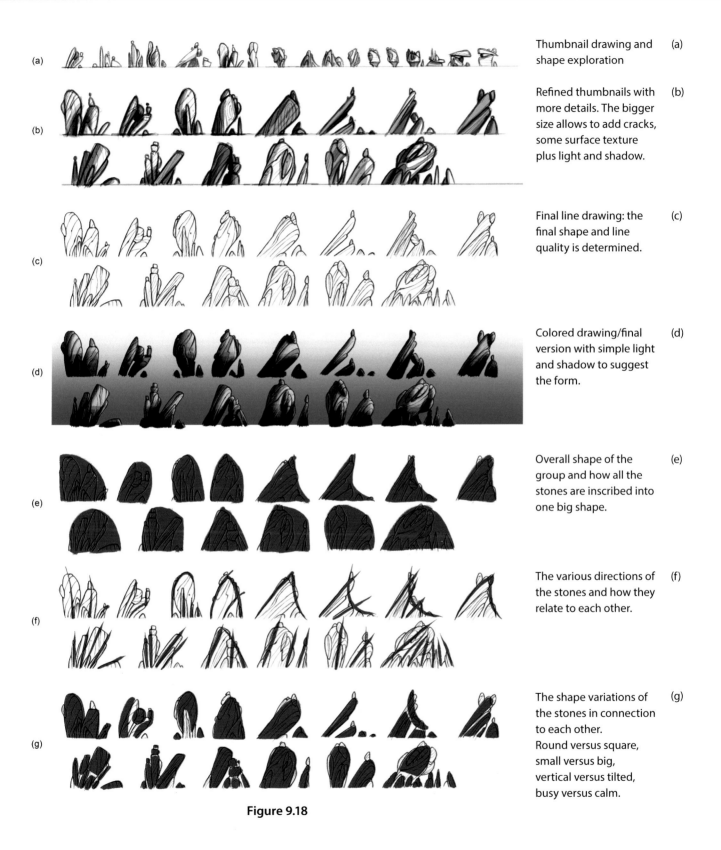

(a)    Thumbnail drawing and    (a)
       shape exploration

(b)    Refined thumbnails with    (b)
       more details. The bigger
       size allows to add cracks,
       some surface texture
       plus light and shadow.

(c)    Final line drawing: the    (c)
       final shape and line
       quality is determined.

(d)    Colored drawing/final    (d)
       version with simple light
       and shadow to suggest
       the form.

(e)    Overall shape of the    (e)
       group and how all the
       stones are inscribed into
       one big shape.

(f)    The various directions of    (f)
       the stones and how they
       relate to each other.

(g)    The shape variations of    (g)
       the stones in connection
       to each other.
       Round versus square,
       small versus big,
       vertical versus tilted,
       busy versus calm.

**Figure 9.18**

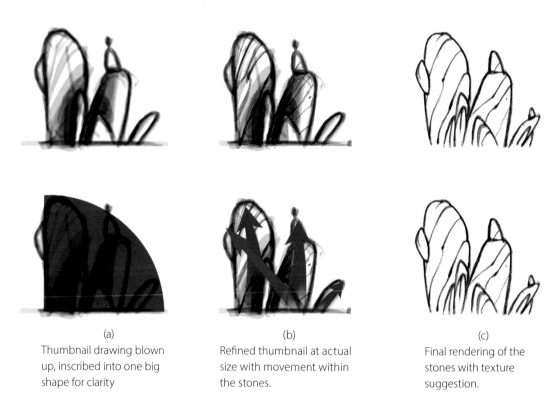

(a)
Thumbnail drawing blown
up, inscribed into one big
shape for clarity

(b)
Refined thumbnail at actual
size with movement within
the stones.

(c)
Final rendering of the
stones with texture
suggestion.

**Figure 9.19**

Figure 9.18a through (c) show in more detail how some of the elements of composition can be used within one of the simple piles of rocks. The first drawing is the thumbnail drawing (blown up for clarity!) already inscribed into a shape (Figure 9.19a), which makes it less busy and organizes its various stones. The thumbnail also already considers a variation in shape, position, direction, and size. The second drawing (Figure 9.19b) takes the "happy accidents" that happened during the drawing process and enhances them if they are interesting enough. In this case the directions (red) of the three stones were slightly exaggerated and to not have them point in one direction only

for a more organic feel. The verticals of the stones' main bodies are juxtaposed by one diagonal graphic vector (blue) that contains various stones in its path. A light texture has already been considered—how its lines could help the overall shape of the piece, either go with it or against it. The flow of the texture, however, should always work with the compositional flow, not against it. The third drawing (Figure 9.19c) is the final drawing, where perspective is added. The stones are rendered three-dimensionally and the texture is refined, breaking up the shapes. The cleanup must never dilute the initial compositional direction but always maintain it.

# CHAPTER 10

# Mood

Mood can be described as the atmosphere and/or emotional expression of an image aside from the character's emotion. It is the visualization of what the architecture, the landscape, or the overall shot or scene emotionally emanate (Figure 10.1).

There is a distinction between the overall mood of the entire feature and its smaller segments. The overall mood, which is sometimes referred to as the *tone* of the film (also touches upon genre) contains the film being a comedy, a horror movie, horror-comedy, a farce, action movie, spy film, etc. But it also includes a more detailed direction of the general speed of the film, its timing, sense of color, the design direction of the film, its style. The next smaller segment is the act: the three different acts in the film each have their own distinct mood, which visualizes the character's journey; those can be broken down further into the mood of each scene or even single shot. The mood of each, however, has to succumb to the overall direction of the entire feature, its tone. Even though *ET: The Extraterrestrial* has comedic elements in it and contains scenes that are more lighthearted, yet others that are serious, a scene with ET dancing and singing a Broadway musical number would completely ruin the already established mood of a fantasy film with mystery, drama, and suspense.

There are three possibilities for how mood can be used creatively in narrative, character, and location:

- The mood of the scene expresses exactly the mood of the main character and reflects it. The surrounding world is therefore the mirror of the character's mental state.

(An example is the ending of Brad Bird's *The Iron Giant* [1999], when the snow starts to fall in the third act of the film and the images are greyer, less saturated, reflecting the dire situation and grave danger of the narrative.)
- The mood is diametrically the opposite of the character's mental state, juxtaposing it. (An example is the scene with the sloth at the DMV in Disney's *Zootopia* [2014]: the moment when Judy Hopps needs to get information quickly, but the slow sloth drags it out painfully. Hopps is eager for the information, but the situation is slow and exactly the opposite of what is needed in that very moment. Even the audience gets annoyed by the slowness.)
- The mood comments on the action critically, ironically, sarcastically (various scenes in *Guardians of the Galaxy* [2014]).

Of course, any mood established in a film will not affect every audience member in the same way, as everyone brings a different background to the film, which in turn tints and affects the viewing experience. There is, for example, the factor of getting accustomed to an artistic device over time. The first time a viewer watches a horror movie with the typical middle-of-the-road horror conventions, it might be exciting and thrilling. The novelty makes it unique and outstanding for the younger audience members. After years of being exposed to the same device, it becomes its own cliché and lacks the thrill; the reaction is then boredom rather than excitement. The trick for the artist is to find a new interpretation of an old problem, while having the target audience in mind. Bringing something new to the table makes the scene exciting again and keeps even those

**Figure 10.1**

DOI: 10.1201/b22148-10

members of the audience interested who have already seen those types of scenes for about 20 years or more. The goal is to find a new interpretation of what *horror mood* can mean from a contemporary perspective, not a perspective that is transferred from the past. An audience would probably not find a murder scene done in the style of Alfred Hitchcock very scary in a contemporary film. New artistic devices have to be found to affect the audience of today in order to have a similar emotional reaction of fear. Film is always an expression of its own time; viewing conventions change and often so does the mood. We will never feel the same feelings an audience member had when watching *King Kong* in 1939, or *Star Wars* in 1977, or *Alien* in 1978. The mood established is still understood today, but it is not felt with the same intensity. Nevertheless there is also the possibility of exposing a younger audience to an older style and mood they usually are not as familiar with, done so successfully in Pixar's *The Incredibles* (2004): a 1960s mood is established through all three features of visual, temporal, and auditory (the three possibilities for mood in film), all following the 1960s spy and secret agent films like the 007 series. The visuals follow the shape-oriented style of the 1960s alongside a 1960s interpretation of the future; the temporal feature follows the slower and stylish 007 films (loosely) and the music clearly is in the footsteps of John Barry's theme to the sixth installation of the 007 series, *On Her Majesty's Secret Service* (1969).[1]

There are three features that contribute to mood in film:

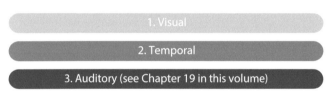

1. Visual
2. Temporal
3. Auditory (see Chapter 19 in this volume)

The visual deals with the image itself and how the artist can create a mood through the content of the frame. The temporal deals with the cinematic temporal use of the shot, its length and arrangement within the scene, and its effect on the mood, and then there is the auditory creation of mood through music and sound.

# 1. Visual

Visual mood deals with everything in the frame that can be seen and includes the background design, the character–background relationship, but also the composition and cinematography. Mood in this regard is what gives a scenery personality, elevates its content from a bare visual depiction of a setting to a place with a unique personality. The background can be a character in its own right and can express comfort or discomfort, happiness

or sadness, friendliness or hostility, or any other human emotion. The visual mood is strongly connected to storytelling, and every emotion of the literal story can be translated into a visual emotion in the set; there is no emotion that couldn't be expressed in visuals in the background. It would not necessarily be understood by the audience in every detail, but it subconsciously affects the emotion that the image emanates. The character is usually the focal point in the scene, though always part of a grander world and never just by themselves. The dialogue and with it the emotional exchange between character and environment is always there. Even in a completely empty setting (like in the TV show *Pocoyo*, in which the main characters always just act in a white void), the emptiness itself affects the character and vice versa. Very similar to a character that has a bland personality, lacking a believable emotional response, a landscape or building is bland without a mood and misses out on much of what visual storytelling can achieve: the emotional interaction between character and setting, but also the interaction between film and viewer. The designer uses the mood of a location to emotionally tell the story but also to relate to the audience on a subconscious level through the aspects of design. A slight change in color and various changes in other aspects can dramatically shift the mood from a rather happy and positive image to a gloomy and mysterious one or vice versa, like Figures 10.2 and 10.3 demonstrate. Both images feel diametrically different in their adjusted version.

The German artists Caspar David Friedrich (1774–1840) and Carl Spitzweg (1808–1885) were both extraordinary in capturing mood in their paintings. Friedrich being more serious and Spitzweg more ironic, in both artist's paintings mood plays a significant role. In Friedrich's work, the sole purpose of the image was to create a mood. He is the representative of German romanticism, where emotions, passion, individuality, and individual sensation were topics that were dealt with artistically. For Friedrich, emotions were an important aspect of his repertoire and he celebrated melancholy, self-reflection, and death as his main themes. As Friedrich's famous quote goes: *Des Künstlers Gefühl ist sein Gesetz* ("The artist's feelings are his law"). He uses nature to represent those emotions, not by merely copying it and pointing out its beauty, but by allowing nature to be grand and overwhelming, giving us the feeling of awe and using nature to represent human emotions. Images of trees, ruins, unusual weather conditions, or contemplative scenes of utter silence are the themes that are depicted and inspiring the viewer to ponder life and death and the perishability of nature and humanity's works. It is the inner world of thoughts and feelings that are exposed in the environment. It was the first time in art that mood was used as a tool to express human emotions through realistic yet stylized natural scenes, and Caspar David Friedrich alongside romanticism influenced what we consider nowadays as mood in Western art. In his most famous painting *Der Wanderer über dem Nebelmeer* (*Wanderer above the Sea of Fog*) from 1818 (Figure 10.4), we see a man looking

---

[1] A more "stylish" version of his interpretation of the original 007 theme by Monty Norman.

**Figure 10.2**

Above are the original (left) and the adjusted image (right) of a temple in Cambodia to have a more gloomy atmosphere, which was achieved by:

- Centering the image
- Darkening the shadows on the path
- Darkening the clouds

- Adjusting the colors by reducing the saturation and brightness and also shifting the hue towards blue
- More contrast

**Figure 10.3**

Above is the original (left) and the adjusted image (right) of the Main Hall of the Forbidden City in Beijing. The adjusted image is cleaner and more inviting, fresh. The changes from the left to the right image included:

- Shadows and sky are much bluer, the sky also has a pink base
- People are removed
- More contrast in the image

- More dominant lines in the roof
- Straightening of the pillars in the front

**Figure 10.4**

Caspar David Friedrich: *Wanderer above the sea of fog* (1818).

**Figure 10.5**

Carl Spitzweg: *The Butterfly Hunter* (1840).

down into a landscape covered partly in fog. Because we see the man from the back and he is in the center of the frame, it is his contemplative state we as the viewer step into: his gaze into the future and the relationship between man and nature. The mood of the picture is very much driven by the unique lighting, the fog that keeps most of the landscape covered and hidden from the view. Friedrich gives us an extraordinary moment of natural silence that stimulates us to gaze and ponder. Much of today's visual development work for film and games goes back in its core to romantic paintings of the likes of Friedrich (or Ivan Shishkin, Johan Christian Dahl, or the Hudson River school). It is the depiction of emotions in any kind of environment and even finding a romantic view in a spaceship or different planet. The works of Paul Lasaine or Maciej Kuciara and many others would not be as strong as they are without the influence of Romanticism.

Carl Spitzweg, on the other hand, is a representative of the German "Biedermayer" era (~1818–1848) whose oeuvre is the exact opposite of Friedrich's. Where Friedrich's paintings are dark and melancholy, Spitzweg is ironic, witty, comedic, with a tendency of romanticizing the daily life of awkward and unique, yet always conservative characters. Friedrich's characters, if there are any, are usually subordinate to nature,

which always plays the leading role in his work. The characters show an overwhelming feeling of wonder towards nature. Irony, however is what drives the paintings of Carl Spitzweg. In his *The Butterfly Hunter* (Figure 10.5), an entomologist is catching insects with a small net in a jungle setting; the jungle has a golden glow that emanates a mysterious mood. The moment is by no means common; it is extraordinary and magical. In front of him, two huge and colorful butterflies cross his path. The irony being that this fully equipped geeky insect hunter with boxes and water bottle, umbrella and backpack, is out to catch tiny insects, but then comes across gigantic magical creatures. The mood in this image is supported by the exquisite lighting situation, which makes one feel the heat and humidity in this lush jungle. One can smell the heavy air! The lighting and handling of the flora renders the image nearly surreal, which fits the story so very well. We see palm trees and bushes, beautifully detailed greenery with little dots of flowers here and there. Sunlight streams into the scene and the butterflies seem to just be there for a short moment until they vanish again into the density of the forest. A magical moment in time indeed. And the hunter himself, with his glasses that reflect the light, is looking himself like an insect. Spitzweg's choice of positioning the two butterflies in the lower left corner is a planned one of course. Being in a corner doesn't allow them to have much free space within the frame. One of the butterflies is resting on a twig and the other one is coming towards it. However, with just a couple of beats of their wings, they will be out of the frame and out of sight very soon, which makes them certainly precious insects. Spitzweg plays with time in his composition and the fleeting moment of seeing those amazing creatures. His depiction of mood in this painting is what makes the moment magical. It is not a common moment in the jungle; it is a special point in time that is emphasized through the light, the colors, the composition, and the overall "feel" of the space with its golden light that everything is bathed in.

Where in one image we only deal with one mood, in a feature film many scenes need to express a mood in the earlier explained hierarchy of visual, temporal and auditory. A feature film that is exceptional in its old-fashioned, yet refined interpretation of an old tale is Roman Polanski's *The Fearless Vampire Killers* (1967), a story in which Professor Abronsius and his disciple Alfred travel to Transylvania to hunt for vampires, where they meet the head of the bloodsuckers: Count von Krolock. The unique mood is established through all three features of visual, temporal, and auditory. The visuals are created through the excellent sets designed by Wilfrid Shingleton, whose interiors are surreal and strange, yet extraordinary in giving the audience exactly what one would expect to see in the Carpathian Mountains (even though most of us wouldn't have a clue of what that would actually look like). Count von Krolock's castle is dusty, old, and filled with heavy furniture, spiderwebs, and stuffy old paintings of a deranged-looking line of ruling-class family members. The inn, close to Krolock's castle, is not only filled with the weirdest characters but also feels dark and old, wry and somehow hopeless. Additionally, the cinematography of Douglas Slocombe gives the world of the film a surreal quality, a mood that is mysterious and fairy-tale-like. The temporal aspect of the mood is then maintained by very long shots, a quiet pace that evokes a different kind of comedy, which is more Buster Keaton than Cartoon Network. The music by Krzysztof Komeda also underlines in its rather quiet eeriness the fairy-tale-like strangeness of the visuals and adds another level to the mood. All three aspects, visual, temporal, and auditory, contribute as a union to the overall exquisite mood of the film.

## Visual mood can be expressed through:

- Color and all other aspects of design
- Background and setting
- Weather and season
- Relationship of background and character
- Composition and cinematography

## Color and all other aspects of design

Figures 10.2 and 10.3 already demonstrated how color affects mood in an image dramatically. However, all the other aspects of design also provide a significant contribution to how a setting "presents" itself. They are obviously part of the background and set design. Some examples:

- Lighting: Light and shadow have not only the power to reveal and hide information, which is widely used in horror movies to create a sense of claustrophobia, but can also paint the scenery in a pleasant light. The lighting in Chen Kaige's feature *Farewell My Concubine* (1993), for instance, or Michael Cimino's feature *Heaven's Gate* (1980) gives a warmth to the sets that transports the visuals into a historical setting. This golden glow of the images also has a romantic feel to it that is often used in commercials (not very different from Spitzweg's painting *The Butterfly Hunter*; Figure 10.5).

- Objects: It is not just the overall architecture or flora that defines a location but also what that location is "furnished" with. Objects not only define the personality of the occupant but also express the needed mood. Why is Sid's room in Pixar's feature *Toy Story* (1995) filled with broken toys? To express the overall mood of a serial killer's hideaway. The colors are uncomfortable and dark; the entire room gives one the creeps. The objects in the room are of course carefully designed in order to create a feeling of despair, desperation, and pure insanity yet also reflect the personality of the character living in the depicted setting.

- Shapes and forms: This point is a bit tricky because in a shot there are so many shapes and forms that contribute to the final image, but, for instance, if shapes are chosen that are roundish, then the image can, with the right colors, create a comfortable feeling. Shapes that are sharp and have spikes can feel more uncomfortable. In Disney's *Lilo and Stitch* (2002), all the shapes are slightly rounded, which has a positive and safe feel to it, contrary to Disney's *Hercules* (1997), in which the shapes in the underworld are all pointy and sharp, rendering it rather repelling. We do not want to touch spiky objects as they seem to hurt, but we can easily grab an object that is rounded and safe. It is obviously a cliché, but it works in the right circumstances.

- Texture and other design aspects: A fluffy world can feel very comfortable with bright and happy colors, like in DreamWorks's *Trolls* (2016), but with a different color scheme can also lead into the opposite within the very same feature.

- Wear and tear versus brand-new: In Henry Selick's *Coraline* (2009), the protagonist's world is old and used, but the Other World, the parallel world she steps into through a little door, is eerily new and shiny, which actually makes it feel fake and unreal, whereas the used and worn reality is a bit depressing and gray. It is the juxtaposition between the two worlds that makes reality seem bland yet truthful, the Other World however dangerous in its alluring perfection.

## Weather and season

The weather plays an exceptionally important role in the creation of mood, as it easily reflects the character's emotional state or the emotional needs of the narrative. For instance, showing a storm merely because it is called for in the script is just one side of the coin. Choosing the storm not just for its physical powers but also the emotional turmoil it can reflect and how it relates to the character's inner and outer journey is the other. Why is it raining heavily when the car stops in front of the *Tyrannosaurus rex* enclosure in *Jurassic Park* (1993)? Would the scene play out as successfully if it were a sunny afternoon? No, it would have played out differently; however, that does not mean that it is necessarily less scary in the sunshine than it is during the rain, as many other artistic elements affect the mood. In *Jurassic Park*, the storm obviously has a much-needed role in the film, as it is part of the overall mayhem, increasing the problems tenfold that the park already has to struggle with. However, it also creates a mood that not only changes the colors of the environment and the overall feeling of the situation but separates nature and human life from each other. It is nature that is out of control in the form of the storm *and* the dinosaurs running wild. The humans literally need to stay indoors to stay alive. The distinction between nature and urban life is keeping them alive … until the barrier is broken down.

Often the moment when weather affects the story visually in a climactic moment is rather controlled and artificial. When Rafiki holds up Mufasa's son Simba in Disney's *Lion King* and at that very moment the sky opens and a ray of sunlight "blesses" the young cub, the religious connotation might be a bit over the top for some viewers. When Bambi's mother dies, it starts to snow at that very moment, which is utterly obvious. When Geppetto is searching for Pinocchio in the heavy rain, the meaning of it seems to be overly pronounced. Surprisingly enough, the general audience usually does not seem to be bothered too much. It is the emotion that counts, the mood that emerges, and weather is just one of the tools used.

Snow, for instance, with its quiet and silencing mood in Zhang Yimou's *Raise the Red Lantern*, is not just a reflection of the emotional coldness of the character's lack of healthy social interaction but also beautifully points out the red lanterns on a white canvas. It is a balance between what is needed visually for the narrative and also what is aesthetically pleasing.

The ever-changing shapes and colors in the sky, the myriad of weather situations, not only provide us with an array of emotional possibilities but also an aesthetic quality that can elevate a scene into a moment that even the heavens comment on.

More on weather in film:

Kristi McKim, *Cinema as Weather: Stylistic Screens and Atmospheric Change*, Routledge, Abingdon, 2013.

**Figure 10.6**

Claude Monet: Rouen Cathedral, *The Portal at Midday* (1893).

**Figure 10.7**

Claude Monet: *Rouen Cathedral at Sunset* (1894).

**Figure 10.8**

Claude Monet: Rouen Cathedral, *The Portal in the Sun* (1894).

**Figure 10.9**

Claude Monet: Rouen Cathedral, *Morning Effect* (1884).

How weather can be used to create mood:

- As a narrative element
- Intellectual element
- Reflective element (for reflecting the character's emotions and/or the narrative)
- Aesthetic element

An excellent study of how weather and light can change the mood of a location, expressed in the most subtle colors yet also artistically exaggerated, is Claude Monet's *Rouen Cathedral* series (Figures 10.6–10.9). He observed the cathedral for 2 years and painted it in over 30 different versions, exploring its change in light and shadow through seasons and the various times of the day, an immensely complex and tedious task.

## Background and setting

Here, the question is not how the location is designed and how it looks, but where and what it is and how it relates to the narrative. What kind of setting is chosen for which effect, a natural setting or an urban one? If the scene asks for a wedding proposal, where would it take place and how does the mood of the place itself express or contradict the narrative? Would the proposal be set in a car garage to express the down-to-earth personalities of the couple, in a mall to show the character's focus on materialistic "stuff," in a quiet forest to show the significance of the moment in a romantic setting, a busy bar to show the characters' urge for

recognition … all of which express the characters' personalities. But one could also choose to interpret the happy situation from a third perspective: a couple who gets engaged in a war zone, where the rubble and destruction do not reflect the characters' personalities but the political upheaval, therefore increasing the seemingly unimportant little step of the loving couple despite the time of crisis, creating a beacon of hope.

## Relationship of background and character

Mood is the emotional state of the environment, and once characters are present there will inevitably be an interaction between the two. Character and background can contradict each other in their emotional expression or agree. Contradicting the emotion creates tension; agreement creates unity. There are of course many shades in between, where the background can comment on the emotional and/or psychological state of the character. Every image has an interaction between characters and set and the characters are never just "in the background"; they are always part of it and communicate with it. There is no image where background and characters are not related; they unrestrictedly influence each other. An exchange and dialogue is always there and has to be considered by the artist to be understood by the audience, either consciously or subconsciously. In animation, the distinction between character and background can be dominant due to technical reasons and reasons associated with the production pipeline of a big studio,

**Figure 10.10**

Robert Wiene's *The Cabinett of Dr. Caligari* (1920).

**Figure 10.11**

often reducing, not on purpose, the strong link between the two, which causes characters and backgrounds to be seen as two separate entities. The character design and background design then easily speak two different design languages and do not fit harmoniously together. However, there are exceptions where the intense liaison between the two is visualized in every little detail.

Pixar's film *Up* has Carl and Ellie Fredricksen's house with its interiors designed in a way that not only expresses the characters' personalities but also their history together, and it also changes through time along with the aging characters. It becomes utterly clear that the house is an extension of the characters' personality rather than just a place to live in. The mood of the characters is reflected in the lighting, composition, and color of the house in an exquisite way. The background serves as the emotional continuation of the character's mental state.

In German expressionistic cinema, a direct translation of German expressionistic painting aesthetics and artistic content into cinematic language, the idea was to express the psychological state of the characters through the environment surrounding them. The scene design became a direct reflection of the characters' mental state, a "background canvas" on which their feelings and psychological inner life could be painted on for everyone to see. In Robert Wiene's *The Cabinet of Dr. Caligari* (1920), the stylistically most aggressive film of German expressionistic cinema, the insanity of the characters is literally painted on backgrounds that are staged like a theatre set. The tilted walls and floors, the crooked windows and doors, the extremely stylized objects in the sets all suggest a demented world where the permanently twisted mind sows mayhem. However, the set design is not just a representation of the characters' emotions, but also a visual guide through the film. Characters' paths are painted on the floor (Figures 10.10 through 10.13), light is painted on the walls and objects, spots of

importance are heightened by painted shapes on the ground. The set literally develops into a blank canvas for the story and its actions in their temporal expansion to be represented visually. Therefore, some shots are visual time lines where we can observe past, present, and future happenings within the set and we can see where important moments will happen during the shot. The set design can be a temporal representation of the entire shot in *Dr. Caligari* (very much like background design with its layout in animation). This overly stylized design has unfortunately disappeared in cinema. Yet as an idea it has survived, just in a much more subtle and delicate way, expressed through light and shadow, color and scene design. The mood in Wiene's *Caligari* is mainly created by twisted shapes and forms, by the questioning of traditional perspectives, and by exaggerated characters, a rather theatrical approach.

Because one of its cornerstones is exaggeration, animation can push the mood to extremes as well and use all aspects of design to their full extent. Tim Burton's stop-motion films *The Nightmare before Christmas* (1993), *Corpse Bride* (2005), and *Frankenweenie* (2012) and Jiří Barta's *The Pied Piper* (1986) were all influenced heavily in their design by expressionistic cinema, which adds visual weirdness to the also odd stories and characters. However, one should be careful to not confuse style with mood without taking the narrative's needed mood into consideration. A style or mood that is used for its own sake does not support the narrative and is therefore null and void!

In animation, there are many examples where the environment has mood, because it is one of the main aspects of background design to create a mood that goes with the scene and its emotion, to strengthen the character's emotional state in the entirety of the frame. In Disney's *Pinocchio* (1940), there is an extraordinary scene that has an ineffable effect on the emotion of the audience. It is the moment when Pinocchio is trapped in a cage in Stromboli's carriage. The lighting and staging, the thunderstorm with lightning, colors and composition, the effects

Figure 10.12

Figure 10.13

and character animation are so immensely emotionally gripping that it haunts one long after the end of the movie because the created mood is so convincing (and again *Dr. Caligari* served as inspiration in its strong light and shadow treatment for this scene). It presents an iconic moment that represents in all its elements Pinocchio's black despair; everything in the frame reflects that mood. Another example with a beautiful visual mood, though much more subtle, is the fireplace in Geppetto's house that Jiminy Cricket warms himself at in the very beginning of the film. The background itself emanates so much warmth, comfort, and snugness, it is not very difficult to follow Jiminy on his way towards the fire and feel the heat warming him and us up. But the comfort in the room is not only there for its heat but obviously reflects also Geppetto's warm personality, which is then extended in the toys he produces, prominently exhibited in the workshop.

Composition can easily create a feeling of open space or claustrophobia, thus affecting the mood more subconsciously. This seriously affects how the audience feels about the space, which in turn affects the felt emotion. The filmmaker can heavily affect the audience's subconscious feelings about a situation by either revealing more space or withholding it. For instance, not showing the establishing shot and thus not revealing the entire space will create an underlying feeling of claustrophobia if the camera is always close to the subjects. However, showing too much space when the character already feels lonely and lost would intensify the scene. Specific shots can make the scene feel cheap or expensive, grand or small, can evoke a feeling of grandeur or the opposite.

Examples of evoking a feeling through composition:

- Size: *Bee Movie* (big versus small)
- Claustrophobia: *The Graduate* (the party scene)
- Open space: *Lawrence of Arabia* (the desert scenes)

## 2. Temporal

This aspect of mood deals with the finished image being used in a time-based manner to creatively evoke or accentuate a mood via editing. The image content is not manipulated, but the arrangement alongside the duration of the various shots are. Via editing, the length and type of shot are arranged for suspense. This goes back to the beginning of filmmaking and the understanding that story, and with it the message that a film conveys, can be influenced through not only the content of the images shown but also the order in which images are presented, their length and arrangement. Continuity style editing has sought a sense of reality on-screen since the early days of cinema. The audience believes what they witness on-screen is actually an illusion of reality and thus they empathize with the characters on-screen. But Lev Kuleshov's and Sergej Eisensteins' theories on montage also come to mind. Kuleshov discovered that the juxtapositions of images not only affect storytelling but also how the content of the image is interpreted. The five methods of Eisenstein's montage are supposed to directly affect the emotions of the audience, and for instance by juxtaposing two seemingly unrelated images, an intellectual connection will take shape in the mind of the viewer, stimulating an idea or emotion that then contributes to the overall mood of the scene.

How the audience feels about a specific setting can be controlled not only by how a setting looks but also by how the setting is presented to the audience. What shots are arranged with what content? For instance, there is a huge, dilapidated industrial park. What does the camera show aside from the actual park? Consider how the following variations tint the feeling the audience has about the park, if the second shot shown is the following:

- A dead cat on the ground that is already decomposing
- A pool of dark oil on the floor
- A pool of green poisonous liquid

- A bushel of blooming dandelions on a corner of one of the dilapidated buildings
- A group of kids playing in the yard
- A loving couple strolling through the park

Each of the shots changes the feeling we have about the place drastically and not only clearly affects the story but also affects how comfortable or uncomfortable we perceive the place to be, whether it is safe or dangerous, interesting, scary, mysterious, insane, delicious, nasty, spooky, intimidating, happy, or anything else. It is therefore crucial for the editor to know exactly what mood needs to be created and how to achieve it.

Editing is not only the art of what to show and when but also what not to show. There is always the effect of images, shots, or whole scenes and their information lingering on in the mind of the viewer and tinting the story of the following visuals/story. For instance, a woman is shown washing her muddy dog because she just came in from a walk in the forest. Right afterwards she sits down for dinner. If we do not get a sense of her having also washed herself, either by wearing different clothes, actually seeing or hearing her washing her hands, or any clue that tells us that she did, we will have in the back of our minds that her hands are still dirty while she is eating her dinner, which evidently affects our perception of her in that very moment. It does not necessarily mean that the audience will be appalled by her being not clean enough, but it can subconsciously evoke a short-term emotion or even just a quick thought. It seems insignificant, but it does have an effect on how we perceive her, how we might see her as a character from then on. Information that is left out therefore also has a significant effect on how the story evolves and how the mood can change in a very subtle way. So the possibilities for creating mood via editing are to control the shot length and also what information is given and what withheld. A very quick cut scene creates the feeling of frenzy and action; a scene with very long shots creates a calm and soothing atmosphere. (Obviously that can be counterbalanced with the action within the shot being frenzied; the content of the shot clearly needs to go hand in hand with the purpose of it being

soothing or exciting.) Steven Spielberg's feature *Indiana Jones and the Temple of Doom* (1984) was considered the fastest cut movie to that point. It created a fast-paced roller coaster (literally) that the audience could not evade. Considering the pacing of certain features today, *Indiana Jones* seems rather slowly paced. The audience's perception changes over time, of course, depending on their exposure.

Films that in my opinion express a noteworthy mood for one reason or another (obviously the list is way too short):

- F.W. Murnau's *Nosferatu* (1922)
- Albert Parker's *The Black Pirate* (1926)
- Carl Dreyer's *Vampyr* (1932)
- Marcel Carné's *Children of Paradise* (1945)
- Yasujirō Ozu's *Tokyo Story* (1953)
- Kenji Mizoguchi's *Ugetsu* (1953)
- Satyajit Ray's *Apu Trilogy* (1955, 1956, and 1959)
- Roman Polanski's *The Fearless Vampire Killers* (1967)
- Stanley Kubrick's *2001: A Space Odyssey* (1968)
- Stanley Kubrick's *Barry Lyndon* (1975)
- Nobuhiko Obayashi's *House* (1977)
- Ridley Scott's *Alien* (1979)
- Stanley Kubrick's *The Shining* (1980)
- Neil Jordan's *The Company of Wolves* (1984)
- Bernardo Bertolucci's *The Last Emperor* (1987)
- Hayao Miyazaki's *My Neighbor Totoro* (1988)
- Katsuhiro Otomo's *Akira* (1988)
- The Coen brothers' *Barton Fink* (1991)
- Zhang Yimou's *Raise the Red Lantern* (1991)
- Jean-Pierre Jeunet and Marc Caro's *Delicatessen* (1991)
- Jean-Claude Lauzon's *Léolo* (1992)
- Jane Campion's *The Piano* (1993)
- Chen Kaige's *Farewell My Concubine* (1993)
- Henry Selick's *The Nightmare before Christmas* (1993)
- David Fincher's *Se7en* (1995)
- Andrew Niccol's *Gattaca* (1997)
- Hayao Miyazaki's *Spirited Away* (2000)
- Michael Haneke's *The White Ribbon* (2009)

# CHAPTER 11

# Size

**Size can be affected by:**

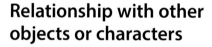

Relationship with other objects or characters

Past experience

Perspective and spacial relationships

Color

Depth of field (see Chapter 12)

Movement

Occupied space in the frame

Shape and design

Figure 11.1

## Relationship with other objects or characters

The size is the relative dimension and proportion of an object and its relationship to the objects around it. Playing with the sizes of objects within a group creates a tension between them and intensifies their relationship but also defines their relative size. Big is much bigger, when placed beside something really small. A muscular man seems more muscular when put next to someone skinny. A skyscraper is huge next to a mouse but tiny next to the planet Saturn. Thus size always depends on its surrounding objects and environment. If an object is on its own on a neutral white ground, there is no comparison that would give any clue about how big it actually is. Only the relationship to another object allows us to make a judgment about its dimensions. The house in Figure 11.1 is, because it is standing on its own and not related to anything close by, impossible to judge on its actual size. Placing it next to bigger house in Figure 11.2 immediately turns it into the "small house." Only through creating a relationship with other objects will it be determined what size house it is supposed to be within the story context. The house itself is neither big nor small, as this is always just a matter of perspective. An object seen very close-up obviously seems big compared to the same object far away, which additionally defines the size of the object in the frame. The object could be tiny, an atom even: if the camera zooms in and it fills the frame, it will appear big to the audience despite it being miniscule (Figure 11.3). The advantage in artistic images

Figure 11.2

is that objects can be shown next to each other with the same size in the frame despite their actual size in reality being quite different. With the use of lenses with a shallow field of depth to avoid blur, characters or objects can be put together in one shot that diminishes their size differences and allows unusual views.

DOI: 10.1201/b22148-11

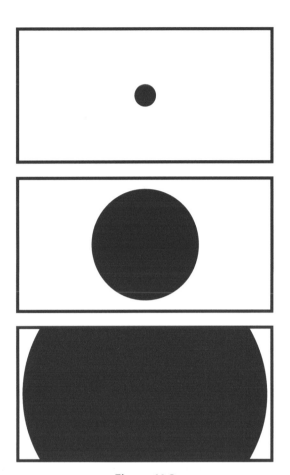

**Figure 11.3**

The *Bee Movie* (2007), for instance, uses many shots where Barry Bee Benson is placed next to florist Vanessa to make their "friendship" feel more believable despite their significant size difference. A shallow field of depth would destroy the illusion of them being "equals" through heavy blurring of either character; every time you focused on a character as small as a bee, the human would be blurred and vice versa.

However, there is not just the (semi-)realistic use of size but the intellectual use of it also. The idea of someone being more important than someone else can also be depicted through size. Often used in art, the size difference between a ruler and his or her subordinates shows that one is more important than the other. On the interior walls of the temple of Abu Simbel, Pharaoh Ramses II is shown slaying his enemies, and he is depicted on a much bigger scale because that makes him appear not only more important but also much stronger, which is proof of his godlike character. The difference in size makes him stand out and puts emphasis on him as a ruler, elevates him beyond mere human status.

There aren't many scenes in animation where the size relationship between the characters and their environment is as drastic as in Disney's *Pinocchio* (1940). There is Jiminy

Cricket, a tiny insect, and we have Monstro, the huge whale as big as a ship. Of course, we already know about the size of Monstro before our heroes reach him (well, he is called *Monstro the Whale* … he is obviously huge), but the image of Jiminy positioned next to Monstro's teeth is still very impressive, as it makes the size difference so much more intense. "The layout men discovered the illusion of great size could only be carried out by paying minute attention to perspective. They drew him (Monstro the Whale) to approximate the scale of a three-story building. Whenever possible, the whale filled up most of the camera field."[1] The layout artists made the size difference between the two believable. First we see the full-scale whale in the ocean with a flock of seagulls flying away from the top of his head. The seagulls are the first size relationship that gives us an idea of how big Monstro actually is. The scale of the smoke that comes out of Monstro's blowhole, the waves and splashes around Monstro and also the speed of movement of the water all contribute to the gigantic size of the beast. Additionally, the size relationship is constantly reiterated and the characters juxtaposed by, for instance, zooming in from Monstro's head and showing Jiminy riding in his bottle between the teeth of the whale into its mouth. There is a constant switch between the three different sizes of Monstro, Geppetto and Pinocchio, and Jiminy Cricket. Their huge size difference is utterly believable.

## Past experience

We see a coin that fills the frame. Our explanation would logically be that the coin is close to the camera because there are not many gigantic coins out there, so the most convincing explanation would be that the coin is at a close distance to the viewer. There would have to be a hint or simple explanation within the story or frame that clarifies that the coin actually is huge; otherwise we usually choose the more plausible explanation, not the more unusual one. This helps us to quickly grasp an image in its perspective and arrangement without getting lost in strange story lines. For example, the house in Figure 11.1: we can roughly determine how tall the house is because we have seen two-story houses before and so its size is fairly clear. However, this only works if it deals with objects that we have actually seen before (we can only judge the house as life-sized if we have a person next to it; without a person the house could be both tiny or huge). If we see a spaceship in space, it is rather difficult to determine its size if there is no clue of a size relationship between it and something we know, for instance, a shuttle with humans in it. Many artists have stunned audiences with size relationships that question our past experiences and shown us sculptures that "just can't be." Ron Mueck, for instance, pushes the idea of natural human-sized sculptures and creates hyperrealistic figures that are either way too big, like his stunning piece *Untitled* (Boy; 1999), a gigantic boy who is squatting; one

1   Popular Mechanics, 1940 Color Shooting in Fairyland, *Popular Mechanics*, Vol. 1, No. 73 (January 1940), pp. 17–24.

would definitely not expect him to be nearly 5 m in height. On the other hand, Mueck also produces miniature figures that are so realistic and utterly detailed that looking at them in person makes one shiver and feel dizzy, because the brain sees something it cannot fully grasp. Reality is shifting and one is confused about the size relationship of the sculpture in the exhibition space. We expect our surroundings to stay the same in terms of the visual laws that we have been experiencing since childhood.

Nevertheless, one can easily be fooled, as size is sometimes just not what it seems to be at first glance. We have seen cars and we know the size of them by heart. Their size is already in our head, and the more realistic they are, the more we expect them to be literally "life-size." In the photographs of artist Michael Paul Smith, however (Figure 11.4), we expect the image to be exactly what it seems to be: actual life-sized cars in front of buildings. There is nothing in the image that indicates that our expectation could not be further from the truth: both cars and street are miniature objects (Figure 11.5), but the buildings in the background are life-sized. Smith mimics the real in his miniature arrangements with such detail and accuracy that we are led to believe his arrangements, exactly because our expectation and what we have learned in the past leads us down the wrong path. The perspective is so cleverly mimicked that our eye cannot see the illusion but can only see it as being real. Smith avoids the perspective lines of the various elements of real and miniature sets meeting. The foreground elements do not mix with the perspective lines in the background architecture, so he avoids the problematic areas altogether and thus creates a perfect illusion, which brings us to the next point of size.

**Figure 11.4**

Michael Paul Smith: *Oil Delivery on a Snowy Day in 1939 (2013).*

**Figure 11.5**

Michael Paul Smith: *Oil Delivery on a Snowy Day in 1939 (2013).*

## Perspective and spatial relationships

Perspective is only then an indicator for size if the perspective lines clearly relate the object in question to other objects surrounding it. A building that is obviously related to other buildings through one-, two-, or three-point perspective gets locked into the perspective grid and thus can easily be judged as to its size. If the building is cut off from the grid, it is only assumed to have the same size, but there is no proof for that. In Figure 11.6, we cannot say how big the ball is; neither can we say if it is behind, next to, or in front of the house, as there is no clear determinant that proves how far away the ball is from

the viewer (we could if it were a 3D viewing experience, but we cannot on a 2D plane). Connecting the ball with its surrounding in Figure 11.7, this clearly defines both the spatial relationship with the house and its size (roughly) as being rather huge.

Where Michael Paul Smith plays with miniature sets to create his illusions, the photographer Joel Sternfeld stuns us with reality and a strong composition to make the size relationship in his image *The Space Shuttle Columbia Lands at Kelly Lachland Air Force Base, San Antonio, Texas* (1979) into a slightly dizzying

**Figure 11.6**

**Figure 11.7**

affair (Figure 11.8). We can see the man in the foreground looking at the Space Shuttle, but it seems like he is Gulliver in Lilliput. The image questions our visual perception, mainly because the platform that the man in the T-shirt is standing on seems to directly expand into the runway with the crowd of tiny people. However, he is actually standing on an elevated platform and the crowd is much lower. The effect is made possible due to the image having a very deep focus, meaning all the elements in the image are sharp and so the crowd, the space shuttle, and the man in the foreground have the same focus. In Sternfeld's image,

if we saw the elevated platform clearly connected to the lower ground, the illusion would be broken. An object therefore has to be locked into the perspective grid or connected to the space via overlap, shadows, and relationships with other objects in order for its size to be determined correctly.

Changing the position of the vanishing points changes the viewing position of the object or building, which also can have an impact on how we perceive the building as either being bigger or smaller (or us being bigger or smaller). The further apart the vanishing points in a two-point perspective, the flatter and more distant the object appears (Figure 11.9); the closer the vanishing points are, the more extreme the perspective is and the taller the object appears (Figure 11.10).

Size is also affected by the object's line quality and thickness. The thicker a line is, the closer it often appears to be, which in turn can be used to either push objects backwards or bring them forwards. Figure 11.11 has the house in the front drawn with a thicker line and the building in the back with a thinner line. This clearly pushes the five-story building backwards.

## Size and color

The only way color affects size is by changing the color attributes of the object to generate color perspective, which can only be fully judged in relationship with objects surrounding it. If color perspective is produced on a small scale that would never have any in the first place, it threatens the

**Figure 11.8**

Joel Sternfeld: *The Space Shuttle Columbia Lands at Kelly Lachland Air Force Base, San Antonio, Texas* (1979).

**Figure 11.9**

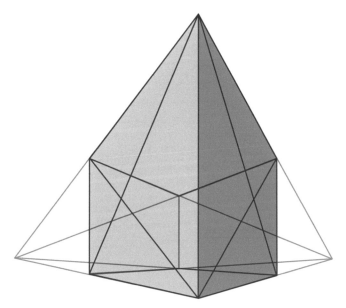

**Figure 11.10**

**Figure 11.11**

**Figure 11.12**

**Figure 11.13**

size of the objects into question. On a more realistic scale of color perspective in the photographs in Figures 11.12 and 11.13, which of the pyramids on the right appears to have a bigger actual size? The pyramid in Figure 11.12 seems to be much bigger in its actual size because of the applied color perspective, which makes it appear further away from the viewer, ergo making it bigger compared to figure 11.13. However, the small pyramid in Figure 11.13 appears heavier, because its darker color feels heavier than the brighter color of the right pyramid in Figure 11.12.

Many painted backgrounds work with heavily exaggerated color perspective to have more depth than would be realistically possible and also to separate two elements through color contrast. This also can have the effect that the foreground elements look smaller than they actually are. For example, in some of the backgrounds of Disney's *Brother Bear* (2003), there is so much aerial perspective that it suggests heavy moisture in the air, though there is also much sunlight. The huge difference of saturation, contrast, and hue between foreground and background, plus the suggested lack of focus in the distant trees, gives the image depth but also changes the size perception of

realistic visual but also helps in separating the two elements that are distant from each other. Color perspective naturally only happens on a scale of large distances, not in short ones. However, in Figure 14.66 there is color perspective despite the short distance between the objects; it does, however, put the

the elements within the frame, which is actually an advantage in the case of *Brother Bear* because it makes it look more playful. It can look like a miniature set because of it.

In recent years, gigantic scale has become more and more convincing in blockbuster movies like *Pacific Rim* (2013) and *Godzilla* (2014). The adding of layers and layers of fog and diffusion makes the sizes of those monsters much more convincing as they step back due to simulated color perspective. The applied "distance fog" simulates depth and with it increases the size of the beast dramatically.

## Movement

When it comes to moving objects, there are three additional aspects that can define size: speed, camera angle, and editing (camera angle is technically part of perspective). Ever watched a giraffe or an elephant move? They are slow and controlled, whereas a mouse is very fast and agile. The bigger the animal or object, the harder it is for it to move fast because it has a much higher moment of inertia. It takes more time for it to get the heavy weight moving in the first place. So the bigger the object, the slower it should be. The big monsters in DreamWorks's *How to Train Your Dragon 2* (2014) or *Monster vs. Aliens* (2009) are slow, very slow. They nearly move in slow motion. This in combination with all the other aspects mentioned earlier gives the illusion of great size—no, enormous, gigantic, insane, and ridiculous size! In *Godzilla*, whenever the monster is shown, it is either from a very low camera angle, an object or architecture for comparison is next to it, or at the end of the film there are flocks of birds circling around Godzilla for size reference. But the cumbersome speed of the beast is what convinces the most.

A formula helps to calculate the speed of an object or character in relationship to its size:

$$24 \times \sqrt{D/d} = f$$

D = dimensions in feet/meters of the big object
d = dimensions in feet/meters of the small object
f  = frames per second (camera frame per second)

For example, a creature is 100 m tall; the frames per second for one stride compared to a human is 178.9 (24 × √100 m/1.80 m), which corresponds to a ratio of 7.5:1, or 7.5 times faster in shooting speed. This results in the actually seen movement of the beast on-screen being 7.5 slower than that of the human. If a human walks with a stride of 1 second, the 100 m tall beast would take 7.5 seconds for one stride.

Nevertheless, the creature has to look convincing and in the end it is always the animator's eye that makes the decision if it works or if it does not. The calculation can only give an estimate.

The camera angle in a scene can make a character or object look bigger than it actually is if the audience is constantly exposed to it being seemingly big, for instance, the character of Rubeus

Hagrid in the Harry Potter movies. This goes along with the editing, which has to combine those shots that reiterate the size differences in order to give the audience the illusion of it being bigger. This was discussed earlier in the case study to Koji Yamamura's *Atama Yama* Chapter 3, where a man has a tree growing out of his head and people come to celebrate underneath it. The editing is done in a way that convinces the audience that life-size people are actually capable of walking onto the life-size head of the man. Yamamura does an exceptional job in us never doubting the logic of the story.

## Occupied space in the frame

Size is relative and it is always ambiguous on its own, but even less so within a clearly defined frame that does not necessarily clarify the distance of the object to the viewer immediately. The following examples, Figures 11.14–11.17, show the changing evaluation of a shape when coupled with differently sized shapes next to it within the frame.

## Actual size and cinematic size

We have already seen in Joel Sternfeld's photograph that size can be manipulated through camera, lens, and composition and how the various elements within the frame are placed in relationship to each other in order to play with the size aspect. This is where the creative advantage of the cinematic composition comes in: the playfulness between the results of camera and lens on the one hand and the distance between objects and camera on the other. The distance of the object to the camera obviously changes its size. A coin close to the camera looks huge, but a hundred meters away it's just a tiny dot.

When playing with shapes in the composition (remember the abstract thumbnail exploration in the section "Composition

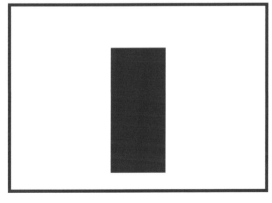

**Figure 11.14**

In this figure, it is open to interpretation how big this rectangle really is, because there is nothing around it that defines its size. We need something to compare the rectangle to in order to estimate its actual dimensions or at least its felt dimensions.

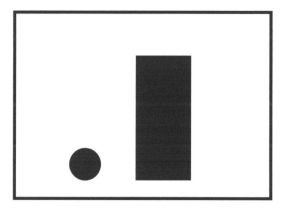

**Figure 11.15**

Putting a very small ball right next to the square makes it feel so much bigger, because now we have an object to compare it to. Objects usually appear in relationship with other objects in the frame (which can be anything really; a carpet or the texture of wood both would help in defining the object's size). This can help to roughly assess its size. Size can also create a feeling of perspective. In this case, it feels like the ball, because of its small size, is either very small and close or huge and very far away. However, because we do not exactly know how big the ball is we can neither say how big the rectangle is or which one is closer; we only have the feeling of one being bigger than the other.

**Figure 11.16**

Positioning an even bigger square next to existing objects all of a sudden makes them shrink in size. The new object influences again the scale of the ones on the left. Now the right square is either the biggest or the closest object.

and Thumbnail Drawings" in Chapter 8, "Directions"), we might need a large shape, for instance, to accentuate an emotion or to balance visual weight in order to express a certain "feel" in the image. In Figure 11.17, for example, the big shape on the right could be a huge wall, but it could also be just a box of matches that is close to the camera. Furthermore, by changing the size, we can change not only the visual weight of the object but we can also affect its significance. But there are two directions.

**Figure 11.17**

Increasing the size of the right rectangle, the space that the ball and the left rectangle occupy is dramatically reduced, and they are cramped into the corner. The huge rectangle is just enormous and feels as if it wants to push the two left objects out of the frame. It is actually growing in size. The further we push that idea, the smaller and more insignificant or further away the other objects feel. They seem to be pushed out by the big weight of the oversized square. This can be the actual size of the object or heavily affected by its position. A very small object close to the camera seems very big, which brings us to the following.

One is to actually put emphasis and importance onto the object and the other direction is to take away the emphasis completely and just use the object for its compositional value rather than its meaning. In Figure 11.18, this composition could, as a combination of the two elements of balloon and house, represent a house full of happiness or playfulness or any other meaning that could result from the two elements (according to the story's needs). However, the balloon could also only be used for its visual weight in the composition and how it makes the house "feel," which is pushed onto, threatened, partly hidden, covered, there is a light weight on the house, etc. The balloon's "meaning" would then be secondary but its compositional weight the main point. However, this has to be done delicately as everything does come with a meaning and does affect the story. Light and shadow, for instance, can help to reduce the importance of an object that is only there for its compositional value. This also works rather well in elements that do not have an immediate meaning to them, are not clearly recognizable, and do not push themselves into the foreground of the story: beams, generic architectural parts, and elements that are so close to the camera that they blur and thus lose their instant perceptibility. The two-dimensional flat cinematic screen allows the play of all elements despite their distance from the camera as elements for the composition (however, depth of field and color perspective can affect it significantly). In a 3D cinematic screen, this is a bit more difficult because the eye can actually determine where each element is located within the space. But even in 3D viewing the visual weight of the object is maintained.

**Figure 11.18**

## Shape and design

Design can impact the feeling of size when its overall shape and also the secondary shapes are inflated, softened, and changed in their relationship to each other. This usually means that important elements are either bigger or smaller in relation to the whole than they should be (Figure 11.19). This is a common design direction for toys for toddlers and smaller children to make the design more "cute" and follow a design that goes along with baby-like features of extreme body ratio and rounded features. It is also widely used in animation design to make objects, characters, and environments more appealing through rounding the shapes. Early Mickey Mouse cartoons or Disney's *Lilo and Stitch* are obvious examples.

By reducing details, eliminating edgy geometry, and rounding edges, architecture and objects do have the tendency to seem to shrink visually. By just taking the same design of the house (Figure 11.20) and rounding all the corners, it already looks smaller (Figure 11.21). The house can be reduced further in size by increasing the size of its secondary elements like windows, door, or chimney. It starts to look like a puppet house (Figures 11.22 and 11.23).

**Figure 11.20**

**Figure 11.21**

**Figure 11.19**

**Figure 11.22**

Films that deal with size in an interesting way:

- Disney's *Pinocchio* (1940)
- George Pal's *Tom Thumb* (1958)
- Joe Johnston's *Honey I Shrunk the Kids* (1998)
- *King Kong* (Merian C. Cooper's 1933 version or Peter Jackson's 2005 version)

- DreamWorks's *Bee Movie* (2007)
- Hiromasa Yonebayashi's *The Secret World of Arietty* (2010)
- Guillermo del Toro's *Pacific Rim* (2013)
- *Godzilla* (Roland Emmerich's 1998 version or Gareth Edwards' 2014 version)

**Figure 11.23**

# CHAPTER 12

# Depth

Depth in an image can be controlled by various aspects to create or avoid it. For instance, in many hand-drawn animated TV shows, depth is avoided for a more graphic look rather than one with three-dimensionality (shows like *Dexter's Laboratory*, *Powerpuff Girls*, and *My Gym Partner's a Monkey* use depth to enhance the flatness or the semiflatness of the space). Depth is therefore also part of a style and can be equally played with in the two- and three-dimensional space.

**Depth can be defined by:**

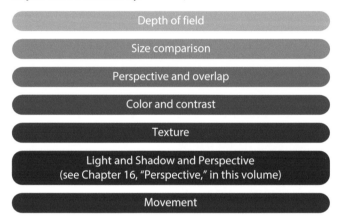

Depth of field

Size comparison

Perspective and overlap

Color and contrast

Texture

Light and Shadow and Perspective
(see Chapter 16, "Perspective," in this volume)

Movement

## Depth of field

Where depth defines the distance from the closest to the farthest object, *depth of field* defines the area between the objects that are visually sharp. This can range from the closest to the farthest

object in a very deep depth of field or deep focus, or just contain one object in the entire frame that is focused in a low depth of field and everything around it is blurred. The human eye only has a small area that is in full focus; the rest of the field of vision is by nature rather blurry. Depth of field and with it the blurriness of the objects or surroundings are a strong indicator of depth, one that immediately makes the eye recognize foreground, middle ground and background. The greater the amount of blur in an object, the further the object gets pushed forward or backward, depending also on the other aspects of color, perspective, texture, and size. Looking at Figures 12.1 through 12.3, the two squares in Figure 12.3 seem to have a greater distance between them compared to the ones in Figure 12.1. Therefore the stronger the blurriness is, the greater the distance seems between focus and out of focus. Even the little blur in Figure 12.1 pushes the upper square away from the level the lower square rests on, either forward or backwards (to me, the blurred squares seem to step backwards, though). The difficulty of deciding if the square is going forward or backward is the lack of overlap, contrast, texture, or color perspective. For instance, changing the contrast between the two squares, does it have the effect of bringing the blurred square closer to the viewer (Figure 12.4)?.

In an image with foreground, middle ground, and background, the possibilities for depth of field are plenty, but the eye will immediately and always go to the area with the sharp focus.

Figure 12.5 shows a bug in a jungle. The focus is obviously on the bug as the concentric composition puts the character in the visual center and there is no depth of field. Figure 12.6 brings

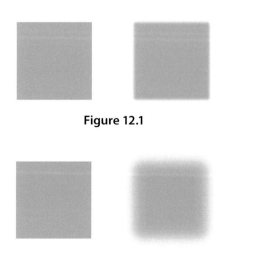

**Figure 12.1**

**Figure 12.3**

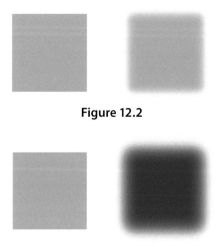

**Figure 12.2**

**Figure 12.4**

Figure 12.5

Figure 12.6

Figure 12.7

Figure 12.8

Figure 12.9

in depth of field and blurs the background, creating more depth, as in Figure 12.5. The focus is literally on the bug and the middle ground. Figure 12.7 additionally has the middle ground blurred, which clearly puts the focus only onto the bug. Even if the eye would like to observe the jungle, one can't, because it is already out of focus, whereas in Figure 12.6 there is at least the possibility for the eye to explore the middle ground. Depth of field puts significance on areas within the frame and the camera chooses what is important and what is not. The more blurry the background is, the less texture, the softer and the more focus is given to the sharp parts in the frame. There is in Figure 12.7 a very clear separation between bug and jungle. If the focus shifts from the bug to the middle ground in Figure 12.8, the eye constantly goes towards the sharp leaves in the middle. The middle layer gets pulled towards the viewer because of the similarity between background and bug in terms of blurriness. However, the overlap of the big leaf's stem clearly positions it closest to the viewer, but

the closeness of bug/big leaf and background, however, pull them towards each other, which causes a visual discrepancy the eye struggles with. In Figure 12.9, with the big leaf's stem behind the middle ground, it clearly moves closer and, despite the smaller leaves, stays in the foreground.

Changing the focus from one element/object/character in the frame to another shifts the viewer's attention from one point in the frame to another, which is an excellent tool for cinematic storytelling, as it does mimic the human eye's ability and natural vision.

## Miniaturization

Exaggerating the blur in an image above the normal level will have the effect of miniaturization (or the opposite: reducing the blurriness in small objects can, under certain circumstances, have

**Figure 12.10**

**Figure 12.11**

the effect of maximizing objects). The eye, being accustomed to a level of blur at certain distances, assumes that the distance is much smaller or bigger than it actually is. For example, in the photograph of New York City in Figures 12.10 and 12.11, we see an aerial view of Manhattan. In Figure 12.10 everything is more or less in focus. But once the image is heavily blurred in the outer parts, the block of houses in the center of Figure 12.11 all of a sudden seems miniscule rather than huge. The same happens with a smaller object like the small Cambodian temple in Angkor Wat (Figure 12.12). The exaggerated blurriness in the background lets the temple shrink down in size (Figure 12.12b).

This can be used, for example, in CG environments to make the set look smaller, like a puppet set, and thus additionally shrink the set.

It is also used in science animation for mimicking macroscopic sizes of elements, molecules, viruses, etc.

## Size comparison

The comparison between two objects whose size is known through past experience is, as we have seen in Chapter 11, "Size," a strong indicator of depth. But the object needs to be locked

within the perspective in order to fully work (see Figures 11.4, 11.6, and 11.7).

## Perspective and overlap

Perspective is another indicator of depth and one that is very accurate in terms of the distances between objects within the frame as long as the constructed perspective is not sporadic but its grid includes all elements in the frame. Without one-, two-, or three-point perspective, only a combination of various factors (size, texture, color, contrast, depth of field, overlap …) gives one a clear judgment for distance. Constructed perspective, however, creates refined depth. A perspective grid into which some elements of the image are locked along with the diminishing sizes towards the vanishing point simulate distances on the z-axis clearly, as we have seen in Figures 11.6 and 11.7. The only proof that an object is in front, on the same level, or behind another object via overlap.

Then there is the relationship between objects and the horizon, which also indicates depth and how far away an object is from the viewer. However, this only is a clear marker of depth if the objects clearly relate to or are standing on the ground plane.

(a)

(b)

**Figure 12.12**

Various objects in various distances from the horizon clarify the perspective rules of the image and thus help the viewer to understand their spatial connections.

## Color and contrast

(Also see Chapter 11, "Size," and Chapter 15, "Color Contrast.")

Contrast between the different levels can also be a strong indicator of depth. Figures 12.13 through 12.15 show how drastically the feeling of depth can change when only the background is changed in value and contrast in relationship to the foreground. In Figure 12.13, the bug seems to be in a lighting that is not too deep. By brightening up the background significantly, the depth is expanded (Figure 12.14) and the silhouette of the character is more obvious; the importance of the bug and the leaf are increased. A lighter background not only opens the space and makes it more "airy" but also pushes the background further away, giving the space depth and clearly light. Darkening the background and reducing the

contrast towards the middle ground flattens the image and obviously, because of the lack of contrast within the entire frame, the image feels flat and dark; its mood even shifts in this case towards melancholy and, if pushed, even sad (Figure 12.15). The less contrast there is in the image, the flatter it is, the more contrast (done in the right way) can produce a deeper image.

## Texture

(Also see Chapter 17, "Texture.")

Figure 12.12a on the left has plenty of contrast, which as we have just seen in the section "Color and Contrast" should produce depth, but the image still feels flat because the texture of the background trees is as busy as the texture of the upper part of the temple; therefore both seem to be on the same level, fighting for dominance. By changing the background from the foreground of Figure 12.12a into Figure 12.12b, giving the background more blur, thus reducing its texture and

Figure 12.13

Figure 12.14

Figure 12.15

darkening it, two levels are created that are clearly different from each other, and the focus is now on the temple and the background steps back in importance. But because of the blurriness of the background, the miniaturization effect occurs and the temple seems much smaller than in the original image on the left.

The size of the texture relative to its distance from the viewer can be a determinant for depth. The closer the object to the viewer, the more coarse-grained the texture can be; the further away the texture, the more fine-grained it appears.

Texture that is too dominant in its visual energy can drag the eye away from the focal point and thus cause a constant back and forth between focal point and texture, like in Figure 12.16, where the house is the focus but the texture in the background is very busy and thus pulls much of the attention. Additionally, it also steps forward and reduces the depth. Reducing the size of the background texture can again allow the focal point to be the center of attention, like in Figure 12.17. Blurring out the background can take away the energy of the texture and allow the foreground to again be the focus. It also makes the image visually more quiet, as seen in Figure 12.18.

Figure 12.16

Figure 12.17

Figure 12.18

# Movement

Movement tells us about the distance of objects to the viewer via parallax, the phenomenon that closer objects pass the viewer with greater speed than objects far away. The sun, seemingly not moving at all when driving parallel to it through a landscape, is therefore obviously extremely far away. A road sign on a highway zips by the car window at high speed; therefore it is very close to the viewer. Depth then is estimated during movement not only via parallax but also through the constant overlap of all the moving elements within the landscape. Closer objects will during the movement constantly overlap objects in the farther distance.

# CHAPTER 13

# Light and Shadow

**Figure 13.1**

The Himalayas before sunset.

## Light, shadow, and form

This chapter is not about the accurate construction of light and shadow, but rather a general observation of it and its artistic impact. An excellent book on the topic of how to render light and shadow is Scott Robertson's *How to Render: The Fundamentals of Light, Shadow and Reflectivity*, Design Studio Press, Culver City, CA, 2014.

Light and shadow are two of the most powerful agents in images. They not only make things visible or invisible but also consciously and subconsciously comment on the content of an image by telling a story, or by creating a unique mood with a subtle and intricate play between the colors, like in Figure 13.1 with the Himalayas in an intricate and rather surreal play of light, color and atmosphere. By denying an area light, its content is covered and mystery is created. Tension and suspense are emotions that go along with shadows and darkness as the audience literally looks into unknown territory where the hidden lures. Primeval fear is what makes us hesitate to step into dark places. Shadows have always had a mysterious feel as they are part of the object, but not the object itself; they represent also parts of the character, being attached to them, but seem to so easily be able to have their own will. Disney's *Peter Pan* (1953) and Carl Theodor Dreyer's *Vampyr* (1932) contain shadows that become acting and reacting characters themselves. Or the terrifying shadow of the vampire in Murnau's *Nosferatu: A Symphony of Horror* (1922) that signals his master's appearance. Light on the other hand often means safety and comfort as nothing is being kept visually from the audience. In Steven Spielberg's *Close Encounters of the Third Kind* (1977) or *E.T. the Extra-Terrestrial* (1982), light is the abstract representation of the alien life-form and is literally a character in its

own right. Nevertheless, light and shadow not only affect the story and illuminate the setting but also give a set, object and character dimensionality.

Light itself is invisible. Its electromagnetic radiation cannot be seen by itself. What can be seen, however, is the object in its path, which gets illuminated and therefore the object lightens up, not the light itself. Shadow on the other hand is the lack of light, the absence of it. Without light everything is flat; light renders shapes into forms. Live-action film or stop-motion animation only exists through the use of light: reality is their basis and reality without light does not exist. Graphic arts like drawing and painting are not dependent on light (other than seeing the physical image of course) as they can freely use the line and shape in any way they please. Light is a possibility, not a necessity. Hand-drawn animation, which is part of the graphic tradition (in its image-making production, not its presentation), does not need light and shadow to convince; it can create its own reality based on lines, colors, and shapes, but not form.[1] Light and shadow can add dimensionality to the two-dimensional (2D) image and render shapes into forms. Nevertheless, in the graphic arts, light and shadow can be separated and used on their own, whereas in live-action or stop-motion animation both are co-dependent. When it comes to hand-drawn animation, light and shadow can cover the whole range from abstract to hyperrealistic, something that live-action cinema isn't capable of doing (as of yet) even in its most stark contrasts. Norman McLaren's masterful animated short

---

[1]  Obviously 2D animation is also part of the cinematic arts, which heavily depend on light in the presentation of the film itself.

DOI: 10.1201/b22148-13

**Figure 13.2**

Norman McLaren: *Pas de Deux* (1968).

film *Pas de Deux* (1968) (Figure 13.2) has, due to shooting with high-contrast film, an extremely short range between light and dark. This is more or less how far live-action images can push light and shadow and create strong blacks and whites. In McLaren's short, there are very few areas where light gives volume to the dancers as the contrast only has fast fall-off shadows that don't allow a long gradient between light and dark. The strong lights from left and right offstage just render the outlines and accentuate the silhouette. *Pas de Deux* is as far as live-action film can push the contrast on film. In the end, the image that is based on reality lives off of light and cannot exist without it.

Drawings, hand-drawn animation, illustration, and all other graphic arts can extend those limits much further to the point of completely eliminating light and shadow in the image itself. A drawing, just consisting of the outline of the character, does not need to have any light or shadow, but just a line that defines shape, not volume. The volume, however, can be suggested through lines, but the lines do not need to render it in its dimensionality to be understood. The drawing of Egon Schiele (Figure 13.3) has only lines that define the nude man; there is no suggestion of any shadow or light. The line itself creates the illusion of dimensionality via the correct placement of the lines with their curvature and overlap. The observing eye fills the gaps and finishes through the knowledge of the human body the image. This is the strength of drawings to leave things open for interpretation and not finish them meticulously, but have the viewers participate in finalizing the drawing in their mind. And here is one important difference in the representation of the objects and characters in drawings and hand-drawn animation versus life action: live-action shows volume, which is only possible with light, whereas shape in a drawing can exist without it. One can light a live-action set evenly and eliminate as much of the shadows and highlights as

possible and have the objects and characters appear flat, but one still has to use lighting to do that. This gives animation and graphic arts a huge range of possibilities to "draw" from, as light and shadow restrict the live-action artist to realism of a certain degree. Any hand-drawn animated line-test proves that there is only the line that describes the body's shapes. We know the volume and perspective in the moving character, because we know how a (human) body looks like and our imagination fills in the gaps. The thickness of the line itself, however, could suggest light and shadow in the drawing. Once we start to introduce color into the image, the situation slightly changes as color itself can be connected to warm or cold, light or dark, which obviously can suggest light but does not have to. 2D animation, existing mostly through color and line, does not therefore need light to be understood. There are many examples of 2D animation where light and shadow do not play a role at all. An example of an animation where the image lacks light and shadow completely is the Chinese animator A Da's short film *Three Monks*, from 1980, produced by the legendary Shanghai Animation Film Studio (SAFS). Landscape and characters are solely rendered by line and color; there is no suggestion of light at all.

The next step toward a more form-oriented visual would be to introduce some light and shadow to provide more volume to the objects, but not reveal where the light is actually coming from. Franz Marc's painting *Little Yellow Horses* (Figure 13.4) gives us the volume of the horses in a basic form, as their bodies are sculpted with light and dark shades of yellow and orange. The light source itself, however, is not revealed; the false suggestion of light is only there for the clarification of volume in its most basic form. There is a hint of dimensionality, underlined by overlap. Gradually introducing more and more light and shadow slowly turns the image more "realistic" and form is rendered more clearly.

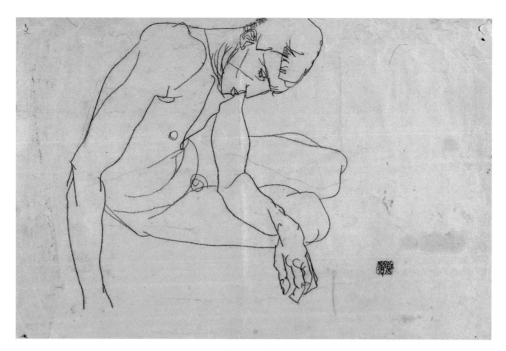

**Figure 13.3**

Egon Schiele: *Nude* (1913).

**Figure 13.4**

Franz Marc: *Little yellow horses* (1912).

# Unrealistic use of light and shadow

Light and shadow do not necessarily have to be rendered realistically, but can be used artistically to either make a story point clearer or to use it as a compositional agent to strengthen the arrangement in the frame. The use of light and shadow in Figure 13.5, for instance, is not realistic at all, but is used to enhance the composition and story. This is where the natural qualities of light and shadow step back and allow its graphic, its metaphorical and story shaping qualities to step forward, which are equally important! The advantage of a more graphic approach is that the image does not require the restrictions

Figure 13.5

needed to render realistically but can use light and shadow freely as an additional creative tool rather than a requirement for realism. For example, the paintings of expressionistic painter Lyonel Feininger (1871–1956) often use the quality of light and shadow for their compositional strength rather than try to render realistically (e.g., *Marine Blau* (1924) and *Gelmeroda Village Pond* (1922)). Also some of the works of futurist painter Tullio Crali (1910–2000), especially his painting *Before the Parachute Opens (Prima che si apra il paracadute)* (1939), deal with light and shadow in a creative and unique way.

**What light and shadow can achieve (aside from illuminating the scene of course and create form):**

Create or enhance the mood

Affect the color-design

Reflect the character's emotional and psychological state

Be the focal point

Serve as a vector towards the focal point

Create layers of information

Address the relationships between character, background and objects

Reflect or comment on the story

Create perspective

The achievements of light and shadow can be examined through the works of N.C. Wyeth (1882–1945), one of the most well-known American illustrators famous for

his romantic images of adventure stories, especially for R.L. Stevenson's *Treasure Island* and *Kidnapped*. His work is often theatrical in order to tell the story clearer and straightforward without much interpretation that might dilute the message. Wyeth studied under Howard Pyle (1853–1911), who is famous for his par excellence pirate illustrations (Figure 13.6) and one of the trailblazers of American illustration at the beginning of the 20th century. In 1900, Pyle opened the Brandywine School for illustration in which he taught a style that N. C. Wyeth, Frank E. Schoonover, and their peers often followed in their own work. Wyeth's illustrations are closely related to that of his teacher's in that they both used very similar techniques and compositions, aside from similar topics. Pyle taught his students the following: "Don't make it necessary to ask questions about your picture. It's utterly impossible for you to go to all the newsstands and explain your picture."[2] To create "obvious" visuals that are immediately understood, not only from a storytelling perspective but also from an emotional one the realistic illustrations are very romantic in their approach and have melodramatic and colorful staging and poses that fit very well the adventurous themes they often deal with. The exaggerated drama is what Wyeth often applies to express the story and that is what makes them theatrical in their core, yet also popular through their easy understandability, however, by no means simple in their compositional complexity, quite the contrary. Wyeth's fame, along with Pyle's, developed because of their embodiment of the adventure–illustration itself. Pyle's work, for example, is what defined the look of what we consider

---

[2] Alexander Nemerov, N. C. Wyeth's Theater of Illustration, *American Art* Vol. 6, No. 2 (Spring, 1992), pp. 36–57.

**Figure 13.6**

Howard Pyle: *An Attack on a Galleon* (1905).

**Figure 13.7**

NC Wyeth: *The Silent Burial* (1907).

to be the typical pirate type and outfit, which we still use today. Wyeth on the other hand achieved the same with his famous illustrations for *Treasure Island* that are continuously referred to as *the* visualization of R.L. Stevenson's famous story. As Wyeth wrote to his mother in a letter after the work on the series of illustrations was done: "Treasure Island is completed! The entire set of seventeen canvases without one break in my enthusiasm and spirit. Better in every quality than anything I ever did." And it clearly shows on every canvas!

Nevertheless, the first two illustrations used for this exploration on light and shadow are not for the novel but are magazine illustrations for another story.

## Create or enhance the mood (Figure 13.7)

This illustration from 1907 *The Silent Burial* of a Native American, from Wyeth's series *The Indian in His Solitude*,

appeared in the *Outing Magazine* (published from 1882 to 1923), which contained articles on outdoor and sports activities. Wyeth paints with a style that though seems realistic is very stylized and exaggerated for theatrical impact. Everything in this illustration is bathed in an otherworldly light that creates a mysterious mood.[3] It fits the cliché of the spiritual native, who is close to nature, just standing still within a spot that appears to have a spiritual significance. The somber mood is very much created by the light coming from straight above the Native American. Nevertheless, it is stylized light that marks the subject and the little pool, and pushes everything else into the background. The light is very much responsible for the strange color and surreal mood. Because the light only illuminates a specific area of

---

[3] Digital representations of artwork can differ quite dramatically in color and contrast; therefore, all statements on color and light are only true to the image presented. A final judgment on color can only be truthfully done in front of the actual painting.

the space, it renders that spot important and with the native Indian and his immediate surroundings becomes spiritual and unique.

## Affect the color design (Figure 13.8)

*In the Crystal Depths*, which is also from the series *The Indian and His Solitude*, beautifully shows how Wyeth uses light and shadow to truly *design* the color direction of the piece. The Indian is in the shadow, which covers most of the picture, but the light is seen on the right in orange and yellow. To juxtapose the golden light, he uses the complimentary color blue in the shadow. He pushes the impressionistic treatment of shadows by painting the left side of the image and the reflection in the river very blue and using it as a strong design element against the sunny side of the rock. The streaks on the river are exquisitely designed and add with the white floating particles to the surreal, mystical, and quiet mood of the piece.

The following illustrations from 1911 are from Wyeth's series for R.L. Stevenson's famous *Treasure Island* (1883) adventure novel and among the most famous depictions of the story.

## Reflect the character's emotional and psychological state (Figure 13.9)

Wyeth said about his own work: "If you paint a man leaning over, your own back must ache." The emotion of the character on the canvas or screen must be felt by the artist to get away from mere visual description and add emotion to the piece. The same then extends into the realm outside of the canvas: the image must evoke emotions also in the viewer. The emotion of the character can be expressed first and foremost through pose and facial expression, but also reflected through the environment, light, and weather. In Figure 13.9, we see Captain Billy Bones, who is in the novel *Treasure Island* a drunkard and seaman of the roughest kind, swearing, yelling, singing, and bragging with bloodcurdling stories about his violent adventures. His description in the novel is of a very uncomfortable and filthy man who everyone tries to avoid. Wyeth shows him standing at the coast, brooding and looking out for someone he is afraid to meet, while his cape is blowing in the wind, giving him a dark

**Figure 13.8**

NC Wyeth: *In the Crystal Depths* (1905).

**Figure 13.9**

N.C. Wyeth: *Treasure Island* (1911).

and voluminous silhouette. The weather condition in this image reflects Bones' personality, who is cold and repelling. Weather is thus an excellent tool for expressing the character's emotional or psychological state as it can stand as a metaphor for character and narrative.

An illustration not necessarily is just depicting one moment of the story, but needs to spark the imagination of the reader. If it reveals too much, the reader's own involvement in the visuals is prohibited. It needs to show just enough for the reader to follow the artist on his path but also be able to expand that path on his or her own. That is exactly what Wyeth gives us: the ground stone for an imaginative world, not the whole world. Light and shadow play a very important role in his work as one will see in the next couple of examples as he likes to hide parts of the image instead of revealing them all.

## Be the focal point (Figure 13.10)

This illustration shows Jim Hawkins, the hero in the story, finally finding the sought-after treasure in Ben Gunn's cave. The light illuminates the scene just enough for the eye to be attracted by Jim's white shirt. The light comes in from an angle that allows

his action to be clear, yet partially covering his face. The light does not have to be a strong shaft that clearly distinguishes light from shadow but can also be a vague light, rendering the objects and characters' forms and allowing a vagueness that supports the imagination of the reader. Images like this are the ones that we associate very closely with Stevenson's adventure story and any other stories about treasures and pirates. Many of Wyeth's images were genre-shaping paintings that very romantically cover the topics in an impressionistic open style yet do not fall into the trap of too much emotion where it can start to be awkward. Much of this is due to his ability to have a focal point but never say too much in the emotional expression of the characters' faces. Eyes are often sunken in and covered in shadows, which allows a certain distance between the viewer and the character. One is never fixated on the eyes, despite their obvious importance.

## Serve as a vector toward the focal point (Figure 13.11)

Ben Gunn, the sailor who has been marooned on Treasure Island for years and seems to have lost his mind, peeks through the woods to see the arriving parties. The streak of

**Figure 13.10**

N.C. Wyeth: *Treasure Island* (1911).

**Figure 13.11**

N.C. Wyeth: *Treasure Island* (1911).

sunlight that falls through the foliage and lights up the trunk in front of him is a clear vector that points down to the focal point: Ben Gunn's face.

## Create layers of information (Figure 13.12)

In this illustration, the character tells a different story than what the shadow suggests. The blind man called Pew tries to find his hat but goes in the wrong direction. His cane is searching at the left of the screen, but the hat is located on the right of the screen. Wyeth's idea is to let the shadow of the cane find the hat. This is the ironic touch in the painting; it tells the viewer through the shadow that Pew is searching for something. The story tells us that he is panicking. Riders are coming down the road and he wants to avoid them. He loses his way on the street, stumbles and is finally being run over by the horses and dies. Without the shadow, it wouldn't be obvious what Pew is actually looking for. Wyeth achieved several goals with his idea: telling a story from various perspectives, trying to find something that is right in front of one's eyes, being ironic, and having a unique composition where not just shapes but also light and shadow are part of the composition.

## Address the relationships between characters, background, and objects (Figure 13.13)

Here Jim Hawkins is leaving home for his perilous journey of finding a treasure on a faraway island. His mother is in the background and is mourning his leaving. Jim is standing in the shadow in the center of the image, while his mother on the left is illuminated by sunlight. The impact is striking because lighting wise the focus is on the mother, story wise and compositionally the focus is of course on Jim leaving. And exactly that is the story the lighting tells us: Jim's future is in the dark and covered by shadows and thus is unknown. His mother's future instead is clear and obvious: she is staying at home in safety. The juxtaposition of composition, light, shadow, and story lets the eye wander constantly from the mother to Jim and gives the image a certain interesting imbalance and movement back and forth. The characters are separated by the light, yet still connected. Their relationship is clear and the story receives a subliminal message through the lighting. Jim is also literally "on the path," whereas his mother is standing next to the path. He is on the move, she is not.

**Figure 13.12**

N.C. Wyeth: *Treasure Island* (1911).

**Figure 13.13**

N.C. Wyeth: *Treasure Island* (1911).

## Reflect or comment on the story (Figure 13.14)

This is the story point in which the pirates and mutineers are cutting out a circle from a page of the Bible due to lack of paper. The circle is blackened with soot on one side and bears a message on the other, which is then given to a traitor as "the black spot," a sign of his upcoming judgment. The black spot that is cut in this illustration is supposed to be given to John Silver, the head of the band of mutineers. He realizes that they had cut it out of a Bible, which, as he tells them repeatedly, is a very bad omen indeed. Wyeth shows us the action of the cutting, but also covers half of the action. We feel the secrecy and thus the wrongness of their action. The lighting situation is referring to the work of Georges de La Tour (1593–1652) (Figure 13.15), with the strong scenes lit by one candle or torch, where the light itself is often hidden by a character, but the effect of the light is overwhelming.

## Create perspective (Figure 13.16)

(This point is going to be talked about much more in the upcoming section "Levels and Lighting" as there is more to discuss).

The image shows John Silver dragging Jim on a rope along with his band of "Gentlemen of fortune" (pirates). The foreground is in shadow, something Wyeth likes to do in his illustrations exactly for the reason of creating a staggered arrangement of levels for

**Figure 13.15**

Georges de La Tour: *Joseph the Carpenter* (1645).

**Figure 13.14**

N.C. Wyeth: *Treasure Island* (1911).

**Figure 13.16**

N.C. Wyeth: *Treasure Island* (1911).

225

producing perspective and depth. Light and shadow are very effective tools to level the information in the image. The levels of light and shadow can also intersect (as is going to be shown in Orson Welles' *Citizen Kane* in this chapter). One can clearly see the very same layering of shadow in front of light in Howard Pyle's illustration *An Attack on a Galleon* in the beginning of this chapter.

When it comes to light and shadow in illustration, we obviously only deal with one image that does not change; however, in the cinematic image, light and shadow can change and thus additionally not only show and comment on a moment in time but also show a development during a certain time frame, thus expanding on the storytelling and, along with all the just mentioned artistic possibilities of light and shadow, also expanding on its metaphorical meaning. The following case study shows an excellent and exceptional example of how light and shadow can be used to its full extent in Pixar's feature *UP* (2009).

## Case study: Light and shadow's effect on story, mood, and emotion in Pixar's *UP* (2009)

Light and shadow should always be visually and intellectually in line with the scene of the script, interpret its meaning, and consider its emotional strength, not merely mimic the natural lighting situation. The emotional or psychological state of the character, as we have seen in *The Cabinet of Dr. Caligari* (Chapter 10, "Mood"), can be exposed in the environment; the weather condition or the architecture of the setting can further refine the union of character and environment. This liaison has to be active and alive as no character is "just" in an environment for no reason. There is always an interaction between the two in a film's theatrical reality. This relationship can be expressed in various ways, although light and shadow are among the most powerful agents. They do not simply illuminate the setting, but they bring emotions to the surface and visualize the character's psychological and emotional state as much as the environment design does with shapes, color, and texture. Light and shadow also affect the color in a setting and can change any location from one side of the emotional spectrum to the other just by changing the intensity, angle, color or type of light. Many movies deal with light in an excellent fashion and it is rather difficult to choose one that should represent light and storytelling. Kenji Mizoguchi's films, especially *The Story of Oharu* (1952) or *Ugetsu* (1953) are beautifully lit black and white masterpieces; Stanley Kubrick's *Barry Lyndon* (1975) is of course famous for its extraordinary way of using natural and realistic light, mimicking a painterly Baroque aesthetic. An even more realistic approach is the previously mentioned film *The Assassination of Jesse James by the Coward Robert Ford* (2007) by Andrew Dominick. Then there is Michael Cimino's stylized and stunning film *Heaven's Gate* (1980) with truly sublime visuals and a golden light, which renders the images in a historical setting of times gone by. *Heaven's Gate* is shot by cinematographer Vilmos Zsigmond, who also shot Spielberg's *Sugarland Express* and *Close Encounters of the Third Kind*. Also, any film of Chinese filmmaker Zhang Yimou is a feast for the eyes in color, lighting, and storytelling, or Chen Kaige's 1993 *Farewell My Concubine*, with its delicate lighting and extravagant and lavish visuals. The examples are plentiful. However, there is one film that I would like to discuss in terms of storytelling and light as it is easily understood in its simplicity and clarity: Pixar's movie *UP* (2009), directed by Pete Docter. In animation, the advantage

is that the lighting in the shot can be controlled to the last little detail as everything is done from scratch and therefore the entire shot can be crafted to perfection. The lighting is incredibly subtle in some shots of *UP* and perfectly represents the story to the minute point. It is especially the first half hour of the film that is masterfully arranged.

The development process of the lighting starts in animation with the color keys for each scene to see the emotional development of the film from a color perspective. Harley Jessup, designer at Pixar, says about the color keys that have been produced by Lou Romano:

> Lou Romano created the colour script, which was very detailed, and then we went back for the lighting studies. We were trying to capture the emotional feeling that Lou put into the colour script. Besides the shape language we have going, there's a very strong use of lighting and colour saturation treatments for different sequences in trying to evoke a mood. We saved certain lighting effects for the climax and then carefully built up to that point. Russell, when he comes on the scene, brings some colour and saturation to Carl's drab, shut-in world. And Ellie has the same effect–of bringing colour to Carl's world.[4]

The main character in *UP*, Mr. Carl Fredricksen, loses his wife at an old age. She had been presented in earlier scenes as the one in the relationship that brought the fun and adventure into their life, that pushed him, the more reserved and conservative type, to enjoy himself. She was the inspired one, whereas Mr. Fredricksen, even as a little boy, was more shy, cautious, and restrained. His tragic loss is visualized in the scene right after her funeral (timecode 00:11:11–00:11:18) with light and shadow creating the needed change of their once happy and colorful home now lacking something that was there before, but disappeared. After the funeral for his wife, Mr. Fredricksen is entering his home in the early evening. The shot (timecode 00:11:18–00:11:32) lacks bright light, has a gloomy atmosphere, and the emotional hole that the death of his wife created is visually present. The time of the day that is chosen to interpret this loss in Carl's life is the sunset, often

---

4  Tim Hauser, *The Art of UP*, Chronicle Books, San Francisco, 2009, p. 84.

standing for old age when life is slowly fading away. Only the right side of the house is partially lit by the setting sun, illuminating the window of the living room, which has the couple's "shrine" above the fire place. The purple setting sun is reflected in both windows, and it is the small light in the left window on the opposite side of the lit house, which is the first to slowly disappear. It seems to represent Ellie's light that has been turned off by her death and soon after, Carl's light on the right also volatilizes: happiness is gone. When Ellie is in the hospital bed in the two shots before, she occupies the left side of the frame and Carl the middle. Cut to the funeral home where Carl is still in the middle and the left is replaced by a huge bouquet of balloons. Dissolve of Carl walking into his house. The left is still occupied by Ellie in our memory, so the left side of the house represents her and the right side represents Carl (if one wants the composition to be interpreted this way). There is a little bit of light left in his life that gave him joy and hope, though once he steps into the house, the light disappears and the sun sets, taking the joy away from the place they built together. The slow disappearance of the light is so exquisite in this shot that it is obviously not only an emotional addition but also the visual representation of the story. Without this subtle performance of light and shadow the story would not read as successfully. Inside of the house in this first shot, right at the spot where the setting sun reflects in the window, we know is the painting of Paradise Falls on the wall that they painted together years ago, which was their desired destination, the depiction of their childhood dream. There is also the wooden bird underneath, a model blimp, the picture of her as a child that is a constant reminder of what they were planning to do as kids. It is like a shrine for their former wishes that were postponed because life got in the way. From the outside we only see a small light in the window that reminds us of this promise they gave each other decades ago to visit Paradise Falls, but the small light connects all the threads of the story in that very moment when he enters the empty house. There is no need for the audience to understand exactly what the light in this image means in detail and how it relates to the overall story. What is important is that the audience *feels* what is emotionally happening with Mr. Fredricksen and how he is dealing with the death of his wife psychologically. What this shot demonstrates is the ability of light to not just express the moment but an entire time-frame. It is the temporal change of the lighting itself that expresses the serious shift in Carl's life.

The next day when he wakes up (timecode 00:11:43), he is in bed and the sun just illuminates the side of the bed his wife used to sleep on. His side is covered in shadow, meaning his life lacks the light it formerly had. But it also shows his own emotional inner state: sadness represented by the lack of light and desaturated color. Our eyes usually go immediately to the lightest and the warmest area in an image; so, the warm sunlight illuminating the empty spot in the bedroom points out his loss immediately though his character makes him the center of the frame from the perspective of the composition. The warm colors and the vector of the sunlight, pointing down at her side of the bed, attract attention first. This creates a nice tension between warm colored light source and cold character because both occupy a different space in the image, although they are nearly symmetrical to the center of the frame. Usually, light not shadow is used to emphasize the focal point, although the opposite can also work if it goes along with the story point. The slight imbalance in the weight of the composition (one side of the bed is empty, while the other side is occupied) points out what is missing and clearly relates both sides to each other. He is the positive space in the shadow, while she is the negative space in the light: a perfect balance in the frame in terms of composition and storytelling. Also, each side of the bed is designed keeping the personality of each one in mind. Mr. Fredricksen is rigid and conservative, represented by the shape of a square. His head is a box, his clock on the bed stand is a box, and the picture frame is a rectangle. Her side of the bed, her being the more flexible type, has round shapes.

The desaturated color direction continues in the film till the appearance of Russel, the little Asian boy that will travel with him to Paradise Falls. As Lou Romano states: "When Carl is forced into the present, he's miserable and the colour is bleak. But as each new character is introduced, we see flashes of life and colour."[5] Russel is bringing with him bright sunlight and saturated colors, a stark contrast to Carl's gloom. The saturation is fully coming into the frame once Carl launches his house into the air, which is the point where Carl's promise to go to Paradise Falls comes true. It is the beginning of his new life, when he takes charge of his own happiness.

5   Tim Hauser, *The Art of UP*, Chronicle Books, San Francisco, CA, 2009, p. 87.

# Case study: Gustav Tenggren's work for Disney's *Pinocchio* (1940)[6]

It is always unfair to praise one artist for the design of a film as there are so many hands and minds influencing the style by working on the project for years. Yet there are some films that at least carry the look of the inspirational artwork into the final film frame to a certain extent. Few films of the Disney Company go back to one artist's style: *Alice in Wonderland* emanates Mary Blair's designs in parts, *Sleeping Beauty* from Eyvind Earl's work and *Pinocchio* has its roots in the Swedish artist Gustav Tenggren's illustrations (1896–1970) and the Swiss artist Albert Hurter's (1883–1942) designs for the interiors of Geppetto's shop. Being of European decent, their work is based on old European fairy-tale illustrations evoking the feel and sensibility of the *old world*, a romantic depiction of contorted alleys and crooked houses. The dreamlike paintings, with old buildings and cobblestone streets in Tenggren's work and the playfulness of Hurter's wooden interiors of Swiss, north Italian, south German, and also Swedish traditional houses, transport one directly into the beautiful cliché of a certain time and place. Not only the illustrations and art pieces both artists have contributed for *Pinocchio* have the illustrative qualities of their artistic personalities, but they are also based in their core on actual architecture. The Disney Family Foundation owns a photostat from the Dean Barickman collection which contains a board with various "General Atmospheric Sketches" by Tenggren. One of those sketches is a view of the German city of Rothenburg ob der Tauber in Frankonia, the northern part of Bavaria.[7] The drawing shows "Das Plönlein," a street corner that Tenggren obviously used as inspiration for the village where Geppetto lives (Figures 13.17–13.20). Also on this photostat we see a sketch of a cant-bay window that we recognize in the "Feuerleinserker," also in Rothenburg (Figure 13.18). Rothenburg was surely not the only influence for Tenggren, but it was a very significant one. Other styles can be detected in his illustrations that seem to derive from additional sources as they don't fit the style of the Franconian architecture of Rothenburg or the area and have more a northern Italian, Swiss or even Russian feel to them. Looking into some of the pictures of Rotherburg that were commercially available in the United States at the time, one stumbles across the images from a publisher out of Detroit: Detroit Publishing Company. At the turn of the century, they published images (between 1890 and 1900) that look very familiar when compared to the images illustrated by Tenggren. The overall textures, the colors, and the "old-feel" have a similarity to Tenggren's illustrations. Much of this is now lost in modern Rothenburg due to renovation, which took away the old feel that those pictures still contain in terms of textures, wall colors, or crooked roofing tiles (Figure 13.20). This of

**Figure 13.17**

Rothenburg: Das Plönlein.

**Figure 13.18**

Rothenburg: Feuerleinserker.

**Figure 13.19**

Rothenburg: Markusturm and Röderbogen.

---

[6] Due to the fact that the Disney Company did not release the copyrights for Gustav Tenggren's illustrations for Pinocchio to be used in this educational section, which would have tremendously helped the understanding of the discussed composition, it is necessary for the reader to find the illustrations either in Disney books or online and then compare them alongside the text to fully grasp the discussed compositions.

[7] Disney Family Foundation, http://www.waltdisney.org/blog/collections-0 (accessed December 13, 2017).

**Figure 13.20**

Rothenburg: Hegereiterhaus.

course does not prove or mean that those pictures have been used as inspiration by Tenggren, but it shows that the images available had the feel and textural qualities of what Tenggren designed. It is an overall quality that is very similar.

Rothenburg ob der Tauber is a tourist destination and famous for its medieval center and therefore many artists have already been in this small Frankonian town to sketch and paint the quaint architecture long before the development work for *Pinocchio* began. Walter Crane, Arthur Rackham, and Swedish artist John Bauer painted watercolors of Rothenburg and all of them were used as style-references for *Pinocchio*.[8] What is surprising for the time of the development of *Pinocchio* is the choice of German architecture for the overall design of Geppetto's town to begin with. Germany's political situation at the time with the staging of its self-confidence within this specific traditional architectural style of German history (in Nürnberg or Quedlinburg), which was to celebrate a German aesthetic, makes one wonder why or how this decision happened. Robin Allen writes, "Tenggren was responsible for the design of the Alpine town in the shadow of the mountains, and it is specifically German in spite of Disney's wish to universalise the setting and to remove the word 'alpine'

from the dialogue."[9] *Pinocchio* is not set in Germany and the choice was just based on a look that satisfied with its quaint architecture, referring to the feel of fairy-tales and old illustration.

Tenggren is obviously technically a brilliant illustrator and throughout his career has had various styles that range from the likes of Edmund Dulac or especially Arthur Rackham in his early work to the shape-driven sensibility of the 1950s that he changed to from the time after he left Disney in 1943. His early work shows his Swedish roots: magical old forests inhabited by trolls; dreamlike atmospheres of a world that is quintessentially organic. Nature is playful and mysterious and the architecture is always handmade and rustic and carries the weight of centuries. Every crack houses an elf and every stone in the forest seems to contain a troll. Tenggren's illustrations recreate the mood of Scandinavian folklore and fairy tales with the sensibility of European late 19th century book-illustration. The inspirational artwork that he created for *Pinocchio* emanates all these abovementioned stylistic points and is still unique in every way. They are not only stunning illustrations that are among the best depictions of *Pinocchio* in general (in this particular style, mind you) but also a technical *tour de force* that proves his knowledge of composition. Most of the artwork that he created for *Pinocchio* is either visually very similar or at least

8   Daniel Girveau, Lella Smith, and Pierre Lambert, *Once Upon a Time: Walt Disney: The Sources of Inspiration for the Disney Studios*, Prestel, Munich, 2006, p. 228.

9   Robin Allan, *Walt Disney and Europe*, Indiana University Press, Bloomington, IN, 1999, p. 78.

close to the final film image which proves the strong influence he had on the look of the film. Not only the characters but also the look of the village, the buildings, the landscape, etc., have a very similar design in illustration and final film; the final film breathes the warmth and comfort of Tenggren's beautiful art. *Pinocchio* was the second feature film that the Disney company created and after *Snow White and the Seven Dwarf*'s huge success and steep learning curve in terms of storytelling, technical advances, character animation, and production, it became the most beautiful feature animation yet. Wooly Reithermann on *Pinocchio* commented: "Because of the success of '*Snow White*,' we went overboard trying to make '*Pinocchio*' the best cartoon feature ever made."[10] One of the major technical feats planned for the film was the greater emphasis on the multiplane camera, which had its premier use at the Disney Studio in the short *The Old Mill* in 1937 and had already given the audience feature film scenes of utmost and spectacular beauty in *Snow White* (also in 1937). Shooting depth to simulate reality in a style that perfectly matched the sensibility of the 2D artwork, the camera itself could zoom in and zoom out, dolly in and dolly out, pan left and pan right and change focus on the various layers that were staggered underneath the camera. Camera tilts were simulated by already working the tilt into the layout design and final painting. In addition to the multiplane camera, the new universal multiplane camera made the camera movements even more spectacular by shooting the huge backgrounds horizontally, not vertically, thus allowing the artwork to be much bigger in scale. Gustav Tenggren's preproduction artwork for *Pinocchio* already incorporated the use of the multiplane camera as every image contains elements that strongly suggest depth in a way that the multiplane camera was especially suitable for. None of his other illustrative works have those elements in their composition and if they do have, then they are not as distinguished in their contrast of foreground elements and background. This leads to the belief that those elements that create depth were specifically incorporated for the advantages of the multiplane camera. Tenggren created for each of the important storypoints in the feature film large illustrations with tempera on board.[11] In all of the illustrations, he achieves a separation of image levels with a strong juxtaposition of lit and unlit elements. Often foreground elements are cast in shadow to bring about depth, which invites the eye to step into the image as one feels the staggering of pieces of scenery very much like on a theatre stage. The contrast of the dark foreground elements in relation to the rest of the image separates the levels from each other into such extent that flatness is eliminated and depth is enhanced. Tenggren uses light, shadow, contrast, and composition to give the image the perfect basis that can be translated with the multiplane camera into film images mimicking space, focus, and depth. Many images that he created as inspirational artwork for *Pinocchio* have that needed contrast that works so beautifully in traditional hand-drawn

animation. That the final film has Tenggren's sensibility is very fortunate in it not having been lost during the production. But there was care taken to retain the fairy-tale mood in the final film as Ken Anderson, an art director on *Pinocchio*, remembers:

> There was a flowering of the layout-department and the background department; everybody flowered on *Pinocchio*. And I think each one [of] us drew on our own individual feeling as much as possible. Of course there was places that you would go to find out the details of architecture if you wanted to see how they really did it, but we kept trying to adapt it to make it more fairy-tale so that you would never find anything exactly the way we did it.[12]

The following examines various examples of Tenggren's work for *Pinocchio* for their composition and narrative visual qualities.

## "Street-scene"

Gustav Tenggren's most famous illustration for *Pinocchio* is Honest John the fox, Gideon the cat, and Pinocchio strolling down a road in the village toward Stromboli's theater.[13] In this specific illustration, Tenggren gives us a lavish camera pan that not only describes one but also two moments of the film. In that regard, this is the perfect artwork for animation, not just being traditional illustration work, but stepping into that specific field of visual development for animation in that he composes the frame with additional filmic language adding time and also movement. But there is also a hint of editing in the image by cutting it into half with the post in the foreground and thus giving us an occurrence during a time frame instead of just one moment.

Tenggren also incorporates two lighting situations for the group. The first one is on the left with the group walking down the shadowy alley toward us. On the right side, the group is also in shadow, but their silhouette reads beautifully in front of the bright, sunlit architecture. This separates the background into two sections: dark left and bright right, which supports the reading direction and the natural urge of the eye to go toward the light.

The left group's direction is unmistakably predetermined by the curvature of the upcoming bent in the alley. The group is surrounded by taller houses creating a canyon-like tightness, that is opened up on the juxtaposing side where Stromboli's theater is located on an open square. The street is defined by heavier and lighter space (Figure 13.24) and thus clearly tells us where the action is heading to: the reading direction from left to right also mirrors the direction in which the space opens up. By putting the shadow on the left side of the architecture, this side is the heavy space, whereas the side across feels light and airy and thus allows the square to be more accessible

10  Gary Arnold, Pinocchio': Disney Animation at Its Peak, *The Washington Post*, December 22, 1978, Friday, Final Edition.
11  Robin Allan, *Walt Disney and Europe,* Indiana University Press, Bloomington, IN, 1999, p. 78.
12  Ken Anderson, *Disney Family Album*, documentary, 1984.
13  You can find this image in Thomas/Johnson's Illusion of Life, page 96-97. Be aware that the image in the book is not depicted in its original width but cut. One should be able to easily find the image online.

**Figure 13.21**

**Figure 13.22**

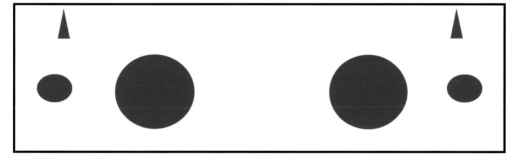

**Figure 13.23**

visually and physically. Also the positioning of the foreground elements reinforces that movement: on the left, containing the covered entrance, stairs, fence, and posts that stretch to the right go parallel with the lower frame and then bend toward Stromboli's theater (the last post of the foreground element is right underneath the entrance of the theater; Figures 13.21 and 13.24). Though all the way to the right, if the last post underneath the theater would be the end of the movement, that started with the stairs and then continued with the mentioned posts, it would stop too abruptly; therefore, Tenggren adds a small round sign-post to smoothen the movement upward (see Figure 13.24). He juxtaposes the round lower corner on the right with the one on the left, creating a vignetting effect with the foreground elements and also creating a border for the alley. The posts themselves have counterparts above them that stress the verticals shown in Figure 13.22, which push the view to the very left and right. That the movement starts on the left and

goes to the right is due to the foreground elements and their distance to each other, plus the lighting situation. This creates an accumulation of visual information on each vertical side of the frame. The business of the left and the right is in stark contrast to the comparatively rather empty middle of the frame, which not only displays the curvature of the street but also makes the image literally bulge forward accentuating the focal points of group on the left and theater entrance on the right, similar to a fish-eye photograph.

Figure 13.23 contains the focal points on each side of the frame and how they perfectly balance each other out. On the left it is the strolling group juxtaposed by the entrance of Stromboli's theater on the very right. The pointy roof of the cant-bay window on the left and the round onion-shaped roof on the right point out the significance of that vertical area. Interestingly, each side of the illustration works also on its own

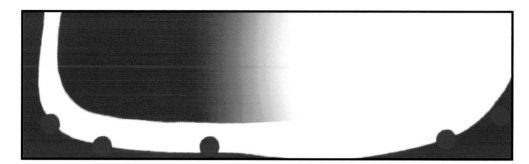

**Figure 13.24**

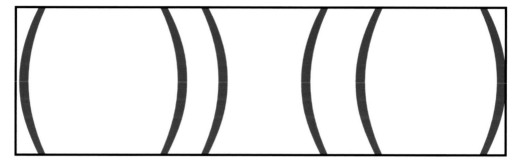

**Figure 13.25**

**Figure 13.26**

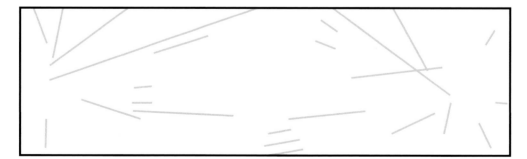

**Figure 13.27**

as the composition on either side accentuates the direction toward its own focal point. Many lines and elements describe through psychological closure curves (Figure 13.25) that keep each illustration contained within brackets and ovals. These ovals within the composition can be found in nearly all of Tenggren's illustrations for *Pinocchio*. They surround the focal area and serve as reoccurring compositional elements (Figure 13.26).

**Vectors**

As with all the other elements in the illustration that juxtapose each other (focal points, directions, weight, etc.), vectors do the same and appear on each side of the illustration in one form or another leading toward the focal point. The street-sign in the middle of the frame has two functions: on the left, it points toward the group (with the laundry line and the perspective of the houses

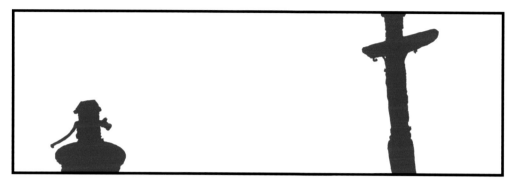

**Figure 13.28**

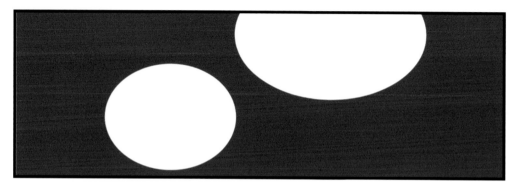

**Figure 13.29**

as its elongation); on the right, it opens up that side of the frame (Figure 13.27) though again all the perspective lines of the architecture go toward Stromboli's theater. The group on the right of Honest John, Gideon and Pinocchio is beautifully contrasted toward the background white of the town. It is not them that is the focal point, but their goal, which is the theater. What a brilliant idea to let them be in the shadow and allow Honest John to point with his walking stick forward toward their destination! The light would not create a stark contrast like that if the surrounding area is still lit the way it is. However, this is obviously done on purpose to allow the composition with its visual goal to overwrite logic and therefore create a working image instead of a realistic one. The two metal shop signs that are pointing left and right are a very unique addition to Rothenburg's architecture and Tenggren uses them as vectors and compositional elements.

There are many more vectors that relate to each other, but it would be slightly tedious to mention them all here.

## "Night scene"[14]

This illustration is similar to the previous street scene in its format, although it contains a very different composition where the focus is only on the group on the left. It is again Honest John, Gideon and

Pinocchio in the village, although this time at night (I keep using the term "village," as it is described as such by Jimini Cricket in the beginning of the movie). An unseen streetlight illuminates the group and bathes them in yellow, warm light. Behind them on the right is a small town square surrounded by buildings. Comparing this illustration again with the images from the Detroit Publishing Company, we find the middle tower with the gateway that is at the very end of the square and its surrounding architecture again in Figure 13.19, showing the Markusturm and Röderbogen. The buildings and the towers changed in shape and are simplified, but the setup is very much the same.

The foreground elements again create depth and once connected form a slanting line between the groups, forcing the eye toward that focal point (Figure 13.28). In this illustration, the perspective lines are not as strong as in the street scene, thus the image feels quieter and does not have the vigorous forces where the eye has to follow the visual path of the street. It is less busy and emanates the quiet of the night, the mysterious mood of a moon-lit silence. The balance is again very strong; however, Tenggren plays with opposites here: the positive space of the group is balanced out by the negative space of the village square, which forms the second focal point (Figure 13.29). To guide our eye toward the dominating focal point with the group, Tenggren uses warm light to drag our attention and cold light to illuminate the secondary focal point, the street square in the distance. The group itself follows in their poses the oval of the spotlight they are inscribed in. The eye of the observer therefore circles from one character to the next and also has the option to

---

[14]  See image on page 176–177 in J.B. Kaufmann, Pinocchio: *The Making of an Epic*, Weld on Owen Incorporated, London, 2015.

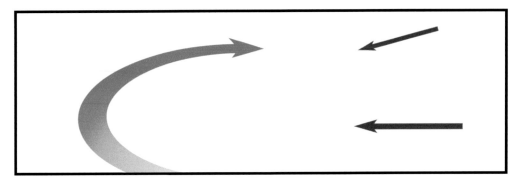

**Figure 13.30**

spiral around the group into the square by following the vector of the well pointing upward into the window above Honest John and the cant-bay window above Gideon into the square (Figure 13.30), which reminds one of the cant-bay windows at the Feuerleinserker in Figure 13.18 from Rothenburg.

## "Stromboli's performance"

In this beautiful illustration of Stromboli's "backstage view" (well, kind of literally), we see him surrounded by all his puppets. We see his huge behind, him wearing yellow knee breeches and a red band around his waist, while bending over above the stage, to play on the other side his marionettes. It is very interesting that Tenggren includes Honest John into the lineup of puppets. Is he like a puppet to Stromboli? Like an "object" he makes money with? That is obviously Honest John's part. Stromboli is playing his puppets and doing his job in a very passionate way. His pose isn't just a standing position but he is dancing with the puppets, light-footed and rather sensitive in his mannerism; slightly different from his brutish behavior in the film, however still flamboyant. His huge behind is right in the middle of the frame and is presented shamelessly. But his light dance makes this unflattering view so very charming. The stage curtain illuminates parts of the interior yellow and separates on- and off-stage space, the glowing magic on stage, and the cold reality behind it, where the marionettes are strung up like corpses, bowing to their master. Even the devil bows toward Stromboli. The foreground elements in this illustration (see Figure 13.31) very much force a sense of depth into the image as there is much contrast between the three different levels: dark foreground, washed-out ochre in the middle ground, and yellow glowing background. The staggering of those color levels drags one into the room.

As Teggren often uses a round compositional arrangement to surround the focal point, here it is the marionettes and Honest John that vignette Stromboli (Figure 13.32). Also, the cloth with the sack above the puppeteer is a compositional balance to his round shape and the cup on the table just above the lower frame. But, it also can serve as a reminder that Stromboli plays a dangerous game and the "sword of Damocles" is always hovering above him. There are many elements serving as vectors in the surrounding circle that make Stromboli's position as the focal point very clear (Figure 13.33). Small details in the puppets, their glance, positioning, or connecting

points create vectors that envelop Stromboli outside of the very dominant yellow shine of the stage curtain. None of those elements touch the puppeteer. There is an aura around him that no one seems to dare to penetrate. It's his personal space that is respected by all of the inferior subjects surrounding him.

**Figure 13.31**

**Figure 13.32**

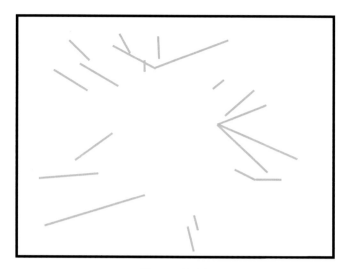

**Figure 13.33**

## "Stromboli and Pinocchio"

Tenggren's illustration for the scene of Pinocchio being in Stromboli's theater is telling two different stories in one image, not to the extent of the first illustration that has been discussed, but still two different perspectives nevertheless. On the right, Stromboli is in conversation with Pinocchio; the puppeteer is in a dominating pose, making clear to the marionette who is the boss. Pinocchio looks as innocent as he could be with a typical little kid pose of bulging tummy and arms behind the back. The room is filled with objects that tell a very interesting story: the objects behind Stromboli are kitchen utensils. The objects Pinocchio is surrounded by are "dead marionettes." The composition is cut into two parts by the foreground element of the dark beam (Figure 13.34). The silhouette of the beam covered in puppets behind Pinocchio is nervous and aggressive, one can imagine an open mouth with teeth, that is about to swallow Pinocchio. The beam feels rather threatening, yet the threat toward Pinocchio is coming from behind him, not from the front as he is still unaware of the upcoming incarceration. The second part of the illustration is the area behind the beam on the left, which depicts what is going to happen to Pinocchio later on: the cage which becomes his prison. Tenggren opens that part of the image through the shape of the beam, which tells us exactly where to look at. The two opening red shapes on the beam in Figure 13.35 open toward the cage and also toward

**Figure 13.34**

**Figure 13.35**

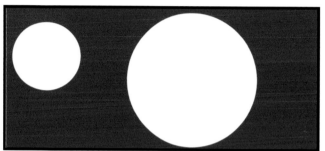

**Figure 13.36**

Pinocchio and the turquoise triangle in the same figure connects the three elements with each other; Stromboli's face is exactly on the same height as the cage. It is apparent that he already knows what he will do with Pinocchio. Stromboli points down to Pinocchio and seems to banish him into the cage. Two actions with one pose! Because of the two separate focal points, each side has its own circular composition (Figure 13.36) where all the objects and elements in the room encompass the three: Stromboli and Pinocchio on the right and the cage on the left.

## "Pinocchio in the cage"

This is another iconic image from the film: Pinocchio, entrapped in the cage, is sitting on a bird's swing, being miserable about his misfortune. It is the very cage and segment of the image discussed before with the same wooden beam angled at the corner. In front of him we see shadows of strung up marionettes. Despite what they actually are, lifeless puppets made from wood, the image seems to suggest a violent death for Pinocchio himself. Figures 13.37 and 13.38 once more show the foreground elements and the oval compositional arrangement to emphasize the focal point. In this case not just Pinocchio in the cage but rather the relationship between him and the puppets is what is visually important. What is unique in this image is the heavy emphasis on shadows and the story they bring forward. The immense advantage of a 2D plane is the connection of all the parts in the image, which also relate to each other, despite their spatial relationship of foreground, middle ground, and background. Pinocchio and the shadows on the wall, that he is obviously not looking at, do relate as the two planes connect intellectually, not spatially. Nevertheless, it seems

| Figure 13.37 | Figure 13.38 | Figure 13.39 |
|---|---|---|

like Pinocchio is actually looking at the real marionettes hanging from the ceiling. The tilt of the shadows on the ceiling and on the bottom of the frame point directly toward Pinocchio in his cage (Figure 13.38) and the bulge of the shadow that runs right behind him on the wall is again part of the oval compositional element that Tenggren likes to apply (Figure 13.39). Everything is related and every line or color serves a greater purpose which is the composition.

## "Shipwreck"[15]

Again an unusual and magical view: this time of Pinocchio walking on the sea ground through a shipwreck. The light of his lantern (let us not ask the question of how the lantern would still stay lit under water) beautifully illuminates the shipwreck and gives us a lit side and a dark side of the wreck, an intriguing pattern of a ship's rib cage. Behind Pinocchio an octopus is hovering, wondering about what it is witnessing … The darkness of the image bathes it in a mysterious mood, playing with the unknown of the deep sea and the danger that lurks beyond the light's safe shine. Not showing what is out there makes it scarier and unpredictable, especially as the audience knows that Monstro the whale is somewhere close by. Walking through the skeleton of the ship, we get the feel of a deeply sad and desolate place, a darkness that Pinocchio's light desperately tries to penetrate. Because he is walking through the ship's remnants, the mood of the ship's corpse is taken over by the whole image and also Pinocchio's journey. His position in the ship's belly reflects Geppetto's own position within the whale's belly and Pinocchio being the one that "walks" both of them out into safety. Tenggren tells us three stories here and makes very interesting connections between the three characters of Pinocchio, his father, and Monstro, linking them with each other through the shapes of the ship's belly.

The composition has a couple of points that are interesting and noteworthy. Pinocchio's position is in the golden ratio and there is a difference of what is behind him and what is in front of him. He has passed the ribs of the ship that are lit by the lamp. All the

ribs in front of Pinocchio are dark. But he is about to walk into the section of the ship that we can't fully see. Something dark and unknown is in front of him literally in the shape of a beam right in front of his face. The choice of Tenggren to pick a shipwreck is a rather successful gambit. There is obviously the connection to Monstro the whale in terms of its size, skeleton, and age (scariness).

This illustration is a truly masterful approach to visual storytelling! The way Tenggren deals with the balance is unique: there is the negative shape on the upper left which is balanced with the same shape rotated and flipped in the lower right corner (Figure 13.40). Pinocchio as the focal point again appears in the oval/round shape that Tenggren often likes to use, this time in the form of the lamp's light. The four corners of the image all

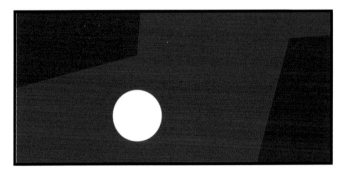

Figure 13.40

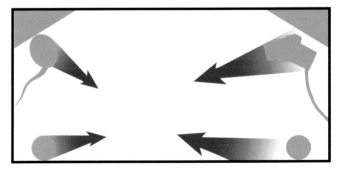

Figure 13.41

15  Page 102–103 in Thomas/Johnson's Illusion of Life.

**Figure 13.42**

have some vectors in them that aim at Pinocchio (Figure 13.41). It is the octopus' eyeline, the upper part of the rudder and all the planks on the upper right; the sandline on the lower right; and the shadow of the ribs on the lower left. That those vectors start from the corners only strengthens them! Figure 13.42 demonstrates how a shape can be created by considering the effects of psychological closure, allowing shapes to form that reflect other shapes from the same composition (in this case, the overall shape of the boat, reappearing again mirrored).

Tenggren in his illustrations for Pinocchio has clearly the leveling of the various elements of foreground, middleground, and background in mind to create via light and shadow a sense of depth, which is in the final film even stronger. Especially, the dark foreground elements invite the eye into the screen.

One can see the same basic compositional elements in variation in all of Tenggren's pieces for the film:

•   Corners create vignettes in combination with shadow areas or light areas, or positive and negative space
•   The focal point is always inscribed into a circle or oval that is created by positive and negative space.
•   Foreground elements are kept dark or in shadow to lead the eye into the image and create depth.
•   The left or right side of the frame contains a strong curve that defines a compositional shape that is either part of the foreground elements to create depth or a negative/positive space combination, balanced out by a similar shape on the opposing side.
•   Very strong tendency toward balancing out not only the major compositional blocks but also small details.
•   Everything in the image succumbs to the main composition and is placed with the focal point in mind: therefore, everything in the image supports the focal point and its direction.
•   There is always a complex layering of compositional frameworks on top of each other to create very pleasing compositions.

After *Pinocchio*, Tenggren changed from his Arthur Rackham style of traditional old European illustration and worked in the 1950s and later in a very different style that was more in line with the shape-driven aesthetics of mid-century illustration. He never went back to this lavish style after *Pinocchio*.

**Books on *Pinocchio*:**

J.B. Kaufmann, *Pinocchio: The Making of an Epic*, Weldon Owen Incorporated, London, 2015.
John Canemaker, *The Lost Notebook: Herman Schultheis & the Secrets of Walt Disney's Movie Magic*, Weldon Owen, Incorporated, London, 2014.

# Levels and lighting or "multiplane lighting"

As we have just seen on the previous pages' case study on Gustav Tenggren's illustrations for *Pinocchio*, light and shadow can create levels of information and highlight parts for storytelling purposes. The question now is how the significance of each level changes according to the changing light situation. In Tenggren's illustrations, it was always the closest level that was cast in shadow, and the middle level was the lit and important one. If the level furthest away is lit instead of the ones that are in the middle, then the emphasis is shifted from the middle to the back. The layers of overlapping shapes in Figures 13.43 through 13.57 have varying light intensities illuminating each level. The examples all contain three overlapping shapes that create perspective plus one shape in the upper left corner that is rather difficult to locate in space as there is no overlap. As the lightest area is most often the one that drags the attention, the other ones usually step visually into the background even if they are in front of the lit layer. In Figure 13.43, the closest level is the brightest and every level further back is cast more and more in shadow. This is the most logical and the simplest solution for lighting and overlap: to illuminate the levels or objects more or less according to their distance from the viewer. This intensifies depth and perspective is already created by the overlap. It also creates movement from the front to the back or vice versa (Figure 13.44). In Figure 13.45, this idea is reversed and the object in the left corner is the brightest, which reverses the focus from the foreground in Figure 13.43 to the corner in Figure 13.45. This is very practical in film where the entire focus can be changed by just shifting the lighting from one level to another and thus guiding the audience's attention. Figure 13.46 has the white L-shape lit and the focus is definitely on that piece despite the overlap. The small square on the upper left has much less significance compared to Figure 13.45. Figure 13.47 has the middle piece lit up and once more the focus clearly shifts to the middle ground. Figure 13.45 has a variation of 13.53, where the movement, because of the continuous lighting change from back to front, is broken. It still has the focus on the bright square, but the flow from back to front is interrupted. The movement in the composition is less smooth. Figure 13.49 reverses the background lighting and the focus is still on the brightest shape in the arrangement, not on the background itself.

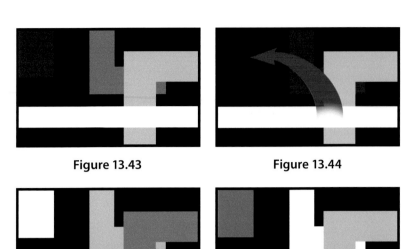

**Figure 13.43**

**Figure 13.44**

**Figure 13.45**

**Figure 13.46**

**Figure 13.47**

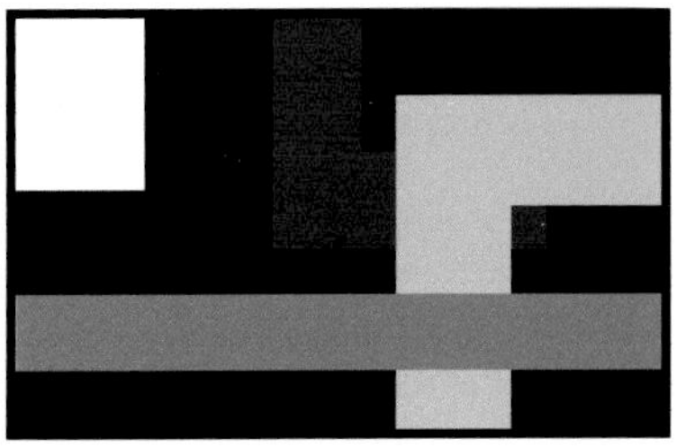

**Figure 13.48**

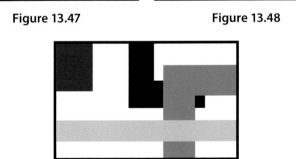

**Figure 13.49**

**Figure 13.50**
Satoshi Kon: *Paprika* (2006).

This concept of lighting levels creates obvious perspective, guides our eyes' focus toward certain parts of the image, and can also separate characters from each other. In the film image, this can be practically implemented like in the screenshot (Figure 13.50) of Satoshi Kon's *Paprika* (2006), which has three different levels: foreground with puppets, middleground with Dr. Chiba on a throne, and background with the guards in shadow. The advantage of creating differently lit layers is, because this specific shot is so filled with characters, they need to be separated from each other to avoid visual confusion. Because of the strong lighting differences, the guards clearly step into the background, though they still populate the screen with their presence without interrupting the importance of Dr. Chiba in front of them.

As we have seen, the lighting can separate one level from another, but it can also single out parts in one layer and/or push back other information on the same layer. Jean-Honoré Fragonard (1732–1806) makes beautiful use in his painting *The swing* (1767) of a rather complex lighting situation (Figure 13.51). The woman on the swing is on the same level as her lover on the floor on the left. She is the center of attention in the shaft of sunlight that is streaming into the frame from upper left; the shadow of the statue on the other hand leaves him in half shadow. The second man on the right, pulling the strings of the swing, is on a level behind the two lovers in the very dark background, completing the triangular composition of the three characters. The woman is swinging in an island of light and is surrounded by an opening in the foliage with a very strong color perspective, tinting

**Figure 13.51**

Jean-Honoré Fragonard: *The Swing* (1767).

**Figure 13.52**

*Jurassic Park III* dir. Joe Johnston (2001).

her immediate surroundings in light blue, which additionally adds contrast to her rose and yellowish colored mountain of ruffles. This accentuates her silhouette which in turn makes her teasing the more obvious. Fragonard is able to play with extremely difficult lighting in a way that still makes the three-dimensionality perfectly clear and allows a dreamlike quality that is nothing short of stunning.

This artistic effect of artificial layering can be achieved in live-action film by adding light to the different levels in order to separate objects and characters from the background. Especially when the background is very busy and the character in the front does not read well, something must be done to achieve clarity. In *Jurassic Park 3*, for instance, the characters spend much time in the jungle, which is a very busy backdrop (Figure 13.52). The character's silhouette does not always read well in front of leafs, trees, and foliage, especially if the lighting situation is not clearly differentiating between the layers. The problem is solved exactly like in Fragonard's painting where the background is slightly taken out in order to make the contrast between background and characters stronger: smoke is added into the air and then lit from above. This causes the smoke to create a curtain of light that diffuses the background and takes out contrast and detail. The effect is unrealistic in this instance, as the scene is shot in the studio where the light is not coming into the scene in parallel rays of light (like sunlight would) but coming in from a light source at the ceiling of the studio,

**Figure 13.53**

Lyonel Feininger: *Church of the Minorities II* (1926).

set, or location. But the goal of separating the characters is achieved and it adds mood and mystery to the mix, a perfect basis for the kind of story that is told.

The separation of levels can also work in a stylized, more abstracted image. It is again the same concept of creating different levels of brightness to achieve contrast and perspective, which does not require a three-dimensional space. Lyonel Feininger's (1871–1956) painting *Church of the Minorities II* from 1926 (Figure 13.53) makes the three-dimensional setup of the space very clear, though still keeping its geometric flatness intact as the various differently colored shapes create contrast and color perspective, nevertheless destroying perspective at the same time with countless tangents and lines. The constructed perspective is also purposefully incorrect and thus flattens the space. It is very clear which level is in the front and which is in the back, due to overlap and color. The image still keeps its root in the 2D plane. Much is possible with the playful layering of light and shadow indeed!

Even if there is no overlap, perspective can still work if the contrast between the differently lit levels is strong enough and the elements work in their size relationship to each other, meaning in the case of the Ankor Wat temple in Figure 13.54, the palm leaf on the top right has to be much bigger in its shape, texture, and size in order to actually step closer to the viewer.

**Figure 13.54**

Angkor Wat, Cambodia.

# Case study: Composition and light in Orson Welles' *Citizen Kane* (1941)

**Direction & Production:** Orson Welles

**Cinematography:** Gregg Toland

**Special effects cinematographer:** Linwood Dunn

**Editing:** Robert Wise

**Art Director:** Van Nest Polglase

**Special Effects:** Vernon L. Walker

**Screenplay:** Herman J. Mankiewicz & Orson Wells

> I wished to make a motion picture which was not a narrative of action so much as an examination of character. For this, I desired a man of many sides and many aspects. It was my idea to show that six or more people could have as many widely divergent opinions concerning the nature of a single personality. Clearly such a notion could not be worked out if it would apply to an ordinary American citizen.[16]

**Orson Welles**

Some films have a status in film history which goes beyond "culturally and historically significant" and reach the level of *legend*. Films like Vittorio De Sica's *Bicycle Thieves*, Ozu Yasujiro's *Tokyo Story*, FW Murnau's *Sunrise: A Song of Two Humans*, or Stanley Kubrick's *2001 A Space Odysee* are not "just" films but cultural phenomena that influenced cinema tremendously. Among those films is Orson Welles' *Citizen Kane*, the cinematic masterpiece of a young and already celebrated Broadway genius. Orson Welles (1915–1985) was one of the great creative minds of the 20th century and because of *Citizen Kane* became one of cinema's masters at the incredible age of 25. Welles had already had great success in theater and radio as an actor, writer, and producer when brought to Hollywood by Filmstudio RKO producer George J. Schaefer.[17] Welles caught the producer's attention after his success with his radio play *War of the Worlds* in 1938, his groundbreaking adaptation of H.G. Wells' famous sci-fi novel of the same name. Welles had produced the play with the Mercury Theater, the New York theater company he had his most important Broadway successes in his early 20s. His theater and radio work was proof of an unconventional creative approach and Hollywood desperately wanted to count this young theater and radio genius among its members, which finally happened in 1938, when aforementioned film studio RKO offered Welles a film contract difficult to reject as it gave Welles not only a financial deal, that was more than generous, but also creative freedom in his work, an unconventional offer at the end of the 1930s in Hollywood. Welles had dealt with film before his move from New York to Hollywood; however, the actual movie business was new to him. This led, due to Welles' lack of professional Hollywood film knowledge, to the unorthodox production that *Citizen Kane* was going to be. The various short films he had shot before were stage shows or dress

rehearsals he had filmed of his theater productions or productions he was involved in. His first feature length film *Too much Johnson* (1938)[18] was produced by and for The Mercury Theater. *Too much Johnson* was, like the aforementioned short films, produced to be projected on the theater stage. Once Welles had moved to Hollywood in 1938, he started right away on his first production for RKO, a film version of Joseph Conrad's famous novel *Heart of Darkness*, which did not get produced due to exorbitant production costs and unfortunately remained in the script phase. His second project, however, was going to be the famous *Citizen Kane*.

Any movie, like a stage play, is seldom the work of one artist alone and neither was *Citizen Kane*. As much credit as Welles rightfully receives, he was after all the director, main actor, producer, and script writer, the same should be given to some other artists as well, as they helped to create the story and its visuals as much as he. The most important artists, next to Orson Welles, were Gregg Toland, the cinematographer of the film, and Herman Mankiewicz, who shared the role of script writer with Welles. As significant as Mankiewicsz is to the film, the focus of this chapter is on Gregg Toland whose "... contribution to the film was the greatest, second in importance only to his own" (meaning Welles).[19] Before Toland signed on to *Citizen Kane*, he had just received an Academy Award for his work on *Wuthering Heights* (1939), directed by William Wyler. Being one of the most creative and artistically forward-thinking cinematographers in Hollywood, he was the best choice for *Citizen Kane* as his creative and unusual work methods and quick results turned out to be the driving creative force between him and Welles.

The studio system in Hollywood at the time was highly controlled and creative experimentation was improbable, as film was defined as a business rather than a creative playground (which makes Welles contract with RKO so unusual). Gregg Toland worked under contract for Samuel Goldwyn, a smaller studio, where the control of the artistic and also technical side of a film was less rigid compared with one of the bigger Hollywood dream machines, in which the studio system did forcefully control every aspect of the creative process and the outcome was not always representative of the director's vision. Samuel Goldwyn loaned out Toland, which often happened during his career at Goldwyn,[20] along with his crew (Bert Shipman, camera operator; W. J. McClellan, gaffer; Ralph Hoge, grip; and Edward Garvin, assistant cameraman). He actually very much wanted to work with Welles and was not assigned the job but asked for it. It was common practice that the cinematographer joined

---

16 Press statement of Orson Welles on Jan. 15th, 1941.
17 Robert Carringer, *The Making of Citizen Kane*, University of California Press, Berkeley, CA, 1985, p. 1.
18 A pristine copy of the film, which was long believed to be lost, was discovered in 2008 in Pordenone, Italy. Dave Kehr: *New York Times*, August 7th 2013 "Early Film by Orson Welles Is Rediscovered."
19 Robert L. Carringer, Orson Welles and Gregg Toland, Their Collaboration on "Citizen Kane," *Critical Inquiry*, Vol. 8, No. 4 (Summer, 1982), p. 652.
20 Patrick L. Ogle, Technological and Aesthetic Influences Upon the Development of Deep Focus Cinematography in the United States, *Screen* Vol. 13, No. 1 (Spring, 1972), pp. 45–72.

Figure 13.55

Figure 13.56

Figure 13.57

the production not long before shooting began, not so on *Citizen Kane*. Toland arrived months ahead of the first day of the shoot to discuss and develop the style of the film with Welles, and also prepare the shooting schedule, design direction, and set design with the crew. The cinematographer being involved in the entire visual style of the film from an early stage on was by no means the norm. In an article, Toland stated that in Hollywood "where most cinematographers learn of their next assignments only a few days before the scheduled shooting starts." the result was that "the photographic approach to *Citizen Kane* was planned and considered long before the first camera turned."[21] Thus, the production from the beginning on can be described as unusual and Welles not only allowed experimentation but outright demanded it and explicitly rejected the typical Hollywood approach. He wanted a new visual style that Toland, and the design department, was perfectly capable of providing. As Robert Carringer so poignantly describes it: "Much of it was openly, blatantly experimental."[22]

Toland had for years perfected a very personal style with new techniques and lenses that he had developed and refined through films like above mentioned *Wuthering Heights* (1939) or John Ford's *The Long Voyage Home* (1940). *Wuthering Heights* had in its cinematography, despite the beautiful imagery, a more "subtle" style compared with the much more experimental *Citizen Kane*, much softer in its images and less extreme in its lighting. There are elements in Tolands earlier films, especially in *The Long Voyage Home*, that show the visual path toward *Citizen Kane*, the film that clearly marks the high point in Toland's visual style, but none of them are as rigorous. Because of the freedom he enjoyed at Goldwyn, Toland was allowed to use the studio's facilities and develop, experiment, and explore new visuals that pushed the traditional idea of what cinematography in Hollywood was capable of. Because of Toland's continuous experimentation at Goldwyn, he had developed many gadgets for his shoots and therefore requested to use his own equipment consisting of special cameras and lenses, which were not in common operation at other studios in 1937/8. This sets his images apart from other cinematographers in Hollywood and gives them an unusual and very personal touch. His eagerness to experiment shows itself in the richness of his work, especially in *Citizen Kane*.[23] Toland and Welles were also able because of RKO's contract (and sometimes lack of knowledge) to develop uncommon visuals for the film, many of which would have been outright rejected by the traditional Hollywood studio system. The list of cinematographic elements used in the film is rather extensive. Robert Carringer, specialist on *Citizen Kane*, sums them up as follows: deep-focus cinematography; long takes; the avoidance of conventional intercutting through such devices

---

[21] Robert L. Carringer, Orson Welles and Gregg Toland, Their Collaboration on "Citizen Kane." *Critical Inquiry*, Vol. 8, No. 4 (Summer, 1982), p. 40.
[22] *Id.* at p. 653.
[23] *Id.* at p. 657.

as multiplane compositions and camera movement; elaborate camera choreography; lighting that produces a high-contrast tonality; UFA-style expressionism in certain scenes; low-angle camera setups made possible by muslin ceilings on the sets; and an array of striking visual devices, such as composite dissolves, extreme depth of field effects, and shooting directly into lights. Most of these elements ran directly counter to the conventional studio cinematography of the time.[24]

Many of the cinematographic techniques used in the film had, as mentioned before, been used already by Toland or others, but in *Citizen Kane* they culminate in one gorgeous firework.[25] Welles with his relatively slim experience in film, nevertheless knew what he wanted to see on screen. Assisted by his theatrical sensibility and the goal of breaking cinematic conventions, he explained it as: "There have been many motion pictures and novels rigorously obeying the formula of the 'success story,' I wished to do something quite different. I wished to make a picture which might be called a 'failure story.'"[26] The Hollywood system had not yet taught Welles what is and what is not *feasible* in cinema and how one has to supposedly shoot a successful studio feature film. Toland taught Welles the basics of filmmaking during those first weeks of planning and the entire production was developed precisely to fit the needs of the unconventional visuals and the ideas of the two artists. There are many aspects in the film that show the theatrical background of the director and that is clearly one of the reasons why the film is not entirely rooted in the Hollywood aesthetic. Long shots, staging that includes characters very far away from the camera, certain theatrical sets like the Grand Hall at Xanadu, and a strong focus on the character development of Charles Forster Kane make this very clear. However, the film makes full use of the toy-box "cinema" and uses all tricks and whistles to bring the story to the screen. This can be seen in the array of visual treats that are spread throughout the film and make us marvel at the screen:

- Miniature sets and special effects (Figure 13.55)
- Simulation of old and scratched newsreels (Figure 13.56)
- Reflections (Figure 13.57)
- Matte paintings (Figure 13.58)
- Deep focus and double exposure (Figures 13.59, 13.61 and 13.62)
- Stunning perspectives (Figure 13.60)
- Unusual lighting situations (Figures 13.63 through 13.66)
- Interesting transitions and superimposed shots
- Meticulously planned compositions.

**Figure 13.58**

**Figure 13.59**

**Figure 13.60**

---

24 Robert L. Carringer, Orson Welles and Gregg Toland, Their Collaboration on "Citizen Kane," *Critical Inquiry*, Vol. 8, No. 4 (Summer, 1982), p. 70.
25 Not everything that Welles' film is praised for is an innovation that happened first in *Citizen Kane*. Andrew Sarris lists various claimed innovations that Kane is famous for and gives their credit to other films, for example, its flashback storytelling structure which he credits to *Power and Glory* (1933). In: Sarris Andrew, Kane: for and Against, *Monthly Film Bulletin*; October, 1991, pp. 1, 6; International Index to Performing Arts Full Text p 20;
26 Press statement of Orson Welles on Jan. 15th, 1941.

Figure 13.61

Figure 13.62

Figure 13.63

## Story

The story of *Citizen Kane* is about Mr. Charles Foster Kane, a newspaper mogul and millionaire and him inheriting a fortune. Kane buys a small newspaper *The Inquirer* and leads it to popularity and success. His marriage to two women and unsuccessfully running for governor reflect what Welles said about his goal of telling a failure story. The question that is raised continuously throughout the movie is the meaning of Mr. Kane's last word on his deathbed: "Rosebud," which in the end is revealed as the word painted on his childhood sled. Orson Welles himself explains in an article from 1941:

> Citizen Kane is the story of a search by a man named Thompson, the editor of a news digest (similar to the March of time), for the meaning of Kane's dying words.... His researches take him to five people who knew Kane well–people who liked him or loved him or hated his guts. They tell five different stories, each biased, so that the truth about Kane, like the truth about any man, can only be calculated, by the sum of everything that has been said about him. Kane, we are told, loved only his mother—only his newspaper—only his second wife—only himself. Maybe he loved all of these, or none. It is for the audience to judge. Kane was selfish and selfless, an idealist, a scoundrel, a very big man, and a very little one. It depends on who's talking about him.[27]

## Deep focus

The most famous and impressive of cinematographers Toland's camera wizardry is the aforementioned deep focus, which is so often talked about when Toland's work is discussed and is part of his bag of cinematic tricks. Deep focus shots have every point in the image in crisp focus, areas close to the camera as well as those far away (e.g., Figure 13.59 or 13.61).

The unusual sharpness and clarity in Toland's deep focus shots is achieved through new technological developments at the end of the 1930s in the area of new film stock, Eastman Kodak's Super XX, new lens coatings, and Mitchell Camera Corporation's new BNC camera.[28] What needs to be kept in mind nevertheless is that Toland did not invent the deep focus shot. Other cinematographers also worked on achieving a deeper focus, like James Wong Howe in *Transatlantic* from 1931.[29] Toland was, however, because of his interest in cinematographic

[27] Orson Welles, Citizen Kane Is NOT about Louella Parsons Boss, *Friday 2*, February 14, 1941, p. 9.
[28] For more information on Toland's use of technical innovations and his collaboration with companies like the Mitchell Camera Corporation or Eastman Kodak, see Robert Carringer, *The Making of Citizen Kane*, University of California Press, Berkeley, CA, 1985, p. 72ff and especially Patrick L. Ogle, Technological and Aesthetic Influences Upon the Development of Deep Focus Cinematography in the United States, *Screen*, Vol. 13, No. 1 (March 1, 1972), pp. 45–72.
[29] Patrick L. Ogle, Technological and Aesthetic Influences Upon the Development of Deep Focus Cinematography in the United States, *Screen*, Vol. 13, No. 1 (March 1, 1972), pp. 45–72.

experimentation and his status in Hollywood, a good candidate to be at the forefront of the technological development in collaboration with camera and film stock companies.

The deep focus shots (e.g., Figures 13.59 and 13.69 and the here discussed shots 2 and 3 in this case study) defy human vision as they present the entire image in sharp focus contrary to the ability of the human eye, which can only focus on the focal point at the center of the visual field. By presenting to us images that are in their entirety sharp, Toland allows our eye to explore as there are no blurry sections that prevent us from satisfying our visual curiosity (the composition and lighting, creating their own center of attraction, however still dominate the path the eye takes through the image). Deep focus shots do not mimic reality as we see it; on the contrary, they allow the audience to see every part of the image clearly. In the traditional cinematic image, the eye sees the blurry parts as being blurry. In the deep focus shot, however, the eye can decide which part to look at and that part will always be sharp and naturally through the eye its periphery will appear blurry.

Focus attracts the eye naturally and in a split of a second our eye can find the sharp area. This is not as easy as in a deep focus shot as there is no focused point that is surrounded by blurriness. Therefore, those shots need other design aspects to guide the eye to those areas that are important for the story. Those devices can be:

- Composition
- Lighting
- Texture
- Staging
- Movement
- Contrast
- Color
- Size

Deep focus shots also have the side effect that they can actually lack the feeling of depth as, logically, everything is in focus, so the natural ability of the eye to judge distance through the degree of blurriness and therefore get a sense of depth through depth of field is missing. This needs to be addressed and compensated by either the composition or lighting (if the film would be in color, color perspective would also help to create further depth). Also, the images' contrast in foreground and background contain the same dark blacks, which also flatten the perspective. Toland's deep focus images create depth through other means than focus, which is, for instance, the use of a strong one-point perspective, which undoubtedly defines the space. The actors are staged in a way to support the vanishing point. The men at the table in Figure 13.59 sit along the perspective lines that lead toward the vanishing point and the dancers in Figure 13.61 even exaggerate through their arrangement the perspective. In addition, it is the element of size perspective that clearly determines what is close to the camera and what

is far away. Size and the accumulation of small shapes toward the compositional focal point or the vanishing point (not the "sharpness" focal point) clearly create perspective and depth (on the next couple of pages, we will see how Toland uses those design aspects to guide the audience's eye).

Another type of shot in the film is often mentioned as a deep focus shot, for example, Figures 13.67 and 13.69; however, they are of a different type and there needs to be a distinction between the above discussed "real" deep focus shots achieved in one take, and special effects shots that simulate deep focus by double exposing the shot. The two kinds have not only a very different technique but also a different storytelling effect on the audiences' visual perception. The stunning image of the special effects shots that also play with the idea of deep focus is achieved by matting parts of the frame, exposing the film stock, then matting the already exposed parts and exposing the formerly covered parts, thereby providing the image with two areas in focus. These shots are exceptional because they also, as the real deep focus shots, contradict human perception, but now by providing two compositional focal points in sharp focus, which establish a relationship and connect the two focused elements of objects or characters. The eye alternates between the two that stand out as being visually relevant. Both shots do come across as "special" shots that drag attention within a scene and point out through their otherness the importance of the current story point.

## Composition and light

Toland created images that were unique and outstanding in every sense of the word. He likes to give us the opposite of what we would expect in the lighting of set and characters, and in his courageous and striking compositions. Many elements reappear in his work and contribute to this unique style. First is the contrast between background and character and its relationship to the character's role and emotional state in that very shot. Because of the stark contrast between black and white, the silhouette of the character steps to the front and simplifies the readability. He also does not shy away from creating unrealistic, or for the search of a better word "uncommon," lighting situations only to convey the story point, not to recreate reality, which goes straight back to German Expressionistic Cinema in which the visualization of the psychological state of the character is of great importance. In Figure 13.66, Kane and Susan are in the dark background; however, the wall behind them is lit. Kane has been caught cheating by his wife on the left; he is the one "shamed," therefore he is the one in the shadow. Nevertheless, once he makes it clear to everyone in the room that he himself is the only one that makes decisions about his life, he steps into the light and thus regains his former strength. Toland and Welles constantly use light and shadow in this strong symbolic form and therefore increase the image's story telling ability.

**Figure 13.64**

**Figure 13.65**

**Figure 13.66**

Various lighting rules can be determined for the film:

- Strong contrast between character and his/her immediate background (which relates to the following point).
- Islands of light can specify the focal point.
- The character's illumination changes during their movement through the set in relationship to their mood and action.
- Light is coming from various directions to create the best possible effect and composition instead of rendering the set realistically. Stylization and theatricality is more important than realism.
- The design of the lighting and its storytelling ability are the most important aspects that overrule realistic recreation of lighting.

Much of the "documentary" style that the story follows can also be seen in the cinematography. The audience witnesses the events like an ongoing news-reel and is part of the action on screen. There are quite a few news-reel shots in the film to underline its "realism" and also the interviews with people that knew Kane underlined this; however, the artistic lighting often goes into a very different direction and gives us highly artistic visuals. One of the most fascinating cinematographic faux pas Toland allowed himself is the scene in the movie theater, where the editor Thompson discusses his assignment in the first act of the film. Toland shot most of the scene against the light source. The newspaper crowd is mostly unrecognizable and thus not described as personalities but literally shot as cutout characters in silhouette, whose specific personalities are insignificant for the events that will follow, but their actions and words are not. Their characters are very much us, trying to figure out the mystery that was Mr. Charles Foster Kane. They are, like the audience sitting in a dark room, watching the events unfold. The idea of shooting the actors in front of light that penetrates into the theatre room from the projection-booth is a brilliant visualization of the previously mentioned lack of importance of the characters/personalities. Especially the invisibility of the facial expressions, which can be seen in Figure 13.64 where we can see the chest of the actor being illuminated but the head is just a black shape, makes us focus on the words, not the face. This extreme light situation is also being used in Thompson's visit to the Library (Figure 13.65), where shafts of light cut into the room, turning the library into a sanctuary or tomb. Again the stark contrast between light and shadow and the resulting silhouetting of the characters shifts the focus toward their action, allowing us to be curious with the editor on that odd paper that has just been taken out of a vault. We are focusing all our attention on the mood and the action, not the facial expressions. These theatrical lighting situations elevate the rather unspectacular story points onto important surreal moments that have visual significance. The set for the library scene is already precisely described in the script: "Everything very plain, very much made out of marble and very gloomy. Illumination from a skylight above adds to the general air of expensive and classical despair. The floor is marble, and there is a gigantic, mahogany table in the center of everything. Beyond this is to be seen, sunk in the marble wall at the far end of the room...."[30] The illumination of the space and therefore its mood is already in the script! Light and shadow carry the mood and story points in Toland's images and thus significantly enhance their meaning and interpretation.

The following discussed shots and scenes are focusing on three different aspects:

- The staging of the actors and the visualization of their psychological state through light and shadow.
- The staging of light and shadow elements to create layers and depth.
- The resulting composition with its story-telling abilities.

In *Citizen Kane*'s shots, the focus lies on unique and unconventional visuals, striking compositions that are constantly changing and never leave the viewer unimpressed. All of it is strictly following the goal of storytelling in all its design aspects. The change of the composition, not just from shot to shot, but especially within the shot, keeps the scenes in a continuous compositional flow and tension. Various shots from the film have been chosen that demonstrate the different topics of staging and set-composition (shot 2) and also their strong amalgamation with light and shadow in Shots 3 and 4. Finally, a pan is discussed in its overall composition in relationship with the large set piece of the Grand Hall of Xanadu.

## Snow Globe and Rosebud (Figures 13.67 and 13.68)

The film opens with Kane's castle, Xanadu, being shown in rather desolate visuals. Those shots anticipate in their mood Kane's failure at the end of his life. The castle and its grounds seem to mourn Kane's upcoming death. Through the surreal superimposition of a snowstorm, we see someone holding a snow globe which gets dropped to the ground, shattering after the dying man whispers the now famous word "Rosebud." A nurse is coming into the room and we see her reflection through the shards of the broken globe (Figure 13.67). Because of this unusual shot, the audience will remember the significance of "Rosebud," which is the key to Kane's life, and only with the understanding of what this word relates to can one understand the film. As Welles explains it:

> The most basic of all ideas was that of a search for the true significance of the man's apparently meaningless dying words.

**Figure 13.67**

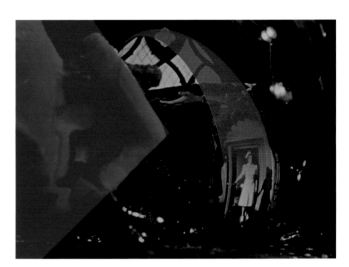

**Figure 13.68**

Kane was raised without a family. He was snatched from his mother's arms in early childhood. His parents were a bank. From the point of view of the psychologist, my character had never made what is known as "transference" from his mother; hence, his failure with his wives. In making this clear during the course of the picture, it was my attempt to lead the thoughts of my audience closer and closer to the solution of the enigma of his dying words. These were "Rosebud." The device of the picture calls for a newspaperman (who didn't know Kane) to interview people who knew him very well. None had ever heard of "Rosebud." Actually, as it turns out, "Rosebud" is the trade name of a cheap little sled on which Kane was playing on the day he was taken away from his home and his mother. In his subconscious, it represented the simplicity, the comfort, above all the lack of responsibility in his home, and it also stood for his mother's love which Kane never lost.[31]

---

[30] Script *Citizen Kane* by Herman J. Mankiewicz & Orson Welles; page 19.

[31] Press statement of Orson Welles on January 15, 1941.

Figure 13.69

Figure 13.70

Figure 13.71

This shot with the broken snow globe is one of the special effects shots mentioned earlier that have deep focus but are not done in one exposure. They are achieved via double exposure with the snow globe being the base image with an area matted out and then exposed again with the nurse being distorted through a diminishing glass in front of the camera (one can see the subtle shaking of the secondary superimposed image).

What drags attention in an image is not just composition or light but also details, texture, and with it focus. In this shot, the nurse is the sharpest element (no pun intended) in the frame. In addition, she is accentuated by the stark contrast of her white dress and the dark background which allows her silhouette to stand out. The architectural element of the curved window above her leads the eye downward and the snowglobe's snow-covered cabin's roof acts as an arrow pointing toward the left and thus also accentuates the nurse (Figure 13.68). A surreal unique shot, the composition of which reiterates the importance of that very moment of the story: the death of Charles Foster Kane and the memory of his parent's house along with his sled, with the brand name "Rosebud," are shattered on the ground and turn into lost memories. Because there is so much going on in this image, it is actually rather difficult to see all the details, for example, Kane's lifeless arm, just underneath the window. The compositional elements of round (window and distortion of the door) and horizontal vectors (the arm of Kane) are slightly fighting with each other. Nevertheless, the round vector of the window and the strong contrast of the nurse's dress in front of the background dominate the composition.

## Susan's attempted suicide (Figures 13.69 through 13.71)

Charles Foster Kane breaks into his wife's bedroom and finds her unconscious in bed after an attempted suicide caused by her failing opera career. She is sweating and breathing heavily and the foreground of the shot blatantly presents the poison she took to end her own life. In this special effects shot, the foreground elements of glass and bottle are in clear focus and extremely crisp; also Kane and a servant in the background are in focus. However, Susan is blurred which results in a shot with two focal points (Figure 13.69).

Because of the focus of bottle and glass in the foreground and then the additional focus of the background characters, both elements seem to be on the same level, having seemingly the same distance from the camera. The characters get dragged forward because of the same focus and the lack of overlap, which would create perspective. For our eye, it makes no sense that there are two focal points in one image and therefore we tend to expect them to be on the same level. Only their size determines the distance between them from a logical standpoint. There is no depth-perception through the lighting situation or the contrast as elements in the foreground have as much brightness or darkness as the elements in the background. What helps us to read the image in its spatial construction is only the size relationship and the few architectural elements in the room. The background characters read again well because of them being silhouetted by the bright background. There are two compositional elements in this shot explained in Figures 13.70 and 13.71. Figure 13.70 has the arm of Kane pointing toward the spoon (the lampshade is right above the vector, accentuating it) and Kane himself is occupying the negative space between the bottle and Susan's head, whereas the butler's body is right above the bottle (Kane's is also taller than the butler reflecting the relationship of glass and bottle underneath). Susan's head is tilted toward the poison, making her "look" at the poison, thus telling the audience the whole incident. As so often, Toland again balances out the glass and the poison with other elements in the frame, this time by mirroring the shapes as seen in Figure 13.71. In addition to the juxtaposing shapes, the wall on the right, because of its brightness, creates a vertical pillar pushing the eye toward the bottle.

The shot starts with just Susan looking at the bottle. We can easily see her because of her slight movement. Once Kane comes in, we have already made the connection between Susan and the poison, so the composition then goes into the next storytelling stage of Kane seeing the incident. The slightly blurry middleground with Susan between Kane and the poison is not the focus of the image anymore: that Kane sees the poison is.

# Shot 1 (Figures 13.72 through 13.81)

The story behind this shot is the suffering and mourning of the former opera singer Susan Alexander, Mr. Kane's second wife. She is sitting in a bar being served by a waiter and interviewed by a newspaper journalist who wants to find out more about Mr. Kane's last word "Rosebud." Susan is obviously distressed and tells the journalist to leave her alone. He goes to a telephone booth to call his boss while the waiter is listening.

Light and shadow in this shot are dominating this dramatic composition. The shadows are so dark, they completely lack definition (on the DVD version of the film; I do not know if the film stock is having some definition in the dark shadows). The journalist in the phone booth is just a black shape. The waiter in the middleground has some light in his face, but Mrs. Alexander is in an island of light, making her the focal point. The complex arrangement of vectors and geometric connections between the actors is despite its full range of visual information quite controlled and ordered. The light and

composition are very clear about who is the actual focus in the shot. It is not the journalist, who is completely in the dark, just serving as a talking prop more or less; the waiter is more important as he shows some compassion for Mrs. Alexander and serves as the mediator between the journalist and Susan, who is the actual focus in this shot. To achieve such strong contrast and depth, a wide angle lens was mounted on the camera and in combination with the high-contrast lighting a sense of depth is achieved that produced this very unusual shot; not just unusual in its depth but especially in its rather unique composition. The light and shadows lead toward Susan (Figure 13.73) and as long as the phone booth is open, the triangular arrangement of the shaft of light between journalist and waiter is also intact (Figure 13.75). When the booth closes, the tilted frame of the doors cut the journalist off from Susan (Figure 13.78). Nevertheless, one light is still pointing toward the journalist: the lamp right above him is like an arrow pointing down (Figure 13.73). The heads of the three actors are arranged according to their relationship with each other in the specific moment of the shot. The waiter is shifting between left and right, depending who he is closer to. In the final frame (Figure 13.81), when he is taking the money from the journalist he has his back turned to Mrs. Alexander reducing the triangle between them to nearly a line. This composition in Figure 13.80 is the one in which Susan is the most lonely as none of the two men on the right relate to her.

Toland furnishes the frame very often with the same or similar arrangement of verticals (Figure 13.79) to create balance in the frame. The action happens in those five vertical stripes, which he fills with characters and positive or negative space (other divisions than the suggested five are obviously possible). In their shots, Toland and Welles never, especially in the very long shots, rely on the story content alone to keep the audience's attention. The composition is constantly changed and moves along the story and the character's psychological state. Every shot surprises with yet another invention that is expressing most poignantly the essence of the story and the relationship between the characters. However, for Toland and Welles the focal point of the image not necessarily has to be in the light or the center of the frame. They switch back and forth never giving the audience what they would expect. Sometimes, the character is lit and clearly visible, sometimes cast in a dark shadow only leaving their silhouette. Merely the voice and the movement of the silhouette let the audience know who it is that is speaking (like the journalist in this shot). It is a powerful tool to take away the visual complexity of facial expressions, casting the face in shadow and allowing the voice and the content take the first row. This gives the eye room to explore the other characters' expressions and how they react to the main characters' actions. There is a continuous dialogue between action and reaction that includes characters, objects, and the set in a manifold of exciting compositions.

**Figure 13.72**

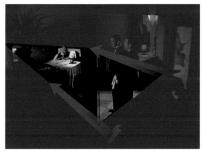

**Figure 13.73**

**Figure 13.74**

**Figure 13.75**

**Figure 13.76**

**Figure 13.77**

**Figure 13.78**

**Figure 13.79**

**Figure 13.80**

**Figure 13.81**

# Shot 2 (Figures 13.82 through 13.91)

Charles Forster Kane's inheritance is explained and along with it the sled, that is going to be so important for the understanding of his life, is introduced. We learn that his mother, after a gold-mine was discovered on her land, arranged for him to get his inheritance at the age of 25 and till then he will be educated far away from his home in Colorado. His father disagrees but his mother makes the decision as the newly gained family wealth is under her name. She signs the paperwork and sends the boy to live with a banker named Thatcher. The scene starts with Charles sliding down a little hill in the snow and the camera dollies back and reveals Mrs. and Mr. Kane and a lawyer, then dollies back further and the characters sit down at a table. All the way in the distance the boy is still visible in the window, serving as a visual reminder, literally between them, that the meeting is in fact about him. He is exactly above the contract that is being singed.

Figures 13.82 through 13.91 show how Toland constantly changes the levels in this shot: first, we only see the boy; then the mother comes in adding a second level; finally, we end up with four characters in the shot, each occupying their own individual level depending on their importance in the shot. The boy, despite being so far way is not unimportant; it is quite the contrary (as we also shall see in the next discussed shot): distance and size are no indicators of importance in Toland's designs! The mother is in the entire shot the dominating character which is shown in her position in the frame and her behavior. The father is the least important one as he obviously has nothing to decide. The strongest composition for this ranking is in Figure 13.88 in which the three characters that are actively involved in this business are inscribed on a curve: the father is not part of this group. The boy is exactly above the signed contract and the lawyer's hand serves as a connector between the two. Toland also likes to use corners as guides for his compositions that he continuously refers to. In this segment of the shot (Figure 13.88), the left lower corner is the one that strengthens the vector of the contract. This connects the mother with the to be signed paper and again leaves the father completely out of it. He is just a bystander. Even when he closes the window, she walks up to it and opens it again: he has stopped caring about the boy, she has not. What is it that makes the boy constantly stand out in this shot despite him being so small in size? It is the window frame that accentuates his importance and also the contrast, as he is so clearly visible in the white surrounding of the snow. There is a subtle light in the middleground just above the mother on the ceiling (Figure 13.88) which gives more contrast to the right side of the frame, rendering it slightly more important, whereas on the other side where the father is standing, contrast is lacking and the ceiling is dark, making him recede into the background.

Figure 13.82

Figure 13.83

Figure 13.84

Figure 13.85

## Shot 3 (Figures 13.92 through 13.99)

This shot shows three characters: Mr. Kane himself; Mr. Walter Thatcher, Kane's legal guardian; and Mr. Bernstein, Kane's friend and employee at *The Inquirer*, the newspaper that Kane had bought. The three deal with the financial losses during the great depression and the effect it has on their business. The arrangement of the three follows Toland's compositional vertical placement in five vertical stripes mentioned before (or four, depending on what elements are seen as being part of the segmentation) and also, like Shot 2 discussed previously, has Kane as a small character in the background, despite being the most significant figure in the shot. It is again Toland's unusual approach of not using big size as the component that signifies a character's importance, but does exactly the opposite, by using a small size for the main character. Kane is perfectly placed between Thatcher and Bernstein and the composition and contrast make him very visible and important indeed.

The shot opens with Mr. Bernstein holding up a contract that is accentuating a triangle (Figure 13.92/13.93), whose core is still maintained after he lowers the paper and reveals Mr. Thatcher in very much the same angle as the contract (Figure 13.95). Once Kane comes into the picture (Figure 13.96), he stands

Figure 13.86

Figure 13.87

Figure 13.88

Figure 13.89

Figure 13.90

Figure 13.91

Figure 13.92

Figure 13.93

Figure 13.94

Figure 13.95

Figure 13.96

Figure 13.97

Figure 13.98

Figure 13.99

# Shot 4 (Figures 13.100 through 13.109)

This shot is a very long one and the complex composition is in constant flux. The three men (later four) in the set switch their positions repeatedly and occupy spaces that are obviously precisely rehearsed to result in a perfect composition, perfection that is rather artificial though highly artistic and convincing. It is interesting that Welles and Toland were going for absolute realism in 1941; their concept for Citizen Kane was to make the audience "feel it was looking at reality, rather than merely at a movie."[32] Looking at the design, lighting, and compositions from today's perspective, this seems like a rather unsuccessful outcome because the finished film is pushed in its style to an extreme so far that everything but realism comes to mind. There are many shots that do follow the style of news reels at the time but the rest of the film is beautifully pushed. Especially, the lighting in this shot is exquisite and unrealistic indeed, yet so effective and nearly surreal. Mr. Kane, Mr. Bernstein, and Kane's friend Jedediah Leland are sitting in the office of *The Inquirer* discussing the further proceedings with the newspaper. Mr. Kane is coming up with his "declaration of principles" that he wants to print on the first page of his newspaper, proof to the public of his social intentions and moral standing. The scene starts with Kane writing on the window; a rather unusual place to write a note to begin with, but it is a spot in the image that makes sense in terms of poses, positions, and story. By writing on the transparent window, he is writing his declaration toward the people of the city that can be seen by everyone. Toland decides to have Kane in the middle of the frame and his two friends left and right; Mr. Bernstein sitting on the left, Mr. Leland very close to the camera on the right. The poses for Mr. Kane are as follows:

- Facing the window writing (Figure 13.100).
- Turning around reading (Figure 13.101).
- Turning off the gas light on his right (Figure 13.102).

in the far distance at the wall in the dead center of the frame, and his position is right between the two. The triangle that was dominating the frame in the beginning of the shot with the brightly lit paper is still there (blue triangle in Figure 13.97), with the upper frame pointing toward the left upper corner, down the perspective line of the panel on the left wall, and on the right side both arms of Bernstein's glasses pointing directly to the lit contract on the table. Kane's head is in line with the eyes of the two (Figure 13.97 red). Kane walks toward the camera and the triangular arrangement changes into a trapezoid one, with the contract, on a vertical line underneath Kane's face; however, the blue triangle is still there (Figure 13.99).

[32] Robert L. Carringer, *The Making of Citizen Kane*, University of California Press, Berkeley, CA, 1985, p. 78.

The lights are turned off with the sentence: "I have to make *The Inquirer* as important to New York as this gas and light." The ironic touch is that he is actually turning off the light right away, despite the importance of the declaration. In the end, he uses his newspaper to manipulate public opinion toward the Spanish American War, so his declaration isn't all what he wanted it to be. It is very difficult to describe the man Charles Foster Kane in his personality because he is a rather complex character that has good intentions, yet over time his decisions are not always having the positive effect intended. Kane turns off the gas lamp and steps forward. Surprisingly he steps into the shadow, his head being completely black. This is the point when Kane reads his declaration and seems to disappear as a person allowing the words to have more impact, as we have seen in other shots before that were discussed. This part of the shot could also be interpreted differently: Kane reads the declaration while his head is in the shadow which causes us to lose trust in him. Is this foreshadowing already what he will be like, to bend the truth for his paper? His friend on the left is still in the light when Kane reads his declaration. Is he Kane's conscience, while Kane is not to be fully trusted?

When he signs the declaration the paper itself is in bright light lifting it out of the shadow and rendering it utterly important (as his friend afterward states that he would like to keep the paper as he has the hunch that this will be like Kane's "declaration of independence"). Once Kane calls his employee to print the declaration on the front page, he withdraws backward into the light and appears again as the businessman Mr. Kane. However, he is not the only one in the frame that changes positions; all the other characters are also part of this complex and continuously changing arrangement. Mr. Leland especially is changing his position and pose in accordance with Kane's, however, always being the subordinate one. In the beginning, he is sitting at the lower left. He changes to the window frame, while the camera is panning to the left (Figure 13.103). When Kane reads his declaration, Leland gets up and stands left of Kane in bright light, juxtaposing the blackness of his friend and balancing the frame. Bernstein is always sitting on his chair frame right. He only shifts a bit and leans forward when the camera pans left, he is obviously the least important character in this arrangement. The camera pans again left when

**Figure 13.100**

**Figure 13.101**

**Figure 13.102**

**Figure 13.103**

**Figure 13.104**

**Figure 13.105**

**Figure 13.106**

**Figure 13.107**

**Figure 13.108**

**Figure 13.109**

the employee steps in to take the declaration with him for print (Figure 13.107); once he leaves, the camera brings Leland back into the frame (Figures 13.107 through 13.109). Toland designs three different group setups—Figures 13.100 through 102, Figures 13.103 through 106, and Figures 13.107 through 13.109—which can be seen as the key frames of the composition. He then brings in little variations between the key frames with small changes in the characters' constellations to achieve more variety and avoid the image to become stagnant.

This shot is also noteworthy for Toland's use of upshots that reveal the ceiling of the room. Usually, in typical Hollywood stage sets, the rooms lacked a ceiling as practical access to the set from above was more important. The lights were above stage and access from the top for the sound boom was needed. The sets in *Citizen Kane* however were all built with an artificial ceiling consisting of a tightly stretched fabric above which the sound equipment was placed. This allowed shots from very low angles that reveal the ceiling and thus create unusual shots with much emotional impact. The lighting situation in this shot is unique and works on so many levels. It is highly artificial, yet has an artistic flavor to it that makes it so very unique.

## Camera pan in shot 5 (Figures 13.110 and 13.111)

In this scene, Kane is at the height of his wealth and power though at a low point in his personal life. His wife Susan is playing jig-saw puzzles day in and day out (oh the irony of it!) and complaining about the boredom in their mansion Xanadu.

They are wealthy though lonely and their conversation is about nothing but the current time in New York, so banal that it is pathetic. Nest van Polglase's set design is spectacular in its scale and grandeur. The vast space, the European gothic entrance, the opulent stairway, and the extravagantly oversized fireplace are adding to the gigantism of Xanadu. Toland does an excellent job in lighting the space and allowing black shadows to dominate most of the image, strengthening the element of discomfort. There are Egyptian statues of sitting Pharaohs, Greek sculptures, a Chinese lion and dragon…. Xanadu is a museum, a collection of treasures that no one appreciates, a place that is already dead and tomb-like. Once Kane steps in front of the fireplace, he seems to have to position himself in a dominating pose in order to defend his space and standing. The huge backdrop frames Kane like a throne and he, the emperor of his mansion, has to guard his castle, pride, and wealth, whether he wants to or not. He is trapped in his own success. The fireplace also evokes images of the open mouth of a huge dragon spitting fire and Kane is stepping into its opening. Susan on the other hand is threatened by a big silhouette of a dragon or monster that towers over her from the right of the frame (Figures 13.114 and 13.115).

The camera pan at the beginning of the shot starts with the Egyptian and Greek sculptures on the left, eliminating the offscreen space on the left. The camera pans to the right and ends up at the fireplace where the dragon seals off the offscreen space on the right, juxtaposing the pharaoh. The reconstruction (Figure 13.110) of the entire shot and set shows the balance of the sculptures left and right clearly and their positioning toward the action. In combination with all the grandness of the architectural

**Figure 13.110**

Pan recreated from various screenshots.

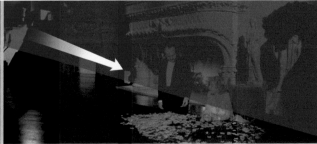

**Figure 13.111**

pieces in between and the stark lighting, the space emanates the claustrophobia of a prison, despite the vast space. It is not so much a spatial claustrophobia than a psychological one, though the lighting intensifies that tightness with its big areas of pure black. If the sculptures left and right would be taken out, the space would feel much bigger, but would lose its space defining borders.

Toland and his crew lights the set in blocks: the sculptures on the left and parts of the Gothic entrance, the staircase, and finally the fireplace are brightly lit. The right half of the Gothic entrance and the portal left of the fireplace on the other hand are dimly lit. This creates a very nice dynamic in the pan in which the visual intensity changes from lit, to less lit, back to lit, etc. Again he does what he did in all the other scenes: create visual interest by always changing the light situation and thus creating a composition in constant flux. This type of lighting is more related to stage lighting for theater than realistic set lighting but is very

visually appealing. Kane himself is walking through the space always in the dark until he stops at the table.

There are two compositional elements that structure the beginning and the end of the pan. The lighting in the beginning of the pan is oriented toward the left, despite the pan moving to the right. The light falling through the portal illuminates the statues and creates a strong vector on the floor to the left. Kane does not follow this vector on the floor but steps over it into the dark, which accentuates his psychological state. The staircase he passes is overwhelming in its direction, also to the left. Once he passes the middle of the stage, accentuated by the candelabra, the direction changes and is marked by the tilt of the portal and fireplace. The set design follows Toland's usual compositions of triangular arrangements in the frame (negative shape underneath the blue shape in Figure 13.111). Now the light shaft coming in through the Gothic gate on the left makes even more sense, as it balances out the mirrored position of the fireplace on the right. There is also

**Figure 13.112**

**Figure 13.113**

**Figure 13.114**

**Figure 13.115**

again the vertical arrangement of elements that balance each other, accentuating the center, the left, and right.

Once Kane stops in front of the fireplace (Figure 13.115), talking to Susan, the actor's position is in the mirrored position from the beginning of the shot, when he steps out of the Gothic arc. Perfect balance is achieved not only within the frame but also during the shot! The strong sweeping curve of the fireplace directly points down toward Susan. The space Kane steps into when talking to her is a perfect visual interpretation of his situation: his background is burning (fireplace) and his ground is shattered (jigsaw puzzle). The jigsaw puzzle is also Susan's life that is in smithereens and she tries to piece it together again (Figures 13.112 and 13.113). Once Kane steps in front of the fireplace in a proud, yet stubborn pose (Figure 13.114), the puzzle is underneath his feet making it look like he is standing on the shards of his personal life.

This set of the Great Hall at Xanadu was built with a lower budget and therefore only the gate, the stairway, and the fireplace were actually built. The rest of the set is either filled with props provided by the prop department or covered by black curtains, very much like the practice on a theater stage. What is interesting in this Xanadu setting is the mentioned theatrical approach to the space in terms of lighting and positioning of the elements that create the apex of the perspective in the middle of the "stage." The architecture is not fully explained and not realistic in its depiction of space but rather a lose assemblage of pieces of art and architecture that suggest rather than explain. They give an idea and a mood which is connected through the light and separated by shadow, creating a rather surreal set instead of mimicking reality.

The final film was not as successful as one would have hoped in 1941 when it was released in the theaters, despite raving reviews. But considering its topic of a newspaper mogul whose life is discussed in detail and who does not seem to find happiness despite his immense wealth did not please the one the film was actually (loosely) based on: William Randolph Hearst (1863–1951), the newspaper mogul who had his own Xanadu at the coast of Southern California in San Simeon: Hearst Castle. Because of him being the one that controlled a big chunk of the newspapers at the time, the movie was not being advertised properly and some cinemas did not play it at all, like New York's Art Deco palace Radio City Music Hall.[33] It was in the decades after, that the film's fame was rising. Especially in the 1950s the film's importance was rediscovered. The richness of its visuals and the complexity of the compositions is something not very often mentioned when the film is discussed, however, it is a big part of what makes *Citizen Kane* so appealing and unique. Despite Toland's and Welles' artistic success of the film and their comfortable collaboration and artistic respect for each other, they would never again get the chance to work together.

**More on *Citizen Kane*:**

Robert Carringer, *The Making of Citizen Kane*, University of California Press, Berkeley, CA, 1985.

33  Richard Armstrong, Some Kind of a Man: Revisiting Citizen Kane, *Australian Screeneducation*, No. 33 (September 2003), p. 125.

# Light, shadows and color

"The sky is the 'source of light' in nature, and governs everything."[34]

**John Constable**

*The following is a study of realistic occurrences that serve as a foundation of artistic interpretation. Learning about how light, shadow, and weather look like realistically helps to understand its complexity and then decide on its use creatively. It is not about copying nature but interpreting it (some artists do not necessarily need to know how nature works, as it of course depends on the style of the artwork and level of realism that is aspired). Because of the vast amount of weather situations, landscapes, and light occurrences in nature, this chapter can only be an interesting foundation for further and more intense personal study.*

Shadows are not just black, they are as versatile as light is and paying attention to one without the other is only half the fun. To learn how shadows work, one must understand light and how light causes shadows and affects them. Shadows are *three-dimensional blocks* that occur due to an elimination or reduction of incoming light. Light that hits an opaque object is intercepted and the rays are reflected from the object's surface. The three-dimensional space behind the object that lacks light is the shadow area or shadow surface. The shadow itself is not falling onto a surface; it is the lack of light that causes the shadow to be visible. Usually, the three-dimensional shadow block itself is invisible (Figure 13.116), appearing only as a contrast between areas that are hit by sunlight and those that lack sunlight. The volume of the block of shadow can be seen if there are particles

(fog, smoke, dust) between the object and shadow surface and only then it appears as the fully three-dimensional form that it is. Shadows themselves have as many variations as light has. It is not "just" a lack of light that defines a shadow but a myriad of other light sources that illuminate and color them. Reflections from other objects and surfaces and the atmosphere itself redirect light rays into the shadows and change appearance and gradient. Shadows on Earth are never completely black, there is always some scattered light that brightens them and makes their appearance colorful and interesting.

**Shadows change their appearance and color depending on:**

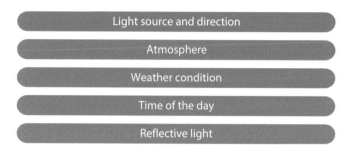

- Light source and direction
- Atmosphere
- Weather condition
- Time of the day
- Reflective light

# Light source and direction

The color and quality of the shadow is highly dependent on the light source, although the shadow of an artificial light is slightly different from a shadow that is caused by natural sunlight.

## Sunlight shadow (Figure 13.117)

The sun is immense in size! We do forget that fact because in the sky it doesn't look THAT big, but it is. And it is the size of the sun that shapes the shadows that it creates. The sun emits rays from its whole surface in every direction, which are not just leaving the sun from one point but from infinite points around its surface. Because of the huge size of the sun, its rays reach Earth from its full wide radius and not only from one imagined point at the center of the sun. This creates two parts of a shadow: one that is the core shadow, the dark part right behind the object called *umbra* (Figure 13.117 U), being the area in the shadow that receives no sunlight at all, other than dispersed rays. The second part is the *penumbra* (Figure 13.117 P), framing the umbra on both sides and being slightly brighter. This is the part that receives some light due to the width of the sun. It is a bit difficult to actually distinguish the umbra from the penumbra as they are blurring into each other. You can usually just see them outside as one shadow that is blurrier on its borders the further it is away from the object that caused it, and darker at its center.

## Construction of sunlight shadows

There are various approaches to this and one needs to use the method that fits the project and the aesthetic, not necessarily

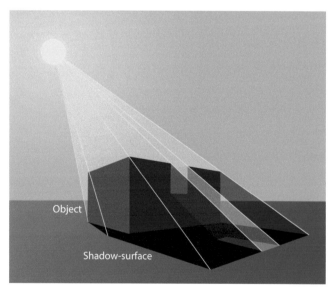

Object

Shadow-surface

**Figure 13.116**

34  Letter to Rev. John Fisher (23 October 1821), as quoted in Leslie Parris and Ian Fleming-Williams, *Constable*, Tate Gallery Publications, London, 1993, p. 229.

Figure 13.117

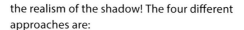

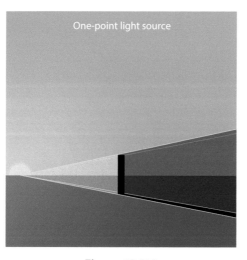

Figure 13.118

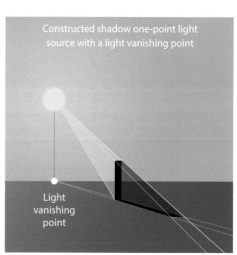

Figure 13.119

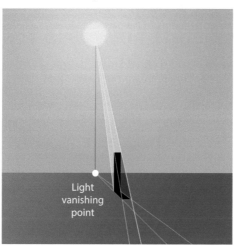

Figure 13.120

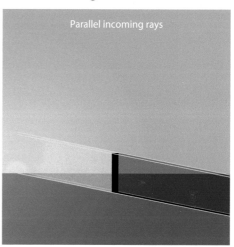

Figure 13.121

the realism of the shadow! The four different approaches are:

1. The sun is reduced to one single point where the light is originating from, shown in Figure 13.118, where the sun is just about to raise itself above the horizon. This produces theoretically a shadow that is infinite; however, it will grow in width the further the shadow is away from its source. Once the sun rises, like in Figure 13.119, we need a light vanishing point for the construction of the shadow, which is determined by dropping a perpendicular from the center of the light-source onto the horizon line (Figures 13.119 and 13.120). The shadow in this construction grows in width the further it is away from the object, which is technically incorrect because the rays of the sun come in nearly parallel, so the width would stay the same.

2. The incoming rays are all parallel and the shadow does not grow but stays the same in its width (Figure 13.121).

3. The rays of the sunlight are leaving the sun's surface from its entire width; therefore, two different points on the rim of the sun's circle need to be incorporated (Figure 13.117). This produces the realistic umbra and penumbra of the shadow.

4. Just do as you please: don't think about realism at all and draw a shadow that feels right and is creating a mood. However, this needs to be in line with the rest of the image's style and should not go against it, meaning a realistic image with a fake shadow might not work (or it might... depending of course on the subject and style).

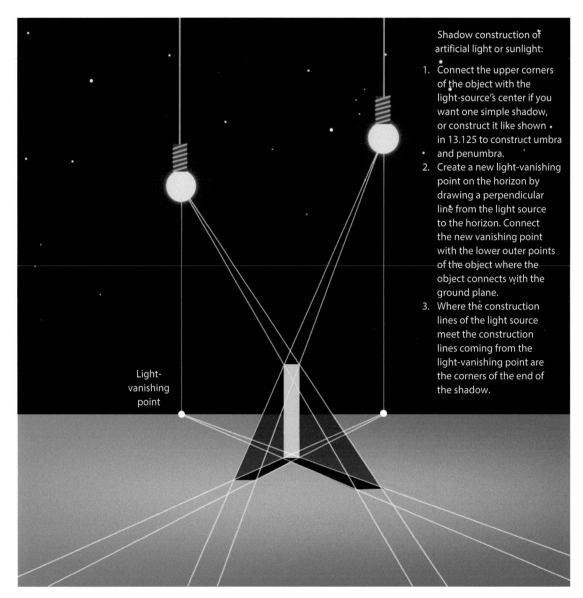

Shadow construction of artificial light or sunlight:

1. Connect the upper corners of the object with the light-source's center if you want one simple shadow, or construct it like shown in 13.125 to construct umbra and penumbra.
2. Create a new light-vanishing point on the horizon by drawing a perpendicular line from the light source to the horizon. Connect the new vanishing point with the lower outer points of the object where the object connects with the ground plane.
3. Where the construction lines of the light source meet the construction lines coming from the light-vanishing point are the corners of the end of the shadow.

Light-vanishing point

**Figure 13.122**

## Artificial light (Figure 13.122)

Technically, artificial light has the same scattering of light as the sun does, but on a much smaller scale. There is still a blur in the shadow but not as much... well, it does depend on the kind of artificial light source. Very small light sources like tiny Halogen lamps have rather clearly defined shadows, whereas a fluorescent tube lamp has a softer shadow, because the light is emitted from a wider surface than from a tiny Halogen lamp. The more light sources are spread throughout the room, the more the shadows get dispersed and multiple shadows start to develop with the overlapping areas of the shadows being darker. This can be seen in a room with lots of ceiling lights where there can be multiple overlapping shadows. To know how to construct the shadows for artificial light, see Figure 13.122.

**More about construction of shadows:**

John Montague, *Basic Perspective Drawing: A Visual Approach*, Wiley, Hoboken, NJ, 2013; Chapter 8: Shadows and reflections

# Atmosphere

The atmosphere is by far the most significant feature on Earth that contributes to the sky's diversity and with it to the distribution of the sunlight throughout the year's recurring cycles. The atmosphere is, compared with the planet's size, a very thin layer surrounding the surface of the Earth and consisting of various gases. Oxygen, carbon dioxide, nitrogen and traces of helium, hydrogen, krypton, methane, neon, ozone, and xenon together constitute the deep blue sky, which we so often experience as the ultimate and infinite depth. Roughly half of the atmosphere's weight is held by gravity below a height of 5.5 km,[35] the other half reaches all the way up into the Exosphere, a height of up to 10,000 km, above which is absolutely nothing—interplanetary space. Weather events or meteorological phenomena mainly occur in the Troposphere, the lowest layer of the atmosphere, which reaches from the ground up to about 12 km in height (with variations between poles and Equator) and contains nearly all the water vapor that causes weather and clouds. In between Exosphere and Troposphere are the following:

- Thermosphere: ~80–800 km height. A layer without any water vapor, so there is no weather happening. However, other visual occurrences appear, like the Aurora Borealis and the Aurora Australis. The temperatures in the Thermosphere are actually significantly high, but because of the gas molecules being very far apart from each other due to the low density of the layer, their impact is extremely low.
- Mesosphere: ~50–80 km height. The upper region of the Mesosphere has the lowest temperatures of the atmosphere, which can reach below −140°C, making it the coldest place on Earth. The only visible clouds in this layer are noctilucent clouds, ice-crystal clouds which are visible only during twilight.
- Stratosphere: ~12–50 km height. This layer is also dry and has very little water vapor; therefore, no weather happens in the Stratosphere either. The only occasional clouds are stratospheric clouds which appear in the polar regions during winter. The Stratosphere also contains the important Ozone layer, preventing most of the Sun's life-threatening ultraviolet radiation from reaching the surface.

Figure 13.123 demonstrates the thickness of the various layers in relationship with each other. The Troposphere just above the surface, being the thinnest, has however the highest temperatures and also the highest air pressure. The further up one goes, the lower the temperature and the lower the air pressure sinks (with exception of the Thermosphere as explained above). Most of the visible action that we can see in the sky happens in the Troposphere, which contains by far the most water vapor and particles, natural and man-made. Not only sand dust, pollen, smoke particles, debris of tornadoes and storms, volcanos, or even small microscopic life-forms but also smog from industries and other human pollutants are part of the mix of particles that cause the myriads of colors and weather situations we observe daily. A clean atmosphere allows the eye to see very far into the distance, like in the Himalayas where there is little human pollution and so far away mountains can be seen very clearly (Figure 13.124),[36] as the air seems nearly transparent. But the atmosphere can also be so polluted with particles, dominant enough to produce a thick layer that covers the landscape like a veil. A gray and brownish belt of sand dust and pollution can be seen as a low hanging layer behind the Djoser step-pyramid in the desert just outside of Cairo (Figure 13.125), or the brown to smoky

[35] Vincent J. Schaefer, *John A. Day: A Field Guide to the Atmosphere*, Houghton Mifflin Company, Dublin, Ireland, 1981, p. 1.
[36] All photographs in this chapter will be available for download in the online folder to this book for precise color reference.

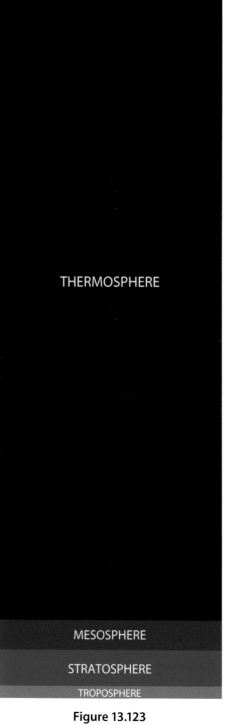

EXOSPHERE

THERMOSPHERE

MESOSPHERE

STRATOSPHERE

TROPOSPHERE

**Figure 13.123**

**Figure 13.124**

Himalayas, Nepal.

blue haze inside Cairo during the very same day (Figure 13.126). However, much sand dust is also part of the atmosphere's mix inside and outside of that location.

The Earth's atmosphere has tremendous influence not only on the distribution of the incoming sunlight and moonlight but also on the distribution of light pollution coming from cities and human settlements. Incoming sunlight hits the Earth's

atmosphere and the direction and strength of the light is changed (or refracted) from the point of entry all the way down to the surface. The change of density, particles in the air, amount of water vapor, and other factors affect the incoming sunlight by spreading its rays, thus slightly blurring it and also altering its color which will be explained in the following sections.

## Airlight or skylight

Figure 13.127 has the top of Mount Everest cast a long shadow onto the lower regions of the atmosphere, the Troposphere, which can be seen as an illuminated orange belt on the horizon that is saturated with moisture. The sunlight just hit the highest point on Earth, top of Everest, casting its shadow onto the atmosphere underneath. However, one can see that the atmosphere despite the lack of direct sunlight is already glowing. Figure 13.128 shows the Nepalese mountains in the morning light. The foreground mountain on the right is in shadow and the background mountain behind it is also in shadow, nevertheless much brighter. Above the mountain we see the sunlight penetrating the air horizontally and lighting up the portion of the atmosphere in the upper part of the image, whereas the part underneath lacks light and is slightly darker. The reason for both is the effect in the atmosphere called *Airlight*, the phenomena during the day where distant objects appear brighter, have less saturation, less contrast, and are more bluish in hue the further away they are from the viewer during the day, orange and red during sunset and sunrise, and grayish/brownish blue during smog, or yellow/red during a sand or dust storm. The accumulating amount of air, with its particles and water vapor, in between the object and the viewer is illuminated by the sun. We can see in Figure 13.129 that the sunlight hits the atmosphere and its rays get slightly dispersed. The rays interact with the molecules and particles and change their direction ever so slightly. The thicker the atmosphere is with particles, the more the light is dispersed. In Figure 13.130, the sunlight that just climbs up behind the mountain peak is illuminating the air itself. It is not the rays themselves that we see but the particles

**Figure 13.125**

Djoser Pyramid, Egypt.

**Figure 13.126**

Cairo, Egypt.

**Figure 13.127**

Longacre, Chris: *Mount Everest, May 19, 2013 at 5:07am.*

**Figure 13.128**

Himalayas, Nepal.

that are lit up. We can also see in Figure 13.128 that there is a color gradient from the peak of the middle mountain to its foot, getting darker the further it is away from the penetrating sunlight. The lit up atmosphere reflects light to the layer of air underneath and brightens it (Figure 13.130). Light rays are bouncing off of particles and get redirected into the darker layer underneath and thus illuminate it. The air itself is glowing. The more particles are in the air the stronger this Airlight appears, so in the early morning when there is much moisture in the air (or in the evening when there is usually more dust in the air), Airlight can be very strong. The lit up accumulated air also reduces the contrast of objects further away from the viewer to the extent where there might not be any texture visible but just a continuous color gradient (Airlight is obviously only visible if there is a significant distance between object and viewer. Though as an artistic device, it can be used for much shorter distances very successfully to mimic distance and depth. In live-action film, this is sometimes simulated with smoke in the air, causing the air to have some substance and visible depth). The particles in between object and viewer form a kind of gauze curtain that covers a clear view. On a sunny day with much water vapor in the air, Airlight can be so strong that mountains in the far distance are not visible at all. The air in between is so filled with particles and light that we only see the atmosphere but not the mountains in the very far distance. When the sun sets and Airlight subsides, the mountains become visible again. Especially in summer when there is dust and sand, due to the dry surface, being blown into the atmosphere, the sky can look rather whitish; once a heavy shower or two has cleaned the air, the sky has again its deep and impressive blue. In addition to the light from above, the atmosphere is also lit up by the reflecting sunlight from Earth's surface. Rivers, the ocean, the entire surface of the Earth bounces back part of the sunlight into the atmosphere and adds to the existing Airlight.

The impressionists were able to depict this light situation and create paintings of surreal beauty. Their understanding of color perspective and especially shadows and their exaggeration

created a new and exciting representation of nature. Light and atmosphere were artistically integrated into the painting and often became the mere reason for the picture. Airlight was a significant part of their aesthetic. In one of Claude Monet's paintings (Figure 13.131) of his series *Charing the Cross Bridge* (1899), we can clearly see how in a highly exaggerating style reducing saturation and contrast result in denser air, in this case more fog. The atmosphere is captured and artistically interpreted through the understanding and control of color in its most subtle extremes to achieve such a delicate painting. One can feel and touch the air!

As mentioned before, the impact of Airlight can also be seen during heavy air pollution caused by dust, fumes, or smoke. For the air to be lit up, it does not matter what particles are dispersed; pollution can be of natural or human causes—the effect is similar but does cause different colors. There is in spring, for example, the high amount of pollen that gets released into the air or in some areas there is dust, sand particles, or just smoke from fires; pollution is not always man-made! However, the particles themselves at some point, if too dense, reduce the amount of incoming light and less light actually reaches the ground. Also, the color becomes more dominant the more the atmosphere is saturated with pollutants. In the aforementioned image of Cairo (Figure 13.126), the pollution is causing a color perspective that is extreme for such a short distance. But it does follow the same rules: reduced contrast toward the distance, reduced saturation, and shift of the hue to blue, brown, yellow, or red (depending on the pollution and situation). For example, in Figure 13.132, the hills around Sheffield in Yorkshire, UK, are rather yellowish; this picture was taken in late spring with lots of mist in the early evening, just before sunset. One can see the stacked layers of the hills, vanishing behind a veil of mist, nearly like layers of flat theater scenes stacked behind each other.

During the day, the sky itself appears brighter toward the horizon (Figure 13.124) because we look through the longest distance of illuminated atmosphere when we look horizontally. The more the

**Figure 13.129**

**Figure 13.131**

Claude Monet: *Charing Cross Bridge* (1899).

atmosphere is saturated with humidity and particles the whiter it appears (the more it is saturated with pollution the more yellow, brownish, or bluish it appears or whatever color the pollutant has). Looking straight up into the clear sky on a sunny day we see the darkest part of the sky during day time as we look through the shortest distance of atmosphere, thus see the least amount of Airlight.

## Airlight and shadows

Airlight does not only lighten up the atmosphere but the dispersed rays of light also brighten up shadows and penetrate darker corners. The rays are bouncing off of particles in the air and therefore get dispersed into different directions. Sunlight does not only come down in parallel rays but also with a lesser degree from no specific direction and reaching objects from all directions, not just from one. This however depends greatly on

**Figure 13.130**

**Figure 13.132**

Outside Sheffield, United Kingdom.

**Figure 13.133**

NASA: *Edwin Aldrin on the moon* (1969).

the weather situation, which will be explained later. Shadows on Earth are never fully black, not even at night.

If there is no atmosphere like on the surface of the Moon, then there is obviously no Airlight and thus no brightening of shadows, as the light is not dispersed. The picture of Edwin Aldrin (Figure 13.133) on the moon from 1969 has Aldrin brightly lit by the sun, but the shadows are pitch black. The surface of the moon though reflects the light from the sun back at Aldrin's suit, which in turn also theoretically would lighten up the shadows, but obviously not enough to be visible. Nevertheless, the shadows on the Moon are not completely black as there is still *Earthshine*. Earthshine is the light that is reflected from Earth's surface onto the Moon, lighting up its shadow side. It is a very faint light obviously, just touching the Moon's surface slightly, nevertheless enough to be visible.

## Airlight and color perspective

Airlight causes the colors to change relative to the distance of the viewer's position. The contributing factors of color perspective are:

*   Time of the day and weather situation (amount of water vapor or pollutants in the air), which will both be explained in the chapters ahead. But color perspective has the same rules despite the conditions of daytime or weather. Color perspective affects all three elements of color: hue, brightness, and saturation, and all three have to be equally

considered when giving the impression of perspective and depth (with exceptions of course):
*   **Brightness:** increases the further the object is from the viewer during the day (however, a pure white close to the viewer would darken at a far distance if the discoloration of the atmosphere is darker than the pure white, during a sandstorm, for instance).
*   **Saturation:** decreases the further the object is from the viewer during the day.
*   **Hue:** shift toward the radiant flux color that is dominant at the specific time of the day (see also Figure 13.135).

Figure 13.136, the back gate of the Forbidden City in Beijing, shows how the colors in background and foreground follow those three rules and either visually recede into the background or come forward. This is true for the colors both in the shadows or light. The hue is shifting toward bluish gray the further the buildings are away from the viewer. On a very clear day, with barely any moisture or particles in the air, close and far objects have a less defined color-perspective, as seen in Figure 13.137, again in the Himalayas. Because of the clarity and crispness of the air, the colors change less dramatically, which not only flattens the image slightly but also makes it very difficult for the eye to judge semiaccurately the distances between foreground and background.

## Atmosphere and color

First we have to understand what happens when the sunlight penetrates our atmosphere to then see what it does to the color of the light. The atmosphere consists of molecules, dust particles, ice crystals, and water droplets. These, once hit by the sunlight, cause the atmosphere to lighten up, which in turn causes our sky to appear bright blue (see the section "The Color of the Sky" for an explanation). While the light penetrates the various layers of atmosphere, its initially fully white composition is affected and with it the color of the light that reaches the Earth's surface.

Usually during a clear day the full spectrum of the sunlight touches the ground, which is white light. The atmosphere of the Earth generally absorbs or reflects certain colors of the sunlight's spectrum if its travelled distance through the atmosphere is very long. Because the sun in the evening and morning stands very low, the sunlight has to travel through a greater portion of the atmosphere in terms of distance compared with the sun that stands high in the sky at noon (Figure 13.134). The higher wavelength of the sun's spectrum, like green or blue, is eliminated in the morning or evening when the distance from the entrance into the atmosphere to the viewer is the longest. The lower wavelengths like red or orange are less affected, which means they more easily pass through directly to the viewer. The more atmosphere the sunlight has to pass through and the denser the atmosphere, all but the red light will be filtered out, which leads to red sunsets and sunrises.

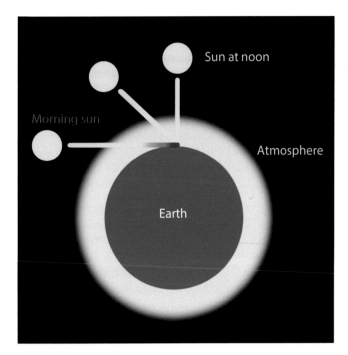

Figure 13.134

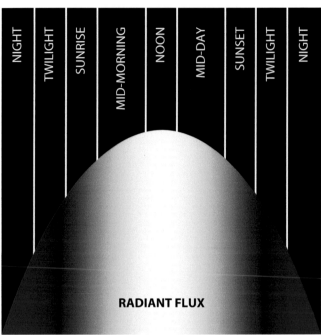

Figure 13.135

Figure 13.136

Forbidden City, Beijing.

Figure 13.135 shows the radiant flux, the energy of the wavelength received by the viewer, and shows which color is reaching the surface during the different times of a cloudless day. Noon has the full spectrum of color (white light) with the most amount of light reaching the surface and the highest radiant power. Toward the evening the light gets more and more red (greens and blues are eliminated) and at twilight the light is purplish blue going into the ultraviolet light (unseen by the human eye) till all (well, not all but most) light disappears at night.

## The color of the sky

Sunlight, as we have seen before, consists of various colors and each has its own wavelength. Red and orange have a very long wavelength and blue has a very short wavelength. Sunlight that penetrates the atmosphere has the rays with a long wavelength pass through more easily, whereas the blue light with its short wavelength is highly dispersed, thus much more blue light reaches our eye when we look into the sky. That's what makes the sky appear blue. However, there is a huge range of colors that the sky can have and it is by no means just the typical blue but ranges from a deep and nearly dark blue to a grayish white and all the colorful possibilities mentioned earlier, such as yellow, orange, red, and purple (plus some situations like dust storms and storms during which it can be brown, rust-red, and even greenish). It is the amount of water vapor and particles in the air that causes the color of the sky to change: the more water vapor (and/or organic or inorganic particles) the whiter/grayer the sky. This does not mean that actual clouds are visible, but the moisture can be evenly distributed. If there is enough moisture in the air to cover the sky with a white layer, but the sun is still strong, then the shadows are blurred and lit

up, but the sun is still being seen, nevertheless the sky is not deep blue, but light blue and seemingly washed out. This is, for instance, happening in Figure 13.154. A sky that is devoid of water vapor, like the typical California blue summer sky, is so deep blue that it often seems unreal (i.e., for someone like me from Germany). But there is also haze, which causes the sky to be more yellowish, brownish-blue, and is solely caused by human pollution.

The air is of course not the same in all parts of the world, and it does contribute to the quality of the sky color. For instance, isoprene, an organic compound produced by oaks, eucalyptus, and poplars, lets the Blue Ridge Mountains, part of the Appalachian mountain range, look more blue from the distance, hence its name.

# Weather conditions

## Sunny day (Figures 13.137 and 13.138)

A shadow on a sunny and crystal clear day is refined and clearly outlined and not blurry in short distances (a cloud would of course cast a blurry shadow on the ground, even on a very clear and sunny day because of its great distance to the ground). The rays of the sunlight are not scattered much and therefore hit the objects nearly parallel, which causes the shadow to be clean and darker with a very narrow blurred border. The further the object is away from the ground though the lighter its shadow on the ground becomes, as some of the dispersed light that is still happening on a sunny day due to the atmosphere's scattering, lightens the shadow. The closer the object is to the ground the darker and more precise the shadow will be. The colors will be at their brightest during noon and the saturation has the tendency to be slightly desaturated in the shadows but the opposite can also

**Figure 13.137**

Himalayas, Nepal.

**Figure 13.138**

Trajan's Kiosk, Egypt.

**Figure 13.139**

Rothenburg, Germany.

happen. The colors will be slowly tinted red/orange toward sunrise or sunset. The contrast between light and shadow is the strongest, it can be during noon on a sunny day.

## Cloudy or rainy day (Figures 13.139 and 13.140)

On a cloudy day, the light rays are immensely scattered due to the thick layer of clouds, filled with water vapor. The rays are getting redirected by hitting water droplets and thus the dispersion is very significant. The thicker the clouds—the more scattering happens—the less refined the shadows are. This happens to the point where defined shadows completely disappear altogether and darkness just appears in corners and covered spaces. Due to the thicker clouds, less light in general is penetrating the atmosphere beneath the clouds and reaching the ground, which causes less brightness overall. The shadows tend to be less dark due to being lit up by the high amount of scattered rays and the contrast between light and dark is much less distinct. Brighter shadows and less overall brightness cause less contrast on a cloudy day. Nevertheless, spaces under cars, for instance, where not much light can penetrate, are usually very dark.

The image of the sky over Sheffield (Figure 13.140) shows a nimbostratus cloud with continuous rain falling in streaks from its base, which has a very dark grayish-blue color. Very little light is penetrating and reaching the surface, which makes the city look dark and gloomy. The clouds further away are brighter again and do not have as much contrast as the ones close by.

## Snowy bright day (Figure 13.141)

Shadows on a snowy bright day have a beautiful blue tint to them and are only dark in the corners, but they often

**Figure 13.140**

Sheffield, United Kingdom.

light up otherwise and reflect the color of the sky. There is so much reflection from the snow itself, because it is pure white and reflects all the colors from the spectrum, that most shadows are rather bright. But the contrast between light and shadow is so extreme due to the whiteness of the snow, that the shadows still seem often dark. Because of the clarity of the air in Figure 13.141, the shadows and the snow itself change little from close to far away. As the snow already is white, it can't get any brighter, but the air in between can darken the snow in the distance just slightly, depending on the pollution in the air. The shadows though get brighter the further away they are from the viewer, thus contrast between snow and shadows is reduced the further it is from the viewer.

**Figure 13.141**

River Main near Karlstadt, Germany.

**Figure 13.142**

Himalayas, Nepal.

**Figure 13.143**

Himalayas, Nepal.

## Heavy snow

Heavy snow is similar to thick fog: objects far away disappear and are desaturated. Everything is slightly grayish/whitish. However, what can be seen clearly does depend on the size of the snowflakes. If the snow is very fine, then it looks rather like fog in the distance. If the flakes are very big, then the colors of objects further away are less affected theoretically. Shadows during heavy snow are nonexistent or extremely blurred out.

## Fog (Figures 13.142 and 13.143)

During fog there is so much water vapor in the air that the little light that penetrates the thick layer is diffused to such an extent that shadows are barely possible and, if found, are blurred extremely. Even under the bridge in the higher mountains in Nepal (Figure 13.142), the stones are still not dark. There are only dark shadows underneath areas that do not get any light at all, in between stones or areas where even the highly dispersed rays cannot reach into. Otherwise, the light is more or less spread evenly. The thicker the fog, the lesser the contrast. Only objects close to the viewer have strong contrast and saturation. As the small patches of grass in Figure 13.142 show, there is less saturation the further away the grass is from the viewer's position, more brightness and slightly more blue in the grass's color. The color perspective is very high, even over shorter distances.

In Figure 13.143, the fog is so dense that even the trees close by can only be seen in a blurry shape with no definition.

## Mist

Mist is technically the same as fog; however, we can see further during mist than fog, so the difference between the two is visibility. Once we can see further than 1 km than we are talking about mist; when we can only see up to 1 km, it is called fog.

## Haze

Where fog and mist have water droplets in the air, haze has dry particles that are usually caused by human pollution. Figure 13.136, the air in Beijing, for instance, has probably to a high degree pollution rather than water vapor.

One of the few short films that deal with the complexity of fog is Russian animator Yuriy Norshteyn's brilliantly executed and told *Hedgehog in the Fog* (1975), a classic and cultural icon in Russia. The cutout animation's story is about a hedgehog that visits his friend the bear every night to drink tea and count the stars. This very evening while the hedgehog decides again to see his friend, he observes a white horse standing in the fog. He ponders about the question if the horse would drown in fog if it went to sleep. Thoughts and curiosity of the hedgehog are

**Figure 13.144**

Mojave Desert, California.
https://commons.wikimedia.org/wiki/File:Desert_Electric.jpg

**Figure 13.145**

Khao Sok, Thailand.

triggered in this surreal environment of the fog and along his way he meets various characters that seem dangerous in their undefined shape in the dense fog but turn out to be harmless. The film is a quiet metaphor that allows many interpretations as its story is rather vague and meanders like the hedgehog himself. It is considered as one of the masterpieces in animation for very good reasons not only because of its storytelling but also its animation technique. The technique of shooting the dense fog was achieved by using a thin transparent piece of paper, whose distance to the camera would be changed in order to blur out the scenes behind it. Various layers of paper and artwork were required to get the stunning results of this complex weather condition. Norshteyn not only uses the fog for its sole mystical appearance and dreamlike quality but also to hide information and make the audience guess, very much like the hedgehog, of what might be hiding. It covers much of what the hedgehog is experiencing and is so dense that he cannot even see his own hands. The white horse, or also a dog, is coming in and out of the fog, appearing and disappearing and changing the perception of real and unreal or what is imagination and what is actuality.

The low contrast in the frames allows sometimes only the hedgehog to be read and sometimes even he is disappearing. The rest of the image is floating in an undefined space. The emptiness allows us to meditate about the meaning of it all and what the hedgehog is experiencing. In the end, he finds his way to the bear's campfire but things have changed: the fog is still on his mind and keeps him guessing, the memory of it and the experienced adventure has left a mark on the hedgehog's consciousness. The encounter with the surreal had a strong impact and compared with the friendly chatter of the bear the hedgehog is absent and like the fog his mind is floating.

## Storms (Figures 13.144 and 13.145)

There is a vast variety of storms and they all can have their specifics of how they develop and produce wind, rain, snow, and hail (for more scientific details on how storms evolve, check Schaefer and Day: *A Field Guide to the Atmosphere*, Chapter 6). Rainstorm, hailstorm, tornado, ice storm, cyclones, cloudbursts, and blizzards, to name just a few, are caused by the huge and threatening cumulonimbus clouds that reach up to 12 km in height, being filled with energy and water vapor, which is distributed throughout the cloud's deeper layers.[37] Storms produce many different colors, from pale to dark gray, dark blues that can shift toward nearly black and sometimes are tinted with yellows, greens, or reds in severe storms. They can also be illuminated by the setting sun like in Figure 13.144, where the falling rain is not gray, but orange, creating a full range of various colors. During severe storms, the light is drastically reduced and shadows completely disappear, leaving only blurry remnants in corners and edges. The saturation can be reduced, colors lose their intensity and everything is tinted grayish and bluish. However, in some cases, the air can also glow yellowish (even in some places into greenish), which gives the atmosphere a rather surreal appearance. When the rain is so heavy that there is a severe downpour, the visibility is obviously dramatically reduced (Figure 13.145). The colors are muted and their freshness is taken out.

## Overcast weather (Figures 13.146 and 13.147)

Overcast weather is insofar interesting as it is just so plain and boring. The sky is covered in a monochrome and even in a blanket of drab monotony. The layer of clouds does not even have to show clear borders of clouds, but just be one undefined layer of stratus clouds. The colors can range from an overall whitish sky, to gray, dark gray, and blue to dark blue, depending on the thickness of the layer (or further layers above). The colors on overcast days are less bright of course and the saturation seems to be reduced due to everything just looking more grayish. The shadows, as can be seen in Figure 13.146, of one of the palace buildings in Bangkok are blurred out and lit up, distinguishing themselves not significantly

---

[37] Vincent J. Schaefer, *John A. Day: A Field Guide to the Atmosphere*, Houghton Mifflin Company, Boston, MA, 1981, p. 194.

**Figure 13.146**

Royal palace, Bangkok, Thailand.

**Figure 13.147**

Sheffield, United Kingdom.

from the other lit areas. The more the light gets scattered because of the thick layer of clouds, the less the difference between light and shadow is. When the sky is heavily overcast and the sun cannot be seen at all during the whole day, it is difficult to distinguish between morning, noon, and afternoon. Figure 13.147 has no real definition in the sky. It can be rather difficult in an overcast sky to judge distances as everything is just the same gray. The upper half of the image just looks completely flat without any perspective. A blue sky is also monochrome, but it has depth and suggests

space, whereas the overcast sky presses down and lowers the perception of an open space.

# Time of the day

There are obvious differences between the various times of the day in terms of color and light, but the question is what contributes to their appearance. There is not just the color scheme but also the light intensity, the difference between lightness and darkness, and the way the shadows fall. There are so many different possibilities and interpretations that this short article can only spur the interest of further exploration!

## Early morning, just before sunrise, also referred to as twilight (Figures 13.148 and 13.149)

The sun has not fully risen yet, so there is no direct light source in Figure 13.148, which shows the desert outside of Abu Dhabi. The sky itself with its Airlight is lighting up the sand dunes with a diffused and very soft light. There are no strong shadows but very blurred and vague ones that are giving a hint of definition of form but not more. The landscape looks rather flat. The light is more bluish and reflects the color of the sky, often with a pinkish or purple tint. The further the sun climbs toward the horizon, the sky itself is slowly being lit red/yellow/white in the east where the sun is just about to rise and dark blue in the west, where the sunlight does not reach the atmosphere of the earth yet. There is low contrast due to the lack of a direct light source. Very early mornings have a soft and mysterious appearance.

This is the time of the day of the arrival of the *Belt of Venus*, which is an atmospheric occurrence that shows itself either before sunrise or after sunset as a pinkish belt just above the horizon where the sun is coming up or just went down. The atmosphere reflects red light of the rising/setting sun and starts to glow.[38] In Figure 13.149, a house in the Himalayas in Nepal, the sun is just about to come up from behind the mountains, so it has already risen above the horizon. Its rays are clearly visible in the sky and illuminate the atmosphere. The scattered light is lighting up the roof and wall of the house just so slightly. The shadows on the wall underneath the overlapping roof are dark and washed out as they only appear in those areas that are difficult for the scattered light to reach. Compared with the hazy morning in the desert (Figure 13.148) where there are obviously also no shadows, the color of the light is different. It is less blue and purple and one can see that there is more particles in the air. A layer of moisture and dust seems to cover the dunes.

[38] John Naylor, *Out of the Blue: A 24-Hour Skywatcher's Guide*, Cambridge University Press, Cambridge, 2002, p. 72.

The light situation in the morning before sunrise is the same as the twilight after sunset; however, there is the tendency for more moisture in the morning and dust in the air toward the evenings.

## Morning, after sunrise (Figure 13.150)

The sun appears slowly from behind the horizon and its rays create very long shadows that are the blurrier the further they are away from its source. The colors are clearly tinted yellow or orange (or sometimes red), as we can see in Figure 13.150, the morning light in Angkor Wat. Compared with the situation before sunrise, the shadows now appear rather dark due to the stronger contrast between light and shadow. They grow shorter and sharper the higher the sun rises. The color of the morning sky therefore can range from a pale gray, to pinkish, through pale yellow all the way to orange and sometimes even reddish. However, the morning sun tends to be less red than at sunset due to more particles having been transported into the air during the day, whereas the air is cleaner and crisper in the morning.

## Noon (Figure 13.151 through 13.154)

The sun stands at its highest and creates very sharp, dark, and short shadows with the strongest contrast during a clear and cloudless day (less scattering of the sunlight around noon due to the shorter distance the light has travelled through the atmosphere). The light is now at its whitest with the full range of the spectrum visible and with its highest brightness. The colors

are at their most saturated during noon on a sunny bright day and the shadows are dark and slightly desaturated; however, some colors are more saturated in the shadows.

The difference between the shadows in Figures 13.151 and 13.152 are rather dramatic. In Figure 13.151, the stone walls of the houses are nearly in full shadow due to the sun being in its zenith, whereas in Figure 13.152 the walls are in full sunlight. A small difference in the angle of the sunlight hitting the wall can make all the difference. However, the few clouds in Figure 13.152 can reduce the sunlight's intensity now and then.

Figure 13.153 shows a couple of houses in a ravine in the Atlas Mountains in Morocco during noon on a cloudless day. The ensemble of houses is located in the mountain's shadow, no direct sunlight falls into the ravine, all is lit up by Airlight. Therefore, no clear shadows happen but just blurry regions that are darker toward corners and where obstructed. There is little contrast between the colors of the wall's shadow or light, for instance.

There is also the possibility for a transparent cover of clouds or a layer of mist that just disperses the light a little, lighting up the shadows and blurring them ever so slightly. In Figure 13.154, the sky is slightly overcast, scattering the sunlight and thus lighting up the shadows under the tree. One can see that because of the layer of clouds the shadow is also blurry at its outline. If the layer of clouds is thicker then no shadows appear and the light is seemingly evenly distributed (Figure 13.156).

**Figure 13.148**

Desert outside Dubai, United Arab Emirates.

**Figure 13.149**

Himalayas, Nepal.

**Figure 13.150**

Ankor Wat, Cambodia.

**Figure 13.151**

Mustang, Nepal.

**Figure 13.152**

Mustang, Nepal.

**Figure 13.153**

Atlas mountains, Marocco.

**Figure 13.154**

Phanom Rung, Thailand.

## Afternoon/late afternoon (Figures 13.155 through 13.157)

The sun starts to lose its intensity, the shadows grow in length again, like seen in the desert in Morocco in Figure 13.155, where the shadows are very long and stretched approaching late afternoon. The colors shift slowly toward yellow and orange. The contrast is reducing and in the late afternoon the sky starts to turn slowly darker in the east. The shadows themselves seem to lighten up again, because the contrast between light and dark reduces. Figure 13.157 shows a couple of pillars in the Luxor temple and the lower parts are already rather dark in their shadows, whereas the top of the shadows are lighter. The underside of the horizontal blocks is much darker, due to the dispersed light not being able to easily reach these areas. What is beautiful is how the orange light bounces off the pillar and tints the underside of this horizontal block.

A very cloudy afternoon, like seen at the famous Scottish bridge over the Firth of Forth (Figure 13.156), has no shadows because the light is so dispersed by the thick layer of clouds that its rays are coming from every direction. The cloudy layer takes away the sun's direction completely and shadows disappear, leaving a slight darkened blurry shape but no defined shadow. The colors are always grayish and less intense.

## Sunset (Figures 13.158 through 13.162)

The sun is slowly disappearing behind the horizon and now its light is colored yellow and orange in a clear atmosphere and golden red in a denser atmosphere, containing particles of some sort. Sunsets as mentioned earlier tend to be deeper in red than sunrises. The shadows are either cold with a dark blue tint or a bit warmer depending on the coloration of the light. The range of colors is very broad and examples can be seen in the five images, ranging from a slightly cold bluish yellow in the desert of Abu Dhabi with a subtle purple mist (Figure 13.158), to a rich purple and pink in the Khao Sok national park in Thailand (Figure 13.159), or even a deep orange–pink with an immense halo around the sun in Sheffield, UK (Figure 13.161), a bluish purple with a tint of orange at a beach in Malaysia (Figure 13.160) to a deep and heavy red in Egypt on the Nile (Figure 13.162). However, the sun is already gone in the last image, which makes this a nautical or astronomical twilight, explained in the section "Twilight"! In the pictures, we see how the color spectrum of the sunlight is also tinting the clouds heavily. The sun, because of its very low position, will at some point illuminate the cloud's base, seen in the deep red clouds above the Nile, which in turn then is reflected in the river. But not only the clouds are shifting in color, the Airlight itself is colored slightly orange or red.

A sunset can also have various colors where sun and surrounding are not the same. In Figure 13.160, the setting sun is deep red and has a gradient toward its base due to the atmosphere, whereas the surrounding is purplish blue toward the horizon. The layer of moisture is so dense, that the sun can be looked at and clearly shows its body without an aura around it.

This time of the day is also called the "golden hour." Filmmaker Terrence Malick shot much of his masterful feature film *Days of Heaven* (1978) during the golden hour, which gives the images a magical touch with soft and pleasant light with no strong shadows.

**Figure 13.155**

Desert in Morocco.

**Figure 13.156**

Forth Bridge, Scotland, United Kingdom.

**Figure 13.157**

Karnak Temple, Egypt.

**Figure 13.158**

Desert near Abu Dhabi.

## Twilight (Figures 13.163 through 13.168)

Twilight happens after sunset, but also before sunrise. There is no difference between the two other than the morning sky being fresher and less filled with particles; therefore, the colors tend to be less intense. After the sun has set below the horizon, its rays cannot directly touch the surface anymore. Nevertheless, its rays still light up the atmosphere and Airlight is therefore the only light source. This is when twilight happens. The sun lights up the atmosphere (see Figure 13.163), which in turn reflects the light into the shadowy side of the Earth. The small light blue area between light and shadow is the area of twilight. As twilight is scattered light without direction, the shadows are diffused and the color shifts from pinkish and purple blue to dark blue. This time of the day is called the Blue Hour and despite no visible light source, there is still plenty of light to illuminate the air in a magical and quiet glow.

Twilight itself is divided into three types:

• **Civil twilight, blue, or magic hour:** when the sun has already set and the sky is illuminated by Airlight. This happens when the sun is 6° below the horizon. Civil twilight is the brightest of the three types.

• **Nautical twilight:** ends at 12° below the horizon. During this time, the stars can be seen with the naked eye, but there is less light than during civil twilight.
• **Astronomical twilight:** the sun's center is between 12° and 18° below the horizon. This is the time when the night sky is not black yet but still has a faint glow.

The length of twilight does vary depending on the position of the observer on Earth. At the Equator, the twilight is shorter than on higher latitudes north or south. There is an area in the inner circles of the polar region where there is twilight all day for a couple of days a year, as the sun is below the horizon continuously, thus the only light is reflective light. This only happens north or south of the polar circle. There are some natural occurrences that also contribute to twilight's intensity, which are volcanic eruptions and, as has been experienced on the 18th and 19th of May in 1910 when the Earth travelled through the tail of Halley's Comet.

Figure 13.164 shows a palace in Potsdam, Germany, in a blue light which does make it look magical and slightly surreal. There are no shadows and the light has already significantly darkened. Figure 13.165, a wall structure in Luxor, has a very

**Figure 13.159**

Khao Sok, Thailand.

**Figure 13.160**

Pankor Laut, Malaysia.

clear sky and there is a hint of purple in the right side of the sky. This is the layer of mist or haze illuminated. The red wall clearly has a purple tint. Figure 13.166 shows a hotel in the desert between Dubai and Abu Dhabi and the twilight here renders all the walls the same. There is just a general very subtle blur from light to slightly darker to be seen

within some of the walls, but most of the structure is rather monochrome, making it fairly difficult to distinguish one from the other, flattening the architecture. The twilight in Hong Kong Kowloon (Figure 13.167) on the other hand has a nearly turquoise tint to it. There is obviously a wide range of colors possible!

**Figure 13.161**

Sheffield, United Kingdom.

**Figure 13.162**

River Nile, Egypt.

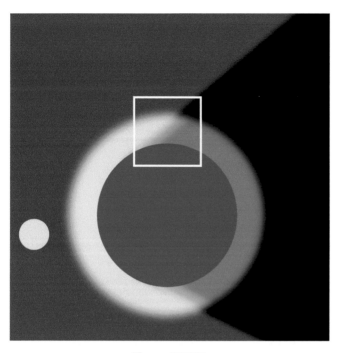

**Figure 13.163**

**Figure 13.164**

Potsdam, Germany.

**Figure 13.165**

Luxor, Egypt.

**Figure 13.166**

Desert outside of Dubai, United Arab Emirates.

**Figure 13.167**

Hong Kong.

**Figure 13.168**

John Singer Sargent: *Carnation, Lily, Lily, Rose* (1885–86).

One of the most stunning paintings of a scene in twilight is John Singer Sargent's *Carnation, Lily, Lily, Rose* from 1885 (Figure 13.168), where we see two girls lighting Chinese lanterns during the Blue Hour, standing in a meadow surrounded by carnations, lilies and roses. The subtle colors of the twilight are superb and we don't have to see the actual sky to feel the tint of blue, purple and rose in the glowing atmosphere. It gives the scene a magical shine, a surreal escapist touch. Sargent painted outside, *En plein air* in the impressionist fashion in the garden where he had arranged the scene with artificial and potted flowers, even after the summer was over and the flowers had already wilted. In order to get the right color that he was seeking he could only paint for about 25 minutes each day, which dramatically lengthened the time for the completion of the painting. The subtleties in the colors are astounding and one can only imagine how difficult it was to get the precision into the color to express this perfect twilight mood. The lighting situation is not only the twilight, but also the relationship between the bluish, purple light and the collaborating light of the lit Chinese lanterns and how the light of both bounces off of all the different surfaces. Sargent so delicately shows the light reflecting off the flora, the lanterns shimmering onto the girls' dresses in this magical scene in which one can literally see the

reflected sky in the blades of grass, in the roses and their leafs and even the sky's reflection in the girl's hair. The air itself seems enriched with light. This delicious yet very short-lived light situation is beautifully complimented by the snapshot-like composition that yet balanced has enough tension to feel organic. This is a true masterpiece that presents itself with ease and yet is an incredibly difficult task as letters from Sargent to his friends stated.[39] For instance, in a letter to his sister Emily he wrote:

> I am still here and likely to be for some time, for I launched into my garden picture and have two good little models and a garden that answers the purpose although there are hardly any flowers and I have to scour the cottage gardens and transplant and make shift. The Millets are most kind and hospitable and although I stop at the Inn, I practically live there. It is in their garden that I work. The two little girls are the children of a painter friend. Fearful difficult subject. Impossible brilliant colours of flowers and lamps and brightest green lawn background. Paints are not bright enough & then the effect only lasts ten minutes.[40]

---

[39] Richard Ormond, *Elaine Kilmurray: John Singer Sargent, Figures and Landscapes, 1883–1899*, Yale University Press, London, 2010.
[40] Sargent to his sister Emily, undated, headed "Broadway/ Worcestershire/Tuesday," private collection. Facsimile of letter ill. Charteris 1927, pp. 76–77.

## Night (Figures 13.169 through 13.171)

During the day, the sky is blue because of the atmosphere being illuminated. We literally see the air being lit up. Toward the night, when the sunlight subsides, this Airlight is slowly disappearing and what was bright and deep blue before is now completely transparent and invisible and allows a peek into the universe. Quite surreal actually! But the night is not completely devoid of light, quite the contrary, as there is the obvious Moonlight but also Skyglow and Airglow.

Moonlight is just sunlight that is reflected from the surface of the Moon, so the color is actually the same white light as during the day. Only because its intensity is much lower (less than one-tenth of 1% of the sun's illumination), it feels like moonlight is more silvery, which is caused by the Purkinje effect: the darker it is, the less the human eye is able to see colors. The very low luminosity of Moon causes the eye to see the night in the bluish range. A photograph with a very long exposure time of a full moon night shows nearly the same image compared to a regular photo being shot during the day. It is the intensity of the light that is

less, not the color. A full moon, when its entire visible surface faces Earth, reflects more of the sun's light and therefore creates visible shadows, which are obviously very dark; however, it can also be lit up again through dispersed light rays. A winter night with snow would have lighter shadows than the same landscape without snow. The painting *In the Wild North* (1891) of a bright night by Russian landscape painter Ivan Shishkin (1832–1898) is a very romantic, yet utterly convincing interpretation of bright Moonlight (Figure 13.169). The shadows are very bright and lit up because of the reflective qualities of snow. But the shadows have a gradient which is darker right underneath the tree and gets lighter the further away it travels from the tree's trunk. Obviously less light is able to penetrate the area underneath its low hanging branches.

At night there are two different light sources that affect the color of the sky and its shadows: the mentioned moonlight (and small amount of starlight) and light pollution from artificial illumination in the vicinity of cities. Light pollution, specifically Skyglow in cities (also Urban glow), consists of light caused by sources from human settlements: streetlamps, buildings, construction sites, advertising, lit major outdoor events, etc. Their emitted light reflects in particles in the air and illuminates them very much the same as Airlight during the day. Light pollution makes it impossible to see star light in major cities. The illuminated layer between the viewer and stars is too dominant in its own glow to allow the star's light to penetrate. In metropolitan areas, this night light often has a yellowish tint; however, it depends on the light used. Cities use either yellow sodium-vapor lamps or blue-green mercury lamps; therefore, it depends on their overall mix of which color will be dominant. Figure 13.170, a long-time exposure and thus a slight exaggeration of the actual situation, shows the harbor in Hamburg after midnight. The sky is illuminated, giving its foggy air an orange glow. In Figure 13.171, the harbor in Shanghai, one can see a faint glow over the city. The more moisture is in the air (or smog), the stronger the Skyglow is.

Clouds also dramatically increase Skyglow, as the light emitted from the city underneath lights up the base of the clouds, bouncing back into the area between city and cloud cover. The city is then hidden under a layer of clouds that is slightly orange or blue-green in its base. Snow also increases Skyglow as the reflective quality of snow is very high in its intensity. In urban areas, an overcast sky will cause the landscape underneath to be much darker than with a clear sky as the incoming light from Moon and stars is blocked or significantly reduced. Starlight is yet another light during the night, though very weak, which is caused by light waves that are either coming from stars or are redirected waves from other planets or even matter in space. Those light waves cause Airglow or Nightglow, which makes the atmosphere light up ever so slightly during the night. Because of Airglow, the night sky is never completely black.

**Figure 13.169**

Ivan Shishkin: *In the Wild North* (1891).

**Figure 13.170**

Hamburg, Germany.

**Figure 13.171**

Shanghai, China.

## Moon-phases (Figure 13.172)

How much of the sun's light is reflected by the Moon is always the same; what is not the same, however, is the position of the Moon in relation to the Earth. From which position on Earth's surface the Moon is being seen affects the type of Moon we observe and thus the amount of light being reflected. Position 1 in Figure 13.172 looks at the Moon from behind; the sunlight illuminates the Moon from the front, but the viewer looking at the Moon observes a New Moon. A viewer in position 2 would see the Moon's surface being fully lit; therefore, it appears as a full Moon. The intensity change of the Moon's light during the month affects the brightness immediately on Earth at night. The lesser the moon, the smaller the amount of light is reflected onto Earth and obviously the darker the night is. It is important to know from which position the sun is illuminating the moon in relation to the viewer's position on Earth. Understanding this will enable

one to place the Sun and the Moon into any constellation and imagine the appropriate lighting situation.

## Sun and Earth's tilt

The Earth travels on an elliptical path around the Sun; however, the Sun is not in the ellipse's center but closer to one end. In addition, the Earth itself is tilted 23.5° while travelling around the Sun. Both, the tilt and the elliptical path cause the four seasons on the southern and northern hemisphere, and also cause the position of the Sun in the sky being different from season to season. Examples A, B, and C in Figure 13.173 not only show how the Earth is tilted on its elliptical path but also show how this affects the exposure of its southern and northern surface to the Sun's rays during summer or winter. Figure 13.173a shows how Earth maintains its tilt during its path around the Sun, which, if one sees the Sun from the Earth's surface, changes the height of the Sun during the year on the horizon.

Example (b) explains the two different hemispheres on Earth and their exposure to sunlight in December and June. In December, the tilt causes less sunlight to reach the northern hemisphere, whereas the southern hemisphere is more exposed. In June, it is vice versa. Illustration (c) shows the position of the sun seen from the northern and southern hemisphere in June and December. Because the Sun has a different position (from Earth's perspective), due to the tilt of the Earth, it appears in the northern hemisphere in summer high in the sky and in winter it appears low in the sky; in the southern hemisphere, it is again the opposite.

## Underwater light
## (Figures 13.174 through 13.176)

The opposite happens with colors under water once sunlight penetrates the water's surface compared to what happens when light enters the Earth's atmosphere: the white light

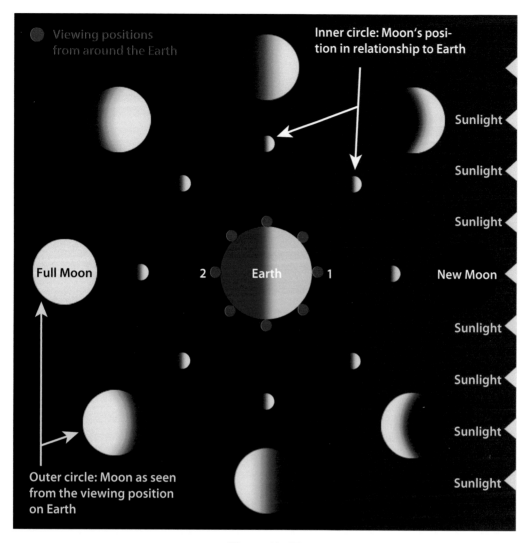

**Figure 13.172**

hits the surface of the water and after a couple of meters already the red light disappears depending on the clarity and of course the color of the water itself.[41] The higher density and different molecular structure of water filters light's rays contrary to air, which is why red gets filtered out first and blue is the last one to remain as shown in Figure 13.174. Even very clear water still has much less visible depth than air does; however, tropical water with no floating particles can be incredibly transparent for many meters, but by no means as clear as air obviously. The last remaining color under water is blue, which is still visible from 35 to 60 m depth. However, the deeper ranges of 60 m are very rare and only happen in exceptionally clear waters. Much less can be seen in coastal areas as the tides often stir up particles, which reduces the

ability of light penetrating. Vertical visibility (how far one can see looking up and down), which changes with depth, is obviously very different from horizontal visibility (how far one can see straight ahead), which has no change of light intensity. The eye therefore can see further horizontally than vertically in water.

For understanding the interaction between water and light, the term "refraction" should be mentioned. Light changes direction or "refracts" when travelling from one medium with a certain density into another medium with a different density, for example, from air to water. In the case of an observer looking directly at a fish below the surface of a pond, the fish appears to be at a more distant location than reality due to the fact that the light being reflected off of the fish is refracted at the boundary surfaces of air and water; or wearing swimming goggles under water also changes sizes and positions of objects, but there are now multiple refractions involved. Refraction changes our visual perception.

41 Steven Davis, *Color Perception: Philosophical, Psychological, Artistic, and Computational Perspectives*, Oxford University Press, New York, 2000, p. 132.

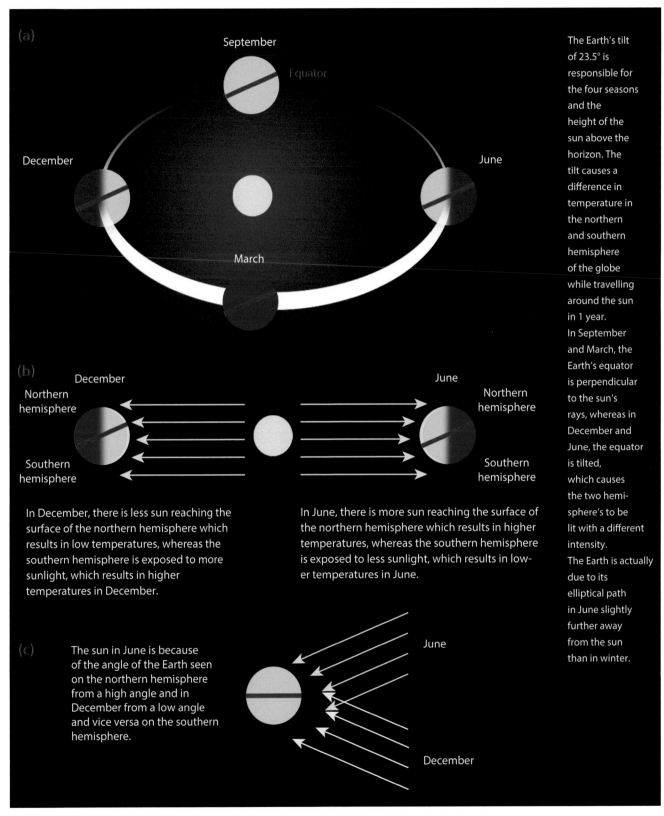

(a)

September

Equator

December

June

March

(b)

December

Northern hemisphere

Southern hemisphere

June

Northern hemisphere

Southern hemisphere

In December, there is less sun reaching the surface of the northern hemisphere which results in low temperatures, whereas the southern hemisphere is exposed to more sunlight, which results in higher temperatures in December.

In June, there is more sun reaching the surface of the northern hemisphere which results in higher temperatures, whereas the southern hemisphere is exposed to less sunlight, which results in lower temperatures in June.

(c)

The sun in June is because of the angle of the Earth seen on the northern hemisphere from a high angle and in December from a low angle and vice versa on the southern hemisphere.

June

December

The Earth's tilt of 23.5° is responsible for the four seasons and the height of the sun above the horizon. The tilt causes a difference in temperature in the northern and southern hemisphere of the globe while travelling around the sun in 1 year. In September and March, the Earth's equator is perpendicular to the sun's rays, whereas in December and June, the equator is tilted, which causes the two hemisphere's to be lit with a different intensity. The Earth is actually due to its elliptical path in June slightly further away from the sun than in winter.

**Figure 13.173**

Underwater light

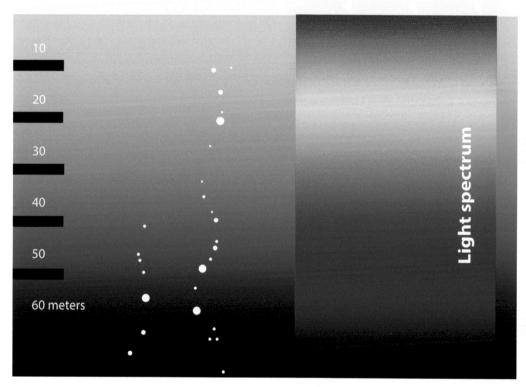

**Figure 13.174**

The light and with it the shadows under water depend on three different aspects:

1. **Incoming light:** the incoming light's intensity and angle are first of all crucial as a low angle allows less light to penetrate the water's surface compared to a high angle. When the light hits the water surface perpendicularly, it allows most of the sunlight to enter the water, whereas a low angle of the light at sunset, for instance, allows the least light to enter. If the incoming light is already highly dispersed (like on a cloudy day), the shadows under water obviously are even more blurred and cannot possibly be precise in their outline. Only a very clear sky with very clear water and a calm surface can produce precise shadows. When we stand at the beach and look at the ocean, what we see is the reflected light from the water's surface. When looking closely towards the water near us, we can observe water in its full depth, and depending on the clarity of the

water, we can even look at the ocean floor. This is due to the refractive properties of water that allow the sun rays to penetrate through and reflect off of the different levels of its collective depth.

2. **Clarity and color of the water:** the less clear the water is, the less precise the shadows are. Visibility in water depends on particles, salinity, and temperature (salinity and temperature are only then important when two layers of different salinity and temperature meet). In very murky waters, shadows are barely visible, which is very similar to the difference between shadows under a clear sky during the day and shadows during a day with heavy fog. What really changes the visibility in water are floating particles, either organic or inorganic materials. Organic materials are, for instance, bacteria and algae that mainly grow in water with less movement during warmer seasons. This can be a natural occurrence or a sign of pollution. Inorganic materials

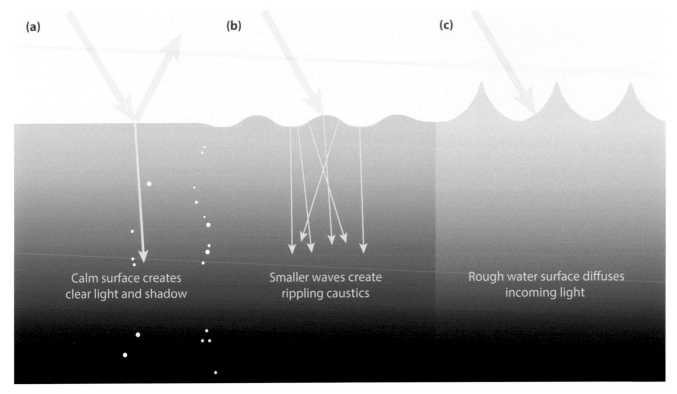

(a)  (b)  (c)

Calm surface creates
clear light and shadow

Smaller waves create
rippling caustics

Rough water surface diffuses
incoming light

**Figure 13.175**

happen, for instance, in coastal areas due to heavy water movement when the tides stir up the ground. The color of lakes or rivers can vary drastically and there are many locations in nature that range from red (Laguna Colorada in Bolivia), brown to yellow (the obvious Yellow River in China), emerald blue (Blue Lagoon in Iceland), turquoise

**Figure 13.176**

Giorgos "The Tiger" Marinou: *Ocean Floor at Konnos bay, Protaras, Cyprus* (2017).

and green (Laguna Verde in Bolivia), acid green (Devil's Bath in Waiotapu, New Zealand), bright pink (Lake Hillier in Australia or Lake Retba in Senegal), or purple (North arm of the Great Salt Lake in Utah), depending on the color of the algae and bacteria, salt content, or the color of the particles or chemicals dissolved. Usually the inorganic particles are solvents from the soil runoff that is washed into the rivers or lakes, but there are also lakes that have high levels of minerals and chemicals (natural or pollutants) that cause a specific unusual color.

3. **Surface movement:** Aside from the movement of the whole body of water stirring up the sediments and causing the water to be murky, Figure 13.175 shows how different surface movements also affect the refraction of the light's rays: a calm surface (a) will allow the light to penetrate very evenly and the scattering is limited, causing defined light and shadow. A slightly wavy surface (b) will create rippling caustics on surfaces under water, the dancing light reflections like that shown in Figure 13.176. A rough sea (c) will disperse the light rays and blurry light and shadow patches are being seen. The clarity of the caustics is absent.

Water can also have a glow very similar to Airlight, which can be seen in the famous *Blue Grotto* on Capri in southern Italy. The grotto has two entrances: a small one above the water's surface and a very big one underneath the surface, which is the main opening for the incoming light. Because of the depth of the second opening, only blue light is penetrating the grotto, illuminating it with an eerie glow. The water seems to be phosphorescent because the space above the water is darker than the water itself. The Blue Grotto was already famous in ancient times and Emperor Tiberius, who had built his luxurious Villa Jovis on Capri, used it already as his private swimming pool.

For an explanation of how water reflections are caused and how light interacts with waves, see Chapter 3, "Water and Light," of Lynch and Livingston's *Color and Light in Nature*.

## Reflected light

For an excellent study of light and shadow and rendering, see Scott Robertson's *How to Render: The Fundamentals of Light, Shadow and Reflectivity*, Design Studio Press, Los Angeles, CA, 2014.

More about weather and colors in the outdoors:

David K. Lynch and William Livingston, *Color and Light in Nature*, Cambridge University Press, Cambridge, 2001.
Marcel J. Minnaert, *Light and Color in the Outdoors*, Springer, Berlin, 2008.

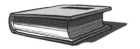

# Clouds and light

We see nothing truly till we understand it.[42]

**John Constable**

The following observation of clouds is to show the variety of shapes, colors, and moods. The point is not to produce a competent meteorological explanation or scientific explanation of clouds, but only to show through one topic the variety of nature's possibilities. It is not an encouragement to replicate nature, but must be seen as a stepping stone for a general understanding that leads to a creative dealing and interpretation with the subject matter.

The variety of clouds in the sky seems vast and endless and they change every moment, giving the sky a different look at all times. Clouds contribute to the mood of a landscape dramatically and also control often our own emotional state. There are sometimes low hanging layers of boring gray soup without any definition, making the landscape look sad and depressing, but then there are also clouds much bigger than skyscrapers, 12 km in height with bright white forms that seemingly reach to the highest regions in the sky; then there are wisps of white clouds, streaks and threads of clouds, hanging cotton-balls and icy clouds in thin layers high up in the atmosphere; the colors are as plentiful as the shapes of clouds and range from the obvious white and gray to purple, blue, and pink to yellow, orange, and red. Clouds can just sit in the sky looking bored or zip across it in a seemingly dangerous speed, boasting with energy. But they also, with their apparent weightlessness, inspire dreams and spur the imagination, yet also help to refer to a state where too much fantasy leads to an unrealistic state of perfection, like being in a *Cloud Cuckoo Land*. The sky is a cacophony of action and breathtaking beauty. Clouds appear in such a vast variety of forms and colors that it is a rather complex subject and in the following I want to simplify the topic slightly as it is helpful to know the basics of how clouds appear in the sky and what the main differences are for our purposes in image making.

Clouds consist of tiny droplets of water vapor or ice crystals floating in the atmosphere and form in up to 12,000 m in height. Various heights can create different types of cloud shapes, which are plentiful but not in their entirety part of this examination of how light affects clouds. For further information on clouds, see the book list at the end of this chapter.

The cloud classification system was introduced by Luke Howard (1772–1864), a British amateur meteorologist, in 1802/1803 and has not much changed since then. We still use the same Latin names for the various types of clouds. One artist who needs to be mentioned when clouds are discussed is the British painter

**Figure 13.177**

John Constable: *Rainstorm over the sea* (1824).

John Constable (1776–1837). A landscape painter, Constable studied meteorology and followed Howard's discoveries and cloud classification, studying the different weather situations in quick oil sketches, which were very unusual at the time when art was produced inside the artist's studio, not in the open field. His painting *Rainstorm over the Sea* (Figure 13.177) shows in very powerful and quick brush strokes a Cumulonimbus cloud with the rain pouring down underneath. Constable was the first artist to study the sky rigorously and painted "skyscapes" just for the sake of studying them. Not many artists have devoted so much energy to the depiction and understanding of the sky and clouds and their interaction with light.

Clouds have two primary groups which are *Heap* and *Layer clouds*.

## Heap clouds (Figure 13.178 left)

Heap clouds or the cumulus clouds (Latin *cumulus* = heap) have three categories, which are all flattish based and have the typical bubbles on its surface, the convection cells, caused by a difference in density within the cloud:

- Cumulus (Figure 13.179): a white, rather small cloud which appears during fair weather, mainly in summer. This cloud does not produce rainfall. Because of the rather calm atmosphere, the cumulus does not reach height levels above 1 km.
- Swelling-cumulus: the cloud grows in width, height, and energy due to a more unstable atmosphere. These types of clouds only produce light rain and might develop into the next stage.
- Cumulonimbus (Figures 13.180 and 13.181): this cloud is very large and reaches into the high levels of up to 9 km, and in some cases even up to 20 km. The top is often shaped like a mushroom or cauliflower and they produce heavy rains, storms, and lightning (Latin *cumulus/nimbus* = heap/rain).

---

[42] John Constable, *The History of Landscape Painting*, third lecture, Royal Institution (9 June 1836).

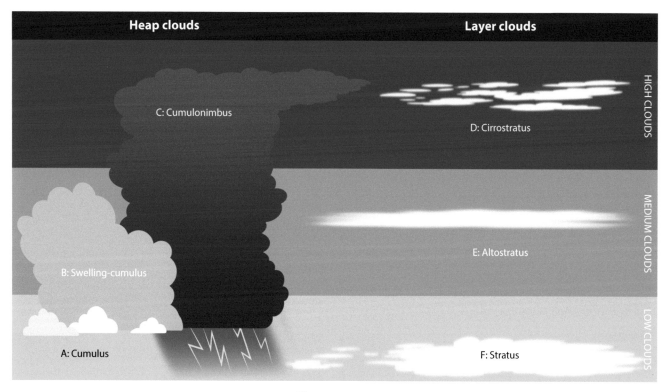

**Figure 13.178**

## Layer clouds (Figure 13.178 right)

Layer clouds or the stratus family (Latin *stratus* = layer) are very flat horizontally and can reach over 1000 km in width, yet rather short in height (0.5–1 km). Stratus clouds do not have the convection cells that give a cloud the cliché shape with the bubbles. They also have three categories: Stratus, Altostratus, and Cirrostratus. All three types, respectively, appear in three different heights in the atmosphere:

- Stratus is actually just what we call fog and spreads on or above the ground in the lower atmosphere. It is white to gray in color and produces light drizzle or rain.
- Altostratus: (Latin *alto* = high) it appears in the middle layer of the atmosphere (~3–6 km). It is gray to darkish-gray in color and carries either water droplets or ice. It can produce a light rain, and also develop into a nimbostratus (from Latin *nimbus* = rain).
- Cirrostratus: it is a stratus cloud that is about 6–13 km in height and has either a congruent body or is fibrous (Figure 13.184).
- A third group of clouds are called *Heap and Layer clouds*, which appear in three different layers of the atmosphere and all three show convection cells: Stratocumulus, Altocumulus, and Cirrocumulus, which are combinations of the earlier mentioned two groups.

There are plenty of more forms and sizes; however, for the purposes of this chapter, this will be enough (for more details on clouds, see Schaefer and Day's *A Field Guide to the Atmosphere*).

The most important aspect of clouds is to see them as three-dimensional forms, but not as 2D shapes. It is our viewpoint that makes us see clouds mostly from underneath or from the side, which causes those huge structures to appear often flat. Once we are in an airplane flying through the clouds, we can observe how they reveal their complex dimensionality and intricate architecture (Figure 13.182). What I want to focus on in the following is how light interacts with clouds and creates a subtle play with light and shadow in the sky and on the surface.

Clouds can be slightly transparent or not at all depending on their density, their water-containing capacity, and their age. It also depends on from which angle the light is illuminating the cloud and how bright it appears. All this determines its color, the light and shadow interaction between the clouds and where the shadow of the cloud itself is seen on the landscape underneath. In Figure 13.183, we can see how the rays of the sun hit the layer of the clouds and either penetrate the cloud and thus get dispersed and reduced in intensity or go through the spaces between the clouds and reach the ground unaltered. In the landscape photograph of the region of Mustang in Nepal (Figure 13.179), the shadows on the ground are rather blurry and not at all clean-cut. The distance between cloud and ground is great enough to cause further scattering of the rays. Figure 13.187 shows how the sun lights up the top of the clouds, but the bottom is in shadow and thus also the entire landscape underneath. The thinner the cloud is the more sunlight penetrates it, which causes the bright patches of light in the sky among the layer of darker cloud base.

**Figure 13.179**

Lo Manthang, Mustang, Nepal.

As clouds during the day are only lit by the sun, the illumination only happens from the top. If the sun is just about to set and is so low that its rays are already underneath the cloud layer, the light situation changes and only the base of the cloud is lit up, not its top part as being shown in Figure 13.201 just after sunset in Singapore (also shown in Figure 13.170). Also a cloud at night can be illuminated either by the moon from above or by city lights from underneath, or of course by both.

## The general color of clouds

The color of a cloud depends on the lighting situation and its age: water droplets in a young cloud are very small in size. There is a huge amount of tiny droplets which cause the sunlight to be reflected back from the cloud's surface, causing the cloud to appear white. Much of the light that hits the cloud is reflected and the whole light spectrum is scattered more or less equally. An aged cloud's water droplets are bigger in size and less in amount (the water droplets have fused), increasing the space

**Figure 13.180**

Phnom Penh, Cambodia.

**Figure 13.181**

Hong Kong.

**Figure 13.182**

Sammy Wolf: *Clouds* (2017).

**Figure 13.184**

Angkor Wat, Cambodia.

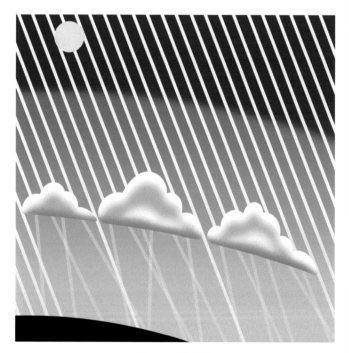

**Figure 13.183**

**Figure 13.185**

Sheffield, United Kingdom.

between the droplets; as a result, more light penetrates the cloud and less is reflected, which makes it look darker. The larger the droplets get, the more likely they are to fall down as rain. Bigger droplets make the cloud even darker. Clouds generally range in color from pure white to gray and dark blue. Supplementary colors occur during sunset and sunrise. Then additionally purple, rose color, and violet to blue, from yellow and orange to red, with all possible combinations can be seen (in some parts of the world, heavy rain clouds turn not only dark blue but also greenish/yellowish just before a very heavy storm, but the reasons are not yet fully understood). The variety of colors can become clear by just comparing all the pictures in this chapter! The color of clouds not only changes due to their age and density, but also due to the distance from the viewer. Airlight causes clouds to have less contrast and more brightness the further they are from the viewer (Figure 13.186). Figure 13.185 shows how the clouds just above the viewer are really dark, but the ones close to the horizon are much less so. During the day cumulus clouds just above the viewer are bright white, but those close to the horizon can be, depending on the level of pollution, from whitish blue to yellowish.

## Clouds and Light

Three factors contribute to the brightness and whiteness of a cloud: density, age, and shadows. A thick cloud will not allow much light to reflect from its body, whereas a thin cloud can even allow the sky behind it to shine through. We can see in Figure 13.181 that one side of the cloud is bright and the other side is darker; obviously the position of the sun modulates the cloud's surface and makes it possible in the first place to actually see its shadows and thus its form. A white cumulus cloud, for instance, that is evenly lit by the sun from right behind the viewer would have no modulation at all and just appear bright white, so shadows are needed to grasp the complexity of the form. However, there are many shadows that describe the various forms and define foreground, middle ground, and background of the cloud. In Figure 13.186, we can see how the base of the clouds is slightly darker than the top, because the bottom is less likely to receive as much light as the top does. The cloud would have to be on top of a reflective surface, like a lake, river, or snow-covered area,

**Figure 13.187**

Ghiza, Egypt.

**Figure 13.188**

to also receive reflected light from underneath. We can also see this happening when we look toward the setting sun in Figure 13.185. The sun illuminates the parts of the cloud that are facing the sun, but the parts that we see are in shadow, like the bottom and the back of the cloud. The same happens in Figure 13.187 on a late afternoon in Giza. The layer of clouds is nearly covering the sky, creating a rather dark gray layer of clouds. But we can see that the upper side of the clouds is brightly lit by the sun, clearly showing the stark contrast between light and shadow.

On a very cloudy day, clouds take away brightness, which makes everything look more gray with less contrast and saturation. The diffusion of light causes the shadows on the ground to be very

**Figure 13.186**

**Figure 13.189**

Alexandria, Egypt.

**Figure 13.191**

clouds in front of the sun. It is again the particles in the air that get illuminated by the rays and lit up, whereas the particles in shadow are less visible (Figure 13.189).

Light and less dense clouds can be so transparent that their shadows show through if the sun is behind them (Figure 13.190). The clouds that are closer to the sun are brighter than the ones that are further away. Additionally, the shadow of the clouds that are layered in front affects the lighting of the cloud on top. Because clouds form in different heights, some clouds on lower levels are covered by shadows from clouds on higher levels.

## Clouds at sunrise or sunset (Figure 13.191 through 13.193)

Theoretically, clouds shift in color the further they are away from the sun at sunset or sunrise. When the sun sets with an orange or red tint, the closer the clouds are to the horizon, the yellower they are; the further away clouds are from the horizon, the redder or darker they are, depending on the color of the sunset.

Figure 13.191 demonstrates in an exaggerated way that the clouds closest to the sun, which is on the right, are obviously the brightest; however, the cloud on the right casts its shadow on the ones behind, darkening them. In Figure 13.192, the sun just sets in front of the viewer and the further the clouds are to the horizon, the brighter and more yellow they are; the closer they are to the viewer, the darker and/or redder they are. Photo 13.193 shows a sunset in Singapore, which slightly shows the clouds closer to the viewer being dark red and purple; the ones further away have an orange- and rose-colored base.

**Figure 13.190**

undefined and blurry and depending on the thickness of the clouds, shadows can disappear altogether.

## The sun behind the clouds (Figures 13.188 through 13.190)

If the sun is illuminating the cloud from behind, then it is the entire rim of the cloud that is brighter and the interior is darker. The brighter the cloud is, the less dense it is, which means that the sun can be seen through a bright cloud, but often not through a dark and dense one (Figure 13.188).

Often what is called "Crepuscular rays" can be seen radiating from the sun and are usually created by light and shadow from

**Figure 13.192**

**Figure 13.194**

**Figure 13.193**

Singapore.

## Illumination and shadow of clouds

Clouds appear on different heights in the sky, from the very low heights of fog up to clouds appearing 12,000 m high. In Figure 13.180, we can see the highly complex structure of a Cumulonimbus cloud that is incredibly voluminous and has occupied immense spaces. The body of those Cumulonimbus clouds is always impressive in scale, and when shun on by the sun, the play of light and shadow is stunning, revealing its massive scope. Additional cumulus clouds on a lower level can be in shadow, whereas the top of the Cumulonimbus is brightly lit by the sun, creating the complex juxtaposition of light and dark. The interplay of which cloud is in shadow and which one in light and which cloud even casts a shadow on other clouds is rather complicated; however, the layering of the different shades of blue, gray, and white makes for very convincing depth and interesting and dramatic visuals. There are all different kinds of options of dark layers being covered by bright layers of clouds or vice versa.

One can be very creative when it comes to clouds as the options are rather extensive as long as it looks convincing it does not necessarily have to be fully scientifically accurate (Figure 13.194). The point is to create convincing and captivating images with a mood.

## The curvature of the earth (Figures 13.195 and 13.196)

Usually the curvature of the earth is not really considered in landscapes, because it is so miniscule that it seems undetectable. Though it is often not considered visually, it should not be forgotten, especially when it comes to clouds. Seeing the clouds being arranged on a curved globe segment helps understand what the viewer is actually seeing from the clouds surrounding them. Clouds are most often just drawn from the side, because it is much easier and looks cartoony, which in animation we often do appreciate. Nevertheless, only a small percentage of clouds show themselves from the side, which are the only ones that are very far away. But all the rest are seen mostly from underneath or something in between side and bottom view. Why is that important? Because it changes the ratio between the bottom of the cloud and its sides: really far away clouds have a thin base line, whereas clouds above the viewer are only base and we can't see any of the cloud's top. Figures 13.195 and 13.196 demonstrate this with the red dot as the position of the viewer. Above the viewer, the base of the clouds is fully exposed, whereas the clouds far away mostly show their sides.

The viewer will see less and less of the open sky the closer the eye gets to the horizon because the clouds that are on the same height cover and overlap each other.

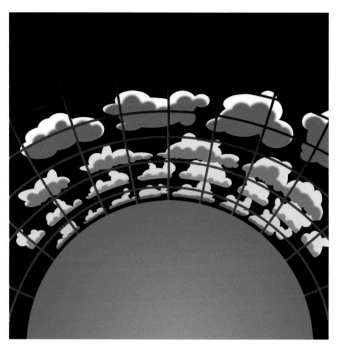

**Figure 13.195**

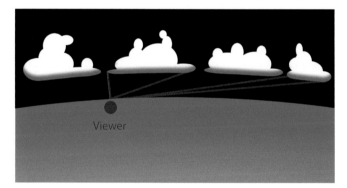

Viewer

**Figure 13.196**

**Much more about clouds and colors in the outdoors:**

Vincent J. Schaefer and John A. Day, *A Field Guide to the Atmosphere*, Houghton Mifflin Company, Boston, MA, 1981.

## Case study: Mountains and streams in *Disney's Bambi* (1942)

*Bambi* is the fifth of Disney's feature films and famous for being the one that elevated character animation to a level of realism. *Bambi* is based on the story of Austrian author Felix Salten who wrote *Bambi, Eine Lebensgeschichte aus dem Walde* in 1923 for an adult audience, published by Ullstein Verlag. In 1928, Simon & Schuster started to sell the translated English version *Bambi, a Life in the Woods*. The book was quite successful in both versions and Salten sold the film rights in 1933 to Sydney Franklin, a director from MGM who wanted to turn the novel into a live-action film. Realizing that life action would not capture the feel of the book, he decided to contact Walt Disney and suggest a collaboration to produce an animated feature film. In 1936, Disney started discussions on the film and the actual production began in 1938.[43] From the beginning there was the clear direction that *Bambi* needed to have a style that represented nature realistically, yet stylized and not fully representational. It was early on understood that in a realistic background of a forest the characters would be very difficult to distinguish from the foliage and myriads of details, so a reduction of visual information in the backgrounds was apparent. Perce Pearce mentioned in a story-meeting at the beginning of the production:

> We should feel the forest rather than see it. I wonder if the way you can best feel nature is just to hint at enough reality and let the rest of it go, leave it to your imagination. In other words keep our general background style simple and not very graphic. We are driving for a certain balance. Nature is very important in this picture dramatically, it's [sic] part of our conflict. Our picture as a whole doesn't just give over to nature but it leaves.[44]

The actual setting of the film was changed from a European forest to one in North America and some of the story elements are also quite different. The original story though provides moments that one remembers from the film, lyrical moments or character situations. However, Salten's original story has more depth to it and lacks the overly cute moments of the film, like the lengthy introduction of Bambi to the animals of the forest. Some characters from the book are gone, like Gobo, the male twin to Faline and other relatives of Bambi. Salten's story beautifully explores the life of a fawn in all its phases and makes the growing up in the forest very believable. Where Disney is cute, the book is realistic to a degree, being based on reality but giving it a human emotional level. The book clearly served as a source of inspiration for the film, yet never meant to be exactly translated into animation.

Finding the actual look of *Bambi* was unsatisfying to a degree as the stylization of the complexity of real forests that were visited and studied by Disney artists in Maine was too busy, too close to reality as it interpreted the forest, but did not eliminate the complexity of the vast amount of details. At the time inbetweener Tyrus Wong decided to submit water color sketches for the film that incorporated everything stylistically and artistically that the crew was looking for. Thomas Codrick saw Wong's work and recognized its potential in his unique approach for the film and suggested it to Walt Disney himself, who decided to put Tyrus Wong (1910–2016) into the position of art director for the background styling (strangely enough Wong is only credited for "backgrounds" in the final film, which he never painted). Tyrus Wong was born in 1910 in Taishan, Guangdong Province, southeast China and left his home with his father at the age of 9 to immigrate into the United States. Wong stated that he was always fond of Song Dynasty landscape paintings, which, being Chinese himself, influenced his personal work. What Tyrus did, which his sketches for *Bambi* are a proof of, was to combine his love for Song Dynasty art (960–1279) with the color-sensibility of Impressionistic and Expressionistic painting. The outcome was unique, very lyrical visuals of surreal and rather distant silence that do not fully reflect the Chinese roots, but have a sensibility and spatial awareness to them that can be clearly seen in Song painting. One of the dominant pillars in Chinese paintings is its landscapes in ink on silk, developed in the Northern Song Dynasty (960–1127). The style of painting is called Shanshui, including both the Chinese character for mountain = *shan* and water = *shui*. Shanshui paintings do not replicate nature but express an idea of the space, a personal exploration of a setting rather than a truthful account. Mountains and seasons are more of a generalization of places and moments instead of giving an exact representation of a place or a time. Chinese landscape painters did not paint what was observed but they painted their true essence of nature, so the paintings are not what we would call photorealistic renderings of nature at all. Shanshui art is not an interpretation of how the artist sees nature and explores it through his art, but about how the artist with his being is experiencing nature, being part of nature. The paintings first stimulate the viewer to see the aesthetic pleasure in the piece; second, they inspire the viewer to mentally travel and thus experience nature directly; and finally, they inspire the viewers to see themselves as part of the whole and contemplate in and about nature itself. The new direction of painting in the Northern Song in the 10th century brought in a lyrical and philosophical moment and elevated landscape painting to its full glory that "dominated eventually the artistic tradition in China."[45] Landscapes became retreats for humans to be marveled at. Man is but a small part of nature, depicted by majestic landscapes with fantastical interpretations of mountains, rivers, and trees. The harmony between man and nature is embodied. The landscape is inviting the viewer to stroll through and experience it in a spiritual dialogue. One

[43] IMDB: Bambi (1942), http://www.imdb.com/title/tt0034492/faq (accessed April 30, 2015).
[44] Bambi (1942), Bluray additional features, documentary *Inside Walt's Story Meetings*.
[45] Michael Dillon, *China: A Historical and Cultural Dictionary*, Psychology Press, Hove, UK, p. 241.

of the leading Chinese masters of the Northern Song was Guo Xi (~1020–1090), painter of the spectacular hanging scroll *Early Spring* (1072), which is one of the most valued treasures of Northern Song art (Figure 13.197). Xi's interests lied in the relationship between man and nature and the changing of seasons in their poetic depiction. He was not only a successful painter at the imperial court of Shenzong but also a theorist on painting. His most notable written work is *Lofty Aspirations among Forests and Streams* in which he explains, for instance, his theory on perspective, or the "angle of totality," among many other topics on Chinese painting.[46] He wanted the landscape to be interpreted through the artist as a being within nature, not necessarily replicating the actual view of the landscape with its mountains and streams. Also important was the interpretation of a mood or a symbolic theme. It is known that Xi's paintings also have a political meaning in that the single mountain stands for the emperor and his might, him being the solid rock in society. However, man himself is but a tiny element within the whole of nature and he is always depicted as such. A diminutive monk, a contemplating scholar, a wandering traveler, a fisherman, and so on are humble characters that themselves either benefit from nature or explore it, yet are never the focus of the image, but small details within the greater picture. One part of Xi's theory is on perspective and the distance between viewer and object, which he calls the "three distances" and which he used within one painting.[47]

The first one is the "high distance," where the viewer is looking up at the mountain from its foot. The second one is the "deep distance," where the viewer is in front of the mountain and looks past it into the distance. The third distance is the "level distance," where the viewer is looking from a nearby mountain at those more distant.[48] The different "distances" of landscapes in Xi's paintings are often separated by clouds and fog where mountains are fragmented and dispersed on the scroll for distance clarity. The lower part of the scroll in *Early Spring*, for example, is denser than the upper part which makes the upper part visually recede into the distance. Xi produces visual islands that float in an undefined ocean of mist, creating surreal landscapes rather than mimicking realistic perspectives. Another point of Xi's theory is the "angle of totality." He stated that though mountains are constant beings, their image continuously fluctuates as the viewer explores them physically by walking through the landscape. Thus, a mountain must never be painted as a solid piece but with a "Floating Perspective," meaning from all angles, not just one.

**Figure 13.197**

Guo Xi: *Early Spring* (1072).

How do the theories and paintings of Song Dynasty in general and Guo Xi in particular connect to the style of *Bambi*? Guo Xi writes in *Mountains and Waters*:

> The clouds and the vapours of real landscapes are not the same at the four seasons. In spring they are light and diffused, in summer rich and dense, in autumn scattered and thin, in winter dark and solitary. When such effects can be seen in pictures, the clouds and vapours have an air of life. The mist around the mountains is not the same at the four seasons. The mountains in spring are light and seductive as if smiling; the mountains in summer have a blue–green colour which seems to be spread over them; the mountains in autumn are bright and tidy as if freshly painted; the mountains in winter are sad and tranquil as if sleeping.[49]

This is what *Bambi*'s core elements are about: the four seasons' change and a profound and deep interpretation of nature through art. Weather and seasons are the foundation of all sequences in

---

[46] Guo Xi's work is of course a step in the development of landscape painting and builds upon earlier theories and paintings. Especially the artistic and theoretical work of Jing Hao (c. 855-915) was hugely influential on Chinese landscape painting.

[47] Wang Yao-t'ing, *Looking at Chinese Painting*, Nigensha Publishing, Tokyo, 1995.

[48] Chong Keng Hua, *Representation of Architecture in Jiehua & Yingzao Fashi: Cognitive Studies on Graphical Representation of Geometric Space*, 2008, http://scholarbank.nus.edu.sg/handle/10635/16522?show=full (accessed December 14, 2017).

[49] Rene Grousset, *The Rise and Splendor of the Chinese Empire,* Barnes & Noble, New York, 1995, p. 195.

*Bambi*. The book's and the film's narrative basis is how weather and seasons shape the life in the forest and affect rhythmically the animal's recurring life cycle. However, the images in *Bambi* only take on the visual ideas of Shanshui, its superficial surface, not the philosophical meaning. In Shanshui, man is just a small part of the grandness of nature, a being within the organic whole. The feature film on the other hand has man as the only creature not being part of the whole, but always entering nature as an enemy, a destructive and disruptive element, which is diametrically opposite of the Chinese Song dynasty's idea of man's position in nature. In Wong's work, nevertheless the animals are often small and seemingly insignificant characters that are harmoniously living in and with nature, exactly like man in Song paintings.

Stripping away the western influences of late 19th and early 20th century interpretation of color and focusing on the backbone of Wong's pieces, they have islands of light and color, of matter and forms floating in an undefined space that does not bind characters and objects, but lets many elements blur into each other in the most unfocused way possible. But then there are always significant elements and characters being refined in line and form-quality to step forward and claim their importance for the story. There is a strong tendency in Wong's work to create through the blurry elements an undefined idea of a space, very similar in Shanshui paintings, where the actual natural setting is never realistically depicted but is the emotional and spiritual expression of the artist's being within nature. In Guo's painting, the mist that reveals only glimpses of the mountain does make the mountains look more awe-inspiring, which was Song landscape painting's general direction of depicting the grandeur of nature rather than intimate moments. Xi writes: "If you want to show the height of mountains, they will appear high if half hidden midway by cloudy forms, but not so if completely exposed."[50] It is this empty space, the mist and clouds, that not only inspires the mind to wander but also elevates the peaks within the painting to ever grander heights. These empty spaces that are filled with mist and cloudy forms are also in Wong's work, not in the same fashion as in Song painting, but as patches of colors that flow into each other, also providing the image with plenty of breathing space and mist. Mist and fog is an important aspect in nearly every background in the final film and Wong's influence is most apparent there; much is shrouded in a layer of fog or just artistic haze. Considerable areas are indistinct, though the focus is still kept where it is important in the staging area. The translation of this kind of mood into the scene in the final film happens on the meadow; when Bambi is introduced to the world outside the forest during a sunny day, its background is mostly blurry and covered in mist, giving it a slightly other worldly feel, an animal feel rather than an image with a human scientific perspective of clarity. Guo Xi writes about atmosphere and spatial recession: "A mountain without haze and clouds is like a spring without flowers

and grass."[51] What remains in Tyron Wong's painting style from the Song paintings is this vagueness of space and the lack of connectedness of forms to the ground plane. The lack of shadows renders the entire ground soft, letting the characters beautifully flow into the ground and into the loose and smooth brushwork, allowing them to truly be part of nature. Wong, as does Guo Xi, uses both islands of forms to create focal points that the viewer is invited to observe. There is never a ground plane that clearly explains the expansion of the space or gives it a dimension that is truly graspable. It is a rather spiritual space that Wong creates, evoking mystical scenes in an Arcadian landscape. David Whitley actually compares the forest in *Bambi* to the biblical Eden, a place without serious predators for the animals.[52] And Wong's sketches often have a spiritual aspect to them. The translation to the final film, however, has less spiritual connotation but still retains its majestic grandeur. Wong also reduces the information to the bare minimum without putting the flow of information at risk. His development work reads perfectly well, not despite their lack of detail, but exactly because of it! There is most often a sincerity in Wong's work that is usually not found in inspirational art for animation, which celebrates the cartoony, the comic, and the entertaining. Wong's work is serious and sacred, giving the characters, the seasonal moments, and nature itself a grace that in part has been transported into the movie.

Wong did not pay too close attention to the specific story points when he painted his inspirational pieces. He said about his approach in an interview with Michael Barrier:

> Mainly it was the mood. If a particular color would give me the mood I wanted, I'd use it. For the spring sequence, everything is light and gay—I was thinking in terms of bright greens and yellows, things like that—uplifting. After the fire, everything's gray—charcoal.[53]

This is also what Guo Xi's philosophy addresses in part: creating a mood rather than a realistic representation of nature and its four seasons. The painting is the artist's invention and creation of a space rather than just a reproduction of a view.

The story in *Bambi* was a naturalistic story, a story that needed a somehow realistic approach to animation in order to work on a level of believability to stay in accordance with the story. Nature and the forest needed to be stylized to allow the characters to read and that goal was beautifully achieved with Wong's semi-translation of Song painting into contemporary development art or illustration. The stylization goes only so far as to eliminate details but still keep the realism intact and create a romantic ideal version of a forest.

*Bambi* for that matter is the high point of Disney's evolution, the pinnacle of the strive for depicting nature "as it could be"

---

[50] Mark Sullivan, The Gift of Distance: Chinese Landscape Painting as a Source of Inspiration, *Southwest Review*, Vol. 92, No. 3 (2007), pp. 407–419, 483.

[51] Guo Xi's Writings on Landscape Paintings; Chapter 8, page 293.
[52] David Whitley, *The Idea of Nature in Disney Animation: From Snow White to WALL-E*, Ashgate Publishing, Farnham, UK, 2013.
[53] Interview with Michael Barrier, on January 13th 1979 http://www.michaelbarrier.com/Interviews/Wong/Wong.html (accessed June 8, 2017).

in animation. What makes Disney's output so enticing and also difficult is its captivating beauty, its undeniable perfection and sheer impossible task of achieving such magical visuals, yet often succumbing to an overly emotional narrative. Disney achieves believability in the perfection of its visuals, the often stunning implementation of the multiplane camera with its perspectives, the masterly use of color and character animation. What one needs to keep in mind is that what Disney produced in the 1930s and the early 1940s was absolutely unique at the time, was a product and an aesthetic, in its moving form mind you, that had never been seen before in that quality or scope. Because of that it needs to be seen as extraordinarily important pieces of film-art and technical achievement without comparison. Undoubtedly, there are many strong moments in *Bambi*, moments of true beauty and natural observation. The steep learning curve of Disney's artists who needed to climb the mountain of understanding movement and anatomy in its realism first in order to achieve such a level of expertise is worth noticing. Paul Wells states it:

> It may be argued that it is the very tension between beauty and banality which informs much of Disney's work, often creating images of profound intensity and technical and artistic achievement, but, at the same time, scenes of great superficiality and over-determined sentimentality.[54]

There is a moment in the book that is very strong in its surreal yet convincing dialogue between two leaves that are about to end their life, falling to the ground just before winter approaches.

The dialogue is, in its written form, a strong statement and one's imagination surely allows it to develop an intense emotional response. However, if compared to the visualization that was shortly considered for the film with the dialogue actually being spoken,[55] the crux of Disney's art becomes apparent: when is the point reached where artistic taste turns into sentimentality or even kitsch? The final film visualizes the moment by just having the two leaves slowly and quietly detach from the branch and fall down and that is that. There is enough time given for the audience to understand the message and the subtlety of the image is truly emotional without a spoken word, it keeps the moment intimate and small. By not having words accompany the images and translating the book into a film, but allowing only the images to tell the story and therefore let much of the meaning of the scene happen in the minds of the viewer, the scene defends its artistic field of animation instead of just visualizing the book. And this is where *Bambi* reveals its emotional strength, because it is also filled with intimate moments, quiet moments of water, puddles, droplets, character movements of silent affection and clear observation that accompany the narrative, often even are the narrative. *Bambi* is not only the story of Bambi but also the story of the forest, the animals being part of the whole, and the seasons' intense impact on the dwellers of the forest. This does just ever so slightly touch upon the Song painting's philosophical approach to nature, which is not just looking at nature, but being part of it and experiencing it aesthetically, physically, and philosophically.

[54] Paul Wells, *Understanding Animation*, Routledge, Abingdon-on-Thames, UK, 1998, p. 231.

[55] Bambi, Bluray additional features, documentary *Inside Walt's Story Meetings*.

# CHAPTER 14

# Color

It is very difficult to actually pin down *color* and define it, as there is just such a huge variety and so very few words with which to describe the individual colors. We can literally see millions of colors with our eyes but only have a couple of dozen words to name them. So we group colors, rather than specify an exact color, when we talk about them in terms like "red" or "yellow," which means a myriad of hues, not really a single color. Sometimes we are a little more precise and say "burgundy" or "light green." This does describe the color slightly more but is still very vague (Figure 14.1). Is it a green that has more yellow in it? Or more blue? How much blue? What kind of blue? The human eye can see between 3 and 10 million different hues, which does not mean that we can actually distinguish one from the other. This is obviously slightly more than we would have names for, and thus describing the exact color is a bit of an issue, so we need to create systems and color models to help us to organize color.

An additional complexity is that color in reality changes and is never really a constant because it is so easily affected by light and shadow, time of the day or the weather situation, which affects the color of an object or the entire landscape dramatically. Then surrounding objects also contribute to the color with their own reflections. All this makes it very difficult to define what color we are actually talking about. But color is also one of the most important aspects when it comes to designing an image and can directly affect the mood of the image, and with it our emotions. Color is not only an agent to make reality in pictures more real by enhancing the various aspects of color through programs like Photoshop. Color can also do the very opposite and render a landscape less real and give the content and narrative a different spin if the colors are subdued or digitally enhanced.

There is never just one color in a picture (well, some pictures do have this, but I guess the exception proves the rule) but myriads of them that relate to each other, creating a symphony of colors, so how can we control all of them to create an aesthetically pleasing whole? Color is additionally also affected by fashion and what color combination is in vogue at the time. What was fashionable in color in the 1940s is by no means the same as in 2018. Color can

also express an emotion and has a meaning. It is easy to say that red is a vibrant and energetic color with a high visual amplitude and should therefore dominate in film scenes or images that require high energy; or that the intense use of red speaks of passion and desire. However, one thing needs to be understood: that film (and with it single images) is not just color and shapes, but most importantly it is a story created through image, editing, narrative, and music/sound. Color, therefore, is just one of the aspects that affects the overall film, but it is by no means the only one. It tints the direction of the film but is never the sole reason for an emotion in a scene. What makes film such a difficult and exciting topic is that there are just so many options for expressing the direction of the story and how all the various elements interact with each other to find the final result. Color assists in how the audience will perceive the flood of information, which can be harmonious or disharmonious, where elements do not agree with each other, which might be exactly the effect intended. It is way too easy to use, for instance, *red* in a scene of passion. What needs to be determined is how this scene of passion is actually positioned as an action within the narrative and what effect it has on the characters' personalities, their relationships, and the overall story arc. What is the meaning of that passionate scene within the development of the character's emotional journey? Is the impact of the passionate scene positive or negative, dangerous or destructive to the character's emotional arc during the film? Feature film is a continuous flow of countless images throughout a period of roughly 1.5 hours, after all, and as we witness the protagonist's journey, color can have a major impact on how we feel about the character's emotional development.

Then there are the specifics of the color and how it "feels" to the audience. Red is warm and blue is cold, which again is way too simple, but it is a start! Is it a warm or a cold red, a red that is slightly more orange or blue, a clean red or a little dirty? Does it sit closer in its hue towards purple or even green? It also changes its "redness" next to other colors. Then there is color theory, which teaches us that blue is complementary to yellow and that those two go well together aesthetically. But that does not specify yet what kind of blue or yellow. Much of color theory simplifies the field of color for better understanding, but achieving harmony of all colors in an image is much more complex, as so many factors contribute to the final image. There are many rules and observations, but there is also the artistic mind, which cannot or should not be limited to a cliché, even if the rules work aesthetically. Isn't it playing with the aspects of design and therefore also color, surprising the audience with the new, that is the purpose of art making?

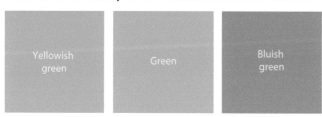

**Figure 14.1**

DOI: 10.1201/b22148-14

# Color in cinema

In cinema, color goes back to the very beginning. There was always the urge to increase the viewing pleasure by adding color to black and white film, which in actuality was not always black and white; quite the contrary. By the early 1920s, roughly 80%–90% of films were tinted or dyed instead of just being black and white. Nevertheless, black and white films have their very own aesthetic qualities, which are not to be dismissed. They do exhibit qualities that cannot be matched by colored images.

Tinting the entire frame with one color was practiced early on in cinema's history for a higher impact of the mood and also to define the time of the day: yellow was used for daytime scenes, blue for nighttime, brownish gold for interiors, red for intense scenes like fires, explosions, or disasters, rose and lavender for romantic scenes, and green for jungle or nature shots, etc. We can see this in a purple-tinted still from Spanish director Segundo de Chomón's short film *La casa hechizada* from 1908, a ghost story that also included some animation (Figure 14.2). This technique, however, tinted and dyed the entire frame, not just parts of it. If one wanted just sections of the frame to be colored, it had to be done by hand and painstakingly, frame by frame. Tinting the black and white strip with brushes was used as a technique to add color to specific elements, despite the laborious and time-consuming process of hand-painting every single small piece (a 10-minute short has, when projected at silent film speed of 16 frames per second,[1] a staggering 9,600 images). The first hand-tinted short film was *Annabelle Serpentine Dance* from 1895 by the Edison Manufacturing Company. We see Annabelle Moore perform the dance, and her wide and floating dress is colored in yellow and orange very effectively. At the very start of the twentieth century, just outside of Paris, George Méliès produced fantastic and adventurous stories and employed in his studio an entire department that painted and stenciled (cut areas from a film frame and used them as stencils) the small frames painstakingly with many colors. However, not every print was painted, as it was a rather expensive procedure, but some of Méliès' colored movies survived, especially his most famous film, *A Trip to the Moon* (1902), which shows to what elaborate extent color was already used in 1902 (Figure 14.3). But painting, dying, or tinting the film image is only one way of adding color to the image, and it never gives a realistic color illusion. So technology needed to invent a system that could record color realistically.

In 1900 Edward Raymond Turner (1873–1903) developed a technique where three strips of separately shot films recorded the colors red, blue, and green, which together created a fairly convincing image of colored film. Turner, a photographer and inventor, had already worked in the first photo studio

**Figure 14.2**

Segundo de Chomón: *La casa hechizada* (1908).

**Figure 14.3**

George Méliès: *A trip to the Moon* (1902).

in London that produced color photographs for still images. Color photography goes back to 1861, when Scottish scientist James Clerk Maxwell and Thomas Sutton produced the very first three-color photograph. The step to the moving image with the same technology is not as easy as it might seem, as the film images have to match in a fast-paced sequence with all three film strips running through the camera at the same time. Turner was unable to finish his technique due to his untimely death at the age of 29 from a heart attack, but he left behind a convincing technology that was discovered and reconstructed in 2012 by the National Media Museum in Bradford, UK (with the help of computer technology), and seems proof of Turner's excellent technique (Figure 14.4). However, his invention at the time was discontinued due to the technical difficulties with the accurate registration of the three film strips. Turner's successor was George Albert Smith, who simplified the three-color strip into a two-strip process that used only red and green and produced films that had modest

---

[1]   The projection speed of silent film did vary greatly, from about 12 to up to 40 fps, because the camera operator alone controlled the speed. The cameras were not standardized when it came to the speed they recorded the images with.

success with its so-called Kinemacolor system from 1908 on. Throughout the 1910s and 1920s, many films had sequences in them in color with processes like Kinemacolor, Technicolor, Multicolor, Brewster Color Process, MagnaColor, Cinecolor, Magnacolor, Pathécolor, Pathéchrome, the Keller-Dorian process, the Handschiegl color process, Prizma, Dufaycolor, Gasparcolor, and many, many others. However, Technicolor was by far the most successful one and proved its capacity for reproducing convincing color by becoming a quality seal for big-budget Hollywood features in bright and saturated colors in the 1930s to 1950s.

## Technicolor

There were four different processes developed by Technicolor starting in 1916, each improving the previous one in recording color that mimics reality. The first process was the two-color Process 1, which recorded two images on one filmstrip by splitting the colors via a prism into green and red; the images were recorded two images apart from each other (red–green–red–green on one filmstrip). Because of exposing two images at the same time, red and green, the film had to be shot twice as fast as regular black and white, which also meant that there needed to be more light for the exposure. The projection was similar: each image needed to be projected through its own lens, so the two lenses had to be adjusted just right for the red and green images to match on screen, which was a difficult task and required a specialist to control the projector. Process 1 used an additive color process (see Figure 14.50), which produced the color by combining colored light and therefore adding light green and red on top of each other, which produced yellowish white light in the overlay. Also the film needed to be recorded and projected with customized projection equipment. Because of its complexity and recording and projecting speed, the process was rather prone to technical problems. The first and only feature that was recorded in this process was director Wray Bartlett Physioc's *The Gulf Between* from 1917, which only survived in frames (Figures 14.5 and 14.6). Because the film could not be presented through a regular projector, it was shown in a road show that travelled through the United States with limited success. The public was mostly enthusiastic, but the technology was not sufficient as of yet.

The next development brought Process 2, which is a subtractive color process and was introduced in 1922. Subtract does the opposite of additive; it absorbs wavelength of light and takes out color, which results in black in the overlapping area, because all light is removed (Figure 14.49). The public was introduced to this process in Chester M. Franklin's feature *The Toll of the Sea* in 1922 (Figures 14.7 and 14.8), the first color feature that could be projected, contrary to Process 1, with a regular projector, as the color is on one film strip, consisting of two strips that were cemented back to back into one. This also made distribution of the film much easier. *The Toll of the Sea* was with Anna May Wong, the first Asian American movie star (who also starred in Douglas Fairbanks' extravagant feature *The Thief of Bagdad* in

**Figure 14.4**

Edward Turner: *Agnes on a swing* (1901/2).

**Figure 14.5**

Wray Bartlett Physioc: *The Gulf Between* (1917).

**Figure 14.6**

Wray Bartlett Physioc: *The Gulf Between* (1917).

**Figure 14.7**

Chester M Franklin: *The Toll of the Sea* (1922).

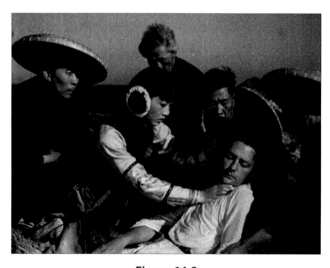

**Figure 14.8**

Chester M Franklin: *The Toll of the Sea* (1922).

**Figure 14.9**

Rupert Julian: *The Phantom of the Opera* (1925).

1924, discussed later on). The filmstrips of Process 2, however, tended to bulge ("cupping"), so the image could be slightly out of focus. Big productions like Rupert Julian's *The Phantom of the Opera* from 1925, for instance (Figure 14.9), used the two-strip Technicolor process for a couple of scenes. The phantom appears as a colorful guest at a masquerade ball in a bright red cape and a death mask that both have an impact that is still to this day difficult to abstain from and frightening in its immediateness. Other features also had colored scenes in them, like Cecil B. DeMille's lavish interpretation of *The Ten Commandments* (1923) or *Ben Hur* (1925), with its famous and influential chariot race. Irvin Willat's *Wanderers of the Wasteland* (1924), however, was yet another feature shot fully in color and was proof again that the process worked not just in specific or important scenes but also in an entire feature (Figures 14.10 through 14.12). However, it also showed that the cemented prints were prone to scratching, much pricier than black and white, and thus not as profitable for the film studios yet. One of the great achievements for Technicolor came with Douglas Fairbanks' swashbuckler *The Black Pirate*, directed by Albert Parke in 1926 and also shot in its entirety in Process 2 (Figures 14.13 through 14.16). It was the first big Hollywood production (*Wanderers of the Wasteland* was a minor production) using this process in its full feature length and was therefore a significant artistic step for Technicolor. Fairbanks had seen *The Toll of the Sea* and, impressed by the possibilities of color, he decided to use Technicolor's Process 2 for his next epic, instead of another of the competitors also providing color techniques. In order to bring the color onto the screen in its full scope, not only as an addition, but relating to narrative and subject matter, extensive studies and preproduction work were developed to achieve the aesthetics of old imagery and interpret the works of illustrators Howard Pyle and N.C. Wyeth, which influenced the contemporary visual style of pirates in the public's imagination. The paintings of the Dutch Masters also had, with their unique use of color, a major influence on Fairbanks' decision to push the desaturated color towards browns and sepia. The outcome was the first color feature that strongly used color design for its narrative interpretation and mood, comprehensively examining the quality of each color already in preproduction.

*The Black Pirate* exudes the feeling of the "old days" exactly because its use of color is not overly bright and saturated, but subtle and restrained. Color does not distract from the actual story, never asks for attention, but quietly supports the image. The result is utterly convincing in its aesthetics and finds its own style. It seemed to finally be the beginning for Technicolor to receive orders for more feature productions from Hollywood; however, technical difficulties with the cemented filmstrips grew during the presentation of *The Black Pirate* and it became clear that this initially temporary solution of cementing the two colored strips together had reached its end. Technicolor did not receive the expected orders and needed to cut down on the planned expansion. However, the company had a goal, which was the representation of the full color spectrum on screen, not just two colors. The two-color process was always considered a step towards full color, never the end of development. Certain colors could not be reproduced, like yellow, purple, or blue, the latter of which could be visually mimicked with turquoise to an extent but was still not fully convincing. Many skies seemed more green than blue. The two colors red and green were initially chosen to simplify the complexity of three colors' much better representation. If two colors could be successfully reproduced without major technical problems, then the next step, three colors and therefore the full range of the spectrum, could be tackled from a photochemical perspective. Also the complex task of engineering cameras and improving Technicolor's processing plant could be developed step by step.

In 1927 the third process was introduced, which used a similar technique to Process 2 in shooting the film in consecutive images of red/green, nevertheless via a complex process including dye imbibition, a dye-transfer technique slightly similar to lithography, through which the final film was printed onto one filmstrip. This removed the problems of the two back-to-back cemented film strips bulging but also made the product cheaper and improved its durability … so it seemed: towards the 1930s, once Technicolor was in higher demand, the process also showed major flaws for increased output, which again caused the industry to lose commercial interest. What needs to be understood is that these processes were highly complicated and contained 15–19 different stages of development, each of which, if slightly faulty, could have a dramatic impact on the image quality. The first full feature film in color shot in Process 3 was *The Viking* in 1928, well received in its colors but not so much in the narrative. The next feature *Redskin* (1929) was to a high degree in color (parts were shot in black and white) and was released at the edge of a new breakthrough that completely changed the landscape of cinema: sound. Sound had been slowly gaining ground in cinema but was finally publicly accepted in the first feature using synchronized and original sound in *The Jazz Singer* from 1927. *Redskin* not only used color but also sound, and the combination shifted the film images further into reality and away from the more detached, yet often artistic, black and white silent images. Technicolor, having struggled through the years after the rejection of their technique by the film studios (*The Black Pirate* had shown the aesthetic qualities but also the massive technical problems of Process 2), had finally reached a point with Process 3 where it had become a popular addition, more affordable and practical. Big studios had started to hire Technicolor's services, which consisted of not only the renting of cameras, but also maintenance, camera operator, assistants, color consultation, and the processing of the film.

The genre that was mainly in color in 1929 and 1930 was the Hollywood musical, which had huge success in those years and color was part of it. Musicals like *Gold Diggers of Broadway* (1929), *Show of Shows* (1929), *Sally* (1929), *Whoopee* (1930), and *King of Jazz* (1930) were very popular with audiences. In the mid-1930, however, this success waned and Technicolor once again saw the demand for its process decrease. In 1931, only three features were

**Figure 14.10**

**Figure 14.11**

**Figure 14.12**

Irvin Willat: *Wanderer of the Wasteland* (1924).

filmed in Technicolor. None were musicals; the public wanted a change. In 1932–1933, two successful features were released by Warner Brothers, which showed that horror movies could also gain a more dramatic mood when shot in color: *Doctor X* (1932) and *A Night at the Wax Museum* (1933). Those two were the last narrative features produced in Process 3. The overall number of features shot in Process 3 is partly proof of its success; however, the Great Depression put a halt to its wider spread until Process 4 was introduced in 1932. Process 4 was made popular through the medium of animation, so let's see first how animation used color before the introduction of Process 4.

## Color in animation

The first animated short in color is from 1920, *The Debut of Thomas Cat* by Bray Pictures, with the Brewster Color Film process, a two-color process, which was not continued for Bray Pictures on another short due to its high costs. Earl Hurd had produced the short for J.R. Bray's company; together they had invented the cel animation practice in 1915, which revolutionized and simplified the animation process.

Lotte Reiniger's feature *Prince Achmed*, the first (surviving) animated feature film from 1926, was fully tinted in various colors and clearly follows the typical treatment of live-action feature film at the time.

The two-color Technicolor Process 3 was first used for an animated segment in the live-action feature film *The King of Jazz* in 1930, animated by Walter Lantz and William Nolan for Universal Pictures. In the feature, a revue film with musical numbers, the short animated sequence explains how Paul Whiteman, band leader of the revue, received his name "King of Jazz." The short is full of animals in Africa, chasing Whiteman, and acting silly; there is even a quick cameo of Oswald the Lucky Rabbit, who was owned at the time by Universal and animated by Lantz. The first animated short film with sound produced in a two-color process was Ub Iwerk's short film *Fiddlesticks* from 1930, the first of his Flip the Frog series, which he produced after having left Disney.[2] It used the Harriscolor process, also a subtractive two-color system. *Fiddlesticks* was released alongside *King of Jazz* and was also produced by Lantz Productions. Any two-color process was by no means fully convincing in terms of representational colors. It was nevertheless a crucial step in the right direction of developing a complex technology that would find its next and final step in the afore-mentioned three-strip Technicolor Process 4, used first on a commercial basis by Walt Disney in his *Silly Symphonies* short *Flowers and Trees* on July 18, 1932.

**Figure 14.13**

**Figure 14.14**

**Figure 14.15**

Albert Parke: *The Black Pirate* (1926).

---

[2]  Ub Iwerks had animated many of the successful Disney shorts, in particular not only designing Mickey Mouse but also animating (with Wilfred Jackson and Les Clark) *Steamboat Willie*. Ub Iwerks was the main animator for Disney's shorts released from 1928 to 1929 and contributed massively to Disney's earlier output.

**Figure 14.16**

Albert Parke: *The Black Pirate* (1926).

Disney met Technicolor representative Herbert Kalmus, one of the main developers of the Technicolor processes and president of the company. He convinced Disney that the full color three-strip process would add spectacle to his *Silly Symphonies*.[3] What needs to be understood is why Herbert Kalmus approached Disney instead of one of the big movie companies in Hollywood, and this goes back to how the three-color process works. The light from a scene travels into the camera, gets split up into its three colors, and via filters exposes three different filmstrips that are green, blue, and red sensitive (actually two filmstrips; one is double-sided). For this process, new cameras and equipment needed to be built to provide the necessary amount of hardware for live-action cinema in Hollywood. Additionally the Technicolor plant needed to be prepared for the new system, which took time. Animation, however, can be shot with just one camera that records the three different colors by shooting each frame three times through a filter (like the recording of Processes 1–3). The different recording technique of animation gave it a technically simpler onset. Having Disney use this process gave Technicolor the advantage of exposing the public and Hollywood to the new system via very popular shorts. It was proof of its successful color technique and quality, and through the colorful cartoons it convinced Hollywood studios that Technicolor's technology had potential for feature films. Filming a live-action feature in full color was an expensive and difficult path, and the industry needed to be convinced that full color was not just a gimmick but a direction that had a dramatic narrative impact. Disney's short *Flowers and Trees* was first shot in black and white, where the color on the animation cels was also painted in black and white tones, and then the tones were carefully removed from the cels, leaving only the inked lines,

and painted again in color. This ensured another existing option in black and white, if the Technicolor result was not convincing in its quality. *Flowers and Trees* was from the beginning on a tryout for both sides, Disney and Technicolor, and only after its commercial and artistic success did Disney sign a contract in 1933 for the sole rights to Process 4. This allowed Disney to use full color until 1935 as the only studio in Hollywood and give Technicolor time to prepare its hardware for the upcoming live-action feature film commissions. *Flowers and Trees* became a huge success, and all other animation studios had to fall back on the lesser quality of the two-strip process by Technicolor or use the color process of another company altogether. The shorts by the Fleischer Studios, for example, used the earlier mentioned two-strip Technicolor system in its series *Color Classics* from 1934 to 1935 (the first of the series, however, was shot with the Cinecolor technique). Charles Mintz produced the *Color Rhapsodies* for Columbia from 1934 to 1949 and used the two-strip Technicolor process until 1935, then switched to full Technicolor. The *Happy Harmonies* were produced by Rudolf Ising and Hugh Harman for MGM from 1934 onwards. In 1935, their short *The Old Plantation* was the first three-strip Technicolor cartoon not produced by Disney. Van Beuren Studios had their Rainbow Parade series, produced for RKO from 1934 to 1946, which used in 1934 the Cinecolor system, then Technicolor two (1935) and three strip (1936). Ub Iwerks produced the ComiColor Series with fairy tale subjects from 1933 to 1936, consisting of 25 shorts using the Cinecolor system.

In 1932, the Hungarian chemist Dr. Bela Gaspar invented Gasparcolor, also a three-color subtractive process, which had an exquisite color range and quality. Gaspar had the process, but he did not have the cameras to film it with. Again the same problem arose of how to use the camera to film the action.[4] Abstract filmmaker Oskar Fischinger, having worked in film special effects in Berlin, developed a camera for Gasparcolor that served animation more than live-action (Fischinger had worked on the special effects for *Frau im Mond/ Woman in the Moon* [1929], directed by Fritz Lang, the first feature that dealt with space travel from a semiscientific perspective). As in the case of Technicolor choosing Disney, animation was again the best technique for Gasparcolor to avoid the issues of live-action shoots with the three-color strips. Animation has no movement during the shooting of the animated frames; therefore the overlap of the three-colored frames is of no concern. Oskar Fischinger produced in Germany various short

---

3  More on this subject in J. P. Telotte, Minor Hazards: Disney and the Color Adventure, *Quarterly Review of Film and Video*, Vol. 21, No. 4 (2004), pp. 273–281. http://dx.doi.org/10.1080/10509200490446150

4  If the three images for red, green, and blue were to be on three different strips of black and white film, then the pictures could be shot at the same time. If, however, the three images followed each other consecutively on the same film strip, then the action could be filmed at the same time if the incoming light were split into three rays. Alternatively, the images could be shot in quick order, one after the other. However, the action needed to be very slow for this option, in order to have the different images receive the same or nearly the same image information for the three-color information to match each other. Very fast action would result in the three consecutive images not overlapping, as the three images in a row show the movement of the object filmed rather than the same exact moment of the action.

**Figure 14.17**

Oskar Fischinger: *Composition in Blue* (1935).

**Figure 14.18**

Oskar Fischinger: *Allegretto* (1935).

films in Gasparcolor: *Kreise* (*Circles*) for instance, which was released in 1933 as a commercial for Tolirag, an advertising agency, and in 1934 a fully abstract revised version was released with a different ending. The colors are vibrant and fresh with a range that must have been impressive, to say the least, at the time of its release. In 1934 the cigarette commercial *Muratti Greift ein* (*Muratti Gets in the Act*), a stop-motion army of dancing and marching cigarettes, also produced with Gasparcolor, became a small sensation in Europe. Also his short film *Composition in Blue* (Figure 14.17) from 1935 showed the exquisite quality of this color system in an exploration of stop-motion animation, real geometric forms, and abstraction. Fischinger really shows a level of expertise and creativity in this short that is dramatically strengthened by the exceptional quality of the color. Abstract animation clearly excels with the addition of

color, as it is such a crucial element of its composition. Gasparcolor became the preferred process for animation and artists like Len Lye (for example, his vibrant and creative commercial *Rainbow Dance* from 1936),[5] Claire Parker and Alexandre Alexeieff, Jean Painleve, and George Pal, who all used Gasparcolor frequently throughout the 1930s for shorts and commercials in Europe. However, because of Nazi involvement and the war situation, Bela Gaspar fled to Hollywood. He could not establish Gasparcolor in the film industry because of Technicolor's own success and so Gasparcolor's patent was finally sold to rival company 3M. Oskar Fischinger recorded the final films in Gasparcolor: *Allegretto* (1936–1943) (Figure 14.18) and *Radio Dynamics* (1943).

## Live-action features in three-strip technicolor

While Disney's short films gloriously promoted Technicolor's Process 4, the development of cameras and technology continued to prepare for the important field of live-action features. In order to not only test the field of color cinematography but also explore its aesthetic possibilities for live-action, Technicolor produced the short film comedy *La Cucaracha* in 1934, to explore what color and mood can do in a film, how it can be used for emotions and composition, but also to serve as a live-action vehicle to convince the studios to join the "color revolution." *La Cucaracha* investigates the field of color in its artistic, aesthetic, and practical use but also explores its metaphorical meaning. The short film was not the first one shot in three-strip Technicolor (it was actually the 11th), but it was the first one that explored color for the narrative and as a design element. Of course, this does not always render the meaning of one color as being absolute and clear in one film, but it has the potential to apply various meanings to one color, especially in the early form of Technicolor, where the range of hues was still limited and subtlety was not yet technically fully achieved. This was refined further in the next couple of years. The first feature film shot in full-color Technicolor was *Becky Sharp* in 1935. There have been other features before that used full color; however, *Becky Sharp* is credited with using color consciously in design and narrative. With the development of the technology, the use of color's aesthetic

**Books on color in cinema:**

Scott Higgins, *Harnessing the Technicolor Rainbow, Color Design in the 1930s*, University of Texas Press, Austin, TX, 2007.

James Layton and David Pierce, *The Dawn of Technicolor, 1915–1935*, Distributed Art Publishers, New York, annotated edition, 2015.

On Gasparcolor http://www.oskarfischinger.org/GasparColor.htm (accessed February 7, 2018).

---

5   Len Lye also used Dufaycolor for his famous short films *A Colour Box* and *Kaleidoscope* for the General Post Office (GPO), British post office, both produced in 1935, and *Swinging the Lambeth Walk* in 1940.

and metaphorical possibilities needed to be explored and that obviously takes time and does come with trial and error. The development of how to use color in cinema is very similar to 3D cinema today. The first films use it as a gimmick, an addition that obviously draws attention through its novelty. A continuous use of the technology then produces a more subtle artistic language and slowly broadens the spectrum. There is always gain and loss when it comes to new technologies and this is also very true for the introduction of full color in film. Where black and white film has a strong impact in distancing the audience from the image and presenting the film image as an obvious interpretation of reality, very much because it lacks color, the black and white image also plays artistically in a different way with composition, light and shadow, and contrast in order to separate the elements in the frame from each other and create depth and a focal point. Black and white film and photography have their own aesthetic and remove the audience from reality, because it is so very different from it. This is similar to the difference between a drawing and a painting. The drawing has its own attraction, which is not less than the painting's but gives another level of otherness. Color added realism and reduced the emotional distance between the action on-screen and the audience, though it was from the beginning heavily used as a tremendous creative opportunity for film, not just for coloring the frame. Various moods could be portrayed through the addition of color, the narrative could be strengthened via color symbolism, connections between characters could be intensified, etc. *Gone with the Wind* and *The Wizard of Oz* are both examples from 1939 of how full three-strip Technicolor bathed the screen in color successfully and used hues and subtleties that truly made color a significant addition to film language, so much so that Technicolor stands for elaborate spectacle and Hollywood glamour in the cultural memory.

## Three-strip technicolor features of interest

- *The Garden of Allah* (1936)
- *The Adventures of Robin Hood* (1938)
- *The Four Feathers* (1939)
- *The Mikado* (1939)
- *The Wizard of Oz* (1939)
- *Gone with the Wind* (1939)
- *The Thief of Bagdad* (1940)
- *The Gang's All Here* (1943)
- *Meet Me in St Louis* (1944)
- *Black Narcissus* (1947)
- *The Red Shoes* (1948)
- *The Pirate* (1948)
- *An American in Paris* (1951)
- *Singing in the Rain* (1952)
- *Scaramouche* (1952)
- *Niagara* (1953)
- *Magnificent Obsession* (1954)
- *The Trouble with Harry* (1955)

# Digital color

The language of color in feature films would continue to be refined and further explored till a new revolution appeared: digital color. Digital color allows a range of control that cannot be achieved with the traditional technique of what was called color timing, done photochemically. However, one needs to be very careful in not considering digital technology as superior to traditional film! "Technicolor is often characterized by a color saturation that is difficult to approximate using modern film stock, let alone electronic media,"[6] Ulrich Ruedel notes. What we watch today as digitally restored films are not necessarily exactly what the audience watched in the movie theatres in the 1930s and 1940s. Modern technology does alter the original, improving it but also changing its initially intended presentation on film, if just ever so slightly.

Digital coloring includes either shooting the film digitally or shooting on traditional film stock, scanning it, then using digital technology to adjust, replace, or control the colors. At the end of the 1980s, digital recording of images started to be developed and towards the end of the 1990s the digitization of film was getting more and more popular, for special effects shots to be included, first in individual shots, but finally entire features were digitized and then color corrected or color adjusted. This process is called *digital intermediate*, which involves digitization but also color manipulation. The range of possibilities in digital color is endless and once again artists and filmmakers needed to learn not only how to use the new technology but also how to discover its artistic opportunities and its strong connection to the narrative. *Pleasantville* (1998), for instance, creates a breach between black and white and intense color, which it expresses not only visually but also in its very story. The twin siblings Jennifer and David find themselves suddenly transported from the 1990s into a black and white 1950s TV show called *Pleasantville*, which they enrich slowly through their actions with color. The technical feat of adding color to the various props and characters could only be done with digital color technology, as it is the only practical and feasible solution. This effect could not have happened in the traditional photochemical process, so digital color allowed this project in the first place.

In 2000 the Coen brothers' feature *Oh Brother, Where Art Thou*, the first film that was color graded in its entirety, used the digital intermediate technology to grade the film and highly desaturate its images, tinting them sepia to achieve an old photography look. Additionally, some of the colors were reduced and/or shifted in hue. Green, for example, was heavily lessened, resulting in a more yellow, dusty, and dry look of the environment. *Oh Brother, Where Art Thou* uses color manipulation not to enrich the story, like *Pleasantville*, where the color is the

6   Ulrich Ruedel, The Technicolor Notebooks at the George Eastman House, *Film History*, Vol. 21, No. 1 (April 2009), p. 47.

actual driving force of the story, but to change the mood and also push the visuals back in time, mimicking a time long past. The new technology allows a level of color control that cannot just alter an image but completely change its mood. The *Lord of the Rings* trilogy (2001–2003) heavily used this technology for its creation of mysterious, otherworldly locations and moods through desaturation, tinting, shifting color levels, and darkening/brightening areas. It is nowadays rather common for films to be digitally adjusted in one form or another, sometimes to an extreme degree like in the latest installments of the *Harry Potter* series, or very subtly to just enhance the image's contrast and color richness. The outcome is often an image that does look "cleaner" than reality itself.

## Attributes of color

The following attempts to make the topic of color as simple yet also as practical as possible. A full study of color and many more aspects of color relationships can be found in the following books, as listed by Kenneth E. Burchett in *A Bibliographical History of the Study and Use of Color from Aristotle to Kandinsky*. Burchett lists 12 essential books on color, of which the first three are historical treatises, less important to the practical use of contemporary color:

1. Johann Wolfgang von Goethe, *Zur Farbenlehre,* Cotta, Tübingen, 1810.
2. Michel Eugène Chevreul, *De la loi du contraste simultané des couleurs et de l'assortiment des objets colorés/The principles of harmony and contrast of colours*, Pitoise Levrault, Paris, 1834.
3. Hermann Ludwig Ferdinand von Helmholtz, *Handbuch der physiologischen Optik*, L. Voss, Leipzig, 1867.
4. Josef Albers, *Interaction of Color*, Yale University Press, New Haven, CT, 1963.
5. Wassily Kandinsky, *Über das Geistige in der Kunst, insbesondere der Malerei*, R. Piper & Co., Munich, 1911.
6. David Katz, *Die Erscheinungsweisen der Farben und ihre Beeinflussung durch die individuelle Erfahrung; der Aufbau der Farbwelt*, J.A. Barth, Leipzig, 1911.
7. Dean Brewster Judd, *Color in Business, Science, and Industry*, John Wiley & Sons, New York, 1959.
8. William David Wright, *The Measurement of Colour,* A. Hilger Limited, London, 1944.
9. Johannes Itten, *Kunst der Farbe; subjektives Erleben und objektives Erkennen als Wege zur Kunst,* Otto Maier, Ravensburg, 1961.
10. Rudolf Arnheim: *Art and Visual Perception: a Psychology of the Creative Eye,* University of California Press, Berkeley and Los Angeles.
11. Albert Henry Munsell, *A Color Notation*, Munsell Color Co., New York, 1919.
12. Arthur Pope, *An Introduction to the Language of Drawing and Painting*, Harvard University Press, Cambridge, MA, 1929.

Color has so many levels that it easily becomes a rather complex and difficult field if someone wants to understand it from a scientific *and* artistic perspective. The scientific side of color can be learned and the artistic side can be practiced. However, color will always have a rather mysterious aura around it because it is such a subtle and delicate matter. How the viewer responds to the colors' relationships can be a challenge, and keeping the audience visually engaged yet also artistically interested and surprised is the goal. It is not only an information exchange going from the artist to the viewer but is also about what that specific color or color combination reminds the viewer of, either in terms of cultural symbolism or personal experiences, and thus subjective memories are also brought into the mixture.

The most practical aspect of color for the artist is the color contrast, as it assists in separating elements from each other and making sense of space, perspective, light and shadow, and characters. Colors can combine elements, make them stand neutral next to each other, or separate them and create a perspective, which I will talk about in the section *Practical Application*. Color assists in placing objects in space, giving them weight and substance, arranging them in the composition, but also creating a mood and establishing on-screen a relationship between object, space, characters, and viewer.

The following needs to be explained first because for our purposes there are two perspectives color can be looked at from. One is the artistic one and one the scientific perspective. The artistic one deals with the practical use of color for artistic purposes; the scientific one deals with the physical, chemical, or mathematical explanations and representations of color. Both are very different and do not always overlap; neither do they always complement each other.

Color theory is yet another rather complex field that is vast and very difficult to oversee; however, for painting, color theory can be studied in Johannes Itten's *Kunst der Farbe* (*The Art of Color*)[7], which still holds mostly true. Not everything is scientifically accurate, but it does give one a very good sense of what color can do and how various colors affect each other. The problem with actual colors, however, is that they do not always follow an exact scientific rule. Itten's theory will be explained in Chapter 14, "Color," the section "Itten's Seven Contrasts."

However, there are some parts of Itten's theory that do not take into consideration the logic and complexity of Munsell's color system, the system that all modern color systems are based on, and thus Itten's theory is not fully scientifically accurate. However, Munsell's system, despite its accuracy and proven scientific

**Book on the history of color:**

Kenneth E. Burchett, *A Bibliographical History of the Study and Use of Color from Aristotle to Kandinsky*, The Edwin Mellen Press, Lewiston, NY, 2005.

7   Johannes Itten, *The Art of Color: The Subjective Experience and Objective Rationale of Color*, Van Nostrand Reinhold, New York, 1973.

truth, is rather complex for painting purposes. His system, and with it all contemporary systems based on it, is not very intuitive for use in painting or the beginning student. These systems are useful for digital and technical purposes and for the advanced practitioner. The scientific aspects of how color works are helpful in understanding what color actually is but are not a replacement for creativity; quite the contrary. Colors are like musical tones that can be arranged in endless ways. No one would claim that the only way to arrange notes is the way Mozart or Beethoven did it. Everyone that wants to conquer color needs to find their own creative expression in this vast field; nevertheless the knowledge of color theory is crucial in understanding color.

Color seems incredibly complex and difficult; nevertheless, children use it in a very playful way and create interesting and unique visuals that defy all color theories and still are often visually engaging (because, to be fair, they usually use a very limited palette). So color is impossibly convoluted yet very simple at the same time, depending what the artist wants to achieve and how deep one wants to go into the complexity of it. There are three different approaches to color in this chapter.

### Technical aspects of color
These are facts that are always true for color. They explain what colors are, how they behave, and how we perceive them. These aspects are crucial in understanding the relationships between colors.

### Artistic aspects of color
These are very subjective and sometimes not graspable. They connect with personal likes and dislikes, one's past, and subjective connotations with the color.

### Intellectual aspects of color
These aspects are social definitions of meanings of color, symbolism, and cultural norms for color. But they also include the meaning of a color that was assigned for one specific art project, which does not necessarily have to overlap with the traditional meaning of that specific color.

## Technical aspects of color and what color consists of:

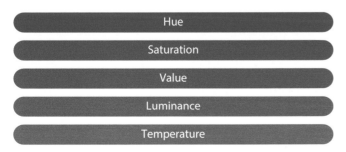

## Hue

*What is usually referred to as red, blue, yellow, green, purple … hue is the "pure" color, untinted by white or black.*

White light, when split through a prism, shows a spectrum of hues that we have grouped into seven colors for simplicity: violet, blue, cyan, green, yellow, orange, and red (Figure 14.19) (in the color wheel, these are then divided into 12 colors).

**Figure 14.19**

The wavelength lower than violet light and higher than red light is invisible to the human eye (for most of us). Red and violet are the furthest apart from each other in the visible spectrum. The visualization of the spectrum is how light appears after it is split through a prism. However, for artistic purposes, based on color theory, the seven color areas are shown in a circle, in which red connects with violet (Figure 14.20). In the color circle, every hue has a hue across, which is its complementary color. The arrangement of the colors has a scientific purpose: mixing two complementary colors with each other results in a neutral gray, like in Figure 14.21 (this works in theory; when mixing actual colors from a tube or bottle this does not always work perfectly because some colors have a stronger impact in dye than others, and thus one will not always end up with a neutral gray). This means that two complementary colors complete each other and create a full range of stimuli in the human eye, which has

three kind of receptors, for red, green, and blue. Complementary colors stimulate all three, thus creating a balanced stimulus (this is the artistic explanation; the scientific one is much more complex). This means that complementary colors are commonly seen as pleasing to the eye (this can be overwritten, of course, by personal preference and subjective aesthetics). Mixing colors with each other that are not complementary results in another hue.

Combining two different hues, their distance on the color wheel to each other has an impact on their tension. The further apart the colors' hues are from each other, the more tension is between them, and the closer they are, the more the two colors unite. There is more tension between red and green (Figure 14.22) than red and orange (Figure 14.23). Despite red not connecting in the spectrum with purple, as purple is the farthest away from red, visually red is closer to purple and has less tension in a grouping (Figure 14.24) compared to red and turquoise blue (Figure 14.25). Complementary colors that are right next to each other also vibrate at their borders, which can be a bit distracting and visually drags a lot of attention. This vibrancy was often used in op art (optical art), which deals with optical illusions between colors and patterns or shapes, to get even more movement into the pictures. Op art was an art movement that started as an idea in the early twentieth century but became more significant as an actual movement in the 1960s.

There is never just a "yellow" or a "blue," but there are countless hues in between that make up the entire spectrum. "Yellow" as a group is a combination of millions of different yellows.

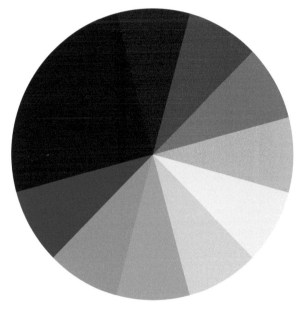

**Figure 14.20**

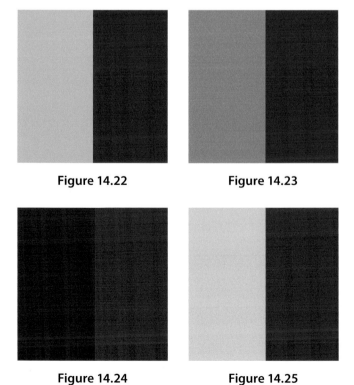

**Figure 14.22**　　　　　　**Figure 14.23**

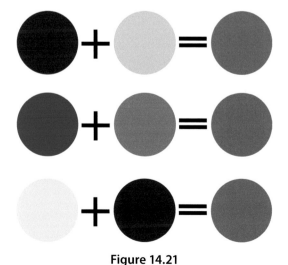

**Figure 14.21**

**Figure 14.24**　　　　　　**Figure 14.25**

Hues can also be mixed with each other, creating new hues. To reduce their possible tension (which they can have if their saturation is very high), both colors can be slightly pushed towards each other by giving both the same addition of a hue. In Figure 14.26, it is ultramarine blue that is mixed in percentages into yellow, green, and red. This takes away some of the tension but also has the negative effect that it reduces the intensity of the initial hue and can change the color dramatically if too much is mixed into the initial color. Yellow, for instance, is very much affected by the addition of blue, whereas for other hues it is less obvious; the green and red still maintain their hue longer than yellow does, which has to do with yellow's luminance. Yellow has the second highest luminance next to white, and adding a small amount of blue, which has a very low luminance, lowers yellow's vibrancy and thus quickly takes away its "yellowness."

Two colors that have a very strong tension between each other, like for example red and green, can also be brought closer to each other by mixing another color in. In Figure 14.27 blue is mixed into the combination of red and green, which results in less tension between the two colors. However, it also again changes the "redness" and "greenness" of the colors and lowers their vibrancy, like we have seen happening with the yellow but much less so. In painting a very thin layer of glaze can do exactly that: bring all colors on the canvas together and reduce their tension.

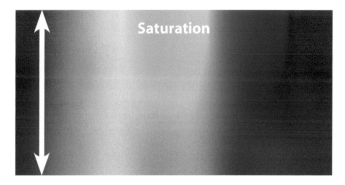

**Figure 14.28**

## Saturation or chroma

*In the Munsell color system there is a clear difference between saturation and chroma, but for our purposes the terms shall be expressing the same color attribute: the intensity or purity of a color/ hue in relationship to its brightness (Figure 14.28).*

100% saturation means that the color is unmixed, there is no additional gray added into the color, and the color is at its most vibrant. A change in saturation changes the "amount of color" in the color. A desaturated color can look weak, faint, pale, and grayish. If all the saturation is taken out of a color, there is only gray left (Figures 14.29 and 14.30).

An actual physical color's saturation can be changed by mixing 50% gray into the color (but that also changes the luminance and value) or by mixing a gray with the same value as the original color, therefore maintaining its luminance and value (to understand this, read the section "Luminance"). However actual physical color is more complex and it always depends on which color is used (type, brand), as all react slightly differently. The color right out of the tube is usually at its highest saturation for that specific color. One can also mix the color's complementary color in and therefore reduce its saturation, but as mentioned earlier it depends on which color is mixed with which complementary color, as colors from a tube do not all have the same chroma. Sometimes this also changes the hue, depending on the color. It is its own complex science, and to fully understand how to mix actual color you need to read one of the mentioned books, like Ian Sidaway's *Color Mixing Bible*.

Digital color does work slightly differently compared to actual physical color when it comes to saturation, as they are both based on two different systems of subtractive and additive colors, which will be explained in the section "Historical Development of the Color Arrangements" in this chapter. When the saturation of digital color

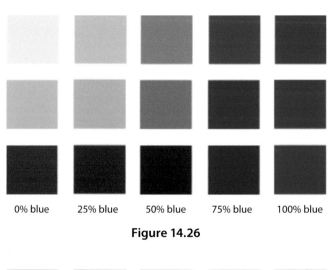

| 0% blue | 25% blue | 50% blue | 75% blue | 100% blue |

**Figure 14.26**

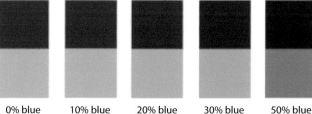

| 0% blue | 10% blue | 20% blue | 30% blue | 50% blue |

**Figure 14.27**

**More on color mixing:**

Sidaway Ian, *Color Mixing Bible: All You'll Ever Need to Know about Mixing Pigments in Oil, Acrylic, Watercolor, Gouache, Soft Pastel*, Pencil, and Ink, Watson Guptill, New York, 2011.

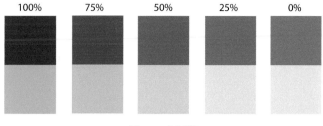

**Figure 14.29**

Desaturation in Lab system maintains luminance.

**Figure 14.30**

Desaturation in RGB system levels values to a 50% grey.

is reduced in, for example, the digital Lab color system, it maintains the luminance of the color and displays two different gray tones (Figure 14.29). The also digital RGB system, however, levels them out and the result is a neutral gray (Figure 14.30). So there is a difference in the saturation of the various digital color systems, which can be rather confusing. But you can also choose to not care and just judge the outcome with your eye rather than be too technical about it.

The relationship between saturated and desaturated colors and their artistic and aesthetic effect:

- Saturated colors tend to be visually important and often step into the foreground and attract attention.
- Desaturated colors tend to be visually unimportant and often step into the background; however, a desaturated red will look much more vivid next to an even more desaturated red. So saturation in an image is relative from an artistic standpoint.
- Saturated colors can often create vibrant effects in their relationships; in particular, complementary colors have an intense vibrancy (Figure 14.32) where the border between the colors seems to move. The less saturated the colors are, the less this vibrancy is (Figures 14.32 and 14.33; because these two examples are printed on paper, the effect of their vibrancy is less dominant than if you replicated the color combinations in your computer and saw the effect on the screen, which would give you a higher vibrancy).
- If saturation is taken out of an image completely, the resulting image will just be black, white, and gray scale (also see Figures 14.32 and 14.33).
- Too many saturated colors can make the image look vibrant and exciting but can also break the image and it can look unreal and fake, even cheap.
- Certain colors suffer from a reduction of saturation. Where all saturated colors have a vibrancy and luminosity, they quickly

**Figure 14.31**

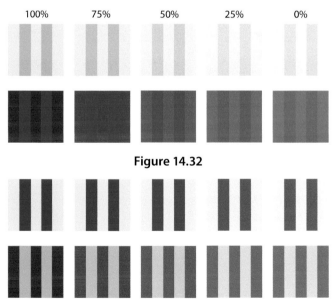

**Figure 14.32**

**Figure 14.33**

lose it when desaturated. Some colors, especially yellows, quickly lose their vibrancy and look dull or even dirty.

- Saturated colors look fresh, strong, new, and intense, whereas desaturated colors look aged, weak, and old.

Very saturated colors can often be found in medieval book illustrations, where the pure colors are shown off as precious and as a sign of wealth. The illustration of the Limbourg brothers (and additional work by Barthélemy d'Eyck and Jean Colombe) in the *Très Riches Heures du Duc de Berry* (~1412–1416) (Figure 14.31) shows the court of John, Duke of Berry, exchanging gifts with friends and dignitaries. The page is a calendar page for the month of January, and we see on the very right John himself in a blue coat, giving and receiving gifts. The ultramarine blue, for instance, one of the most expensive colors at the time, is just extraordinarily vibrant and draws most of the attention in the image. Ultramarine blue was derived from the mineral lapis lazuli, mostly mined in Afghanistan, which was ground into fine powder, mixed with binder, and then used for coloring. Not mixing the precious color with other colors or white released its full vibrancy and allowed this single color in the picture to shine and show the wealth of its principal, the Duke of Berry. Combined with painted gold, the effect is stunning when the illustration is seen in its original.

We have also seen at the beginning of this chapter in the section on Technicolor that Douglas Fairbanks opted for a desaturated color, slightly tinted sepia, in his feature *The Black Pirate* to achieve the look of old paintings and illustrations. So saturation has an impact on what is dragging attention in the image but also can affect the "style" and can make a color look young and fresh or aged and old.

## Value, lightness, and tone

*Value, lightness, and tone define how bright or dark a color appears, how much white or black is mixed into the color (Figure 14.34).*

When adding black or white to a color to change its brightness, the color's saturation also changes but not its hue (Figure 14.35). The hue, or where the color is located on the spectrum, stays the same (imagine a vertical line in example Figure 14.34: all the colors on that line have the same hue, as they originate from the same hue in the middle, shown by the black horizontal line, which contains all the different hues with full saturation; going north or south of that hue gives one brightness and darkness of the same hue).

More brightness in the overall image takes away the contrast between all the colors. For example, Claude Monet's painting *Ice Floes* (1893) (Figure 14.36) has only light colors with a very weak saturation and the faint hues can only be guessed at. The image shows the depth of winter where the freshness of spring and summer is completely absent. The colors are just various shades of white, which feels cold and distant, lacking life. The painting is rather light in its visual weight, meaning it "feels" like it weighs much less than the painting in Figure 14.37. Bright colors lack visual weight and feel washed out, weak, and also, like desaturated colors, tend to step backwards in an image, thus lacking visual

importance. Saturated colors and also dark colors in a rather light image would usually immediately draw attention to themselves. With contrast in the image, however, bright colors can also step forwards, like highlights or painted light sources in dark images.

Darker colors have more visual weight and create contrast when combined with bright colors. The two paintings of Monet next to each other with the earlier mentioned *Ice Floes* shows how the *Palazzo Contarini* (Figure 14.37) is much heavier in visual weight but also feels more real, has more substance, whereas *Ice Floes* feels distant and ethereal. What makes Monet's paintings generally so exciting is the interplay between the colors. The water is not just painted blue, but there is also cyan and purple in there and some darker green. This complex interplay between the colors makes them work with each other and interact, giving the

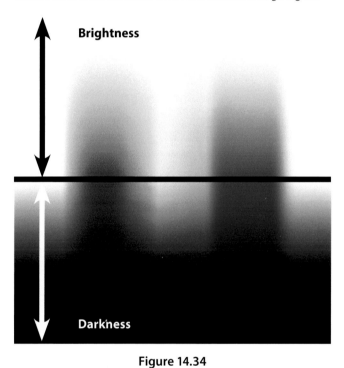

**Figure 14.34**

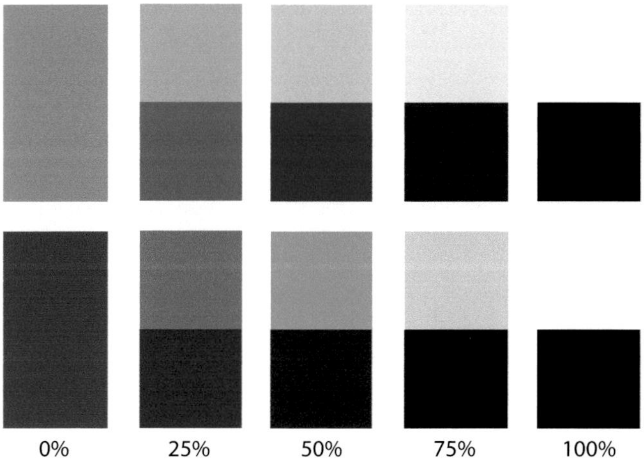

| 0% | 25% | 50% | 75% | 100% |

**Figure 14.35**

**Figure 14.36**

Claude Monet: *Ice Floes* (1893).

**Figure 14.37**

Claude Monet: *Palazzo Contarini* (1908).

surface a vibrancy and movement that a solid color cannot have (a fully saturated color has a very different vibrancy to it).

When painting with actual color, white and black will change the color dramatically when brightening or darkening it, and sometimes this effect is not wanted. Therefore, do use white and black sparsely and use other colors to brighten or darken with. For instance, adding white to a red to brighten it also takes away the warmth of red and lowers the saturation. Try adding orange or yellow to get a brighter red, thus maintaining its saturation.

## Luminance

Luminance is the perceived brightness of a color, how much light a color or an object emits, and how bright it appears to be (compared to *brightness*, which describes how much light a color/object receives). Every hue has its own luminance, which is related to white, with a luminance of 100. For example, blue is much less luminous than yellow (Figure 14.38). With a neutral gray (luminance of 50) in the middle, we can see that the blue is slightly less luminous, yet yellow is much more (90) (see Figure 14.39). Black has the least luminance with 0, and white, as mentioned, has the highest.

Desaturating the color has an impact on the luminance, if it is desaturated with a 50% gray. This means that a color very high in luminance, like yellow (90) would, if desaturated, lose luminance and slowly go towards that of the 50% gray (50). However, this can be prevented if the yellow is desaturated with a gray with the same luminance. The chart in Figure 14.39 gives an idea of the different luminance of the various colors. Some colors like red stay practically the same if desaturated with a medium gray; others, like blue and purple, gain luminance, because their luminance is lower than medium gray. Brightness affects all colors the same and increases their luminance as all colors go towards white; the same with darkening the colors, which lowers the luminance until it is zero, black.

Vincent van Gogh's painting *The Starry Night* (1889) (Figure 14.40) has the moon and stars and their aura seem to emit light. The yellow of the moon and stars is unmixed and has full saturation, which makes them appear warm; they shine and with the interplay of the less luminous blue surrounding their aura through their dynamic brush strokes develop a vibrancy in the painting. The contrast between the blue's and yellow's luminance support the glow.

Luminance is judged in paintings rather roughly, as there are so many colors interacting with each other and it would be tedious to go into every color and check them for their luminance. The eye is a sufficient judge!

**Figure 14.38**

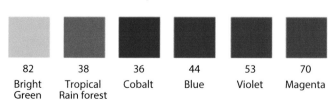

| 54 | 56 | 61 | 73 | 90 | 85 | 82 | 38 | 36 | 44 | 53 | 70 |
|---|---|---|---|---|---|---|---|---|---|---|---|
| Red | Coquelicot | Safety Orange | Chrome Yellow | Canary Yellow | Spring Bud | Bright Green | Tropical Rain forest | Cobalt | Blue | Violet | Magenta |

**Figure 14.39**

**Figure 14.40**

Vincent van Gogh: *The Starry Night* (1889).

## Temperature

Color also has a felt temperature, either feeling cold or warm. Simply spoken, warm colors are red, orange, and yellow; cold colors are green, purple, and blue. However, mixing cold and warm colors can result in warm blues or cold reds and oranges. Colors are on a sliding scale and there is much overlap, as can be seen in Figure 14.41, where the red is warm on the right when mixed with orange, yet cold towards the left when mixed with purple. Blue feels slightly warm with yellow but even colder with a bright blue. Warm colors tend to attract the eye, and cold colors have the tendency to step backwards in importance. This can be used for the composition by giving the focal point warm colors, for instance (of course, this depends on the story being told and the mood created, as the opposite can also work). Additionally, warm colors can feel closer and cold colors more distant, which can also be used in the composition to support depth.

However, this is only a tendency of the color to feel close or further away. In Figure 14.42, the warm color surrounds the characters, which gives the movement stability and puts focus onto the middle of the composition (from a color perspective) compared to the illustration in Figure 14.43, where the warm colors in the front of the running group additionally drag the

**Figure 14.41**

**Figure 14.42**

**Figure 14.43**

characters towards the right, enhancing the movement (the shape of the frame also accentuates the stability in Figure 14.42 and the movement in Figure 14.43).

In Van Gogh's painting *The Starry Night* (Figure 14.40), the moon itself is painted in a warm yellow; however, the glow of the moon is mixed slightly with blue, which causes the aura of the moon and stars to feel cold. There is more attraction to the shape of the moon, rather than the light it is surrounded with.

# Historical development of the color arrangements

Color is not an actual property of an object; it is part of human visual perception. What we call color is how humans see color and how color shapes our visual field, but it is by no means a universal truth. Color also does not have one common principle that fits all areas in society where color is used. Artists use color and how it works in a different way than physicists or chemists, printers or TV engineers do. Every group has their own description of color, which is true for their field but not necessarily for everyone else's. Additionally, it also depends on what kind of color is being used, oil or watercolor, felt pen or digital color in a computer. They all work differently and all that can make color an extremely confusing and complex topic that seems easy on the surface, but the deeper one digs the more tangled and convoluted it becomes.

To understand color one needs to first look into how color is formed and perceived; for this we need to go back to the rays of light and their interactions. The light with its full spectrum hits

an object's surface. The surface allows certain rays (with their specific color sensation) to be reflected and others not, which means for instance that a green apple only allows green rays to be reflected, but red, yellow, blue, and purple are absorbed. So our eyes can only see the color green, which makes the apple appear green. A red apple reflects only the color red; a white surface, like this paper, reflects the whole spectrum; but a black page would not allow any rays of the spectrum to reach our eyes, so it appears black because all the colors are absorbed.

Due to the vast number of colors a system needs to be in place to help with their arrangement; thus color models are needed to categorize and group colors, to make it easier to understand their relationships. Since Aristotle, scientists and artists have examined color and developed dozens of different systems that all try to control the endless amount of color possibilities within one system. Only some of the more important historical models shall be introduced here, as there are way too many to discuss them all.

## Newton's Color Theory (~1665)

Isaac Newton (1642–1726), an English scientist and mathematician, discovered the dispersion of white light via a prism into its various colors. The start of this would be the simple color spectrum, which places the hues next to each other: red–orange–yellow–green–cyan–blue–purple. The next step was to see the relationship between red and purple and connect the two, arranging the colors therefore on a circle, not a line. This started out with a simple color wheel, a two-dimensional representation of color where just the hue was displayed (Figure 14.44). This visualizes the main relationships between the colors, which ones are the primary colors that once mixed produce the rest of the spectrum. Two-dimensional wheels are limited in what they can show of the variety of color and cover only hue, or hue and saturation or hue and lightness.

## Goethe's Theory of Colors (1810)

Johann Wolfgang von Goethe, a German writer, poet, and art critic, arranged the colors in a two-dimensional circle; his theory was more a collection of phenomena rather than a theory. His wheel gives attributes and human traits to the colors, like yellow—"good," orange—"noble," red—"beautiful/fine," purple—"unnecessary," blue is "common," and green "useful" (see Figure 14.45). All six colors are also associated with the four human areas of spirit and emotional life: yellow and green are mind, green and blue are sensuality, purple and red fantasy, red and orange reason. This is a very different approach to Newton's, as Goethe's sees it not only from a scientific perspective but also an aesthetic one. However, not everything in his theory was convincing and only the "Physiological color" part received acclaim.

## Phillipp Otto Runge's Color Sphere (1810)

Both Newton's and Goethe's colors were arranged solely on a two-dimensional wheel, and its two-dimensional use lasted

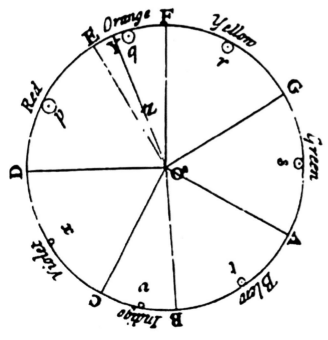

**Figure 14.44**

Isaac Newton's *Color circle* (1665).

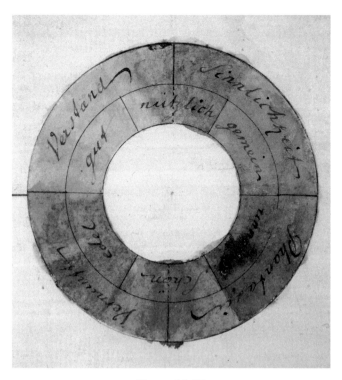

**Figure 14.45**

Johann Wolfgang Goethe's *Farbkreis/Color circle* (1810).

until 1810, when German painter Philipp Otto Runge proposed a sphere in which the colors were presented three-dimensionally, including all three properties of color (there have been many different forms proposed by others) (see Figure 14.46). Runge's sphere had the hues arranged around the equator and the sphere's axis had a gradient of gray, with its bottom black and its top white. Other systems followed, like Michel Eugène Chevreul's hemispherical system of 1839, for instance. Still, they all lacked one element, and then finally came the system that every modern color system and measurement is based on: the Munsell color system, introduced in 1905.

## Albert Henry Munsell's Munsell Color System (1905)

Albert Henry Munsell, an artist and color theorist, took one important step in his model: there are three properties in Munsell's system: hue—value—chroma. All three are arranged in a three-dimensional system that is not a globe but expands outwards depending on the human perception of the various colors. That means that not every color has the same horizontal growth in chroma as other colors. The human eye does not recognize all colors equally but is more receptive, for instance, to the differences between purples and reds than it is to the variations in green.

Hue in Munsell's system is easy: the actual color, red, yellow, purple, etc., is displayed in the system in concentric circles

(see Figure 14.47 and 14.48). What Munsell calls "value," which is displayed vertically, consists of the relationship between brightness and lightness. The distinction between brightness and lightness takes into consideration human perception and the theory that we see objects based on their lightness rather than their brightness. Brightness is the absolute perception of the amount of light, whereas lightness is the relative brightness of an object. The color of an object is seen relative to the brightness of another object that appears white under the same lighting situation. A white paper will appear white to the human eye under strong sunlight but will also appear white in the shadow. It is a different white, but nevertheless our eye recognizes it as white and puts everything else in relationship to that white.

> A typical newspaper, when read indoors, has a certain brightness and lightness. When viewed side by side with standard office paper, the newsprint often looks slightly gray, while the office paper appears white (the newsprint appears darker than the office paper because it has a lower lightness). The amount of light reflected from the newsprint outdoors might be more than a hundred times greater than the office paper was indoors, yet the relative amount of light reflected when comparing the two has not changed with the change in illumination. Thus the difference in brightness between the two papers, or their lightness, has not changed. The Munsell value scale is a scale of lightness.[8]

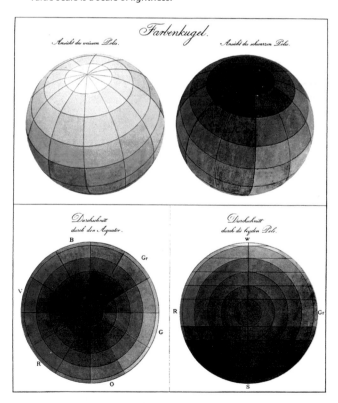

**Figure 14.46**

Phillipp Otto Runge's *Farbenkugel/Colour sphere* (1810).

---

8   Edward R. Landa and Mark D. Fairchild, Charting Color from the Eye of the Beholder, *American Scientist*, 2005, Vol. 93, p. 440.

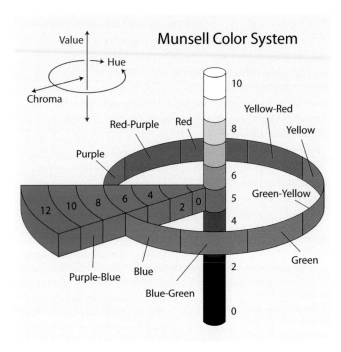

**Figure 14.47**

*Munsell Color System* (Courtesy of Wikimedia Commons, https://upload.wikimedia.org/
wikipedia/commons/d/d5/Munsell-system.svg).

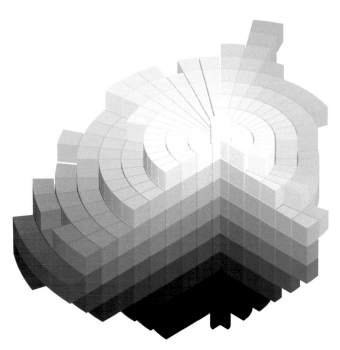

**Figure 14.48**

Albert Henry Munsell's *Munsell Color System* (Courtesy of Wikimedia Commons,
https://commons.wikimedia.org/wiki/File:Munsell_1929_color_solid_cylindrical_
coordinates.png).

He also realized that what was earlier called "saturation or colorfulness" was actually more than just that: saturation also changed under different lighting situations and needed to be explained and refined as brightness and lightness had. So Munsell introduced "chroma" as the third color property and displayed it in his system horizontally. Chroma is the difference of an object's color from that of a neutral gray under the same lighting situation. Colorfulness/saturation is an absolute perception; chroma always relates to a neutral gray. A red pen will look more vibrant under sunlight compared to the same pen indoors with lower light, which results in the same pen looking more muted. However, its chroma is about the same in both lighting situations, outdoors and indoors.

In Munsell's color system, all colors are arranged in a globe-like structure: the further one goes upwards to the "north pole," the brighter the color is; the further to the south pole, the darker the color is. The various hues and also the strongest saturation of the color is around the equator and gets less vibrant towards the globe's core. The Munsell system allows a very accurate standardization of color and is widely used as such.

Contemporary color systems are mostly based on Munsell's system, like the CIELAB system from 1976, based on Richard Hunter's color system Lab from 1948 (based on yet another system … it just never ends). In the Lab system, the colors are arranged in a cube and with four horizontal directions of the cube being assigned to red and green, represented by the letter *a*, and blue and yellow by the letter *b*. The letter *L* is assigned to the lightness of the color. The Lab system is device independent and used for translating color information of RGB and CMYK into a system that contains both, as Lab has the widest range of colors.

## Subtractive and additive color

The colors that can be mixed with each other on a canvas or paper or that can be printed belong to a subtractive color model (Figure 14.49). The colors for printing are applied in three main colors: red—blue—yellow (or today in magenta—cyan—yellow).

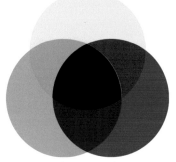

Subtractive color

**Figure 14.49**

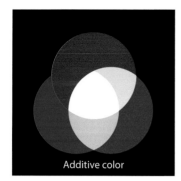

**Figure 14.50**

Through overlap the light is subtracted and certain wavelengths are filtered out, resulting in additional colors. Blue and yellow overlapping create green, for instance. All three main colors overlapping create black, which can be seen in the middle.

Where subtractive color deals with actual paint, additive color (Figure 14.50) is produced by light or by the rapid succession of two or more colors (for instance, yellow and blue on a spinning wheel mixing into green). Additive color is produced in digital screens, digital photography, and television, where three different electrodes release red, blue, and green light and mixed proportionally produce the secondaries of magenta, yellow, and cyan. The overlap of all three colors produces white.

# RYB, CYK, RGB and color mixing

The RYB color wheel has red, yellow, and blue as the main colors, which are called the "primaries." They are the three colors from which all other colors can be mixed. Mixing the primaries with each other results in the secondaries: red + yellow = orange; yellow + blue = green; blue + red = violet. Mixing the secondaries with the primaries results in the tertiaries (see Figure 14.51).

What color *is* a primary color, however, depends on the color model that is used. There are usually three kinds of color models, each of which already have the primaries in their names.

- **RYB: Red Yellow Blue**
  This subtractive color model is used in printing and painting (see Figure 14.52).
- **RGB: Red Green Blue**
  This additive color model for display purposes of television and digital screens mimics the human perception the closest, as the human eye also has three receptors for red, green, and blue (Figure 14.53).
- **CMYK: Cyan Magenta Yellow Key (= Black)**
  This is a subtractive color model for printing (Figure 14.54).

We can see that RYB and CMYK are both subtractive color models, whereas RGB is an additive color model, for digital applications.

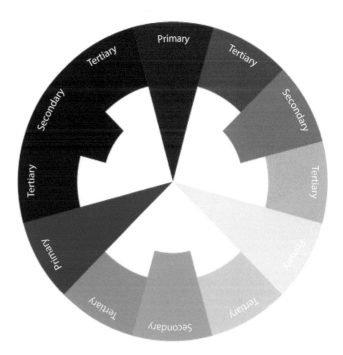

**Figure 14.51**

# PANTONE colors

In the mid-1950s a system was developed by the company PANTONE to refer to colors with a name and number in a chromatic arrangement that allows the matching of colors. The system is widely used for printing. Over 1,000 colors are printed in catalogues and each is given a name. This catalogue, owned by designer and printer, makes it possible for a color being, through comparison with the catalogue, named and correctly printed, as both designer and printer have the exact color in their catalogue. In 2007 Pantone started with a new color system called the *PANTONE Goe System*, which has 2,058 chromatically arranged solid colors, nearly twice as many as the older PANTONE system.

# Color harmony

This is a vast topic that is just bound to be difficult and nightmarishly confusing, because it has elements in it based on taste and subjective appeal and is endless in its scope. Myriads of books and treatises have been written on color harmony and aesthetics, and they all make sense in their own little universe, but once one has accepted and understood one harmony, the next one already proves its invalidity and suggests another theory that is also convincing in its own realm. Is there a common direction in what "looks good" and what does not? Is or should there be a rule of how to combine colors that then always look pleasant? What I find personally pleasant and original as a combination of colors today, I might find in 10 years banal and pedestrian, because a prolonged exposure to certain color combinations will obviously take away

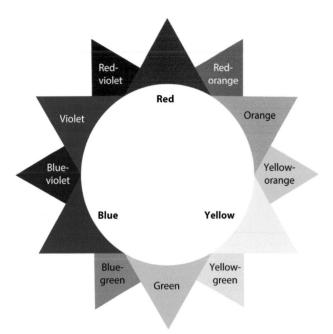

**RYB (red-yellow-blue) color wheel**

This is the oldest of all the color wheels and thus the one that is the most well known. It is used primarily for painting, graphic design and art-education and for the use for painted color; oil-, water-, acrylic-color that consist of pigments or dyes. The RYB wheel is a subtractive color system that pre-dates modern color science, which shifted the primaries to magenta, cyan and yellow, instead of RYB having red, yellow and blue as the primaries. However it is still in wide practical use in painting as painters don't really use magenta, cyan and yellow for mixing colors for canvases. Those three colors are for printing rather than painting. Paint comes in different colors and only because color-theory teaches us that yellow and blue result in green does not mean that this always works with pigments that are in a tube. It depends on which pigment is used and in what percentage the colors maintain their qualities. Therefore painters need to figure out for themselves what is the right mix to get the results they need.

**Figure 14.52**

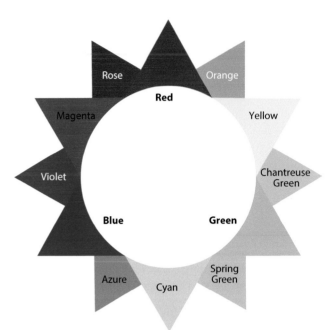

**RGB (red-green-blue) color wheel.**

This model is an additive one which is used in digital technology. The RGB color model arranges all the colors in three-mensional system in form of a cube with red, green and blue (RGB) being the corners of the cube. Red is the x-axis, green the z-axis and blue the y-axis. This color system is widely used for digital cameras and computer graphics.

**HSL and HSV mode**

Both systems are a three-dimensional representation of the RGB system, arranging the three color attributes in a cy- lindrical form. Hue is on the outside of the cylinder, going towards the center the saturation is reduced; the vertical ar- rangement is lightness in HSL and value in HSV/HSB.
**HSL**: Hue, saturation and lightness.
**HSV or HSB**: Hue, saturation and value (or brightness).

**Figure 14.53**

their initial excitement. The problem already arises in defining what the purpose of the color harmony is: fine art, comics, interior design, architecture, graphic design, illustration, images that render realism, images that avoid realism, abstract art, sculpture, photography, paintings, animation … each individual field approaches color from a slightly different perspective. Do I see color in a psychological, mathematical, philosophical, physical, art historical, chemical, historical, social, perceptive, commercial, or artistic context? It's indeed a bit of a pickle. Nevertheless, does this mean that anything goes and it's all just up to the artist to knock themselves out with the craziest combinations of color? Yes and no, because it always depends on how it's done. There are two different viewpoints on color harmony: the scientist's and the artist's (and yes, they do

overlap sometimes). The scientist tries to find a logic in the use of colors, explores it from every angle to find its laws and rules, the mathematical, physical, chemical explanation of color. Then there is the visual perception of color and how the viewer reacts to it, sees it, experiences it, and finally understands it. The artist, on the other hand, wants to create something new and unique, so laws can be followed closely or are only there to be broken or not cared for at all, to express a unique perspective.

The artistic exploration of color harmony is not an easy one because it is based on subjectivity in much of its field. Many color harmonies have been written over the years and it is impossible to claim one is better than the other, as it depends on one's own

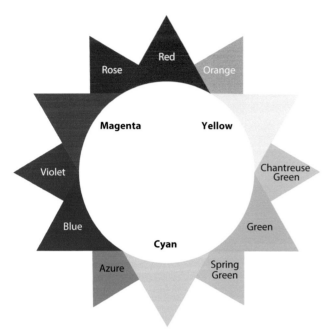

**CMY (cyan-magenta-yellow) color wheel**

This color wheel is also a subtractive model which is used mainly for printing. The CMY color wheel is very similar to the RYB color wheel, the only difference is that its primaries are magenta, yellow and cyan. The intensity of the cyan and magenta make the colors more intense in their printed and digital form. For the actual printing the CMY model has K added for 'key', which is black, resulting in CMYK.

**Figure 14.54**

preference which aesthetic is the right one. However, there are some that Kenneth E. Burchett mentions.[99]

What I personally find helpful, because it is straightforward and easily allows personal exploration, are Johannes Itten's seven contrasts of color, which are the most simple yet practical suggestions of what color can do (the following is a reduced version of Itten's explanations, which can be read in his book *The Art of Color*). Those seven contrasts are not rules or laws; they just describe the tensions between colors and how they react to each other. There is no guideline for how to use them, which keeps it open to the artist to play with those contrasts creatively.

**More books on color:**

Augusto Garay, *Color Harmonies*, (N. Bruno, Trans.). University of Chicago Press, Chicago, IL, 1993.

Lois Swirnoff, *Dimensional Color*, (2nd ed.). Norton, New York, 2003.

Karl Gerstner, *The Forms of Color: The Interaction of Visual Elements*, (D. Q. Stephenson, Trans.). MIT Press, Cambridge, MA, 1986. (Original work published as Die Formen der Farben).

Zelanski, Paul J., & Fisher, Mary Pat, *Color*, (4th ed.). Prentice-Hall, Upper Saddle River, NJ, 2003.

Becky Koenig, *Color Workbook*, Pearson Education, Upper Saddle River, NJ, 2003.

Hazel Rossotti, *Color. Why the World isn't Gray*, Princeton University Press, Princeton, NJ, 1985.

---

9   Kenneth E. Burchett, *A Bibliographical History of the Study and Use of Color from Aristotle to Kandinsky*, The Edwin Mellen Press, Lewiston, NY, 2005.

# Itten's seven contrasts[10]

- 1. Contrast of pure color
- 2. Contrast of warm and cold colors
- 3. Simultaneous contrast
- 4. Contrast of proportion
- 5. Contrast of light and dark
- 6. Contrast of complimentary colors
- 7. Contrast of color quality

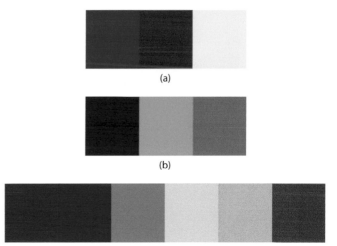

(a)

(b)

(c)

**Figure 14.55**

## 1. Contrast of pure color

Two colors of various hues contrast each other. The strongest contrast between three colors is between the primaries, red, blue, and yellow (Figure 14.55a); between two colors it is the complementary colors that have the strongest tension, which also is the most colorful. The tension decreases in the secondaries (Figure 14.55b) and again in the tertiaries (Figure 14.55c). So blue—red—yellow have the strongest tension in three colors, blue and yellow as complementaries for two colors, whereas colors that rest closer to each other have less tension. Also see how Itten's Farbkreis (Figure 14.62) reflects this contrast clearly.

**Figure 14.56**

## 2. Contrast of warm and cold colors

Colors can also be categorized into two groups: cold and warm colors. Cold colors are blue, purple, and green, whereas red, orange, and yellow count as warm colors. However, blue can also be warm and red cold depending on what color is mixed in. If a hint of blue is mixed into yellow, the yellow starts to feel cold; a blue that is slightly mixed with orange can feel warm (this obviously depends on what kind of warm and cold color is mixed; this does not work equally in every case). The example in Figure 14.56 shows that red feels still warm with orange, but does not feel as warm with purple. Cyan, a cold color, feels warmer with a hint of orange but even colder with a bright blue. The contrast between warm and cold can be subtle yet still very effective.

Warm colors also have the tendency to attract the eye and drag the attention in a composition.

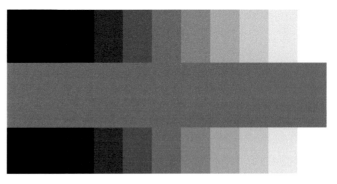

**Figure 14.57**

## 3. Simultaneous contrast

Michel Eugène Chevreul was the first to explain simultaneous contrast as an optical phenomenon between colors. Two colors will affect each other's appearance in hue, saturation, and value if they are in close proximity. In the example with the gray fields (Figure 14.57), the neutral gray band feels brighter when surrounded by dark tones and darker when surrounded by brighter tones. When color is introduced, the

[10] Johannes Itten, *The Art of Color: The Subjective Experience and Objective Rationale of Color*, Van Nostrand Reinhold, New York, 1973.

eye is exposed to different stimuli at the same time in the form of colors next to each other; their relationship will be tinted by their complementary color. The example in Figure 14.58 shows that the red band feels slightly more blue towards the orange and more yellow towards the violet. The red in Figure 14.59 is more violet towards the yellow and more orange towards the blue. (The simultaneous contrast can be experienced only when exposing the eye to a clear stimuli without much distraction. To fully experience it, keep your eyes very close to the example and focus or replicate the example on a digital screen.) Now compare the two red stripes in Figures 14.58 and 14.59 with each other. Are they perceived as being slightly different?

A color can never stand on its own, because it is always surrounded by other colors and thus is affected by them. What we see in all the other design aspects, where the size of an object changes depending on the size of the object next to it, or light changes its intensity if the shadow next to it changes its darkness, the same is true for color. This effect has to be taken into consideration when painting: every color that is put onto the canvas will affect the look of the whole image. Therefore, the colors have to always be adjusted to every new color that appears on the canvas. For instance, the warmth of a red influences the temperature of the whole. This can have a major impact onto the picture or be a very subtle difference but significant enough to be relevant in a painting.

## 4. Contrast of proportion

How much of a color is present in an image also has an impact on the overall tension or balance. Two properties contribute to it: the size of the color and its luminance. The higher the luminance, the less color is needed to have an impact. For example, in a combination of blue and yellow: in order to create a balance between the two, much less yellow needs to stand next to more blue to be balanced. Figure 14.60a is after Itten the aesthetically pleasing relationship between yellow and blue, whereas Figure 14.60b would be out of balance as there is too much yellow.

## 5. Contrast of light and dark

This is a very important contrast, as it gives the image depth and form and assists in separating elements from each other. No contrast in light and dark makes an image feel flat and plain and it lacks a focal point. Figure 14.61a feels light in its weight, whereas adding darkness gives tension and also adds weight (Figure 14.61b). The blue squares immediately drag attention and the eye goes straight towards them. However, in an image with mostly dark colors, the light ones will stand out.

This does not include all images, as we have already seen in Monet's painting *Ice Floes* in Figure 14.36, where there is barely any contrast at all, but this is the very point of the image.

Figure 14.58

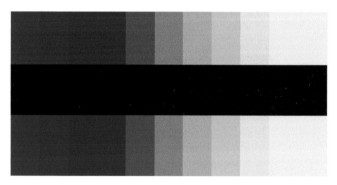

Figure 14.59

(a)

(b)

Figure 14.60

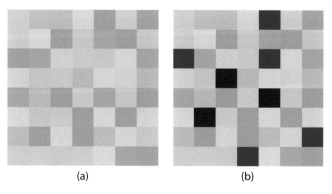

(a)                    (b)

Figure 14.61

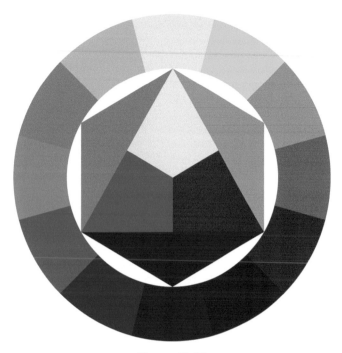

**Figure 14.62**

Johannes Itten: *Farbkreis/colour wheel* (1961).

**Figure 14.63**

## 6. Contrast of complementary colors

Complementary colors are colors that oppose each other on the color wheel. That means that it depends on the color wheel used which colors actually do rest across from each other. For the RYB color wheel, red is complementary to green, orange to blue, yellow to violet in its primaries. One can also use Itten's color circle or "Farbkreis" (Figure 14.62), developed in 1961, which includes the three primaries of red, yellow, and blue in the middle. The mixed primaries result in the secondaries of orange, purple, and green, which then lead to the full color circle with the additional tertiaries. What is significant to note is that in Itten's Farbkreis the colors are arranged in order of luminance: yellow with its high luminance is on top and then further down are the colors with less luminance. This color circle is one that also has found a wide distribution in painting due to its simplicity.

Complementary colors, as the name says, "complement" each other, meaning they will produce a neutral gray if mixed equally and only if they are truly complementary. The four digital examples in Figure 14.63 show that mixing yellow with blue does create a color that is closer to neutral gray, as does mixing red and cyan, magenta and green. Red and purple, however, do not create neutral gray, because they are not complementary to each other (you also will get a neutral gray if the primaries are mixed equally; however, with actual paint it isn't as easy, as some colors are rather strong and easily overpower every other color, so the percentage might change). Complementary colors also have the strongest tension between each other, because they are the furthest apart on the color wheel.

## 7. Contrast of color quality

This is the contrast of the quality of the color, which includes changes in saturation. Colors that are desaturated can appear saturated on their own but appear desaturated next to saturated colors. Saturation is therefore only detectable by the eye in relationship with other colors.

Johannes Itten, *The Elements of Color*, Van Nostrand Reinhold Company, New York, 1971.

# Practical application

Separation and connection of color

Perspective and depth

Color and focal point

## Separation and connection through color

A pile of spaghetti in the sand of the Sahara is difficult to see; a pile of spaghetti with tomato sauce in the sand of the Sahara is a very different matter! Thus one option for color is to distinguish elements from each other so that they separate and do not connect or blend into each other. The colors should be contrasting enough to render the object different from its surroundings (or do the opposite, depending on the need in the image). With the three aspects of color, saturation, brightness, and hue, the colors can either not bring a specific element forward, like in Figure 14.64a, where the monochromatic image does not allow any element to be the actual focal point from a color perspective; background and foreground seem to be on the same or a similar level (don't think about the overlap, but just the color). This creates a rather calm and quiet design. In Figure 14.64b, there is so much going on that every color begs for attention and the eye does not really know where to look at. This creates tension and is visually rather loud. The third possibility in Figure 14.64c allows only one element in the composition to step forward and therefore be the focal point. The pink flower pot is dragging attention because it is lighter, warmer, and more saturated than its surroundings but also just different in its hue than all the other colors. The fourth option is to group specific parts of the image together via color and connect them like in Figure 14.64d, where the purple color of the two flower pots connects the two clearly (remember the gestalt theory in Chapter 5, "Composition").

How are these rules now implemented in a painting (see Figure 14.65)?

- The main point in using color from a technical perspective is to either separate elements from or connect them with each other. For instance, by placing the shadow of the sitting policeman in the middle of Figure 14.65 behind the man's half cup, the contrast between foreground and background is increased, which then makes this part a strong focal point within the composition. The bright colors of the cup are much brighter in front of a darker background.
- The foreground character is more saturated than the poster behind him.
- The poster is brighter and desaturated to show an older print.
- The darkness of the policeman's outfit makes him stand out from the brighter background, pushing him forward in this color relationship.
- All colors separate where it is important and do not where there is/should be no focus (the flowers on the poster

(a)

(b)

(c)

(d)

**Figure 14.64**

aren't crucial to the story, so their importance is lowered by "blending" them into the background, reducing their contrast).
- Warm colors in the character; cold colors in the poster.
- Simultaneous contrast: provide a range of colors that derive from the whole spectrum, not just a few (if it does not conflict with the mood).

**Figure 14.65**

(a)

(b)

**Figure 14.66**

- Contrast of color quality: the foreground is saturated and bright, the background slightly less so.
- Contrast of light and dark is especially strong in the face, which is the focal point of the image.

## Perspective and depth

We have seen in Chapter 13 in the Section "Airlight" that colors change depending on the distance to the viewer. The further away the object is, the less saturation it has, the brighter it is during the day and the more it is affected by the color of the radiant flux. However, this is a natural observation, not an artistic "must." Obviously color can be played with and explored creatively.

What works in a vast landscape that has huge distances where airlight actually has an impact can also be used on a small scale to suggest distance via airlight where there technically is none or at least none that the eye can see. Figure 14.66a and b show how the change in color and contrast affects the position of the object relative to the viewer. The airlight is obviously exaggerated, but in a room situation a slight change in color perspective can have a significant effect, as we have seen in Figure 14.65 with the difference of foreground character and background poster. An increase of airlight in short distances is often also used when characters are miniscule or to create a certain mood.

## Color and focal point

The following examples give options for how color can be used in a practical way to enhance composition and narrative. Its focal point can be supported by:

- Warm and cold colors (Figure 14.67a): the orange pot clearly steps forward.
- Saturated/desaturated (Figure 14.67b): the purple pot again steps forward (this is probably less pronounced in the printed version of the book).
- Bright and dark (Figure 14.67c): again the purple pot is the focus.
- Light and shadow (Figure 14.67d): the purple pot is in the light, thus marking the focal point in this composition (however, if only the pot were in shadow, it could also become the focal point because of its "otherness").

(a) Warm and cold

(b) Saturated and desaturated

(c) Bright and dark

(d) Light & shadow

**Figure 14.67**

# Options for the artistic use of color:

Be subjective

Support a style

Support the mood

Avoid or enhance realism

Create a harmonious whole

Use of color concept and color composition

Use of color sketches

Use of a color bible/ color script

## Be subjective

Color does not have to be "realistic" in order for the image to read or for the content to be understandable. As always, there is the artistic freedom of doing whatever the artist wants to explore. Color can be interpreted from a very personal point of view to express a subjective angle, which is of course a valid direction. Whether it works or does not, whether it expresses the goal and purpose of the piece is ultimately also a subjective reaction from the audience to either accept it or not. Image making and with it film should also challenge the audience aesthetically and not just please. However, the more realistic the image needs to be, the more it needs to obviously adhere to the rules of optics and color.

## Support a style

Certain color combinations can be part of a style. Every decade has its own color aesthetics and one can clearly distinguish a 1960s color sense from a 1970s one. There is the possibility to use color in supporting an entire time frame if this is part of the overall concept of the piece. Using a famous piece of art, for instance, and taking its color direction to guide the color design of the entire project is a possibility to give the film a congruent color style. Also every era has its own color aesthetic. What was in vogue 10 years ago seems a bit old-fashioned today. There are many ways of interpreting color and every new decade has a different sensibility for it, which is affected by what the artist is/ was influenced by politically, socially, artistically, and of course his or her own congenital color sensibility.

Wes Anderson's films are very distinct in their sense of narrative and color. The films express a childlike optimism in which the problems of the adult world exist but the characters are always dealing with them in a playful fashion, are a bit odd, a bit eccentric, and themselves, like the backgrounds and sets, stylized. The colors support this direction gleefully. *The Life Aquatic with Steve Zissou* (2004) or *The Grand Budapest Hotel* (2014) play with color design that is so grandly exaggerated that it pushes the

**Figure 14.68**

*Laika's: Coraline* (2009)

film into a kind of contemporary fairy tale for ingenuous adults in a forgotten film from the 1960s or 1970s. Anderson's films reference design mostly from the mid-twentieth century and recollect Jaques Tati and the stylish artificiality of many sets in Tati's *My Uncle* (1950), *Playtime* (1967), and *Traffic* (1971). Color is obviously just one element of the design of Anderson's films; he also is very keen on using strong symmetrical compositions or miniature sets. The overall feel is of a cosmos of its own. The color palettes have a strong impact through a wide range of pastels in *Moonrise Kingdom* (2012) or a heavy use of blues and turquoise in *The Life Aquatic with Steve Zissou*; a light rose and heavy purple in *The Grand Budapest Hotel*. Precisely because the style does not recreate the present but artistically interprets the past in a stylized fashion, Anderson's films do not recreate an exact time frame or place; they are rather ambiguous even when they state a specific time frame like *The Royal Tenenbaums* (2001). The audience can bathe a little bit in nostalgia with innocent enthusiasm.

## Support the mood

Figure 14.68 shows a screenshot of Laika's *Coraline* (2009): an overcast sky tinted gray. The sunlight does not break through the clouds, which desaturates the landscape and gives it a melancholy that expresses the story point of Coraline just having moved into the new house, which is seemingly boring, plain, and depressing. On a cloudy day, the shadows are blurry and the contrast is reduced between shadow and light; the color's quality is clearly associated with the weather condition. In the second image (Figure 14.69), modest sunlight gives all the colors' hues a shift towards yellow and orange, a marginally warmer, more comfortable, and friendly color scheme. The slightly stronger saturation, due to the sunlight not being filtered and tinted by clouds, results in a happier color mood. The house is inviting and

more jovial than in the previous image, where the melancholy could not be evaded. Because weather has such a huge impact on the lighting and thus on the color in the outdoors (and partially indoors), it always needs to be in relationship with the narrative and chosen rightly for its effect and impact.

However, this is obviously only one side of the coin; the other side is a mood that is not based on reality and where the intuition of the artist paints a mood that hopefully expresses the emotion needed.

## Avoid or enhance realism

Color is also a strong contributor towards or against more realism. A green sky would obviously immediately evoke either an otherworldly feel or render the environment strange, odd, different, cartoony, unreal. There are two options for how colors can be used in images: representationally and nonrepresentationally. Representational color depicts objects the way we see them in a realistic and natural way and therefore support realism; nonrepresentational colors depict objects in an unrealistic fashion and play with color artistically and usually subjectively. Representational color was used for instance in Disney's *Lion King* in most of its scenes; nonrepresentational color was used for instance in UPA's *Gerald McBoing-Boing*. Disney's *Hercules* has many backgrounds that have highly exaggerated and stylized colors next to more representational ones, which supports its cartooniness. However, this needs to go along with all the other aspects of design; otherwise it will just look wrong. If all colors are nonrepresentational then the entire place can look strange, surreal, illustrative.

## Create a harmonious whole

In order for an image to not appear cluttered with colors, they need to be arranged in a color composition, where all the colors

**Figure 14.69**

Laika's: *Coraline* (2009).

either have importance when they support the focal point or lack importance for the opposite. The arrangement assists in structuring the image, improves the overall composition, adds perspective, strengthens the focal point, and thus enhances the clarity of the image. The grouping and arrangement of certain colors into areas of importance keeps the image from nervousness and provides order and easy readability. This would be the color harmony in the image, where the colors are part of a pleasant whole. However, not every color design needs to be harmonious, as this depends on the concept of the piece and its emotional and artistic goal. Because color is not always objective, certain color combinations are pleasant for one viewer and unpleasant for another. Balancing out the colors with each other and having a concept of the use of the colors (that also follows, for example, Itten's seven contrasts of color or any other color theory or harmony) creates a pleasant image where every color has a purpose that supports the overall aesthetic quality of the design. If the narrative requires an uncomfortable mood, a lack of color harmony can support that.

## Use of color concept and color composition

Learning to use color is a process and as the pioneers of color film had to learn from scratch how to use their technology for aesthetics and storytelling in their movies, so students have to learn what color can achieve and how to use it creatively with their own sensibility. Color should not just be used to fill the frame or finish the design but should be used with care and thought. How all the colors are arranged and how they interact with each other is important insofar as it prevents the image from being cluttered and all over the place, but it also assists the development of the story over the time period of the film. To arrange the colors accordingly and successfully, there is the need for a color concept and a color composition. Both share some points but are disparate in their responsibilities.

Where the color concept is the intellectual approach in relationship to the narrative, meaning, message, or theme, the color composition focuses more on the individual set, shot, and scene and their impact.

## Color concept

The color concept visualizes the development of the overall color throughout the duration of the film and its relationship to the narrative. The purposes for it are as follows:

- To create an overall mood for the film; this is not about the mood of the scenes and sets, but an overarching mood. For example, Disney's *Lilo and Stitch*'s general direction for the color is saturated and bright, reflecting a happy and positive world in Hawaii; Pixar's *Up* is generally also saturated and bright, with colors that express excitement, although some scenes are darker and desaturated. The last instalments of the *Harry Potter* series are very desaturated and often tinted bluish to further push the feeling of dread.
- To allow the narrative and the story arc to be interpreted through color.
- To support an overall style, historical setting, time frame, or fashion sense.
- To develop color metaphors/symbolisms that work for the entire feature.
- To create a color bible, color script (see below).

For instance, Tim Burton's *Corpse Bride* (2005) has the world of the dead in bright colors, which expresses happiness and joie de vivre; the world of the living is the exact opposite and has a desaturated sense of color, which reflects a lack of life, a restrained social construct with a negative Weltanschauung. This color concept is then refined for the overall story arc and how the color might change throughout the feature, then additionally considered in its impact on the various scenes of the film. Color in the concept has a narrative meaning and also a metaphorical and overarching arc.

## Color composition

The color composition, on the other hand, deals with how the color affects the composition of the various sets in the film and/or the individual shots or scenes. Which color within the set and characters should dominate to support the composition? What kind of color should be used for a certain narrative effect? These decisions deal with the technical and artistic effects of the color rather than the meaning of it (but obviously the meaning always has an impact on the technical side of the composition, too).

For the color composition in each shot/scene to work, the following points need to be kept in mind:

- What or who is the focal point?
- What should be pushed forward, what backward through color?
- Does the color support perspective, depth, and contrast?
- Which area attracts attention first?
- Does the character separate from the background?
- Does the character read within the environment?
- Do the colors serve as vectors for the focal point?
- Do all the colors support mood, weather condition, and lighting situation?

**Figure 14.70**

## Use of color sketches/color thumbnails

Color sketches are the foundation for every painted image (Figure 14.70). Like thumbnail drawings, color thumbnails are essential for the process in *finding* the right mood for the image. The emphasis is on the word *finding*! It is not about just doing it and painting one color sketch, but exploring the color possibilities, allowing all options to be considered, and then picking the one that fits the direction of the piece. As mentioned in the section on thumbnail drawings, small color sketches reduce the complexity of the innumerable color decisions that have to be made during the painting process of the final piece and allow an overview of the entire image on a small scale. It makes it much easier to arrange the important colors in an order. Small scales force the eye towards the overall color composition of the entire frame instead of getting lost in the details. Every image has to have a color organization that assigns all colors their place and purpose within the composition. The color thumbnail needs to express the mood of the final image

with the lighting situation, which has to be clearly expressed. The size of color thumbnails depends on the artist's preference and can range from miniscule frames of 1 cm in length to 10 cm. A bigger size would defeat the purpose of a color thumbnail.

## Use of color bible/color script

Natalie Kalmus, the color consultant and color supervisor for all Technicolor processed films from 1934 to 1949, wrote in 1935 about the awareness of color in her article "Color Consciousness," concerning the effect color has on the audience. In early color films, Technicolor was already considering the impact of color mood on the story and thus its dramatic effect. Kalmus writes:

> In the preparation of a picture we read the script and prepare a color chart for the entire production, each scene, sequence, set, and character being considered. This chart may be compared to a musical score, and amplifies the picture in a similar manner. The preparation of this chart calls for careful and judicious work. Subtle effects of beauty and feeling are not attained through haphazard methods, but through application of the rules of art and the physical laws of light and color in relation to literary laws and story values … When we receive the script for a new film, we carefully analyze each sequence and scene to ascertain what dominant mood or emotion is to be expressed. When this is decided, we plan to use the appropriate color or set of colors which will suggest that mood, thus actually fitting the color to the scene and augmenting its dramatic value.[11]

The Technicolor company used a method of evaluating each scene in its emotional impact and had a representational color for each scene. This seemingly logical procedure unfortunately led to many directors being rather annoyed by Natalie Kalmus, as she felt that her decision of what fit the mood and what did not was to be strictly followed, because she was not only the authority on color but also the representative of Technicolor. However, the directors did not want anyone telling them what was possible in color and what was not, despite it being in the beginning a new and rather unexplored asset to the production of movies.

Walt Disney was the first to land a contract with Technicolor's three-strip full-color process and produced the first full-color animated short *Flowers and Trees* in 1932. That color from then on had a major impact on Disney's shorts was to be expected, as he saw the public's reaction to his first colored short, which was more than positive. It received an Academy Award in 1932 in a newly created category for animated short subject. Disney from then on produced all *Silly Symphonies* in Technicolor. The most famous character of Disney's universe at the time, Mickey Mouse,

---

[11] Natalie M. Kalmus, Color Consciousness, *Journal of the Society of Motion Picture Engineers*, Vol. 25 (1935), pp. 139–147.

had his shorts produced in color from 1935 on, with *The Band Concert* being the first one. In the early years of colored short films, color is used as representational instead of emotional color. The gradual change of the use of color throughout the 1930s in Disney's short films can be clearly traced. What is impressive in the company's output throughout the 1930s is the continuous improvement that can be seen from short film to short film. The early shorts are concerned about learning the process and understanding what color can do for a film. Very visible changes came in the mid-1930s, when dramatic impact was explored in order to prepare the field for their first feature film *Snow White and the Seven Dwarfs*. Attention was given to the emotional effects that color can have on various scenes. One of those short films was *Three Orphan Kittens* from 1935, which has more visual depth compared to the shorts from just a year before. The image looks richer and has more weight exactly because there is a more thoughtful use of color. *Three Orphan Kittens* has more contrast in the colors than any of the shorts that precede it. The color is still representational; nevertheless this would not change for quite a while. In the early Disney features the artists, because of the groundwork they had done on the shorts, were more and more aware of color and emotion being tied together, and they created scenes that represented perfectly the mood through color instead of representing a mere semirealistic situation. *Snow White* was a huge leap forward, made possible by the experimentation in the short films. The mood was developed through color, composition, animation, and the extensive use of dramatic light and shadow. Another step after *Snow White*'s premiere was the short film *Ferdinand the Bull* from 1938. Former animator Ken Anderson was at that point art-directing the short and said about the development of the rich colors in the backgrounds:

> I went to Europe and I was just slayed by the beautiful colours and the beautiful architecture and the people and everything particularly in Spain. The hot colors and here was a chance on a new picture, it was *Ferdinand the Bull*, it was in Spain to really have some color in it. Prior to this time it was uneconomical and actually the word was out that Walt didn't want any painting he wanted tints so that he could unroll a long roll of paper and just put blue tints for the sky and no matter where the character went they were going to read. Spain was a hot country, had reflective lights and the light bounced off the ground even in the shadow and showed under the areas and shadows and it was hot color hot country; it should be painted. So to do what I was proposing to do you had to carefully make sure that where ever these characters went they worked with these paintings if we can paint these backgrounds. Well, the head of the background department let it be known that Walt hated it, through a fact that he was certain that Walt hated two things: purple (never use anything purple) and also don't paint it. It can't be painted, there is no way it's gonna work. At the time Walt was gone, Walt was in Europe; and so Walt came back and he saw it and he loved it.[12]

[12] Ken Anderson, *Disney Family Album*, documentary, 1984.

*Pinocchio* made yet another leap forward, raising all of this to new heights, and was more illustrative and slightly less concerned with realism, *Fantasia* and *Dumbo* even less so. *Fantasia* was a film that put realism on the sidetrack and even stylized the sequence of Igor Stravinsky's *The Rite of Spring*, an interpretation of the development of life on Earth, which is richly decorated with emotional color that pushes the story much further instead of just illustrating it, despite it being a "documentary" on nature's development. The mood in the scene in a late Cretaceous swamp, through which hadrosaurids and other smaller dinosaurs are roaming, is stunning in establishing a mood that had not been seen before in color. It is utterly convincing in its contemporary scientific accuracy. It took Disney only 7 years to be in total control of color and its emotional impact, which is a massive achievement.

The use of color really starts to change again with UPA and the color design of its shorts in the 1950s. The realistic or semirealistic color is replaced by nonrepresentational color that interprets an emotion through color and gives it a meaning. The images have a unique and modern color aesthetic and design that is often a subjective and rather personal approach. In the UPA short *Rooty Toot Toot* (1951), for example, the color changes slowly from red to blue when the attorney is shot dead and he literally cools down while twitching on the floor. The color in the beginning of the shot represents the passion between the attorney and Nelly Bly through the color red, and then his death is described in blue, which takes away the passion and replaces it by him cooling down in temperature of color and body. The color is therefore not just a vehicle for mood but a representation of an intellectual idea of passion and death. The concept of color change through scenes or the entire movie was taken to the next level in the "second golden age of animation" at the end of the 1980s when *color scripts* were developed to give color a stronger role in the conceptualizing of animated films. The emotional impact of color, not just in a single scene but throughout the whole movie, was visualized in color boards that explained mood and emotion from scene to scene and thus presented the entire movie in its color progress according to the script.

The color script, the way animation productions use it today, developed through various stages and as a tool got more and more refined over the years. The process usually starts with color sketches that are sometimes based on approved initial artwork (inspirational artwork, visual development art) or done from scratch, based on the script. An assemblage of all the color sketches then forms the basis for the color script, containing all the shots and scenes where the color either changes or is significant. Richard Vander Wende did the color script for the Disney production of *Aladdin*. Vander Wende designed a color scheme for the feature that defined the character's personalities and their environments through colors that had a determined meaning to them and interpreted the character's traits in hues that were mainly associated with that one character or set. In *Aladdin* there are two directions: Jafar's and Aladdin's. Jafar, being the villain in the film, is associated with colors that are more saturated, have a darker value, and are hotter in temperature. His colors move more towards red. Aladdin's palette is more towards blue-yellow, which signifies "good, idealistic, romantic, cerebral, creative" in this film.[13] The visualization of the characters' personalities through color helps to connect characters subconsciously with each other. The audience will feel that relationship. In Roman Polanski's *The Fearless Vampire Killers*, Count von Krolock, the vampire lord, wears a blood red coat, signifying obviously him being a blood-sucking vampire. Alfred, the apprentice of Professor Abronsius, also wears a blood red jacket from the beginning of the film. He does not yet have any connection to the vampires, but at the end of the film he is the one that will carry the evil into the world by himself being turned into a vampire. His jacket being bloodred from the beginning on already tells the observant audience member that there is a bond between Alfred and the Count and also makes it clear who is going to end up as a vampire. This is a very subtle yet clear message. Sarah, the daughter of the innkeeper Yoine Shagal and the love interest of Alfred, does not wear red in the beginning but she has bright red hair. Color makes characters and locations relate to each other. The color script gives an idea of how colors change from warm to cold, from saturated to desaturated, from bright to dark, and how all this reflects the storyline and the characters' emotional journey. For example, action sequences could have high energy whereas more quiet scenes can have a desaturated color scheme. Following the idea that highly vibrant red always marks danger, though, limits the possibilities in animation. Harley Jessup, art director for films like *James and the Giant Peach*, *Monsters Inc.*, and *Ratatouille*, says, "Sometimes the climax could be black and white or it could be colored very cool, and still get across the sort of climactic emotions that you're supposed to be feeling."[14] A well-balanced color script makes a film more visually diverse and interesting and prevents it from being monotonous. It also distinguishes one scene from another and provides each sequence with its own visual direction and personality. One wants a range of colors to dominate the frames and not the same color from beginning to end.

The color script of Blue Sky's *Horton Hears a Who* (2008) is a nice example of how color can guide the story along. Lead color designer Daisuke Tsutsumi created a color language for the film where specific colors stand for narrative moments. Pink is used for disaster and devastation, for the climactic ending of the film; yellow, being the complementary color of magenta, pink, and

violet, stands for resolution and peace. Relating certain hues to a story point gives you a starting position for the color design and allows exploration within that scheme.

Because of the digital possibilities in film, color can be slowly changed as a dramatic and subliminal aid to lead emotions throughout the whole feature. In traditional 2D animation it was not that easy to change the color throughout a scene or sequence, because the background color could not be changed easily within one shot. It could be changed from shot to shot, or scene to scene. However, with the rise of digital productions the continuous change of color became more feasible, as the color can now be controlled through time; it would be possible to have a completely desaturated frame in the beginning and let the saturation slowly rise through the entire length of the film until the last frame with highly saturated colors. The overall color of digital film can be adjusted in all its separate elements (background, characters, effects …), which adds an immensely important tool to the temporal development of the mood in a full feature, sequence, or scene.

# Intellectual possibilities of color:

> Have a meaning

> Support the narrative and dramatic direction

## Have a meaning

Why is a certain color chosen and what does it say about the character, the environment, the mood, and the narrative? A color should not just be random, but chosen for a reason. Is the character extroverted or introverted, aggressive or calm, open-minded or close-minded? Is the landscape inviting, hostile, does it express the character's emotion, or connect or disconnect with the character … all of it can be expressed through color; the audience is probably not going to clearly read the color's meaning but can hopefully, with all the other contributing elements, sense its meaning. Next to the color's explanation of characters and environment, it can also visualize elements of the story and be a metaphor for a story point or the entire theme of the film.

Krzysztof Kieślowski's three feature films, which are loosely based on the three colors of the French flag, *Blue* (1993), *White* (1994), and *Red* (1994), deal with the meaning of their three colors, which are blue for freedom, white for equality, and red for brotherhood. Because the film title already clearly defines a color, and the viewer is obviously aware of the importance of that color when buying the movie ticket, the eye is constantly drawn to everything blue, white, or red in the film, seeking its meaning and searching actively for an interpretation. But in the feature *Red*, for instance, objects, clothing, cars, books, posters, furniture, and entire rooms are red, which does not give a meaning to

---

[13] John Culhane, *Disney's Aladdin, The Making of an Animated Film*, Little, Brown and Company, New York, 1992, p. 89.

[14] Amid Amidi, *The Art of Pixar: 25th Anniversary*, Chronicle Books, San Francisco, CA, 2011, p. 13.

each single object but gives an overall aesthetic that recalls the color's various meanings, which are of course brotherhood, but also blood, love, passion, anger, etc. The color in *Red* does not just deal with the meaning of the French flag but goes much further and creates a world of its own where reality is just ever so slightly lifted into a magical world where past, present, and future are strangely entangled. People meet and their destinies are interwoven, a place where history repeats. Red serves as a placeholder for various ideas and meanings, not just one.

For the meaning of a color there are two choices. The first one is to use the socially accepted meaning of a color in a certain cultural setting and what that color stands for, which can vary significantly amongst cultures; this would be color symbolism. For instance, purple can stand for emancipation; for mourning; for reflection or penance in the Christian color code; or it can mean arrogance and vanity or have dozens of other meanings depending on country, time frame, and society. The second choice is to apply a certain color meaning just for that one film or project. For example, a character moves to a new town. He was always a die-hard fan of a certain soccer club that had the color blue in their symbol. However, the new city's soccer club's color is orange. The character does not warm up to the new environment, as he has still not accepted being part of a new city now, so the color blue being associated with him could visualize that. At the end of the film, however, he dresses in an orange shirt, which symbolizes that he has now fully accepted the new city and is also proudly publicly showing it. Another example: a couple met at the beach and the image of the beach with its deep blue is now the metaphor for their love. Blue is not a color one would traditionally connect with love and passion; quite the contrary. But because the audience can connect blue with the couple's backstory, for that one film blue would stand for love despite its traditional meaning. The color therefore does have a meaning that is part of the social and cultural code, but that can also be overwritten if established correctly and clearly.

The Chinese director/former cinematographer Zhang Yimou is famous for his extensive use of color in his features. Films like *Raise the Red Lantern* (1991), *Ju Dou* (1990), *Hero* (2002), and his feature film take on a famous theatre play, *Curse of the Golden Flower* (2006), bathe in color and bring an operatic grandeur to the screen that is nothing short of stunning. For instance, the story in Yimou's famous feature *Raise the Red Lantern* is clearly reflected in the color red, already in the title. The protagonist, 19-year-old Songlian, seemingly steps into fortune when entering the house of wealthy Master Chen as his fourth mistress in 1920s China. There is a power struggle between the wives, which is constantly reiterated through the red lanterns, lit or unlit, as the wives compete for who is going to receive Master Chen's affection that night. The chosen one is honored by the red lanterns being lit in her courtyard. Red represents in Yimou's feature passion and love but also betrayal and death. The color red in Chinese culture mostly stands for luck, good fortune, and happiness. The discrepancy between the traditional

use of the color red and the contrasting struggle in the Chen household makes red seem to mock the narrative, as all comes with a price. Often the rooms are filled with deep and rich red light; for instance, when Master Chen is clearly having an affair with Songlian's servant, Yan'er, the room is bathed in blood red, showing on the one side the passion between Master Chen and Yan'er, but also Songlian's realization of being betrayed and her understanding of her own miserable situation. Aside from the meaning and symbolism of the color red, there is the aesthetic and compositional quality of red in *Raise the Red Lantern*, as the red lanterns separate dramatically from their surroundings, which are either grayish stone or pure white snow, sometimes tinted in deep blue light during twilight or night. The juxtaposition between the red lanterns and often more neutral backgrounds makes a stunning visual with deep impact.

## Support the narrative and dramatic direction

Color is such a difficult aspect to grasp and creating a list of meanings for colors that always works is counterproductive to creativity, which was already established at the beginning of the three-color Technicolor revolution. Natalie Kalmus, who I mentioned earlier, was the head of the color control department (Color Advisory Service) of Technicolor, a position that was responsible for not only the quality control of the films but also for the aesthetic and narrative implications of color. The department was created in the beginning of the two-color Technicolor system to aid film companies with their use of color, to not overwhelm the audience with too much color that could pull the audience's attention from the narrative. For the three-color Technicolor system, the department was deemed even more important because there was now a much broader and more sophisticated color design possible, and Technicolor had to make sure that its product was implemented with the help of expertise and a color sensitivity. Natalie Kalmus with her colleagues created color guidelines for Hollywood that suggested a connection between color, story, and characters, where color was seen as having an impact on the dramatic effect and having the subconscious potential of driving the narrative, but mustn't draw attention to itself. The department would advise on all productions that used the Technicolor system, producing color charts that considered all scenes, sets, and characters. Technicolor thus had control over the aesthetic output of all films that used its system and encouraged color's strong relationship with the narrative, securing in the long run the quality of color as a dramatic agent assisting storytelling. Natalie Kalmus suggested in an article in the *Journal of the Society of Motion Picture Engineers* from August, 1935: "White represents purity, cleanliness, peace, marriage … White uplifts and ennobles …" This is somehow true in Western societies, but that does not make it a common fact, as white in China, for instance, stands for purity and cleanliness but also for death and funerals, and therefore it has a very different connotation to the Western meaning. This is true for all other colors. Their meaning is rather ambiguous. It is too easy to claim "green stands for envy," as green can also stand for nature, for growth, and even something evil, disgusting, foreign, alien, and weird. So color has strength in representing a meaning, but that meaning can be difficult if only seen from its social perspective. An acid green does not always stand for nature and neither does a dirty green. Kalmus describes, for instance, the "serenity of a blue sky," which again is true, but in a film the addition is a narrative and the narrative will tint the meaning of the color depending on subtle editing, the story development, and all the complex interactions of the characters that lead to that point in the film where the color blue in the sky is present. For instance, a brutal murder happens at the beach. The background is a perfectly blue sky, which in this case does not necessarily say "serenity" but might actually say the opposite and through its perfect blue depth mock the scene it witnesses. Color only works artistically if all the other elements of composition and storytelling, all the elements of design, work together harmoniously or contradict each other to evoke exactly the emotion that fits that very scene. It is the range of possibilities that is endless and thus it is impossible to create rules for using color for the narrative other than the traditional rules for painting and observation.

Kalmus is correct in stating

> In the preparation of a picture we read the script and prepare a color chart for the entire production, each scene, sequence, set, and character being considered. This chart may be compared to a musical score, and amplifies the picture in a similar manner. The preparation of this chart calls for careful and judicious work. Subtle effects of beauty and feeling are not attained through haphazard methods, but through application of the rules of art and the physical laws of light and color in relation to literary laws and story values. In the first place, this chart must be in absolute accord with the story action. Again, it must consider the art, principles of unity, color harmony, and contrast.

However, we must not forget that development in art has also "allowed" us to do the exact opposite.

There are some technical rules in color that, if followed, make it much easier to understand the image from a technical perspective, read the characters, and just more easily perceive the image's content. That is the technical aspect of color:

the simplification of the image's content for the viewer. But then there is the artistic use of color and this is a very different game altogether. Yes, colors that are opposites on the color wheel do go well together and are aesthetically pleasing, but that does not necessarily mean that all colors that go well together express exactly the narrative of the story point.

Kalmus writes:

> We plan the colors of the actor's costumes with especial care. Whenever possible, we prefer to clothe the actor in colors that build up his or her screen personality. In a picture which we recently completed, two young girls play the parts of sisters. One is vivacious, affectionate, and gay. The other is studious, quiet, and reserved. For the first we planned costumes of pink, red, warm browns, tan, and orange; for the second, blue, green, black, and gray.

Again she is correct in color evoking emotions in the audience, but one should not just follow this rule strictly, as it will limit creativity and ultimately end in a cliché.

In animation the use of color as a dramatic agent is very common and its use can be overly obvious and interrupt the narrative flow because of its blunt simplification. When for instance Simba fights Scar at the end of *The Lion King*, Pride Rock is bathed in deep red from fire and lava; when Ursula grabs Ariel at the end of *The Little Mermaid*, she does it after the sun has set and the sky is bathed in a deep, dark red. This can be seen as an obvious and not very subtle choice of color despite its emotional impact. Using red for instance to accentuate a high activity scene or a strong emotional one obviously works very well and has been done in plenty of features and TV shows; however, it also serves as a cliché, as it does not necessarily play with color creatively but uses it as a predefined rule out for the effect rather than creating a new and unique color metaphor. (However, the narrative also falls into the same trap of using locals and situations that are there for the effect. Why is the pinnacle of the story arc often interpreted through fire and explosions? Well … because it works! That doesn't mean it's original.)

Color does increase the dramatic direction of the narrative and is crucial for expressing it visually, but it can also, when used bluntly, interrupt the narrative flow and pull too much attention towards itself.

# Case study: Nonrepresentational color in UPA's *Rooty Toot Toot* (1951)

When UPA started to create cartoons in the late 1940s, their
goal was to distance themselves artistically as far as possible
from what Disney and many other studios created at the time.
Their first short film, *Hell-Bent for Election* (1944), already showed
a new direction, not yet fully developed, but with an obvious
urge to try something new. The visuals are still rooted within
1940s aesthetics, but some images allow a glimpse into what is
about to come. In their next short, *Brotherhood of Man* (1945), the
idea of pushing visuals into a different direction is much more
obvious. Modern aesthetics that had been explored in fine art
for decades slowly dripped down into illustration in a simplified
way and finally reached animation at the end of the 1940s.
UPA brought those modern visuals that had been out there for
30 years already onto the screen and played more freely with
color, shapes, movement, and cohesive designs that changed
the animation landscape from then on. Where Disney's designers
at the time tried to imitate nature or slightly stylize it, where
Warner Brothers cartoons pushed the timing and the sanity of
their characters to brilliant heights, UPA started to approach the
whole design and story aspect from a different angle. Their
artists took references mainly from other sources than animation
or comics. The art scene shaped the design language of
contemporary illustration, which UPA used as a basis for their
developing style. The visual and artistic achievements of fine
arts movements of expressionism, cubism, futurism, Dadaism,
surrealism, and some other *-isms* can be seen in various cartoons
of UPA. For animation, this unique approach was revolutionary
and had a huge following in the decade to come, because it
presented animation in a modern package and tremendously
pushed the development of character design and movement.
In terms of color, UPA went in the complete opposite direction of
what had been done in animation, though all those innovative
ideas that UPA introduced into animation had been developed
in the other art forms for nearly 30 years. UPA translated the fine
arts language into movement and animation on-screen.

One cartoon, however, had been experimenting with a very
different kind of character animation in the beginning of the
1940s: Chuck Jones' Warner Brothers Cartoon *The Dover Boys
of Pimento University* (1942). In this short Jones invents what is
later referred to as "limited animation." By reducing the actual
movement of the characters and replacing it with precisely
planned timing and thoughtfully designed poses that are often
still, the poses themselves express their strengths and receive in
strong key poses more screen time. The single pose is important
and contains all the information of that narrative moment. The
character animation gains in precision, speed, and often wit,
because of the pushed timing. The character's movement in *The
Dover Boys* adds stylization to the cartoon's design that is fresh
and so very different (Tex Avery had already experimented with
different timing in his shorts). Warner Brothers' *The Dover Boys* is
a unique and extraordinary short that anticipated much of what

**Figure 14.71**

**Figure 14.72**

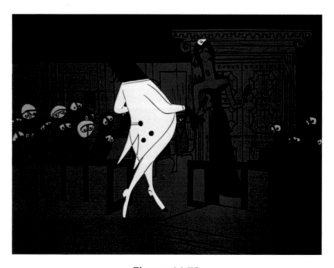

**Figure 14.73**

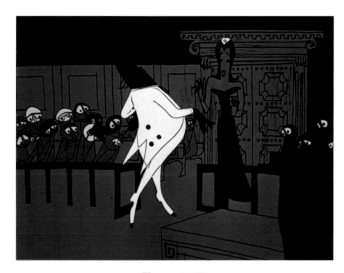

**Figure 14.74**

**Figure 14.75**

**Figure 14.76**

UPA later reinvented and refined in a new animation sensibility. Though *The Dover Boys* lacks the aesthetic qualities of the UPA shorts, its backgrounds, as nice and creative as they are, have a cold and sterile feel to them. The gags, on the other hand, are to this day precise and hilarious. There was a relationship between people who worked on *The Dover Boys* and UPA. Animator Robert Cannon was to become one of the main directors at UPA and Chuck Jones directed UPA's first short film *Hell-Bent for Election*. One of UPA's achievements was the interpretation of the character movement in unison with the design, as the studio put emphasis on every part of the short being stylized and artistically interpreted. Movement, character design, background design, storylines, and color were emotionally and intellectually visualized. The goal was to find a visual representation for emotions through color and shapes and let those tell the story. UPA's approach to color was very different from any other studio in Hollywood or New York. It has more in common with expressionism, cubism, or abstract expressionism (very loosely stated!) than American animation at the time. The idea behind it was to not use color as a mere representation of the color as it appears in nature, but to find the color that represents the emotional state of a scene, setting, or character. This is obviously a very subjective approach to color, but if done right it has the strength of evoking emotions in the audience rather than giving the audience a representational color scheme. Since around 1905 expressionistic artists had already dealt with the connection of color and emotion and its expression on the canvas. Later on, these ideas spread into sculpture and film. That animation was not very influenced by the visual development of art movements from the 1900s until the end of the 1940s might seem surprising, though considering the purpose of animation as being mostly entertainment compared to being fine art, it is understandable. Additionally, animation had to explore its own technique first with animation cels to separate background and character, sound, color, and the principles of animation. Animation also developed out of newspaper comics, and the draftsmen who later worked in the animation industry did not produce art in the fine art sense, but commercial art. There were obviously artists who did not work for the big studios and developed animation art that explored new ground from an artistic perspective rather than a technical perspective (Oscar Fischinger, Walter Ruttmann, Viking Eggeling, etc.), but the bigger percentage was focused on commercial animation in bigger studios, and many of them did follow the aesthetic direction of Disney.

UPA cartoons are a joy to watch exactly because of the strength in their design. Every short has a very personal look that is unique to that specific short. It is never repetitive and UPA's oeuvre is a neverending source of inspiration and ideas. The range is immense and always surprising. For example, *Rooty Toot Toot* has a very illustrative look to it, whereas *Fudget's Budget* (directed by Robert Cannon), a short about how a family calculates their budget, a seemingly rather dry topic, has an inventive stylization.

*Rooty Toot Toot* was directed by animation genius John Hubley, who had worked for Disney for years as a background and layout artist until he left during the Disney strike in 1941. His contribution to animation is unprecedented and he was without a doubt one of the creative forces behind UPA. After UPA he continued with his wife Faith Hubley putting out short films annually that are still considered as the highlights of independent American animation, amongst which *Adventures of an \** (*Adventures of an asterisk*) (1956), *Tender Game* (1958), *Moonbird* (1959), and *Windy Days* (1967) are animation art. *Rooty Toot Toot* from 1952 was Hubley's last short at UPA, after having directed various films with Columbia's characters of the Fox and the Crow: *Robin Hoodlum* (1948), *The Magic Fluke* (1949), and *Punchy DeLeon* (1950). He is also the creator of the character of Mister Magoo and directed the first Magoo shorts. *Rooty Toot Toot* was the film where Hubley could fully experiment with every element of the short and was not bound to either a company's characters or to following a unique character like Mister Magoo, who is a very unusual type, but still, despite the charming narratives about an old, half-blind man, is still stylistically more traditional in a way.

*Rooty Toot Toot* is different from every angle: it is clearly not a film for the entertainment of children, as it is about drinking, smoking, betrayal, sex, passion, and murder, but it also deviates stylistically from many animated shorts before. It really does explore further the less charted territory in design, narrative, and character animation, which all has already been touched upon in its possibilities in *Gerald McBoing-Boing* in 1950 and UPA's other output before. But *Rooty Toot Toot* does push these elements even further.

The story is about Frankie, who is being charged for the murder of Johnny, her then–piano playing boyfriend. The case is told from three different perspectives: the barman's in whose bar Johnny was shot while playing the piano and practicing with Nellie Bly; from Nellie Bly's perspective, who was with Johnny when he was shot, and from Frankie's perspective, who is described by her attorney as honest, pure, and demure. At the end of the trial, Frankie is released from the case as being innocent but out of jealousy shoots dead her attorney Honest John, who was just about to passionately leave the court room with Nellie Bly.

Hubley chose Paul Julian for color and design because he wanted a different style. Julian's backgrounds turned out to be rather experimental in color, depiction of space, and texture. Much of the texture was done with an "oddly corroded gelatin roller,"[15] which gave most backgrounds a nervous ground on which then the line drawings and additional texture/shapes of the backgrounds rest (Figure 14.78). The background color does not suggest perspective or space; it is rather a monochrome, evocative ground plane on which the line drawing and

Figure 14.77

Figure 14.78

Figure 14.79

15 Adam Abraham, *When Magoo Flew, The Rise and Fall of Animation Studio UPA*, Wesleyan University Press, Middletown, CT, 2012, p. 96.

architecture/furniture is placed. Color here visualizes mood and emotions, but not space and depth. The color choice of red at the end of the short film reflects, for instance, the verdict of "not guilty" leading then straight into the kiss Frankie places on her attorney's cheek, followed by the passion between Nellie Bly and the attorney, to finally end with the same blood red background in Frankie shooting her attorney (Figure 14.79). The color red thus represents the three emotions of celebration, passion, and bloody aggression. The dimensionality is very much broken up by only giving snippets of spatial and architectural information that together suggest a space that is slightly deconstructed. Individual architectural elements might hover in space, yet define a wall, for instance, or a window. For the backgrounds that accompany Honest John's narrative perspective of the events, there is no texture at all as everything is clean, pristine, and white to reflect Frankie's innocence. The color here shifts to pink, purple, and rose colors, whereas in the other tales there are darker tones. Everything goes against a realistic depiction and uses nonrepresentational colors to express a mood instead of an actual realistic space.

The characters can also change the mood of the backgrounds. For example, when Nellie Bly enters the room the background color changes gradually from a warm ochre to a cold blue. The background is therefore a reflection of the character's emotions and not *just* a backdrop.

The short *Rooty Toot Toot* is filled with unique and new creative ideas to such an extreme that they might have even felt odd at times. Characters dance ballet and sing, some are half transparent, others change their colors according to the narrative. The characters also do not strictly follow the traditional technique of colors just filling in the empty spaces on the animation cel between the outlines, but there are various stylistic choices that enrich the unique character lineup with innovative ideas. The character of the barman, for instance, has an underlay of a colored shape that follows him rather than the color being a fill-color of the outline. The characters' skin colors are also nonrepresentational, as they interpret the personality rather than reality. Nellie Bly is bathed in a cool blue, Johnny is black and white, and the attorney is white and dark red; nevertheless,

the colors can change when the emotion and mood changes. The characters as much as the backgrounds are reduced to their necessities, and their shapes are decisive and precisely express their personalities. Every character has a very distinct design element that is unique.

A very interesting design choice happens at the end of the short. After the trial, Frankie, who was accused of the murder of her pianist lover Johnny, shoots her attorney out of jealousy with the very same gun, Exhibit A, seconds after she was granted a full discharge by the court. Her attorney was flirting with one of the witnesses, the singer Nellie Bly. The defense attorney approaches Nellie Bly after the trial to leave the court room with her. The color of the background is deep red, which reflects the passion of the couple, and additionally Frankie's jealousy and rage. Once Frankie shoots the attorney three times in the back (the same number of shots Johnny received into his back), the color shifts slowly to blue: the passion is gone, the image turns cold. The attorney dies and himself turns blue, once he is "cold" (Figures 14.71 through 14.77). The impact of this color change is gripping: warmth disappears and the cold of death slowly creeps in. To change the color of the attorney at the end of his life to blue gives us the actual visual and emotional impact of the lifeless corpse turning cold. The poignant character animation in the end, though, is topping off the joke. The pathetic twitching of the attorney's legs is just a small addition to the character animation, but it makes all the difference.

After finishing the short, Hubley was forced to leave UPA because he refused to disclose the names of people related to communism in front of the House Un-American Activities Committee. From 1952 on, he was blacklisted in the industry and not allowed to work on films where his name would be mentioned. So he worked on commercials and also started his own studio Storyboard Studios with his wife Faith, and together they produced short films for *Sesame Street*, commercials, and also personal films, some of which received Academy Awards and are still counted amongst the most important short films from the 1950s, 1960s, and 1970s.

# Case study: Walt Peregoy's background styling and color keys for Disney's *101 Dalmatians* (1961)[16]

In 1959 *Sleeping Beauty* was finally released into the movie theatres and the response to the film was a critical success, though the financial blessing the company had hoped for and needed to pay for the $6 million film wouldn't come. It was after all an extremely expensive film compared to Disney's usual output, and to recoup those kind of expenses is not an easy task. So, it was decided that the next feature film would be produced on a much lower budget and a simpler style compared to the lavish backgrounds and style of *Sleeping Beauty*. That next film was to be based on the book *The Hundred and One Dalmatians*. In 1956 Dodie Smith had published her children's novel, which caught the attention of Walt Disney, who bought the rights one year later to turn it into an animated feature film. The man for the job of styling the new feature was to be designer Ken Anderson, who is credited in the film for production design and art direction and had been at Disney since the early 1930s, first as animator and then designer. He had already been credited as the production designer on *Sleeping Beauty* and was again to be the designer on this next feature. Because of the financial restraints and the overwhelming design influence that Eyvind Earle had on *Sleeping Beauty*, Ken Anderson was to design a very different look for *101 Dalmatians*, one that will be considered as one of Disney's most beautifully designed features. Walt Disney himself at the time was very busy with Disneyland, its development, and preparation. It opened in 1955 and was still growing in size and popularity. He was also occupied with TV appearances on ABC for his *Mickey Mouse Club*. Where he was loosely involved in the production and the design of *Sleeping Beauty* (at least signing off on designs, not so much on the actual crucial decision-making on pushing the film forward), for *101 Dalmatians* Walt Disney himself was even less involved in the design, which led to the aesthetically unique film.[17]

Ken Anderson chose artist Walt Peregoy to work with him on the background designs, developing a style that turned out to be diametrically the opposite of the previous film. Peregoy seems to have been a bit of an enfant terrible at the studio, having a very strong opinion on art and his own work, even being considered "opinionated." Audiences had already seen his work in the backgrounds for the short *Paul Bunyan* (1958) and he was also the head of background painting on *Sleeping Beauty*.

Alongside Eyvind Earle, Marc Davis, and Joshua Meador, Peregoy had appeared in Disney's documentary *4 Artists Paint 1 Tree: A Walt Disney "Adventure in Art"* from 1958, which was originally a segment of the April 30, 1958 episode of *Walt Disney's Wonderful World of Color* (1954) airing on ABC TV.[18]

About being chosen by Anderson for the feature, Walt Peregoy stated: "Ken Anderson said I was the guy who is going to do the style and Ken knew me and nobody tells me what to do. If I want to wipe out a line I wipe out a line. Nobody controlled what the finished product will be."[19] In another interview he stated:

> … But the reason I was chosen by Ken Anderson is that if he put me as a color stylist, he knew I'd do it, I'd create something, not just another Disney background. He knew it would be me. Now all the artists at Disney in key positions suffered the same thing—they knew all rocks had to be round and all trees had to look like trees and the sky had to have fluffy clouds and they're all done with airbrush, right from the beginning. And I always asked myself, how come their idea of realism is completely contradictory to a duck or a mouse or a baboon talking? That's not realism, it's satire. It's freedom. These animals say things that people don't want to say and they're put in situations—so, why the hell does a flower have to be put next to an airbrushed rock? I could never understand this. One Hundred and One Dalmatians was not a fairy tale and all of the artists realized now here's the chance to do what we want to do. Some in subtle ways and others absolutely divergent from a Disney look.[20]

Peregoy designed the colors and the painterly style that was used behind the background drawings. A more painterly and slightly cartoony and even a hint abstracted treatment was very in vogue in the 1950s in painting and illustration; however, it finally found its way into animation and can be rightfully celebrated as a great achievement in the aesthetics of animation. It was UPA's *Rooty Toot Toot* that paved the path for a new view on style in animation in 1951, 10 years before *101 Dalmatians*. The director, John Hubley, was one of the masters of animation and pushed the art form to new heights; his short film *Rooty Toot Toot* is an important stylistic turning point in animation design and its groundbreaking influence cannot be overestimated. But the Disney Studios were not yet ready for this kind of artistic tour de force in its feature in 1960, which despite its beautiful and utterly successful design did not push itself to the artistic heights of UPA's short. The final feature film 101 Dalmatians is very much a Disney film, with representational backgrounds

---

[16] Due to the fact that the Disney Company did not release the copyrights for Walt Peregoy's background styling and color keys for the feature 101 Dalmatians to be used in this educational section, which would have tremendously helped the understanding of the discussed composition, it is necessary for the reader to find the illustrations either in Disney books or online and then compare them alongside the text to fully grasp the discussed compositions. Many of his color keys can be found online.

[17] Bob Miller, Walt Peregoy, Interview Jan. 1992; published in *Walt's People*, Vol. 5, edited by Didier Ghez, Xlibris, Bloomington, IN, 2007, p. 294.

[18] 4 Artists Paint 1 Tree: A Walt Disney "Adventure in Art" (1958), http://www.imdb.com/title/tt0263015/?ref_=nm_flmg_slf_2 (accessed April 5, 2015).

[19] The Making of 101 Dalmatians; 101 Dalmatians, Disney DVD bonus material

[20] 20Didier Ghez, *Walt's People Volume 9 Talking Disney with the Artists Who Knew Him*, Xlibris, Bloomington, IN, 2010, p. 283.

and semirealistic characters. The character design still has some extraordinary original personalities, especially the three villains, Cruella de Vil and her two sidekicks Horace and Jasper, who are all deliciously evil. The only character that does not fit as well into the human lineup is Anita (who looks very much like a stylized version of the early Julie Andrews, but is supposedly only based on actress Helene Stanley, who acted as the live-action reference for the animators). Marc Davis designed Anita and, after Walt Disney did not approve of her look, Milt Kahl then pushed her design to arrive at the final character. With her design, the male Disney artists again fell into the trap of designing a beautiful woman instead of a character with personality, whereas the male character is more pushed in his design and the typical goofball that gets the pretty girl. He is much more of a cartoony character than she is. The size of his nose is overly exaggerated compared to her cute little button nose. The character animation is of course mostly excellent, as expected from a Disney film, though it never invents its own style. It presents beautifully executed movements yet lacks originality in also creating a new style of movement or an artistic interpretation of the movement alongside the given design. One of the negative points of typical Disney character animation, despite its visual splendor, complexity, and technical bravura, is the missing playfulness with movement. There is not much difference in the character animation from film to film (the character animation style in *Sleeping Beauty* is more or less the same as in *101 Dalmatians*, aside from the obvious less angular design of the latter). The only one who pushed character animation and explored its possibilities within the restrictions of the Disney style was Ward Kimball; the others left Disney and blessed the animation world with their explosive creativity elsewhere, like the brilliant Robert Cannon or Art Babbitt, animating for instance on *Rooty Toot Toot*. Parts of the character animation in *101 Dalmatians* is too much based on the live-action reference material and therefore fights the slight stylization of the backgrounds with its very realistic movement. It is rather obvious when the animators were following the reference too closely and when not. That is again where UPA understood design in all its facets: design is not just the look of the background and characters, but also the style of character animation and how the movement interprets the level of stylization of the short in its own artistic possibilities.

## Xerox: The magical solution that changed animation

There was always the animator's discontent that their actual line work of their character animation on paper never showed up on-screen, as their work went always through the ink and paint department, where much of the appeal of the character animation's initial line aesthetic and dynamic was traced away. This was obviously necessary in order to bring the lines and colors onto transparent cels, which then are put on top of the painted backgrounds, a technique invented in 1915 by the two animation producers John Bray and Earl Hurd. Since then the

tracing of the animation drawing on cel greatly reduced and eliminated the, for some people, special appeal of 2D animation: the visible, organic line of the animator. The inking and painting of the cels had traditionally been done by women at Disney Studios and they did absolutely stunning work, especially on *Sleeping Beauty*. But their valued and highly sophisticated work would soon be obsolete. In the 1930s there had been a process invented at the Fleischer Studios to transfer live-action footage onto cels and it had been used occasionally; even Disney used "process cels" in *Pinocchio* in some shots (shots that unfortunately do not want to fully fit into the style of the final film, like the moving trailer of Stromboli in the rain), but the technique was not practical in a large-scale production.[21] One invention was about to change that: the technology of Xerox, which would drastically change animation over the next decades. In the Xerox process, a lens takes a picture with bright light of the black and white animation drawing and passes it onto an electrically charged plate with a photoconductor covering it. The positive charge of the electrically charged plate underneath is changed into a negative one in the black animation lines, which results in the drawn lines of the animation drawing now being on the photoconductor as electrically charged negative lines. The plate is then dipped into black toner, which is itself charged positively. The photoconductor only holds the powdered color where the drawn line had been (negative line on the conductor holds the positively charged toner). The toner is then transferred onto an animation cel and fixed with heat and pressure. The first time this process was used at Disney was in *Sleeping Beauty* in the dragon sequence; however, it was not the first use of this new technology. Smaller studios and UPA had already employed it in commercials and TV productions. *Sleeping Beauty* animator Burny Mattinson remembers:

> Actually, Woolie Reitherman was directing the sequence of the dragon fight [in *Sleeping Beauty*] and he used the Xerox process for the first time on the dragon. I think they went back over the Xerox line with ink and paint, but he did use the Xerox process for enlarging and reducing her in the frame as an experiment. That actually was the start of Disney using the Xerox process in animation. It was a very crude process—we used an omega 8×10 enlarger as our camera and we had these old aluminium inking boards. We coated those with the Xerox material. It was very crude, but by the next picture, we had a first class operation with Xerox.[22]

The first short film that fully took advantage of the Xerox technology was Disney's *Goliath II* from 1960, a bit inconsistent in its design, though with a very charming story of a miniscule elephant who proves to his gigantic father how courageous he really is. The technology obviously worked on *Goliath II* and the animators' lines, even sometimes the

---

[21] Michael Barrier, *Hollywood Cartoons; American Animation in its Golden Age*, Oxford University Press, Oxford, UK, p. 566.
[22] Didier Ghez, *Walt's People—Volume 7 Talking Disney with the Artists Who Knew Him: Burny Mattinson interview*, Xlibris, Bloomington, IN, 2007.

construction lines, finally showed up on-screen, to the delight of the animators. The elimination of the inking process was initially of course a money-saving cut in the overall animation process, as inking and painting the characters on cels is a costly process and plans for getting rid of the inking had often been considered. There was just not a practical solution in sight for how to get the drawings onto the cels. After *Goliath II*'s technical success it was decided to use the new technology in the next feature film: *101 Dalmatians*. However, the use of Xerox in this feature should not be solely seen as a money-cutting solution but as a creative tool in its design that widened the possibilities in animation, as the limitation of Xerox was actually turned into its strength. Ken Anderson says about the line of the animator:

> … You start to make a drawing (as an animator) and that drawing has life because it is drawn right out of your mind. You are not thinking about the technique, your hand or anything else, it is just the whole picture coming to life out of your hand. If somebody including yourself is given the chore of tracing that, immediately it becomes dead.[23]

This is of course true, but it is seen from the perspective of the character animator (which Ken Anderson was in the early Disney years). One needs to remember that all these statements about the animator's line come from animators, of course, and they naturally want their line to be seen on-screen. Not many artists from the inking department are ever asked about their opinion on the aesthetics of using the black xeroxed line on-screen instead of their highly specialized and trained skill and also their ability to merge character and background with intricate line work of the highest skills in color. When one is looking at a cel from the earlier feature *Sleeping Beauty*, one is simply flabbergasted because of the complexity of the line coloring. There has never been a film with such intricate and complex line work and such an amount of color. There is a stark contrast between having a film with the most complex line work in animation history being followed by a film with just a black character outline. Compared to the cells of *Sleeping Beauty*, which had dozens of different colors in the characters' lines, the Xerox technique allows only one color, which is usually black. That indeed was a huge change in aesthetics, which makes one understand the significance of story artist Floyd Norman's statement: "We were all very excited about it and mainly because it was so different. It was so different from what had been done at Disney before. It really broke new ground for Disney's animation department."[24] The inking department lost many artists because of the Xerox technique, which from that point on eliminated the inking altogether. A whole branch of animation production broke away and the lush visuals of traditional Disney animation were a look of the past. The Xerox technique was used as mentioned as a tool in the film, which included

not only the transfer onto cels but also the multiplication of the characters on-screen to achieve those 101 Dalmatians to begin with. In the title sequence there are literally dozens and dozens of Dalmatians in a size that would have been impossible to animate on that scale. Xerox made those shots possible by downsizing the characters and copying them onto the cel. Also there are many shots in the film where the multiplication of the dogs was made possible by copying them over and over to achieve the number of dogs needed. The copying via Xerox onto the cel is a huge simplifying factor but cannot be the mere reason for the accomplishment of the film. The new modern direction for Disney Studios was not only expressed in the design but also in the music that was used for the film. For the studio's past features, more conservative music was the usual choice, but in *101 Dalmatians* the contemporary modern design was underlined by a less traditionally orchestrated score. It had a jazzy feel to it, a direction that was not present in Disney's oeuvre but very much so in Max Fleischer's films from the 1930s and 1940s, who used contemporary jazz music for his short films with Betty Boop, for example. Also the use of a TV on-screen in *101 Dalmatians* with the deliciously over-the-top Kanine Krunchies commercial pushes Disney visually into the twentieth century. All their previous features had been either interpretations of nineteenth (or earlier) century European stories or films that visually reminisced an art style that was more nineteenth than twentieth century illustration (including *Fantasia*, which rarely touched upon artistic explorations of the early twentieth century, nor did most of the short films: they were all still rooted in for the most part representational aesthetics). *101 Dalmatians* was the first Disney film with a contemporary story and a mid-century aesthetic.

The Xerox technique preserved, as mentioned, the animator's line. Reading the statements of contemporary Disney animators witnessing for the first time their own character animation on-screen, unchanged through inking, one feels their excitement and their approval of the new technology. Animator Marc Davis: "The Xerox process was a delight for the animators at least we felt at the time. It was the first time we saw our drawings on the screen."[25] There is of course the loss of the subtlety and beauty of the inked line but also the gain of the animators' vibrant work. However, the claim that the line quality of the animator was preserved in the final film is only half the truth, as it is the cleaned-up drawing that is preserved, which is unfortunately much less "lively" than the original line of the more appealing rough animation.

**More on the Ink & Paint Department at Disney:**

Mindy Johnston, *Ink & Paint: The Women of Walt Disney's Animation*, Disney Editions, Glendale, CA, 2017.

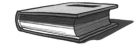

[23] Ken Anderson, *Disney Family Album*, TV documentary, 1984.
[24] *Redefining the line: The making of 101 Dalmatians*, DVD documentary.
[25] DVD documentary Redefining the line: The making of 101 Dalmatians.

In *101 Dalmatians*, Ken Anderson and Walt Peregoy developed the perfect aesthetic for the Xerox technology to work with the background style. The brilliant idea they had was to treat the backgrounds exactly the way the character animation is treated, by separating color and line and placing the line drawing of the background over the painting, whereas in all of Disney's films before, the line in the background was never seen as it was just used as a guideline for the painter but then eliminated. This new style is not only aesthetically very pleasing but also allows a different interpretation of three-dimensional space. Layout stylist Ernie Nordli went over the layout drawings and made everything a bit more stylized, shifting some of the geometric elements, making them slightly crooked, adjusting the line thickness, overall changing the realism of the space and its objects. Depth in the background is achieved through a different thickness of the line depending on the distance from the camera. In some backgrounds, however, in the dense London fog the line seems to completely disappear and only the painting suggests the buildings in the far distance. The interesting approach of the background's stylization is that the line drawing is three-dimensional though the color treatment behind it is absolutely flat, only slightly suggesting color perspective here and there. This allows the background to follow exactly the design that Disney's character animation had followed for decades in the rendering of the characters on cel, which produced flatness in the color but a dimensionality in the movement. That is why the use of the Xerox technology for the background treatment is one perfect interpretation of the Disney character animation style into a background. Peregoy had already worked on various productions and knew the significance of the background for the final film: "A background creates a world for animated characters. It's the ambiance. It's not an attempt to make (though it is now) a live-action representational background that literally looks like a backdrop behind vaudeville animated characters."[26] This is an important aspect of the films of that period: that the stylization of the characters and backgrounds are an interpretation of reality, not a representation of it. Animation therefore plays with reality but isn't there to copy it. This is where *101 Dalmatians* develops an interesting interpretation of Peregoy's earlier statement: its background drawings and perspectives are actually rather realistic with a slight stylistic shift, but the coloring gives it an additional twist that removes it very much from realism, flattening the perspectives and adding an important level of "abstraction" (in the widest possible meaning of the word, that is), which tremendously affects the drawn overlay. Disney himself supposedly hated lines and therefore he pushed the inking department to use colored outlines that would then disappear in the adjoining shapes, painted in the same color. This makes the character melt into the background instead of separating from it, as the colored outline does not interrupt the color flow from character into

background. Ken Anderson affirmed that Disney "inherently hated lines … He was the one who really pushed us into cel paint ink lines, where the ink line is the same color as the area it is encompassing … So he was very upset when he saw what was happening on *Dalmatians*."[27] *101 Dalmatians* surely broke new ground for Disney.

## Peregoy's color keys

Walt Peregoy explains his role as a background stylist:

> It's important that the stylist be well immersed in the animation film business. And if he has been in the business, he should have empathy for film. Painting backgrounds is a very, very special and unique approach. It's not illustration. It's not painting pictures. It's creating ambiance and a world for the animated moving characters to live in, to work in. The more integrity that the backgrounds have, the more integrity the film has. And it's obvious: the more integrity the background stylist has, the more integrity the film will have.[28]

The style that Peregoy developed for *101 Dalmatians* along with Ken Anderson is a two-edged sword, if you will, because it is comprised of two complete opposites, two very contrary approaches that, despite their extreme otherness, still work together and are actually a perfect background solution for Disney's character animation at the time. There is on the one hand the line drawing that defines the actual background in its spatial expansion and its decoration. And then there is Peregoy's unique color work underneath the intricate line work. For the background paintings Peregoy developed color keys for important shots, which are exciting visually in their own right and play with shapes and color in a free and uninhibited way. Peregoy's color sketches can be called "modern" as they step into a fine art approach, disassemble the image, and add a slight cubist touch to them. Cubism deconstructs the image's dimensionality and presents the viewer various viewing angles of the objects and space depicted. Peregoy is not using the actual intellectual fundament of what cubism means; he only uses the visual element of the color design and breaks it apart. His use of color is mostly realistic; however, sometimes he adds an unexplained shape of color to question the logic of the space, destabilizing its realism. Only in some backgrounds nonrepresentational, or rather heightened, exaggerated colors are used to enhance the mood. The paintings of Peregoy have something in common with the visible brush textures and the reduction of forms to simple geometric shapes of Nicolas de Staël's work (Figure 14.80); however, where Staël stays mostly abstract, Peregoy applies the necessary realism as a black line work on top of the paintings. His remark "I've never been influenced at any time ever by anything that's contemporary or

---

26 Bob Miller, p. 291.

27 Michael Barrier, *Hollywood Cartoons, American Animation in its Golden Age*, Oxford University Press, Oxford, UK, p. 566.
28 Bob Miller, pp. 291–292.

**Figure 14.80**

Nicolas de Staël: *Méditerranée (La ciotat)*, 1952.

otherwise," seems rather questionable, as his work is so rooted in the 1950s aesthetic that it couldn't be more of a representation of the time.

There are many shots in the feature film where the richness of the color is courageous, notably in the Blu-ray version of the film, which has a vibrancy that is stunning. For example, the scene in the old mansion of the de Vil family, where Jasper and Horace keep the 99 puppies, is rendered in bright red when Pongo and Perdy are rescuing the puppies with the help of the old Colonel. The use of nonrepresentational color in these shots obviously underlines the drama of the narrative. But most of Peregoy's work uses color that renders the backgrounds realistic to a degree. Studying his loose, sketchy work, one wishes the final film had had a similar, slightly more loose approach in the line drawings of the backgrounds instead of the overly accurate lines that render the backgrounds, though this might in turn clash with the accurate character animation.

The boldness and simplicity of Peregoy's shapes in the color keys still allows the narrative to read perfectly well. The color, which explains the environment with a 1950s/1960s color sensibility, slightly muted, with often low saturation, and the subtle, convincing moods he creates are what makes these color sketches so strong and exciting. They suggest and invite the viewer's imagination into finishing the image, which are their strength. The final backgrounds, on the other hand, present a stage for the characters with convincingly constructed, three-point perspectives that do not allow any interpretation; they determine but do not suggest, which of course has its own appeal and value, as they allow the character animation in its dimensionality to fit in. In Peregoy's color work, the touch of modernity is significant and it clearly translates into the

final film. What brings the drawings into the 1950s/1960s is solely the underlying color, which breaks the restraints of Disney's traditional perspectival construct and flattens it through colored shapes going *against* the perspective or not fully supporting it. There are no gradients or excessive highlights; nor are there textures in the background paintings other than brush work. Often objects are not separated in color contrast from their surroundings, which leads to additional flattening of the space. Also, the color is not confined to the initial shape it belongs to but can flow out of it. This implementation of color correlates with the modern sensibility already introduced much earlier in illustration and then used as a stylistic element by Hubley in *Rooty Toot Toot*. The separation of the design aspects of color, form and shape, line, light and shadow, time, etc., is what makes modern design so exciting. The deconstruction of the various elements and then the free assemblage of it in a new way is the core idea that has been explored in the arts of the twentieth century. Disney explores the mere surface of it and uses it in a commercial, yet beautifully crafted design. In some backgrounds this is much more successful than in others, as some of them do not follow strictly the established design rules and fall back into Disney realism. Especially the nature backgrounds in the winter scenes often have more realism and dimensionality than is good for them. Also, some representations of skies with rather fluffy clouds mimic reality more than they should be and therefore create depth that is unwanted if they are to fit into the film's remaining visuals. It is to a great extent the influence of the underlying color that adds the overwhelming success to the film's backgrounds and style, giving them the needed "modern" touch that greatly affects the intensely rendered drawings. The interesting juxtaposition of traditional Disney style with modern visuals is what is surprisingly convincing.

## Conclusion

After being asked about the input that Walt Disney himself had in the design and production of the film, Peregoy answered in an interview that there was no input in the style by Disney and that he "disliked it immensely after it was done."[29] The film itself became a very big success both critically and financially because it *was* different and had a contemporary feel to it. As mentioned before, the Xerox technology was not about to go; quite the contrary, it was going to stay for the next decades and shape the look of hand-drawn animation tremendously, not only for TV but also for features. Where the included aesthetic of Xerox in the design was so successful in *101 Dalmatians*, its use afterwards in films like *The Sword in the Stone*, *The Jungle Book*, or any other Disney feature in the next 20 years, was often less convincing. The amalgamation of background and characters does not work in the later

29 Bob Miller, Walt Peregoy, Interview Jan. 1992, published in *Walt's People*, Vol. 5, edited by Didier Ghez, Xlibris, Bloomington, IN, 2007, p. 295.

features because the backgrounds do not follow the same design rules the character animation does. The dimensionality in the painted jungle backgrounds in *The Jungle Book* is in stark contrast to the flat, xeroxed characters, which often do not melt with their surroundings but always stand out in front of them as a separate layer not wanting or not being able to merge with them. *101 Dalmatians* did mark a preliminary end to successful and well-designed animated features at the Disney studios and it should take a long time till it produced again features with a design quality of the same caliber. What came afterwards is partly entertaining, has some stunning character animation pieces, but never comes close to the feature with the many dots. The Disney Company lost touch with the artistic development that was happening all around

them and allowed their features to tend to be repetitive aesthetically, as they did not reinvent themselves, despite some of the amazing characters they still invented. Character animation with a lack of successful design or a good story, a concept that is unique, and a production that seems exciting seems pointless because it is a technique celebrating itself but not really developing the art form further. The quality of the features that were produced after *101 Dalmatians* was plain in comparison. Whenever you fall into the trap of producing a formula, you need to step back and do the opposite to *not* repeat yourself. *101 Dalmatians* marks the end of an era of creative outpour from a company that had every feature film look different from the previous one; however, what a beautiful and gorgeous end it is!

# CHAPTER 15

# Color Contrast

## Contrast

*Contrast* is described as "the state of being strikingly different from something else in juxtaposition or close association."[1] Contrast appears therefore in every single element of an image and its narrative. There is contrast in shape (for example, round versus squared), the juxtaposition within any of the various design aspects discussed, and contrast in the character's design (see Volume 2, Chapter 32, "Contrast"), but contrast is also as relevant in sound, music, or the narrative in the form of the different types of characters, for example (see also Volume 2, Chapter 4, "Personality," the section "Different Types of Characters"). Additionally, there is contrast in color, as we have already seen in Itten's seven contrasts of color.

Color contrast is what gives the relationship between the miscellaneous colors tension and separates them from each other, which is the very point of color contrast: to show that one color is different from another. The more contrast there is, the more the colors differ. A red looks much redder next to a green than next to an orange; a saturated blue looks bluer next to a desaturated blue. Color contrast provides an image with tension and with a wider range of possibilities; thus it can make the image overall more interesting, creating depth, and subtleties.

Contrast in color can be achieved in all five aspects of color:

## Contrast in hue

The further the colors are apart from each other on the color wheel, the more contrast they have. Therefore, the colors

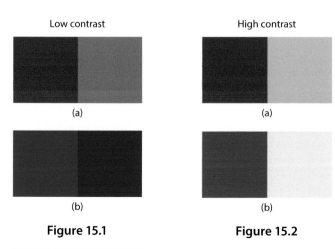

Figure 15.1        Figure 15.2

next to each other on the wheel have the lowest contrast (Figure 15.1a and (b)) and the colors that oppose each other diametrically on the wheel have the highest (Figure 15.2a and (b)). The more contrast they have, the more vibrant they are in their full saturation, like this vibrancy can be seen much more clearly if the colors are recreated on a computer screen.

## Contrast in saturation

Low contrast in saturation makes the colors separate less and their otherness is often not significant enough to make them stand out (Figure 15.3 a and (b)). High contrast in saturation, on the other hand, makes the saturated colors stand out and step forward in significance (Figure 15.4a and (b)), whereas the desaturated ones step back. Colors with high contrast in hue but contrasting saturation also follow this rule that the saturated color will step forward, like in Figure 15.4b, where the highly desaturated yellow is much less "important" than the saturated purple.

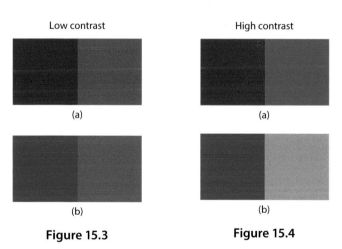

Figure 15.3        Figure 15.4

## Contrast in brightness

Low contrast in brightness like in Figure 15.5a and (b) makes the slightly brighter colors on the right stand out and attract attention. Colors with very high brightness can feel a bit washed out and because of the visual weight of the low brightness of the colors in Figure 15.6a and (b), the darker colors can step forward in importance. However, this does depend on the contrast of proportion (see Itten's seven principles of color) and how much of each color is present, as the otherness of a color can also attract attention.

---

[1] Oxford Dictionaries: Definition of Contrast, https://en.oxforddictionaries.com/definition/contrast (accessed September 5, 2017).

DOI: 10.1201/b22148-15

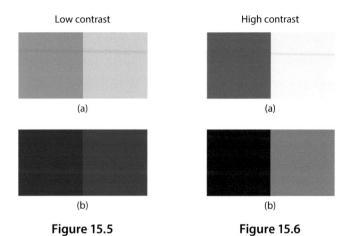

Low contrast

(a)

(b)

**Figure 15.5**

High contrast

(a)

(b)

**Figure 15.6**

## Contrast in luminance

Colors with high luminance attract attention and with low luminance step backwards. Again, however, the contrast of proportion is important. In Figure 15.7a and (b) the luminance between the two colors is similar, which results in low contrast; in Figure 15.8a and (b) the luminance between canary yellow (90) and cobalt blue (36) produces the highest

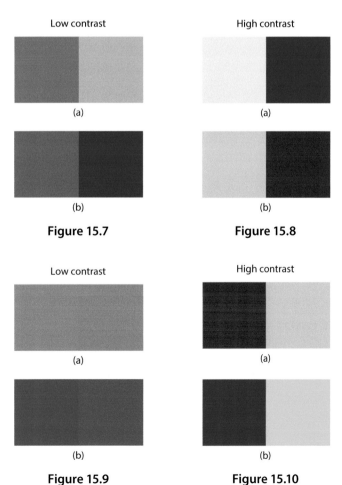

Low contrast

(a)

(b)

**Figure 15.7**

High contrast

(a)

(b)

**Figure 15.8**

Low contrast

(a)

(b)

**Figure 15.9**

High contrast

(a)

(b)

**Figure 15.10**

contrast (white with 0 and black with 100 have the highest possible contrast in "color"). Contrast in luminance, however, is not easy to detect with the human eye and thus does step backwards in importance when it comes to contrast.

## Contrast in temperature

With low contrast in temperature (Figure 15.9a and (b)), the warm orange in Figure 15.9a only attracts slightly more attention than the slightly warm pink right next to it; in Figure 15.9b the warmer blue on the right seems actually slightly less important than the colder blue on the left. High contrast in color temperature, however, pushes the warm colors forward and the cold ones back. The stronger the contrast (Figure 15.10a and (b)), the more intensely the warm color will attract the eye.

## Practical use of color contrast

Color contrast is important at any stage of the image-making process and needs to be considered at all times when using colors in their complex relationships. It is also one of the aids that help to distinguish one object from the one right next to it and thus create depth, visual weight, and subtleties in texture and details. The human eye is very acute to the perception of contrast. As much as the light situation might change during the day, the eye will adjust and see the images as relatively similar in contrast and color.

Before starting out with a color sketch, one can do a tonal study of the composition and explore where the tones need to be darker and where lighter for all the elements to read and also to clarify the lighting situation. Of course, this does not mean to make it realistic! It means to see what is aesthetically pleasing for that specific image, style, and narrative. Figure 15.11a has very low contrast between the objects and background, which makes everything bland and not read well. Figure 15.11b has the outline already darker, which helps with the definition of each object; however, the object's tones are still too similar to distinguish from each other. Figure 15.11c has the tones arranged in such a way to show that each object is different from the next. There is a good range of dark to bright in the image.

One artist who continuously experimented throughout his life with color contrasts and the relationships between objects was Giorgio Morandi (1890–1964), an Italian painter who mainly focused on painting still lifes, which were very restrained in their composition and choice of colors, always subtle, and often very subdued. He explored in a minimalistic fashion simple arrangements of the same objects and his colors are often rather low in contrast, testing how far one can go while still reading the image clearly. In his still life from 1957 (Figure 15.12) most of the objects, the table, and also the wall are white. There is barely any shadow that would help to create more contrast. But still the objects all clearly read because there is enough contrast

(a)

(b)

(c)

**Figure 15.11**

here and there to separate all the elements from each other. The bottles that read most clearly are the two blue ones on the right, because their darkness has the strongest contrast to their surrounding white. In his painting from 1947–1948 (Figure 15.13), the contrast is dramatically reduced and the objects clearly melt together with the background, creating more of a unit compared to the previous painting. The range between light and dark is much less refined and thus the image overall also feels lighter in this instance.

Let us see how we can practically use color contrast in painting. Figure 15.14 has an arrangement of two bottles that don't read at all because the contrast in the entire image is very low. The bottles' shapes blend into the surroundings and there is no strong color anywhere. Every color has a color next to it that is very similar in brightness, hue, and saturation.

Increasing the contrast ever so slightly in Figure 15.15 by adding, for instance, a darker shadow line where bottle and table meet, the bottle not only gets heavier but also separates as an object from the table. Also lightening up the area around the bottles and darkening the bottles themselves increases the contrast and makes the objects stand out more and gain more visual weight. Making one element too dark, however, destroys the balance between all colors and drags too much attention to itself! Only because the bottles now read better doesn't necessarily mean that they read well enough. Depending on one's personal preference, more contrast might have to be added to find a level that is acceptable for one's own taste and/ or the needs of the image's mood or style. Figure 15.16 makes the mistake of bringing warm color into the background, which pulls it forward and makes it look very odd. The bottles should be warm in color if perspective is wanted or, like in Figure 15.14,

**Figure 15.12**

Giorgio Morandi: *Still Life* (1957).

**Figure 15.13**

Giorgio Morandi: *Still Life* (1947/1948).

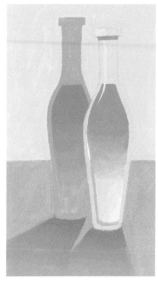   

| Figure 15.14 | Figure 15.15 | Figure 15.16 | Figure 15.17 |

everything should be treated with colder colors, which keeps the entire image congruent, yet flat. The distinction between warm and cold colors is so strong that background and bottles don't seem to be in the same space. Figure 15.17 additionally adds a dark and warm-colored horizon line, which is so strong in its contrast compared to all the other colors that it drags all the attention and pushes itself into the foreground, being stronger than the overlap of the bottles, a mistake that ruins the entire image.

What makes contrast a bit difficult to discuss is the range of possibilities and personal style, preference, and aesthetics. Giorgio Morandi's paintings show that an extremely low contrast image is also an aesthetically pleasing option (or Claude Monet's painting *Ice Floes* discussed earlier; Figure 14.36) and has as much validity as one with high contrast. The question is what the purpose of the image is and what mood is needed. Creating a balanced color contrast in a painting can be a long process!

The overall color contrast deals with the maximum range of the image's brightness and color and also the relationship between the objects' distances to each other and their relative brightness and range of color. An image with medium contrast ranges from white to black and/or all its hues, containing the whole range of brightness and darkness and all the shades in between (Figure 15.18), which makes the image appear crisp and fresh, clean, and more solid in its visual weight. Objects look heavier and more real and have a better perspective as the range of brightness in the foreground is much wider compared to the background, which separates both foreground from background. With contrast the contents of the frame have more visual weight, more details, texture, and a wider range of hues.

If the contrast is too low or decreased (Figure 15.19), the image gets dull and flattens out, loses its freshness. Depth, weight, the range of hues, and details disappear, which causes for instance the background to mostly vanish; the image loses life and solidity. From an emotional standpoint, images with medium contrast are inviting and visually appealing. Low contrast makes them unattractive and less inviting, somehow dull and plain.

If the contrast is increased, the shift goes towards black, white, and solid, over-saturated colors (Figure 15.20). Gray scales and the entire field between brightness and darkness disappear and the colors start shifting towards full saturation, eliminating the subtle hues between the primary and secondary colors. Details and textures disappear, color subtleties vanish, and the image loses its color perspective, its textural perspective, and its mood; however, it gains in contrast between foreground and background and silhouettes read better due to the elimination of all midtones. Pushing the contrast even further results in only black and white with fully saturated primary and secondary colors (Figure 15.21).

## Low contrast

Details and texture start to disappear. They are the very subtle parts in an image created by the variation of brightness and color and are affected immediately by any change in the contrast. Those details start to vanish if the contrast is reduced. The wide range of hues dissipates.

- Less contrast means less depth perception, which leads to a flatter image.
- The crispness of the image is reduced. The loss of range of color flattens the image and reduces its crispness by emitting highlights and evening out shadows, reducing the object's dimensionality and form.

- The image loses weight. A wide range of brightness allows the objects to be seen in their most natural form, which leads to a realistic depiction of weight and solidity. Less contrast, however, reduces the shadows and the overall visual weight of the objects, which makes them appear less three-dimensional and lighter.
- If the image is completely reduced in contrast, it will lead to a 50% gray.

## High contrast

- Figure 15.21 has extremely high contrast, where there are absolutely no midtones left and only the black, white, and highly saturated colors are left.
- The color's saturation gets more intense the higher the contrast, allowing some of the colors to be unrealistically vibrant.
- Details are more visible in the subtle areas of the picture, because the differences between light and dark are increased. Details and textures in the midranges intensify and are more visible, yet start to be unrealistic and stylized.
- The object's visual weight increases as the colors have more brightness and saturation and black starts to dominate.

- White starts to bleed out and the bright areas lose details and texture.
- If the image's contrast is pushed to an extreme, the colors shift to maximum saturation and brightness, resulting in heavy blacks, whites, and primary and secondary colors with no details.

## Contrast and weather

Figure 15.22 shows a bridge in the mountains of Nepal in dense fog. The particles in the air take out most of the color's saturation, hue, and values and level them out, turning the landscape slowly into a plain gray. The more fog, the less contrast during the day. Increasing the contrast in Figure 15.23 makes the fog seem to recede and increases the weight of the various elements in the picture.

The more clouds there are covering the sky, the less contrast the landscape underneath has, compared to the same landscape with few or no clouds. The closer the object is to the viewer, the more contrast it has; the further away, the less contrast. Mountains in the far distance would have very little contrast even on a sunny day.

**Figure 15.18**

**Figure 15.19**

**Figure 15.20**

**Figure 15.21**

**Figure 15.22**

In Figure 15.22, the contrast is as it was shot with the camera. The fog is dense and swallows the shadows.

**Figure 15.23**

In the Figure 15.23, the contrast has been increased digitally, which reduces the fog in the foreground immensely and additionally intensifies the colors.

# CHAPTER 16

# Perspective

The vast field of possibilities within perspective makes this a rather exciting topic, of which the typical construction of a three-point realistic perspective, which is often very daunting, if not outright scary to construct, is only a very small portion. But there is a full range of possibilities, of which one option is actually having no perspective at all, then the one-, two-, or three-point perspectives, but there are also some aspects of design that suggest and support perspective, like gradient and overlap, size, color, texture, contrast, focus and field of depth, light and shadow, and foreshortening. They are all valid contributors to representations and/or interpretations of perspective and even a mixture of all of them can be developed into an exciting style. This does not mean that the best choice is an accurately constructed three-point perspective because it represents our vision most closely. After all we are dealing with art making, which means the *interpretation* of reality, not just the representation of it. It depends on what perspective style fits the content of the story and also the visual ability of the target audience. Only because it looks realistic does not make it more complex in terms of its artistic visuals or value and neither does it make it more sophisticated in its content. The ability to represent reality "as it is" is only one direction, not the ultimate goal of image making. If we repeatedly followed this direction of representing reality, the development and the core idea of art, to evolve, would be lost and art *per se* would be stagnant. Thousands of years of art production

of hundreds of cultures cannot be reduced to the idea of three-point perspective being the pinnacle. Perspective is, as any other aspect of design, one that needs to be played with in all its shades and possibilities. If one only considers the vanishing point perspectives of one, two, or three points as an option, one misses out on so many other exciting alternatives to create space or even do the opposite and avoid space. A completely flat design has as much artistic worth! One can even use perspective purposefully wrong to create an interesting visual effect. Art is a playground that has to be explored in all its shades. The construction of perspective with different vanishing points produces a convincing image through the illusion of space, but it is still only an approximation of it. Every culture has its own system of how it sees its environment and there are myriads of ways of depicting the space we live in. The following just explores four very different interpretations of space from four different cultures.

## Egyptian: Green room in the north palace at Amarna

"Egyptian art seems flat and horizontal, lacking perspective and depth!" Obviously this is not true, as we cannot or must not see art from today's viewpoint only but have to see it from the viewpoint

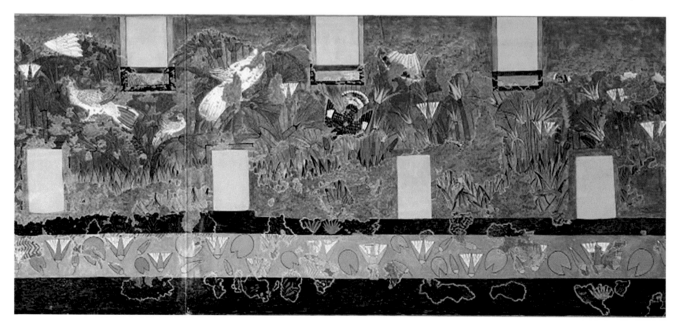

**Figure 16.1**

Facsimile painting from the "Green Room" in the North Palace at Amarna, Egypt (ca. 1353–1336 B.C.); artists: Nina de Garis Davies (1881–1965) & Norman de Garis Davies (1865–1941).

DOI: 10.1201/b22148-16

of the culture that created it (which we can't really, but we can at least try). The Egyptian world is mostly shown horizontally, in stripes of information. There is often a stacking of stripes and they can also flow into each other and overlap, but in general the arrangement is a horizontal orientation in clearly arranged stripes. Egyptian art always has a very defined, even mathematical order and clarity, the elements are carefully arranged and do not seem to allow the slightest deviation from tradition and norm. Art is not just a creative expression, which is actually a rather modern invention; it is often a political and social tool to record and spread information. For people who cannot read, visuals can also be an extension of language. That language has to have its rules and its traditions in order to be understood. Egyptian art is built and created to last, to praise the achievements and beliefs of a people for eternity, and the main objective is order and clarity. The pharaoh's purpose is to maintain the order of the realm and with the help of the gods make sure of the annual cycle, the reoccurring annual flood of the life-giving river Nile, which guarantees the harvest and thus survival. This order is reflected in the art and with it its perspective, which never shows visual depth and only suggests perspective through overlapping characters and objects. The size relationship between people is never a sign of distance but always one of hierarchy. The bigger characters are the pharaoh or gods, the smaller ones the pharaoh's subjects or enemies. The strict convention of all Egyptian art was followed from the famous Narmer Palette from 3100 BC until the country was ruled by outside forces, which influenced and loosened the traditional conventions but also ended several thousands of years of continuity. The only time period when Egyptian art did see a major change was during the Amarna period, during Pharaoh Akhenaten's reign (1351–1334 BC) and shortly into Tutankhamun's short reign. The art was more personal, private, even intimate; it included more movement in the characters and images. Overall, there is a sense of emotion compared to the more reserved pieces before and after the Amarna

period. Figure 16.1 shows a wall painting from the Green Room, the residence at the North Palace of one of Akhenaten's daughters, with a lavish painting of papyruses, birds, and a small canal with water and water lilies, depicting marsh life on the Nile. The horizontal orientation of the traditional Egyptian viewpoint is still very much maintained and the scene is bursting with life. Though there is no perspective in terms of depth, there is still a very clear sense of what is in the front and what is behind through overlap. The horizontal stripe of the canal is seen from the top, which actually gives two different views: the side view of the papyrus and then the top view of the water with two stripes of dark stretches and plants. However, all are strips of information, rather than actual depictions of reality. They are pieces of information that are designed and arranged instead of mimicking the actual look of the marshland. This style of depicting nature on the Nile is of course not an invention of Amarna art but has a very long tradition; an exquisite example can be seen in the reliefs in the mastaba of Kagemni, an official during the reign of Pharaoh Teti (2345–2333 BC), a thousand years prior to Amarna art. The mastaba is located in Saqqara and offers stunning details showing the daily life of fishermen, for instance (Figure 16.2). The scene displays a reed boat with three fishermen on the Nile. In the stripe underneath the boat we see fish, so the stripe clearly shows water, but the fish extend all the way to the top in front of the men. The Nile is either seen in a side or top view. Behind the men are vertical stripes in front of which we can see flying birds. The pictorial ground is divided into water and air, which do not at all follow the perspective we are used to but present a very unique interpretation of a three-dimensional space into a two-dimensional plane. The Green Room and the scene with the fishermen both show how Egyptian space is seen: as horizontal arrangements of information. A similar approach can be seen in many of the old cultures in which horizontal stripes are the main compositional tool. Overlap is therefore often the only aspect that suggests perspective.

**Figure 16.2**

The mastaba tomb of Kagemni (2345–2333 BC).

**Figure 16.3**

Cubiculum (bedroom) from the Villa of P. Fannius Synistor at Boscoreale (50–40 B.C.).

## Roman: Villa of P. Fannius Synistor at Boscoreale, Italy

This example shows the interior of a wall painting in a cubiculum (bedroom) from the villa of P. Fannius Synistor at Boscoreale, a small town outside of Naples. The cubiculum was painted around 50–40 BC during the Late Republic and preserved due to the eruption of Mount Vesuvius in 79 AD (Figure 16.3). The two long sides of the room are mirrored in their depiction of two idyllic landscapes, which seem to have been inspired by theatre stage designs.[1] The painting shows a view through pillars above a socle into a townscape with gates, vegetation, round temples, and various houses with balconies and windows. There are no people in the scene, just a quiet assemblage of architectural elements. The two facing holy gates in the middle of the long walls of each side of the room contain statues. On the left we have an archaic statue of Artemis-Hekate, left and right of which are wilding trees and vegetation; on the right wall is an unidentified statue

surrounded by healthy trees.[2] Left and right of these holy gates are views of architectural elements that each in their overall arrangement are oriented towards the wall's centers, which are the statues. But because both statues are facing each other it is the center of the room that is the most important viewing point. This clear direction is at first glance seemingly a one-point perspective with the vanishing point in the absolute middle, the statues; however, the details of the architectural elements do not follow the perspective but sometimes even go against it, showing for example a downward view onto a roof (Figure 16.4). We can see depth and clear form in the individual elements and each on its own is convincing enough, but as a group they feel slightly thrown together from today's sense of perspective. The form and depth are supported by shadows on the sides of the buildings and gates. Also a hint of color perspective is achieved by the furthest buildings in the background being the brightest, but within the assemblage of the architectural elements this color perspective is not applied.

---

[1] Aoyagi Irelli and Pappalardo De Caro, *Pompeijanische Wandmalerei*, Belser Verlag, Zurich, 1990, p. 218.

[2] Aoyagi Irelli and Pappalardo De Caro, *Pompeijanische Wandmalerei*, Belser Verlag, 1990, p. 254.

All the walls are richly painted with architectural elements that a person sitting or lying in the bedroom looks "out towards." One gets the impression of being in an open kiosk with a low socle, on which pillars carry the roof. The viewer looks into a fantastical and romantic landscape on all sides. The paintings are an illusion to make the viewer believe he or she is in a theatrical setting rather than just in a bedroom. The city is not an actual depiction of a real city, but a fantasy. The space of the room expands into the fantastic, opening the confined space of the bedroom into a much bigger realm. It invites the viewer to break down the walls and imagine a grander space.

## Chinese: *Along the River During the Quingming Festival*

This Chinese scroll contains one, if not the most, treasured painting of Chinese art: *Along the River During the Qingming Festival* (Figures 16.5 and 16.6, showing part of a long scroll). Painted by Zhang Zeduan (1085–1145) at the end of the Northern and beginning of the Southern Song dynasty (remember the article about Guo Xi, see Chapter 13, "Light and Shadow," Case study: Mountains and streams in Bambi (1942), Same time period!). Zhang Zeduan was a court painter during the reign of Emperor Huizong, who was also an artist in his own right. Zeduan's massive genre painting of over 5 meters in length depicts daily life along the banks of the Bian River in the twelfth century, in the capital Bianjing of the Northern Song dynasty (today's Kaifeng, Henan, East China). The river runs south of the Imperial Palace and the part Zhang Zeduan painted is southeast of the two outer walls of Bianjing. The bustling city is filled with

**Figure 16.4**

Cubiculum (bedroom) from the Villa of P. Fannius Synistor at Boscoreale (50–40 B.C.). Detail of the east wall.

**Figure 16.5**

Zhang Zeduan: *Along the River During the Quingming Festival* (1085–1145); detail.

**Figure 16.6**

*Zhang Zeduan: Along the River During the Quingming Festival (1085–1145); detail.*

an herbal drink stand, a fabric store, a storyteller's stall, a wine shop, a butcher, a doctor, sales offices, a carpenter's workshop, a barbershop, a camel caravan, a temple, a sesame pancake shop, a firewood store, a tavern, fortune-teller, restaurant and bakery, teahouse and inn, bridges and gates, houses and boats, and so much more. All this is filled with about 500 men and women (mostly men), children, officials, artists, merchants, and travelers. The depicted Qingming festival is an annual event that is celebrated at the beginning of April and commemorates ancestors, while also being an opportunity to go on a spring outing. However, whether the scroll really depicts this specific festival or even the city of Bianjing is debated. It could also be an idealized and romantic version of the city, not an actual realistic view.[3]

The Biang River marks the center of the painting and all the elements, buildings, bridges, houses, are loosely arranged, not following one defined perspective standing position of the viewer, but many. So following the scroll from right to left, the viewer walks into the city, starting at the scenes with willow trees, then passing the peasant's houses and village dwellings, and slowly reaching the town's vibrant, bustling markets and center of its economic wealth and trade. Readers of the scroll change their viewing perspective along with the scroll. Every small scene has its own personal perspective space, so viewers are always, wherever they are looking, right in the action. The scroll's horizontal orientation invites continuous walking of the eyes along the river banks and the perspective does not favor one area over the other. One needs to keep in mind how the

scroll would be viewed: it is unwound and only the section that is in front of the viewer is seen, whereas the unseen parts are rolled up. The viewer tracks along the scenery. The scroll is after all over 5 meters long and a defined standing position of the artist, with a Western perspective, would have clearly rendered the view differently, not inviting a horizontal stroll through the painting, but presenting a view fixed in one standing position. It is similar to the difference between a camera track along the city in which the camera physically moves along the city (which is Zeduan's technique in this one scroll), compared to a camera pan where the camera does not physically move and because of the camera's standing position favors that one point and renders it significant (Western perspective). In Zeduan's painting the entire length is of visual importance exactly because of the lack of one clear vanishing point. Chinese landscape paintings provide islands of perspective, not an overall perspective where everything succumbs to one or two vanishing points.

Chinese architectural perspective used axonometric perspective, where the viewer is usually way above eye level, the ground floor is tilted about 45°, and all vertical and horizontal lines are parallel or perpendicular to the horizon. All the depicted elements in *Along the River* are constructed with a parallel or nearly parallel perspective; however, some of the houses do taper towards the back side or the front side. Much of the architecture shows the right side panel of the building (like in the gate in Figure 16.6, where we can see the right gate entrance of the tilted gate), instead of the left one. This gives the entire composition a slight tilt and continuity that stimulates the unwinding of the scroll.

Zeduan uses the so-called jiehua technique, which is for Chinese art the accurate perspectival depiction of architecture and objects (like boats, bridges, etc.) done with precision, measurements, and rulers to ensure straight lines when needed. Despite its accuracy, the painting is very likely not a realistic depiction of the city but an idealized illustration of an event.

At the end of the Tang dynasty and beginning of the Song dynasty lived an artist and art theorist called Jing Hao (~855–915). He wrote a narrative called *Bifa Ji* (*Notes on Brushwork*), which is a conversation between a young man (Hao?) and an old man, a sage, who teaches him about the theories of painting. In this conversation, the old man says after being asked about what is lifelikeness and reality: "Lifelikeness means to achieve the form of the object but to leave out its spirit. Reality means that the forces of both spirit and substance are strong. Furthermore, if spirit is conveyed only through the outward appearance, and not through the image in its totality, the image is dead."[4] Clearly, there is much more to an object than just its surface. The point of the image is never to replicate what is being seen, but to enhance, to paint with emotions, knowledge, and spirituality.

[3] See article by Valerie Hansen, The Mystery of the Qingming Scroll and its Subject: The Case against Kaifeng, *Journal of Sung Yuan Studies* Vol. 26 (1998), pp.183–200.

[4] Stephen West, *Ways with Words; Writing about Reading Texts from Early China*, University of California Press, Berkeley, CA, 2000.

# European Baroque: Ceiling in the Würzburg Residence, Germany

The baroque is famous for its movement, its explosive action, and grandeur on a scale that often baffles. Perspective was one of the tricks of baroque art and often used to expand the interiors, especially in the illusionistic ceiling paintings, also called *quadratura*. They open up the view towards a marvelous sky and reveal architecture, myriads of characters, animals, allegorical figures, angels, puttos, and cherubs flying and frolicking in fantastical scenarios and colorful clouds. The painted architecture always extends the existing architecture, blending the two harmoniously. The grandest ceiling painting of them all, of approximately 580 m², was painted by Giambattista Tiepolo (1696–1770), which he painted with his son Giandomenico in the grand staircase of the Würzburg Residence, Germany, in 1750–1753 (Figure 16.7). Tiepolo was a Venetian painter at the end of the baroque, beginning of the rococo, and one of the leaders of his trade in Europe. The four sides of the ceiling in Würzburg show the four continents Africa, Asia, America, and Europe, each represented by an allegorical woman accompanied by an animal she is riding on. In the middle of the ceiling we see Apollo flying in the sky surrounded by the gods of Olympus, the four seasons, and other allegorical figures. Tiepolo uses architectural elements behind the rows of characters in the front and then accentuates the thrilling depth through color perspective in the characters and them receding into the layers of clouds. Size perspective amongst the characters assists the feeling of depth. Banners, sticks, architectural pieces, and the arrangement of the characters all strive towards the sky, creating a dizzying feeling of movement and tension. One of the most successful elements that support the believability of the perspective illusion is the perfect handling of foreshortening in the figures. Their flawless rendering and accurate bottom view makes the illusion complete. How the light streams into the actual staircase in Würzburg was also considered by Tiepolo and integrated into the painting, pushing the illusion of reality and painting. The purpose is to extend the view and make the already impressive real architecture even bigger through the illusionistic painting.

The four examples of Egyptian, Roman, Chinese, and baroque approaches shows how different cultures used perspective for different purposes and to express their diverse thoughts. All are obviously valid approaches even today.

The following explores those aspects that support and create perspective. Linear perspective, for example, clearly creates an

**Figure 16.7**

Giambattista Tiepolo: Ceiling of the grand staircase (1750–53).

illusion on a two-dimensional plane for perspective, but other aspects like gradient and contrast just support perspective. Some of those create a feeling of depth, rather than perspective, but nevertheless still support perspective.

**Aspects that create perspective:**

No perspective, 1, 2 or 3 point perspective

**Aspects that support perspective:**

Gradient

Overlap

Size relationship

Color perspective

Textural perspective (also see Chapter 14, "Color," the section "Practical Application," the subsection "Perspective and Depth")

Contrast

Light and shadow

Focus, Field of depth (see Chapter 12, "Depth")

Foreshortening in characters (see Volume 2, Chapter 24)

# No perspective, 1, 2 or 3 point perspective

## No perspective

Having no perspective in the image is a very valid and actually visually attractive direction that has in the time of CG animation stepped into the background as a solid and powerful interpretation of space. It is often connected to the work of children, because children's drawings usually have no perspective at all. No perspective seemingly represents a design direction that is basic and lacks the sophistication of a photorealistic, three-point perspective. Nevertheless, nothing could be further from the truth! It is one thing to draw "wrong" because one does not have the skills or knowledge to draw it right (like children draw without the restrictions of trained knowledge), yet a totally different one if drawn wrong on purpose and with the knowledge of design and its effect on the viewer in mind. The difference between naive and purposeful design is that the latter is created with the expertise of design and the will of interpretation in mind. The avoidance of space in its dimensional expansion has exciting visual possibilities that interprets rather than represents. The movie *The Secret of Kells* (2009) plays with some of these options when flipping the ground plane vertically and mimicking a medieval portrayal of space, and it does this very successfully and visually convincingly. However, how often have I heard in class the comment when showing old art or art from other cultures: "Oh they didn't know any better … they didn't know how to get it right yet." There is always the possibility of the artist not wanting to do it differently because it wasn't important to them to represent nature realistically. The idea of art developing from "unsophisticated" Stone Age idols to a so-called "sophisticated" three-point perspective is ludicrous. Art has a development that is ongoing, yet is also in constant flux. There is no high or low point; there is only change. Art is always a representation of its culture and time.

In zero-point perspective, there is no visible system in the object's or landscape's lines being either parallel or perpendicular to each other. The various sides of the object are not depicted in their actual geometry. The object can, like in Figure 16.9, be shown from different viewpoints at the same time and still be convincing as a box, as we know what an actual box looks like. None of the depicted lines need to be parallel to each other to be understood as an actual box because we know what a box is, so our mind already understands what it is supposed to be.

**Figure 16.8**

Charlie O'Sullivan: *Tales of Love.*

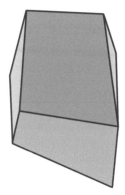

**Figure 16.9**

**Figure 16.10**

**Figure 16.11**

For instance, cubism and deconstructivism both use this as the basis of its art and architecture (Frank Gehry, for example).

In Charlie O'Sullivan's painting (Figure 16.8) *Tales of Love*, we have a more or less complete lack of perspective yet a creative and unique painting that describes a dreamlike landscape filled with surreal plants and pattern. She uses colors and shapes to achieve this emotional rather than descriptive feel of an environment. Her color palette is soft and subtle, does not fully represent natural or realistic color, yet doesn't deny it either. The perspective in this little landscape happens in the overlap of some of the trees and in the equal distribution of contrast. The trees do overlap here and there and sometimes their crown takes over the shape of the fields behind them, replacing the fields with the actual crown: an interesting play between positive and negative space (Figure 16.10). This flattens the painting and destroys the very idea of overlap creating perspective. Her use of shapes, colors, textures, and very interesting pattern create an unusual and personal space that invites one to linger and enjoy the playful relationship between all these elements and how they affect one's mood and emotion. The range of artistic choices and ideas is what makes her pictures appear rich. For example, she allows the pattern of the ground to flow into the trunk of the tree to represent the bark (Figure 16.11), or the silhouette of a character appears next to a tree, suggesting a surreal space (Figure 16.12). O'Sullivan developed a style that does not need perspective in order to achieve its goal; quite the contrary. The lack of perspective helps it to be even more surreal and invite us into a world that is gentle, friendly, and detached from reality. There are various views in the image: trees and plants are seen from the side, streets and fields are seen from the top, which in the end provides the viewer with more information than a regular, perspectively correct depiction. We do know how a landscape is supposed to look and how its elements are arranged. O'Sullivan gives us more, because she adds a unique interpretation to the landscape, which causes emotion and a new viewing sensation.

The object in Figure 16.13 is an extension of the one in Figure 16.9. It has some perspective to it, which is mostly

**Figure 16.12**

rendered through light, shadow, and simple gradient. The perspective seems impossible, but it is the gradient that suggests twisted planes; therefore it could actually be physically built. Adding to the same object the wrong lighting and gradient makes it more inconceivable and abstract (Figure 16.14), yet it still

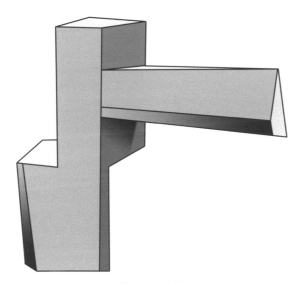

Figure 16.13

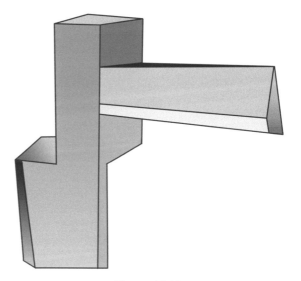

Figure 16.14

has a definite dimensionality to it despite lacking constructed perspective. By changing the elements of the object, perspective can be eliminated or achieved, but it can also, like in Figure 16.14, be a visual cheat so the viewer thinks there is perspective where there actually is none.

Taking all the aspects of perspective out of the image we end up with a surface with objects scattered around or arranged that have no size relationship to each other, where color does not suggest perspective at all, where contrast does not allow a separation of foreground, middle ground, and background, and gradient is nonexistent.

Aspects to consider when suggesting no perspective:

- *Overlap*: This aspect obviously shows what is in front and what is behind. To break this aspect, we can have the character or object be transparent and only appear in line work, then the overlap is put in question.
- *Size*: Size can obviously be changed in order to break perspective and show the opposite of what one would expect. The character in the front is small; the one in the back bigger.
- *Color*: Using color against its color perspective qualities, thus avoiding perspective. Also saturation, brightness, and hue can define foreground, middle ground, and background in an opposite fashion.
- *Texture*: The texture close to the viewer is fine; texture far away is coarse. Or texture is evenly distributed in its granularity throughout the picture.
- *Gradient*: Going against the perspective strength of the gradient.
- *Light and shadow*: Using light and shadow only to differentiate planes from each other, but not having it use its realistic form-giving qualities.
- *Field of depth*: Field of depth *per se* has the tendency to create foreground and background, though this can be broken with

determined overlap of focused elements versus out-of-focus elements.
- *Contrast*: Strong contrast in the image will attract the eye and create perspective; the lack of contrast will render the area unimportant and flatten that section.

## Suggestive perspective

The other kind of "no perspective" would be the one that is undetermined in its depiction of dimensionality, being more suggestive than descriptive. This includes all the aspects of perspective mentioned above, though not necessarily in the "correct" perspective-producing fashion. For example, overlap could happen but not in combination with the right size, or the overlapping shape can be transparent, imbricating yet questioning at the same time. A very good example of this direction is Juan Gris' (José Victoriano Gonzalez, 1887–1927) painting *Still Life with Checked Tablecloth* from 1915 (Figure 16.15), belonging to the synthetic cubism movement, which lasted from 1913 until the early 1920s. Gris had studied painting in Madrid and worked drawing comics strips until he moved to Paris in 1906, where he continued to illustrate for magazines. In 1911, he shifted seriously to painting and produced his first cubist works.[5] In the beginning he focused on the dissection of objects and in 1914 moved towards synthetic cubism, focusing on the playful reassembling of the pieces, which he interpreted with a more colorful spectrum that was also more decorative or designed compared to many of the other artists in the same movement. Amongst the objects that are arranged on the table with the two-colored checked table cloth are two teacups, the newspaper *Le Journal*, a bottle of ale and one bottle of red wine, a large white-footed fruit compote, and a guitar. A variety of oblique angles dominate the composition and make it

---

5   Giulio Carlo Argan, *Propyläen Kunstgeschichte. Die Kunst des 20. Jahrhunderts 1880–1940*, Propyläen Verlag, Berlin, 1990.

exciting and dynamic; however, they clearly show an arrangement of the objects into a triangular shape. Gris rearranges the various elements into a composition that resembles a bull's head with the cups as nostrils and the guitar as horns, and one can even see two eyes staring at the viewer.[6] On close observation one can also see that Gris has scratched the wet paint of the tablecloth to mimic the threading of the cloth, which adds to the texture in the painting tremendously. In *Still Life with Checked Tablecloth* Gris gives the illusion of perspective through overlap and light and shadow to create form. There is also a hint of color perspective, as some elements come forward due to their brightness while others recede. In particular, the white fruit compote pushes itself into the foreground due to its continuous overlapping stand and the dominant grapes behind it that very much drag attention because of their realistic rendering. Gris also uses false perspective in the table itself, where we can see the legs of the table with its top in false but still semiconvincing perspective; however, the tablecloth in its checked pattern puts the perspective into question. The left corner of the table creates a tangent with the frame, sabotaging the dimensionality of the space. All the objects on the table are stacked on top of each other with overlap; however, they do also penetrate each other's forms and shapes, interrupting the levelling of the objects. The guitar on the left and the two cups are shown in their white silhouette, the most basic depiction of an object on the two-dimensional plane; however, the grapes are painted in a realistic fashion. Juan Gris gives us a broad range of possibilities indeed.

**Figure 16.15**

Juan Gris: *Still Life with Checked Tablecloth* (1915).

# Case study: No perspective in UPA's *Fudget's Budget* (1954)

Director and animator Robert Cannon was one of the most creative and also most radical amongst the character animators and directors in the 1940s and 1950s. His work not only helped to pave the path towards the famous UPA style but the whole industry. His creativity and inventiveness with movement and shape is astounding as animator and director alike. Cannon started his career at Leon Schlesinger Productions (which later in 1944 became Warner Bros. Cartoons, Inc.). He worked for the major studios in the 1930s and 1940s: he briefly worked for Disney, though mainly animated for Warner and assisted animators Bob Clampett and Chuck Jones in their short films for the *Looney Tunes* and *Merry Melodies* series. At the end of the 1940s he worked for Tex Avery's animation unit at MGM on *Droopy* shorts and on one of Avery's masterpieces, *Little Rural Riding Hood* (1949). One of the shorts where his work as character animator is outstanding is the character animation in Warner Brothers' *The Dover Boys of Pimento University, or the Rivals of Roquefort Hall*, directed by Chuck Jones in 1942, on which he worked alongside animators Ken Harris, John McGrew, and Ben Washam. Warner Brothers' goal at the time was to

lead its animation department away from the ever-so-popular Disney style and find its own expression, and Chuck Jones was the one for the task. The animation in the final short of *The Dover Boys* is so very different from others at the time that it left its mark in animation history, if not immediately, but in the mind of animators of what is possible in this medium. Robert Cannon is noted as the primary animator on *The Dover Boys* and he obviously pushed the animation into never-before-seen territory in terms of timing and animation technique. (Smear animation was used successfully in the short to show characters moving extraordinarily fast. The inbetweens were replaced by a smear that gave the characters incredible speed in going from one pose into another.) Much of the animation is very different from what had been done at the time in Hollywood: dainty Dora Standpipe, for instance, the love interest and fiancée of

---

6   Emily Braun and Rebecca Rabinow, *Cubism: The Leonard A. Lauder Collection* (Metropolitan Museum of Art), Yale University Press, London, 2014, p. 135.

the three Dover Boys, is apparently a damsel in distress. She moves like her name suggests: she is so very uptight that instead of walking she smoothly floats and yet does not move at all.

The characters go from pose to pose and otherwise stand often still, which is the precursor to what would become "limited animation" under UPA in the 1950s, which Robert Cannon was part of. *The Dover Boys* already shows Cannon's never-ending ability to invent and to push character animation further and further. However, when *The Dover Boys* was finally screened the executives at Warner were not very amused by the short film and wanted to fire Jones (they ultimately didn't, because no replacement could be found; of course not: it was Chuck Jones!).

In 1945 Cannon joined Steven Schwartz to produce shorts for the Private Snafu educational films for Signal Corps. Cannon had already worked on quite a few Snafu shorts while at Warner Brothers: the short *Spies* (1943), *Infantry Blues* (1943) *Private Snafu vs. Malaria Mike* (1944), *A Lecture on Camouflage* (1944), *Gas* (1944), in which Bugs Bunny briefly appears, *Outpost* (1944), and *Going Home* (1944) were all directed by Chuck Jones (and also a non-Snafu short film for the US Office of War Information: *Point Rationing of Foods* from 1943). Warner had won a bid against Disney to produce the Snafu shorts for the government. The shorts were only screened for the military and meant for the education of the forces on various topics like hygiene, military behavior, or even money spending. Only long after the war did the shorts become publicly available. When Cannon left the Chuck Jones unit at Warner Brothers and started at UPA, Steve Hilberman stated about Cannon joining the company: "We were lucky in having a man like Bobe Cannon, who wanted to push *animation* in different directions."[7] The short *Quick Facts: Inflation* (1944) was the first Snafu short produced by UPA and directed by Steven Schwartz, which already looks different from the shorts that Chuck Jones directed. Where Jones is very dimensional in background and animation and of course follows the Warner style, Schwarz's Snafu is flat and graphic in the backgrounds and dimensional in the character animation. He pushes this much further in the next short, also produced by UPA and again animated by Cannon: *A Few Quick Facts: Fear* (1945). The animation in this short varies significantly from the first short on inflation as having a very stylized beginning that uses black and white contrasting silhouetted characters with very graphic movement rather than dimensional movement. The trumpeters of the castle are stylized and shift in the frame to the right, then join into one line that moves to the left gracefully and unfolds again into the three trumpeters (exactly like the movement of the short film *Fudget's Budget*, which will be discussed!). Robert Cannon animated this section and it is truly stylized animation, not just in the design, but in the movement, which is a very important aspect! Modern influences on character animation

**Figure 16.16**

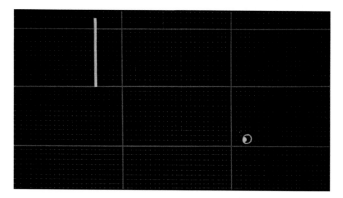

**Figure 16.17**

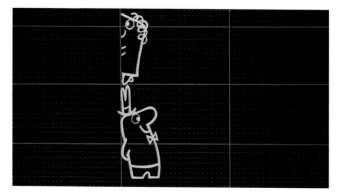

**Figure 16.18**

and animation design were not sudden but developed over years as David Hilberman, one of the three founders of UPA, stated in his interview with John Canemaker from 1979:

> There is the impression that part of the strike at Disney[8] was because people were unhappy about the (film's) design. That's a lot of crap. The change from the, quote, Disney classic animation

7   Adam Abraham, *When Magoo Flew, The Rise and Fall of Animation Studio UPA*, Wesleyan University Press, Middletown, CT, p. 57.

8   In 1938, the Screen Cartoon Guild was formed and animation studios started to join the union. Disney, being the last of the studios in Los Angeles that hadn't joined yet in 1941, had a strike of many of its employees despite Disney paying the highest wages of the industry. Dissatisfaction was high amongst the artists due to unpaid bonuses, promised promotions, and other situations they considered unjust. In addition, job security was a concern.

**Figure 16.19**

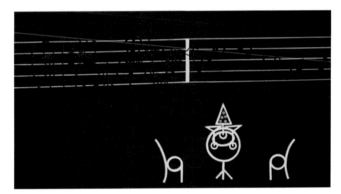

**Figure 16.20**

**Figure 16.21**

the first studio that was run by design people, and we were talking to an adult audience, to our peers. Not the family audience, not the kiddies. So given that the design just came out. The limited animation grew out of our need to economize on budget. Also, the two dimensional characters we were designing didn't lend themselves to a fully acted-out Disney emotion. We didn't have that kind of story and there wasn't demand for the personality actor or animation.[9]

Cannon worked as an animator on various short films at UPA and did so while still working for Warner, animating in his spare time in the very beginning. Most of the early films from UPA have him in the credits for character animation: *Hell-Bent for Election* (UPA's very first short from 1944, directed by Chuck Jones), *Robin Hoodlum* (1948), *The Sailor and the Seagull* (propaganda short film from 1949), *The Magic Fluke* (1949). However, Cannon is mentioned as the director on *Brotherhood of Man* from 1945, a short film about tolerance amongst all cultures. This short film again pushed the style further, being much more stylish and flat in all its elements. According to Adam Abraham,[10] he shared the actual job with John Hubley, Cannon being responsible for the character animation side of the short. The creative leader at the studio at the time and director of most of the before-mentioned shorts was John Hubley, who worked for UPA until 1952, when he was forced to leave his position after he withheld names from the House Un-American Activities Committee.

In 1950, Cannon directed a short story for UPA (with John Hubley as supervising director) by Ted Geisel, "Dr. Seuss," which became the very first big success of the company: *Gerald McBoing-Boing*, a story about a little boy who couldn't speak words but only spoke in sounds. The design was done by Bill Hurtz and color by Jules Engel and Herb Klynn. Everything in this short film pushes the boundaries and follows one strict design concept. From backgrounds to character animation or color design, simplicity is used as an aesthetic, which goes back to the rules of Bauhaus: *form follows function*, just translated into the moving animated image. There is no unnecessary decoration in the image and every part of the design is reduced to its core elements, expressing the story point without excess visual information. *Gerald McBoing-Boing* received an Academy Award for best animated short film in the same year. Robert Cannon continued directing and created stunning short films like the delightful *Willie the Kid* (1952), *Madeline* (1952, nominated for another Academy Award), *Christopher Crumpet* (1953), and *Christopher Crumpet's Playmate* (1955). Cannon's work at UPA mostly names him as the director of shorts, not the animator. However, his eagerness to experiment in the field of character animation can surely be seen in the shorts he directed. His character animation credits start again with the work he did from 1957 on for John Hubley and his wife Faith's Storyboard Studio.

came over a period of about 2 or 3 years. Early on Chuck Jones at Warners experimented. He had a fella named McGrath who was quite a design man and he had experimented with some design in The Dover Boys. Bobe Cannon was involved (as animator) and beginning to reach out for animation style. Screen Gems under Frank Tashlin after the strike brought in as many of the top strike people as possible. So you had those early design ideas happening before UPA came into being. It was simply that you had designers who had art training who were beginning to push out and feel their oats. People who know who Picasso was and could recognize a Matisse across the room. And here they were at Disney, Warners, working with this really corny, cute stuff. They were ready. UPA was

9   John Canemaker and David Hilberman, Supergraphics, *Cartoonist Profiles* Vol. 48 (December 1980).
10  Adam Abraham, *When Magoo Flew, The Rise and Fall of Animation Studio UPA*, Wesleyan University Press, Middletown, CT, p. 65.

## Fudget's budget (1954)

In 1954 Cannon directed UPA's *Fudget's Budget*, animated by Gerald Ray, Frank Smith, and Alan Zaslove. It boasts originality in its character animation as much as in its design done by Thornton Hee (designer) and Jules Engel (color artist). The short film is one of UPA's most consequential style achievements. Everything in the short follows a strict concept that is never broken and spreads out in front of us literally like a spreadsheet. The short tells the story of the Fudget family's financial problems and their struggle to deal with a self-imposed budget. It was inspired by Thornton Hee's own financial struggles at the time.[11] *Fudget's Budget* pretends to be a semi-educational short film that points out to the audience that the trouble the family is in is due to their excessive spending. The entire economic basis of the story can clearly be seen in the concept of the film, which is visualized to the point in the backgrounds and the characters. The backgrounds have ledge paper as a basis most of the times, which gives them a "calculated" feel of stiffness and clarity. It does make the image unusually clean and organized, exactly what the story is about: calculation of numbers and budgets. The foreground elements in the form of the character animation are as clear and precise. There is no brush stroke or overly organic line to be seen; only clean, precise, thick lines. The black backgrounds make the characters and objects read very well, only in a few images the black is replaced by another color to increase the image's temperature; for example, the couple dancing in front of a reddish background. The characters themselves are so reduced in their overall body shape that they nearly resemble the number 1. Man, woman, and kids have the same shape and are only distinguished by their clothing, hair or hats, and size. What makes this short film exceptional compared to others at the time is its extraordinary style and how far Cannon, Hee, and Engel pushed modern design. It is not reality that is pushed or even slightly abstracted but an intellectual concept that is spiked with abstracted simplified objects and characters that don't necessarily follow the laws of physics and are as removed from reality as the backgrounds are. The abstracted objects are always just a substitute for the "real thing," never the actual object itself. The house is not an actual house but just an outline and so is the boat in the storm. They are there as clichés to fill the visual gap the audience needs to understand the story and what the narrator is explaining. The design never attempts to be or never really needs to be more realistic, as the story with its visuals develops as much in the mind of the audience as it does right there on-screen. There are plenty of moments in the film where a visual cliché or a very graphic substitute of an object is enough to tell the story:

- When the Fudgets buy a new car, we only see the shape of what is considered an old car and then it's replaced by a streamlined car that even speeds on a colorful highway, suggesting the fun in the fast lane the new car brings to the life of the Fudgets (Figure 16.22).

**Figure 16.22**

**Figure 16.23**

**Figure 16.24**

- When the Fudgets dance in a club, we see the band playing on a scale in the background.
- At the house, the fence and the TV antenna appear in the shape of a dollar sign. The Fudgets literally plaster their house with money (Figure 16.19).
- Later on when they are in serious financial trouble, the SOS signal shows up as $0$ (this can also be read as $Zero$), which brilliantly combines the idea of rescue needed due to lack of finances (Figure 16.26).

Those visual clues tell the story in an efficient way, very much what the story itself is about.

11 Adam Abraham, *When Magoo Flew, The Rise and Fall of Animation Studio UPA*, Wesleyan University Press, Middletown, CT, p. 112.

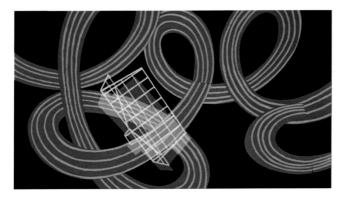

**Figure 16.25**

**Figure 16.26**

The designers of the short also take significant story points and translate them into respective compositions: when the Fudget's budget is sufficient, the composition is calm, quiet, and balanced: life is in order. Once the budget is out of control, the composition also goes mayhem: the business of the frame very much accentuates the financial trouble of the family.

*Fudget's Budget* is from 1954, produced just 9 years after *Brotherhood of Man*, the first film Cannon directed for UPA, and the differences are obvious. *Brotherhood of Man* still has one foot in the character animation style of the 1940s with volume, form, and three-dimensionality of the characters. However, the backgrounds and the overall design are already breaking perspectives, flattening out images, and in some backgrounds appear as a true UPA cartoon. It paves the way for what is about to come. The designs for *Brotherhood of Man* done by John Hubley and Paul Julian are the opposite of everything that animation had been striving for to that point: dimensionality, illusion of life, convincing emotions through stylized yet realistic visuals. Hubley and Julian finally achieved their goal of a new direction in animation. However, the character animation of the short is not yet on the same level. Robert Cannon is also credited as animator alongside with Ken Harris and Ben Washam. The inventiveness in the character's motion is not as in *The Dover Boys*, for instance. The characters in *Brotherhood of Man* move semirealistically and have full form, despite their very

modern design. However, it is a very different kind of short with social–political content, not a comedy like *The Dover Boys*. That the character animation takes a step back in its actions and "loudness" might have been a reason for the subtleties and I would consider it a strength, as it allows one to focus on the story with its message instead of the character animation.

The traditional Disney style produces films that can envelope the audience in their splendor and make them believe that the characters on-screen are actually alive with their emotions. UPA's characters, trying to be exactly the opposite of that naturalism, have a more difficult time expressing emotion to the full extent of Disney's animation, as their stylization makes subtle expressions a bit more difficult, though obviously not impossible. A three-dimensional approach allows every kind of emotion and pose, as it easily mimics the human form, whereas a flat and two-dimensional approach reduces the possibilities in favor of the design. That does not limit the kind of stories you can tell; it just limits the emotional expression in the characters' realistic poses and movements, which can of course be replaced by other means in the animation: colors, composition, music, sound … or, as in many of the UPA's shorts, the inventiveness of the movement. However, the limitation of realism, on the other hand, opens up movements that one could not use in a realistic character, as shown in Mr. and Mrs. Fudget turning into straight lines when turning around. Limitations open up new possibilities! *Fudget's Budget* is nearly as far as one can go in terms of stylization and simplicity. It has stunning designs and incredible ideas that are based on a strong intellectual visual concept. In particular, the visualization of the storm is a treat. It is not in the least an actual storm that is portrayed, but an abstract interpretation of one in the most unique way possible. Its swirling bands that intertwine (Figure 16.25), its blue transparent matter with parallel white lines represent the concept "storm" (Figure 16.26 and 16.27). It is not what a storm might *look* like but is what a storm *feels* like. Waves and rain are similarly treated: rain is just shown as parallel lines and wave peaks simply move up and down. This is the crucial difference between the animation of the 1940s and what UPA developed to bring animation into the 20th century: allowing animation to make the transition from a realistic though stylized image towards an intellectual idea that is visualized in various artistic styles.

The character design of the short pushes many of the character styles of other shorts produced at UPA even further. Mr. and Mrs. Fudget are completely transparent aside from their outline, a style that Cannon had already used in the ingenious short *Christopher Crumpet* (1953),

**More on UPA:**

Adam Abraham, *When Magoo Flew: The Rise and Fall of Animation Studio UPA*, Wesleyan University Press, Wesleyan University Press, Middletown, CT, 2012.

also designed by Hee and Engel, and in moments of Hubley's *Rooty Toot Toot* (1951). Nevertheless, the Fudgets are pushed further and are much simpler in their shape language and details. They show volume in parts but also can "turn into" a single line when turning around. Their transparency continuously shows them being trapped on and in the ledger paper that they are acting on. Money and calculation is what their life is about! They are not to be seen as separate entities from their background but as part of their life-affecting calculations. The background does remind one of prison bars the characters are acting in.

Robert Cannon kept directing shorts at UPA and created memorable characters in shorts like *Gerald McBoing-Boing*, *Willie the Kid*, *Madeline*, *Ballet-Oop*, and others. After leaving UPA, Cannon and Emery Hawkins worked on John and Faith Hubley's short *Adventures of an \** and further pushed the envelope of what character animation was capable of, in a short film of an artistic quality seldom seen in animation. It is a pleasure to watch this short with its baby character changing shapes and bouncing around in childlike moves; it is one of the true masterpieces of 1950s animation and in my opinion one of the best animated short films ever produced! The little kid is not acting like a little baby; the character is interpreting the movements of little babies to the highest degree in the abstract shape of an asterisk. The essence of that movement is depicted, not the realistic movement itself. There have not been many animators who were able to take character animation to that level of abstraction and still be fully convincing and understandable in what the character is actually doing. Cannon pushes it even further in the relationship between the two lovers in Hubley's next short film, *Tender Game* (animated by Ed Smith, Robert Cannon, Jack Schnerk, and Emery Hawkins). The character animation is extraordinary in its simplicity, yet overwhelming in the emotion that all the animators bring onto the paper, with simple yet poignant movements that pointedly express to the point the essence of particular actions and affections with perfect timing and poses between two lovers. The animators do not care about accuracy in their animation in terms of the traditional animation style. Some parts of the animation are rather rough yet always playful and free. Nevertheless, the animation never fails to be understood and melts together with the background, creating a perfect amalgam where movement and background become one in style and texture.

**Figure 16.27**

**Figure 16.28**

UPA's *Fudget's Budget* (1954).

Robert Cannon also worked on *Moonbird* (1959), which received an Academy Award in 1959, and *Children of the Sun* (1960), both directed by the Hubleys, and on *The Cosmic Eye*, released in 1986 by Faith Hubley, 22 years after her husband's death in 1964.

After UPA, Robert Cannon worked on commercials for Playhouse Pictures, a commercial studio in Los Angeles, and had a tenured senior appointment in the anthropology department of the San Fernando Valley State College. "His first anthropological film experiment combined live action, stills, animation, stop-frame, multi-screen, time-lapse, etc., imagery, with the mime clown Lotte Goslar creating a world totally free from three-dimensional perspective."[12] He obviously kept the UPA spirit alive in terms of experimentation and perspective-free visuals and explored other creative fields outside of animation.

[12] Edmund Carpenter, Robert Cannon 1909–1964, *American Anthropologist*, New Series, Vol. 67, No.2 (April 1965), pp. 453–454.

# Parallel perspective

The next step towards "more" perspective is parallel perspective, in which all lines are parallel to each other (Figure 16.29). All horizontal and vertical lines are perpendicular and all diagonals are parallel. There is no tapering of the object in space, and all relating surfaces have the same dimensions despite being close to the viewer or further away. The illustration in Figure 16.31 underneath is constructed in parallel perspective strictly from the front: there is no vanishing point and all the lines are technically parallel. The viewing position is in front of the tall house in the middle, which

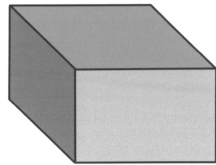

**Figure 16.29**

**Figure 16.30**

**Figure 16.31**

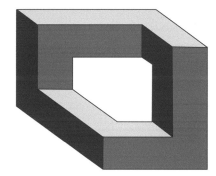

**Figure 16.32**

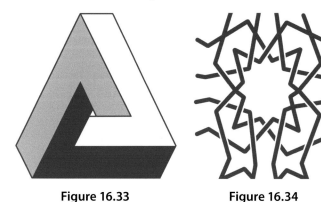

**Figure 16.33**                    **Figure 16.34**

gives a bit of form to the houses, suggests dimensionality. The contrast of light and shadow areas on the front of the houses is more important than the correct lighting. The reduction of the perspective to a parallel perspectival approach allows a playful handling of the light and shadow and color.

Another example is in Figure 16.30, where we see a man looking at his house, which was just cut in half. It has a similar approach as Figure 16.31 in following a parallel perspective. The horizontal lines do not allow any top view of the furniture on the left to underline the image's simplicity and let the flat composition speak instead of the perspective. The construction of the shadow is again incorrect, but it gives enough contrast to render form and mimic a dimensionality that is not really there. Gradients in the color help to further suggest dimensionality and realism. The image looks slightly odd, which is the point of the whole composition.

Parallel perspective cannot depict real depth or size relationships, as there is no vanishing point that would let the object shrink with increasing distance from the viewer (however, various sizes can be used incorrectly to mimic depth). In correctly constructed parallel perspective, an object close-up has the same size as an object very far away. Because it is impossible to determine a point in three-dimensional space and show size in parallel perspective, images can be created that logically do not work like the object in Figure 16.32. This limitation can be seen as an advantage to create impossible architectures with a surreal and disorienting feel, as many of the illustrations of M.C. Escher's (1898–1972) dizzying architectural phantasies proof, by confusing the viewer with their impossibility. The Penrose triangle (Figure 16.33) is part of these impossible constructions that work on a two-dimensional plane but not in a three-dimensional one. This geometric impossibility goes back as far as the twelfth century in the Girih pattern of Persian and Arabic architecture (or even further, into the late Roman period). For example, the learning institution of the Abbasid al-Mustansiriya Madrasah in Baghdad, Iraq, has a pattern of complex intertwining geometric lines (shown in Figure 16.34), a line rendering where interweaving lines suggest overlapping dimensional bands.

is seen straight on. The side panels of this house cannot be seen. This view would look rather flat and in order to still give the house some feeling of depth, light and shadow and gradient are used and also the side panels of the curved roof seem to go backwards, suggesting perspective. The houses on the left and right frame the middle one not only because of their position but also because they open towards it in their own parallel perspective, pretending therefore a vanishing point behind the house in the middle. The arranged houses only show their distance from the viewer through overlap and being on differently lit levels. The exact form of the houses and hills can only be guessed but not precisely determined. The incorrectly constructed shadow situation in the architecture

## Case study: Between no perspective and parallel perspective in animation in UPA's *Willie the Kid* (1952)

UPA's *Willie the Kid* was directed by the aforementioned Robert Cannon in 1952 and tells the story of Willie, a little boy, and his friends playing the imaginary roles of cowboys, ladies, robbers, thieves, and a sheriff, with a dog serving as their horse. Their imagination turns the little neighborhood the kids are living in into a Wild West setting of an old town in the desert with cactuses and a spiky entertaining story. T. (Thornton) Hee, the designer of the short, and Cannon wanted to create a new educational show for kids and decided to visit a classroom in a nearby school. This did not turn out as planned because of bureaucracy issues and instead the theme for the short was discovered afterwards in a nearby parking lot, where a little boy was playing cowboy. The artists who worked

in the unit for Cannon brought their kids to his house and they played cowboys and Indians.[13] The kids' voices are as funny as the character animation. The short film boasts creative unique ideas and the juxtaposition of the two realities of the world of the grown-ups versus the one of the kids is absolutely believable. The penetration from one into the other in short moments just reminds one of the make-believe of the kids' imagination but is never distracting. More

---

[13]  Adam Abraham, *When Magoo Flew: The Rise and Fall of Animation Studio UPA*, Wesleyan University Press, Wesleyan University Press, Middletown, CT, 2012, p. 112.

**Figure 16.35**

**Figure 16.36**

**Figure 16.37**

**Figure 16.38**

UPA's Willie the Kid (1952).

of this and it would have taken away the believability of the Wild West. The film was yet another step forward in terms of perspective and modern depiction of space, one that would be pushed further in *Fudget's Budget* 2 years later. There are two different worlds in *Willie the Kid*: one is the depiction of the real suburbs and one the imaginary Wild West town and its desert. The suburbs are very flat and devoid of all perspective other than overlap; the Wild West has suggested perspective that once in a while slightly mimics a one-point perspective, but there are always elements in the architecture that break that direction again. The difference between the vertical and horizontal suburbs (Figures 16.35 and 16.36) and the imaginary world of the kids makes it more visually exciting when we get into the Wild West town rendered in pink and also playing with diagonals (Figures 16.37 and 16.38). Whenever the perspective takes over and gives too much space in the image, lines either come in that are wrong or important perspective lines are taken out to flatten the image again. There is a constant shifting and pushing of oblique lines that provide the image with tension. Involvement of the audience with the creation of space happens as "things aren't what they are supposed to be" and thus the eye is fooled and kept alert at all times. The chosen architectural elements that are visualized only serve as glyphs that stand for elemental information needed to understand the image, but they are never there for any decorative purposes. The information is reduced to the bare minimum. However, the arrangement of the elements in the frame are very well designed, following a modern simplicity of reduced basic points. There is nothing in the frame that is not absolutely crucial for the understanding of the space and its mood.

In the screenshot in Figure 16.36, the objects are tilted in a semicubist fashion and show the front and the top of stove and table at the same time. However, the chairs are in slight parallel perspective. The toaster and the coffeepot are also shown from different angles and added onto the vertically tilted surfaces (the surface of the stove is more tilted because the heating elements are oval, not round).

The character animation, done by Bill Melendez, Frankie Smith, Roger Daley, and Grim Natwick, follows the style of *Gerald McBoing-Boing* from 2 years earlier, especially in the animation of the parents, who are all rubbery and without joints. Because the characters do not have a solid ground connection in form of a shadow, they fit perfectly into the twisted world. The connection is assumed, yet never explicitly expressed (if a shadow had been added, the directions of the shadows would have needed to be carefully considered to not add more dimensionality and contradict the flatness of the backgrounds). However, the characters themselves do have some dimensionality to them, and their animation is accepting the given space not in its flatness, but its dimensionality, to a degree. The characters use all three directions for their actions and also are three-dimensionally constructed. However, they never clash with the backgrounds, because the animation constantly goes against realism with holds and unique creative ideas to break every possible relationship to realism.

*Willie the Kid* is very congruent in its concept and execution and there is no element that does not clearly follow its design direction. The color, done again by Jules Engel, is nonrepresentative in typical UPA fashion but also modern and edgy (if not strange). It never suggests a dimensional space but always seems to deliberately go against it. The backgrounds are flat, only showing traces of perspective; the animation supports this with holds. The short is therefore yet another excellent exploration of space and characters in animation, creating an artistic and intellectual space rather than just following a generic path of dimensional construction.

**More on UPA:**

Adam Abraham, *When Magoo Flew: The Rise and Fall of Animation Studio UPA*, Wesleyan University Press, Wesleyan University Press, Middletown, CT, 2012.

# Linear perspective

Linear perspective consists of the geometric construction of space on the basis of vanishing points. Linear drawings have the following possibilities for perspective: one, two, and three point. These deal with the three different directions of space: *x*, *y*, and *z* in relationship with the corresponding three sets of lines of a simple cube: height, depth, and width (see Figure 16.39):

1. One-point perspective has four sides of the object, the lines that define depth, tapering towards one vanishing point (which is located on the horizon line).
2. Two-point perspective has eight sides of the object tapering towards two vanishing points (also located on the horizon line), depth, and width (four sides to each).
3. Three-point perspective has all 12 sides of an object taper towards three vanishing points, depth, width, and height. The third vanishing point is located either above or below the horizon.

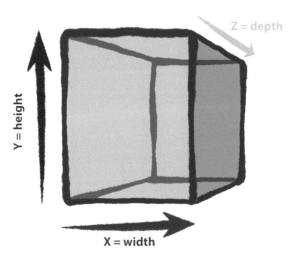

**Figure 16.39**

# One-point perspective

Euclid (mid-fourth to mid-third century), a mathematician from ancient Greece, was the first, as far as we know, to offer a mathematical approach to perspective in the third century BC in his treaty *Optica*, which took on the topic of perception, seen before mostly from a philosophical standpoint, and suggested a geometrical approach. For example, he observed correctly, "Objects increased in size will seem to approach the eye". With Euclid's geometry, Greeks and then Romans had already developed a system with one vanishing point to construct perspectives; however, they did not fully comply with its need for consistency, as not all architectural lines strive towards the vanishing point in the surviving frescoes. (We have seen in the example of the fresco in Chapter 16, "Perspective," in the section, "Roman: Villa of P. Fannius Synistor at Boscoreale, Italy," how some parts of the buildings taper towards one vanishing "area," but not all lines succumb to the suggested system).

The following can only be a very rough and rudimentary account of the complex development and construction of perspective. For further reading, the following book is highly recommended:

John Montague, *Basic Perspective Drawing, A Visual Approach*, John Wiley & Sons, Hoboken, NJ, 2013.

Nevertheless, the concept of the vanishing point was understood and it was already placed on the eye level of the viewer.[14] Pompeian wall decorations are proof of the use of one vanishing point, whose further development and knowledge were however lost or not deemed important in the following centuries and needed to be rediscovered later on. The next main steps in defining optics and visual perception was written by Ibn al-Haytham (Abū ʿAlī al-Ḥasan vibn al-Ḥasan ibn al-Haytham, ~965–~1040; or simply referred to by his Latin name, Alhazen), an Arab scientist whose work was highly regarded in the West and was very influential on the further development of perspective during the following centuries.[15] The use of mathematics to construct perspective that mimics the human vision developed (or was redeveloped and refined) in the fourteenth and fifteenth centuries and was the one that then dominated the Western art world for over 400 years, during which it was refined to perfection until it was again put in question in the nineteenth and twentieth centuries. Its development was driven in the early Renaissance by artists like Giotto, Ambrogio Lorenzetti, Filippo Brunelleschi, Masonlino da Panicale, Piero della Francesca, Paolo Uccello, Donatello, Battista Alberti, and many others, who all contributed to perfecting perspective to the complex system used today. It was the combination of science and art that in the early Renaissance pushed artists and scientists alike to "understand" the complexities of the visual world and use mathematics and geometry to solve the problem of convincing perspective, based on the work of Euclid and others.

In the early fourteenth century, Giotto (1266/7–1337) had already demonstrated a simple use of the concept of one vanishing point but did not yet fully grasp the importance of it for the entire image, rather drawing it intuitively but nevertheless convincingly to an extent. One-point perspective was the first step in developing linear perspective in the Renaissance, and Filippo Brunelleschi (1377–1446) is seen as the (re)discoverer of linear perspective. Brunelleschi was an architect in his own right and most famous for the technical brilliance of his overwhelmingly successful design

---

[14] Christopher W. Tyler, *Perspective as a Geometric Tool that Launched the Renaissance*, Smith-Kettlewell Eye Research Institute, San Francisco, CA, 2000.
[15] Thomas Frangenberg, The Image and the Moving Eye: Jean Pélerin (Viator) to Guidobaldo del Monte, *Journal of the Warburg and Courtauld Institutes*, Vol. 49 (1986), pp. 150–171.

**Figure 16.40**                    **Figure 16.41**

Masaccio: *Trinity* (between 1425–1427); Santa Maria Novella, Florence.

of the dome of the Cathedral of Santa Maria del Fiore in Florence (1420–1436), which today is still considered an architectural and engineering marvel. His perspective discoveries did finally allow such works as Masaccio's fresco *Trinity* (between 1425 and 1427) in the church of Santa Maria Novella in Florence, a tall illusionistic fresco that has the viewer look up at the group of characters into a classic architecture (Figures 16.40 and 16.41). The eye is fooled into believing the painted scene is actually deep space. The one vanishing point in Masaccio's piece is at eye height, making it seem like one is actually looking up into the barrel vault with coffers. Masaccio's piece was one of the first that demonstrated true linear perspective. He also integrated into the perspectival view of the chapel slightly foreshortened characters, who are realistically painted with believable form, fabrics, and anatomy, enhancing the overall illusion of a realistic space. The dimensionality and rendering of the entire painting adds realism to the piece that had never been seen before to that degree. We see the Holy Trinity of God,

the Holy Spirit in the traditional form of a white dove above Jesus' head, and Jesus himself on the cross. Underneath the Virgin Mary is standing on the left, pointing towards her dying son and Saint John on the right praying. Then just above the level of eyesight are the two donors of the painting. Underneath them rests a skeleton on a sarcophagus, above which reads in translation "As I am now, so you shall be. As you are now, so once was I." A clear *memento mori* stating that death is unavoidable, serving as a reminder to everyone stepping in front of the fresco that life is short. However, the point is not just to live life to the fullest but to prepare for one's afterlife by believing in the Trinity. Mary even points up towards the Trinity and looks at the viewer at the same time, reminding them that through her son's sacrifice and God, one reaches eternal life in heaven. The perspective is not there for its own sake, but the purpose of the fresco is the religious background and its imbedded message. The realistic space nevertheless enhances the grandeur of the image along with the message for the viewer of the Renaissance.

Masaccio was born in 1401 and died very young in 1428 at the age of 26 or 27. What he painted was a very innovative and contemporary image at the time and new from many perspectives, literally. Not only were the architectural arrangement and style new, but also the clothing was contemporary; in particular, the donors appear in their "Sunday best." This is important insofar as it changes our perspective on how to see the image. It is not just an old painting; it is a revolutionary idea that in the best Renaissance fashion bows to ancient Roman and Greek architecture but also transports it into the fifteenth century and proposes a new and exciting visual people at the time could easily relate to.

Brunelleschi developed the one-point perspective, but he did not write it down in a treatise; this happened in 1435–1441, when Leon Battista Alberti (1404–1472), himself a famous architect, poet, and writer, published the mathematical construction of one-point perspectives with one vanishing point and released his work to the public in his very important work *De pictura*. Once Brunelleschi had, so to speak, "opened Pandora's box," the development of perspective throughout the early and high Renaissance continued to be refined. Melozzo da Forli (1438–1494) is famous for his exquisite use of perspective and especially the foreshortening in the characters. Similar to Forli's work is Andrea Mantegna's

art (1431–1506). Mantegna was a court painter for the ruling family of Gonzaga in Mantua, Italy. His exquisite work included extreme perspectives, but his famous painting *The Lamentation of Christ* from ~1480 (Figure 16.42) shows his foreshortening skills, exquisitely illustrating the dead Christ from a rather dramatic viewpoint at his feet. It seems as if the painting was a personal devotional piece for Mantegna himself or a rejected commission, as it was found after his death amongst his belongings. There are no images from earlier periods that include perspective with such drama and perfection, not only showing a different viewpoint but also using perspective for its storytelling impact. We see Jesus lying on a slab of marble, with a slightly raised head. At his side is John, Jesus' mother Mary, and behind her we can just see a bit of Mary Magdalene, all mourning the tragedy. By placing the viewer towards the feet of Jesus, there is much intimacy created, because we are now part of the mourners, not just passive bystanders. We actually kneel in front of the dead Messiah and look at his corpse from a low perspective. His wounds are dominantly presented to us, with his wrists tilted so that we can clearly see his sacrifice. The viewer is not just looking *at* a picture but is part *of* the picture, a significant difference that opens up so much more of what pictorial storytelling is capable of! This low position of the viewer is energetically increased by the composition for the viewer of the

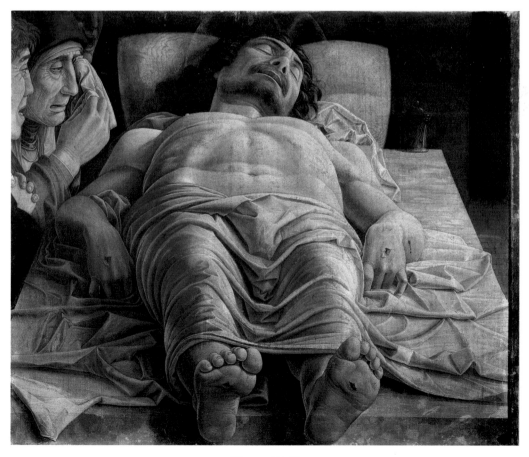

**Figure 16.42**

Andrea Mantegna: *Lamentation of Christ* (~1480).

Renaissance and is still for us today, offering a revolutionary new visual that draws much attention. However, the perspective does seem odd in parts, because Jesus' feet are way too small and his head is too big if we compare it to "realistic" foreshortening. The reasons for this could be that the smaller feet compositionally attract less attention but the face draws more, shifting the focus to Jesus expression rather than his feet.

Mantegna's illusionistic skills paved the path for artists in the Renaissance like Antonio da Correggio (1489–1534), who likewise experimented with perspective and visual illusions in fresco and painting, created some of the most sensuous works of the high Renaissance, and with his skillfully rendered characters and excellent chiaroscuro anticipated the art of the baroque and rococo. Correggio's ceiling fresco *The Assumption of the Virgin* (1526–1530) in the cathedral of Parma (Figures 16.43 and 16.44) is a celebration of space, an illusionistic heaven with characters in complex foreshortening, which itself was so influential that it was a fabulous precursor of what was to come in the baroque's and rococo's grand ceilings. Correggio's ability to paint an illusion that is absolutely believable can for instance be seen in the squinch's decoration with garlands, which look so very realistic (Figure 16.44). Also, St. John the Baptist is dimensionally modeled to such a superb degree that one can see him actually stepping out of the surface

of the wall. Correggio also makes strong use of color perspective and contrast to exaggerate the feeling of depth in the dome, which you can see in the different renderings of the close and distant characters in Figure 16.43, which shows the Assumption of the Virgin, part of the central dome fresco. However, the floating figures demonstrate Correggio's ability to create perspective via characters, not just architecture; characters who are perfect in light, shadow, anatomy, and foreshortening create the depth and space that Correggio seemingly so effortlessly creates.

The culmination of the use of one-point perspective in Renaissance art is seen in Raphael's fresco *The School of Athens* from 1509–1511 (Figure 16.45), which not only stuns the viewer with a complex arrangement of the classical philosophers and contemporary artists but also uses a setting that is nothing short of spectacular in its spatial expansion and believability. It is still a one-point perspective, but the additional aspects of pushing the illusion with color, form, and anatomy create this apex of Renaissance fresco. The development throughout the Renaissance of depicting space in a way that mimics human vision was not a quick one, but a process to which many artists contributed with not only architectural perspective but also the perspective of the human body with its foreshortening, as well as artistic contributions to illusionistic paintings. However, Renaissance art

**Figure 16.43**

Antonio da Correggio: *The Assumption of the Virgin* (1526–1530) detail: the virgin and the angels; dome.

**Figure 16.44**

Antonio da Correggio: *The Assumption of the Virgin* (1526–1530) detail; St. John the Baptist; squinch.

**Figure 16.45**

Raffael: *The School of Athens* (1509–1511).

only focused on one vanishing point, despite sometimes having various one-point perspectives combined in one image, which might give the illusion of two vanishing points.

## Construction of one-point perspective

In one-point perspective, all horizontal and vertical lines are perpendicular to each other; the horizontal lines are all parallel to the horizon, the vertical ones perpendicular to the horizon. The horizon line is the line of our eye height and the vanishing point is either on the horizon line or above/underneath it. The height of the horizon determines from which height we are looking at the subject. A viewer who looks at the tall box in Figure 16.46 from a very low position, with the eyes closer to the ground, will see the lower part of the box at the same height as the horizon (Figure 16.46a) whereas a person who views it from eye-level will see the upper part of the box at the same height

as the horizon (Figure 16.46b). If for example I am looking at a subject that is slightly to my right, then the vanishing point is on the subject's left, as shown in Figure 16.47a. If I move to the subject's right side, then my vanishing point also moves with me (obviously because my eyes are changing position, my vantage point changes), as shown in Figure 16.47b. Seeing the change of the object's perspective from the eye's point of view, we actually see Figure 16.48, where the world around us is shifting but the eye position is the same, so Figure 16.47a and (b) actually have the same vanishing point, but the object's position changed. Therefore, an object that is located above the horizon will reveal a bottom view, underneath the horizon a top view, and an object that is on the horizon will only show a front view (Figure 16.49).

In one-point perspective, both front panel and back panel of a box diminish in size the closer they get towards the vanishing point and the lines that define depth taper (Figure 16.50).

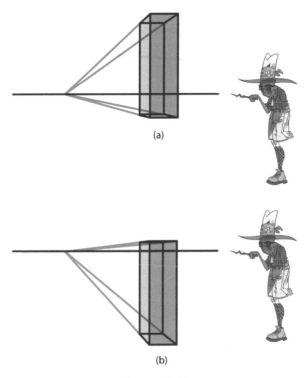

(a)

(b)

**Figure 16.46**

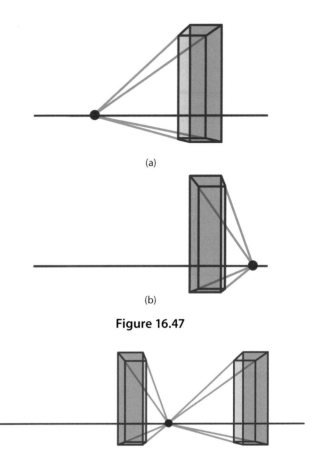

(a)

(b)

**Figure 16.47**

**Figure 16.48**

In one-point perspective it depends on where the vanishing point is located in relationship to the horizon line: either on the horizon line or away from it. If the vanishing point is on the horizon line (Figure 16.50a and b), the ground plane of the object is parallel to the horizontal ground plane. If the vanishing point is not on the horizon line, then the object is floating in midair and not related to the horizontal ground plane (Figure 16.50c), thus it has its own vanishing point unrelated to the horizon. Its front and back panels, however, are still vertical and in their orientation

parallel to the horizon line. In Figure 16.50b the object looks like it is in perspective and we believe that the box is tapering towards the vanishing point. The result looks convincing. If we turn the object in space too much and move the vanishing point to the left of the object, it causes it to change its shape and

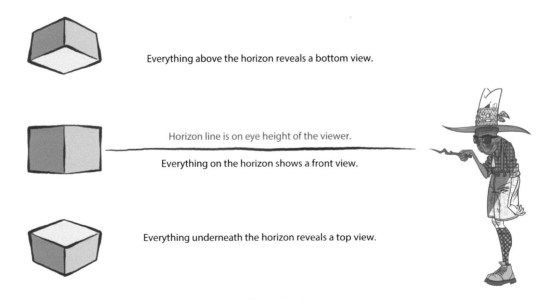

Everything above the horizon reveals a bottom view.

Horizon line is on eye height of the viewer.

Everything on the horizon shows a front view.

Everything underneath the horizon reveals a top view.

**Figure 16.49**

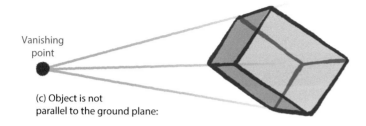

Vanishing point

(c) Object is not
parallel to the ground plane:

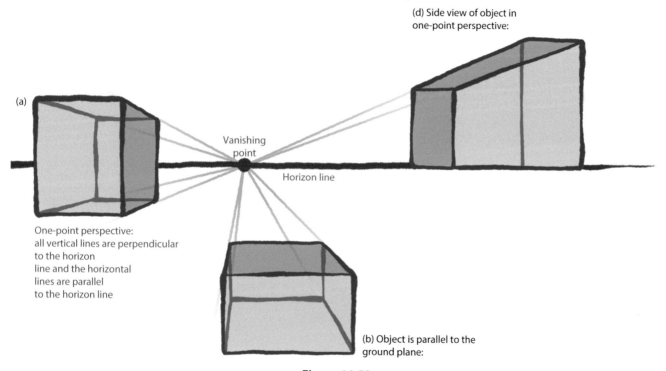

(d) Side view of object in
one-point perspective:

(a)

Vanishing
point

Horizon line

One-point perspective:
all vertical lines are perpendicular
to the horizon
line and the horizontal
lines are parallel
to the horizon line

(b) Object is parallel to the
ground plane:

**Figure 16.50**

reveals the limitations of one-point perspective. The mistake
in Figure 16.50d is that the vanishing point cannot be used in
front of an object, only behind it ("behind" means the vanishing
point is in the infinite, as in Figure 16.50a). The trapezoid shape
of the upper and lower panels in Figure 16.50b are convincing
as tapering towards the vanishing point, in Figure 16.50c it is
not anymore. Also the ground plate of the box is exactly on the
horizon line, which additionally makes it look odd. Both lower
lines of the side and front panels sit on the horizon line, which
flattens the lower part of the box. But this "wrong" approach can
also be used to construct the architecture wrongly on purpose,
like in Figure 16.51. The vanishing point is not behind the object,
where it logically should be, but in front of the object to the left.
This makes the front panel actually smaller than the back panel.

Figure 16.52 has a whole house in one-point perspective and,
despite being correctly constructed, it can look a bit awkward in
some of the details because the front side is always flat, which
can conflict with the perspective of all the other elements.
However, it also gives a simplified playful appearance, which is
kind of like a slightly dimensional version of "flat." In its boxiness
and geometric simplicity, it does look like a LEGO construction.

**Figure 16.51**

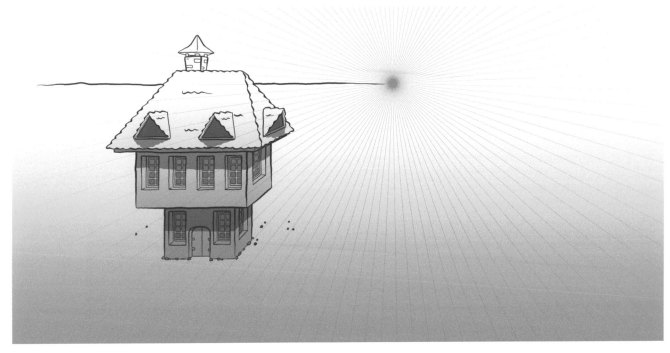

**Figure 16.52**

## Two-point perspective

Two-point perspective was first mentioned in the book *De artificiali perspectiva* by Jean Pélerin (also called *Viator*) in 1505. The knowledge of the construction with two vanishing points had been known before and was not invented by Pélerin; however, he was the first to publish a printed compendium on perspective that contained the use of two vanishing points. The practical use of this system was not popular until the middle of the seventeenth century and was then used extensively by Dutch painters with astonishing accuracy. Painters of interiors like Gerard Houckgeest (~1600–1661) constructed complex architectural structures that are not only convincing through their geometrical precision but also because of their demonstration of light and shadow and realistic color. The stunning interior space of the New Church in Delft (Figure 16.53) is of such quality that even the small distortions in the outer regions of the tile work are nearly negligible. Houckgeest produces an architectural view that makes it very difficult to believe it is actually painted on a panel of wood.

**Figure 16.53**

Gerard Houckgeest: *Ambulatory of the New Church in Delft, with the tomb of William the Silent* (1651).

In Italy, Canaletto (1697–1768) (see Figure 16.54) was one of the most excellent painters of the use of very precise two-point perspectives in his convincingly realistic depictions of cityscapes, especially his famous views of Venice and London. (However, he was obviously not the first one to use the subject matter or technique, just the most famous one.) Canaletto's views of the cities stun with their intricate accuracies and details not only in the architecture but also in the characters who populate the scenes. Aside from the geometric construction of perspective, he also used the camera obscura to achieve his realistic paintings. Canaletto was to be the most successful painter of cityscapes and part of a group of Italian painters creating what is called *vedute*. The goal of this type of scenic painting is not just the precise representation of the architecture but also the handling of light and shadow and creation of a mood, an emotion. Like Canaletto, who was trained as a painter for theatrical stages, Giovanni Battista Piranesi was also a trained theatre stage designer, an occupation that lent itself to spectacle and visual experimentation via perspective.[16] Stage design had the purpose of illusion, so a profound knowledge of perspective was crucial. Piranesi excelled in the representation and fantastical interpretation of the remnants of ancient Roman architecture, which he documented in great detail in Rome, and his work to this day is important evidence for the scope and conservation status of the famous buildings at that point in time. Piranesi also created fantastical "prison" etchings (Figure 16.55), which show dark underground architectural places filled with stairs, bridges, and machinery. Their dark tone and surreal subject matter is partly so convincing because of his ability to open up a surreal space and give it depth through light and shadow and convincing perspective with a fresh and even sketchy looseness.

**Figure 16.54**

Canaletto: *The Entrance to the Grand Canal, Venice* (1730).

## Construction of two-point perspective

Two-point perspective allowed artists to find different viewpoints and turn objects and buildings more convincingly in space, thus replicating and interpreting a much wider space than with just one vanishing point. Two vanishing points allow two sets of lines to taper towards either one of the vanishing points. All verticals in a two-point perspective construction are parallel to each other and perpendicular to the horizon; all other lines taper towards either one of the two vanishing points.

We do see the world around us in a three-point perspective, but usually two points will do. For example, in Figure 16.56 the Gyeongbokgung palace building in Seoul, South Korea, is so far away and at eye level, that the third vanishing point can be neglected; however, it is clear how all the lines taper towards the two horizontal vanishing points.

**Figure 16.55**

Giovanni Battista Piranesi: *The Drawbridge* (1761).

16  Joanna Barbara Rapp, A Geometrical Analysis of Multiple Viewpoint Perspective in the Work of Giovanni Battista Piranesi: An Application of Geometric Restitution of Perspective, *The Journal of Architecture*, Vol. 13, No. 6 (2008), 701–736, DOI: 10.1080/13602360802573868

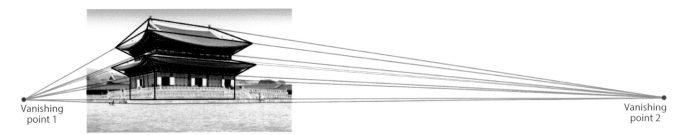

Vanishing
point 1

Vanishing
point 2

**Figure 16.56**

Now that we have two vanishing points, let us see what they actually do in their position on the horizon line. Again, the boxes constructed below the horizon give us a downward view and the ones above the horizon an upward view. The two vanishing points are always on the horizon line.

Figure 16.57 explores some possibilities of what happens with the perspective of a box if the vanishing points are shifted on the horizon line. In Figure 16.57a, the vanishing points are very close

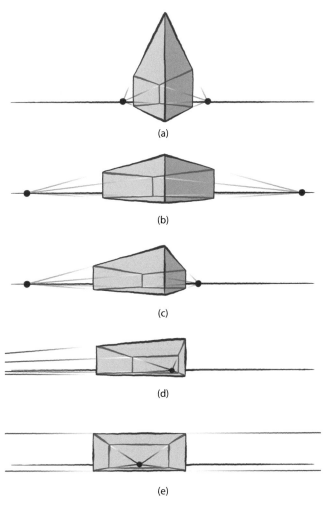

(a)

(b)

(c)

(d)

(e)

**Figure 16.57**

to each other, which squeezes the object (or we can also see it as a building) and makes it look like we are very near to it; it either is big and tall or we are small in size in front of it.

In Figure 16.57b the vanishing points are far apart, which reduces the distortion, and we are further away from the building. When shifting the vanishing point in Figure 16.57c (or when shifting the box between the two vanishing points), the object itself turns and we get an image like Figure 16.56, where the palace is slightly turned. Pushing both vanishing points even more, the right one now behind the box and the left vanishing point further to the left outside of the picture frame, the box's side panels disappear and we can only see the front in slight perspective, shown in Figure 16.57d. Figure 16.57e shows the extreme of the turn, where we now see only the front of the box and the one vanishing point from the right is now in the center. The left vanishing point is in the infinite, so the upper and lower lines of the box are parallel: we have again a one-point perspective. (In reality, all lines curve slightly due to our vision being warped. But this is often ignored due to the complexity of the construction.) If you follow the position of the two vanishing points from Figure 16.57b through (e), you can see an animated movement: the object turns in relationship to the also moving vanishing points. This might help you to understand the liaisons amongst the various elements in perspective better.

Figure 16.58 shows how the constructed boxes change in perspective, depending where they are in relationship to the vanishing points. All the boxes that are inside of the "Cone of Vision," the light blue circle, are believable in their perspective construction. The objects that are outside of the Cone of vision start to be distorted, and the further away from the cone, the more wry they look. Nevertheless, this of course does not mean that everything outside of the cone is going to be wrong; it just means that every drawing needs to be judged upon the distortion being acceptable or not. The Cone of Vision covers about 60% of the space between the two vanishing points. But in some instances a very harsh perspective is the goal, so the Cone of Vision is a guideline only.

Figure 16.59 has a downward view of a building in two-point perspective, with the roof being above the horizon. Make sure that none of the architectural elements directly collide

**378**

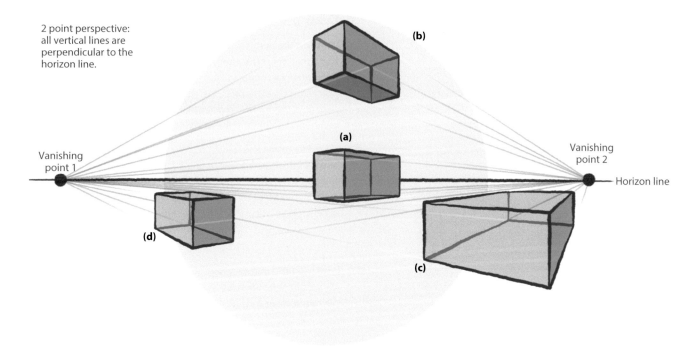

2 point perspective:
all vertical lines are
perpendicular to the
horizon line.

(b)

(a)

Vanishing
point 1

Vanishing
point 2

Horizon line

(d)

(c)

**Figure 16.58**

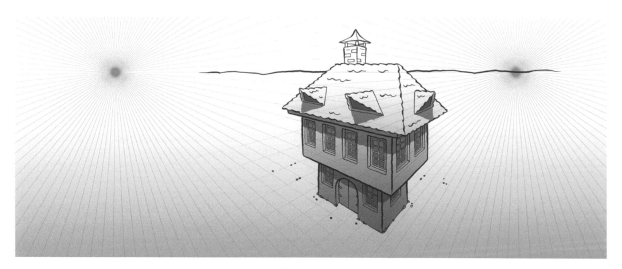

**Figure 16.59**

with the horizon line, as that creates tangents and the feel
of perspective will be reduced due to an awkward clash of
background and foreground, causing the perspective to flatten.
The rooftop in Figure 16.59 is just a little bit above the horizon
to separate the two.

Playing with the two vanishing points can give us some odd
outcomes that are nevertheless interesting possibilities.
Figure 16.60 has one vanishing point on the horizon and one far
above, so the second vanishing point is not on the horizon line as
it is supposed to be. This creates a strong distortion that can be
used creatively in the design.

**Figure 16.60**

## Draw a square and circle in perspective

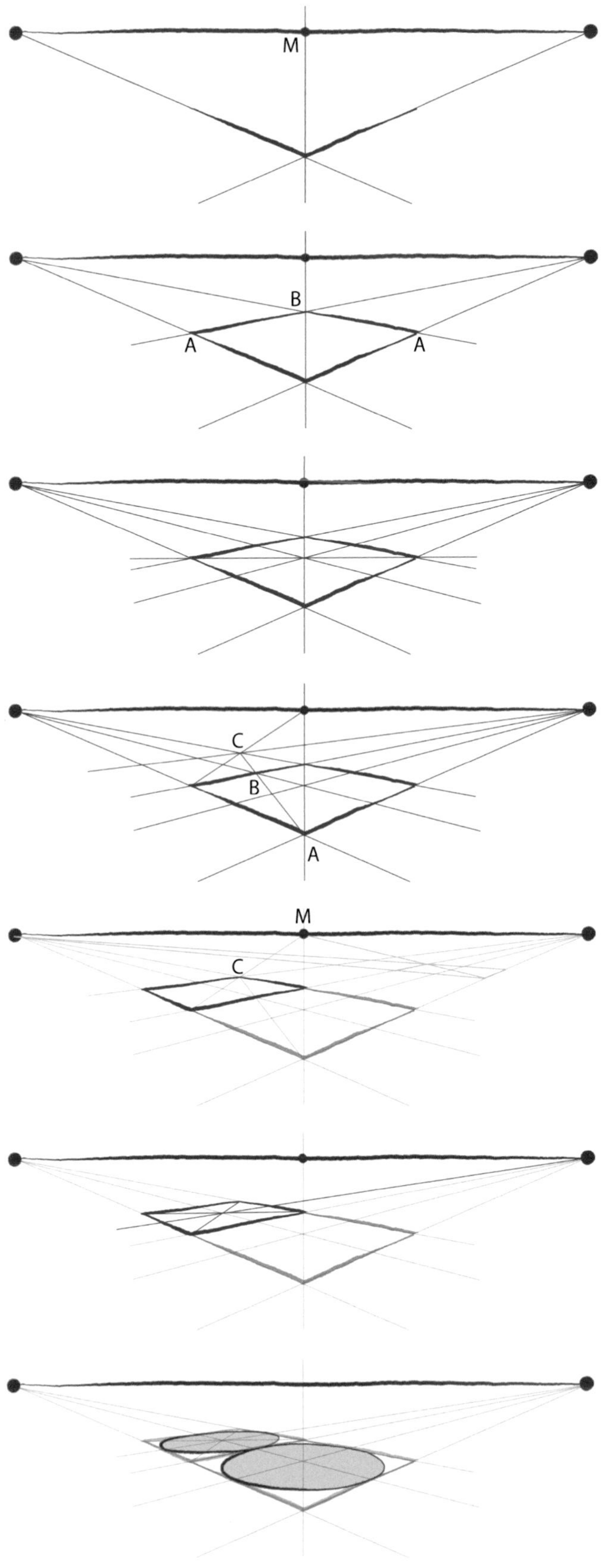

We know that a square's diagonals are on a 90° angle. We also know that the point where one of the square's diagonals is exactly perpendicular to the horizon line is right between the two vanishing points, which is the vanishing point M. So this is where we'd start. Construct the vanishing point M, right between the two vanishing points, and determine the position of one edge of your square.

Now determine the length of the square's side, by connecting one vanishing point with a point A (any point is fine if the length seems OK). That will also result in point B, which is the crossing point between the diagonal of the square and the side of the square. Draw a line through the vanishing point and point B to construct the opposite point A.

Construct the middle point of the square by just connecting its diagonals. Now we have a square that is however in a 45° angle. We might want to shift it in space.

We construct another foreshortened square right next to the one we already have. Connect point A with the intersection B, which results in point C, shown in red.

Connect the vanishing point with point C and you have another square in perspective.

You can also see that the point between the two vanishing points M, if connected with C, directly ends up in the corner of the newly created square. So once we have M, we can now draw the square in any position of the ground plane (green).

To prepare for the circle, we have to find the middle points of the square's outlines. Again, connect the diagonals and you'll have the middle point. Connect the vanishing point with the middle point and the outlines are cut in half.

Now construct freehand a circle into the square. This whole procedure can be done very easily in Photoshop, by using the Line tool. Then construct on the side a regular square with a circle inscribed and with the Transform ˃ Distortion tool, the square with the circle can be easily imbedded into the constructed square's perspective.

**Figure 16.61**

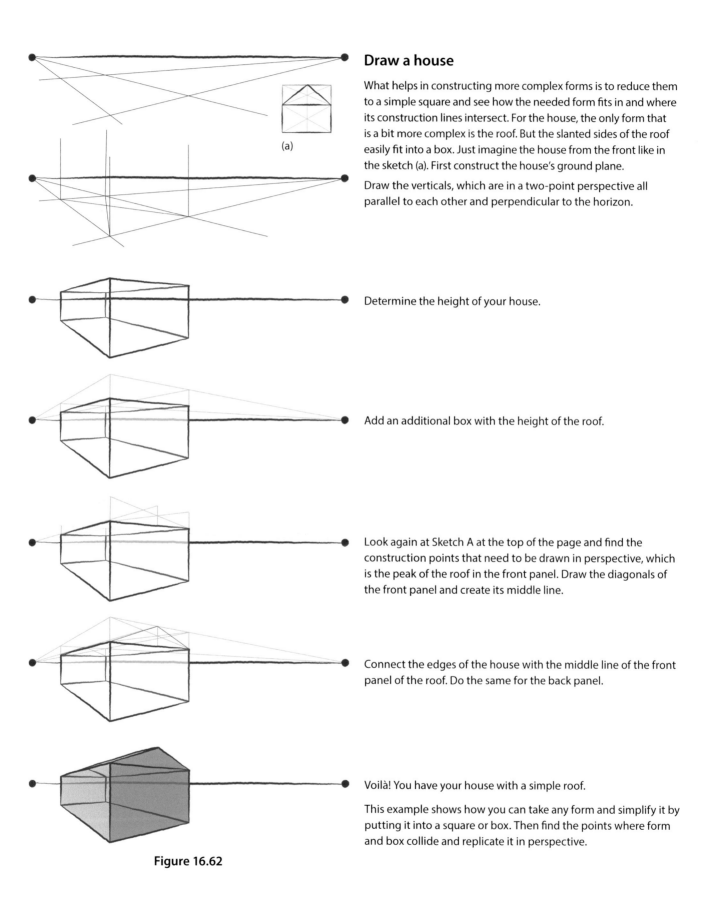

## Draw a house

What helps in constructing more complex forms is to reduce them to a simple square and see how the needed form fits in and where its construction lines intersect. For the house, the only form that is a bit more complex is the roof. But the slanted sides of the roof easily fit into a box. Just imagine the house from the front like in the sketch (a). First construct the house's ground plane.

Draw the verticals, which are in a two-point perspective all parallel to each other and perpendicular to the horizon.

(a)

Determine the height of your house.

Add an additional box with the height of the roof.

Look again at Sketch A at the top of the page and find the construction points that need to be drawn in perspective, which is the peak of the roof in the front panel. Draw the diagonals of the front panel and create its middle line.

Connect the edges of the house with the middle line of the front panel of the roof. Do the same for the back panel.

Voilà! You have your house with a simple roof.

This example shows how you can take any form and simplify it by putting it into a square or box. Then find the points where form and box collide and replicate it in perspective.

**Figure 16.62**

# Three-point perspective

Three-point perspective is the final step in full realism, or better mimicking full human vision as closely as possible in drawing. This method was not used in images until the middle of the nineteenth century. At the end of the nineteenth century, artists started to question the realistic depiction of images and began to deconstruct them again. Vanishing points disappeared and the visual world again began purposefully falling apart. Paul Cézanne and Vincent van Gogh were some of the pioneers of what was to come. The twentieth century then was the time when in art all the elements of composing images were challenged and a multitude of different visual interpretations developed. Breaking apart the elements that pictures consist of allows the artist to fully understand each element's power and ability. Art concepts like cubism, synthetic cubism, surrealism, futurism, fauvism, suprematism, Dadaism, abstract expressionism, pop art, etc., not only questioned the visuals themselves but also the concepts and ideas behind those visuals. The realistic depiction with an accurate three-point perspective was not what twentieth century painting was trying to do (with exceptions of course, like photorealism). Photography was very well able to create visuals that depicted the world in its accurate dimensions since the mid-nineteenth century. So photography became an able tool for realism and a replacement of the realistic depiction that painting and drawing had been striving towards for centuries. Both slowly started to distance themselves from realism towards the end of the nineteenth century, exploring more the possibilities of image making photography was not able to.

However, accurate three-point perspective was and still is for instance crucial for matte painting in visual effects for film to give a perfectly constructed scenery the believability it needs to convince on screen. It is also clearly being used in other applied arts like comics, animation, or illustration. However, nowadays many computer programs make it much easier to construct architecture, and the painstaking and time-consuming procedure of drawing the complex structures is very much reduced.

Some artists played with complex perspectives in a very creative way and invented visuals that showed the three-dimensional space but also questioned it. Immediately the work of Dutch graphic artist M.C. (Maurits Cornelis) Escher comes to mind (1898–1972), whose impossible perspectives still confuse the viewer and show surreal images with mathematical accuracy. In addition, Salvador Dali (1904–1989), the main representative of surrealism, did in his later work use traditional construction of perspective to give his images the needed believability. He also used traditional painting techniques and combined them with a new aesthetic and infused it with his interest in optical illusions and mysticism. For instance, his piece *Christ of Saint John of the Cross* from 1951 (Figure 16.63) offers a perspective never seen before when depicting Jesus on the cross. The viewer

**Figure 16.63**

Salvador Dali: *Christ of Saint John of the Cross* (1951).

takes on the position of God to gaze down at Jesus. Traditionally Jesus is looked at from a low perspective, which is the more "humble" position of the mourner. One cannot see Jesus' facial expression of pain and suffering. This lack of personal connection with Jesus' face expresses an eerie silence and quiet, supported by the surreal landscape. Dali's interpretation uses three-point perspective but literally flips it around and combines two different visuals into one. He readdressed the topic of the crucified Christ again in 1954 in his painting *Crucifixion (Corpus Hypercubus)*, in which the cross is replaced by a hypercube in perspective, and in *The Ascension of Christ* (1958), which with its depiction of Jesus being seen from the feet up reminds us of Mantegna's *Lamentation of Christ*, discussed earlier.

**Figure 16.64**

**Figure 16.65**

Felipe Varini: *Huit rectangles* (2007).

The end of the nineteenth century refined perspective, yet also questioned it; the twentieth century deconstructed it or played with it and created visuals that put to question our visual perception in paintings, architecture, sculpture, installation, but also in film and of course animation. The point in twentieth century art is often to make the viewer doubt reality by offering an alternate interpretation of space. For instance, the work of Swiss artist Felipe Varini (1952–), who paints simple shapes into architectural spaces, whose true image can only be seen from one specific viewpoint within the room, whereas all other vantage points will break up the two-dimensional image into pieces. His installation *Huit rectangles* (Figure 16.64) from 2007 was painted onto the walls at the Musée des Beaux Arts in Arras, France, and shows the flat image of red squares on top of the three-dimensional hallway. Moving away from the one point that provides this view deconstructs the overlaid red squares and one will see something like Figure 16.65. Varini's piece not only flattens the architecture into a "picture" with an overlay of red squares, but it also makes it difficult for the brain to make sense of this juxtaposition between one and the other, which are both extremes in their own right: the ornate architecture with the deep corridor and the tiled floor, which so poignantly reminds one of the first Renaissance depictions of floors in one-point perspective, and on the other hand the most flat and simple twentieth-century artistic exploration of color and shape: a square. Both nevertheless strangely enough complete each other. This breaking up of traditional spaces is even more clearly seen in contemporary architecture in deconstructivism[17] and parametricism.[18] The traditional space that has been developed over centuries is avoided and harmony, repetition, or simple shapes like square, circle, or triangle are averted. The space and architecture created is organic, asymmetrical and futuristic. The works of Lebbeus Woods, Zaha Hadid, Rem Koolhaas, Daniel Liebeskind, the Coop Himmelb(l)au, and Frank Gehry should be studied, as their work explores the complexity of contemporary architectural form and space.

In animation, the rise of 3D animation has in the last decades put extraordinary pressure on depicting space dimensionally, as the computer likes the three-dimensional space; it will continue to do so until the technology is potent enough to again start questioning the space and suggest new and more innovative interpretations of space rather than correct representations of it.

---

[17] Deconstructivism (from ~1980 onwards) literally deconstructs architecture and assembles it again in various forms, avoiding traditional aesthetics and harmonious arrangements. Main contributors are Frank Gehry, Daniel Liebeskind, Zaha Hadid, Peter Eisenmann, Coop Himmelb(l)au or Rem Koolhaas.

[18] Parametricism (from ~1990 onwards) deals with the computational advances in the construction of urban design, architecture and interior design and is in its style rooted in digital animation techniques. It is the calculation of complex structures with the aid of algorithms and computer programs. It avoids repetition, simple shapes as squares, circles or triangles and creates spaces wherein all elements relate. Main contributors are Zaha Hadid, Coop Himmelb(l)au,

## Construction of three-point perspective

The third vanishing point is actually two different ones: one is above the horizon and one is below the horizon (Figure 16.66). In order to construct a perspective that is convincing enough with the third vanishing point, the point needs to be very high up or down to not have extreme distortions. Because of the distance of the third vanishing point, it is a rather impractical method to draw by hand and very complex and tedious to accomplish. Often a two-point perspective with parallel verticals is sufficient for the depiction of architecture. However, with the use of computer programs the technical implementation is more feasible, and Photoshop does offer some practical tools that make the construction much easier; 3D programs like Maya, AutoCAD, and SketchUp Pro are all programs that make a fully realistic rendering of architecture more practical.

The vanishing points in three-point perspective are the same as in two-point, sitting on the horizon line; we only add the two vanishing points that deal with the distortion of the height of the object. The third vanishing points deal with the tapering of the views up or down and therefore are located either above or underneath the object. Three-point perspective has none of the sets of lines that make the object parallel or perpendicular to the horizon line. All lines taper towards one of the three (actually four) vanishing points. As in two-point perspective, the further the vanishing points are away from each other, the less pronounced the perspective is; the closer the vanishing points are, the closer we seem to be to the object and the stronger the distortion is.

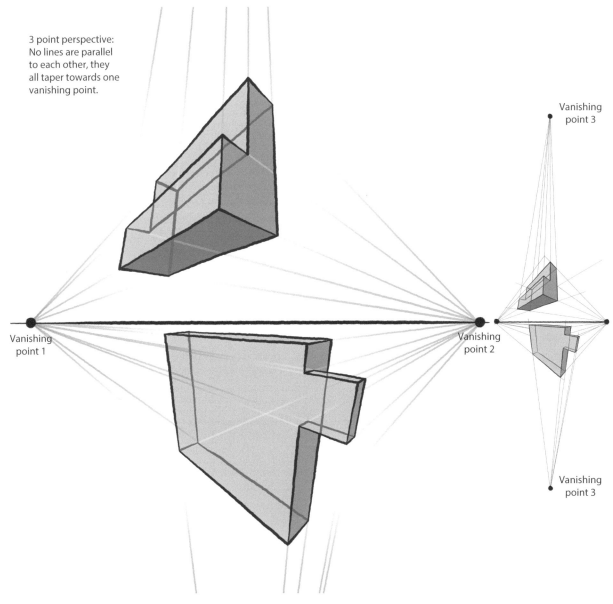

3 point perspective:
No lines are parallel
to each other, they
all taper towards one
vanishing point.

Vanishing point 1

Vanishing point 2

Vanishing point 3

Vanishing point 3

**Figure 16.66**

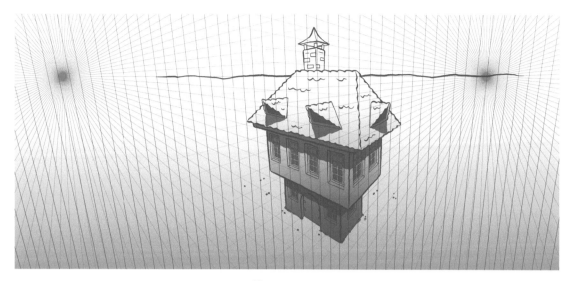

**Figure 16.67**

To construct a three-point perspective can be a rather daunting task and not everyone is up for the challenge. One solution can be to construct a two-point perspective and then distort the image digitally in Photoshop. This will obviously cause additional unwanted distortions, but they can sometimes be acceptable as minor mistakes. In this example the house looks much longer compared to the original two-point construction, as the height would visually be reduced due to the foreshortening of the third vanishing point.

**Figure 16.68**

Roy Lichtenstein: *House III* (2002).

However, there is one problem, as you can see in Figure 16.66: an object that is located on the horizon line cannot be constructed, as the vertical lines would go to the vanishing point above and below. Only a curved line can accomplish this. This issue can only be solved with slightly bent lines. In animation, when having a camera tilt up and down a building, the entire perspective needs to be curved to provide a smooth, continuous line (also see the next case study on the short film *Cannon Fodder*,"

Case Study, "Katsuhiro Otomo's *Cannon Fodder*"). The complexities of a three-point perspective can be plentiful and sometimes a simplifying "version" of the real construction also does the trick, as can be seen in Figure 16.67: if it works, it works.

There are options for playing with the three vanishing points from a creative perspective; they do not necessarily have to be correctly used. The advantage in 3D space is that with knowledge

Figure 16.69

Figure 16.70

and expertise the viewing expectations of the audience can be dramatically played with and thus affect the emotional impact of the space. For instance, Roy Lichtenstein's sculpture *House III* (Figure 16.68) from 2002 uses perspective in a very unique and interesting way. The perspective is inverted and the vanishing points are in front of the object, not on the horizon line behind it. The three-dimensionality of the object is obviously wrong, yet it is still convincing in giving the visual information needed to know what it is, despite its "inside-out" design. Walking past the sculpture creates an optical illusion that makes the house turn in front of you because of the mirrored perspective. It turns against the expected correct direction and the mind is confused.

The possibilities that 3D design is capable of in terms of deconstructing the object in a creative way are endless, and 3D is not only there for depicting characters, objects, and the environment in a realistic form but invites us to play with visual perception in 3D in all its facets, even combining all types of perspective into one interesting visual design.

The concept of vanishing points can also be used for prop design, where the object tapers towards one vanishing point without it defining the perspective but being part of the actual design, like in the spaceship example in Figure 16.69. All forms in the spaceship taper towards a point that is underneath the ship. This can alter the direction of the object or its relationship to its surroundings.

In addition, more than one of each of the vanishing points can be introduced, to result in an image like Figure 16.70, where there are actually two different third vanishing points above. This results in a crooked architecture that looks like Diagon Alley in the Harry Potter feature films. Be creative with vanishing points and do not just use them religiously to replicate reality.

It took our artistic buddies from the past over four centuries to figure out perspective, so give it some time to practice and don't expect perfect results in an hour!

## Case Study: Katsuhiro Otomo's *Cannon Fodder* (1995)

*Please watch the short film before or after you read the following!*

Katsuhiro Otomo is a Japanese illustrator, comic book author, and director who first became famous for his groundbreaking manga *AKIRA*, published from 1982 till 1990.[19] The manga is a massive achievement not only in its scope but also in its

storytelling. Otomo very much borrows from film language and his manga reads as easily as an excellent storyboard. *AKIRA* was then made into an animated feature film in 1988, also directed by Otomo. The film became hugely influential in its aesthetics and style and is still an outstanding example of Japanese film.

In 1995 Katsuhiro directed one segment of the feature animation *Memories*, consisting of three vastly different stories with

---

[19] After having published his first Manga, *Domu: A Child's Dream*, which ran from 1980 to 1981.

completely disparate styles. All three stories are based on Otomo's manga shorts. Satoshi Kon (*Tokyo Godfathers* [2003], *Paprika* [2006]) was also involved in writing the first story, *The Magnetic Rose*. The third short, *Cannon Fodder*, was written and directed by Otomo himself.

*Cannon Fodder* is a stylistically very different film compared to the other two shorts of *Memories* and does not attempt to fit into the general stylistic direction of anime in either its design or its story. It is a rather dark narrative about a young boy living in a Orwellian society and learning how to be a "good soldier." He lives in a city that is surrounded by walls and everyone is working on the defense of the city, which is constantly under threat by yet another neighboring, yet never seen, city. The boy's father is a worker in one of the many buildings that house enormous cannons. His job is simply pushing the shells into the cannon with a whole group of other men, all looking rather gaunt and sickish. The little boy's fascination with war and the enemy is a disturbing detail, as it is clear that his infiltration and education will cause him to also join the war effort. Interestingly enough, the enemy is never seen and one does not even know if there is an enemy at all or if the government just pretends to keep the economy going.

What makes this short animation such a gem of Japanese anime is the artistic direction in its design but also its interesting concept of not having a cut throughout the entire short. This might seem like it's not a big deal, but in animation this is a complex task on a huge scale. In traditional 2D animation, a simple horizontal pan was what the camera was capable of, where the camera just follows characters from point A to point B horizontally. The character could of course also walk into the *z*-axis direction (depth), but a three-dimensional camera movement was extraordinarily difficult. From one shot to the next, the camera of course can change (pan and zoom), but a three-dimensional camera movement within one shot was technically not feasible or just very, very difficult. Some films do play with this problem; in particular, Richard Williams' feature *The Cobbler and the Thief* had some shots that dealt with excruciatingly complex camera movements. However, the norm is to keep the layout of the shots fairly manageable. What makes Otomo's short so special is that many shots have a three-dimensional camera movement already planned into the background painting. The level of calculation and knowledge needed to plan these shots is nothing short of astounding. The camera is literally not bound to the two-dimensional plane but freely explores the space, flies through windows, and moves seemingly easily from one location to the next. The short has to be seen a couple of times and studied in order to be fully understood in its complexity. When and where Otomo overlaps one background with another in order for the illusion not to be broken is stunning, to say the least!

# Foreshortening in one-point perspective (Figure 16.71)

(a)

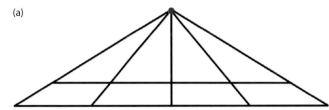

The floor panel is tilted in perspective and its single tiles reduce in size towards the vanishing point.

(b)

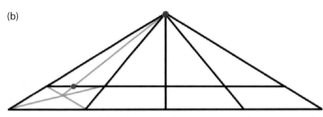

Construct the middle of one tile by connecting the edges, and connect it with the vanishing point. A new point is created (purple).

(c)

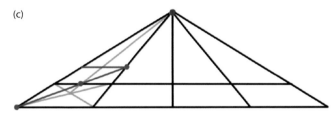

Connect the new point with the lower left corner and the intersection creates yet another new point, which determines the new width of the tile in perspectival foreshortening.

(d)

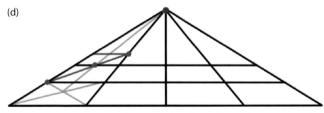

Repeat the same procedure and the tiles will get shorter towards the vanishing point.

(e)

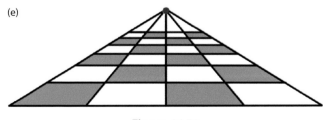

**Figure 16.71**

# Foreshortening in two-point perspective (Figure 16.72)

a. The box in perspective needs to be reduced in size towards the left vanishing point.
b. Construct the middle of the front panel of the block by connecting the edges and connect it with the vanishing point on the left. A new point is created (purple).
c. Connect the new point with the upper left corner and the intersection creates yet another new point, which determines the new width of the block in perspectival foreshortening.
d. Repeat the same procedure and the blocks will get smaller towards either vanishing point.

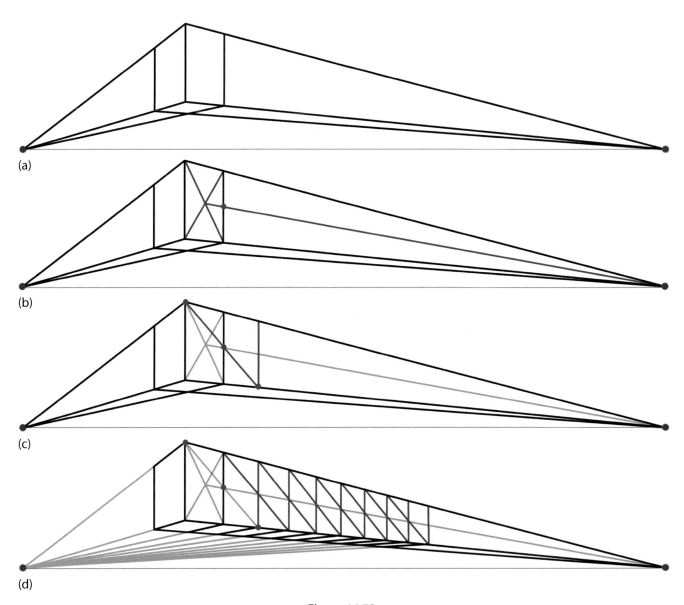

(a)

(b)

(c)

(d)

**Figure 16.72**

# Foreshortening in three-point perspective (Figure 16.73)

Use the same procedure as in two-point perspective. The only difference is that the vertical lines are not parallel anymore but taper towards the third vanishing point.

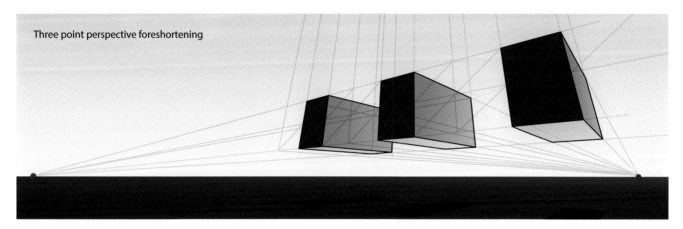

**Figure 16.73**

# Reflections (Figures 16.74–16.77)

**Figure 16.74**

A side view or nearly side view just mirrors the image, though there is a slight perspective change there that is not taken into consideration in the image. This is the easiest way of creating reflections. It is convincing but only works to a certain extent; then the perspective change that is needed, but not constructed, becomes apparent.

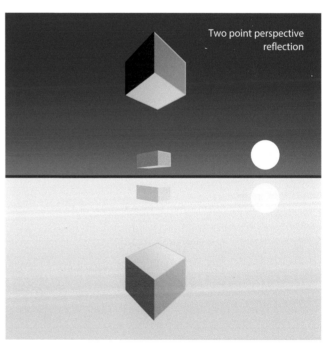

**Figure 16.75**

The reflection of a geometric object like the depicted cubes above is rather simple. The object is just flipped with the horizon as the symmetrical axis. The closer the object is to the viewer, the more of the bottom side of the object is revealed in the reflection.

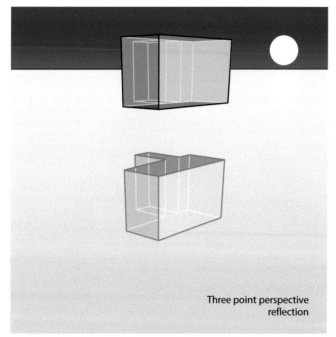

**Figure 16.76**

**Figure 16.77**

Only a (semi-)photorealistic image requires accurate construction of the reflection; a stylized image needs an understanding of the reflection, which then is convincingly interpreted. For geometric objects like the ones above, this is a fairly easy task to construct: the horizon plane is the mirror axis for the reflected image. We see more

of the downward view of the box in the reflection than we see in the original piece. Once we see the object at an oblique angle, more of the underside is revealed; then the reflection has to be properly constructed to make sense. In the images above, only the reflection reveals parts of the object that are hidden in the original view.

**For more complex reflections go to:**

John Montague, *Basic Perspective Drawing, a Visual Approach*, John Wiley & Sons, Hoboken, NJ, 2013. Shadows and reflections: Chapter 8.

**Figure 16.78**

Concept art by Errol Le Cain for *The Thief and the Cobbler*.

## Case study: Perspective and design in Richard Williams' *The Thief and the Cobbler*

*Richard Williams*: "The reason I started animation is when I saw what you can do with it. When you are a Rembrandt today you wouldn't be able to resist animation. Instead of doing etchings he would be making stuff move. I would think … but it's a remarkable medium, you can do anything. And you can change it, you see … if you are playing a chorus, if you are improvising on an instrument, you have to do it then and then: that's it! But with this stuff [Williams reaches over to his animation paper] you can keep fixing it. You can improvise, you can plan it, you have total flexibility with animation. It's just that nobody has really outside the early Disneys and a few interesting short lived excitement, who knows, I am just making one picture. One big picture with all the stuff I know packed in, like a triple deck of sandwich … it's just jammed.'[20]

Richard Williams' *The Thief and the Cobbler* is an exceptional animated feature on many levels. It is the most elaborate feature film in animation history and its scale is unprecedented, being animated in its entirety on ones instead of twos and having an aspect ratio of 2.35:1 Panavision widescreen format, which clearly adds to its grandeur. It is also one of the very few animated features that never got finished in its intended form. Its entire production length of an astounding 31 years makes it also the second-longest film production in film history (live-action and animation). As of 2012, Williams' film was surpassed in production time by Yuriy Norshteyn's *The Overcoat* (based on a short story by Nicolai Gogol), which Norshteyn had been animating since 1981.

In 1962, David Lean stunned the world with his undeniable masterpiece *Lawrence of Arabia*, a feature in Super Panavision

70 (aspect ratio 2.20:1 or 2.35:1) that in scale was epic, to say the least, and boasted extravagant and lavish visuals composed to perfection. Where David Lean's film is set in Arabia, Williams' film *The Thief and the Cobbler* is set across the Euphrates River in the imaginary Golden City[21] of Persia. Williams also shot his film in Panavision (2.35:1), for reasons of obvious opulence and grandiosity. He always stated that this feature film would be his masterpiece, *the* masterpiece in animation … and a masterpiece of unprecedented scale it became, but not the way Williams anticipated it.

After having much success with his first short film *The Little Island* in 1958, Williams opened his own animation studio in London, where he had moved in 1955 from Toronto, Canada (via Ibiza in 1953). The short film *The Little Island* was so successful that it won Williams the BAFTA Award (British Academy of Film and Television Arts Award) for best animated film. This gave him the starting position for his London studio to produce commercials for national and international clients. The quality of Williams' studio was well known, as it not only boasted complex visuals that often used experimental techniques, like paint on glass, but also highly rendered colored pencil pieces that mimicked reality. Some of the commercials were nearly realistic and had an accuracy similar to today's computer animation. For example the famous commercials from the 1980s for the German building society Schwäbisch-Hall had their mascot Schlauer Fuchs ("Sly Fox") rendered with astounding accuracy and form

---

[20] Dormer Mike, *Richard Williams and The Thief who never gave up*, Thames Television, 1982.

[21] In the Miramax version of the film, the Golden City is referred to as Baghdad. Williams himself never mentions the city's name in his version of the film.

**IN PRODUCTION:**

# The Amazing Nasruddin

RICHARD WILLIAMS'
FULL-LENGTH EASTERNCOLOUR ANIMATION FILM OF
IDRIES SHAH'S FAMOUS CHARACTERISATION OF
'MULLA NASRUDDIN' THE LEGENDARY FOLK HERO

Style and colour of the film is based on Persian miniatures and Williams refers to it as a 'banana skin Ali Baba' or 'Slapstick 1,001 Nights'.

**Figure 16.79**

First page of Pat Williams' article in The Observer, February 21, 1965.

and were proof of the extent to which Williams' artists could push hand-drawn animation. Also, the lion mascot of the Samson tobacco commercials is unbelievably complex and at the same time beautifully rendered. However, most of his commercials suffer from the same problem: despite the visual splendor the character animation very often lacks flow. The characters morph from key frame to key frame rather than the key frames being ironed out by shifting elements of the movement and adjusting the spacing.

But Williams wanted more than just to produce commercials and had the dream of breaking into the animated feature film business, which at the time was not flourishing. Animation was being reinvented in the 1960s and 1970s, for instance with the Hubleys' famous award-winning shorts, but also George Dunning's supremely weird feature *Yellow Submarine*, which stunned audiences with a very new and different look designed by German illustrator Heinz Edelmann. Dunning's film paved the path in feature animation for an adult audience in 1968. Ralph Bakshi, on the other hand, surprised with his version

of Robert Crumb's comic *Fritz the Cat* in 1972, opening animation to adult themes of drugs, sex, and political awareness, so there was much exploration being done and Williams' feature clearly expresses these aesthetic explorations. *The Thief and the Cobbler*'s "fertilization" started in 1964 when Williams contributed illustrations for Idries Shah's book series on the famous stories of Mulla Nasruddin, a Sufi wise man from the thirteenth century, famous throughout the Middle East and Persia as the wise fool (also known under the name of Effendi in Turkey and China[22]). Idries Shah's brother, Omar Ali-Shah, was an early producer for Williams' company and also, like Idries, a teacher and writer on Sufism. While Williams was working on the illustrations of Mulla Nasruddin, he simultaneously started development on a feature film based on the famous Islamic character and had two of the staff members of his studio design inspirational illustrations and backgrounds that would depict the world of Nasruddin. Designer and layout artist Roy Naisbitt[23] and illustrator Errol Le Cain, credited as "background stylist" in what would turn into *The Thief and the Cobbler*, were the ones who created the Persian-looking Golden City's interiors and exteriors. From early on, it was decided that Persian miniatures would be the design base for the feature. On February 21, 1965, *The Observer* had an article on Richard Williams' animation studio, located at 13 Soho Square in London (Figure 16.79). In the article, Williams talks about his new project *The Amazing Nasruddin*, the feature's working title at the time. Even the famous Woody Allen was quoted in the article as saying: "See Dick run. Dick Williams is the new Disney. Dick is in the position now that Disney was in when he was making his first feature. Dick's *Snow White* is called *Nasruddin*."[24] Other works were also produced at the studio and in 1971 Williams received the offer to produce an animated TV special after Charles Dickens' *A Christmas Carol*. The animation of the finished product is impressive and elaborate for a TV production, especially in certain passages where Williams and his artists use transitions that were quite unique at the time. However, the character animation is often stiff and there is much morphing going on in the character's movements where key frames melt into each other. Nevertheless, the film received much praise and won him the Academy Award in 1972 as best animated feature. (This did not happen without major discussion, though, as the film was initially produced for TV but then released into theatres because of its high quality, which did enable it to be submitted for the prestigious award. Because of this, the Academy of Motion Films

---

[22] In 1979 Shanghai Animation Studios produced *The Story of Effendi*, directed by Qu Jianfang and Jin Xi, a stop-motion film that is still one of the most beloved and famous animated films in China.

[23] Roy Naisbitt is an animator and mostly layout artist who has worked on *Who Framed Roger Rabbit*, *Balto*, and *A Christmas Carol* (amongst others). He is especially known for his breathtaking background layouts and complex perspectives in camera pans. The sequence of Roger Rabbit flying through the kitchen and the layout of the last sequence with the war machine in *The Thief and the Cobbler* are some of his stunning achievements.

[24] Pat Williams, Evolution of a Studio, Richard Williams, *The Observer*, 21st February 1965.

and Sciences decided that films that had already been shown on TV must not be eligible for its awards.)

Williams had been working on *Nasruddin* for years, only interrupted by the Dickens TV special. He already had a whopping 3 hours of animated *Nasruddin* footage unedited. How could that be? What again would happen decades later with *The Thief and the Cobbler* already had happened with *Nasruddin*: surprisingly enough there was no consistent story line. Williams had so much animated footage that was supposedly unique and overwhelming in quality, but what it lacked was a continuous story line with characters that developed throughout the film. Not that a film needs a consistent story line; it can be an episodical story that has small clips of happenings, like in Studio Ghibli's *My Neighbors the Yamadas*, which works perfectly fine without an uninterrupted story line. In particular, this could be expected for a character the likes of Nasruddin, who is based on a compilation of short anecdotes to begin with. However, this obviously only works if the feature is intended from the beginning to be episodical, which Williams supposedly never did. The project of *Nasruddin* was cancelled because Idries Shah demanded 50% of the profits and his sister claimed all the rights to the stories, which for Williams was unacceptable. Shah left Williams some of the characters he had designed for the illustrations and the film, but Williams had to write a new story, if he wanted to continue with some of the characters he had created. In 1973, 1 year after his Academy Award win, Williams announced

> *Nasruddin* was found to be too verbal and not suitable for animation, therefore Nasruddin as a character and the Nasruddin stories were officially dropped as a project. However, the many years work spent on painstaking research into the beauty of Oriental art has been retained. Loosely based on elements in the Arabian Nights stories, an entirely new and original film entitled *The Thief and The Cobbler* is now the main project of the Williams Studio. Therefore any publicity references to the old character of Nasruddin are now obsolete.[25]

That was the actual birthday of the feature *The Thief and the Cobbler*, at the time called *Tin Tack*, whose story treatment was written by Howard Blake.[26] The thief, one of the characters that Williams was allowed to keep, was a side character in *Nasruddin* and appeared unchanged in *The Thief*. Zig-Zag and Princess Yum-Yum's nurse were also transferred to the new production. There were some scenes that made their way into *The Thief*— Yum-Yum's nurse beating up the thief at the beginning of the film, the laughing camel at the waterhole, and the dying soldier pierced with arrows, fleeing from the battle field of One-Eye reaching King Nod's palace.[27]

The story of *The Thief and the Cobbler* in the version available today is as follows: There is a cobbler by the name of Tack, who lives

in the Golden City; there is also a thief, "who shall be unnamed," who also lives in that very city, which has three golden balls on its highest minaret just begging to be stolen by the thief, which he obviously achieves. However, a prophesy of the ancients has stated that if the balls are stolen, the city will fall to destruction to the evil and mighty One-Eye; but the mystics had also stated that the city might be saved by "the simplest soul with the smallest and simplest of things." Then there is also King Nod, his daughter Yum-Yum, and the king's grand vizier Zig-Zag, who is in love with Yum-Yum. There is a witch, there is Yum-Yum's nurse, a whole band of brigands, a laughing camel, and many other characters odd and funny. In the end, Tack the cobbler fights the mighty One-Eye, defends the city, and finally marries Yum-Yum, whereas Zig-Zag gets what he deserves. The End …

In 1973 Williams was approached by Broadway producer Lester Osterman to be the animation supervisor of the feature film *Raggedy Ann & Andy*, based on the books by Johnny Gruelle. After some consideration, Williams agreed to direct the film as he could reinvest parts of the money earned back into *The Thief* and could also hire some famous animators for the production who then could benefit both films with their knowledge of traditional animation techniques and expertise.[28] Art Babbitt, Grim Natwick, Emery Hawkins, and Tissa David created memorable characters for *Raggedy Ann & Andy*, for instance the Camel with the Wrinkly Knees. The film definitely tried to invoke the Disney animation style, not in its design, which was done by Corny (Cornelius) Cole, but in its technique of full animation, which it succeeded at, bringing very complex characters and situations in full animation onto the screen. The production seems to not have been an easy one and in the end the film was heavily over budget and also over time (an issue that Williams would run into quite a bit in his career). After the film was released in 1977, despite its impressive animation in some parts, the public did not receive it well, as the story had some flaws. It did not really seem to be about Raggedy Ann and Andy, but more about the odd places that they visited and the characters they met along the way. Some of the animators who worked on *Raggedy Ann & Andy* switched over to William's other production[29] and *The Thief* proceeded slowly whenever there was time between commercials. One year later Mohammad Feisal, Prince of Saudi Arabia, was interested in financing *The Thief* due to its content of Sufism and thus he heavily invested in it. He offered US$100,000 for a 10-minute sequence, which Williams used

---

More on *Raggedy Ann & Andy*:

John Canemaker, *The Animated Raggedy Ann & Andy*, Bobbs-Merrill Company, Indianapolis, IN, 1977.

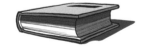

---

[25] Michael Dobbs, An Arabian Knight-mare, *Journal Animato*, Vol. 35.
[26] Kevin Schreck, Persistence of Vision, 2012 documentary.
[27] 27See footnote no. 25.

[28] 28John Canemaker, *The Animated Raggedy Ann & Andy*, Bobbs-Merrill Company, Indianapolis, IN, 1977, p. 107.
[29] 29John Canemaker, *The Animated Raggedy Ann & Andy*, Bobbs-Merrill Company, Indianapolis, IN, 1977, p. 286.

to finish the infamous battle sequence at the end of the film. Unfortunately the 10-minute long test sequence, produced to convince the Saudi prince about Williams' ability to finish on time and on budget, cost in the end about US$250,000.[30] It took more than a year to finish and was a tour-de-force of effects animation of unprecedented scale that cannot be described, but has to be experienced to be believed. Although Mohammed Feisal was impressed by what he saw, he withdrew his offer as Williams had not followed the given deadline … twice. The project was reduced in scale in 1979 and was again only worked on in production downtimes during commercials. During the 1980s Williams had two more producers who helped him finance the film: Gary Kurtz and Jake Eberts, who later financed the film with US$10 million, which was also not enough to finish The Thief.

Steven Spielberg saw finished parts of The Thief's final battle sequence and knew that Williams would be the right animation director for his upcoming production of Robert Zemecki's Who Framed Roger Rabbit. And the right man for the job Williams was! His work on Roger Rabbit gained him two well-deserved Academy Awards, one for best visual effects and a special achievement award for his outstanding animation direction. Through his work on Roger Rabbit, Warner Brothers was convinced that Williams was indeed capable of finishing a project, as he had just proved on the highly successful Roger Rabbit. Warner made a deal to finance The Thief with $25 million for the completion of the film and an additional $25 million to promote the finished film.[31] Finally The Thief was back in full production in 1989, and it looked promising for it to be finished in the given 2 year time frame. However, Williams kept changing and changing and extended scenes quite often, which lengthened the entire film significantly and with it of course the budget. A storyboard was finally produced (after over 25 years of production!) to show the investors a version of the film that showed its pacing and overall story line. Production was in full gear but everyone knew that because of the changes it would be barely possible to finish the film on time. The final deadline for submitting the finished film to Warner Brothers was missed and in 1992, on Friday, May 15, the film finally got taken away from Williams by a completion bond company,[32] which was part of the initial contract between the two parties, Williams and Warner. The contract stated that if Williams were unable to deliver the product on time, a third party, the bond company, would step in and take over production. The bond company hired Fred Calvert to finish the film in the cheapest way possible. The finished film is different from Williams' version, has added unbearable song tunes, speaking characters with cheesy lines (some of the initial

characters were silent), and additional character animation that is of very low quality, never even coming close to the original high-quality animation style from Williams' animators. This was the unfortunate end of this epic masterpiece of animation (for now).

Williams had lost everything he had worked on for over 30 years! It is very understandable that financiers want to see a result and do not want to be told that the film isn't yet finished and needs another couple million to be completed, over and over again. It is ironic that if the completion bond company had just given Williams the money to finish the film, there would have been a much better chance of recovering some of the expenses, as the film would have surely been further worshipped by animation fans and would have probably appealed to a certain degree to the general audience just because of its unprecedented scale. The additional costs would have been similar, but the gains probably higher (but then again: who really knows). This was a seemingly poor business decision by the completion bond company. As easy to comprehend as their reasons are, they lack logic looking back. But who would not run out of patience? After all, Williams had spent US$28,000,000[33] on the production of The Thief and the Cobbler.[34]

To really judge the film, one does not want to watch the theatrically released version, but there are other ways to enjoy the film as it was intended. The feature is unfinished and lacks the final touch of finished animation, editing, and music and can only be seen in the latest so-called Recobbled Mark 4 version, an approximation of the original. The Recobbled versions are scenes and shots from various sources, storyboards, copies of the film, test footage, line tests, and finished scenes from The Thief and the Cobbler edited together by Garrett Gilchrist, a fan of the feature, dedicated to recreating the most accurate version of the film. There is also a DVD collection, with the documentary Persistence of Vision by Kevin Schreck from 2012, which contains the most accurate version of the film on a separate DVD, based on the original 1992 work print of Richard Williams, presented in its entirety. Despite all this, one feels the struggle for grandeur in the unfinished version where the animated shot counts more than the overall story structure. The emphasis always lies on the animator's ability to pack the shot full of ideas and spectacle, irrespective of whether it furthers the story or not. For animators who only see the technique of character animation, the film is a masterpiece; for people who want to see a story unfold, with strong characters that develop on-screen, the film is challenging; for those who enjoy design, the feature is often a visual feast with magnificent aesthetics … The Thief and the Cobbler is thus a rather difficult film to pin down, as it stuns one in every scene

[30] Kevin Schreck, Persistence of Vision, 2012 documentary.
[31] Animator Michael Schlingmann in Kevin Schreck's Persistence of vision, documentary 2012.
[32] Robert Welkos, Oscar-Winner Loses 'Dream'; 'Roger Rabbit' Artist sees his 'Arabian Knight' Seized after Decades of Work, Journal: Austin American Statesman, p. E.5.

[33] The film already had a financial backing through producer Jake Ebert in the middle of the 1980s, which was US$10 million. Additional money was constantly poured into the production by Williams' company over the years and an additional $25 million from Warner would have brought the estimated final budged far above the $28 million mentioned in Mike Dobbs' article in Animato! magazine.
[34] See footnote 32.

and one tries to grasp how the animation was done in its complexity and one also mourns at the same time due to its continuous defiance of the rule of animation of preparing a storyboard to help to get a logical shot flow and consistency into the film. On the other hand, one cannot stop thinking about the passion that all the artists put into the project and the years and years of hard work that show in every single frame on-screen. But then there is also the blame for Williams' inability to follow the basic rule in animation of planning ahead and being able to structure the film, planning the cost of the entire production, and also planning its completion. Williams was in that regard very similar to Walt Disney, for whom money was always there to be spent. It was up to his brother Roy to find it. Williams' production technique was never one that focused on a budget but focused on the artistic outcome. It is about the art form of animation for him. In that regard, he is a true "artist," so involved in his work that real life with its finances are of no concern to him. He lacks understanding that for most companies that finance a project, the art side is not really the point of why they put money into it to begin with, but the possibility of increasing the initial investment. For Williams, however, there is no higher power than art itself. He wants to make the scenes and shots as perfect and visually stunning as he possibly can and then give it some more. Some of the shots that Williams has designed and animated with his staff of artists surpass anything that was possible at the time in live-action cinema, nor had it been seen in animation. The breaking of the camera restrictions are spellbinding, especially the famous dizzying chase through the palace with the cobbler and the thief in an op art–inspired environment; and obviously the final 10 minutes with the war machine breaking down is tiring in its grandeur. Williams creates visuals that were not feasible in any other medium at the time than animation. He raises animation to a visual level that it has never been before. But his inability to step back and see the entire production caused much distress and financially questionable actions. The famous card-game shot with Zig-Zag playing card tricks in front of One-Eye (also see the case study of this shot in Volume 2, Chapter 12, "Shape") took a painter about 3 months to finish with traditional paint on animation cels. There is a full set of cards, with each card showing the precise images of spades, hearts, diamonds, and clubs, which in terms of detail is an incredibly time-consuming task. After it was done, Williams did not approve of the used colors and all of it had to be painted again. "He must have spent thousands and thousands and thousands on stuff that was never used."[35] It is rather painful to read about Carl Gover's production work for Williams and the problems during the production.[36] Williams expected everyone to work at their very best and very often the very best was not good enough. Sixty-hour weeks were expected, which of course pushed

everyone to work very hard and put overtime into the production only to please the boss, from whom much could be learned. This was not always a downside, as many of the animators who worked on the feature remember how much they learned on this specific production and how it was one of the very few places in animation worldwide where one could actually dive into character animation of formidable quality. Williams wanted his animators to improve and learn and some famous animators had been hired to animate and teach the staff and bring much sought-after traditional animation skill and knowledge into the company. Emery Hawkins, Art Babbitt, and Grim Natwick, three legendary animators who had worked on animation during the golden age of American animation and had literally had a hand in the development of character animation as an art form came over to London to work on *The Thief* (after the production of *Raggedy Ann & Andy*). Art Babbitt was animator of the famous drunken mouse in Disney's *The Country Cousin* (1935), leading animator/animation director on *Snow White*, *Dumbo*, and *Pinocchio*, animation supervisor of the segment "The Pastoral Symphony," and animator of "The Nutcracker Suite" in *Fantasia*. He was also the head of the Disney strike in 1941. After he parted with Disney he brought the unique characters of UPA to life and pushed animation further as an art form that celebrates movement. Art Babbitt joined Williams' company in 1973. Grim Natwick started out as the animator on *Betty Boop* at the Fleischer Studios (he was also the designer of Betty's original look) and then worked on the prince and princess in *Gulliver's Travels* (1939), Fleischer's first feature. At Disney, he was the lead animator on the character of Snow White, went back to Fleischer to work on shorts, then switched to Walter Lantz Studios and Warner Brothers. He also worked at UPA on John Hubley's *Rooty Toot Toot* as animator. The third master of animation, Emery Hawkins, started out at Screen Gems Studio as an animator on the short *Let's Go* in 1937[37] and after another short film went on to work for MGM's director Fritz Freleng. In 1939 Disney became his employer and he animated Donald Duck and characters in other shorts. Afterwards, in 1941, he went back to Screen Gems and also worked for Walter Lantz and then finally Warner Animation. He also was part of UPA's *Hell Bent for Election* and Hubley's *Adventures of an*\* and *Tender Game*. Hawkins represented the Warner animation style, and Williams hired him as animator and teacher for his studio. What Williams did was preserve the knowledge of these talented animators who were partly responsible for the golden age of American animation and allowed the younger generation to learn from the old masters the secrets of the trade and the knowledge needed to produce high-quality character animation. One can see the excellence of the work being done in such a production with the input of these specialists alongside Richard Williams' tedious comments

[35] Kevin Schreck, *Persistence of Vision*, documentary 2012.
[36] The Thief: Carl Glover, Part 2; posted February 7, 2008. http://thethief1.blogspot.com/2008/02/in-meantime-after-lot-of.html (accessed February 27, 2015).

[37] *Let's Go* is a rather odd short about bees from Prosperity, the "town of industry," that drop honey-bombs onto famished and weak grasshoppers, which gives them enough strength (without eating the honey!) to build a prosperous town themselves.

**Figure 16.80**

*The Thief and the Cobbler*: Screenshot of the messenger riding back to King Nod's palace.

and critiques. The work had to be redone over and over with an accuracy and detail that was just not common in animation at the time anymore and therefore stood out as something very special. Nevertheless, this also came with a downside at the Williams' studio, as animator Richard Burdett stated in an interview: "The more experienced you got the more work was thrust on your lap." Burdett also speaks about the situation at the studio:

> I think some of them (the staff) were a bit amused by the fact that he (Williams) kept changing the script. I mean that was ongoing for the ten years I was there; and when I left they were still going through the same hoops. You could never get time off. I mean my wife had meningitis and he wouldn't give me time off to go and see her. So I had to go during my lunch hour to see my wife in the hospital. And that was basically I guess what turned me on thinking about working for myself. And to be honest I was fed up working there because the pressure was just mounting all the time.[38]

Williams is brilliant as an animator and inventor of extraordinary movement and artistic entertainment. But in a production there is little time at some point for experimentation, and constant changes or continuous redoes are not the norm for very good reasons. His "vision" of a spectacle of thousands and his unswerving goal of epic visuals is of course possible in animation if one has the money to spend and already Disney realized in *Pinocchio* how expensive those exemplary images can get. However, Walt already understood through his brother Roy that these visuals in animation come with a very high price. Animator Michael Schlingmann, who had worked on *The Thief*, says:

> If a scene would work out nicely he (Williams) would just make it longer. I think the dying soldier (Figure 16.80) started off as a 15 second shot or something. Then it turned into a 20 second

shot, then 30 seconds and then ended up a minute long. It's one of those things where he had seen the line tests and say: "This is just too nice to stop it here," and then extend it and that happened to many scenes. So the film was constantly getting longer. So there is absolutely no telling where we were at the time basically.[39]

This work method is unacceptable in a major feature production. It is a very good method for short films and that is what *The Thief* basically is: an assemblage of astounding short pieces. Expanding the shots constantly during production kills the rhythm of the overall film and constantly interrupts the story flow, because the elongated shots in *The Thief* drag attention to themselves instead of keeping the focus on the main story. Following the success of *Who Framed Roger Rabbit*, when production was finally again in full bloom for *The Thief*, Williams started to add the stunning animated backgrounds that had never been seen before in animation on this scale (however, he had already used some animated backgrounds in *Raggedy Ann & Andy*). He seems to have been his own worst enemy in the production, never being able to allow the film to actually get finished, especially because he repeatedly convinced himself of his vision of producing a "100 minute Panavision animated epic feature film with a hand drawn cast of thousands."[40] *The Thief and the Cobbler* was always meant to be a visual experience very much like Stanley Kubrick's *2001: A Space Odyssey*, a film whose sometimes psychedelic visuals are more escapism than straightforward storytelling, more art form than entertainment. It is at its core a celebration of the art form of animation despite its shortcomings in story. It might also be interesting precisely because of those shortcomings, as one does not get what one expects in an animated feature film.

[38] Kevin Schreck, *Persistence of Vision*, documentary 2012.

[39] Michael Schlingmann in Kevin Schreck's *Persistence of Vision*, documentary 2012.
[40] Michael Dobbs, An Arabian Knight-mare, *Journal Animato*, Vol. 35.

## Story

Scripts in animation are usually changed throughout the production in order to improve the story and fine-tune it for a better outcome. This is the editing process of a live-action film, only done not at the end of the shoot but during production. Story changes are rather common up to the very last possibility of change, but only changes that do not affect the already finished parts of the film are the norm. Changes that affect finished sections are usually only done when there is absolutely no other solution to fix the story. Animation is in dire need of a structure, and when Williams states that animation can be changed over and over again in his statement right at the beginning of this article, and that this is what makes animation the perfect medium, these are only half the facts. Of course it *can* be changed if someone has the money *to* change it. The main problem of *The Thief*, as it appears today, is its lack of what is commonly considered a good story. *The Thief* surely does not follow the conventional Hollywood approach that is easy to understand and very clearly structured. There are many moments in the film that are just there for the vanity of the character animation itself. Many scenes do not contribute to the overall story, but hinder its flow because they put emphasis on themselves rather than supporting the main plot. This is not necessarily a problem if it is planned this way from the beginning on and does not hinder the understandability of the story. Williams' film suffers from continuous repetitions and animated scenes that are just too long for most of the general audience members to enjoy. They are beautiful to look at, boast ideas and creativity, and no doubt are a pleasure for the animation enthusiast to watch and enjoy. However, in a feature film they do affect the patience of the viewer and as a student of mine commented, after having seen the film, on the thief's actions of trying to steal the golden balls from the tallest minaret: "I can see that you want to get the golden balls. We know that you will get the balls. Would you just get on with the story!" Some viewers enjoy this repetition and others cannot stand it. Many scenes in *The Thief and the Cobbler* are not easy to sit through when compared to commercial feature animation. But then one has to ask whether it is necessary for a film to follow the typical animated feature film formula or whether there is also the option of creating a totally new style of animated feature, that focuses on the art of animation instead of the art of common entertainment. I myself find it very interesting that the film is different and not easy to digest, which is exactly what a film should be. Film is an art form and does not have to follow a formula in order to entertain visually or intellectually; entertainment is not the same for everyone. Not everyone is entertained by *Snow White and the Seven Dwarfs*, as strange as that might seem …. However, if one wants to create a blockbuster film that costs quite a few million, the unique artistic approach is not always the best solution to drag people of all ages into the theatres.

The main complaint about *The Thief and the Cobbler*'s story is the pacing and the disconnectedness of different scenes. It is also the question of the necessity of whole sequences appearing in the film. What is the reason that the cobbler is chosen to be the guide through the desert? Are the brigands really important? The group of the cobbler and Princess Yum-Yum are going into the desert to find the witch but come across the brigands, whom Yum-Yum orders to be their safety guards; however, in the end they don't really have anything to do with the outcome. Is it wise to have a group of about 30 complex characters in the film who have no particular purpose other than making the film grander and costing quite some money to draw? Characters with rather cut-out personalities like Princess Yum-Yum or others who lack personality make it difficult for the audience to connect with the characters emotionally in the story. The entire film has few characters that invite identification—even just caring for them is difficult as we are never involved in the story emotionally. We do not really care for the loving bond that develops between the princess and the cobbler; neither do we care about the thief's miraculous journey through the war machine, from which he escapes unharmed. We do not care because we do not have any emotional connection with the characters, as they are only presented to us on a stage that the animator Williams uses to present his artistic abilities and technical skills. Williams' characters are comparable to Buster Keaton's silent characters, but the difference is that in Keaton's films there is an emotional connection from the beginning on, as the introduction of the character is always on a personal level that the audience can identify with. We care for the character because we feel an emotional bond. Whenever Williams introduces a character, he impresses us with his craft, not with a personality that drags us into the story and creates some kind of affection. All of the introductions of his main characters are masterpieces in character animation and they all portray the character's personality beautifully. Nevertheless, when he introduces the cobbler we see him sleeping and sewing in stunning three-dimensionality; afterwards he falls down the stairs and shortly thereafter is standing in front of King Nod. We are already in the middle of the story and don't really know much about the main character despite the masterful animation. When he introduces Princess Yum-Yum we see her holding flowers that take all attention away from her, because Williams stuns us with his ability to create a three-dimensionally turning flower. On the other hand, the thief is introduced in all his greed beautifully; Zig-Zag's introduction via his walk is also extraordinary and unique, and all of the character animation represents his personality along the splendor of the scene. Those two characters, the thief and Zig-Zag, come across from the beginning on as valid personalities. The execution of the introductions drags attention to their technique and extravagance rather than the personality of the character. This would not be an issue if throughout the film the personality of, for example, the cobbler or the princess, were further developed and the characters went through some emotional development, which then would help us to understand the characters' actions. But that unfortunately does not happen. The characters make decisions that seem random and are always unexplained, as they often act without a reason. Zig-Zag is the only one who really has a reason for his actions and an agenda. Williams is brilliant in his ideas and his ability to make small scenes extremely entertaining. For example, the polo game and the thief's unintentional involvement in it is beautiful but what is the point of the scene other than it being stunning, which it truly is? It does not contribute to the story at all; does it contribute to the thief's personality? No. The whole scene repeatedly pounds the idea that the polo ball is following the thief and he is trying to escape from it. It is the only time in the film that an object follows the thief and he actually does *not* want it. Does it hinder the story from flowing? Probably … Is it entertaining? Very much so. The question arises, why *not* have a scene like the polo game in the film? In animation we learn over and over about exactly how a story has to be told; that the logic of the story needs to be in every shot and everything has to contribute to the flow of the story. We sometimes forget improvisation as a valid form of entertainment. Animation is so obviously the opposite of improvisation, so much so that it is difficult to let the creativity freely flow in the work process because everything has to be planned so meticulously and tediously, up to the last miniscule detail. What Williams gives us is a bit of lighthearted improvisation, where not just the trunk of the tree is important but also the branches, not just the main story line, but also the little side actions that make the life on-screen more vibrant. That is where Williams' film withdraws itself from easy critique, as it is a piece of art, not only a piece of entertainment, and thus plays by its own rules and establishes a new direction for animation. Whether it is successful or not lies in the eye of the beholder.

## Storyboard

Williams wanted from the beginning on to create the grandest animated feature in film history, which is a rather bold plan and sounds more like a vanity project for the artist himself. He also wanted absolute control over the editing of the film, which in animation is a unique demand. Animation is not live-action and every shot that is painstakingly finished is too expensive to just be cut out of the film and thrown away if it does not fit the story. In live-action if a shot lands on the cutting floor it does not really matter as much, as there are usually many other shots that cover a similar view and content (if it is not an entire scene for which a huge set had to be built). The director and editor have multiple takes to choose from to assemble a scene in a live-action film. Animation does not have that luxury because it is an extremely expensive medium that has to be planned out from the beginning to the end, and therefore the funds available have to be used with proper and accurate planning, which is partly done via storyboard. For most of the production Williams did not use any storyboards, as he felt that it would restrict his creativity and was too controlling; therefore in 1988 he had about 2.5 hours of pencil tests for his feature.[41] A project that lacks a storyboard

is unheard of in the field of commercial animation feature film. Once a shot goes into the production of character animation or even painting, the director should be very confident that the shot is exactly what is needed for the scene to read; otherwise, money is wasted if it needs to be reworked for whatever reason. The final storyboard was drafted for specific scenes but not the entire film until way into the production (decades). Many shots in the final film, which is available in the *Recobbled Mark 4* version or Williams' own work print copy of 1992, have problems with continuity style editing, the predominant editing style in film. Continuity style editing pays attention to the temporal and spatial continuity in scenes and the overall logic of the story from shot to shot. Williams' storyboard in the existing version does not always follow the cinematic needs of logic, especially when it comes to space and character placement. Spatial continuity also deals with the character's eyelines matching from shot to shot and the characters not changing sides in the frame from one shot to the next despite the camera moving. However, one needs to keep in mind that the existing versions of the film are either reconstructed and not yet finished or a work-print also not yet finished, but are by no means the final and finished version of the film! What the final film therefore could have looked like is difficult to say. Problems in continuity can be seen in the following scenes:

- In the sequence when Yum-Yum and the Cobber visit the witch in her "hand castle," there is no continuity in the space itself. The tower is a hand from the outside, but once the witch is flying around the tower on a rope there is all of a sudden another wall of hands on the left that was not there in the establishing shot of the hand. She might be flying between the fingers of the hand?
- A wide shot shows the arrangement of the characters on the hand castle, which changes in the shots afterwards, not only in orientation but also direction. The witch looks down at the chest with gold that she has received as payment from Princess Yum-Yum and then looks up to the left → cut to the princess looking down. So we expect the princess to be really close to both chest and witch because of her eyeline. But the witch in the next shot is running to the left and there is no princess to be seen.
- Afterwards, the witch checks the cobbler's heart with a stethoscope; Princess Yum-Yum is looking to the right, despite the cobbler being on her left.

All these issues in continuity are not major problems by themselves but they add to the continuous disorientation of the audience not knowing the exact arrangement of the characters and the dimensionality of the location and set. The disregard for directions is spread throughout the existing version of the film and strikes one as odd in a $28 million production. Some scenes or shot combinations are excellently crafted, and others are clumsy and full of weird shot decisions. It comes across as unprofessional and unrefined, and all these problems can easily be avoided by producing a proper storyboard that helps

---

41  See footnote no. 40.

to design the scenes and make sure that all the directions are correct, the eyelines match, and the entire scene is easily understood. Williams' not "believing in storyboards" had a major disadvantage aside from not being able to plan the movie financially and story-wise: the continuity suffered heavily and thus the understandability of the entire film. The director wanting final control is of course understandable, as he can change scenes left and right if they do not fit his "vision." But it is the director's job to know what the vision is before he releases the shots into production. Ideas are not the problem most of the time; the money to produce those ideas is the issue and that has to be calculated right if one is eager to finish a film.

## Persian miniatures

As mentioned, the design of the film is mostly based on Errol Le Cain's work intricate development work (Figure 16.78) interpreting the style of Persian miniatures, which had been used as inspiration since the feature *Nasruddin*. The design direction for *Nasruddin* is what Williams called "banana skin Ali Baba" or "Slapstick 1.001 nights."[42] It was decided early on where to look for inspiration when it came to the design of the film. The historical Nasruddin lived during the thirteenth century in what is today central Anatolia in Turkey and what was at the time of Nasruddin Turkish–Persian territory. However, the most beautiful and visually appealing designs of roughly that area and time frame (very roughly) are Persian miniatures; therefore, the style of both films, *Nasruddin* and *The Thief*, derived from Persian manuscripts of the Safavid dynasty,[43] which ruled from 1501 to 1722. It was a period with great emphasis on the arts, especially architecture and the manuscript art. What needs to be understood is the substantial influences on Persian painting from China's art. After the Mongol invasion of Persia in 1219 and the takeover of not only Persia but what is today Iran, Iraq, Azerbaijan, Turkmenistan, Turkey, Georgia, Pakistan, and Afghanistan, the Mongol rulers established their capital in today's Iran and brought with them Mongol artists who were trained in the Chinese style of painting. The coexistence of the Mongol artists with Persian artists influenced the style of Persian art greatly, and this can be seen in the Safavid miniatures to a great extent. Many aspects of Chinese painting can be recognized in the Safavid miniatures in characters, landscapes, animals (especially horses), and rendering of nature. This created a basis for the artists and was the beginning of the development of Persian painting, though the basis was very strong as it affected not only the depiction of natural objects and characters but also the depiction and interpretation of space itself. Chinese space does not provide a three-dimensional perspective but parallel perspective and axonometric projection, in which the architecture is tilted in such a way that the axis of the object depicted is not parallel to the projection plane. Axonometry does not have a vanishing point and therefore the image is not optically distorted like in one-, two-, or three-point perspective. This interpretation of reality can be seen in Chinese art of the tenth century and then found its way via Mongol invasion into Persian art. What is interesting is what Persia did with the perspective and how it incorporated it into its religious belief system. There are five principal states of being, referred to in Sufism as the "five divine presences."

1. *Nasut* or *Mulk*: The human world is real and all-comprehensive.
2. *Malakut*: Realm of royalty, which dominates the physical world or the sensory is an intermediate world
3. *Jabarut*: Heaven and the human intellect (supernaturally natural paradise, which we carry within us) or the world of the archangelic
4. *Lahut*: Realm of the spiritual, the world of the divine names and qualities
5. *Dhat* or *Hahut*: the infinite self or the divine[44,45]

The states above Jabarut are without form or formal manifestations, which is dominant in Nasut and Malakut. The imaginal third presence is in between the mundane and the divine; it has its own time, color, shape, and form and is its very own world, the world of imagination. Miniature paintings depict this world in their interpretation. They cannot portray it in a realistic three-point perspective, as this would reduce the imaginary world to the world of the mundane, or Nasut. The miniatures are interpretations and visuals of the imaginary, not replicas of reality. This is a very important point in order to understand the use of perspective in the paintings. The basis of this is, as mentioned before, derived from Chinese paintings; however, it fits the philosophical needs of Sufism. Miniatures are therefore the representation of the sensory and the joy of paradise. Around the fourteenth century, the Shiraz school of painting introduced another aspect of perspective to miniatures: the horizontal arrangement of characters, where the lower levels refer to characters that are close to the viewer and the upper levels are reserved for those far away. Carpets and floors

**More on persian miniatures:**

Marianna Shreve Simpson, *Sultan Ibrahim Mirza's Haft Awrang*, Smithsonian Institution, Washington, 1997.

Sheila R. Canby, *The Shahnama of Shah Tahmasq, The Persian Book of Kings*, Yale University Press, London, 2014.

Eleanor Sims, *Peerless Images, Persian Painting and its Sources*, Yale University Press, London, 2002.

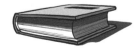

[42] Pat Williams, Evolution of a Studio, Richard Williams, *The Observer*, February 21, 1965.
[43] Williams Alex, *The Thief and the Cobbler*, http://www.awn.com/mag/issue1.12/articles/williams1.12.html (accessed March 6, 2015).
[44] Frithjof Schuon, *Form and Substance in the Religions*, Indiana University Press, Bloomington, IN, 2002, p. 53.
[45] Seyyed Hossein Nasr, The World of Imagination' and the Concept of Space in the Persian Miniature, *Islamic Quaterly*, Vol. xlll (July-September 1969), p. 132.

**Figure 16.81**

Shahnama of Shah Tahmasbi (King's Book of Kings) (~1522–1537); Painter of this specific folio is Sultan Muhammad: *King Gayumars and his court*.

**Figure 16.82**

Shahnama of Shah Tahmasbi (King's Book of Kings) (~1522–1537); Painter of this specific folio is Sultan Muhammad: *King Gayumars and his court*; detail.

are vertically flipped and seen from above.[46] This horizontal arrangement goes along with the interpretation of architecture in parallel perspective or axonometric projection. Space in the miniatures is not reality and never attempts to be a replica of it, but rather an alternate spiritual space that gives the viewer a glimpse into another realm. This also goes along with the natural world that is depicted, which shows nature in a much more lush and Arcadian light than anything that is present in the more dry climate of Iran. Overabundant nature is to be seen in the famous Persian gardens, which boast of flora and water. The presence of rich nature in most of the miniatures makes the idea of the visualization of paradise even more believable and convincing.

The miniatures themselves, most often painted in royal workshops, are usually not created by one specific painter, but by a group

of artists who worked together on one book, which makes the provenance of who painted which page sometimes difficult, but of course there are exceptions. What makes Persian and also Mughal miniatures so unique is their extreme focus on detail and pattern. There are miniatures that are more detailed than others, and the designs for Williams' film stay between the two extremes, nevertheless having rather big patterns compared to the famous manuscripts with their extremely miniscule details and overwhelming styles. The manuscript is one of the most important pieces of Islamic art production, and the ones of the Safavid period are particularly celebrated for their high level of artistry and complexity. The details in their floral and geometric patterns are stunning. An example of one of the most important Persian manuscripts is the *Shahnama of Shah Tahmasbi* ("King's Book of Kings") from ~1522 to 1537, which boasts exquisitely detailed illustrations and richly decorated pages of unsurpassed extravagance. All of its pages are luxuriantly covered in gold sprinkles around the text, and the entire manuscript contains a

---

[46] David Talbot Rice, *Islamic Painting. A Survey*, Edinburgh University Press, Edinburgh, 1971, p. 87.

**Figure 16.83**
Sultan Ibrahim Mirza's Haft Awrang:
*Majnun approaches the campe of in Layli's Caravan* (1556–1565).

called *Freer Gallery Haft Awrang of Jami* (1556–1565) (Figure 16.83). Consisting of about 300 folios and 29 full-page illustrations, the *Haft Awrang*, or in translation "The Seven Thrones," is a celebrated piece of Persian literature, a collection of seven poems by the Persian poet Mawlana Nuruddin Abdul Rahman Jami (1414–1492), who wrote it between 1468 and 1485. Three poems are allegorical romances, three are didactic discourses, and the last one discusses the two mentioned genres.[48] The page "Majnun Approaches the Camp of Layli's Caravan" (Figure 16.83) is one of the most elaborate and well-known pages of the manuscript and is rather strange in its composition. Six tents and canopies overlap each other at various angles, which makes it a very busy and lively composition indeed. In between, we see various characters, horses, and camels engaging in camp life. The overall logic of the space is not fully clear and the patchwork of fabrics also does not support a dimensional space, which leads to the overall arrangement of elements being placed nearly in the form of a collage rather than following a traditional composition. However, this is exactly what makes this page so enticing and exiting. This magnificent miniature of Mirza's manuscript shows the playfulness, the various textures, the bright colors, and use of light blue and rose colors that are so dominant in Williams' film. These two manuscripts are only examples from a wide range of illustration styles that are present in Persian manuscripts, as there were many artists working on the books for years and years. Both manuscripts, and others from the same period, are abundant with nature and social life. The versatility of its flora, with trees, bushes, and flowers, the multitude of outfits of the characters, and the sheer endless invention of decorative pattern for architecture, carpets, fabrics, etc., is truly impressive. These examples give an idea of the scope and richness of Persian miniatures; they are by no means *the* inspiration for the film *The Thief and the Cobbler* but suggest the inspirational materials at hand for the designers. What is striking in the film's design is its adamant devotion to its Persian art source. This makes his film unique in its entire design, as it is clearly in awe of its source material.

## Design direction and space

Both mentioned manuscripts show the unique color combinations that are reflected in the final film, which also uses the Persian interpretation of space and composition. The space that Williams' artists invent very closely relates to the different possibilities of the miniatures' perspective: parallel perspective and axonometric projection in its backgrounds. Aside from a couple of exceptions, the architecture is either flat or axonometrically depicted. Most backgrounds are of enticing and unique design, translating the source material into animation, like the stunning backgrounds during the chase between Tack and the thief through King Nod's palace (Figure 16.84). The space itself is a mixture of Persian axonometric perspective but also with a twist of op art to confuse the audience. But then there

staggering 258 illustrations and 759 folios.[47] In particular, folio 20v of painter Sultan Muhammad (Figures 16.81 and 16.82) is exceptionally beautiful and is considered his masterpiece, not just in its details, exquisite composition, and color, but also in the technique of how he renders stone with colors melting into each other. It shows Iranian king Gayumars and his court just being informed by an angel of his son's looming death by the hand of Ahriman. The color in this painting is sensitively balanced and the blue in the stones and rocks, interspersed with streaks of purple make the entire page glow. Merely the detail can show its real quality in color and craftsmanship (Figure 16.82). Miniatures of that quality and detail can only be appreciated in their original form in person, as it is barely possible to reproduce the intricacy of the original. Another spectacular example of Mughal miniatures is *Sultan Ibrahim Mirza's Haft Awrang*, also

[47] 48Sheila R. Canby, *The Shahnama of Shah Tahmasq, The Persian Book of Kings*, Yale University Press, London, UK, 2014, p. 16.

[48] Marianna Shreve Simpson, *Sultan Ibrahim Mirza's Haft Awrang*, Smithsonian Institution, Washington, DC, 1997, p. 18.

**Figure 16.84**

**Figure 16.85**

Screenshot *The Thief and the Cobbler.*

are other backgrounds that are rather odd. For example, in the shot when King Nod and his daughter Yum-Yum are running down the stairs in the palace (Figure 16.85), the background falls apart—the stairs are flat, the background panel is flat, but its pattern is slightly tilted, which is an odd choice for a geometrically oriented design style, and one asks oneself where the stairs are actually coming from, as the perspective between the stairs and the yellow patterned panel is not convincing in its distances. The feeling of space is especially unclear in the throne room of King Nod and many other parts of the palace. They give snippets of information that work visually, but the overall spatial expansion of the space lacks often clarity.

Strangely enough, though, there is a constant discrepancy between two- and three-dimensionality in the feature. Where most of the backgrounds are so true to Persian miniatures in their vertical planes, Williams also gives us three-dimensionally rendered architecture, fully animated in perspective, like the Golden City in the beginning of the film. This is somewhat odd, as where the rest of the film underlines its own flatness and

devotion to Persian space, those shots always stand out as "see what I can do" and are distracting from a conceptual view.

The treatment of the background of the Persian illustrations can easily be translated into a painted background for animation. The flatness and rejection of three-point perspective in these miniatures is a perfect ground for a 2D animation design, as they follow a similar aesthetic.

There are some common design rules that Persian miniatures from the Safavid period generally follow despite their origin or date (there are obviously differences between the schools in the various cities and also differences between the artists, though they are not considered as too important in this paper). The production chose a rather general Persian miniature style and created a design that mostly expresses "Persian" but not a specific century, area, or artist. Some of the rules in the design of Persian miniatures that also appear in *The Thief and the Cobbler* are

- The surfaces of the paintings provide many flat and vertical planes with the ornamental decoration of flowers

**Figure 16.86**

*Fountain of the Lions*, Alhambra, Granada, Spain.

**Figure 16.87**

Fountain on the market place, screenshot *The Thief and the Cobbler*.

and grass, trees, carpets, or tiles underlining the verticality of the frame.

• The artificial floor or ground plane is almost always flat and depicted from a 45° angle. In *The Thief*, there are top views (Zig-Zag's march into the Golden City) but also tilted ground planes with various geometric pattern of tiles and carpets. Natural settings have two possibilities: one with uneven ground (the polo game) and one with flat ground (the gardens of the palace, for instance). Nevertheless, both have decorative floral elements enriching the plane with an arranged yet organic pattern.

• There is a very strong emphasis on pattern and geometric designs in every part of the image. Walls, sculptures, fabrics, even within trees or bushes, pattern plays an important role in the style.

• The perspective is constructed with the use of parallel perspective or axonometric projection. Only the three-dimensional moving backgrounds use three vanishing points for their construction.

• All fauna is very decorative and two-dimensional.

• Clouds, fog, and mountains follow Chinese style and design. What Williams adds to the design is the utterly convincing translation of the cloud design into animated movement.

• Strong emphasis on shape and its exaggeration (also due to Chinese influence, very dominant in the horse design).

• The flatness of the vertical planes is often enhanced by lack of size perspective, which goes along with the Safavid miniatures' depiction of space: grass blades, for example, are placed in an arranged pattern on the monochrome surface with the same sizes, underlining again the verticality of the plane (parallel and axonometric perspective in general lack size perspective in the architecture, which of course could be added in the characters).

• The lighting is of no concern in the miniatures; however, in *The Thief* it is often kept to a minimum, and many shots and backgrounds lack it altogether. When light appears, it is mostly devoid of an exact light source, which keeps the

image overall more flat. Nevertheless, some backgrounds do have a strong emphasis on light and shadow, like the introduction of the thief, with a strong morning light casting the town square half in shadow. However, the composition and shadow still keep the image flat.

• The architecture is often shown with inside and outside in the miniatures, very similar to Chinese painting where the two spaces are linked and not separate.

• Background, middle ground, foreground, and characters always receive the same attention to detail; therefore, the image lacks textural perspective, supporting its flatness.

• The characters that are closer to the viewer are lower in the frame; the ones further away are higher. This is used in some shots in the feature: for example when Zig-Zag enters the Golden City he is shown on a vertically tilted ground plane with characters underneath and above him. It is not really a downward shot, as the perspective of the characters is from the side rather than above, which perfectly translates the Persian miniature into animation.

• The characters' faces always have a three-quarter view in the miniatures; that is one of the points that is obviously changed in Williams' character animation, as he favors mostly three-dimensional character animation. However, the three-quarter view is given preference.

• The horses' shapes are clearly derived from Chinese horse designs. The famous horses from the Tang dynasty are obviously the models that the Persian miniatures had in mind when recreating their shapes and designs. Williams adopts this design in the horses, whose legs are extremely thin and the skull elongated.

• Characters' heads are almost always round in the miniatures, which in the feature is reflected by the two main characters of Princess Yum-Yum and the cobbler. All other characters are expressed in very exaggerated shapes, fitting the general exaggeration of animation design.

**403**

- The image of Sultan Ibrahim Mirza's *Haft Awrang* (Figure 16.83) contains a mix of different patterns in various colors, which makes the image appear like a quilt: a mix of geometric and floral patterns that feel even busy in some accounts but have a richness that draws one into the image. In Williams' film the use of pattern can be distracting at times due to the flickering effect of the background.

The decorative pattern in the film, the composition and perspective, the colors and arrangements of space to the extent of even allowing itself to be awkward in a "modern" compositional arrangement, constantly refers to the

miniatures. Obviously, much research was done, and it is apparent in every one of the development and final film images that the foundation is Persian. Roy Naisbitt was responsible for most of the background designs of the palace (and the layout of the film), and he created some truly unique visuals. However, the final film does have a rather incoherent and inconsistent look at times and feels a bit like patchwork; in particular, some sequences do not want to succumb to the Persian style, especially the scene in the desert with the brigands and also the scene with the old witch and the hand tower. The locations lack the ingredients of Persian design. Because there is not one Persian style or artist predominant

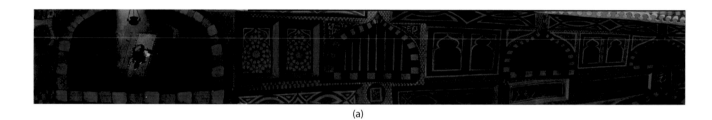

(a)

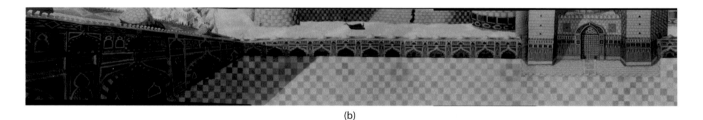

(b)

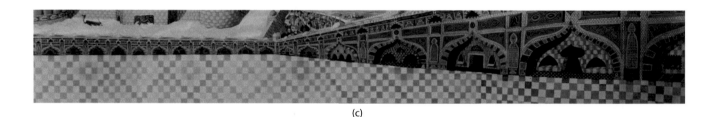

(c)

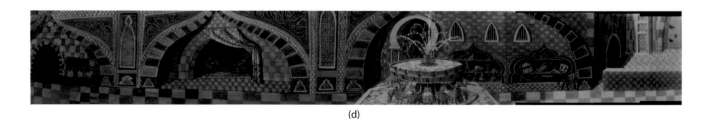

(d)

**Figure 16.88**

The reconstructed background of the first scene of the film in its entire length. The beginning of the pan has the cobbler sleeping in his workspace, and at the end of the pan the thief appears from behind the wall. The immense scale of the square is similar to the Naqsh-e Jahan Square (built between 1598 and 1629) in Isfahan

(Figure 16.89), with its palace building Ali Qapu, the great portal, at the frontage of the square. The setup of Williams' square is very much the same, having a grand square with a rectangular layout, two stories with lower stories for shops, and a big gate on one side of the square.

**Figure 16.89**

Jameh Mosque of Isfahan, Iran, is an example of Persian architecture, with intricate tile work covering completely the walls of the inner courtyard. The two stories with the upper smaller windows are also part of the architectural interpretation of Williams' square, which can also be seen in Naqsh-e Jahan Square, also in Isfahan, built during the Safavid era.

in the film's design but rather a general Persian feel, some of the images do not go together and seem to refer to different visual styles from the same Safavid period. A very interesting approach indeed because similar looks are to be seen in the manuscripts painted by different painters, too. Some backgrounds directly refer in style to specific painters of Safavid miniatures, like the shot of the messenger riding back to King Nod's palace. The design of the mountains during that scene is clearly hinting at a very personal style, which goes back to Chinese style painting.

Naisbitt uses well-known architecture as reference, like the famous Courtyard of the Lions in the Alhambra in Granada, Spain. This landmark (Figure 16.86) was obviously the model for the fountain in the main square of the Golden City at the beginning of the movie. The fountain, dating to the eleventh century (compared to the courtyard itself, which was constructed in the thirteenth century) has very much the same design concept in Williams' film. The shapes of the lions' jaws, the fish-scale pattern of some of the manes, the floral pattern on the fountain bowl, the geometric ground plane and bowl, etc., are all to be seen in Naisbitt's interpretation (Figure 16.87, a closeup of the background painting in Figure 16.88d). The inside of the fountain is covered in blue concentric circles that give the water surface above much additional movement; what a beautiful idea! The colors

are exquisite in the background painting and express the freshness and crispness of a summer day in an imaginary Persian city. The square itself seems to have its basis in the famous square of Isfahan and the attached Jameh Mosque with its stunning blue tiles (Figure 16.89). The double-tiered structure with the kiosks and curved arches is very much the same in Naisbitt's extremely long background (Figure 16.88a through d). Many architectural similarities to the Jameh Mosque can be found.

The Soltaniyeh Mosque in northern Iran (Figure 16.90) seems to have been the inspiration for the Golden City's introduction shot right at the beginning of the film (Figure 16.91). The arches in the Golden City and in the palace often have the very iconic pattern of the Cathedral of Córdoba (Figure 16.93). But not only real architecture was used to inspire the artists. Inspiration was also drawn from one feature especially: Douglas Fairbanks' 1924 extravaganza *The Thief of Bagdad*. For instance, the main entrance gate of the Golden City, with its spikes and all, is directly taken from Fairbanks' famous feature.

Nevertheless, as mentioned in the storyboard section, some locations and backgrounds don't feel spatially resolved when they appear shot after shot in the scenes and it is very difficult to grasp the actual setup of the space. It creates an awkward feeling if one is not able to visualize the architecture in its spatial expansion or if the continuity of the space is in some shots

**Figure 16.90**

Soltaniyeh Mosque (beginning of the thirteenth century) in northern Iran seems to have been an influence for the Golden City's main building on top of the hill (Figure 16.91). Where Soltaniyeh Mosque is octagonal in its floor plan, the mosque in the animation is hexagonal and has a small cupola on its dome, which the original lacks. This shot in the film is one of the fully dimensional renderings where the entire architecture is turning in space.

**Figure 16.91**

This rather odd decision defies all the rules that seem to be established for the design of the film and is obviously different from the rest of the film. These inconsistencies in the design are difficult to grasp. They always feel like a challenge for the animator to prove what can be done instead of having the visuals serve the design and story.

disregarded and walls or floor designs change in follow-up shots. This might have been done for design reasons but can be distracting. For example, the polo game: because we never really see an establishing shot that explains to the audience the spatial relationship between the cobbler, the thief, and the group of Zig-Zag, King Nod, and Yum-Yum, the characters as a group do not seem to be located in the same space; they feel very much as if they exist in separate locations. In this scene, there is also a very strong disconnectedness in the overall mood, with the color and design of the space changing from one shot to the next. Whenever the thief is shown, the sky color is umbra and the surrounding environment earthen in tone, which makes the shots look overcast and gloomy; when Williams cuts to Zig-Zag, King Nod, and Yum-Yum, the sky is bright blue and warm and the colors of the characters are saturated. Of course, this could express the different emotional states of the two groups, but it does confuse slightly. Another example of spatial logic is in the scene where the cobbler is fixing Princess Yum-Yum's shoes in her room and the thief is climbing up the pipes on the outside. Behind the cobbler, through the window one can see the pipes, through which the thief is crawling upwards, and it seems like the thief is climbing through the pipes horizontally and then cut to the pipes outside, where there is no pipe in front of the window. These are minor inconsistencies that unfortunately can have a major effect on the audience by subconsciously

adding confusion. There are many examples like the ones described where the continuity of the space is disregarded. This happening once or twice does not really matter in a feature film, but in *The Thief and the Cobbler* it happens rather frequently and at the end of the film one feels exhausted, not only because of the visual splendor and grandeur of the images but also because of the spatial inconsistencies.

## Character–ground connection

The vertical floor planes of the Persian miniatures have the characters not standing in their surroundings from a dimensional perspective, joining the planes in their orientation, but have them floating in front of them. The ground is tilted vertically and the characters are shown from the side, presenting themselves in a slightly more voluminous form. So the juxtaposition between the view, often from a 45° angle, onto the ground and the view of characters from the side fight each other logically but are successfully solved in the miniatures, as objects, architecture, and also characters mostly follow the same design concept of axonometric projection. All characters are usually depicted from a three-quarters view and seldom from a side or a three-quarters back view. In some of the illustrations, the character's feet are horizontally oriented and the legs have nearly the same length, showing little or no perspectival foreshortening. Also the

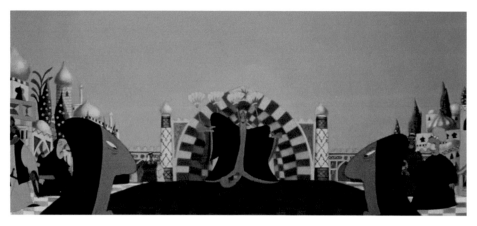

**Figure 16.92**

Screenshot *The Thief and the Cobbler*. Zig Zag's entrance into the Golden City. The curved arch behind him shows the shows the voussoirs of the semi-circular arches in alternating white and red stripes.

**Figure 16.93**

Mosque–Cathedral of Córdoba, Spain. The backgrounds of The Thief often show the voussoirs of the semi-circular arches in alternating white and red stripes, which are so famous from the designs of the Cathedral of Córdoba in Spain, deriving from the Dome of the Rock in Jerusalem.

characters are usually arranged in loose horizontal stripes and don't overlap each other too much. There is some overlap here and there, but not to an extent that would defy the flatness of the image. In the flat illustration, the connection of character and background is very convincing, as the real third dimension is never touched upon and thus everything in the image follows the same design rules. Nevertheless, in some illustrations there is definitely a continuous fight between elements in the frame, some pushing themselves forward and others backwards, which is at the same time interrupted by other elements trying to keep everything flat. This stark tension can be slightly disorienting to contemporary eyes. However, once the character starts to move in the animated interpretation, with the same design elements that appear in the illustrations, the separation of character and background happens immediately. The character steps out of its flat realm in the illustration and enters the dimensional space in front of the background. In order to prevent this from being too dominant, either the character animation has to be adjusted to

**Figure 16.94**

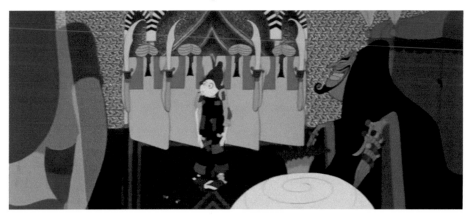

**Figure 16.95**

**Figure 16.96**

Screenshots *The Thief and the Cobbler*.

the flatness of the background and stay flat itself (like in most of the UPA animation) or the background has to receive some depth and perspective even though it is not a fully constructed, correct two-point perspective. The backgrounds in *The Thief* have slightly more dimension and form than in the Persian illustrations, though Williams is not too adamant about being consistent in every single background. Some backgrounds have parallel perspective; others have none. In Williams' interpretation of the Persian

style into animation, he evidently needs to add movement to the characters. This creates a conflict in the visuals, as Williams' moving characters have a different dimensionality compared to the rather flat backgrounds, because he prefers a voluminous and form-oriented animation style instead of keeping the characters completely flat. As Alexander Williams, Richard's son, describes the film's style: "The use of Persian motifs lends the film a graphic two-and-a half-dimensional quality which defies normal physical laws."[49] The more stylized and flat the characters are in design and movement, the better they fit into the flat backgrounds. Flatness in some areas of the character animation helps the characters to connect with their surroundings. This does not always work in Williams' film, as much of the animation focuses in most of his characters on full form and volume. There is sometimes a stark discrepancy between the two, depending on the shot and character. Generally, each shot in the beginning planning phase needs to be evaluated on its perspective and composition in terms of the character movement within the background and then a decision has to be made on how to proceed with the character animation's perspective if you deal with a design like the one in *The Thief*. The main problem with a completely vertical ground plane in 2D animation is the immediate connection of the character with the floor. How does the perspective of the feet, which are usually drawn in perspective in Williams' animation, connect with the flatness of the ground, which is often shown tilted and from an angle? When the character is interpreted in a three-dimensional way, but the background is flat and denies the character its full movement within the space (because the flat space itself is spatially limited and thus limiting), creative solutions have to be found to place the character convincingly into the space so that the two parts of feet and ground are not fighting each other. Williams finds solutions that are sometimes very convincing and sometimes not as much, but are always creative and fitting. There are four different ways he allows the characters to interact with the background:

- Horizontal orientation, where the feet are placed on the horizon line, seen from the side view (Figure 16.94).
- The character is drawn in perspective with the feet also in perspective, but the background is flat and totally vertical (Figure 16.95).
- The character and ground plane are in perspective (Figure 16.96).
- The connection between feet and character is not shown in the frame either due to overlap, camera position, or the character's design.

All of these different options give Williams enough to work with to allow the character to be rooted in space without fighting too much with the unconventional perspective. He chooses which shots he wants to be in perspective and which he does not. The polo game has the shots with the thief in perspective, where even the grass and hills are animated dimensionally and other shots are flat. This back and forth makes the film look a bit disconnected at times, as the space itself alternates between shape and form, making it difficult to really get consistency in the depiction of the space as a whole. This is only a problem if you see it as a problem. It can also be seen as an advantage, creative solution, or simply a style decision that accurately follows the Persian lead.

---

[49] Alex Williams, *The Thief and the Cobbler*, http://www.awn.com/mag/issue1.12/articles/williams1.12.html (accessed March 29, 2015).

## Character movement within the shot

**Figure 16.94**: The background buildings of the town square, shown in side view, are overlapped with the vertical tiles of the foreground. The characters are on top of that tile element, which has no perspective at all. This results in a visual conflict between the two, where the dimensional characters fit the architecture, yet the flatness of the ground plane juxtaposes them. The character animation in those shots usually stays within a horizontal stripe, underlining the composition's horizontal orientation.

**Figure 16.95**: The ground plane is completely flat, showing no perspective, and the character movement is mostly on the z-axis, staying within the compositional confinements given by the background design. The carpet design follows the vertical orientation.

**Figure 16.96**: The 45° tilt of the ground plane is reflected in the character animation's 45° direction towards the lower right. The diametrically tilted tent and the carpet design pushes the characters forward towards King Nod on the right.

## Complex architectural animation

There are a couple of multiplane shots with different levels in the film but they are very subtle: for example the lion fountain on the main square just before the appearance of the thief is on a separate layer and moves at a different speed when the camera passes by to end at the introduction of the thief. Then there are quite a few multiplane shots at the end of the film in the destruction of the war machine. Those are shots that are impressively grand. However, the multiplane shots are not necessarily the most remarkable shots in *The Thief*, regardless of their splendor; the hand-animated backgrounds are actually the ones that stun, despite not necessarily fitting into the perspectival concept. The film starts with a very long dolly shot through the desert and ends with a complex turnaround of the Golden City. Other animated backgrounds are during the introduction of Princess Yum-Yum, the moving hills in the polo game, the op art chase through the palace, the camera flight through the air into One-Eyes, and one shot where Zig-Zag walks down the tower from his room through a spiral staircase. Williams uses these heavily animated and complex shots frequently throughout the film. They are even more dimensional than any multiplane shot could be and thus create a three-dimensionality that not even *Pinocchio* has to that extent. He animates architecture in perspective, moving and turning with the characters, sometimes moving inside of the turning location. This destroys the flat space that has been so tediously and beautifully created in the still backgrounds. The illusion of flatness is completely abandoned and replaced by a full staircase, for instance, that the camera swirls through, a whole city that turns in front of the camera, an entire landscape that the camera flies through to reach the base of One-Eye. All these examples are shots that drag attention because they are so elaborate and elegant. Williams wants to showcase his craft, which

Figure 16.97

Figure 16.98

Screenshots *The Thief and the Cobbler*.

is undeniably there. Those shots are stunning to say the least; they are sometimes even magical because one raises quietly the question: How? But that question is already too much; it throws one out of the escapist moment of the film and reminds one that it is handmade animation. The magic evaporates and puts Williams the technician and craftsman into the spotlight, where the characters' emotional expression or the film's mood should be.

There are some shots in the feature that seem excessive, to say the least. They are beautiful to look at if one can actually see them in the film. One of the many that come to mind is the flight of the thief with the palm leaves as wings, when he flies by the witch's tower, which is adorned with hands. While the thief is passing, the hands move and reach out for him, opening and closing their fingers. It is a two-dimensional interpretation of a three-dimensional zoetrope. This dazzling idea and execution creates a vibrating background interacting with the character in a surreal way, if one can actually see it in the quick background flying by. One would hope that this idea wouldn't just be used once but would actually be part of the concept of the tower. Unfortunately, it stands alone in the scene and has no other shot accompanying it that explores this idea further and thus would make it part of the actual tower, not just a quick (stunning) gimmick.

## Visual trickery

Williams loves to stun his audience with visual wizardry and complex spectacle, and he succeeds undoubtedly many times in *The Thief*. One of the most famous scenes in this regard is the cobbler chasing after the thief, who just stole Princess Yum-Yum's sandal out of the hands of the cobbler. Tack, the cobbler, finds himself in an op art–like environment that might put Victor Vasarely and Bridget Riley to shame. One scene has both of them slide down a complex staircase, with the stairs animated in perspective (Figure 16.97). This scene is a highly polished remake of a sort of a similar scene in Williams' *Raggedy Ann & Andy* where Ann, Andy, the camel with the wrinkled knees, and Sir Leonard Looney also slide down a twisted staircase and then slither on a black and white checkered floor, very much the same that happens to the thief and the cobbler. The backgrounds of the scene are made up of patterns and squares in every shot that play with perspective and our perception of it. We are constantly fooled and proven to be wrong. It is a surreal Escher-like feast of optical trickery. In one shot, Tack runs along a wall with a circular pattern on a wall that turns one way and when Tack changes directions the pattern also starts to turn the other way (Figure 16.98). This is such a complex task and so exquisitely executed, it baffles one! It was always known that the stroboscopic effect was to be taken very seriously in animation as it can destroy movement when not paid attention to, usually in the movement of the backgrounds in relationship to the characters. The logic behind the stroboscopic effect in 2D animation is the distance between the frames and how that results in movement, especially in wheels and camera pans. If a wheel is to be animated (Figure 16.99), the inbetweens have to be placed correctly in order to get the direction of the movement correct. We want the black wheel in Figure 16.99a to turn clockwise. If the inbetweens (red) are right in the middle of two key frames (Figure 16.99b), there is no movement but only a flickering between the key frames (black) and the inbetweens (red). In order to get a rotating motion, the distance between key frame and inbetween has to be different. In Figure 16.99c, inbetween 2 is actually closer to Spoke 3 than to Spoke 1, which means that the wheel would rotate backwards instead of forwards. If one wants a movement to be clockwise, the inbetween spoke has to be closer to Spoke 1. In an actually moving wheel that speeds up, the distance between the moving spokes changes as the speed increases, which results in a seemingly forward–backwards movement within the wheel. The same can happen in a panning movement when the camera pans over a background (Figure 16.99d). At a certain speed, the background will flicker instead of moving smoothly. Williams uses this visual phenomenon as an advantage for this shot of Tack changing directions in the palace (Figure 16.98). The difficulty of this feat is greatly reduced by animating on ones instead of twos, as the distance between the spokes is smaller than if animated on twos. Williams proves that even the ever "scary" stroboscopic effect can be handled with artistic bravura and actually used to advantage.

## Comparison between Disney's *Aladdin* (1992) and *The Thief and the Cobbler*

That the Disney artists watched *The Thief and the Cobbler* before they worked on *Aladdin* is more than obvious when one watches both movies. It is not only the setting but also partly the storyline, shots that are taken from *The Thief*, the characters, even entire gags and ideas are taken from Williams' movie. There are flabbergasting similarities between Williams' character of Zig-Zag and *Aladdin*'s character of the genie by Erik Goldberg and Jafar by Andreas Deja. That Zig-Zag inspired the Disney artists is more than obvious and understandable, as Zig-Zag was a unique and different character compared to anything that Disney had done before. The blue skin color appears again in the genie and the overall shape language of the grand vizier's body and attire appears again in Jafar. Jafar's strange mouth shape also strikes one as odd coming from Disney's animators at that time. It does not at all fit the other character animation, as it is flat, "experimental," and very different from all the other design in the film, which is typical Disney form-oriented character animation. However, when comparing it to

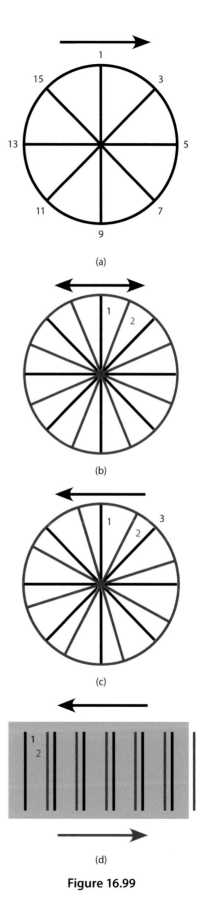

**Figure 16.99**

Williams' character of the grand vizier, one can see similarities in the interpretation of the mouth shapes. Moreover, the grand entrance sequence of Zig-Zag in One-Eye's palace is interpreted in the musical sequence of Aladdin meeting the genie. There are also the many shots of Aladdin flying, jumping, and hurtling through the air and through window awnings. That is exactly what happens to the thief when he tries to steal the golden balls from the minaret and falls through clotheslines and awnings. There is the scene of the thief trying to get an emerald out of a bottle, whereas Aladdin's monkey friend Abu in the cave takes a ruby from a statue. Of course, all of this does not just happen by mistake or by chance. The artists at Disney obviously saw the quality and the importance of Williams' achievement and were so impressed by it that it influenced their creative output. But when Aladdin was produced (before 1992), Williams' film was still in full production, so the artists at Disney must have known that both films would compete on the market, as The Thief was supposed to also be finished in 1992. Why did the artists at Disney use elements of The Thief so bluntly? There is always the option to reference or be inspired by a movie. It is a very different approach altogether to be inspired too much without even considering the underlying design language and design logic of both films. Watching The Thief and right afterwards watching scenes from Aladdin is a very strange experience because one can see the grandeur and mastery in the first and then the empty visuals in the latter. Williams did not want to pursue the matter, as he just wanted to finish his own film and then have proof of his abilities.

Aladdin is obviously a very different film from The Thief and has scenes in it that are a delight to watch, characters that are beautifully animated, and a design that is very consistent, though it does not bring anything new to the animation table. It is technically extremely well done entertainment, but it never reaches the artistic and creative heights that Williams' film is lifting itself onto. One is pure entertainment; the other is an artistic tour-de-force with obvious flaws, but nevertheless a piece of true art.

Slowly the film has been receiving more and more recognition and has been newly reconstructed from its original work print. Screenings in Los Angeles and London and Kevin Schreck's documentary Persistence of Vision from 2012 about the fascinating production of the film have brought the discussion of the film again to the public's attention. However, finishing the film is at this point probably not going to happen anymore, as the technology has changed so much and finding animators who are capable of working on complex shots like the ones in The Thief is not going to be an easy task if the quality is not to be sacrificed.

From the beginning of the film's production in the early 1970s, Williams stated that he would produce his masterpiece. His continuous obsession with creating "masterpieces" is kind of disturbing. It's not for the artist himself to decide which piece of his is a masterpiece; it is for critics and his audience to decide. He is still talking about creating a masterpiece at the age of 80. In an interview with Dan Sarto, he stated: "Now I'm able to do anything I can think of. So, we'll see if I can stretch this thing out [his life] because I'm now doing my masterpiece." What should be considered is that a masterpiece has nothing to do with the amount of work you put in or how complex the scenes are or whether you animate on ones or twos. Perfection is not proof of genius. Spending the money of others for your own production of a masterpiece is just self-indulgent. Feature animation is a collaborative and extremely expensive endeavor and needs to be controlled financially throughout all the stages of its production. It is too easy to claim that the bankers and financiers of the project aren't able to see and judge real art. Well, they are financing the project with other people's money, who are mostly not in it for the artistic aspects but for making a profit. If one is interested in making art, then the format of a short film might be a better solution. And in Williams' film, the details are better than the whole. His short segments in The Thief are clearly amongst the most beautiful and complex pieces of 2D animation ever produced, bursting with ideas and creativity. They are gems that one can enjoy over and over again and never get tired of because one asks the continuous question of "How did they do it?"

Williams' shortcomings caused the film's completion to fail. The final film really shows its journey through 30 years and feels a bit like a quilt of 2D animation, a patchwork of various ideas that came up during its long production time. Williams was so obsessed with getting the character animation right, where he should have also paid attention to the story and the characters. There are gems in the film left and right, but they never culminate in a fully coherent piece. Williams' inventiveness in the animation and compositions, the neverending push of what animation can do, the defying of the rules that animation supposedly has, the exploding passion of an artist who loves the medium exactly because it allows one to ignore reality and use animation to its most elegant and escapist extremes are what makes The Thief and the Cobbler a delight to watch over and over again. Its being unfinished can also be seen as an advantage, as it awakens our curiosity of having found an archeological gem that is broken but sparks our imagination about a time long gone. Its unfinished state is exactly what makes it stand out from all the other finished animated feature films, which is exactly what Williams wanted: to create a film that stands out and is talked about. He very much succeeded in the end, creating with his armada of animators and artists a triumphant visual experience.

**More on *The Thief and the Cobbler*:**

Kevin Schreck, *Persistence of Vision*, documentary film, Kevin Schreck Productions, 2012.

# Aspects that support perspective

## Gradient and perspective

We have already talked about gradient in the sky due to air light as can be seen in Figure 16.100, a view into the Nepalese mountains (also see Chapter 13, "Light and Shadow," the section "Airlight or Skylight"). The closer to the horizon we move our eyes during the daytime, the lighter the sky's

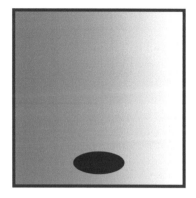

**Figure 16.102**

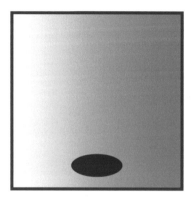

**Figure 16.103**

**Figure 16.100**

Himalayas, Nepal.

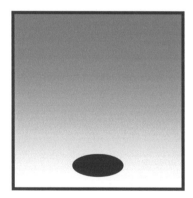

**Figure 16.104**

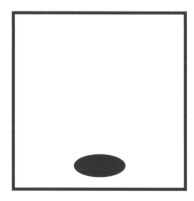

**Figure 16.101**

**Figure 16.105**

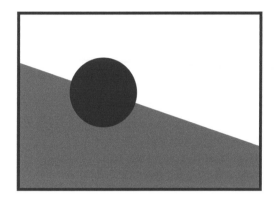

**Figure 16.106**

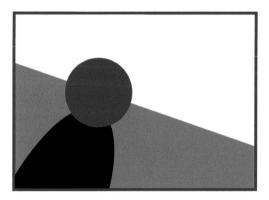

**Figure 16.107**

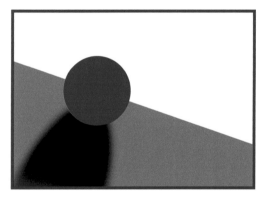

**Figure 16.108**

**Figure 16.109**

color becomes. The sky is a dark blue right above the viewer, because the depth of the atmosphere the light is travelling through is the shortest. Right at the horizon, where the blue is very bright, the light travels through the greatest distance of atmosphere filled with water vapor and particles. Gradient in the sky signifies distance on a grand scale. Gradient in general, however, gives an image more complexity, variation, and realism. It also supports perspective, as it suggests a more complex lighting situation by additionally rendering the space. Figure 16.101 has no gradient, just a blue oval in a flat space. The space itself does not feel dimensional, has no apparent depth (with a story involved, however, this feeling can change, of course). The four gradients in Figures 16.102 through 16.105, on the other hand, have a feeling of space, undefined really, but still there is some expansion. It does not really matter which direction the gradient has; it will always create space and imply some change of light. If we push the idea of creating perspective through gradient and additionally use light and shadow for rendering, we create solid form and space. In Figure 16.106, we have a grey plane on which rests a blue ball. There is no gradient and no light; thus the image is very flat, lacking depth. We cannot say with certainty whether the ball is actually resting on the surface or floating above it. There is some perspective because of the overlap and contrast, but there is no form and no volume. Figure 16.107 has a shadow that clarifies that the ball is on a surface and the position of the light source is suggested as being behind the blue ball. The shadow itself gives us depth as it comes towards us, defining the image in its three-dimensional space. Figure 16.108 only adds a blur to the shadow with a slight gradient at the end, which renders it and the image more realistic, clearly separating the material from the ball and the shadow from the table. The shadow is more clearly defined as a shadow and the ball feels more three-dimensional, despite it being exactly the same as in Figure 16.107, but the blurry shadow does push the ball further towards us. Figure 16.109 finally has more form in the ball, a gradient in the background and table, which dramatically increases the feeling of depth and spatial expansion. The gradient in background and table react to the light source and thus become active members in the arrangement. Gradients can also suggest a light source outside of the frame and therefore include the offscreen space.

## Overlap and perspective

Overlap is the most obvious indicator of perspective, one that very rarely fails, as the only visual explanation of an object covering another object is that it is in front of it. Figure 16.110a has two objects next to each other and one cannot say which one is closer to the viewer. Figure 16.110b has both objects touching each other, creating a tangent, which does not define the exact position of each object in space either. A tangent contains three options in their spatial setup: the objects are actually touching

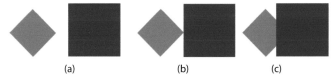

(a)                (b)                (c)

**Figure 16.110**

**Figure 16.111**

and have the same distance from the viewer, or they are in front of or behind each other, just visually but not physically touching. In Figure 16.110c the objects overlap and it is very clear that the dark blue square is in front of the light blue one. As tangents are to be avoided when perspective is wanted, overlap should be sought after for the same reason of creating perspective.

In the photograph of a palace building in the Forbidden City in Beijing (Figure 16.111) the dark foreground element, a stone fence, that covers the top of the frame is touching the roof riders. The touching makes it seem like both stone element and roof are on the same level. The connection, a tangent, between the two elements destroys perspective and depth. All of a sudden the palace and the stone fence melt into one layer. It can create

a stunning and surprising effect if used with a purpose, but it can obviously ruin the depth of an image. The photograph in Figure 16.112 has a stone element right next to the palace and it overlaps the roof ever so slightly on its right. Nevertheless, the bit of overlap is enough to make it clear which element is in front and which in the back. In this photograph, the perspective is obvious and the feeling of depth is maintained because we can see that one is in front of the other. However, if the roof is partly in front of the dark pillar (Figure 16.113), we immediately recognize the mistake and the image does not make any sense. The roof ostentatiously and immediately pushes itself into the foreground and the eye has problems seeing it any other way, as the stone is now huge in size and behind the building, but strangely connected with the ground in front of the palace.

## Size and perspective

The only way of making sense of Figure 16.114 is to push the pink spaceship into the far distance of the space and have the large spaceship in the front. Another explanation would be secondary as it seems the less likely one: the small ship is a toy ship and a realistically sized one stands next to it. We always relate one size to the other, immediately find the visual relationship between the two, and then evaluate the story and meaning: we choose, however, the most logical explanation first. Of course, a different story changes the image. If the story were that the big spaceship was for mom and the smaller one for her daughter, then the story would completely turn the perspective around.

What size always requires is a comparison with other objects. By deliberately ignoring this and bringing in objects that do not specify their size on-screen, the audience can be confused. The two spaceships could be huge or teeny-tiny, depending on an object that we add and whose exact dimensions we know. The relationship then would give us some indication of the size of the spaceships. Overlap or color perspective are very helpful tools for an approximate size evaluation and can definitely help to clarify the two spaceships.

**Figure 16.112**

**Figure 16.113**

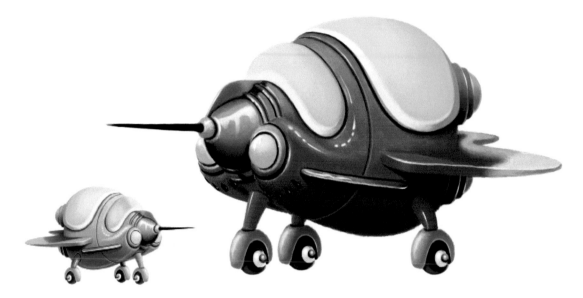

**Figure 16.114**

## Textural perspective

Texture has the ability to bring objects forward or push them back, depending on the scale of the texture used. The size of the texture in Figure 16.115 does exactly that: the texture in the vertical strip in (a) feels like the one closest to the viewer and (c) the one furthest away. They do because they also relate to each other. If we only saw (c) on its own, then it would not feel as far away (probably; if I see it as the surface of the moon the distance can easily become dramatic).

The photograph in Figure 16.116 has the texture of the wall of the Forbidden City in its regular size and in Figure 16.117

in a size that is too big for the wall. The bigger the texture, the closer the wall seems to the viewer. Having both pictures next to each other, it is impossible for the eye not to see Figure 16.117 as being "zoomed into the wall." The distance between viewer and wall is undeniably different in both examples. But not only the wall is being zoomed into; the building also seems much closer in Figure 16.117. However, the texture is always in a relationship with the other textures surrounding it and that relationship is also of importance. A very busy texture can negatively affect perspective, because it will step into the foreground and therefore destroy the intended depth.

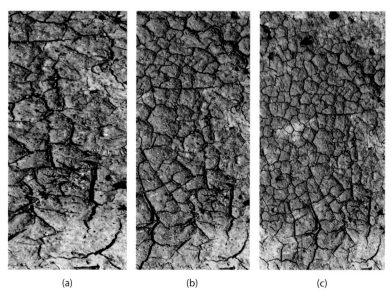

| (a) | (b) | (c) |

**Figure 16.115**

Figure 16.116

Figure 16.117

## Contrast and perspective

An object also differentiates itself from other objects or its surroundings through contrast in color and texture. Figure 16.118a through (c) shows how contrast affects the separation between object and background. Figure 16.118c has the strongest contrast of the three and therefore the black dot sets itself apart from its surroundings the most. Elements in the background usually (in a realistic and natural setting) have the least contrast and elements in the foreground the strongest contrast, which adds to perspective and depth.

Contrast is obviously always dependent on the juxtaposition of different elements with each other. In Figure 16.119a through (c), the contrast of the background changes drastically from (a)

having the strongest contrast to (c) the weakest, whereas the contrast of the foreground element stays the same. The easiest to read is (c) because the background does not contain any black or white; therefore the geometric shape reads well. (a) has much black and brightness in the background, so the shape does not read well at all. However, (a) has more depth in the background itself, whereas (c) has none. (b) has plenty of contrast in the background yet the foreground element still reads well enough. So (b) would have depth in the background and contrast in the foreground, which would be the best solution in this case to create depth and support perspective. The more contrast there is between background and foreground, the more easily the elements can be distinguished from each other and in turn enhance perspective.

(a)                              (b)                              (c)

Figure 16.118

 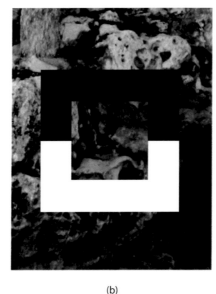 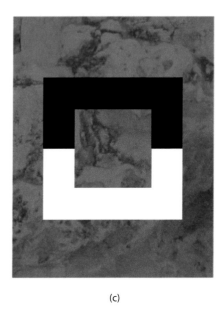

(a)  (b)  (c)

**Figure 16.119**

## Light and shadow and perspective

Light and shadow can be used as very strong indicators for perspective or for the lack of it. The following examples show how light and shadow develop space in its dimensionality from flat to three-point perspective. If there is only light and shadow that follows a horizontal orientation and underlines therefore the flatness of the space, perspective is neglected, like in Figure 16.120, in which the horizontal x-axis is the dominant factor in the plane. With a gradient in the shadow, the space takes on a very different dimension and widens (Figure 16.121). The slow disappearance of the shadow at its end gives the space dimension and, despite being still flat, lifts it seemingly from the two-dimensional and graphic plane into a slightly three-dimensional space. In Figure 16.122, the shadow suggests a distance between the object and the viewer but does not define the three-dimensionality of the space; however, its very flatness and the vertical y-axis are dominant. If the shadow itself has a gradient, like in Figure 16.123, there seems to be more

dimensionality to the overall space and the ground plane tilts at an angle upwards, rather than being vertical on the picture plane. The z-axis is suggested.

In Figure 16.124, there is a monochrome diagonal shadow that describes the tilt of the ground plane along the z-axis but also goes along with the flat image plane. It is both two- and three-dimensional. Figure 16.125 gives a much clearer idea of the dimensional space with the added gradient. Now the shadow clearly steps out of the two-dimensional plane and renders the space three-dimensionally. In Figure 16.126, the perspective is the most complex of all the previous examples. Nevertheless, the shadow as such still expresses a flatness through its color, but also clearly defines a moving surface with depth. In Figure 16.127, with the gradient in the shadow, the surface structure of the plain is further explained in its depth and the dimensionality of the ridge can be seen throughout. Therefore: shadows support perspective and with gradient the space's dimensionality can be clearly enhanced.

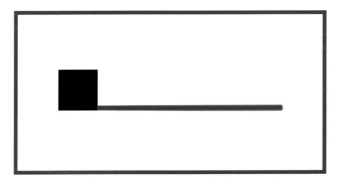

**Figure 16.120**

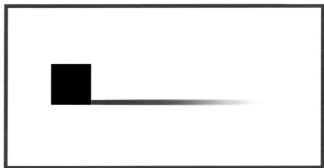

**Figure 16.121**

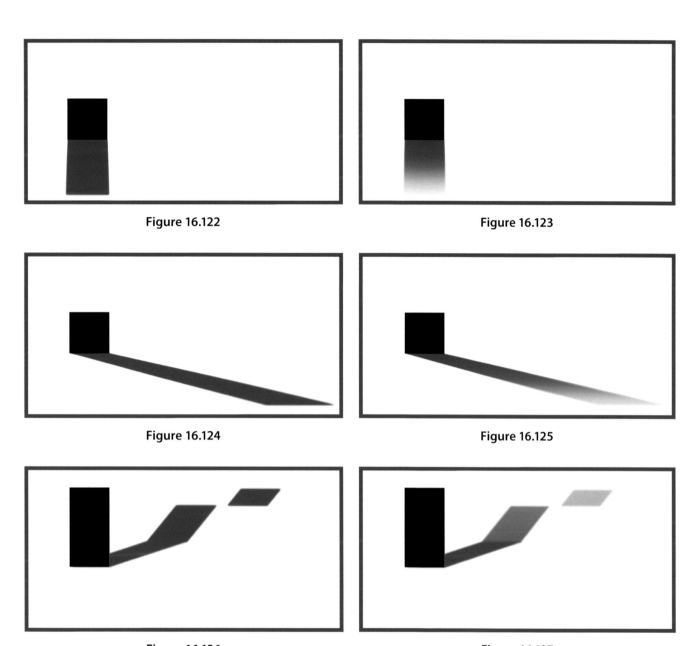

Figure 16.122

Figure 16.123

Figure 16.124

Figure 16.125

Figure 16.126

Figure 16.127

# CHAPTER 17

# Texture

Imagine you touch an object with closed eyes and you have to determine how it feels just based on its texture. Is it rough or smooth, moist or dry, wooden or metallic, soft or hard? We often neglect the haptic feeling of an object, because we focus mostly on the visuals. However, taste, smell, and touch are still an integral part of how we perceive everything around us. Textures define objects' surfaces and transport lots of information that we can use creatively to give the objects, characters, or the environment that we design personality and a story. There are two different ways of perceiving an object and its texture: haptic sensation and visual sensation. The haptic senses allow us to feel the object's weight, its surface, temperature, size, and actual texture. This is the most direct approach of experiencing the texture, by touching it. Of course we don't always touch everything. There are lots of things we wouldn't dare to touch because we can imagine how it would or might feel. We don't have to touch a tarantula to know how the hairy legs would feel on our skin and how the bulgy body would weigh in our hands. We don't have to touch dog poop to know that it's soft and warm and yucky.

Then, there is visual sensation, where we can see the texture and know or expect how it feels or what it stands for in terms of dry–wet, hot–cold, rough–smooth, etc. Watching a movie makes us imagine things and it leads us to believe in something that is not real, especially when it comes to animation, where everything is possible and even a house made of jelly is an option (like in Sony Picture Animation's feature *Cloudy with a Chance of Meatballs*). For our imagination to flourish, moods need to be created in films and textures are one part of the image that can change the feel and with it the mood of an environment completely. The designer has to choose what kind of object attributes would trigger stronger feelings in the audience and still fit the story line. Choosing a texture just because it is pretty might work once in a while but also might give out the wrong message, lead to misinterpretations, and therefore hurt the story. The overall concept and feel of the movie has to go hand in hand with the choice of textures. In a film that is supposed to have a warm and comfortable feeling, textures that are cold and hard might not be right, but cloth, fuzzy textures, wood, and organic textures might be a better choice ("might," as all of this of course has to be weighed out with the other elements of design). A great example of the creative use of textures is DreamWorks' feature *Trolls* (2016), where the world of the trolls is completely made out of colorful felt (Figure 17.1). The texture of the felt is so soft and fluffy, so comfortable and cuddly, that one just wants to live in that world with the bright colors and happy shapes. However, giving the felt a slightly different color and making it seem oily and dirty, we quickly switch from the comfortable world of the trolls to the sad and drab world of the Bergens.

**Figure 17.1**

Dreamworks' *Trolls* (2016).

DOI: 10.1201/b22148-17

| Figure 17.2 | Figure 17.3 | Figure 17.4 | Figure 17.5 |

Texture has an immense impact on how the audience responds to the visuals, because it can remind them of puppets, of childhood, of teddy bears and plush toys, or of filth, dirt, and grime and everything in between. In particular, computer animated films that do not pay attention to the power of textures can feel cold and slick, where the haptic senses are not involved and something is missing while watching the film. The objects lack not only believability but also life. In this regard, *Trolls* did an excellent job in making the audience constantly want to touch the characters and squeeze them because they are just so darn cute! To fully understand texture we need to first group texture into its different types.

## Types of textures:

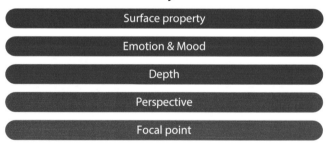

Natural textures

Artificial textures

There is a gap on purpose as artistic textures are not part of reality, which the first two textures are.

Artistic textures

- *Natural texture:* Any organic and also inorganic matter that exists in nature.
- *Artificial texture:* Any texture that is man-made and therefore always inorganic.
- *Artistic texture:* Any texture that is artistically produced and interprets or invents textures.

All three types of textures can again be subdivided into *regular* (Figure 17.2) and *stochastic* (irregular) textures (Figure 17.3).

## Visual magnitude of texture

The two textures in Figures 17.4 and 17.5 show two variants of a simple wood texture. Figure 17.4 is calm and simple, whereas Figure 17.5 has within the texture another smaller, busy organic pattern that makes the overall square busier, giving it more visual magnitude, which defines its overall level of details and shapes, its granularity, but also its contrast and color. Texture with exceptionally high visual magnitude distracts and always

seeks attention, whereas low magnitude allows a texture to be subdued. Nonetheless, a texture with high magnitude can be used as an advantage to drag the viewer's eye towards the focal point or it can also be a disadvantage if the texture takes the focus away from the center of attention. In this way, textures are like colors: they need to be balanced out with each other and need room to "breathe," to avoid overwhelming the entire image. A very smooth polished surface has a much lower visual magnitude in its texture than, for example, marble or old tree bark. One is calm and quiet, whereas the other is busy and loud. Too much marble texture in an image and one does not know where to look because the texture is just taking over. Two extremely busy textures right next to each other drag so much attention that they either need to be reduced in their strength or a calm texture needs to be placed in between them to allow both to express their importance.

## What texture conveys:

Surface property

Emotion & Mood

Depth

Perspective

Focal point

### Surface property

This point captures the haptic characteristics of surfaces, which include the granularity, whether the surface is smooth or rough, moist or dry, sticky or not, soft or hard, its surface temperature … It is the qualities of the object that we perceive by touching its surface. The surface property also gives us information on how dirty or clean it is, which affects our response to the surface. Is it safe to touch? Or how old or new it is; is it solid or crumbly? The surface can also give us a hint about the weight of an object. A ball with a stone texture is probably going to be heavier than a ball of felt. Before choosing a texture, one should ask what the object/environment is supposed to express, what mood it should have, and what story point it supports. Then the textures that fit this direction or concept are chosen, not just to express a material but to express an emotion, which leads us to the next point.

## Emotion and mood

An emotion is developed by giving the object a story; however small and insignificant that story might be, it will affect our emotions towards that object. A dusty old photograph evokes different emotions than a brand new, clean, and shiny one. This emotion is not necessarily always objective, but there are enough overlapping areas that make it clear to most people how they react to a surface. The dusty old photograph, for instance, feels drier because of the dust, which will stick to our hands when we touch it. The paper probably feels a bit softer, its edges are slightly frazzled, there are crinkles in there, maybe even some stains. The new photograph is much cleaner (probably), the paper is different from the old photo, there are no wrinkles, and the edges are clean-cut. But the question still is, what do we feel when we see the picture? Of course, what first affects our reaction to the picture is the story. If the picture shows proof of a nineteenth century ghost and is part of a horror story, then we would reject the picture and with it all its properties (or be utterly fascinated by it, not being able to take our eyes away from it). If, however, the picture shows a romantic version of one's ancestors, then the emotion towards the picture would be much more positive. Of course, it is way too easy to claim that certain textures always have this or that effect. It depends on the story that is being told and how those object properties, and with it the textures, fit into the story. For example, Pixar's feature *Up* from 2009 targets a certain age group and style. This style, mostly connected to kids' animation or animation for young audiences, likes to oversize objects slightly, make them appear bloated. This causes objects to look toylike and applied to the whole environment creates a world where the cartoony characters fit right in. The shape language of the characters goes hand in hand with that of the environment. The texture used must not contradict the cartoony look. But what is a cartoony texture? The textures are, as much as the shapes and forms, all slightly oversized. For instance, Mister Fredrickson's trilby hat and his jacket are obviously very rough and suggest a style that is outdated, reminiscent of the 1960s, with a texture that is heavily exaggerated in size and therefore rather large. The effect is that the objects look smaller than they are; the oversized texture and shape/form language shrinks them down significantly. Additionally, the materials are all thicker than they realistically would appear: paper, cloth, wood, metal, and the rim of Mr. Fredrickson's hat, all feel thicker and bolder. The feel of scale of course isn't *just* caused by texture and size but also by the shapes and forms, the relationship of all the applications, the style and cut of the characters' clothing, the characters' who wear it, Mr. Fredricksen's oversized hands and head, etc.; it should never be just one aspect that causes any effect but the ensemble of various aspects. Every shape/form and texture in the feature film

is larger in scale; even the blades of grass are larger. The entire ensemble of design aspects in the feature *UP* creates the look and feel of a toylike world.

Questions that should be answered when choosing textures are as follows:

- What is the overall concept for the textures in the entire film? (In the case of *Up* it would be texture that is oversized to create the in tendency toylike world.)
- What is the textural concept of a single scene? Does it go along the overall textural concept of the entire feature and additionally support the needs of the scene?
- What is the textural concept of the single object, and does it support the mood of the shot or scene, while at the same time still succumb to the feature's and scene's textural concept.
- You can see a strict hierarchy going from the textural concept of the entire feature defining its overall feel and mood, to the submissive textural concept of the scene, and ending in the textural concept of the single object.

## Depth

Because of the change of size of the texture's granularity in relationship to distance, depth is created. A rock close by has more details compared to a rock very far away, where details disappear. The density of textures far away is compressed, which often leads to details blending into each other and creating a seemingly smoother texture. Also, less contrast in textures far away reduces the visual magnitude of textures in the distance. We can clearly see that in the two examples of the wood grain in Figures 17.6 and 17.7: the one texture is clearly further away than the other.

Nevertheless, this can get a bit more complex if one zooms into a texture that seems rather smooth in a close-up; zooming then even further, it can get again more granular in a macro-zoom.

## Perspective

The surface texture always helps in strengthening perspective, as the tilt of the texture in space is important for us to perceive the object correctly in its spatial expansion and orientation. We can immediately recognize if the texture and the perspective do not match in an object. Depth, orientation, and perspective are therefore closely related. In the four examples in Figures 17.8 through 17.11, it is fairly clear how the texture is positioned in space.

## Focal point

Textures with a high visual magnitude always attract attention. It can even overwrite color and light and shadow if the texture is very busy and its granularity too dominant. The two examples with the table shows exactly that: the stone surface on the floor is so busy in Figure 17.12 and has such a high visual magnitude

Figure 17.6

Figure 17.7

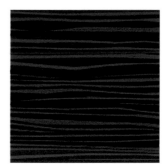

Figure 17.8

Figure 17.9

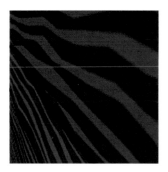

Figure 17.10

Figure 17.11

that it really drags the eye's attention away from the table, which is supposed to be the focus of the frame, not the floor. Reducing the visual importance of the floor's texture, it recedes into the background and allows the table to be the focus (Figure 17.13). However, it should be done to an extent where the texture on the ground is still there and seen, but just less obvious.

Obviously, in CG animation texture can play a very important role in giving the image weight and realism and all the necessary information for the object to read clearly. Texture is a very strong visual clue in describing environments, objects, and characters. Subtlety and balance is always the way to go. A busy and strong texture right next to a similar busy one creates visual disturbance and tension that does not help either surface, as both swallow each other (exceptions make the rule). A subtle and calm texture next to a busy one allows both of them to express their "otherness" and therefore both read much better. Every image needs some areas that are quiet and others that are more "loud" to create tension. Too much of one shifts the needed balance. The amount of information that texture gives us should never compete with any other information in the image, meaning that the texture should always be informative but not dominant. It must not drag all the attention because of its business or granularity (unless there is a purpose, of course). For example, in Figure 17.14, the focal point of the spaceship is the window of

Figure 17.12

Figure 17.13

the cockpit. Putting a high magnitude texture at the back of the ship in Figure 17.15, the front loses its importance and the eye is dragged to the tail, where there might not be any action (the action obviously always happens in the cockpit!). The texture must not compete with the overall composition of the piece! It also obviously has to fit the size of the object and not be too big or too small. However, sometimes this is wanted to suggest a different scale, as we have seen in *Up*. Stylized design usually requires stylized textures or exaggerated textures. Realistic forms and cartoony textures usually do not go well together. However, this is not a rule but rather a challenge for the artist to find a solution that works.

In animation there is the option of replacing diegetic with nondiegetic sounds to enhance the impact of the moment and give the already cartoony scene an also cartoony sound. The animated image is already detached from reality by designing and animating it in the first place. Adding sounds to it that detach it even more from reality makes sense. The same principle is true for textures. Replacing a realistic texture with a texture that "feels" right and expresses something that is more emotion than realism makes sense in a cartoony realm. It is about finding the right texture that says exactly what the object needs to express in that specific scene or set. Why not have the entire design in the film be made out of soft, fuzzy cloth if it is meant to be comfortable and cozy? The limitation is the imagination of the artist. CG animation still tries to copy reality, not realizing that by doing so it cuts out a huge part of the artistic expression that it could have. This artistic expression could affect the emotional impact of the scene and thus the emotion of the audience. This point leads us to artistic textures.

# Artistic textures

## Artistic textures can be divided into:

- Actual texture
- Simulated texture
- Implied texture
- Invented texture

Artistic textures are obviously endless and there is no limit of how to interpret the textures with different painting techniques or even collages or found objects. Additionally, the actual texture of the painted surface, what the painting is painted on (rough burlap, smooth wood, polished metal), significantly affects the overlaid texture. The painted surface has a huge impact on the feel and look of the painting. The extraordinarily smooth texture of a painting by Jean-Auguste-Dominique Ingres (1780–1867) is very different from the rough texture of a painting by Lucian Freud (1922–2011), whose thick impasto brushwork is an important part of the painting's surface structure and also the emotional effect it has on the viewer. In drawings, it is the texture of the paper that needs to be considered and how its own texture affects the drawing itself. Some papers hold the pencil or charcoal dust much better than others; therefore, the actual drawing differs greatly from paper to paper. Also, ground textures can be created to be painted and drawn on, to provide a texture that then shines through the thinly layered paint on top.

Painted textures, however, all fall under one of the mentioned points above.

**Figure 17.14**

**Figure 17.15**

### 1Actual texture

The *actual texture* refers to the texture of the object itself, not a mimicked one. In a painting, it would be the texture of the burlap canvas or the paint itself. In sculpture, the texture of the surface of the stone, the clay, the metal, or in sculptures that use objects for its body, then the objects themselves (Nam June Paik, for example, who uses various objects like TVs in his sculptures, the textures of which give the pieces a slick and modern feel and carry a certain "futuristic aura" with them).

### Simulated texture

This is texture that pretends to be something that it is not. For example, in drawings or paintings the texture mimicking the actual texture in a realistic way is simulated texture. The fabric of the complex carpets in a painting by Jan Vermeer (1632–1675) is not the actual rippled texture of the fabric but a smooth, painted surface on the canvas. The painted texture only gives the impression of it being the actual texture.

### Implied texture

This texture does not directly mimic the actual texture but finds other representations that are close to it and follows the direction of the original, staying in the vicinity of its visuals.

### Invented texture

Invented texture is object unrelated and creates texture that has no basis in reality; therefore it often appears in abstract works that do not mimic or interpret reality but develop their very own visual spaces.

## Case study: Texture and the connection of foreground and background elements in Hubley's *Moonbird* (1959)

Faith and John Hubley had an illustrious career in the animation industry for decades and can easily be called one of the most creative forces in animation from the 1950s onward. Together they received three Academy Awards (and were nominated for eight) for their short films and created some of the most significant animated films of independent American animation. The couple also did work for *Sesame Street* or commercials like the Marky Maypo kid for Maypo instant oatmeal. In their work, they often used unscripted dialogues of their kids or friends, which they then utilized for their unique aesthetic.

John Hubley worked for Disney in the 1930s as a background painter for features like *Snow White, Pinocchio, Bambi, Dumbo,* and *Fantasia* and left Disney after the famous company strike in 1941. He joined UPA as a director and created memorable shorts like *Mr. Magoo, Rooty Toot Toot, Gerald McBoing-Boing,* and many others. At the beginning of the 1950s, he was forced to leave UPA due to his refusal to release colleagues' names to the House Un-American Activities Committee, which blacklisted Hubley in the film industry for years. From then on, he worked on animated commercials, as there was no mention of his name. After his liaison with Faith Hubley, whom he married in 1955, the couple opened their own studio, Storyboard Studio, and aside from commercials worked every year on one short film of their own, creating superb personal films that are amongst the most creative works in US animation history. Their very first short film, *The Adventures of an \** (1957), which they produced for the Guggenheim Museum in collaboration with the museum's director, James Johnson Sweeney, pushed animation to its limits in the 1950s. It is the story of a rambunctious little boy who explores the world and convinces his rather annoyed and bored father that having fun is more important than being "adult." The extraordinary character animation was done by Emery Hawkins and gleefully plays with shapes and movement in the most loose way possible. The boy is reduced to simple shape variations of an asterisk and bounces throughout the frame, which is a pleasure to watch. The music by Benny Carter is as fluffy and happy as the boy's actions. The short exudes the lust for life and shows a strict dissociation from mainstream animation, going in its visual style more towards contemporary fine art and illustration than referring to traditional animation styles, even aesthetically pushing the work that Hubley had been doing at UPA. It is more Picasso than traditional animation, and Hubley always saw it as a goal to delineate from the traditional animation style and the imitation of life and incorporate more contemporary artistic developments into his work, something he surely did achieve. *The Adventures of an \** was the beginning of a long and fruitful collaboration between John and his wife, Faith. This short not only marked the starting point of their Storyboard Studio's personal work but also set the aesthetic direction. The shorts' textures are clearly given

**Figure 17.16**

**Figure 17.17**

**Figure 17.18**

**Figure 17.19**

**Figure 17.20**

**Figure 17.21**

dominance in their importance and every frame boasts a variety of overlaid brush textures that create depth and give the images weight and body. The images are strictly two-dimensional but use the layering of textures and transparency of the various animation and background layers to create depth, a technique they kept going back to throughout their career. The use of textures was a very important element of contemporary art, and painters like Picasso, Jackson Pollock, and Miro had an aesthetic where textures were one of the key elements of the exploration of art at the time.

The personal shorts of the Hubleys also stepped into new narrative terrain as they told stories that were about social interactions, relationships, fantasy from a child's perspective, and also political ideas. (In 1962, for instance, the couple produced a short film called *The Hole*, a 15-min dialogue between two workers at a construction site in New York, discussing the possibility of a nuclear attack. *The Hole* also won an Academy Award in the same year.)

In 1959, the Hubleys created their fifth Storyboard Studio production, *Moonbird*. The film's story is based on a recording of the couple's two sons playing a make-believe story they came up with on the spot (remember the UPA short *Willie the Kid* from 1952 where Robert Cannon also used kids' recorded voices for the soundtrack). Mark, age 7, and his 4-year-old brother, Ray, are refreshingly creative with their ideas for trying to find the Moonbird during a night of exploration. Faith Hubley recollects: "We heard the boys plotting to go to the park and find a bird. We all went to the studio with a bird cage, a bag of candy, and a shovel, and taped the sound track in 3 hours. Three months later, it won an Oscar."[1]

The story in this exquisitely designed short is of two boys who go out at night to hunt a bird. They carry around a small cage and some candy for bait with which they try to trap the bird. After a while, they eventually stumble upon one, which is large and friendly, slightly awkward, yet playful.

This simple story is told from the perspective of secrecy, as the boys have to hide and be quiet in order to not chase away their prey; nevertheless, they scream and yell, sing and argue all the way through their night adventure. The main design guidelines are secrecy, a night mood in various shades of ultramarine and Prussian blue, and a looseness in the painting and drawing style that reminds one of children's artwork.

From the beginning, the Hubleys visually give us the meaning of secrecy by making the night rather dark and not showing everything, but only revealing parts that seem important. The compositions and camera shots are very selective and often cover parts of the frame with elements, mainly foliage

[1] Legendary animator carries on tradition. By: Saccoccia, Susan, Christian Science Monitor, 08827729, 11/24/95, Vol. 87, Issue 252.

and flora, or leave big parts of the frame just empty, allowing shadows or silhouettes of the characters to tell the story. This generates the feel of us spying on the two boys, who themselves are trying to not be seen by their parents or by the bird they are trying to catch. The Hubleys' decision to let the characters be semitransparent supports that visual interpretation of secrecy. The characters melt into the background and become one with it, auditorily by trying to be quiet and visually by the audience seeing the background through their opaque bodies. They sometimes nearly disappear while sneaking through their backyard. Their ghostlike appearance makes them shadows walking through the night. In some shots, the characters can only be seen in light silhouettes, adding to the feel of magic and otherworldliness that the night provides.

In mainstream animation, the characters are most often in full color and therefore jump out of the frame for what they are: overlays on top of the background. There are various technical and artistic tricks that can help the two images, character and background, to form more of a unity instead of visually separating, for instance with colored outlines or treating background and character with a similar style, like in Disney's *101 Dalmatians*, or applying shadows and light rendering on the characters. This for sure reduces the gap between character and painted background but does not eliminate it. Or the colors of the outlines can help to let the character coexist with the background, not fighting the connection, like in *Sleeping Beauty*, where the elaborate color scheme of the outlines allows the characters in their complexity to stand their ground alongside the extremely complex backgrounds. However, most of the time, the characters in hand-drawn animation do separate from the background simply because of their existence on acetate sheets instead of paper and their rather sharp-cut silhouettes. The background, on the other hand, is painted and has a complex color scheme; the characters are flat in color and usually don't have too much light and shadow shading in them, due to the complex and very expensive procedure of adding complicated shadow work on every animation cel. There are of course exceptions where the flatness in color of the characters can also be found in the backgrounds. In particular, UPA or Warner Brothers cartoons from the 1950s have that very pleasant correlation between characters and background elements.

Hubley's idea of making the characters often transparent and therefore letting them melt into the background is a very enticing move. The characters are now part of the painting instead of just sitting on top of it. It is a very illustrative approach of high visual beauty. (This can also be seen in Te Wei's short films like *Where is Mama?*, in which the characters are so much part of the design by precisely mimicking traditional Chinese ink paintings that you can barely see them as characters on a different animation layer but as being part of the overall image.)

**Figure 17.22**

**Figure 17.23**

**Figure 17.24**

**Figure 17.25**

**Figure 17.26**

The layering of the background or overlaid elements, which are sometimes opaque, creates interesting effects of depth and space. It is not an imitation of reality that the Hubleys are after at all, but a feeling of a very unique space, a child's space for adventure, not a grown-up space. It is the lack of precision that makes this short so charming and again and again refers to a child's artistic aesthetic rather than an adult one. The painterly treatment of the background and foreground elements are also the aesthetic basis of the visual style for the character animation, which is as creative in the use of line and shape as the background. Its (by traditional animation standards) inaccurate shapes, its texture that allows the brushwork to be a major part of the texture, the looseness of the whole image are what drive the visuals of the characters. In particular, the bird, with its body consisting just of wiggly organic lines (Figure 17.25), is reminiscent of the "anything goes" aesthetic of children's drawings. The characters have obvious pencil, brush, or other textures and their handmade look is never hidden or covered up; it is actually an advantage in their design to let the drawing tools be part of the final look. The character animation itself is more about the movement and its feel than the realistic depiction of weight and solidity. And throughout the short, the characters also change their color slightly without it being a distraction. It is unusual and strikes one as strange in the first place, but it's

easily accepted as a style and as a look (also often caused by the animation layer split into two different layers, which changes the opacity of each layer).

The Hubleys use a visual style that is very illustrative and translate it seamlessly into animation. The texture of the brush is what gives the images depth and life. Much of the actual brush texture is seen in the final background and sometimes there are multiple layers of transparent foliage stacked on top of each other, showing a beautiful dimensionality despite the flatness of the individual elements. The texture of the brush itself affects the color and gives us shades of dark and light, which in turn makes the painted surface interesting and vibrant, giving it movement and dynamism.

In very subtle ways they let us discover the story by never putting it there bluntly but giving story elements away as little snippets of information; the story loosely unravels but is as much covered as the images are. For instance, the camera shows the two boys at night going through the yard, but we see the scene from the boy's bedroom (Figure 17.19). This shows us where the boys are supposed to be: in bed. But who wants to be in bed when fun can be found outside by playing with a big Moonbird?

For more information on textures, please see also Chapter 33, "Texture," in Volume 2.

# CHAPTER 18

# Movement

Film is all about movement, exists only because of it, and especially for animation movement is its own art form, as we are able to control movement like no other artist can. There is no other art form that goes so much into the detail of movement as animation does, because we control it to the individual frame. However, this chapter approaches movement more from a general and overall perspective when it comes to the design of the frame and how movement leads the eye through the image. There has already been an explanation on how the changing focal point can be dealt with from one shot to the next in Chapter 5, "Composition." This chapter expands on that.

There are two different ways of seeing motion: one is to recognize the motion itself and be aware of it happening, yet not follow it with the eyes; the second way is locking one's eyes onto the object in motion and following it in a *smooth pursuit*.[1] Being aware of movement does not necessarily mean that we will follow its path with our eyes. Standing at a highway, we do not follow each car that passes but focus on what is important at that very moment. However, if something penetrates our peripheral visual field quickly, out of reflex, we follow it and then decide if it is important to continue pursuing it. We either look away if it is not of interest or keep our eyes locked onto the moving object if it is significant. When it comes to moving images, the reflex of being distracted by sudden movement has to be taken into consideration, as it can seriously disrupt the concentration of the viewer. Movement itself will always overwrite composition, no matter how strong the composition itself is or how visually attractive. The magnitude, speed, or size of the moving object does not matter; the eye will see an object that enters the frame without hesitation. The eye instantly turns, even if the movement is only seen in the periphery of the vision. This instinct allows us to immediately recognize potential threats in an otherwise calm environment. It is actually very difficult not to follow this instinct! When sitting in a restaurant with a TV turned on, it is a struggle for us to not watch the TV, as the movement, even in the corner of our eyes, will drag our attention. Figure 18.1 (Video 18A) demonstrates this point: the very strong composition of the background, which puts the focus into the center of the frame,

is not strong enough to keep our eye focused on its center once the moving shape comes in. We have to follow the ball and our eye struggles to go back to the center. We can actually use this instinct to our advantage in shots to drag the attention from one focal point to another just by adding movement. For example, two characters are talking to each other. One character is sitting still but is just talking. The other character moves, does some random action, like straightening a hat or smoking. We will look at the character who is moving, not the one who is talking, even if it's just for a second. This can be the movement of the character itself or an object that moves, a car or anything else that will change the focus from one area in the frame to another. As long as the focal point is less interesting in its own movement and the moving object obvious enough, we will switch focal points unconsciously.

## Focal point switches left and right

The eye can always only focus on one section of the image, moving or not. When there are two moving objects with nearly the same attributes, we constantly go left and right without

**Figure 18.1**

1 University of Pennsylvania, Understanding Smooth Eye Pursuit: The Incredible Targeting System of Human Vision, *ScienceDaily*, July 5, 2007. www.sciencedaily.com/releases/2007/07/070702145312.htm (accessed on January 15, 2018).

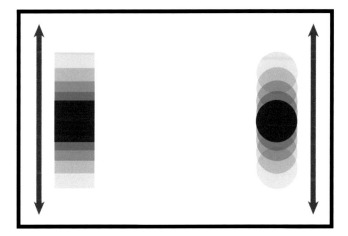

**Figure 18.2** 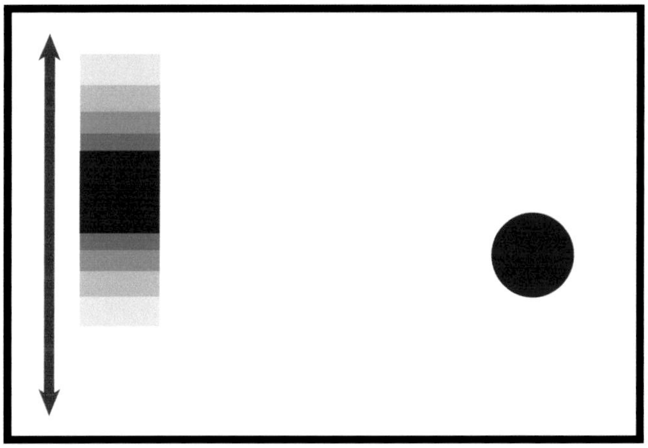                                        **Figure 18.3**

exactly knowing where to look at (Figure 18.2 or Video 18B). The two moving points are equally important and our eye cannot decide which one to give its full attention. The last part of the movie clip, however, has the square move up slightly faster than before, which immediately catches our interest and the square shifts in importance. So with the aspects of design and/or the object's attributes, the importance can easily be shifted to either one of the shapes, rendering it more important.

Equal objects that move at the same or similar speed are observed without distinction. None of the objects signify to the eye that they are more important than the others. This can be changed by letting one object move while the other one rests and vice versa, as shown in Figure 18.3 or Video 18C. The left square moves, while the white dot on the right stands still and vice versa; they stand and move alternately. The result is that the focal point constantly shifts. The movement drags our attention and we will look at the shapes that move. This seemingly obvious occurrence is very important when it comes to character animation, for example: movement should

always happen in the character that the audience is supposed to focus on. Two moving characters cannot be observed at the same time. In the design of the moving frame with several focal points, this back-and-forth can be used in a very subtle way to force the eye from one area to another.

## Speed

High speed creates more visual energy than low speed (Figure 18.4) (Video 18D). Therefore, the eye will look at the faster moving square rather than the slower moving circle. We still see the square and look back at it once in a while, but the visual importance definitely lies in the circle. However, at some point the eye gets tired and will look away from hectic action.

## Size and speed

The bigger the object, the more it attracts the eye (Figure 18.5) (Video 18E). The speed of the object, however, overrides size. Even the tiny dot on the black background is more a focal point

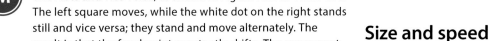

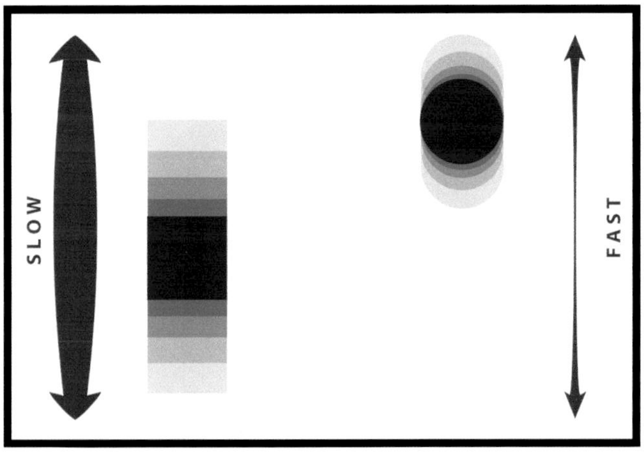

SLOW                          FAST

SLOW                          FAST

**Figure 18.4** 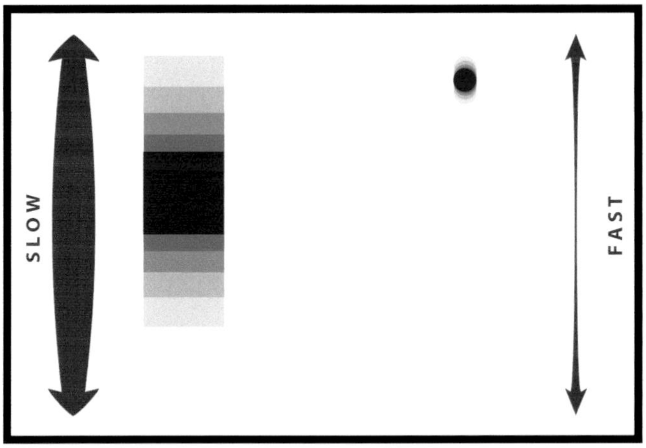                                        **Figure 18.5**

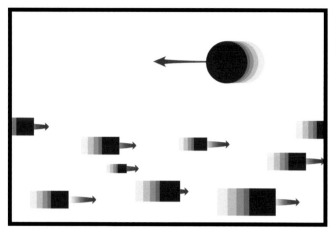

**Figure 18.6**

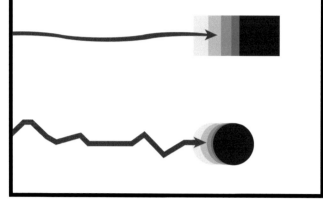

**Figure 18.7**

than the bigger square. The high magnitude of the small square's movement attracts the eye constantly. The faster it is and the higher its magnitude, the more we are attracted to it.

## Reading direction and size

An object moving in the opposite direction from all the other objects in the frame pushes itself into the foreground (Figure 18.6) (Video 18F). Its size only heightens its magnitude (as speed also would). In the example shown in Figure 18.6 we can see that even the number of squares on the bottom of the screen cannot fight against the size of the bigger circle above. Additionally, the lower movement of the squares is one continuous movement, but the incoming ball interrupts with its otherness and therefore also becomes more interesting. However, color, speed, or any other element of design could override size if it renders the object more important than the others. If the ball is much smaller than the group of objects underneath, it can still attract the attention, if its magnitude is much higher and its "otherness" is clear.

## Straight path versus nervous path

The two shapes in Figure 18.7 and Video 18G move on a different path: the upper square moves on a smooth curve, the lower ball on a nervous path. The nervousness and quick actions of the lower ball drags the attention. The eye still goes up to the smooth rectangle once in a while but is immediately drawn back down towards the nervous object. The eye is aesthetically drawn to the smooth arc; nevertheless, the more nervous arc drags the attention. The more uneven the path, the higher its magnitude.

All these points are extremely important for how the viewer will respond to the action on screen and how the eye is able to follow it from one significant informational point to another. Not paying attention to how the eye responds to movement will cause confusion, because the viewer's eyes will wander through the image, not knowing what is and what is not important. Pay attention at all times to where movement leads the eye and whether that coincides with the focal point!

# CHAPTER 19

# Music and Sound

Sound shows us the image differently than what the image shows alone, and the image likewise makes us hear sound differently than if the sound were ringing out in the dark.

**Michel Chion[1]**

Because of the sheer scope of the topic of sound, I cannot possibly cover it in a thorough manner in this book. Therefore, please also refer to the book suggestions in each section.

Silent movies were never really "silent," as there was always some kind of music or sound effect played during the presentation of the film to increase the action and drama and comedic value on-screen. However, there was always the goal of having music and sound be part of the actual film strip to streamline its presentation and be in full control of the artistic possibilities and their emotional effect on the audience. From the beginning of the development of film technology, accompanying sound was also delivered, but the technology was not able to deal with the accurate amalgam of image and sound until the end of the 1920s. The first public sound presentation happened in 1900, in film's infancy, at the Paris Exhibition. These sound presentations of the Gratioulet-Lioret system, the Phonorama, and the Théâtroscope system were the first exposure of the public to the combination of sound and film (not the first one in general, however, as a couple of years earlier other sound–film systems had been developed but were not publicly displayed). These early systems also revealed the main difficulties for the amalgam of sound and film: the synchronization of image and sound, locking the recorded sounds precisely and accurately to the images. Because both were recorded by different devices, playing back both caused slightly different speeds, which put the two out of synch. Additionally, the low quality of both the recording and presentation sound systems at the time, along with the low volume of the presentation, caused it to not be very practical for bigger venues. One possibility for early sound was the sound-on-disc system, in which a record with the soundtrack and musical score was connected to the projector; although the system worked, it was not practical or viable for a general widespread application as of yet. Over the years a huge number of sound systems were developed, some of which were the Kinetophone (1895), Cinemacrophonograph (1899), Phono-Cinéma-Théâtre (the Gratioulet-Lioret system, 1900), Chronophone (1901;

introduced by the French film company Gaumont, which used records for the sound, as described), Elgéphone (1908; developed by Léon Gaumont himself), Cameraphone (1909), Movietone (Fox Film Corporation's sound system, first used in 1927 in Murnau's Sunrise), Photophone (RCA's sound-on-film system, which was first used in 1929), and many, many others. However, most were not good enough in their sound quality for a big audience or financially practical for wide distribution. What changed was the invention of the soundtrack not being played on a separate device or medium but being projected as an optical soundtrack directly onto the film strip, left of the image. American inventor Lee de Forest developed this technique in 1919, which was publicly presented in short films in 1923 as DeForest Phonofilm. The connection between image and sound was now solid and the problem of one or the other not being in synchronization was finally overcome, despite the low quality of the sound. Phonofilm was only used at the time for short subjects, while other sound systems were still being developed and refined, of course. The actual era of sound began in 1927 with the American feature The Jazz Singer, which was released on October 6, the first successful feature with synchronized sound, using the Vitaphone sound system by Warner Brothers, an analog sound-on-disc system, where the record that contained the soundtrack was connected to the film projector, ensuring perfect synchronization. Warner Brothers had already shot and presented five films with the Vitaphone system previously (Don Juan being the first one in 1926), but it was The Jazz Singer that had songs, music, sound effects, and a little bit of dialogue, whereas the previous features had only music and sound effects. The success of The Jazz Singer was not due to it being the "first sound film," because it clearly was not, but to the more extensive track and the feature's main actor and singer, Al Jolson, portraying protagonist Jakie Rabinowitz. Al Jolson's popularity drew audiences into the cinemas and made the feature a huge success for Warner and the official start of sound in cinema.

Sound was now here to stay and film language had to be adjusted to a new way of storytelling. What needed to be learned was how to develop or discover a new aesthetic, one that did not rely on silent characters, was cinematic in nature, but used sound as an additional tool. For example, the characters who are talking do not necessarily have to be seen by the audience; they can talk offscreen and still support the narrative. Just as every new technological innovation needs to be learned and explored in order to discover its strengths and artistic possibilities, film artists had to learn how to creatively use sound. This of course came with some awkward and not-so-perfect beginnings.

[1] Chion Michel, *Audiovision, Sound on Screen*, Columbia University Press, New York, 1994, p. 21.

DOI: 10.1201/b22148-19

The movies right around the start of sound in film do not always show this switch in the most positive light. The high sophistication and visual complexity of silent films that had developed over 30 years was all of a sudden questioned and a new aesthetic developed over the next years, often relying on simple dialogues too much to transfer information rather than finding a visual representation like the silent features did so very well.

## Sound in animation

Animation can create visuals that are beyond reality, are uncoupled from the confinements of nature, and can create any visuals imaginable: literally. It is only the creativity of the artist that limits the visual grandeur of animation, and sound is very much part of this vast creative field that animation provides. Sound had a very impressive start in animation with Charles Fleischer's sound experiments in his *Ko-Ko Song Car-Tunes*. The film *Come Take a Trip in My Airship* was the first animated short film with sound, produced in March of 1924 with the earlier mentioned Lee de Forest's Phonofilm sound-on-film process. Fleischer's *Song Car-Tunes* also introduced the sing-along to the world in the form of the bouncing ball, where the audience participates in the singing of the songs on-screen: early karaoke! Out of 57[2] *Song Car-Tunes* Fleischer produced 38[3] shorts with the Lee de Forest sound system. A very charming one is *Jingle Bells* from 1927, in which a simple white line drawing of an elf serves as the bouncing ball and shows the lyrics of the song "Jingle Bells" to the audience. On October 14, 1928, Paul Terry released *Dinner Time*, his first short film with sound, produced by Van Beuren Studios, which was also, like the Fleischer Studio, stationed in New York City (Disney Studios was in Los Angeles). *Dinner Time* is part of Van Beuren's *Aesop's Fables* and had Paul Terry's famous character Farmer Al Falfa as the protagonist. Terry used the RCA Photophone system; nevertheless, the short *Dinner Time* was not successful enough to raise awareness of its use of sound. On November 18, the same year, Disney released its first short film with sound, *Steamboat Willie*, starring Mickey Mouse, a short that plays with the title of Buster Keaton's famous and stunning feature *Steamboat Bill, Jr.*, released in May of 1928. Disney used Pat Powers' Cinephone system (which was clearly based on the Lee de Forest's Phonofilm sound process, but de Forest was financially not able to sue for patent infringement). *Steamboat Willie* was not the first animated short with sound, but it was the most successful one and the one that convinced audiences that the characters on-screen produced some of the sounds themselves rather than the sound being a song or a band.

What Disney understood was how to use sound specifically for animation purposes and how sound allows the characters on screen to feel more alive if used correctly. *Steamboat Willie* became one of Disney's most successful shorts at the time and most definitely helped in making *Mickey Mouse* a household name. The sounds Disney chose for his characters and the music on-screen were by no means realistic but already what we would call "cartoony." The synchronized sound effects and Mickey's whistles and voice make it so much more believable that those drawn characters have a life of their own. Sound therefore adds another level of realism but also pushes the cartooniness of the characters and actions.

Hugh Harman and Rudolph Ising had both already worked for Disney in Kansas City and animated on Disney's *Alice Comedies* and then in Los Angeles on *Oswald the Lucky Rabbit*. After they left Disney and joined George Winkler to produce more *Oswald* shorts, they developed a character they called *Bosko*. Bosko was a black American boy, who had his first appearance in May of 1929 in *Bosko, the Talk-Ink Kid*, a short film produced to promote and present the character to movie studios interested in producing a series. Carman (Max) Maxwell, also an animator who had worked at Disney's Laugh-O-Gram Studio in Kansas City, was the early voice of Bosko, and his voice was recorded before the character animation was produced. Unlike the Mickey Mouse shorts, in which the mouse was voiced by Walt Disney himself and which mainly relied on music and sound effects in the first sound shorts and less on actual dialogue, Bosko performed as a fully talking and thinking character having a dialogue with one of his creators, Rudolph Ising, who appears in live-action shots in the short. Bosko's voice being synchronized with the animated lip movement is an excellent piece of work, considering the novelty and complexity of the medium. Warner Brothers, via Leon Schlesinger, was the one to take Bosko under contract and his first official short film *Sinking in the Bathtub* was released the following year in 1930, the first short of the long-lived and beloved series called *Looney Tunes*.

Sound quickly became the norm in Hollywood after 1928 and audiences expected shorts and features to come with sound, a not-insignificant additional expenditure for the studios. Sound then surely changed animation and feature film and was for a short while the driving force in animated short films until the novelty wore off and became a regular accompanying agent. Nevertheless, the use of sound in animation always played a very special part in sound design, as the sound can be completely

More on sound in film and animation:

Richard Abel and Rick Altman, *The Sounds of Early Cinema*, Indiana University Press, Bloomington, IN, 2001.
Donald Crafton, *The Talkies: American Cinema's Transition to Sound, 1926–1931*, University of California Press, Berkeley, CA, 1999.

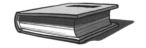

---

2  Fleischer Studios: Filmography, 2018. Fleischer Studios, Inc. and TM Fleischer Studios, Inc. http://www.fleischerstudios.com/filmography.html; (accessed July 4, 2017). This webpage is a very interesting source for information on the Fleischer Studios!

3  Out of the Inkwell films, Filmography. http://www.imdb.com/company/co0068397/?ref_=tt_dt_co (accessed July 4, 2017).

detached from the original sound–object relationship and still be convincing. Walter Murch rightly stated:

> In fact, animation—of both the "Steamboat Willie" and the "King Kong" varieties—has probably played a more significant role in the evolution of creative sound than has been acknowledged. In the beginning of the sound era, it was so astonishing to hear people speak and move and sing and shoot one another in sync that almost any sound was more than acceptable. But with animated characters this did not work: they are two-dimensional creatures who make no sound at all unless the illusion is created through sound out of context: sound from one reality transposed onto another. The most famous of these is the thin falsetto that Walt Disney himself gave to Mickey Mouse, but a close second is the roar that Murray Spivack provided King Kong.[4]

But sound also had another advantage for some studios. Warner Brothers for example saw with pleasure the success of its first series *Looney Tunes* and asked Leon Schlesinger to start yet another series, based on songs Warner owned the rights to. Warner had unsuccessfully tried a live-action series, kind of like an early music video, to promote the songs of their extensive music and song library and promote them to their eagerly waiting and money-spending audiences. Five shorts had been produced, in which double-exposed live-action footage of sets and cut-outs were overlaid by the footage of the performer of the respective song. However, the series was soon replaced by the fully animated series *Merrie Melodies*, which also heavily used the songs Warner owned. For example, in 1936 Warner released the feature film *The Singing Kid* with Al Jolson (the very same from the earlier mentioned *Jazz Singer* from 1927), an extremely popular performer at the time. In this feature, the song "I Love to Singa" was sung three times and Warner again had approached Leon Schlesinger to produce an animated short based on this song. So also in 1936 they released the animated short *I Love to Singa*, in which a young owl wants to sing jazz despite his father teaching him classical music. Disappointed in his son, the father kicks the young owl out of the house, who then wanders about only to find a talent radio show, on which he performs jazz to everyone's delight. *I Love to Singa* was one of director Tex Avery's first shorts as a director and some animation enthusiasts even like it.

Another short film that should be mentioned when it comes to sound is UPA's *Gerald McBoing-Boing* from 1950, directed by Robert Cannon. In this short the character Gerald's voice is replaced by sounds, as Gerald cannot speak words, but makes the sound *boing-boing-boing* instead. Gerald's emotions and "words" are car horns, explosions, train whistles, or the sound of a cuckoo clock. That Gerald makes those sounds is absolutely believable in animation, because the visuals are already so far removed from reality that any additional oddness is more easily

accepted by the audience. Animation can obviously freely play with any of the elements it contains, and sound is one that really can push the film onto a rather surreal level, one that is detached from the laws of physics and nature, where sound can be used in the most outrageous and creative way, where the noises, hisses, rattling, the scratching and swallowing, the squeaking and scuffing are the sounds of communication.

One more exceptional example is Chuck Jones' short film with Daffy Duck, *Duck Amuck*, from 1953. In it, Daffy is constantly interrupted in his "job" as a professional actor, which of course he fails at performing on a continuous basis. *Duck Amuck*'s uniqueness lies in the fact that it freely plays with all aspects that animation has to offer: space, timing, on-screen and offscreen space, sound and the lack of it, and the acceptance of the character himself that he is acting in an animated short, which is painted and hand drawn. In one scene Daffy is literally erased by a gigantic eraser and only his voice keeps on yapping. The interesting part of this scene is that Daffy can actually live without his body. His voice is still there in the void talking after the body is completely erased by the mighty pencil. Cartoon characters can obviously be erased without disappearing completely. Their physical bodies, which consist of nothing other than pencil and paint, are the part that can be controlled by the artist. The personality and "soul" of the character exist without it and live in the voice. In another scene, the sound of a guitar is replaced by the sound of a machine gun, an old screechy car horn, a pistol, and the cry of a donkey. Daffy then tries to yell but can only voice the cry of a rooster and some chicken sounds, a laughing kookaburra, and finally a pathetic little squeak, which then outraged the duck. Sound can therefore be detached from the cartoon character and live on its own, but the character can also be detached from his or her voice and other odd sounds can be attached to the character.

More on *Duck Amuck and its deconstruction:*

Paul Wells, *Understanding Animation*, Routledge, London, 1998, pp. 39–43.

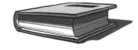

Because animation is such a visual medium, too often the artist only thinks in visuals and forgets that sound can also "paint pictures." Sound can add visuals that the image itself is incapable of showing. Just look at an image of a leaf without sound and one with sound that contains birds, wind, water, branches breaking, or the call of a fox. The image will immediately grow, sprout, and add space that goes beyond any space the artist could possibly paint. Sound develops its own reality and space, which is impossible to create through images, as both have their own unique strengths. Much of what happens on screen can be withheld as visual information from the audience and replaced by sounds in order to give the images more tension or variation from shot to shot. Especially when it comes to storyboarding, sound is one element that can dramatically enhance suspense but is not used to its full potential exactly because animators

4   Walter Murch, Stretching Sound to Help the Mind See; Sound Design: The Dancing Shadow, in *Projections 4*, 2000. http://filmsound.org/murch/stretching.htm (accessed on January 15, 2018).

(students mostly) too often think only about the visuals, not the various options of visual and auditory stimulation in the final film. There is a huge difference between the image of an explosion accompanied by lovely and pleasant, calming music, one with the actual sound of the explosion, one with the sound of a much bigger explosion, and one without any sound at all. Using sound is not just about replicating reality (and in this regard it is creatively exactly like all the other aspects we have been discussing) but about playing creatively with the expectation of the audience and the mood that is established. Sound can do the very same, just in a more hidden and sneaky way that the audience isn't immediately aware of. Sound paints and opens the space around the image in a nearly limitless way. It breaks down the frame of the image, allows the outer world to penetrate the restrictions of the frame and bring in a "felt" reality, which can be artificial or realistic. Does the image need sound to work? Of course not … for 35 years there was only limited sound and the moving yet semisilent images from yesteryear still inspire the imagination of the audience today. It depends on how much someone is willing to accept and emotionally invest into the artistic creations of the first 30 years of filmmaking. Silent movies are a task to watch for audiences nowadays, as the viewers feel like they are not "entertained" because they have to bring their own imagination and often patience to the show. By contrast, in a contemporary blockbuster movie everything is presented on a plate without the audience having to be bothered to imagine the possibilities or to accept another, less perfect reality. Of course, that does not mean that silent movies are better than "talkies." But the silent movie approach offers another creative possibility, another option that can be used in today's shots and scenes for the film's own benefit, which is the incorporation of the audience's own completion of the given story. I remember having seen Pixar's stunning film (well, the first 30 min, that is) WALL-E (2008) in the theatre. In one scene halfway through the feature, we see Eve and WALL-E fly through space in the most romantic way possible. The audience member goes along with the two characters emotionally and with goose bumps secretly wipes away a single tear from his cheek (yes, I proudly did!), when all of a sudden the onboard computer explains after being asked by the captain: "Dancing … a series of movements involving two partners where speed and rhythm … " Why do I need to hear what I can already see on-screen? The only effect it has is that I am taken out of the emotional experience of giving in to the incredibly well-executed and surreal moment of Eve and WALL-E dancing through space. It interrupts the movie experience, only reminding the audience that it is just pixels on a screen. Sound and images do not always go hand in hand and dialogue in particular seems to tap into another part of the brain than music and sound effects do. It often brings the story to a logical, semirealistic level, whereas music and sound effects tell the story on an emotional level. Sound and especially dialogue is not always the only way to tell the story; sometimes it is beneficial to not say anything at all and just let the visuals do the job … with a little bit of sound effects and music if needed.

# Different types of sound for film
## Diegetic sound

This is the actual sound in the character's world, the sound that both the character on-screen and the audience member can hear. This would be, for instance, a car driving by the character, the birds chirping in the location, or the dialogue between the characters but also music playing from a radio or sounds from a television set. Diegetic sounds are all the sounds and noises from the location the character is in.

## Diegetic sound source connected and source disconnected

What needed to be learned in the late 1920s, when sound finally became not only a simple addition to film but an artistic device that fundamentally affected film language, was how sound could be used in film creatively. Sound, despite being locked to the image, can be edited and played with. Two people are talking to each other; the camera shows Character A talking and her voice is heard as she is speaking. Then the camera cuts to Character B and he is talking. But we can also, as long as we have seen both characters talk to each other, just stay with Character A and see her reaction, while we hear Character B talk offscreen. The source of the sound does not necessarily have to be seen on-screen to be understood. Sound coming from an on-screen source is therefore "source connected," whereas sound coming from a source that is located offscreen is "source disconnected." This is a crucial creative device that allows the sound to play independently of the image, a device that gives the image–sound relationship an organic feel rather than being rigid and confined if the sound is just constantly locked to the visual. If you watch a film where the sound, especially in a dialogue scene, is continuously source connected, the scene easily feels very cheap and plain. Constantly shifting between the various sound options also brings in variation!

## Nondiegetic sound

This is sound that only the audience can hear but not the characters on-screen. The musical score, for example, is only heard by the audience in the theatre; the voice of the narrator or voice-over, sound effects that are part of the score to create a mood are all never part of the character's realm, but only part of ours. Diegetic and nondiegetic sound, mostly music, can melt from one into the other. The music can start out as nondiegetic music that plays loudly and covers all the diegetic sounds on-screen, but as the scene progresses it is lowered in volume, maybe even the quality changes, and it becomes apparent that the song is actually playing on the car radio of the protagonist.

# There are three elements that contribute to sound:

- Voices and characters
- Sound Effects
- Music and score

## Voices and characters

Good voice actors for animation can make or break a character and there are myriads of animated characters that are unique exactly because of the talent and creativity of the voice actors who invented them. It would be too easy for the character designer to take the credit for the invented character, but it is the voice that gives it its life and spirit. The voice is then the stepping stone for the character animator and the better the voice and the more nuanced, the more it serves as a boost for the animator's own creativity to invent unique and creative performances. Animated characters need voices that create a character in the listener's mind without it being seen on-screen. As *Duck Amuck* proved to us in 1953, the animated character is not just the character on-screen, but it is a voice that lives on without the body, has a life of its own, and is already a character before being interpreted by the animator. Voice acting is a very different art form than acting, as the voice actor has to be convincing without a body, without the visuals, has to create a voice that has timing, timbre, personality, and uniqueness and paints a character in the audience's mind, with one of animation's most important pillars: exaggeration. For a couple of decades now, actually since Robin Williams voiced the Genie in Disney's *Aladdin* in 1992, it has been the norm rather than the exception to hire famous actors for the job of voice acting in animated features (not TV though), which in my opinion often greatly reduces the quality of the characters' personalities. There are clearly many actors who are capable of an excellent voice acting job; however, voice actors are trained to create and invent unique characters especially for animation and games, whereas actors are usually hired not only for their own voice but also for publicity. That famous actors are hired for the job of animation voices often does show in the outcome: many voices in today's features are rather bland and lack the specific qualities of *animated characters*. Unfortunately, often the design of the characters then follows the look and mannerisms of the actors, which I witnessed in DreamWorks's *Bee Movie*, where Barry Bee Benson's design is close to Jerry Seinfeld's look. The animation then becomes a vehicle for the stardom of the actor, rather than an artistic field in its very own right. One of the few animation companies that has refrained from this habit is Pixar (aside from their *Toy Story* series, which is very much excusable because it was their first feature and they needed all the publicity they could get). For voice acting, it is not the name that is connected to the character that is important but the quality of the voice itself. That there are some excellent voices by actors is of course a given, like Jason Bateman's memorable voice of Nick Wilde in Disney's *Zootopia* (2016). Nevertheless, we know it is Jason's voice; it is not a fully new character personality that we are listening to, like Homer Simpson, voiced by Dan Castellaneta, who created the simple, lazy, and yet somehow charming character of Homer out of nothing, which is true creative voice acting. Dan and any other talented voice actor can invent new characters, which is the very point of the job, not merely using an existing voice.

It is very easy to forget while we watch our favorite characters on-screen that actual voice actors are behind the animated characters and not enough credit is given to those voices that express so precisely those invented personalities, especially in TV productions. There are obviously many voice actors who need to be mentioned when one talks about voice acting for animation; however, only a few should be named. It is actually interesting once in a while to look into the work of the actors who are responsible for the characters we love so much. It is seldom a convincing character if there is no talented voice attached, a voice that creates the character with all his or her traits, quirks, mannerisms, and zaniness (I know this following list is utterly unfair, as every country has myriads of talented voice actors that many people have literally never heard of, but for the sake of simplicity I go down the path of mostly American animation, which is the one most of us are familiar with. Also this list is just a little push for you to look into who actually voiced your own favorite characters, which in my case is German actor Hans Clarin, who voiced the famous characters of the kobold Pumuckl and Hui Buh, the ghost with the rusty rattling chain; or Eartha Kit's insane voice for the villainous Yzma in Disney's *The Emperor's New Groove*):

- First and foremost, "the man of a thousand voices," Mel Blanc. He was responsible for all the voices of the male characters of the Warner Brothers animation universe and voiced Bugs Bunny, Daffy Duck, Yosemite Sam, Porky Pig, Tweety and Sylvester, Foghorn Leghorn, Marvin the Martian, Pepé Le Pew, Speedy Gonzales; he was even the voice of Gideon the Cat in Disney's *Pinocchio* (yes, I know it's only one hiccup), voiced Barney Rubble in the *Flintstones*, and many others in animation and commercials. Mel Blanc was the first voice actor who actually received screen credit for his work.

**Books on voice acting:**

Terry Apple, *Making Money in Voice-Overs: Winning Strategies to a Successful Career in TV, Commercials, Radio and Animation*, Lone Eagle Publishing, Los Angeles, CA, 1999.
Tom Blakemore, *Recording Voiceover*, Routledge, London, 2015.

- *June Foray:* Foray was the voice of Warner Brothers' Granny, the owner of Tweety Bird; she also voiced Rocket J. "Rocky" Squirrel from the *Rocky and Bullwinkle Show*, Jokey Smurf, and in Disney's *Cinderella* she voiced the vicious cat Lucifer. She spent decades lobbying the Academy Award to create a Best Animated Feature category, which was established in 2001. She was a voice actress for 84 years!
- *Tom Kenny:* the voice of SpongeBob SquarePants. His portrayal of SpongeBob, a mixture of Pee-Wee Herman, Jerry Lewis, and Laurel and Hardy, creates a unique character that is always pure emotion: either over-the-top happy and positive or just completely crushed. SpongeBob is emotion times ten, and Kenny perfectly expresses it with a voice that is nasal and squeaky but has perfect timing, which is so helpful for animation purposes. Kenny has also voiced the Ice King in *Adventure Time* and the Mayor in the *Powerpuff Girls*, amongst many others.
- *Dan Castellaneta:* the voice of Homer Simpson, Grampa Simpson, Krusty the Clown, and others for the long-running show *The Simpsons*. Castellaneta's voice for Homer is slow, deep, and sounds cerebrally challenged, yet warm and comfortable. The uniqueness of the voice is what makes the character of Homer so endearing in his stupidity and complete lack of fatherly qualities, as he is selfish and lazy, always making the wrong decisions. Amongst many other characters Castellaneta also voiced Dr. Emmett Brown in the *Back to the Future* animated series.
- *Betty Lou Gerson:* Cruella de Vil from *101 Dalmatians* is one of Disney's all-time best villains. Gerson was an American actress and voice actress for radio, film, and television. She was the narrator in Disney's *Cinderella* (1950) and appeared in *Mary Poppins* (1964) as the Old Crone. She was also the voice of Frances Albacore in *Cats Don't Dance* (1997).
- *Ed Wynn:* the memorable voice actor who gave the Mad Hatter in Disney's *Alice in Wonderland* his insane personality and impeccable timing. Ed Wynn was a comedic performer in the Ziegfeld Follies, a vaudeville and revue theatre show in New York, which Wynn performed for in 1914 and 1915. He was also on TV in 1936, for an experimental broadcast. In the 1950s he had three television shows at NBC and CBS, including one of the first variety shows for TV in 1949–1950. He was nominated for an Academy Award for his dramatic portrayal of dentist Dr. Fritz Pfeffer in *The Diary of Anne Frank* in 1959. He also portrayed Uncle Albert in Disney's feature *Mary Poppins* (1964).
- *David Jason:* a British actor who was responsible for such extraordinary characters as Danger Mouse, Mr. Toad in the beautiful stop-motion series *Wind in the Willows*, the BFG himself, and Count Duckula, a vicious vegetarian vampire duck, amongst many others!
- Daws Butler
- Bill Thompson
- And many, many others …

## Narration and voice-over

The voice-over in film is a rather odd thing, because the audience does not see the person who is talking. The speaking voice remains just that: a voice, which often is more of a presence than an actual character. Of course, one of the protagonists of the film can be the narrator, but more often than not it is an omniscient "higher power," who tells the story on-screen from a perspective of distance and knowledge about what will happen or has happened. Of course, it also depends on who the narrator is and how he or she talks, what he or she says. In Terrence Malick's feature *Days of Heaven* (1978), for instance, the narrator is a young girl, innocent yet still aware of the happenings, more than the adults that are actually driving the action.

The narrator of a film is usually the storyteller, the one who knows the story and tells it to the audience, commenting on it. In Stanley Kubrick's *Barry Lyndon* (1975), the narrator accompanies the viewer throughout the entire movie and explains Barry's rise from a poor Irish farmer's son to the social elite in a matter-of-fact fashion. The omniscient narrator in the film tells Barry Lyndon's story, contrary to the source material, William Makepeace Thackeray's novel *The Luck of Barry Lyndon* (1844), where Barry himself is the narrator. Contrary to the book, in which Barry boasts of his honesty and morals, clearly to the reader a complete misinterpretation of his own personality, the film has a rather neutral narrator, who neither comes across as comical, as in the book, nor boasts of Barry's accomplishments but rather clinically narrates Barry's life.

A very different type of narration that goes against the traditional voice-over of "telling the story" is used in director Terrence Malick's films, which are lyrical and often devoid of extensive dialogues; therefore, the voice-over provides not only needed information for understanding the plot but also gives insight into the thoughts and contemplations of the characters. In his feature *The Thin Red Line* (1998), he has not just one narrator but various characters from the narrative express their reflections and thoughts, read letters, and have inner monologues and thus Malick creates a complex patchwork of images, sounds, music, and voices, which force the viewer to grasp the story far beyond the mere narrative happenings on-screen but to see it from a broader, philosophical perspective. The voice-over elevates the visuals onto an intellectual level, which the mere images would not be able

Books on voice-over:

Sarah Kozloff, *Invisible Storytellers, Voice-Over Narration in American Fiction Film*, University of California Press, New York, 1989.
Chion Michel, *The Voice in Cinema*, Columbia University Press, New York, 1999.

to reach. Malick's films are not narrative films in the traditional sense that they explain the story from beginning to end, claiming to be reality. His films feel like memories of the characters on-screen that the viewer is invited to witness. There is always a sense of surrealism and otherworldliness that is only accentuated by the voice-over.

Spoken words will direct the viewer's attention towards certain thoughts and ideas connected to the visuals, which Michel Chion calls "text added value." For example, we see a little girl crying on the sidewalk. Without words, we all have a reason in mind why the girl might be crying. However, if a voice were to comment on it and say "She is lost," then obviously we all would pity her; if the voice says "It's not nice to murder your father!" then we would have a slightly different story to the exact same shot. So the spoken word definitely leads the story of the visuals in a chosen direction and the audience will interpret the image and with it its content and emotional expression differently. Images do not always tell the whole story and sound can either change the direction of the visuals or can also enrich the visuals with unexpected information.

## Sound effects

Sound effects are the artificial sounds added to the film after it has been shot, either to emphasize, clarify, or to redo the entire soundscape of the film. Sound effects consist of four elements.

- *Hard sounds:* These are sounds that are recorded outside of the studio: slamming doors, car sounds, etc., sounds that are not yet synched with the visuals.
- *Ambient/background sounds:* Background noises that give the space volume. City noises, forest sounds, the humming of air conditioners, or simply white noise to take away the silence and "emptiness" of a space.
- *Foley:* All the sounds that can be created by the Foley artist in the studio, like footsteps, rustling noises of fabrics, prop sounds. Foley sounds are synched to the visuals during recording (compared to the hard sounds, which are not yet synched).
- *Design sound effects:* These are sounds that are created from scratch, like a laser gun or the sound of a dinosaur—sounds that do not occur in nature and cannot be simply recorded but have to be created artistically. The audience has no idea what an actual dinosaur sounded like, so the sound needs to be convincing enough but can actually be anything as long as it does not make the audience giggle or question why the *Tyrannosaurus rex* sounded like a rabid chicken instead of a vicious, dangerous, and bloodthirsty beast of hell (however, the former would actually be really funny).

## Music and score

Composition of the musical score is usually started once the film is edited; the music is then written for the final edit. However, another possibility is that the music leads the visuals and the film is edited to the musical flow.

Songs are commonly not part of the score but part of the soundtrack and serve as a verbal communicator of the narrative or its themes, whereas the musical score is generally, aside from choirs, nonverbal (of course, exceptions occur).

### Leitmotif
The leitmotif is part of the musical score. It is a German term meaning "leading motif" and is a musical representation of a character, an emotion, an object, or a theme, idea, or situation. The leitmotif can introduce characters, and whenever they appear or are referred to in the narrative the leitmotif accentuates this and/or their emotional or psychological state. The first composer to use the leitmotif extensively was German composer Richard Wagner (1813–1883), whose four-opera cycle *Der Ring des Nibelungen* (*The Ring of the Nibelung*) (1848–1874) is famous for its use of musical themes and leifmotifs. The leitmotif is a very common device for film music, which appears throughout film in various versions and emotional tints. For example, in Steven Spielberg's *Close Encounters of the Third Kind* (1977), the theme of the film's score, written by John Williams, is a five-tone motif, which serves as a greeting to the alien visitors, as music is seen in the film as the only communication device between humans and aliens abstract enough to express a common ground. This motif appears over and over in the film in various forms and moods and its simplicity is easily recognizable. One film can have many motifs, as many as the film has important characters if the composer chooses this path. John Williams' themes for *Star Wars* (1977) are plenty and Howard Shore used even more themes in the *Lord of the Rings* trilogy.

**Books on sound design:**

Stanley R. Alten, *Audio in Media (Wadsworth Series in Broadcast and Production)*, Wadsworth Publishing, Belmont, CA, 2013.
Zettl Herbert, *Sight Sound Motion, Applied Media Aesthetics*, Thomson Wadsworth, Belmont, CA, 2008.
Batcho James, *Sound for Independent Audiovisual Storytelling*, Sanshin Publishing, 2013.
Chion Michael, *Audio-Vision: Sound on Screen*, Columbia University Press, New York, 1994.
Beauchamp Robin, *Designing Sound for Animation*, CRC Press, Boca Raton, FL, 2013.

**Books on film music:**

Kassabian Anahid, *Hearing Film, Tracking Identifications in Contemporary Hollywood Film Music*, Routledge, New York, 2001.
Kevin J. Donnelly, *The Spectre of Sound: Music in Film and Television*, British Film Institute, London, 2005.

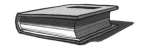

# The possible purposes of sound:

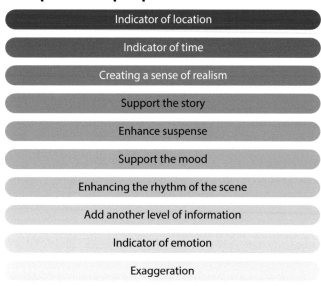

Indicator of location

Indicator of time

Creating a sense of realism

Support the story

Enhance suspense

Support the mood

Enhancing the rhythm of the scene

Add another level of information

Indicator of emotion

Exaggeration

Create a sense of comfort, suspense, excitement, or alertness

## Indicator of location

The camera is very close to a person sitting in a chair and there is no visual clue in the image where that person is sitting. Sounds of an airport with noises and announcements clearly define the location as an airport. The sounds of a coffee maker and an oven door opening locate the character maybe at home and in a more private setting. But the sound could also be futuristic and therefore place the character into a science fiction location. There are common audible clues that often define a location; they serve as commonly accepted and understood markers of spaces—the sounds of a typical office, a typical restaurant, a typical train station. They are generic, but they work. In many films the cliché eagle's cry to audibly support the picture of the vast outdoors becomes a bit silly at this point, because it is even used in natural locations where eagles don't live (and honestly: how often have you actually heard an eagle cry in the outdoors?). Cliché they might be, but they do work, and because much of sound is not fully consciously listened to, there is a broad creative field to be played in.

Sound also connects locations from one shot to the next or separates them. For example, we see a person sitting at a cafe, reading a newspaper. The sound of a coffee machine is heard, chatting people are in the background, some quiet music is playing. If we now cut to a person sitting in a library and the sound of the cafe just continues uninterrupted, we would either feel that it is actually the same space, just another room of the café, or the sound, and with it the space of the cafe, has some impact on the person in the library. The sound connects both places either physically or intellectually.

## Indicator of time

The sound of milk being poured into a glass, the sizzling sounds of frying eggs and bacon clearly say that it is breakfast time (usually); chirping birds point towards daytime and an owl could signify nighttime. Sounds can indicate time and seasons. Nevertheless, there can be a discrepancy between sound and image when it comes to time, where the sound can be continuous in its time but the image is not or vice versa. This happens in a montage sequence when the music is one continuous piece but the visuals show a series of moments during a prolonged period of time. The music has the effect of grouping the visuals into one scene, making one statement rather than many.

## Creating a sense of realism

Adding realistic sounds to an image lifts it up immediately and provides it with a sense of space; it takes away its two-dimensional flatness and opens it up into a three-dimensional space that, depending on the style of the visuals, can be realistic or semirealistic. The flat film image without sound is a glance into another reality, a peek into a box, which is however always confined to the screen. With realistic sounds added, the image grows and the viewer is involved in the action on-screen, becomes part of it, and is surrounded by it. The slightly surreal nature of the silent image can be removed by just giving the image some ambient sound and it will open up. But of course the opposite can also be achieved, by denying the film image realistic sounds and thus pushing it towards a surreal, strange, or even comical aesthetic.

## Support the story

This is the most obvious point for using sound, to support the story at its most basic level. A car drives through the frame and we hear the sound of the car engine. The sounds simply explain and refine what we see on-screen. We hear the characters talk to each other, hear the sounds and the music of their world. The sound is a supporting element of the story and helps the audience understand the narrative.

In order to understand the story, there can also be nondiegetic sounds that help us to grasp what is going on with the characters, which might not be clear yet from the mere images on-screen. For example, a narrator can support the story by just explaining the actions.

## Enhance suspense

What auditory information is revealed and what is withheld is crucial for the development and maintenance of suspense, and by "suspense" I not only mean the typical suspense in a horror movie but suspense in any kind of scene. For example, a character is not seen but only heard, because she is offscreen. This causes the audience to want to know who that character is, what she does, how she acts and reacts. Not seeing that character but only hearing her increases the suspense of the scene.

## Support the mood

Sound is a major contributor to the mood of a film and background sound effects give a location some personality. How we perceive a space has much to do with the sounds that space is connected with. A plain room with the sound of an air conditioner humming is sterile and uninviting; the same room with the quiet background noise of city life suggests a social environment outside of the confinement of the room. However, there is not only realistic sound but also sound that artificially creates a mood, sounds that do not belong into the room, the nondiegetic sounds, like wood creaking or strange, eerie artificial sounds that are part of a soundtrack to evoke discomfort or comfort, depending on the creative direction of the scene. Sound has the ability to subconsciously evoke a feeling about a space or situation. In the feature *Barton Fink* (1991) by the Coen brothers, the sounds of the hotel room are an important aspect of the visuals insofar as they exaggerate the scenes and give each object personality. The furniture squeaks more than usual, the door makes a sucking noise when opened, the peeling wallpaper makes a moist and sticky sound, the hallways have a quiet humming sound; the entire universe of *Barton Fink* is just slightly heightened to give it a hint of surrealism and oddness, enough to point out the warped story. Sound is very effective in manipulating the audience's emotions subconsciously.

## Enhancing the rhythm of the scene

The rhythm of a piece of music or sound design has the ability to push the scene forward, not only accompanying the scene but with its rhythm impelling it. The sound's rhythmical beats usually dominate the scene rather than the visuals themselves or the edit. There are various options for this:

- *The rhythm of the sound does not match the rhythm of the visuals (Figure 19.1):* this can create a disharmonious scene that has however a dynamic structure to it. As an additional option, both sound and visual can align in their rhythm for short moments and then again move away from each other.

**Figure 19.1**

- *The rhythm goes with the visuals (Figure 19.2):* the visuals can be either edited to the sound, so the cuts happen to the beat of the track (as shown in Figure 19.2), or specific actions within the shots can align with the sound (like in the two case studies below). Because in animation we have such a high degree of control of every little element within the frame, we can for example time the beats of the soundtrack to an eye-blink of the character or time it to any other significant part of the action.

The audiovisual amalgamation is fully controllable. Too much harmony, where the rhythm of the music matches the rhythm of the edit exactly, can be awkward and forced, lacking an organic structure. If for instance the whole scene is cut exactly to the beat of the sound it can be boring or artificial (can, but does not have to be!). Nevertheless, a continuous rhythm in the sound can also stimulate a sense of an upcoming change, an event, or a sudden action. This is often used in scenes of suspense or horror films: the continuous rhythm of the musical score or even just the heartbeat of the protagonist are enough to expect something to happen.

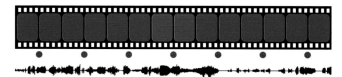

**Figure 19.2**

## Add another level of information

We have seen in Kenneth Anger's short film *Scorpio Rising* how sound can have various levels of information, changing the meaning of each shot dramatically (see Chapter 6, "Character Staging and Film Language," the section "Editing," the subsection "Montage"). The added musical track with popular songs from the era affects the visual narrative of the images and gives it a meaning that goes beyond the meaning of the initial visual.

## Indicator of emotion

It is not just the musical score that reflects the emotions of the characters or the entire scene, but it can also be sound effects and a general audible mood that describe how the characters feel. For example, a character is in a forest and feels happy. We hear the birds chirp and the bees hum. Then the cellphone rings and the character receives a horrible message. To reflect the change in her emotions, the entire forest can now take part in her sorrow and the previously happy sounds subside or are muted and other sounds sneak in that aren't as positive. The audible world surrounding the characters is not a fixed one; it can change according to the mood and the emotions of the characters and the needs of the narrative.

## Exaggeration

Of course, in animation the *swoooosh* sound is one that supports a fast action, being an indicator of speed, and the exaggerated sound of a hammer on an anvil in a Tex Avery cartoon is just pushing the hitting force to a comical extreme. Animation plays so much with exaggeration that of course sound has a huge role in amplifying the visuals and often is the gag itself.

However, it is not just the cartoony exaggeration that is of importance but exaggeration of any kind that enhances or further describes a situation, a character, or an object. This can be a bullet that penetrates a body with a hard thud, making the audience nearly feel the hard impact, or just a subtle breeze that is slightly enhanced to make the invisible being felt and of course heard on-screen.

Sound can also push the action forward or slow it down by speeding up the sound or beats, but it can also slow down the action.

## Create a sense of comfort, suspense, excitement, or alertness

Just remember a train ride when you were really exhausted and right next to you, sitting or jumping up and down, was a couple of kids, and a crying and screaming baby was driving nails into your brain. More and more sounds piled up and it became very difficult for you to focus on your novel or just to keep calm. Sounds can create a cacophony of audible stimuli that are sometimes impossible to absorb, thus creating a high level of stress. The opposite of course also happens: the lack of noise or sound can create a sense of ease and comfort or even creepiness and expectation. The soundscape produced for a film thus can either stimulate the audience's mood or calm, excite, or scare them. High-pitched sounds have the tendency to cause the listener to be alert, whereas low-pitched sounds can have the opposite effect.

## Case study: Rhythm in scene 3B of Disney's *Snow White and the Seven Dwarfs* (1937)[5]

**Animators of the sequence:** Ham Luske with assistants Errol Gray and Don Lusk, Eric Larson with assistants Jack Bradbury and Don Lusk, Bernard Garbutt with assistant Lynn Karp, Tony Rivera.

**Director:** Perce Pearce, Ham Luske

**Assistant director:** Hal Adelquist.[6]

In order to understand the complexity of this shot discussed in this section, you have to watch it various times with and without sound to fully grasp the imbedded rhythm of character animation, camera work, and music. The discussed shot in Scene 3B has the timecode 00:12:15–00:12:29.

On the 27th of December, 1937, *Time* published an article called "Mouse & Man" in which they wrote about Walt Disney's latest feature and newest toy:

> In a typical Disney cartoon, the action and sound move according to an intricate schedule in which the frames of the film are synchronized with the musical beat or sound effects. The animation cels are assembled, together with backgrounds and other cels of intermediate background, and taken to the camera. In Snow White, the $75,000 multiplane camera is the one chiefly used—it is much like any other movie camera, except that its action can be governed to expose one frame of film and then stop. Regular cinema cameras run at the rate of anywhere from eight to 64 frames per second. What makes the Disney camera unique is its towering, 14-ft. framework. The camera peers vertically down from the top of this iron structure through several levels, set below it like the grooved shelves in a baker's pie-wagon. On the lower levels, various elements of back ground drawn in relative perspective may be superimposed, one over the other, imparting an illusion of depth in the finished print. Above these backgrounds the animation cels are grouped. In this process an average 750-foot Disney short takes two weeks to be photographed. After that it is taken to the Technicolor plant for processing, and made ready for final release.[7]

*Snow White and the Seven Dwarfs* has often been praised as one of cinema's greatest achievements and as Disney's most successful film. The shot in the scene labeled 3B, the moment when Snow White is led by a group of animals through the forest to then arrive at the dwarfs' cottage, is one of the most technically and aesthetically complex moments of this film, one that expresses all that animation can achieve in terms of artistry and expertise in Disney-style animation. In this shot (00:12:15–00:12:29), rhythm plays the most important part in the movement of image and camera and both beautifully support each other. As surprisingly complex as this shot is for Disney's first feature film, it shows one of the most congruent shots in all of 2D feature films. The artistry and collaboration between the various departments are very much visible on-screen and prove that the Disney artists were capable of creating magical moments in cinema that had never been seen before with that level of expertise, sense of color, and technical knowledge. One easily forgets nowadays what an impact *Snow White* had on its audience at the time and how impressed many critics were by the visuals and the animation. As was stated in the movie critique of *Snow White* in *Time* magazine in December of 1937:

> … Technicolor is used with simpler and stronger effects than ever before in motion pictures, giving a vital, indelible reality to the fairyland locales. Skeptical Hollywood, that had wondered whether a fairy story could have enough suspense to hold an audience through seven reels, and whether, even if the plot held up, an audience would care about the fate of characters who were just drawings, was convinced that Walt Disney had done it again. *Snow White* is as exciting as a Western, as funny as a haywire comedy.

5   Due to the fact that the Disney Company did not release the copyrights for screenshots and layout images of the feature *Snow White* to be used in this educational section, which would have tremendously helped the understanding of the discussed shot, it is necessary for the reader to check and compare the shot from the movie with the text to fully grasp this case study.
6   J.B. Kaufman, *The Fairest One of All: The Making of Walt Disney's Snow White and the Seven Dwarfs*, Walt Disney Family Foundation Press, San Francisco, CA, 2012, p. 287.

7   Mouse & Man. Time, 0040781X, 12/27/1937, Vol. 30, No. 26.

It combines the classic idiom of folklore drama with rollicking comic-strip humor. A combination of Hollywood, the Grimm Brothers, and the sad, searching fantasy of universal childhood, it is an authentic masterpiece, to be shown in theatres and beloved by new generations long after the current crop of Hollywood stars, writers and directors are sleeping where no Prince's kiss can wake them.[8]

Though of course it was not all praise, there were few critiques of the character animation of the humans and their realism. For some, it was not realistic enough; for others, too jerky or too realistic, depending on what the critics were looking for. Generally, though, critics were seeking even more realism at the time.[9] What needs to be considered when watching *Snow White and the Seven Dwarfs* today is the film's outstanding quality when watched in Blu-ray version. The digital restoration of the feature's 119,550 frames in 1992[10] gave the image back its original quality, which is truly outstanding. The film was the first one to be fully digitally scanned, cleaned, and then again recorded back on film in 4K resolution. The images were restored by removing scratches, dust and specks, and inconsistencies in color. Of course, this does not change the content or the story but has an impact on the pristine look of the feature today.

The feature might seem in some scenes slightly awkward today and outdated in terms of the character animation in Snow White's case, or the dwarfs' character design, which is very different from Snow White herself in terms of body ratio and cartooniness; also the flow of the story is at times a bit bumpy, as much time is spent on the introduction of the dwarfs. Nevertheless, *Snow White* still has an immensely important place in film history that must not be underestimated and its achievements are outstanding. It is a film that proves that Disney Studios not only improved its skill level at a speed that seems nothing less of stunning but also was very capable of creating scenes that even today make one wonder how they could have handled the complexity on such a scale. In particular, in the discussed shot from scene 3B, the complicatedness was beyond anything animation cinema had seen up to the day of *Snow White*'s release; nevertheless, it looks so graceful and easy. The interconnectedness between Snow White's and the animals' movements in the shot has an immense impact on the smooth flow of this shot, and the animals not only guide the path for Snow White in an utterly organic and seemingly uncontrolled way but also succumb to the musical beats. The music itself accompanies this scenic rhythm by underlining it in a subtle and gentle way.

The layout of the background, foreground, and middle ground is the foundation of this exceptionally crafted shot and was meticulously planned out for the perfect composition for each stage of the shot. The complexity of the liaison of movement

and background elements, the interplay of light and shadow, the intertwining relationship of the characters moving from background elements to foreground and back, the timing of the scene that carries us in waves through the setting, all create what is usually called the "Disney magic," which I personally would call "an exquisite piece of animation art." Skillfully, the artists involved in this shot allow every single component of the shot's composition to be part of its rhythmical structure. Background, layout, color, character animation, music, and camera movement all follow the same goal: the rhythm of Snow White running through the forest.

## Analysis of the shot in scene 3B

The positioning in the entire shot of many background and foreground elements that lean towards the left give the layout a tilt that supports the movement to the left (however, this cannot be seen in the initial layout drawing but only in the final shot). Trees and bushes are all tilted to assist Snow White and the animals in their movement towards the cottage on the left. Only the beginning of the shot (timecode 00:12:15) shows a round composition, from which Snow White steps out, in return just reflecting the end of the previous shot.

During the main shot of Scene 3B, there are numerous ways in which Snow White walks and skips. This provides the variation needed so we aren't bored watching her just "walking to the dwarfs' cottage." Variation is what makes the whole shot breathe and come alive with such strong force and keeps us alert to what happens on-screen, as the action and with it the entire visuals are continuously exciting in even the most mundane action of Snow White walking to the cottage. In her first steps in the shot before the main shot (timecode 00:12:07), she is being dragged by the birds to screen left into the forest. She hesitantly walks left and peeks through the birches. After the cut she lightly hops up a path rather daintily (timecode 00:12:15) and disappears shortly behind a tree (timecode 00:12:18). When the music turns more gently, she slows down her walk and gets caught in a tree with her cape (timecode 00:12:24). The cape gets stretched, and this creates tension and anticipation that is released with her running slowly up the path (timecode until 00:12:28). The music then, right before the cut, comes to a high point, when she herself reaches the top of the rise. After the cut, the music returns to the theme of her skipping up the hill. She rests a short moment to take in the environment and then goes into the dark thicket that then opens up to the view of the dwarfs' cottage. The music describes this audibly by quieting down and finally stopping when the cottage is visible. Snow White's various ways of walking, skipping, slow and fast, getting caught and being released, the interplay of tension and release give us a new experience in every moment of her action and make it an ongoing pleasure to watch this shot, never repeating itself.

However, it is not just Snow White's movement that is compelling but the running and skipping of all the animals that really carry the rhythm and complexity of this scene. The rhythm of the animals'

8   Mouse & Man. Time, 0040781X, 12/27/1937, Vol. 30, No. 26.
9   Jonathan Frome, Snow White: Critics and Criteria for the Animated Feature, *Film, Quarterly Review of Film and Video*, Vol. 30, No. 5 (2013), pp. 462–473.
10  Fisher Bob, Off to Work We Go: The Digital Restoration of Snow White, *American Cinematographer*, September 1993, p. 48ff.

- Snow White SW
- Rabbits R
- Brown Squirrels BS
- Grey Squirrels GS
- D=Deer; YD=Young Deer
- Chipmunk C

**Frame 49**
The deers pass SW, who stops for a couple of frames while we hear a cymbal.

**Frames 31–34**
The young deer follows the movement of SW. She bends backwards because of her stuck cape and at the same time the deer jumps up and lands during the follow-through of her skirt.

**Tension and anticipation through SW's stuck cape**

| 49 | 48 | 47 | 46 | 45 | 44 | 43 | 42 | 41 | 40 | 39 | 38 | 37 | 36 | 35 | 34 | 33 | 32 | 31 | 30 | 29 |
|---|---|---|---|---|---|---|---|---|---|---|---|---|---|---|---|---|---|---|---|---|
| SW | | | | | SW | SW | SW | SW | SW | SW | | | | SW | SW and | SW | R | SW | SW | |
| | R | | R | | | | R | | R | | R | | | YD are | R | | | | | |
| | | | | BS | | | | | BS | | BS | | BS | resting | BS | | BS | | BS | |
| | | BS | | | GS | | | | GS | | GS | | | in their | | | | | | |
| D | | D | | D& | | | | | | | D | D | | YD | movement YD | YD | | YD | | D |
| | | C | | Coff | | | | | | | | | | | | | | | C | |
| animation speed | | | animation speed | | | animation speed | | | animation speed | | | animation speed | | | animation speed | | | animation speed | | |

The soundtrack here is shown running from right to left. One can see that the major beats of the track coincide with the steps of animals and Snow Whites alike, allowing all elements to subtly intertwine.

**Figure 19.4**

...ne 26
...w White's
...e get's
...ght in the
...nch

Frame 20
The brown squirrel on
the right tree jumps
down to the ground
to a point of emphasis
in the music.

Frame 10
The brown
squirrel jumps
from one tree
to the next.

Frames 7–13
The young deer jumps up to a significant
note in the music (the grey squirrel on
the ground lands on that note), follows
that rhythm and lands on the same note
a couple of steps/measures later.

Frames 2–5
The brown squirrel on
the right tree jumps
down and hops on
the ground in the
rhythm of the music.

Frame 1
SW and
most of the
animals are
doing their
first step.

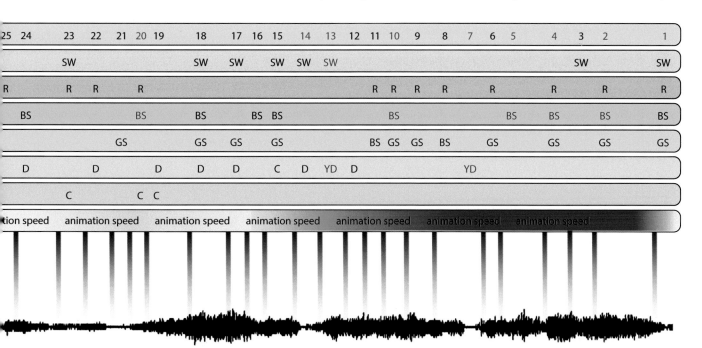

447

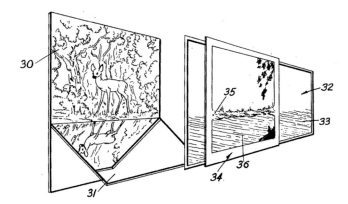

**Figure 19.3**

steps coincide with the steps of Snow White and with certain rhythmic beats in the music. The animals either mimic the flow of the music with their movement or they hit certain beats with their steps.[11] The number of characters is already stunning to begin with, but the choreography of the animals is nothing short of spectacular in its complexity and the result it achieves, which feels so light and effortless. All this time, the animals and Snow White are mirrored in the rippled water of the river in the foreground. The effect of the mirroring was achieved by a polished plate of tin that was mounted in an angle underneath the actual character animation,[12] which can be seen in the original drawing for the patent in Figure 19.3. The reflection of the character animation and the background is visible in the angled plate and the added sheet of rippled glass provides the water effect. This was an effect patented as US2314629, "Method of Creating Illusions." The method was filed by Leonard B. Pickley on December 18, 1939 and was granted on March 23, 1943, for Walt Disney Productions. The effects include the reflection of Snow White in the well in the beginning of the feature and the reflection of the animals in the river shown in Scene 3B.

## Diagram in Figure 19.4

Again: to understand the diagram one has to watch and study the mentioned shot fairly often with and without sound; otherwise, the complexity will not be grasped!

The diagram in Figure 19.4 explores the steps of animals and Snow White in relationship to the music. There is an obvious correlation between the characters' footsteps and the rhythmic beats of the music. The footsteps slow down before the tension and speed up after the tension. This rhythmical beat of the steps gives the shot an underlying structure that one can feel and its accompaniment by the camera movement and zoom creates the perfect harmony between all the elements.

---

[11] The characters' movements not only hit the musical beats exactly but also are slightly offset for a couple of frames sometimes. This allows the character animation to feel more organic instead of being rigid and stiff.
[12] J.B. Kaufman, *The Fairest One of All: The Making of Walt Disney's Snow White and the Seven*, Walt Disney Family Foundation Press, San Francisco, CA, 2012, p. 123.

## Examples of rhythm in the scene

The character animation mimics the musical pattern:

- (time-code 00:12:15): A dark brown squirrel at the very right of the frame jumps from the tree down to the ground and hops towards the left. Its very path visually describes the movement of the music and introduces us into this shot as the action on the very right draws our attention. The squirrel's initial jump is taken over by the gray squirrel in front of it, which hits the next point in the musical rhythm, and afterwards by the brown squirrel in the tree jumping to the left. It's the moment when the brown squirrel lands on the tree that another musical beat hits.
- (time-code 00:12:21): When Snow White slows down and hides by the tree in the middle of the shot, the music has a slow and more hesitant moment where all the animals, especially the two grown-up deer, are crouching slightly down, visually interpreting the music and also of course avoiding the low tree (was the layout designed with the music already in mind?).

The character hits certain notes of the music:

- (time-code 00:12:17): The young deer right behind Snow White follows her movement with its head and when it jumps up it hits precisely an accent in the music and when it lands hits that very same rhythm again.
- (time-code 00:12:28): The deer at the very end of the shot hits with its left front hoof a moment in the music where we can hear a high cymbal tone, like an accent in the score.

The animal character reacts to Snow White's action:

- (time-code 00:12:25): The young deer reacts to Snow White being caught in the branch with her cape. The deer's reaction emphasizes Snow White's action and makes it more important by mimicking it (or doubling the action).

Camera movement:

To fully appreciate this shot, it is crucial to also study what the camera is doing at any moment of the shot and how all the characters react to that. When Snow White is caught by the branch, there is a very subtle interaction between her and the young deer. Where the deer is prancing around her while she is caught, the camera is slightly ahead of her position and the older deer are leaving the frame. Then she catches up with the camera and the grown-up deer, surpasses them. The shot ends with all of them reaching the top of the hill. This interaction allows her to be in charge of the movement of the group. It is her who leads the shot; despite leading her to the cottage, the animals are actually led by her movement.

The camera itself is not just a passive bystander but an active part of the shot that knows at all times what is happening and supports the emotional impact with zoom and speed.

During the shot, the camera pans left, parallel to the forest's path. The shot starts out with a full shot of Snow White stepping slightly forward into the setting and then running to the left. The camera pans with her and first simulates her movement towards us by slightly zooming out. There are two moments where the camera zoom goes with the movement of Snow White: zoom out right at the beginning of the shot and then zoom after the cape is released until the end of the shot, both of which accentuate the music and the character animation.

## Background and animation layers

The six different layers used in this shot of Scene 3B all perfectly mimic parallax:

- Background layer with blue blurred-out trees and rocks painted very loosely and out of focus.
- *Second background:* contains the path the characters are walking on. At the end of the shot this layer becomes the dominant layer in the shot and the other layers vanish.

- *Animation layer:* contains all the characters in the shot.
- *First overlay:* contains all the trees, roots, bushes that the characters are passing behind. All of the trees are in focus.
- Water effects layer (a rippled sheet of glass that is overlaid on top of the mirrored animation, then a rippled sheet of glass adds the water effect by dragging it horizontally along the animation).
- *Second overlay:* this layer contains the parts that pass by the camera very close, like trees and branches with leaves or a bushel of mushrooms.

**More on *Snow White*:**

J.B. Kaufmann, *Snow White and the Seven Dwarfs: The Art and Creation of Walt Disney's Classic Animated Film*, Walt Disney Family Foundation Press, San Francisco, CA, 2012.

Martin Krause, Linda Witkowski, Stephen H. Ison, *Walt Disney's Snow White and the Seven Dwarfs: An Art in Its Making: Featuring the Collection*, Hyperion Books, New York, 1995.

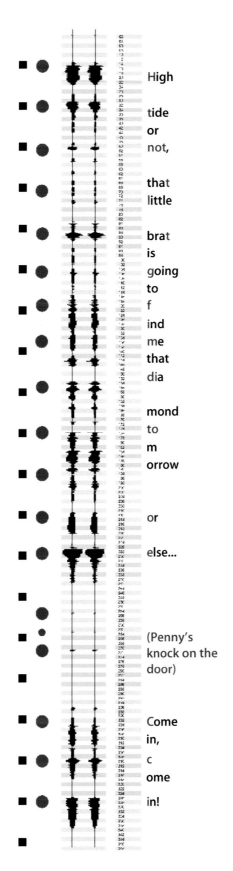

High

tide

or

not,

that

little

brat

is

going

to

f

ind

me

that

dia

mond

to

m

orrow

or

else...

(Penny's
knock on the
door)

Come

in,

c

ome

in!

**Figure 19.5**

## Case study: Rhythm in the character animation of Disney's *The Rescuers* (1977)[13]

**Directors:** Wolfgang Reitherman, John Lounsbery, Art Stevens

**Art director:** Don Griffith

**Directing animators:** Don Bluth, Milt Kahl, Ollie Johnston, Frank Thomas

When I was a kid or student and was watching animation, once in a while a shot or scene came along that was seemingly different from the rest, had a quality that I knew was there, but I did not really understand what it was that made that specific shot so graceful and unique, so utterly aesthetically pleasing, like the shot of *Snow White* just discussed. I learned that very often it had to do with the imbedded rhythm within the character animation and sometimes it was an amalgam of animation timing, poses, and dialogue that perfectly interpreted that rhythm. One of the very best scenes where rhythm plays such a crucial role is from Disney's feature *The Rescuers* from 1977. The scene (timecode 00:51:10 – 00:51:23) was animated by Milt Kahl and is one of the most famous characters and scenes of his career and outstanding Disney villains. Kahl gives the character of Madame Medusa such extreme poses and ugly expressions that one has to despise her. She is pure selfish evil, packed in a soft bag of tissue! Madame Medusa's role in the feature *The Rescuers* is selfish with a tad of sociopathic behavior. She wants the "Devil's Eye" diamond that only Penny, an orphan girl she abducted, can bring from an old pirate's cave. Two mice from the Rescue Aid Society learn of Penny's abduction through a message in a bottle and help to rescue her with a group of animals.

*The Rescuers* was similar to the feature *101 Dalmatians* in bringing a more contemporary story onto the screen instead of the popular fairy tales or stories that were set in the past (*Sword in the Stone* or *The Jungle Book*) or recent past (*Aristocats*).

When Cruella de Vil was animated by Marc Davis for the feature *101 Dalmatians* in 1961, Milt Kahl was supposedly jealous of the character and then animated Madame Medusa in this extreme fashion, pushing her character to pleasurable heights of a despicable nature.[14] Her personality on-screen is so believable and (in-)human, with all the complexities of a character who does not just act but thinks and is deceptive. The moments when she tries to talk Penny around

---

[13] Due to the fact that the Disney Company did not release the copyrights for screenshots used in this educational section, which would have tremendously helped the understanding of the discussed shot, it is necessary for the reader to check and compare the shots from the movie with the text to fully grasp this case study.

[14] *101 Dalmatians* Blu-ray, documentary.

and puts on fake emotion have incredible power and are utterly convincing.

What makes this scene so easy to watch and gives it flow is that the whole scene follows an imbedded rhythm that is so brilliantly interpreted by voice actress Geraldine Page. It is her take and interpretation of Medusa's sentence that puts emphasis on certain words and provides the whole sentence with a musical flow that pushes the animation forward with its imbedded rhythm. Milt Kahl used this rhythmic flow for his character animation and gave those moments extreme poses and impeccable timing to increase the scene's overall impact. From the beginning to the end of the sentence, every word more or less follows a measure.

The following can only be fully understood by repeatedly studying the shot with and without sound!

Here are the rhythmic points that appear in the sound clip (emphasis on certain sounds is in red; also see Figure 19.5 for the visualized soundtrack):

"**H**igh **t**ide or **not**, tha**t** **l**ittle bra**t** is **g**oing to **f**ind **m**e that **d**iamond **to**morrow, **or** e**l**se … [knock on the door] … **c**ome in, **c**ome in!"

Even Penny's knock on the door fits into this rhythm. The advantage of following a rhythm in the voice acting (as obvious as this one here from Geraldine Page that follows a clear beat, or a less obvious rhythm that can be found in any well-spoken sentence) is that the character animation adopts and visually interprets the emphasis of the sentence's beats, thus strengthening each other's impact. Both have to work together, not against each other. Though like in the previously discussed *Snow White* scene the character animation does not strictly follow the beat to the frame, it follows it enough to let the audience feel the rhythm in the sentence very clearly. By not being a slave to the frame, the shot retains its organic structure and feels less rigid.

It might seem tedious but the rhythm in a shot is extremely important in order to get a flow into the movement and give the shot that special something, a musical beat that provides it with a solid foundation on which to then build on. Rhythm can elevate a common shot to a great shot!

Milt Kahl's character animation hits the beats with poses and a timing that is very significant. First, Medusa's behind wiggles outrageously to the beat of "High tide or not …," hitting the *H*, *T*,

*O*, and *N*, where "high" gets two beats, "tide" also two; "or" and "not" each receive one. The next major beat is the word "brat," which is striking, at the same time as Medusa slams the stool on the ground, a very strong pose and perfect timing, to emphasize Medusa's hatred towards Penny. "Brat" expresses that with her hitting the stool and she says it right at the moment when her head does a follow-through due to the action of the slamming of the stool. The next beat is the word "going," which is the point of an extreme follow-through action of Medusa sitting down and the anticipation of her hopping on the stool towards the mirror. The following beat is her stool hitting the ground again and her saying "fff(ind)" very intensely. The *f*-sound is obvious and forceful and happens again at the same time as the follow-through of the hop. This makes three follow-throughs of the head in a row that all hit the beat. The next beat is more silent and there isn't much action (but creates tension between action and less action), but it leads towards the strong pose of her leaning into the mirror with a nice line of action towards her face. The composition in this shot is very successful, as we don't really see her full expression in the three-quarter view, but with the mirrored face we can see all of her hideous facials, which are so much fun in their extremes.

The beat for "to(morrow)" is intensified by her throwing down her earring, and Kahl keeps the pose at the end of "tomorrow" very long to lead into the "or else," which again has lots of movement and action. Milt Kahl constantly shifts between phases of action and phases with less action to make each read better, and the contrast allows each to be more extreme (a quick pose is quicker between two slow moments). The word "or" is accompanied by heavy head-shaking with lots of movement and "else" with a strong facial expression. Both are intense in their movement, so the next pose is nearly a still: her hearing Penny's knock on the door. Then her whole mood changes drastically and she is just "charming" in the most fake way possible. The sound of "come in, come in!" has a musical ring to it and her head does exactly that: she mimics the tones of the words with her head by shaking it back and forth.

The film is based on Margery Sharp's *The Rescuers*, a series of books that started in 1959; however, Disney's film is primarily based on the second book in the series, *Miss Bianca* (1962). In 1990 Disney released *The Rescuers Down Under*, which continued the story of the two mice, Bernard and Miss Bianca, this time going to Australia to rescue the boy Cody from Percival C. McLeach, another totally over-the-top villain.

# CHAPTER 20

# Variation

There is a reason for why *variation* is the last point of the design aspects in this book, because it needs to be considered at all times and concerns each individual aspect of composition; it is so to speak an overarching aspect. Variation in visuals with colors and shapes, in editing, in motion and sound, all aspects benefit from variation. It is *the* significant aspect that prevents the film from being repetitive and becoming plain. Film then only uses its full potential if every single element is constantly explored in its various options to cover the widest range possible, within the boundaries of its concept. Film and design becomes uninspiring when it repeats itself and does not allow its possibilities to spread and open up every single path. This is true for the shape variation in character design to suggest a wide range of character personalities and body types, but aside from the overall shape there is an endless amount of variety within the characters' secondary shapes, like head, feet, or hands, and the shapes in the even smaller sections like eyes, fingernails, etc. The same is true for the characters' attire, the decoration and pattern, the poses and expressions, and even its character animation. Variation in each part broadens the options dramatically and allows us to shift between styles but also makes the outcome look more organic, if that is what is wanted or needed for the narrative. In a storyboard, if the same composition is repeated over and over again, the audience very quickly gets bored and loses interest in the story; if the mood is the same, the color the same, the form of the architecture or the furnishing of the set repetitious, then the piece lacks originality and the audience will lose visual interest. To avoid this and provide the director and art director with the widest range

of possibilities in the development process, variation is one element that is crucial and serves as a very helpful tool to expand on one's own designs. Especially for visual development work an expansive spectrum must be presented for the director and art director to choose from. Diversity is what makes the artist explore his or her own field. The danger with variation, however, is if the suggested designs are so different from each other that they do not follow the same style direction; then variation has been pushed too far.

A simple sapling has seemingly nothing really to be designed. But of course every part of the sapling can be changed to make the design different and unique. For example, the lineup of the saplings in Figure 20.1 shows just a plain sapling (Figure 20.1a) with the leaves having the same size and height. In Figure 20.1b the height is changed, in Figure 20.1c the size, in Figure 20.1d a little sprout is added, in Figure 20.1e the shape of the leaves is a bit more edgy, Figure 20.1f is taller and the leaves are drooping more, Figure 20.1g has a thinner stem and different pattern on the leaves, Figure 20.1h is thicker and the sprout lacks leaves, Figure 20.1i has differently shaped leaves as does Figure 20.1j, Figure 20.1k has a very shape-oriented approach, Figure 20.1l is very stylized … you get the point. By changing all these various elements, you extend your ideas dramatically. Everything can be changed and explored. This helps to find a version that fits the style. Additionally, the line quality can change, as well as the color, texture, and all the other aspects of design. The primary elements for variation are shape and ratio! Explore!

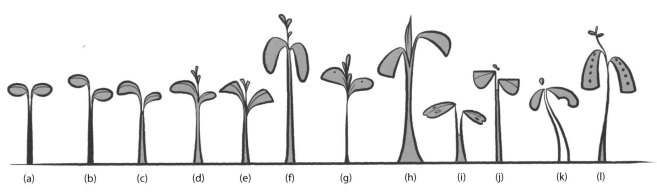

(a) (b) (c) (d) (e) (f) (g) (h) (i) (j) (k) (l)

**Figure 20.1**

DOI: 10.1201/b22148-20

Figure 20.2

Figure 20.3

Variation is needed to keep the audience interested and the design exciting. The following can help you to see the possibilities of variation in all of the elements of composition:

- Big versus small
- Round versus squared
- Bent versus straight
- Geometric versus organic
- Composition inscribed into various geometric shapes (see Figure 20.3)
- Fast versus slow
- Busy versus calm
- Textured versus smooth
- Tall versus short
- Heavy versus light
- Rough versus sleek
- Hairy versus hairless
- Hot versus cold
- Loud versus quiet
- Beautiful versus ugly

- Close versus far
- Cramped versus open
- Tight versus loose
- Bright versus dark
- Comfortable versus uncomfortable
- Aesthetically pleasing versus aesthetically challenging

Constantly bring something new to the design to entertain not only the audience but also yourself in the process. Once the artist is bored, the outcome is seldom very exciting. For example, Figures 20.2 and 20.3 show an exploration of exaggerated trees to find possibilities within the framework of odd shapes and ideas. These are not final designs but explorations to see how far the ideas can be pushed. Start out with thumbnail sketches (the top row of Figure 20.2) that already vary in shape and composition. The red overlay in Figure 20.3 shows how the thumbnails deal with shape, composition, weight, direction, and variation, which are then refined and expanded in the next step underneath the thumbnails. Of course, too much variation makes the style fall apart!

# Additional Reading

## Animation history

Balakirsky Katz Mayaa, *Drawing the Iron Curtain: Jews and the Golden Age of Soviet Animation*, Rutgers University Press, New Brunswick, NJ, 2016.

Barrier Michael, *Hollywood Cartoons: American Animation in Its Golden Age*, Oxford University Press, Oxford, 2003.

Bendazzi Giannalberto, *Animation: A World History: Volume I—III*, Focal Press, Waltham, Massachusetts, 2016.

Bendazzi Giannalberto, *Cartoons: One Hundred Years of Cinema Animation*, Indiana University Press, Bloomington, IN, 1995.

Cohen Karl F., *Forbidden Animation: Censored Cartoons and Blacklisted Animators in America,* McFarland & Co, Jefferson, NC, 2004.

Crafton Donald, *Before Mickey: The Animated Film 1898–1928*, University of Chicago Press, Chicago, IL, 1993.

Culhane Shamus, *Talking Animals and Other People*, Da Capo Press, Boston, MA, 1998.

Ghez Didier, *Walt's People: Volume 1–19: Talking Disney with the Artists Who Knew Him*, Theme Park Press, 2014–2017.

Giessen Rolf, *Animation Under the Swastika: A History of Trickfilm in Nazi Germany, 1933–1945*, McFarland & Co., Jefferson, NJ, 2012.

Klein Norman M., *Seven Minutes: The Life and Death of the American Animated Cartoon*, Verso, New York, 1996.

Koyama-Richard Brigitte, *Japanese Animation: From Painted Scrolls to Pokémon*, Flammarion, Paris, 2010.

Laqua Carsten, *Wie Micky unter die Nazis fiel: Walt Disney und Deutschland*, Rowohlt Taschenbuch Verlag, Berlin, 1992.

Lehman Christopher P., *The Colored Cartoon, Black Representation in American Animated Short Films, 1907–1954*, University of Massachusetts Press, Amherst, MA, 2007.

Neupert Richard, *French Animation History*, Wiley, Hoboken, NJ, 2014.

Pointer Ray, *The Art and Inventions of Max Fleischer, American Animation Pioneer*, McFarland & Co., Jefferson, NC, 2017.

## Animation theory

Furniss Maureen, *Art in Motion, Revised Edition: Animation Aesthetics*, John Libbey Publishing, Barnet, UK, 2008.

Leslie Esther, *Hollywood Flatlands: Animation, Critical Theory and the Avant-Garde*, Verso, New York, 2004.

Wells Paul, *Animation and American Society: Cartoons to Computers*, Keele University Press, Keele, UK, 2002.

Wells Paul, *Understanding Animation*, Routledge, London, 1998.

## Visual perception

Arnheim Rudolf, *Art and Visual Perception: A Psychology of the Creative Eye*, University of California Press, Berkeley, CA, 2004.

Arnheim Rudolf, *Visual Thinking*, University of California Press, Berkeley, CA, 2004.

## Composition

Arnheim Rudolf, *The Power of the Center: A Study of Composition in the Visual Arts*, University of California Press, Berkeley, CA, 2009.

## Film history

Monaco James, *How to Read a Film: The World of Movies, Media, Multimedia: Language, History, Theory*, Oxford University Press, Oxford, 2009.

## Drawing

Enstice Wayne, Melody Peters: *Drawing: Space, Form, and Expression*, Pearson Education Inc., New York, 2013.

Hampton Michael, *Figure Drawing, Design and Invention*, Michael Hampton, 2013.

Mattesi Mike, *Force: Animal Drawing: Animal Locomotion and Design Concepts for Animators*, Focal Press, Waltham, MA, 2011.

Mattesi Mike, *Force: Dynamic Life Drawing*, Focal Press, Waltham, MA, 2006.

Robertson Scott, *How to Draw: Drawing and Sketching Objects and Environments*, Design Studio Press, Culver City, CA, 2013.

Robertson Scott, *How to Render TP*, Design Studio Press, Culver City, CA, 2014.

Stanchfield Walt, *Drawn to Life: 20 Golden Years of Disney Master Classes: The Walt Stanchfield Lectures—Volume 1 & 2*, Focal Press, Waltham, MA, 2009.

## Storyboarding

Katz Steven, *Film Directing Shot by Shot: Visualizing from Concept to Screen*, Michael Wiese Productions, Studio City, CA, 1991.

Katz Steven, *Film Directing: Cinematic Motion: A Workshop for Staging Scenes*, Michael Wiese Productions, Studio City, CA, 2004.

# Editing

Murch Walter, *In the Blink of an Eye, A Perspective on Film Editing*, Silman-James Press, West Hollywood, CA, 2001.

# Cinematography

Alton John, *Painting with Light*, University of California Press, Berkeley, CA, 1998.

Kenworthy Christopher, *Master Shots Vol 1–3: 100 Advanced Camera Techniques to Get an Expensive Look on Your Low-Budget Movie*, Michael Wiese Productions, Studio City, CA, 2003.

Mascelli Joseph V., *Five C's of Cinematography: Motion Pictures Filming Techniques*; Silman-James Press, West Hollywood, CA, 1998.

Mercado Gustavo, *The Filmmaker's Eye: Learning (and Breaking) the Rules of Cinematic Composition*, Focal Press, Waltham, MA, 2010.

# Animation techniques

## 2D animation

Culhane Shamus, *Animation: From Script to Screen*, St. Martin's Griffin, New York, 1990.

Gilland Joseph, *Elemental Magic, Volume I & II: The Art of Special Effects Animation*, Focal Press, Waltham, MA, 2009 & 2011.

Thomas Frank and Johnston Ollie, *Illusion of Life: Disney Animation*, Disney Editions, Glendale CA, 1995.

Webster Chris, *Action Analysis for Animators*, Focal Press, Waltham, MA, 2009.

Whittaker Harold, Halas John and Sito Tom, *Timing for Animation*, Focal Press, Waltham, MA, 2009.

## Stop-motion animation

Gasek Tom, *Frame-By-Frame Stop Motion: The Guide to Non-Puppet Photographic Animation Techniques*, CRC Press, Boca Raton, FL, 2017.

Lord Peter, Sibley Brian and Park Nick, *Cracking Animation: The Aardman Book of 3-D Animation*, Thames & Hudson Ltd., London, 1998.

Pettigrew Neil, *The Stop-motion Filmography: A Critical Guide to 297 Features Using Puppet Animation, Volume I & II*, McFarland & Co., Jefferson, NC, 2007.

Purves Barry J.C., *Stop-Motion Animation: Frame by Frame Film-Making with Puppets and Models*, Fairchild Books, London, 2014.

Shaw Susannah, *Stop Motion: Craft Skills for Model Animation*, Focal Press, Waltham, MA, 2017.

Ternan Melvyn, *Stop Motion Animation: How to Make & Share Creative Videos*, Barron's Educational Series, Hauppauge, NY, 2013.

# Experimental animation

Russett Robert and Starr Cecile, *Experimental Animation*, Da Capo Press, Boston, MA, 1988.

# Computer animation

Kerlow Isaac V., *The Art of 3D Computer Animation and Effects*, Wiley, Hoboken, NJ, 2009.

# Special effects

Duignan Patricia Rose, *Industrial Light and Magic (Into the Digital Realm)*, Del Rey Books, London, 1996.

Smith Thomas G., *Industrial Light and Magic*, Ballantine Books Inc., New York, 1992.

# Game design

Schell Jesse, *The Art of Game Design: A Book of Lenses*, CRC Press, Boca Raton, FL, 2008.

# Matte painting

Cotta Vaz Marc, *The Invisible Art: The Legends of Movie Matte Painting*, Chronicle Books, San Francisco, CA, 2004.

"If, however, you do not sit quietly at ease, sitting at a clean table by a bright window, a stick of incense beside you and every anxiety suppressed then you will not perceive the beautiful lines and the fine meanings. You will be unable to imagine the elusive feelings and the flavors of beauty.

How can the primary significance of painting be easy to maintain? Circumstances must be ripe, and the mind and hand mutually responsive. Then, when you begin, you will freely achieve excellence, taking from all sides and "penetrating to the source."[1]

**Guo Xi (1020–1090)**

[1] Dora Emily Pollak: *The Cosmos in Ink, Spirit Resonance and Correlative Realms in Early Chinese Philosophy of Landscape Painting;* Reed College, 2009, p.109.

# Index